The Wiley Handbook of Psychology, Technology, and Society

The Wiley Handbook of Psychology, Technology, and Society

Edited by

Larry D. Rosen, Nancy A. Cheever, and L. Mark Carrier

WILEY Blackwell

This edition first published 2015
© 2015 John Wiley & Sons, Ltd.

Registered Office
John Wiley & Sons, Ltd, The Atrium, Southern Gate, Chichester, West Sussex, PO19 8SQ, UK

Editorial Offices
350 Main Street, Malden, MA 02148-5020, USA
9600 Garsington Road, Oxford, OX4 2DQ, UK
The Atrium, Southern Gate, Chichester, West Sussex, PO19 8SQ, UK

For details of our global editorial offices, for customer services, and for information about how
to apply for permission to reuse the copyright material in this book please see our website at
www.wiley.com/wiley-blackwell.

Library of Congress Cataloging-in-Publication Data

Rosen, Larry D., editor.
  The Wiley handbook of psychology, technology and society / edited by Larry D. Rosen,
Nancy Cheever, L. Mark Carrier.
    pages cm
  Includes index.
  ISBN 978-1-118-77202-7 (hardback)
1. Social psychology. 2. Internet–Social aspects. 3. Internet–Security measures.
I. Cheever, Nancy D., editor. II. Carrier, L. Mark, editor. III. Title.
  HM1025.W55 2015
  302–dc23

                                            2014048335

A catalogue record for this book is available from the British Library.

Cover image: © John Lund / Getty Images

Set in 10/12pt Galliard by SPi Publisher Services, Pondicherry, India
Printed and bound in Malaysia by Vivar Printing Sdn Bhd

1 2015

Contents

About the Editors

Larry D. Rosen, PhD, is Professor and past Chair of the Psychology department at California State University, Dominguez Hills. He is a research psychologist with specialties in multitasking, social networking, generational differences, parenting, child and adolescent development, and educational psychology, and is recognized as an international expert in the "psychology of technology." Over the past 30-plus years, Dr. Rosen and his colleagues have examined reactions to technology among more than 50,000 people in the United States and in 22 other countries. In addition to editing this handbook, he has written five books including: *iDisorder: Understanding Our Obsession With Technology and Overcoming its Hold on Us* (2012); *Rewired: Understanding the iGeneration and the Way They Learn* (2010); *Me, MySpace and I: Parenting the Net Generation* (2007); *TechnoStress: Coping with Technology @Work @Home @Play* (1997); and *The Mental Health Technology Bible* (1997), and writes a technology column for the newspaper *The National Psychologist* and regular blogs for the magazine *Psychology Today* and the *Huffington Post*. He is currently working on his next book, which concentrates on why we get so distracted from the dual perspective of brain science and psychology, which will be published in 2015. Dr. Rosen has been featured extensively in television, print, and radio media and has been a commentator on *The Daily Show*, *Good Morning America*, NPR, and CNN. He has been quoted in hundreds of magazines and newspapers including *USA Today*, *The New York Times*, *Newsweek*, *Time*, *Chicago Tribune*, and *Los Angeles Times*. He maintains an extremely active research program and his most recent investigations include: generational differences in technology use and multitasking; the distracted mind from the dual perspectives of psychology and neuroscience; the impact of technology on health and sleep; integrating technology in education; the impact of social networks on adolescents and parents; online empathy; the impact of task switching during studying and in the classroom; and the impact of texting language on English literacy. Further information is available at DrLarryRosen.com.

Nancy A. Cheever, PhD, is a Professor and past Chair of Communications at California State University, Dominguez Hills. She is a research psychologist, writer, teacher, and consultant who specializes in media psychology. As the Chair of the Communications Department from 2011 to 2014, Dr. Cheever oversaw the operations of a department with more than 500 majors and minors, and 20 faculty members. Dr. Cheever is a founding mentor of the George Marsh Applied Cognition Laboratory at the university, where she and her colleagues engage students in primary research associated with technology and psychology. A former newspaper journalist and magazine editor, Dr. Cheever's vast research interests examine emerging and existing media technologies and their content and how they impact people's thoughts, attitudes, opinions, and behaviors. Her latest published research was an experiment measuring people's anxiety levels with and without their smartphones. In addition to editing this handbook, she is the co-author of two books: *Rewired: Understanding the iGeneration and the Way They Learn* (2010), and *iDisorder: Understanding Our Obsession With Technology and Overcoming its Hold on Us* (2012). Dr. Cheever regularly has presented her research at dozens of conferences, has been the subject of magazine and newspaper articles, and a featured guest on radio and television programs including NPR and PBS. Dr. Cheever teaches communications research methods, news writing and reporting, media psychology, and capstone courses. She received her BA in Communications from California State University, Dominguez Hills, where she was awarded the Outstanding Journalism Graduate; her first MA (communications) from California State University, Fullerton, where she won the Top Scholar Award from Kappa Tau Alpha, the national communications honor society; her second MA (media psychology) from Fielding Graduate University; and her PhD in media psychology from Fielding Graduate University.

L. Mark Carrier, PhD, has been a Professor of Psychology at California State University, Dominguez Hills (CSUDH), for more than 15 years. He has a bachelor's degree in cognitive psychology from the University of California, San Diego and a master's degree and a PhD in experimental psychology from the same institution. His research interests center on the psychology of technology, especially with regard to human multitasking. As Chairperson of the Psychology Department from 2006 to 2014, Dr. Carrier managed 1,200 majors and 40 instructors. He is co-founder of the George Marsh Applied Cognition Laboratory and of the Brain Imaging Laboratory at CSUDH. He has published articles in scientific journals on topics related to human cognition. Dr. Carrier has co-authored two prior books about the psychology of technology: *Rewired: Understanding the iGeneration and the Way They Learn* (2010) and *iDisorder: Understanding Our Obsession with Technology and Overcoming Its Hold on Us* (2012). In *iDisorder*, Dr. Carrier and his colleagues described many different ways in which the overuse and abuse of personal technology can affect how people think, feel, and behave. In 2010–2011, he was named the Outstanding Professor at CSUDH. Mark participates in national mentoring programs to train students for careers in scientific research and serves on a large number of campus committees related to student learning. In the past, Dr. Carrier served as the Co-Team Leader for the American Psychological Association/ National Institute of General Medical Sciences Project, an effort to increase the number of underrepresented students in the biomedical sciences.

List of Contributors

Karin Archer is currently in the final stages of completing her doctoral studies at Wilfrid Laurier University. Her research interests involve examining educational applications related to technology use. Specifically, her research has involved identification of key variables that predict disclosure when engaged in social networking. In addition she has been involved in the development of instructional interventions directed at promoting an understanding of disclosure and privacy online. Her current research program investigates early introduction to mobile devices and parental instruction in that context.

Miriam Bartsch, Dipl.-Psych, is research assistant at the Institute of Media and Communication at the University of Hamburg, Germany (with Prof. Dr. Uwe Hasebrink), where she is studying the effects of mass media, currently focusing on media repertoires. Before that, she studied media effects such as those of online advertisements, including neuropsychological methods such as EEG or eye-tracking, at Hamburg Media School. For her final thesis she conducted an empirical online study on impression management and privacy concerns on Facebook and is planning to do her doctoral degree in media sciences as well. Ms. Bartsch studied psychology at the University of Hamburg, where she focused on media psychology and media and communication sciences as well as on communication psychology (with the distinguished communications psychologist Dr. Friedemann Schulz von Thun). She also earned a certificate of media psychology with Dr. Sabine Trepte and a certificate of problem- and conflict consulting with Dr. Alexander Redlich. She was a visiting scholar with Dr. Kaveri Subrahmanyam at the Children's Digital Media Center @ Los Angeles, CSULA/UCLA (California State University Los Angeles, University of California Los Angeles). Additionally, she worked as a student research assistant in media psychology at the University of Hamburg and in medical psychology at the University Hospital Hamburg-Eppendorf.

Fatih Bayraktar, PhD, is an Assistant Professor of Developmental Psychology in the Psychology Department, Faculty of Arts and Sciences, Eastern Mediterranean University, Famagusta. He received his PhD and MA in developmental psychology from Hacettepe University and Ege University of Turkey, respectively. He began studying cyberbullying during his PhD education and wrote his dissertation on this subject. He continued to study cyberbullying while he was working at the Institute for Research of Children, Youth, and Family at Masaryk University, Czech Republic as a postdoctoral research fellow. He contributed to the international project COST ISO801 "Action on cyberbullying: Coping with negative and enhancing positive uses of new technologies in relationships in educational settings" as a member of the

Czech team, and he wrote a paper titled "Cyberbullying: The discriminant factors among cyberbullies, cybervictims, and cyberbully victims in a Czech adolescent sample" by using COST data with this team. He continues to work on cyberbullying in an international project titled "Adolescents' perceptions and experiences with bullying and cyberbullying: A cross-cultural examination," which includes the United States, Czech Republic, North Cyprus, India, China, and Japan.

Chelsey Beaney, BSc, is a research assistant who has been working on projects investigating the role of new digital technology to support children's learning and development in the School of Management at the University of Bath.

Olivia N. Berch is an undergraduate student at Iowa State University. Her plan is to graduate in 2016 with a double major in psychology and child, adult, and family services. She is also planning to graduate with honors. Currently, Ms. Berch is working as the undergraduate manager of a research lab in the psychology department. After graduating, Olivia plans to attend graduate school and obtain a PhD in clinical child psychology or developmental psychology. Ms. Berch's passion is to have a positive impact on those children most affected by emotional and intellectual disorders. She has started these endeavors by devoting her time as a respite and supported community living provider for those in need due to intellectual or physical handicaps. While not working, she also delights in spending time with her family, friends, and co-workers who support her during all of her adventures as a student and future researcher.

Vickie Bhatia, MA, is a fifth-year doctoral candidate in clinical psychology at Stony Brook University. Her broad research interests involve examining the relationship between mental health and interpersonal functioning among adolescents and emerging adults as well as the mechanisms underlying these associations. More specifically, she is also interested in examining how individual differences (e.g., personality traits, cognitive biases, emotion regulation skills) may influence the association between romantic relationship functioning and depressive and anxious symptoms. Her research on the association between poor social networking interactions and mental health problems is guided by interpersonal models of depression and she seeks to extend the current literature to a novel, but extremely salient, interpersonal platform.

Chris Bigenho, PhD, is the Director of Educational Technology at Greenhill School in Dallas, Texas. He received his PhD in educational computing from the University of North Texas and his master's in educational technology from Pepperdine University. As an independent researcher, his research interests include emerging technologies in learning environments, and the cognitive aspects of technology in learning environments with a specific focus on dual-tasking and cognitive load. He also works in the fields of games for learning and self-regulatory practices for learning. Dr. Bigenho owns an educational consulting practice and is a frequent speaker and presenter on the topics of education and technology. He has spoken at schools and conferences across the United States and South America.

Vanessa Black, BA, graduated with a bachelor's in psychology and a minor in criminal justice from California State University, Dominguez Hills in May 2012. Since then she has been working as a lab manager for the CARES Study at the Los Angeles Biomedical Research Institute (LA BioMed) at Harbor-UCLA Medical

Center. Ms. Black is interested in forensic psychology and is planning to pursue graduate education.

Jorge A. Blanco-Herrera is a second-year graduate student in social psychology and human–computer interaction at Iowa State University. He is managing and studying in the Media Research Lab under Dr. Douglas Gentile. Mr. Blanco-Herrera received his bachelor of arts in psychology at the University of Nevada, Las Vegas, where he worked in the Human Memory Lab under Dr. Colleen Parks and the Reasoning and Memory Lab under Dr. David Copeland. His area of focus lies at the intersection of psychology and technology, specifically, the cognitive, social, and developmental effects of video games. Mr. Blanco-Herrera's current line of research explores the effects of video game mechanics, player interactions, and content design, particularly their relationship to skill and competency attainment, attitude change, and education. Mr. Blanco-Herrera is especially interested in the positive potential of video games and other forms of play, as inherently engaging sources of learning, as well as vessels for otherwise unattainable vicarious experiences. His interest in video game addiction notes the extremity of this engagement in some gamers, as he hopes to create more balanced experiences. Overall, Mr. Blanco-Herrera seeks to expand on current research and advocacy in an environment of collaboration between researchers and industry professionals seeking to advance the field.

Deborah A. Boehm-Davis, PhD, is Dean of the College of Humanities and Social Sciences and a University Professor of Psychology at George Mason University. She received her graduate degrees from the University of California, Berkeley. Prior to joining George Mason in 1984, she worked on applied cognitive research at General Electric, NASA Ames, and Bell Laboratories. More recently, she served as a Senior Policy Advisor for Human Factors at the Food and Drug Administration's Center for Devices and Radiological Health. Dr. Boehm-Davis has served as President and Secretary-Treasurer of the Human Factors and Ergonomics Society (HFES) and as President of Division 21 (Applied Experimental and Engineering Psychology) of the American Psychological Association (APA). She is co-author of the textbook, *An Introduction to Humans in Engineered Systems*, and co-editor of the forthcoming *Handbook of Human-Systems Integration*. She has served as an associate editor for *Human Factors* and the *International Journal of Human-Computer Studies* and on the editorial boards of several journals. She is a fellow of the HFES, APA, and International Ergonomics Association. Dr. Boehm-Davis was awarded the Franklin V. Taylor award for career achievements from the APA and the Award for Scientific Achievement in the Behavioral and Social Sciences from the Washington Academy of Sciences. She has testified before Congress, and served on numerous panels for the National Research Council, National Research Foundation, Transportation Research Board, and NASA. She was a member and chair of the Federal Aviation Administration's Research, Engineering, and Development Advisory Committee, as well as their Human Factors Subcommittee. She was a member of the Air Force Scientific Advisory Board and the Transportation Security Administration's Scientific Advisory Board.

Laura L. Bowman, PhD, earned her undergraduate degree in psychology from the Ohio State University in 1983 and her PhD in experimental psychology with a focus on cognitive psychology from Kent State University in 1989. She is currently a professor in the Department of Psychological Science at Central Connecticut State University (CCSU) where she has just completed a term as Department Chair. Her research centers on cognitive processes including memory and attention. She has published several articles on the distractibility of media multitasking and she and her colleagues are continuing to examine factors that relate to attention and electronic media use. In 1997 Dr. Bowman traveled to Malaysia as a Senior Fulbright Scholar at the Universiti Malaysia Sarawak where she taught and did research examining Malaysian university students' perceptions of research ethics. She returned to Malaysia more recently to the HELP University in Kuala Lumpur to teach and conduct a cross-cultural comparison of Malaysian and American university students' distractibility, multitasking, and electronic media use. Dr. Bowman regularly teaches undergraduate courses in cognitive psychology, research methods, environmental psychology, and co-teaches an honors course in world cultures. In 2006 she was a semi-finalist for the Teaching Excellence Award at CCSU. In her 25 years at CCSU, she has been an active member of many departmental and university committees and has co-authored multiple posters/presentations at professional conferences such as the Association for Psychological Science and the American Psychological Association.

Mark Brosnan, PhD, is a Reader in Psychology and Director of Research for Psychology at the University of Bath. He is a chartered psychologist with the British Psychological Society (BPS) and a member of the Cognitive Psychology Section and the Division of Neuropsychology. Dr. Brosnan's current research projects examine how children with an autism spectrum disorder (ASD) can be involved within the design of a computer-based assistive technology. His team has developed protocols for "participatory design" that effectively support children with ASD to be active design partners. This has informed a series of design principles that have guided the development of a mathematics tutor and an iPad application to reduce challenging behaviors – both designed by people with ASD for people with ASD. Dr. Brosnan has a long-standing research interest in how technology is used, and has written a book on "Technophobia." This explores how and why people can become fearful of using technology. Recently this has extended into social media and Dr. Brosnan teaches a cyberpsychology course in the Second Life virtual world. Of particular interest is how these new online environments can facilitate communication in people with ASD. Dr. Brosnan has published extensively within the fields of both ASD and cyberpsychology research and focuses upon how technologies can be developed to support the deficits in social communication and interaction associated with ASD.

David M. Cades, PhD, received his doctorate in human factors and applied cognition from George Mason University in 2011. He specializes in investigations of vehicle operator behavior, including perception response time, vision, nighttime visibility, and distractions. Dr. Cades has expertise in the testing and analysis of how interruptions and distractions affect performance. He has investigated the negative effects of distractions in environments, including, but not limited to, driving, commercial aviation, health care, offices, and classrooms. He has applied this knowledge to see how distractions can cause errors that lead to accidents. Dr. Cades also has expertise in evaluating and designing graphical user interfaces including devices for use in automobiles and aircraft. He has investigated the effects of manual and voice-activated infotainment devices in automobiles. For commercial aircraft, he has worked with pilots, air traffic controllers, and airline operations in support of the Federal Aviation

Administration's NextGen initiative. Dr. Cades has investigated vehicle operator behavior of automobiles, trucks, bicycles, motorcycles, and aircraft. He has evaluated the adequacy of warnings on products and in their manuals and he has applied his experience to projects involving safety- and health-related user behaviors of industrial equipment, kitchen appliances, video game entertainment systems, home theater products, and personal protective equipment.

Keith W. Campbell, PhD, is a Professor of Psychology at the University of Georgia. His work is primarily on the topic of narcissism, ranging from understanding narcissism as a trait and disorder to narcissism as a cultural phenomenon. He is the author of more than 100 scientific journal articles and book chapters, and the books *When You Love a Man Who Loves Himself: How to Deal with a One-way Relationship*; *The Narcissism Epidemic: Living in the Age of Entitlement* (with Jean Twenge); and *The Handbook of Narcissism and Narcissistic Personality Disorder: Theoretical Approaches, Empirical Findings, and Treatments* (with Josh Miller). He and Jean Twenge also have a personality textbook, *Personality Psychology: Understanding Yourself and Others*, to be published in 2015. His work on narcissism has appeared in *USA Today, Time*, and *The New York Times*, and he has made numerous radio and television appearances, including *The Today Show* and the *Glenn Beck Program*. He holds a BA from the University of California at Berkeley, an MA from San Diego State University, a PhD from the University of North Carolina at Chapel Hill, and did his postdoctoral work at Case Western Reserve University. He lives in Athens, Georgia, with his wife and daughters.

Emily Christofides, PhD, currently holds a joint postdoctoral position at the University of Guelph and Wilfrid Laurier University. She completed her master's degree in consumer behavior and her PhD in social psychology at the University of Guelph. Her research has focused on privacy as a psychological concept and the social effects of new media. In her research on privacy theory she has contributed to our understanding of the personal and situational factors that impact privacy decisions. This research highlights the complexity of privacy as a concept and helps to explain some of the inconsistencies between privacy beliefs and behaviors. Dr. Christofides has also investigated the factors that explain peoples' tendency to disclose or protect their information online. She has examined this issue from a number of different perspectives including: the differences between age groups in the factors that predict online disclosure and use of privacy settings; the way in which being a member of a profession or a professional-in-training impacts online disclosure decisions; how online information sharing impacts romantic relationships; how exposure to relationship-relevant information online impacts information-seeking behavior; and how the information that one discloses, gender, and medium of disclosure affect the way others judge the discloser. More recently, her research has extended into the health domain, particularly around health decision-making and consumers' understanding of the privacy issues related to purchasing genetic tests from companies that provide direct-to-consumer genetic testing through their websites.

Candrianna Clem, MA, is a doctoral student in sociology specializing in demography at the University of Texas-Austin and examines the social implications of technology on college students' academic and social experiences. Ms. Clem's primary research interests use quantitative methods to analyze how racial and digital inequality impacts educational and occupational outcomes. Her research focuses on how race is linked to residential segregation, poverty, STEM (science, technology, engineering, and math) literacy, and unequal access to technology. Of primary interest is determining the implications of these inequalities on educational experiences and outcomes, identifying strategies for increasing diversity/inclusion, and closing achievement gaps in education. Her most recent work uses digital textbook analytics data to explore the ways that age differences in online reading behavior influence academic performance. She is currently a member of the Education and Transition to Adulthood Group (ETAG) at the Population Research Center at the University of Texas-Austin, which studies the pathways through education and how they interact with family life and work. In particular, this group's focus includes STEM preparation and careers, with a primary interest dedicated to the diversity in experiences, and disparities according to gender, race and ethnicity, social class, as well as disability, immigration, or language minority status.

Joanne Davila, PhD, is a Professor of Psychology and the Director of Clinical Training at Stony Brook University. She has published widely in the areas of adolescent and adult psychopathology and interpersonal functioning. Her current research focuses on the interpersonal causes and consequences of depression and anxiety disorders, including social networking experiences, risk factors for the early development of romantic relationship dysfunction in adolescents, the role of attachment representations in interpersonal functioning, and well-being among LGBT individuals.

Michelle Drouin, PhD, is an Associate Professor of Psychology at Indiana University-Purdue University, Fort Wayne. She has been a faculty member there since 2005, after completing her bachelor's degree in psychology at Cornell University and her DPhil in experimental psychology (with a concentration in developmental psychology) at the University of Oxford. Dr. Drouin regularly teaches courses in human development, including social and personality development, language development, child psychology, and development across the lifespan. Additionally, she runs an active research laboratory, mentoring undergraduate research assistants in psychological research. Her primary research examines innovations in technology, such as texting and social networking, and the effects of these innovations on communication, literacy, relationships, and human development. She also studies the roles of technology in teaching and learning. Dr. Drouin's research on sexting and mobile phone addiction has attracted international attention, and she regularly does interviews for television, radio, newspapers, and magazines. Her research has been cited in a number of prominent news sources including CNN, NPR, MSNBC, CBS News, *The New York Times*, *Huffington Post*, Reuters, *Men's Health*, *Parenting Magazine*, and *Psychology Today*. Most recently, she has had articles published on the effects of Facebook on committed relationships, unwanted but consensual sexting, and solicitation of and communication with back burners (relationship alternatives) via social networking.

Brian A. Feinstein, MA, is a sixth-year doctoral candidate in clinical psychology at Stony Brook University. He has several related research interests, including the relationship between interpersonal functioning and mental health; stress and coping; and lesbian, gay, and bisexual (LGB) health. Specifically, he is interested in the extent to which people's interpersonal experiences influence their well-being and the mechanisms underlying these associations. He is also interested in how LGB individuals cope with stress related to their sexual orientation as well as risk and protective factors related to psychopathology among LGB individuals. He has received support for his research from the American Psychological Association of Graduate Students, the National Science Foundation, and the Society for the Psychological Study of Social Issues.

Jeff Gavin, PhD, is a Senior Lecturer in the Department of Psychology, University of Bath, and an Adjunct Lecturer in the School of Law and Justice at Edith Cowan University, Australia. As a critical social psychologist, he has established a program of research examining how identities are constructed and negotiated through online communication. His current research explores social media and young people's relationships, online health support, and Internet stalking and other forms of online harassment. As these areas cut across several academic fields, Dr. Gavin's research is often interdisciplinary, involving collaborations with computer scientists, forensic psychologists, and healthcare professionals, as well as industry partners, such as uDate and Match.com. This work involves both textual and visual analyses of online interactions, as well as the design and implementation of online support in collaboration with colleagues in human–computer interaction. On the basis of his own research experience, as well as roles on various university research ethics committees, Dr. Gavin has also co-authored several scholarly articles on online research ethics.

Adam Gazzaley, MD, PhD, obtained an MD and a PhD in neuroscience at the Mount Sinai School of Medicine in New York, completed clinical residency in neurology at the University of Pennsylvania, and postdoctoral training in cognitive neuroscience at the University of California, Berkeley. He is the founding director of the Neuroscience Imaging Center at the University of California, San Francisco, a professor in neurology, physiology, and psychiatry, and principal investigator of a cognitive neuroscience laboratory. His laboratory studies neural mechanisms of perception, attention, and memory, with an emphasis on the impact of distraction and multitasking on these abilities. His unique research approach utilizes a powerful combination of human neurophysiological tools, including functional magnetic resonance imaging (fMRI), electroencephalography (EEG), and transcranial magnetic and electrical stimulation (TMS and TES). A major accomplishment of his research has been to expand our understanding of alterations in the aging brain that lead to cognitive decline. His most recent studies explore how we can enhance our cognitive abilities via engagement with custom-designed video games, and how this can be bolstered by closed loop systems using neurofeedback and TES. Dr. Gazzaley has authored more than 95 scientific articles, delivered more than 350 invited presentations around the world, and his research and perspectives have been consistently profiled in high-impact media, such as *The New York Times, New Yorker, Wall Street Journal, Time, Discover, Wired*, PBS, NPR, CNN, and *NBC Nightly News*. Recently, he wrote and hosted the nationally televised, PBS-sponsored special *The Distracted Mind with Dr. Adam Gazzaley*. Awards and honors for his research include the Pfizer/AFAR Innovations in Aging Award, the Ellison Foundation New Scholar Award in Aging, and the Harold Brenner Pepinsky Early Career Award in Neurobehavioral Science.

Douglas A. Gentile, PhD, is an award-winning research scientist, educator, author, and an Associate Professor of Developmental Psychology at Iowa State University. His experience includes more than 25 years conducting research with children and adults. He is the editor of the book *Media Violence and Children*, and co-author of the book *Violent Video Game Effects on Children and Adolescents: Theory, Research,* *and Public Policy*. He has authored scores of peer-reviewed scientific journal articles, including studies on the positive and negative effects of video games on children in several countries, the validity of the American media ratings, how screen time contributes to youth obesity, and what is being called video game and Internet "addiction." He is the creator and host of the radio show *The Science of Parenting* (and also has a nationally syndicated comedy music radio show, *The Tom & Doug Show*). His work has been featured on National Public Radio, the BBC World Service, CNN, *Good Morning America*, and *The Today Show*, as well as *The New York Times*, *Washington Post*, *Los Angeles Times*, and hundreds of other newspapers and television stations internationally. In 2010, he was honored with the Distinguished Scientific Contributions to Media Psychology Award from the American Psychological Association (Division 46). Princeton Review named him one of the top 300 professors in the United States. Dr. Gentile earned his doctorate in child psychology at the University of Minnesota.

Abbie Grace, PhD, is a lecturer at the Wicking Dementia Research and Education Centre at the University of Tasmania. She recently completed a PhD at the University of Tasmania examining university students' use of text messaging language, specifically their use of textisms (such as *y* for *why*, *btw* for *by the way*, and emoticons such as :o) and :-D). Dr. Grace also investigated the links between students' use of textisms and a variety of factors such as literacy levels, gender, phone technology, opinions on the use of textisms, as well as the year and country in which messages were composed. This doctoral work showed that the use of textisms does not degrade young adults' literacy skills, and that, in fact, students used phone technology quite creatively to enhance the expressivity and efficiency of their phone-based communication. Dr. Grace is now working as a lecturer in the newly created Bachelor of Dementia Care at the University of Tasmania. She is enjoying the opportunity to help students to understand the underlying biological and cognitive processes involved in neurodegeneration, and to learn ways of improving the lives of people experiencing dementia and those who care for them.

Christopher L. Groves, MS, is a third-year graduate student studying social psychology at Iowa State University. He currently works under Dr. Craig Anderson as a member of the Aggression Research Team and regularly collaborates with Dr. Douglas Gentile and his Media Research Lab. Chris received his BA in psychology and English literature at Silver Lake College, at which time he worked as an autism line therapist applying behaviorist techniques to improving the behavioral functioning of children diagnosed with autism spectrum disorder. He received his MS in cognitive-affective psychology from the University of Wisconsin, Oshkosh, working under Dr. David Lishner and Dr. Quin Chrobak. During this time, he conducted research on violent media effects and false memory development. His current research involves examining the influence of media on outcomes such as aggression, moral disengagement, prosocial behavior, problem solving, and attributions regarding success and failure. Most recently, his research has focused on the identification processes at work when viewing violent media that give rise to increases in aggressive behavior. He has co-authored several book chapters on topics including violent media effects on aggression, attention, risk behaviors, prosocial behavior, and video game addiction. Mr. Groves plans to complete his PhD in 2017, at which time he intends to apply for a tenure-track university faculty position.

Anne Jelfs, PhD, is head of the Learning and Teaching Development Team at the UK Open University's Institute of Educational Technology. Dr. Jelfs has 20 years of experience conducting evaluations and her research interests include the application and evaluation of technologies in education. She has published refereed journal articles in this area and also has an interest in the accessibility of educational technology. Her other interests are in the quality assurance of distance education, and her PhD was on stakeholders' conceptions of quality in distance higher education. Her PhD research used a qualitative approach termed phenomenological phenomenography, and qualitative research methods are key to her research designs. Her current work is in two areas: accessibility of disabled students to high-quality learning and teaching and the use of institutional data to support quality assurance processes.

Richard Joiner, PhD, is a Senior Lecturer in the Department of Psychology at the University of Bath and for the past 20 years he has been investigating the impact of gender on the uses of and attitudes toward new digital technology. He has published more than 20 papers in this area and recently has looked at whether the changes in technology (e.g., social networking sites and micro-blogging) have ameliorated or exacerbated the old gender digital divide.

Reynol Junco, EdD, is a social media scholar who investigates the impact of social technologies on college students. Dr. Junco is an Associate Professor of Education and Human–Computer Interaction at Iowa State University and a fellow at the Berkman Center for Internet and Society at Harvard University. Rey's primary research interest is using quantitative methods to analyze the effects of social media on student psychosocial development, engagement, and learning. His research has also focused on informing best practices in using social technologies to enhance learning outcomes. For instance, Rey's research has shown that technology, specifically social media such as Facebook and Twitter, can be used in ways that improve engagement and academic performance. He recently published a book entitled *Engaging Students Through Social Media: Evidence-Based Practices for Use in Student Affairs* with Jossey-Bass.

Daren Kaiser, PhD, is an Associate Professor in the Department of Psychology at Indiana University–Purdue University Fort Wayne (IPFW). He joined the faculty at IPFW in 2003 after spending four years as a visiting professor at East Carolina University. He teaches courses in learning and behavior, biopsychology, psychopharmacology, research methods, and elementary psychology. He received his PhD in experimental psychology with an emphasis in animal learning and cognition from the University of Kentucky in 2000. Since then he has continued his research in animal cognition, publishing papers on the flexibility of animal timing using rats as an animal model. Having broad interests in psychology, he has also collaborated with Drs. Michelle Drouin and Dan Miller, also of the IPFW Psychology Department, in the area of technology and human behavior (particularly as related to cell phone usage and texting). In his free time he enjoys canoeing, and fishing the beautiful northeastern Indiana natural lakes with his wonderful dog Josey.

Nenagh Kemp, PhD, is a Senior Lecturer in Psychology at the University of Tasmania. Her broad research interests lie in the acquisition, development, and use of spoken and written language, from infancy to adulthood, as it occurs both typically and atypically. She is particularly interested in spelling development in children, and the use of spelling strategies in adults, and her doctoral thesis was on these topics. In recent years she has become fascinated with the fast-changing nature of the written language of digital communication. Dr. Kemp enjoys working with students and colleagues to investigate the links between "textese" use and other skills, and to examine the ongoing evolution of this new style of written language. She is currently looking at how people change their use of textese to suit their message recipient. She is also interested in the linguistic and social role of Australian diminutive word forms, such as *arvo* for *afternoon* and *footy* for *football*. Dr. Kemp is an associate editor for the *Journal of Research in Reading* and *Reading and Writing*, and a member of the editorial board of *Scientific Studies of Reading*. She received her bachelor of arts at the University of Tasmania, and her PhD at the University of Oxford.

Mike Kersten is pursuing his doctoral degree in experimental social psychology at Texas Christian University (TCU). He graduated summa cum laude from California State University, Dominguez Hills (CSUDH) with a bachelor's degree in psychology. Working from the perspective of terror management theory (TMT), his research interests focus on how people construct and maintain meaning in life as well as the wide array of social behaviors that people perform in response to existential threats. Some of his work, for example, has examined how thinking about mortality motivates people to unconsciously initiate communicable synchronization (e.g., language style matching) with others as a means of managing existential anxiety. More recently, Mr. Kersten has explored the benefits associated with nostalgia, the sentimental longing for the past. Specifically, his research examined nostalgia's proclivity to increase health optimism, which in turn promotes people to place more importance on their health-relevant goals and engage in greater health behaviors. Mr. Kersten previously served as President of the CSUDH Psi Chi chapter and as an invited member on Psi Chi's Executive Leadership Committee. In 2012, he was awarded Psi Chi's Kay Wilson Leadership Award for Outstanding Chapter President, led his Psi Chi chapter to receive the CSUDH President's Award for Outstanding Academic Achievement, and was named the Outstanding Psychology Student of the Year at CSUDH.

Robin M. Kowalski, PhD, is a Professor of Psychology at Clemson University. She obtained her PhD in social psychology from the University of North Carolina at Greensboro. Her research interests focus primarily on aversive interpersonal behaviors, most notably complaining, teasing, and bullying, with a particular focus on cyberbullying. She is the author or co-author of several books including *Complaining, Teasing, and Other Annoying Behaviors; Social Anxiety; Behaving Badly: Aversive Behaviors in Interpersonal Relationships; The Social Psychology of Emotional and Behavioral Problems; Cyberbullying: Bullying in the Digital Age;* and two curriculum guides related to cyberbullying. Her research on complaining brought her international attention, including an appearance on NBC's *The Today Show*. Dr. Kowalski has received several awards including Clemson University's Award of Distinction, Clemson University's College of Business and Behavioral Science Award for Excellence in Undergraduate Teaching, the Phil Prince Award for Excellence and Innovation in the Classroom, Clemson University's College of Business and Behavioral Science Senior Research Award, Clemson University's Bradbury Award for contributions to the honors college, and the Clemson Board of Trustees

Award for Faculty Excellence. She is a 2013 and 2014 finalist for the South Carolina Governor's Professor of the Year award.

José M. Lara-Ruiz earned his BA in psychology at California State University, Dominguez Hills (CSUDH). He is currently pursuing his MA in clinical psychology at California State University, Northridge. Upon completing his MA, Mr. Lara-Ruiz plans to pursue a doctoral degree in clinical psychology. His research interests include the biopsychosocial factors associated with post-traumatic stress disorder (PTSD). In addition, Mr. Lara-Ruiz is interested in the cognitive sequelae of PTSD and traumatic brain injury. He aspires to conduct research investigating this phenomenon and contribute to treatments that may result in improving functional outcomes in military and non-military populations. Mr. Lara-Ruiz became a member of the George Marsh Applied Cognition Laboratory in January 2013 under Drs. Larry Rosen, L. Mark Carrier, and Nancy Cheever and has assisted in several research projects, including his senior project investigating the effects of PTSD on academic performance and the use of technology as a maladaptive coping mechanism of traumatic events. Moreover, he has assisted in research utilizing functional near-infrared spectroscopy (fNIR) to examine prefrontal cortex activation during tasks of executive functioning. Additionally, Mr. Lara-Ruiz is a research assistant at the Neurocognitive Equipotentiality Recovery and Development Laboratory, at LA BioMed, Harbor UCLA Medical Center. He served as the CSUDH Psi Chi Chapter President and Student Co-Chair of the Ninth Annual CSUDH Student Research Day.

Jessica A. Latack, MA, MS, is a fourth-year doctoral candidate in clinical psychology at Stony Brook University. Her research focuses on psychosocial sequelae of female sexual victimization, and in particular the ways in which sexual trauma affects women's romantic relationships and sexual risk behaviors. More specifically, she is interested in two seemingly opposite subgroups of sexual victims, those who become sexually avoidant and those who engage in increased sexual risk behavior. In an effort to examine the underlying mechanisms between the experience of sexual trauma and subsequent risk behavior, she has begun to investigate potential markers by leveraging attentional and neural measures in response to sexual stimuli.

Ann Lewis, MA, is a second-year doctoral student at Iowa State University. She received both her master's and bachelor's degrees in linguistics at Brigham Young University. Previously, she studied under Dr. Ross Flom in the Brigham Young University Infant Development Lab. Currently, Ms. Lewis studies under Dr. Douglas Gentile in the Iowa State University Media Research Lab and Dr. Kevin Blankenship in the Iowa State University Attitudes and Social Cognition Lab. Her research focuses on the intersection of quantitative communication studies, linguistics, and social psychology. Ms. Lewis' interests cover a broad scope of judgment, concept, and behavioral research. Her previous graduate work focused on the psycholinguistics of prosociality and aggression, as well as the effects of selfish vs. cooperative advertising language on customer service evaluations. Current lines of work include the role of identification and vicarious experience in narrative-based media; the formation, maintenance, and structure of value and attitudes systems; and relationship management through conversation. Ms. Lewis has industry experience in industrial/organizational psychology as a research associate in a corporate communications and behavior change training firm, focusing on trainings for speaking up in high-risk contexts. Ms. Lewis is interested in video gaming both as a method of communication between real people through multi-player modes and as a form of either developer- or player-generated narrative. It is a rich opportunity for both beneficial and destructive learning with the potential for long-term effects on interpersonal relationships and cognitive habits.

Laura E. Levine, PhD, received her PhD in developmental and clinical psychology from the University of Michigan. She worked with children and families at the Children's Psychiatric Hospital and in private practice for 10 years. She is currently a Professor in the Department of Psychological Science and has taught child psychology and lifespan development for 20 years at Central Connecticut State University. She has authored two textbooks: *Child Development: An Active Learning Approach* and *Child Development from Infancy to Adolescence: An Active Learning Approach*. Her research has focused on how media use shapes attention and has been published in the *Journal of Applied Developmental Psychology*, *Computers and Education*, *International Journal of Cyber Behavior, Psychology and Learning*, *American Journal of Media Psychology*, and *CyberPsychology, Behavior, and Social Networking*. Her work on the scholarship of teaching and learning has been published in *New Directions for Teaching and Learning*, *College Teaching* and *International Journal for the Scholarship of Teaching and Learning*. She also studies the social development of toddlers and this work has appeared in *Developmental Psychology* and *Infant and Child Development*. Currently she is combining her interests in early childhood and media with research on the impact of mobile media use by infants and toddlers.

Lin Lin, EdD, is an Associate Professor of Learning Technologies at the University of North Texas. Her research lies at the intersections of technology, cognition, and education. She has conducted research on the design of effective online and blended learning; the impact of media multitasking on cognition and learning; and the power, motivation, ethics, and usability issues related to game-based learning. Lin has published in dozens of academic journals, including the *Proceedings of the National Academy of Sciences* and *Computers and Education*. She has been cited and interviewed by magazines and newspapers such as *Le Temps*, *Ingeniøren*, *Scientific American*, and *Fort Worth Star-Telegram*. Lin received her doctoral degree from Teachers College Columbia University.

Shea McCowen graduated cum laude from Iowa State University in the spring of 2014 with a BA in psychology and a minor in women's studies. She spent several years at ISU working as a research assistant in a variety of laboratories exploring topics such as the effects of media with Dr. Douglas Gentle, and romantic relationships alongside Dr. David Vogel. Additionally, she spent many years as a Community Friend to an individual with a cognitive disability and Prader-Willi syndrome and as a volunteer wildlife rehabilitator. She is currently attending the University of Northern Colorado in Greeley, Colorado, pursuing a master's degree in counseling with a focus on marriage, couples, and family therapy. Once Ms. McCowen has graduated, her highest goal is to open up her own private practice and become a therapist for the community. She intends to offer therapy that provides a focus on positive and healthy sexuality as a space for personal growth and strength, ultimately working to dismantle barriers surrounding issues such as mental illness, sexuality, sexual/gender orientation, and heteronormativity. In her free time Ms. McCowen enjoys spending time with her friends, family, and cat, baking, and supporting local social activism groups.

Aimee D. Miller, MA, obtained her BA in psychology, with honors in the major and her MA in clinical psychology from California State University, Dominguez Hills (CSUDH). Ms. Miller plans to pursue a PhD in clinical psychology with an emphasis in neuropsychology. She aspires to obtain tenure at a research university, where she can conduct research and teach courses in psychology. Her research interests include substance-related disorders and youth risk behaviors. Ms. Miller has been a member of the George Marsh Applied Cognition Laboratory since May 2012, where she has assisted with multiple research studies. She recently completed her master's thesis, which investigated the individual risk factors that increase the likelihood of recruitment, trafficking, and victimization on the Internet. In addition, she has examined the effects of everyday multitasking and media use in the Net Generation, as well as the role of technology in sleep disruption, and assists with research utilizing functional near-infrared spectroscopy to examine executive functioning. Ms. Miller is the former treasurer of the CSUDH Psi Chi chapter and has served as a research assistant, lab manager, student leader, and teaching assistant. She has presented her research at numerous national and regional conferences, and has been the recipient of several academic awards, including the 2014 Outstanding Psychology Student Award; several research awards, including first place at the 2012 and 2014 CSUDH Annual Student Research Day competitions; and scholarships, such as the 2013 Promoting Excellence in Graduate Studies, Student Travel Scholarship from CSUDH.

Daniel A. Miller, PhD, is an Associate Professor in the Department of Psychology at Indiana University–Purdue University, Fort Wayne, where he has been a faculty member since 2005. He teaches courses in elementary psychology, stereotyping and prejudice, statistics, and industrial organizational psychology. Daniel completed his PhD at Purdue University and his undergraduate studies at Ohio State University. His main research interests lie in the area of stereotyping and prejudice and social cognition; in particular, he is interested in the emotional aspects of collective actions in response to social injustice. However, in recent years he has begun collaborations with Drs. Michelle Drouin and Daren Kaiser, also of the IPFW Psychology Department, in the area of social networking and human behavior. In his ever-vanishing spare time, Daniel enjoys Ohio State football, classic cars, and good food, drinks, and live music. Daniel is married to his high school sweetheart and they have two daughters. Daniel has never had a cavity.

Jyoti Mishra, PhD, is an Assistant Professor of Neurology at the University of California, San Francisco (UCSF). She also serves as a Senior Scientist at the Brain Plasticity Institute at PositScience Corporation. Her training is in the field of human cognitive and computational neurosciences, with an emphasis on neural mechanisms of attention and cognitive control. Jyoti's current research focuses on developing and evaluating novel neurotherapeutic tools that enhance cognition in healthy individuals, with further applications in individuals with cognitive impairments, including children with attention deficit disorder (ADHD), underprivileged children with an early life history of stress and abuse, and older adults. These neurotherapeutic tools integrate the latest in software, hardware, and

Internet technologies and their efficacy is rigorously evaluated in randomized controlled trials, conducted in the United States and worldwide via research collaborations in global mental health. In recognition of her work, Dr. Mishra has received the Sandler Biomedical Breakthrough award, the NIH/Fogarty International Clinical Research Fellowship, a National Academies Keck Futures Initiative (NAKFI) grant shared with Dr. Adam Gazzaley, and a UC Global Health Basic Science Award, among other honors.

Megan A. Moreno, MD, MSEd, MPH, is an Associate Professor of Pediatrics at the University of Washington School of Medicine. She is PI of the Social Media and Adolescent Health Research Team (SMAHRT) at Seattle Children's Research Institute. Dr. Moreno's training includes an MD from George Washington University, a master's in education from the University of Wisconsin-Madison, and a master's in public health from the University of Washington. Dr. Moreno's research interests focus on the intersection of technology and adolescent health. SMAHRT is a transdisciplinary research team with emphasis on trainee mentorship, collaboration, and member diversity. Dr. Moreno and her research team focus on three core research areas: innovative approaches to adolescent health using social media, Internet safety education, and measuring technology use and misuse. SMAHRT places emphasis on the development and dissemination of ethical and sound research practices using innovative technologies. Dr. Moreno has provided presentations and served on committee and advisory boards both internationally and nationally regarding adolescent health and social media. Dr. Moreno currently serves as an executive committee member on the American Academy of Pediatrics Committee on Communications and Media. An important aspect of her research is in translation of research findings into practices and tools for use in communities by parents, educators, and providers. She is author of a parenting handbook for Internet safety based on research and collaborations with the American Academy of Practice.

Amanda Nosko, PhD, obtained her doctorate in social and developmental psychology at Wilfrid Laurier University. Her research focuses on disclosure and privacy practices in social networking sites and interventions aimed at promoting safe and effective use of social media for social and educational purposes. In particular, Amanda's research looks at how and why people are so drawn to social media, and whether usage differences exist as a function of various factors including, but not limited to, age, gender, experience, education, and peer culture. Currently, Amanda works as an instructional designer and instructor at Wilfrid Laurier University and the University of Waterloo. She has a well-developed knowledge of effective learning strategies (i.e., adult learning theory) and technologies, and has extensive experience with designing and instructing both in-class and online courses at the post-secondary level.

Beverly Plester, PhD, is a retired Senior Lecturer in Psychology and Honorary Research Fellow at Coventry University. She completed her PhD at the University of Sheffield, and has conducted research into children's use of textspeak and its relationship with traditional literacy measures. She has also studied children's spatial cognition and understanding of aerial photographs, and children's understanding of the speech act of promising.

Sara Prot, MA, completed her master's degree at the University of Zagreb in 2009 and is currently a doctoral candidate at Iowa State University. She is working with

Drs. Craig Anderson and Douglas Gentile, conducting research on aggression, prosocial behavior, media effects, and intergroup conflict.

Megan A. Pumper is a clinical research associate with the Social Media and Adolescent Health Research Team (SMAHRT) at Seattle Children's Research Institute, and she has been with SMAHRT since 2009. She graduated from the University of Wisconsin-Madison in 2012 with degrees in psychology and zoology and is looking to pursue graduate school in the future. Megan's research interests include substance use dependence and mental health predispositions such as depression, specifically how older adolescents are talking about these on social media. She is interested in differences in health displays across the variety of social media websites to which adolescents have access. Ms. Pumper has a particular interest in working with high-risk and international populations.

John T. E. Richardson, PhD, is a Professor of Student Learning and Assessment in the UK Open University's Institute of Educational Technology. He taught psychology for many years at Brunel University and has many publications in that field. He has spent the last 14 years as an educational researcher at the Open University. He specializes in large-scale quantitative surveys on various aspects of the experience of students in higher education (i.e., their approaches to studying, their academic engagement with their courses, and their perceptions of the academic quality of their courses and programs), as well as their academic attainment. He is a fellow of the British Psychological Society, a fellow of the UK Society for Research into Higher Education, and an academician of the UK Academy of Social Sciences.

Karen Rodham, PhD, is a Professor of Health Psychology at Staffordshire University. Her research explores the coping strategies employed by people when they are facing complex and/or chronic health-related problems. The questions that interest her most are those that require an in-depth qualitative approach to answer. More recently her focus has been on exploring how the Internet might be a means of obtaining/providing support for groups who are marginalized, perhaps because they have a taboo health issue (e.g., self-harm) or because they have mobility issues. In addition to her academic role, from 2006 to 2013 Karen was a practicing health psychologist in the National Health Service (NHS). During this time, she worked with people who were living with complex regional pain syndrome (CRPS), known more commonly in the United States as reflex sympathetic dystrophy (RSD). Her interest in ethics stems from her research and practice work that often involved sensitive issues, as well as from her experiences of serving on an NHS ethics committee as an expert panel member and chairing university faculty ethics committees.

Jeffrey Rokkum, MA, is the first in his family to attend college, and received his MA in clinical psychology in summer of 2014. Mr. Rokkum holds a special interest in the study of belief formation and how technology interacts with beliefs. Currently he mentors psychology undergraduate students in the George Marsh Applied Cognition Laboratory at California State University, Dominguez Hills while working on his independent projects under Drs. Larry Rosen, L. Mark Carrier, and Nancy Cheever. He maintains an active research role and just finished conducting a study on technology usage and fantasy proneness predicting magical beliefs. When he isn't attached to his various technologies (or attempting to acquire more technologies), he spends time outside hiking or photographing the wilderness.

Andrew Richard Schrock is a PhD candidate at the Annenberg School for Communication and Journalism at the University of Southern California (USC). His research focuses on practices and politics related to emergent media, particularly mobile communication, social media, and open data movements. Andrew received his BA in computer science from Brandeis University, successively working as a software engineer and freelance journalist for five years. At the University of Central Florida he taught applied courses in the Digital Media Department and wrote a thesis on habitual use of MySpace. Upon arriving in California he taught at CSU Long Beach and USC while serving as a research assistant to danah boyd at the Harvard Berkman Center for Internet and Society. He is currently part of several research groups including Civic Paths, the Annenberg Innovation Lab, and Open Data LA.

Nancy Signorielli, PhD (University of Pennsylvania, 1975), is Professor of Communication and Director of the MA program in communication at the University of Delaware. Beginning with her dissertation research, an in-depth methodological examination of television characters, she has conducted research on images in the media and how these images are related to people's conceptions of social reality (cultivation analysis) for the past 45 years. She is an original member of the Cultural Indicators Research Team. She has written and/or edited eight single- and co-authored books and published more than 100 journal articles and book chapters, as well as numerous research/grant reports and encyclopedia entries. She has made more than 150 presentations at invitational conferences as well as the annual conferences of the discipline's major organizations. She testified in May 1993 at House Energy and Commerce committee's subcommittee on telecommunications and finance oversight hearing on television violence and its impact on children. Her current research focuses on portrayals of aging, gender roles, occupations, minorities, and violence on prime-time network television. Dr. Signorielli teaches courses on mass communication, research methods, children and the media, and media message analysis. She has served on the editorial boards of several communication journals, and serves as an ad hoc reviewer for numerous journals. She has been noted as a prolific communication scholar, named a Centennial Scholar of the Eastern Communication Association in 2009, and received the Distinguished Scholar Award of the Broadcast Education Association in 2010.

David Šmahel, PhD, is an Associate Professor at the Institute of Children, Youth, and Family Research, Masaryk University, the Czech Republic. He directs the Interdisciplinary Research Team on Internet and Society workgroup, which researches social-psychological implications of the Internet and technology. His current research focuses on adolescents' and adults' Internet use, the risks and online problematic situations of children and adolescents, the construction of online identities, virtual relationships, and online addictive behavior. He is editor of *Cyberpsychology: Journal of Psychosocial Research on Cyberspace* and has co-authored the book *Digital Youth: The Role of Media in Development*. Dr. Šmahel led a cross-cultural qualitative investigation in nine European countries within the EU Kids Online III project and is author of the relevant report, *The Meaning of Online Problematic Situations for Children*. Dr. Šmahel has also published in several international journals such as *Developmental Psychology*, *Cyberpsychology and Behavior*, *Zeitschrift für Psychologie*, *European Journal of Developmental Psychology*, and others. He is also author of several book chapters in anthologies, including the *Encyclopedia of Cyber Behavior*,

Encyclopedia of Adolescence, Internet Addiction: A Handbook and Guide to Evaluation and Treatment, and *Gesundheit und Neue Medien*.

Caroline Stewart, BSc, is a research assistant in the School of Management at the University of Bath and has been working on projects investigating the role of new digital technology to support children's learning and development.

Kaveri Subrahmanyam, PhD, is Professor of Psychology at California State University, Los Angeles and Associate Director of the Children's Digital Media Center @ Los Angeles (UCLA/CSULA). In 2013, she was a recipient of the CSULA Outstanding Professor Award. Dr. Subrahmanyam is a nationally recognized expert regarding the effect of interactive media on children and adolescents. She also conducts research on dual language development, and studies Latino children's learning of Spanish and English. Dr. Subrahmanyam studies the cognitive and social implications of interactive media use. She conducted one of the first training studies showing the effects of computer game use on spatial skills. Subsequently she studied the developmental implications of chat rooms, blogs, social networking sites, and virtual worlds (e.g., Second Life) with a focus on the development of identity and intimacy. She is currently studying the relation between digital communication and well-being, the cognitive implications of digital media and multitasking, as well as the relation between Latino pre-school children's home media use and their oral language development. Dr. Subrahmanyam has published several research articles and book chapters on youth and digital media and has co-edited a special issue on social networking for the *Journal of Applied Developmental Psychology* (2008) and a special section on interactive media and human development for *Developmental Psychology* (2012). She is the co-author (with Dr. David Šmahel) of *Digital Youth: The Role of Media in Development* (2010).

Jean M. Twenge, PhD, is a Professor of Psychology at San Diego State University, the author of more than 100 scientific publications, and author or co-author of two books: *Generation Me: Why Today's Young Americans Are More Confident, Assertive, Entitled – and More Miserable Than Ever Before* and *The Narcissism Epidemic: Living in the Age of Entitlement* (co-authored with W. Keith Campbell). Dr. Twenge frequently gives talks and seminars on teaching and working with today's young generation based on a dataset of 11 million young people. Her audiences have included college faculty and staff, high school teachers, military personnel, camp directors, and corporate executives. Her research has been covered in *Time, Newsweek, The New York Times, USA Today, U.S. News & World Report*, and *The Washington Post*, and she has been featured on *The Today Show, Good Morning America, CBS This Morning, Fox and Friends, NBC Nightly News, Dateline NBC*, and National Public Radio. She holds a BA and MA from the University of Chicago and a PhD from the University of Michigan.

Ludivina Vasquez was a member and research assistant at the George Marsh Applied Cognition (GMAC) Laboratory at California State University, Dominguez Hills (CSUDH) from 2010 to 2012. As an undergraduate, Ms. Vasquez was also a member of the Minority Biomedical Research Support Research Initiative for Scientific Enhancement, which afforded her the opportunity to present her research at both regional and national conferences on topics related to risky online and offline behavior. Ms. Vasquez was also a teaching assistant for several upper- and lower-division psychology courses at CSUDH and was a member of both Psi Chi, the National Honor

Society in Psychology, and the Honor Society of Phi Kappa Phi. She graduated from CSUDH with honors and was awarded both the Presidential Award for Personal Perseverance and the Presidential Outstanding Student Award. Currently, Ms. Vasquez is a graduate student at the University of Tulsa where she is earning her master's in clinical psychology. She is a member and research assistant at the Study of Prevention, Adjustment, and Resilience to Trauma and Adversity research lab and the University of Tulsa Institute of Trauma, Adversity, and Injustice. After graduating, Ms. Vasquez hopes to work in a school setting, preferably with at-risk or disadvantaged youth.

Petra Vondráčková, PhD, is a lecturer at Charles University in Prague and General University Hospital in Prague, First Faculty of Medicine, Department of Addictology, Czech Republic. She is a co-author of an online self-help program for people with Internet addiction. As a clinical psychologist and psychotherapist she has rich experience in working with people with mental illness. Her current research interests include Internet addiction and attachment.

Bradley M. Waite, PhD (Kent State University), is an experimental psychologist. He is Professor and former Chairperson of the Department of Psychological Science at Central Connecticut State University. He has long been interested in the ethics of research, and served administratively as the Chairperson of the CCSU Institutional Review Board where he had oversight of university research ethics compliance processes for more than 20 years. He has studied the impact of media and taught courses in media psychology for nearly 30 years. Dr. Waite also teaches courses at the graduate and undergraduate level in developmental psychology and research methodology. His primary research interests are in media psychology. His perspective is embedded in developmental psychology. Dr. Waite's research focuses on the impact of electronic media use on individuals by examining connections among media use, multitasking, and psychological dimensions such as cognition, attention, distractibility, and aggression. Dr. Waite is also interested in "real-life" issues associated with the ethics of research and in exploring the uses of *in situ* research strategies. He believes in the efficacy of collaborative research endeavors with colleagues and students and regularly serves as a research mentor to graduate and undergraduate students on a broad spectrum of media-related topics. He is an active member of several professional organizations including the American Psychological Association, the Association for Psychological Science, and Public Responsibility in Medicine and Research.

Sam Waldron, BSc, graduated from Aston University with a BSc in human psychology in 2010. She has since been working as a researcher based at Coventry University, within the Centre for Research in Psychology, Behaviour, and Achievement. Her research interests focus mainly on the impact of new technologies upon language skills in both children and adults. To date she has co-authored several journal articles examining the impact of text messaging and textism use upon spelling and grammatical abilities in primary school, secondary school, and undergraduate cohorts. These studies have been published in several journals, including the *British Journal of Developmental Psychology, Computers and Education*, and the *Journal of Reading and Writing*. She is currently looking at the impact predictive text use has upon both textism use and grammatical ability. She also intends to extend her work by examining the differences between intentional and unintentional texting errors. She is also interested in attitudinal differences between traditional and digital reading formats.

Nicole E. Werner, PhD, received her doctorate in human factors and applied cognition in the George Mason University Department of Psychology. Her research focuses on interrupted and multiple task management, communication and team coordination, error analysis and prevention, as well as applying human factors to improve patient safety and healthcare systems. She has studied interrupted task performance in a variety of settings including the laboratory, the pharmacy, in nursing, and in trauma resuscitation teams. Her research has focused on bridging theoretical concepts related to interrupted task management developed in the laboratory into real-world settings. Ms. Werner is also a research analyst at the Johns Hopkins University School of Medicine in the Division of Geriatric Medicine and Gerontology as well as the Johns Hopkins University School of Nursing Center for Innovative Care in Aging, and a member of the Johns Hopkins Medicine Armstrong Institute for Patient Safety and Quality. She is a Telluride Patient Safety Roundtable Scholar and recipient of the 2014 Human Factors and Ergonomics Society Student Member with Honors award.

Elizabeth Whittaker is a student at Clemson University majoring in psychology with a focus on statistics. Elizabeth's primary research focus is on cyberbullying and the use of social media in cyber aggression.

Clare Wood, PhD, is Professor of Psychology in Education at Coventry University and the Director of the Centre for Research in Psychology, Behaviour, and Achievement. Her research interests over the last 20 years include the early identification and remediation of literacy difficulties in children, the relationships between speech and written language skills, and the educational potential of technology. In 2000 she was awarded the Reading/Literacy Research Fellowship by the International Reading Association and in 2006 she received the British Psychological Society's award for Excellence in the Teaching of Psychology. She is committed to developing more integrated theoretical accounts of literacy attainment and understanding the ecology of reading difficulties.

Eileen Wood, PhD, is a Professor in the Department of Psychology at Wilfrid Laurier University. With degrees in both developmental and instructional psychology, her primary research interests involve examining how children, youth, and adults (emerging through older) acquire, maintain, and reproduce information in educational contexts. One of her research programs investigates traditional instructional strategies that facilitate learning and memory. A second program investigates the use of technology as instructional tools and its impact on instructors and learners. This research examines new instructional technologies relative to traditional instructional strategies, and as unique instructional opportunities. In addition, she examines the use and impact of using computers, digital technology, and mobile technologies for social purposes both in and out of the classroom. She has published numerous research articles, chapters, and textbooks. She has been recognized for her strengths as an instructor and researcher. She is the recipient of the University Teaching Excellence Award, the Hoffman-Little Award for Teaching Excellence, and the OCUFA Teaching Excellence Award. She is also the recipient of the Research Professor Award. In addition, two of her textbooks were awarded Book of the Year awards. She is currently investigating on-task multitasking when using technology in the classroom and parent–child social interactions with mobile devices.

David A. Ziegler, PhD, is a postdoctoral scholar in the Department of Neurology at the University of California, San Francisco. He completed his PhD in systems neuroscience in the Department of Brain and Cognitive Sciences at the Massachusetts Institute of Technology where he took a cutting-edge multimodal neuroimaging approach to examine the effects of healthy aging and Parkinson's disease on cognitive control systems in the brain. The current focus of his research is on unmasking the neural mechanisms that account for age-related changes in cognitive control and to translate these basic neuroscience findings into cognitive neurotherapeutic interventions to alleviate impairments in attention in diverse populations. He has a particular interest in merging complementary approaches, such as meditation and yoga, with neuroplasticity-based interventions to improve cognition while also enhancing overall well-being. Dr. Ziegler has received numerous awards including a UCSF School of Medicine Technology Transformation Grant, a Human Brain Mapping Trainee Travel Award, the Angus MacDonald Award for Excellence in Undergraduate Teaching at MIT, the Denison University President's Medal, and was a two-time recipient of the Harvard/MIT/MGH Advanced Multimodal Neuroimaging Training Program Fellowship. His research has been featured in *The New York Times*, the Faculty of 1000, the MIT Spotlight, *Nature Outlook*, and in numerous regional media outlets.

Lucia Zivcakova is a PhD candidate in the developmental psychology program at Wilfrid Laurier University working under the supervision of Dr. Eileen Wood. Dr. Zivcakova examines how numerous educational tools and practices impact student behavior, with special interest in examining the impact of technology use on students' learning behaviors. More specifically, her primary research focuses on examining how students use technologies to supplement more traditional learning methods, and how such media multitasking behaviors in and outside of the classroom impact their learning. Lucia's secondary research investigates students' understanding, perceptions, and behaviors regarding academic integrity and misconduct. Dr. Zivcakova is especially interested in designing academic integrity interventions and examining the effectiveness of these interventions with regards to lowering levels of academic misconduct, increasing awareness, and creating a campus atmosphere of the high importance of academic integrity.

Preface

In the beginning (*c.*1969) there was the ARPANET, which provided an interconnected network for Defense Advanced Research Project Agency (DARPA) to connect universities that had defense department contracts and other professionals doing government work. Initially, only a couple of universities were online but more came quickly. Before long ARPANET split into MILNET for military work and NSFNET and several other government-based networks and in a matter of less than 20 years, the Internet was born. What followed was quite literally an explosion from connecting over a 300-baud-rate modem where you placed your phone in a rubber coupler, listened to the beeps and buzzes, and then watched as character after character emerged slowly on a dot matrix printer. To someone who was there it was magic.

People who had the Internet in the early 1980s were able to access ARCHIE, GOPHER, MELVYN, and USENET and find information and people far and wide. The communication was slow, but it was thrilling. Principal investigators working on grants were able to connect online in an ongoing discussion. Wading through many lines of old messages was required in order to get to the new ones, but it was amazing to be able to leave a message for another PI and find a response a day or so later. It has been an interesting ride from the early 1980s to current day and those nearly three decades have seen the slow buildup of the text-based Internet through the 1980s until the development of the World Wide Web and Mosaic in the 1990s, which allowed us to use a graphical environment to go far beyond the simple line-based system that we had just grown accustomed to in the past decade. Mosaic turned into Netscape Navigator – which also included a simple tool to build your own website – and Navigator begat a string of browsers, each with their own quirks and possibilities. Browsers needed a means of finding information and so search engines were born. Search engines such as Alta Vista and Lycos and other metasearch engines such as WebCrawler and Dogpile provided a means to search the Internet by searching the search engines. Eventually, in the late 1990s Google was introduced and all the other search engines that followed provided intense competition for our eyeballs and questions.

All of what people could do online needed to be done on a rather large, by today's standards, desktop computer, which began with the IBM PC and Apple series until the desire to have a computer that was portable led to laptops such as the IBM-PC Convertible, Apple PowerBook, and entries into the portable computing field by Compaq, Toshiba, Commodore, and others. As demand for portability increased, smaller and smaller "laptops" emerged including Netbooks and eventually Chromebooks. When even smaller devices were desired, personal data assistants (PDAs) emerged on the scene, including the early versions of the Palm Pilot and the BlackBerry, which allowed Internet access and other functions typically done on a computer system.

But that was not enough for us and when in 1999 the Japanese company NTT DoCoMo released a "smartphone" that incorporated the qualities found in a cell phone or mobile phone – which had been in existence for several years but did not allow Internet access – the world changed dramatically. While the Japanese embraced their smartphone, it was not until Research in Motion released the BlackBerry that smartphones took off in America in the early 2000s. And took off they did! Within a scant 10 years we have gone from a society that embraced the Internet on machines that either resided semi-permanently on a desk or sat somewhat uncomfortably on a lap to a small device that nearly every person in America carries in their pocket or purse. While cell phones – those without all the advanced features of smartphone – were the standard until the early 2000s, the smartphone has become increasingly more popular. According to Statista,[1] a company that compiles statistics from around the globe, 11% of the 2008 U.S. population owned a smartphone and that has increased to 81% in 2015. eMarketer,[2] a digital marketing, media, and commerce company, estimates that there are nearly 2 billion smartphone users in the world and that two-fifths of all mobile phone users own a smartphone. eMarketer predicts that by 2017, 50% of mobile phone users worldwide will be using a smartphone.

The smartphone has certainly been a game changer in our world and because so many of us now carry a powerful Internet computer – complete with dozens of applications that do anything from shop to play music to provide video to literally anything you can imagine – all day long and, for many, all night long, too. The purpose of this handbook is to provide a snapshot of how this ubiquitous online access to information, communication, entertainment, products, and so much more has affected us on a variety of levels. The literature on the psychology of technology is too broad to cover in one publication, even one with 30 chapters. Nonetheless, the chapters that follow examine the impact on all aspects of our lives and provide, in many cases, an outlook for the future and, in others, a prescription for maintaining mental and physical health. We have ventured around the world to provide readers with the most up-to-date research and scholarship from Australia, Canada, the Czech Republic, Germany, the United Kingdom, and the United States.

Our authors are most prestigious and have won numerous awards and accolades, including the following:

- Dr. L. Mark Carrier, Dr. Larry D. Rosen, and Dr. Kaveri Subrahmanyam won Outstanding Professor Awards on their campuses.
- Dr. Adam Gazzaley: Pfizer/AFAR Innovations in Aging Award, the Ellison Foundation New Scholar Award in Aging, and the Harold Brenner Pepinsky Early Career Award in Neurobehavioral Science.
- Dr. Douglas Gentile: Distinguished Scientific Contributions to Media Psychology Award from the American Psychological Association (Division 46).
- Dr. Robin Kowalski: Clemson University's Award of Distinction, Clemson University's College of Business and Behavioral Science Award for Excellence in Undergraduate Teaching, the Phil Prince Award for Excellence and Innovation in the Classroom, Clemson University's College of Business and Behavioral Science Senior Research Award, Clemson University's Bradbury Award for contributions to the honors college, and the Clemson Board of Trustees Award for Faculty Excellence.

- Dr. Clare Wood: British Psychological Society's award for Excellence in the Teaching of Psychology.
- Dr. Eileen Wood: University Teaching Excellence Award, the Hoffman-Little Award for Teaching Excellence, and the OCUFA Teaching Excellence Award.
- Dr. David Ziegler: UCSF School of Medicine Technology Transformation Grant, a Human Brain Mapping Trainee Travel Award, the Angus MacDonald Award for Excellence in Undergraduate Teaching at MIT, the Denison University President's Medal, and was a two-time recipient of the Harvard/MIT/MGH Advanced Multimodal Neuroimaging Training Program Fellowship.

Our authors have also been active in research and other scholarly activities, publishing literally hundreds, if not thousands, of journal articles, edited journals, and have written seminal books in this field:

- Dr. Deborah Boehm-Davis is co-author of the textbook *An Introduction to Humans in Engineered Systems* and co-editor of the forthcoming *Handbook of Human-Systems Integration*. Served as an associate editor for *Human Factors* and the *International Journal of Human–Computer Studies* and on the editorial boards of several journals.
- Dr. Mark Brosnan published a book entitled *Technophobia: The Psychological Impact of Information Technology*.
- Dr. W. Keith Campbell is the author of more than 100 scientific journal articles and book chapters, and the books *When You Love a Man Who Loves Himself: How to Deal with a One-way Relationship*; *The Narcissism Epidemic: Living in the Age of Entitlement* (with Jean Twenge); and *The Handbook of Narcissism and Narcissistic Personality Disorder: Theoretical Approaches, Empirical Findings, and Treatments* (with Josh Miller). He and Jean Twenge also have a personality textbook, *Personality Psychology: Understanding Yourself and Others*, to be published in 2015.
- Dr. L. Mark Carrier co-authored *Rewired: Understanding the iGeneration and the Way They Learn* and *iDisorder: Understanding Our Obsession with Technology and Overcoming Its Hold on Us*.
- Dr. Nancy A. Cheever co-authored *Rewired: Understanding the iGeneration and the Way They Learn* and *iDisorder: Understanding Our Obsession with Technology and Overcoming Its Hold on Us*.
- Dr. Douglas Gentile is editor of *Media Violence and Children: A Complete Guide for Parents and Professionals*, and co-author of the book *Violent Video Game Effects on Children and Adolescents: Theory, Research, and Public Policy*.
- Dr. Reynol Junco is the author of *Engaging Students Through Social Media: Evidence-Based Practices for Use in Student Affairs*.
- Dr. Robin Kowalski is the author or co-author of several books, including *Complaining, Teasing, and Other Annoying Behaviors*, *Social Anxiety*, *Aversive Interpersonal Behaviors*, *Behaving Badly*, *The Social Psychology of Emotional and Behavioral Problems*, *Cyberbullying: Bullying in the Digital Age*.
- Dr. Laura Levine co-authored *Child Development: An Active Learning Approach* and *Child Development from Infancy to Adolescence: An Active Learning Approach*.
- Dr. Larry D. Rosen is the author of *Me, MySpace and I: Parenting the Net Generation* and co-authored *TechnoStress: Coping With Technology @Work, @Home,*

@Play, The Mental Health Technology Bible, Rewired: Understanding the iGeneration and the Way They Learn and *iDisorder: Understanding Our Obsession With Technology and Overcoming its Hold on Us.*

- Dr. David Šmahel is editor of *Cyberpsychology: Journal of Psychosocial Research on Cyberspace* and co-authored the book *Digital Youth: The Role of Media in Development.*
- Dr. Nancy Signorielli authored or co-authored *Violence and Terror in the Mass Media: An Annotated Bibliography* and *Violence in the Media: A Reference Handbook.*
- Dr. Kaveri Subrahmanyam co-authored *Digital Youth: The Role of Media in Development.*
- Dr. Jean Twenge authored *Generation Me: Why Today's Young Americans Are More Confident, Assertive, Entitled – and More Miserable Than Ever Before* and co-authored *The Narcissism Epidemic: Living in the Age of Entitlement* and *Psychology of Personality.*

Although our authors are clearly exceptional, some have been honored as being top in their respective fields:

- Dr. Douglas Gentile was named one of the top 300 professors in the United States by Princeton Review.
- Dr. Megan Moreno is an executive committee member on the American Academy of Pediatrics Committee on Communications and Media.
- Dr. Nancy Signorielli testified in May 1993 at the U.S. House of Representatives Energy and Commerce committee's subcommittee on telecommunications and finance oversight hearing on television violence and its impact on children.
- Dr. Deborah Boehm-Davis served as a Senior Policy Advisor for Human Factors at the Food and Drug Administration's Center for Devices and Radiological Health. She has also served as President and Secretary-Treasurer of the Human Factors and Ergonomics Society (HFES) and as President of Division 21 (Applied Experimental and Engineering Psychology) of the American Psychological Association (APA). She has testified before Congress, and served on numerous panels for the National Research Council, National Research Foundation, Transportation Research Board, and NASA. She was a member and chair of the Federal Aviation Administration's Research, Engineering, and Development Advisory Committee, as well as their Human Factors Subcommittee. She was a member of the Air Force Scientific Advisory Board and the Transportation Security Administration's Scientific Advisory Board.

Finally, many of our authors have appeared on and/or in numerous national and international programs and publications including *The Today Show*, CNN, MSNBC, PBS, NPR, *The Wall Street Journal*, BBC World News, *The New York Times*, *Scientific American*, *Dateline NBC*, *U.S. News & World Report*, *The Washington Post*, and *The Daily Show with Jon Stewart*.

This handbook is divided into sections that cover this title's major areas of study. While certainly not exhaustive, the handbook provides an excellent overview of the field.

Part I: The Psychology of Technology

The first section includes chapters that encompass broad areas of research such as the impact of technology on the brain, generational similarities and differences in technology use and values, Internet credibility and information literacy, ethical concerns in online research, and issues of age and gender. In "The Acute and Chronic Impact of Technology on our Brain," David A. Ziegler, Jyoti Mishra, and Adam Gazzaley present a review of the existing literature on how technology affects the human brain. They write that it is "unquestionable that innovations in technology and media will continue at a lightning pace, resulting in new methods for interacting with our worlds and bringing with them new sources of distractions, as well as potential avenues for enhancing our lives." How these technologies affect our brains is complicated and often controversial. The literature points to both positive and negative effects of using technology on the brain, including some "profoundly promising aspects of how new technologies might be harnessed to enhance cognition in at-risk populations, leading to better lives."

In the next chapter, "Similarities and Differences in Workplace, Personal, and Technology-Related Values, Beliefs, and Attitudes Across Five Generations of Americans," handbook co-editor Larry D. Rosen and José M. Lara-Ruiz present a research study that examines values, beliefs, and attitudes among members of five generations of Americans. Beginning with an introduction to how researchers have conceptualized generations in the past, Rosen and Lara-Ruiz provide data on more than 2,500 people who provided an assessment of their personal, work, and technology-related values, beliefs, and attitudes as well as their use of technology. Drawing on generational comparisons and trend analyses, this chapter argues that technology has altered our understanding of generations and that due to the rapid pace of technological change, we must consider that generations no longer span 20 years but instead form mini-generations of half that length.

Handbook co-editor Nancy A. Cheever and Jeffrey Rokkum examine the literature and significance of Internet source credibility and information literacy in the chapter "Internet Credibility and Digital Media Literacy." They write that as technology continues to expand people's access to information, the variability of accuracy and believability (or credibility) of that information increases, and policies to verify Internet content are practically nonexistent. They conclude that while people do understand differences in credibility exist among Internet sources, they tend to judge websites based on the way they look rather than their content. Digital media literacy is a process and a skill that is developed over time. Research into programs to increase awareness of credibility issues and enhance digital media literacy points to a need for greater content assessment and teaching the process of evaluating sources rather than simply teaching people how to search for information.

Next, in "Gender Digital Divide: Does it Exist and What are the Explanations?" Richard Joiner, Caroline Stewart, and Chelsey Beaney from the University of Bath present three studies that track the differences in uses of the Internet by men and women through studies performed at a variety of UK universities over a 10-year period. The authors present an excellent and interesting case for the continuing existence of a secondary digital divide that still exists to this day and conclude that much of this rests on the differential uses of the Internet by men and women, where women use it primarily for communication and men for entertainment.

John T. E. Richardson and Anne Jelfs review the basis of data and opinion about differences between digital natives and digital immigrants in "Access and Attitudes to Digital Technologies Across the Adult Lifespan: Evidence from Distance Education." The authors chose to use a large sample of distance education students who are less likely to be typical college students but also more likely to need to use technology to complete their studies. The authors describe their study of a large sample of students of different ages and make comparisons by age of response rates, use of and access to different technologies, attitudes toward technology use, and approaches to studying. Results are described in tables and in the text and conclusions are drawn about how there may not need to be a distinction between digital natives and digital immigrants in this environment.

Finally, in "Navigating Psychological Ethics in Shared Multi-User Online Environments," Jeff Gavin and Karen Rodham explore the challenges of privacy and confidentiality in online research. They write that the Internet has become an invaluable resource for researchers interested in contemporary social and psychological practices. The expansion of psychological research into the online milieu brings with it new ethical challenges, particularly in terms of consent, privacy, and confidentiality. As a consequence, a number of authors have written about practical and ethical considerations with regard to online research. Current guidelines do not address the ethical and methodological challenges posed by the changing trends in Internet use, which now include multi-author and multimedia sites such as Facebook, Twitter, MySpace, and YouTube. The authors draw from their experience as researchers of online identities, support, and coping to explore how decisions about public and private spaces, informed consent, and anonymity are addressed in online environments containing several layers of text, image, and audio-visual input from multiple sources across multiple, linked sites.

Part II: Children, Teens, and Technology

The second section of the handbook examines the impact of technology on youth and young adults. In "Executive Function in Risky Online Behaviors by Adolescents and Young Adults," a research team from the George Marsh Applied Cognition Laboratory at California State University, Dominguez Hills presents an empirical research study examining the link between executive function and risky online behaviors. Based on their research, the authors conclude that executive function is a relevant factor when considering the causes of risky online behaviors by teens and young adults. They suggest that "more research is needed in order to examine the possibility that the act of going online itself leads to changes in executive function," and that "more information is required to understand the details of how individual differences in executive function affect risky online behaviors." They write that "acknowledging developmental differences in executive function can also help to improve prevention work in adolescents and young adults by building on their existing executive function" skills. The authors suggest that "software and website designers should put safeguards into programs and online environments where possible and allow for parental controls."

In the review chapter "Cyberbullying: Prevalence, Causes, and Consequences," Robin M. Kowalski and Elizabeth Whittaker cover the definition of cyberbullying, compare and contrast cyberbullying with traditional bullying, relate the characteristics of victims and perpetrators, and list the consequences of cyberbullying for victims and perpetrators. Cyberbullying encompasses a range of aggressive behaviors that involve the use of electronic communication technologies. Although cyberbullying and traditional bullying share three primary features of aggression, power imbalance, and repeated behaviors, cyberbullying differs from traditional bullying in the anonymity that surrounds the behaviors and in the increased accessibility of the victim. Several person and situational variables are related to victim and perpetrator involvement in cyberbullying, including social intelligence, hyperactivity, and risky online behavior for victims and empathy, narcissism, depression, and anxiety for perpetrators. Victims of cyberbullying experience several negative physical and psychological problems, while being a perpetrator is associated with a range of negative factors. Kowalski and Whittaker presse for more research on defining and measuring cyberbullying and more longitudinal research on cyberbullying.

Next, in "A Step Toward Understanding Cross-National and Cross-Cultural Variances in Cyberbullying," Fatih Bayraktar is interested in understanding variations in cyberbullying and cybervictimization rates across nations and cultures. He proposes that part of the explanation for the variations is found in two key psychological constructs whose values depend upon one's nation or culture. The two key constructs are femininity/masculinity and independent/interdependent self-construal. Using data collected from a sample of university students, Bayraktar tested two different models of the relationship between the constructs and cyberbullying/cybervictimization. The author suggests that masculinity and independent self-construal are strongly associated with respect to cyberbullying and that independent self-construal is a protective factor against cybervictimization in those with strong femininity.

In "Sexual Communication in the Digital Age," Michelle Drouin reviews the known research on the topic of "sexting," defined as the transmission of sexually explicit material via cell phone and the Internet. The chapter begins with a description of the various electronic avenues that people use for sexting, discusses the prevalence rates of sexting, reviews research on the content of "sext" messages, considers the motivations, risk factors, and consequences of sexting, and ends with brief summaries of new directions in sexting research. The new directions include sexting compliance and coercion, and couples using sexting for computer-mediated sexual communication.

Drouin and her colleagues Daren Kaiser and Daniel A. Miller tackle "Mobile Phone Dependency: What's All the Buzz About?" In this chapter, the authors discuss the phenomenon of problematic mobile phone use (a.k.a. mobile phone dependency), defined as "mobile phone use that causes problems in a user's life." The authors summarize the literature on problematic mobile phone use, noting that the differences in the existing findings partly might be attributable to differences in socio-cultural, historical, or methodological factors. The possible effects of prolonged text messaging use are described, including decreased face-to-face socializing, increased anxiety and dependence, and phantom vibrations. New directions for research are presented, two of which are the recognition and treatment of problematic mobile phone use and using mobile phones as mechanisms for behavior change.

The next few chapters look at text messaging. In "Assessing the Written Language of Text Messages," Abbie Grace and Nenagh Kemp explain that the twentieth anniversary of the first text message was celebrated in December 2012. In 2012, 8.5 trillion messages were sent. The development of a text messaging "language" during this rapid growth has prompted researchers to observe a rapidly forming and changing style of communication and to investigate the factors that influence its development. The authors explain that "the ability of texters to participate in textism-rich conversations and to further develop text messaging language style can be seen as an addition to, not a deletion from, their overall set of literacy skills." The authors discovered that textisms have little or no negative effect on conventional literacy skills, and in fact the use of textisms seems to have communicative value unique to the informal social and technological environment in which it is situated.

In "Texting Behavior and Language Skills in Children and Adults," the research team of Sam Waldron, Nenagh Kemp, Beverly Plester, and Clare Wood provide a literature review of the connection between texting behavior and language skills. The authors summarize the results of studies that look at reading ability, spelling ability, phonology, grammatical ability, and general writing. Additionally, the writers note several methodological problems in running texting studies, including problems with self-report measures and issues related to how textisms are measured. The review concludes that the relationship between texting and language skills depends on the age bracket considered, with some evidence suggesting that texting might be beneficial for children. For adolescents and adults, there is not a clear relationship between the behavior and language skills.

Finally, in "Are 'Friends' Electric? Why Those with an Autism Spectrum Disorder (ASD) Thrive in Online Cultures but Suffer in Offline Cultures," Mark Brosnan and Jeff Gavin discuss the ways in which participation in online communities by people with autism spectrum disorder can enhance their interpersonal relationship where they may otherwise struggle in offline communities. The authors present research projects involving persons who use Facebook and self-identify as having ASD. The first study established that persons with ASD have a preference for online communication over offline communication. The second study established that emotion is expressed online by those with ASD. The third study showed that persons with ASD can engage in empathic interactions online. In summary, the authors found that persons with ASD engaged in "normal" communication and interaction in an online context.

Part III: Social Media

Part III examines the phenomenon of social networking platforms from a variety of perspectives. In the review chapter "Social Networking and Depression," Brian A. Feinstein, Vickie Bhatia, Jessica A. Latack, and Joanne Davila present an examination of the association between social networking site (SNS) use and depression. The authors present a thorough review of the existing literature on SNS use and depression, and explain its prevalence and associated risk factors. The authors conclude that negative experiences and social comparisons on SNSs as well as using the Internet to the point of experiencing negative consequences in one's offline life are both associated with depressive symptoms, while *only* the amount of time using SNSs is not related to depression. It is the quality, not the quantity, of social networking that better predicts depression.

In "Sex, Alcohol, and Depression: Adolescent Health Displays on Social Media," Megan A. Moreno and Megan Pumper review the issue of adolescent health risk behavior on social media from an explanatory perspective using previous empirical research. The authors present an overview of health risk displays such as alcohol use, sexual activity, and depression, and the consequences relating to such behavior. "Exploring Disclosure and Privacy in a Digital Age: Risks and Benefits" explores issues of privacy and disclosure in social networking, offering an overview of the area from face-to-face communication to contemporary digital settings. Karin Archer, Emily Christofides, Amanda Nosko, and Eileen Wood focus on risks and benefits, with practical advice for discouraging over-disclosure and maximizing privacy. In the next chapter, "The Emergence of Mobile Social Network Platforms on the Mobile Internet," Andrew Richard Schrock examines mobile social networking from a variety of perspectives, first summarizing the developments leading to mobile social network platforms and then explaining how these platforms represent a shift from traditional desktop to mobile social network paradigms. The author then examines three specific mobile social network platform characteristics: constant contact, the importance of place, and locational privacy.

The next chapter in this section looks at impression management issues. In "Technology and Self-Presentation: Impression Management Online," Miriam Bartsch and Kaveri Subrahmanyam present a comprehensive overview of impression management from a historical perspective as well as embedding it into issues of privacy. The need for privacy and the need for self-presentation are viewed as two sides of the same issue. The authors find that while users engage in online impression management that is part-and-parcel with self-presentation, they also are concerned about privacy. Finally, "Narcissism, Emerging Media, and Society" provides a literature review of the connection between emerging media and narcissism exploring the range of studies done that attempt to connect the two. W. Keith Campbell and Jean M. Twenge provide a comprehensive chapter that covers a vast array of literature that will assist the professional reader in gaining a handle on this interesting topic.

Part IV: Multitasking

Extensive use of technological devices leads to media multitasking as well as frequent interruptions in task flow. These issues are explored by the chapters in Part IV. In "Searching for Generation M: Does Multitasking Practice Improve Multitasking Skill?" L. Mark Carrier, Mike Kersten, and Larry D. Rosen present an empirical research project that examines whether more multitasking among young people leads to improved multitasking skill. The authors present a literature review examining multitasking behaviors, ultimately showing that while Generation Mers believe they can multitask efficiently, little evidence shows this to be true. The authors present two general hypotheses: that extreme Generation M multitaskers will report having the same difficulty combining tasks as moderate and low multitaskers and those in other generations; and that extensive practice on a task will not make that task easier to combine with other tasks than others. The authors conclude that more multitasking does not lead to improved multitasking skill.

In "Multitasking and Attention: Implications for College Students" Laura L. Bowman, Bradley M. Waite, and Laura E. Levine review the evidence related to media multitasking in college students and/or young adults. The evidence shows that people are media multitasking frequently, with impacts upon academic performance and attentional skills. Additionally, the writers discuss the effects of media multitasking while engaging in driver and pedestrian behaviors. The experimental literature on divided attention is summarized, indicating clear limits in people's ability to do more than one task at a time. The authors end the chapter with several lists of recommendations regarding how individuals and agents involved in media multitasking environments can make improvements to minimize the negative impacts of media multitasking.

Next, Eileen Wood and Lucia Zivcakova set out to review what is known about how multitasking affects students during the learning process in "Understanding Multimedia Multitasking in Educational Settings." In the beginning part of the chapter, scientific research and theory that delineate how multitasking works are presented. It is shown that multitasking generally involves performing only one task at a time, but can be true multitasking (i.e., parallel processing) under certain conditions that are unlikely to take place during real-world learning tasks. The writers then go over the existing empirical research on multitasking that is "on task" and multitasking that is "off task" (i.e., related or unrelated to the learning goals). The authors conclude that multitasking, when well integrated into the learning context, can have positive outcomes, but, when it involves off-task use of technologies, can lead to learning decrements.

In "Multitasking, Note Taking, and Learning in Technology-Immersive Learning Environments" Lin Lin and Chris Bigenho describe the intense multitasking environment that exists in today's classrooms due to the presence of computer-based technologies. The chapter investigates how multitasking in this environment might impact long-term learning. In order to understand the answer, the authors divide classroom multitasking into two kinds: multitasking with compatible tasks and multitasking with non-compatible tasks. Compatible tasks are those that have goals that are similar to the primary learning goal. Non-compatible tasks have goals that distract the student from learning. In reviewing the research on these situations, the authors explain a variety of models from cognitive psychology and from educational psychology that can be applied to the multimedia learning environment.

Finally, in the review chapter "Multitasking and Interrupted Task Performance: From Theory to Application," Nicole E. Werner, David M. Cades, and Deborah A. Boehm-Davis present a thorough examination of the theory and research related to task interruptions. The authors offer a definition of interruptions and explain the differences between interruptions, multitasking, task switching, and distractions. The chapter covers work interruptions, task performance, errors, interruption and resumption lag, and so on and describes the current findings and future goals of related research.

Part V: The Media's Impact on Audiences

The final section examines how media and technology use and content affect people in a variety of ways. Nancy Signorielli offers the latest research on cultivation research in "Cultivation in the Twenty-First Century." In this chapter Signorielli examines the historical significance and new research surrounding cultivation theory, which posits that long exposure to televised images and narratives can cultivate attitudes about the real world that match the common themes that television presents. Signorielli, part of the original "cultural indicators" team headed by the late George Gerbner, presents a thorough examination of cultivation theory and research from its inception in the 1970s to the present. Though not a new technology, television continues to garner more advertising dollars and viewers' time than any other medium, making it perhaps the most pervasive and influential mass medium that can be seen from a variety of platforms, including newer technological devices such as smartphones and tablets. As a socializing agent, television presents shared cultural stories that influence people's thoughts and opinions. The chapter presents a detailed description of how cultivation is conceptualized and measured, examining the various constructs that researchers have tackled.

In the next chapter, "Internet Addiction," Petra Vondráčková and David Šmahel explore Internet addiction from historical and contemporary perspectives. The authors provide the classification and definition of Internet addiction, its primary measurement tools, the major related scholarship, prevalence rates and correlates, and the associated problems and treatments. The authors explain how Internet addiction fits with the DSM criteria, and the various schools of thought surrounding its inclusion or exclusion as a stand-alone disorder. The authors conclude that much more research is needed in this area, and that more accurate definitions and diagnostic criteria, including longitudinal studies, are needed to fully understand this phenomenon.

In "Smashing the Screen: Violent Video Game Effects," Ann Lewis, Sara Prot, Christopher L. Groves, and Douglas A. Gentile present an examination of violent video game effects from both the theoretical and empirical perspectives. The authors review the existing literature on the topic through a number of sections including their related theoretical frameworks, cognitive and behavioral outcomes, helping, empathy and desensitization issues, sexual socialization, racial and ethnic stereotyping, school performance, and issues of attention, addiction, and cognitive control. The authors conclude that the wide body of research in this area generally points to violent video game play associated with negative effects, though a multitude of variables both exacerbate and mitigate the salience of these effects. The authors also note that video games themselves are generally not problematic, and that some video game play has prosocial and other positive outcomes.

More information about video games is offered in "What is Known About Video Game and Internet Addiction After DSM-5." A research team from Iowa State University presents a literature review of a subject that has been extensively studied and is now finally in the Appendix of the new DSM-5. This makes this chapter a very powerful addition to the handbook as it sets the stage for what research needs to be done to further move Internet gaming addiction to the future DSM-6. Finally, in the last chapter, "The Future of Technology in Education," Candrianna Clem and Reynol Junco explore the existing research on technology use in education, and specifically examine online modalities, flipped classrooms, social media, and use of tablets in the classroom. The authors conclude that the most effective methods of using technology in education match course objectives with the specific modalities and that educators who are highly motivated and trained to use these technologies will produce better outcomes.

Notes

1 See www.statista.com for the latest statistics within the U.S. and around the world.
2 "Smartphone Users Worldwide Will Total 1.75 Billion in 2014," at http://www.emarketer.com/Article/Smartphone-Users-Worldwide-Will-Total-175-Billion-2014/1010536 (accessed November 21, 2014).

Acknowledgments

Putting together this book required the assistance of several people whom we would like to thank. Stacey Glick from Dystel & Goderich Literary Management was always there for us to help guide the book through the negotiation process. Andrew Peart was the publisher for Wiley who first approached us and has maintained his sense of humor in spite of our numerous questions and concerns. An extension was requested and granted, graciously, by the publisher, as we finalized the content of the book and made last-minute adjustments to the organization of the chapters. Karen Shield served as project editor for Wiley and always answered our emails immediately and clearly. Editorial assistance was provided by Amy Minshull from Wiley. In addition, Nancy Cheever's work was partially supported by the Dean of the College of Arts and Humanities at California State University, Dominguez Hills. We would also like to thank the members of the George Marsh Applied Cognition Laboratory for tolerating the absence of their mentors – or at a minimum their preoccupation – as we concentrated on editing this handbook. We would also like to thank our chapter authors for being timely and finding ways to produce high-quality work in spite of their obviously busy lives. As you read their bios you might wonder how they manage to juggle everything they do. This is why they are tops in their field!

Larry D. Rosen, Nancy A. Cheever, and L. Mark Carrier

Part I
The Psychology of Technology

1

The Acute and Chronic Impact of Technology on our Brain

David A. Ziegler,[1] Jyoti Mishra,[1] and Adam Gazzaley[2]

[1] *University of California, San Francisco*
[2] *Mount Sinai School of Medicine*

Our modern-day environments are technologically richer than ever before. There is no better example of the pervasiveness of technology and media in our daily lives than a brief survey of the annual International Consumer Electronics Show. The 2014 event was dominated by innovations such as smartwatches, earbuds that measure heart rate (and vary your workout soundtrack accordingly), and even a navigation jacket that integrates wirelessly with mobile GPS devices. Such wearable electronics are the perfect examples of how media and technology have become ubiquitous in our daily lives. While there has been much discussion and debate over the potential positive and negative societal implications of technology (Ling, 2004; Rosen, Carrier, & Cheever, 2013), an equally important but relatively unexamined question is what effect these new technologies have on our brains.

With each new wave of technological advancement, we are faced with new streams of sensory inputs from myriad modalities that challenge our brains and require us to adapt to an ever-changing information landscape. This burgeoning set of new information brings with it novel forms of irrelevant distractions and interference, which can disrupt performance on goal-directed activities. Further, this information overload imposes greater cognitive demands on our neural systems to selectively attend to sensory inputs that are relevant to our immediate goals, while ignoring the interfering sources. Over the past decade, research in our laboratory has focused on unraveling the neural mechanisms underlying our capacity to selectively attend to goals in the face of interference (Clapp, Rubens, Sabharwal, & Gazzaley, 2011; Gazzaley et al., 2008; Gazzaley, Cooney, Rissman, & D'Esposito, 2005; Zanto, Rubens, Bollinger, & Gazzaley, 2010). In this chapter, we will review what is known about how our brains cope with technologies such as television, Internet, email, digital and social media, video games, and mobile devices, how multitasking with multiple technological devices affects neural processing, and will consider the possibilities for harnessing new technologies for personal cognitive benefit.

The Wiley Handbook of Psychology, Technology, and Society, First Edition. Edited by Larry D. Rosen, Nancy A. Cheever, and L. Mark Carrier.
© 2015 John Wiley & Sons, Ltd. Published 2015 by John Wiley & Sons, Ltd.

Usage and Attitudes Toward Technology Across the Lifespan

While an ever-increasing pool of new technologies and digital media appears to be an inevitable phenomenon, there is no clear consensus as to whether the impact of this on our brains is positive or negative. Proponents of technological innovation cite increases in productivity, flexibility, and control over how we accomplish our goals (Hill, Hawkins, Ferris, & Weitzman, 2001; Valcour & Hunter, 2005), but the majority of the existing research literature tends to focus on negative aspects of technological media innovation in our daily lives. Email and text messaging provide an instructive case in point. While they both enable flexible, immediate communication from any place, and at any time, there is increasing evidence that such forms of communication are a primary source of chronic stress in our lives (Barley, Meyerson, & Grodal, 2010), ultimately leading to increased workload and a widespread sense of overload (Boswell & Olson-Buchanan, 2007). Converging evidence suggests that the unpredictable nature of email and text messaging via mobile devices leads to a highly rewarding reinforcement schedule that engages the dopaminergic reward systems of our brains (Berridge & Robinson, 1998; Small & Vorgan, 2008). Indeed, a recent study that used an ecologically valid experience sampling method determined that the desire to use various forms of media (e.g., social networking, checking email, or surfing the web) were among the hardest urges for people to resist (Hofmann, Vohs, & Baumeister, 2012). Given that email and Internet access are inexpensive and virtually omnipresent, self-control failures in regulating one's media consumption have the potential to escalate into pathological media abuse (LaRose, 2010; Song, LaRose, Eastin, & Lin, 2004), a condition sometimes referred to as "Internet Addiction Disorder" (Ng & Wiemer-Hastings, 2005).

Attitudes Toward Technology in Young Adults

Additional insight about how we perceive the impact of technology comes from considering how interactions with media vary among people in different age groups. Perhaps not surprisingly, tech and media usage currently tends to be highest among the "Net Generation" (Rosen, 2007) and younger generations, such as the iGeneration, who have followed (Rosen, Carrier, & Cheever, 2010), who have grown up in a rapidly evolving culture of computers, Internet, smartphones, and gaming platforms. A survey study found that high school students reported the greatest amount of media use (particularly in the realms of texting and online chat), whereas middle school students were the most frequent video game players (Rosen et al., 2013). While both media use and video gaming were somewhat lower in college students (Rosen et al., 2013), tech usage by this population is undeniably pervasive, with 73% of college students reporting that they feel unable to study effectively without some form of technology accompanying this activity (Kessler, 2011). Self-reported attitudes toward technology are overwhelmingly positive among teens and young adults, with the vast majority feeling that tech improves the quality of their lives (Rosen et al., 2013). An interesting paradox emerges, however, when such attitudes are juxtaposed against repeated observations of negative correlations between academic performance and time spent using tech and social media (Kirschner & Karpinski, 2010; Rosen et al., 2013). Other research suggests that many of the negative effects of media use stem from multitasking or task-switching costs that come as technologies compete for limited attentional and cognitive resources (Junco & Cotten, 2012; Sana, Weston, & Cepeda, 2013; Wood et al., 2012), although one study found a positive relationship between media multitasking and multisensory integration (Lui & Wong, 2012). Such complexities highlight the need for a greater understanding of how our brains deal with technology and multitasking if we are to devise effective strategies for coping with an increasingly complex landscape of consumer technology. We will address this topic in the second section of this chapter.

Concerns About Media Exposure in Children

When it comes to technology and media use by younger children, and even infants, most discussions reflect a desire to limit early life exposure to television, video games, and the Internet out of a fear that overstimulation will have long-lasting negative consequences, such as violent behavior, distorted body images, susceptibility to harmful advertising, and even obesity (Cheng et al., 2010; Christakis, Zimmerman, DiGiuseppe, & McCarty, 2004; Johnson, Cohen, Kasen, First, & Brook, 2004; Lumeng, Rahnama, Appugliese, Kaciroti, & Bradley, 2006). More recently, critics of new media cite evidence from the neuroscience literature pointing to the potential for "negative neuroplasticity" in which television and Internet consumption might lead to a detrimental rewiring of children's brains in maladaptive ways, leading to impairments in attention, learning, and self-regulation (Ball & Holland, 2009; Derbyshire, 2009; Small & Vorgan, 2008). While such potential negative outcomes merit consideration, a more nuanced examination of the empirical effects of media and technology on the developing brain is warranted. Indeed, new studies provide support for an emerging view that, when managed properly, healthy media usage by infants, toddlers, and preschoolers can have beneficial later-life outcomes, promote positive plasticity, and even enhance learning in children with ADHD (Choudhury & McKinney, 2013; Obel et al., 2004). In the third section of this chapter we will review the existing literature on neuroplasticity as it relates to childhood media exposure.

Technology in Aging Populations

The lightning pace with which our tech landscapes are changing poses a unique challenge for a growing population of older adults. Many older adults are part of a generation that did not grow up carrying cell phones, playing immersive games on home video game consoles, or even watching television in color. Simultaneous interactions with multiple streams of media are often not second nature for people in this age group, and in some cases the onslaught of new technology can leave older adults feeling discouraged, out of touch, and overwhelmed. An additional challenge for older adults is the fact that media multitasking tends to rely on similar neural networks and cognitive functions that have been shown to decline with age (Hasher, Zacks, & May, 1999; Healey, Campbell, & Hasher, 2008; Waterston, 2011). A decreased ability to suppress distracting inputs (Gazzaley et al., 2005, 2008) and to multitask (Clapp et al., 2011) may create a hurdle for those older adults who would otherwise enthusiastically embrace multiple new technologies. At the same time, when older adults are able to get connected and adapt to new technologies, they find at their fingertips an array of positive benefits, such as being able to easily connect with old friends and family via social media and videoconferencing, increased personal productivity through the use of organizational apps or voice recognition software, or even using home gaming consoles to boost their physical activity (Grobart, 2011). In addition, advances in technology are now leading to a potential revolution in cognitive neurotherapeutics designed to remediate cognitive deficits in otherwise healthy older adults. We recently demonstrated that older adults could reverse some age-related cognitive declines by training with a multitasking video game and that this training was associated with brain activity patterns typically observed in 20-year-olds (Anguera et al., 2013). These and other studies, which we will describe in more detail in the last section of this chapter, offer hope that we might be able to harness advances in media and technology to yield cognitive and social benefits.

Effects of Technology and Multitasking on the Brain

While considering group-average differences in perceptions and attitudes toward technology and media can give us a broad societal perspective, we must consider individual differences in technology interactions to begin to understand their specific effects on our brains and cognition. One of the few studies to examine brain structural correlates of media interactions found that online social network size (i.e., number of Facebook friends) predicted gray matter density in the superior and middle temporal gyri and medial temporal lobe structures – regions that have been linked to social cognition and associative memory (Kanai, Bahrami, Roylance, & Rees, 2012). This finding mirrors studies of real-world social networks, which also report correlations between network size and amygdala volumes (Bickart, Wright, Dautoff, Dickerson, & Barrett, 2011), as well as intrinsic functional connectivity between the amygdala and cortical networks subserving perceptual and affiliative aspects of social cognition (Bickart, Hollenbeck, Barrett, & Dickerson, 2012). While these neuroimaging studies are not able to tease apart causal effects, it is interesting to note that several key aspects of real-world social network size have been found to be heritable (Fowler, Dawes, & Christakis, 2009; Fowler, Settle, & Christakis, 2011), suggesting that genetic factors may explain individual differences in how people choose to interact with media and technology and may mediate some of their neural effects.

Cognitive Profiles of Media Multitaskers

As mentioned earlier, one of the primary consequences of increased availability of new technologies in our daily lives is the tendency to attempt to attend to multiple streams of content simultaneously, a behavior commonly referred to as media multitasking (Rideout, Foehr, & Roberts, 2010). Much research has attempted to elucidate the acute and chronic effects of media multitasking on a variety of cognitive functions, including learning, memory, and attention (Kirschner & Karpinski, 2010; Lin, 2009; Lui & Wong, 2012; Ophir, Nass, & Wagner, 2009), and these works are described in greater detail in other chapters of this book. A natural prediction would be to expect that those individuals that engage in heavy media multitasking would be particularly good at task-switching, given their normal tendency to rapidly switch back and forth between streams of content. In contrast, Ophir and colleagues (2009) found that heavy media multitaskers were actually worse at task-switching, when compared to low media multitaskers, and specifically on tasks that required them to focus their attention on a particular subset of information. In other words, high media multitaskers had difficulty filtering out irrelevant information, and instead distributed their attention almost equally to both relevant and irrelevant items (Ophir et al., 2009). This finding suggests that these individuals, relative to low media multitaskers, tend to rely more on a breadth-biased form of cognitive control or bottom-up attention processes (i.e., attention driven by salient events in the environment instead of voluntarily set top-down goals; Cain & Mitroff, 2011; Lin, 2009). When bottom-up attention mechanisms dominate, distractibility increases, translating into a decreased ability to maintain selective attention and impairments in goal-directed activities (Kanai, Dong, Bahrami, & Rees, 2011).

These results, while seemingly counterintuitive, are consistent with other studies that have examined individual differences in traits associated with multitasking and distractibility. Questionnaire-based indices of susceptibility to distractions have been found to be highly heritable, with approximately 50% of interindividual variability being attributable to genetic factors (Boomsma, 1998). These same indices of distractibility are quite stable over time (Broadbent, Cooper, FitzGerald, & Parkes, 1982) and predict susceptibility to distractor interference under conditions of low perceptual load (Forster & Lavie, 2007). Based on these results, one might expect other trait-level characteristics to correlate with susceptibility to distraction. By collecting both laboratory-based measures of actual multitasking ability and reports of participants' self-perceived multitasking ability, one study revealed a negative correlation between actual and perceived multitasking ability (Sanbonmatsu, Strayer, Medeiros-Ward, & Watson, 2013). That is, those individuals who were most capable of successful multitasking were less likely to actually engage in such behaviors. This study also found that the tendency to engage in media multitasking was most strongly associated with personality traits of impulsivity and sensation seeking, and was inversely related to measures of executive control. Similarly, Minear, Brasher, McCurdy, Lewis, and Younggren (2013) found that high media multitaskers reported being more impulsive than low media multitaskers, and exhibited lower levels of fluid intelligence. At the same time, they found no experimental evidence that high media multitaskers were deficient in their ability to suppress task-irrelevant information (Minear et al., 2013).

It is important to note, however, that such results remain correlational and do not speak to the issue of causality. That is, media multitasking may not necessarily lead to detrimental changes in cognitive control, but rather could reflect a propensity for those individuals with a better capacity for distributing attention to be more likely to engage in media multitasking behaviors (Sanbonmatsu et al., 2013). Indeed, other results have complicated the straightforward notion that media multitasking has only negative effects on cognitive control abilities. Consistent with the conclusions of Ophir et al. (2009), subsequent studies have reported converging evidence that high media multitaskers tend to rely on a breadth-biased form of cognitive control (Cain & Mitroff, 2011; Lui & Wong, 2012). However, using a modified visual search task in which target detection is enhanced by integrating visual and auditory information, Lui and Wong (2012) demonstrated that the degree of media multitasking correlated positively with the ability to benefit from multisensory integration. Such findings are particularly intriguing in light of research in our lab investigating the interaction between top-down attention and multisensory integration (Mishra & Gazzaley,

2012). In a rich stimulus environment with a constant stream of visual, auditory, and audio-visual stimuli, we found that the ability to discriminate stimuli is enhanced when attention is distributed across the auditory and visual modalities, in contrast to when attention is focused onto one or the other modality. Further, this ability to distribute attention onto multisensory inputs was found to be associated with greater efficiency in the neural processing of sensory signals in both visual and auditory cortex. This ability to distribute attention across the auditory and visual senses was also found to be preserved to a large extent in older adults (Mishra & Gazzaley, 2013). Putting these results in context with those of Lui and Wong (2012), the brains of high media multitaskers may perform more efficient processing and generate superior performance under multisensory rather than unisensory (visual or auditory alone) settings.

Interference Resolution in the Brain

While relatively few studies have directly examined the neural processing associated with media multitasking, much can be gained by considering the broader literature on the neural mechanisms underlying multitasking, regardless of the medium. Inherent to engaging in media multitasking is an increased susceptibility to interference coming from multiple streams of content. For more than a decade, research in our laboratory has sought to understand the impact of distractions and interruptions on goal-related activity and to characterize the neural mechanisms underlying successful resolution of interference, which has led to a recently proposed framework for the characterization of interference (Mishra, Anguera, Ziegler, & Gazzaley, 2013). Our research has revealed that top-down control consists of a complex balance between enhancement of goal-relevant inputs and suppression of irrelevant inputs, which can be classified as "distractions" and "interruptions" (Clapp & Gazzaley, 2012; Clapp et al., 2011; Gazzaley et al., 2005, 2008; Zanto et al., 2010). Distractions are sensory information that should be ignored, like the background chatter when working at a café. Interruptions are external stimuli that need to be attended to, but which are of secondary priority to achieving our overarching goals. Interaction with interruptions while attending to primary goal-relevant stimuli qualifies as multitasking, such as may occur when responding to a text message while driving.

To understand the behavioral and neural costs associated with external interference, our laboratory has pioneered a multi-methodological approach, coupling fMRI and EEG with novel cognitive paradigms and analytical techniques. Our approach has led to new conclusions regarding spatial and temporal mechanisms of top-down modulation in the setting of external interference, the neural networks that underlie them, and the changes that occur in this system with normal aging (Berry, Zanto, Rutman, Clapp, & Gazzaley, 2009; Bollinger, Rubens, Masangkay, Kalkstein, & Gazzaley, 2011; Clapp & Gazzaley, 2012; Gazzaley & D'Esposito, 2007; Gazzaley, Rissman, & D'Esposito, 2004; Gazzaley et al., 2005, 2008; Wais, Rubens, Boccanfuso, & Gazzaley, 2010; Zanto et al., 2010). In a series of studies, we have shown that in the presence of external distraction, early modulation of stimulus processing minimizes distraction cost (Clapp & Gazzaley, 2012; Gazzaley et al., 2005; Rutman, Clapp, Chadick, & Gazzaley, 2010) and resistance to the negative impact of distraction on memory involves maintaining functional connectivity between the prefrontal cortex

(PFC) and visual cortical regions (Gazzaley & D'Esposito, 2007; Gazzaley et al., 2004; Rissman, Gazzaley, & D'Esposito, 2004).

Interference in Working Memory

More recently, we studied the effects of simultaneously displaying overlapping relevant and irrelevant stimuli on working memory performance (Chadick & Gazzaley, 2011). Using functional connectivity fMRI measures, we found distinct and dynamic connectivity between sensory areas and PFC based on task goals. Relevant stimuli engaged neural connections between visual and PFC networks, while irrelevant stimuli simultaneously coupled sensory areas to task-irrelevant networks in the brain. In another set of experiments, we demonstrated that working memory performance within individuals was related to the extent of neural interference suppression (Berry et al., 2009). Zanto et al. (2010) then used a transcranial magnetic stimulation-induced perturbation of a frontal region to confirm a causal link between PFC-mediated modulation of visual activity during stimulus encoding and working memory performance. This finding is consistent with other studies that also found this region of PFC to be a critical site for cognitive control of interference (Brass, Derrfuss, Forstmann, & von Cramon, 2005; Bunge, 2004).

Clapp and colleagues (Clapp & Gazzaley, 2010; Clapp et al., 2011) used a different experimental design to probe both distractions and interruptions, each introduced during the delay period of a working memory task. Performance measures revealed that working memory accuracy was significantly reduced in the setting of distraction and even worse when interrupted by another task. Neural data showed suppressed early visual processing of ignored distractions in young adults. In contrast, neural activity to interruptions, which served as stimuli for a secondary discrimination task, was enhanced. Recently, we replicated these findings for intrasensory interference during auditory working memory (Mishra, Zanto, Nilakantan, & Gazzaley, 2013). A subsequent study found that interruptions disrupted activity in a memory maintenance network, as measured by functional connectivity between visual association cortex and the middle frontal gyrus, and dynamically reallocated neural processing to the attended interrupter (Clapp et al., 2011). The memory maintenance network was then re-engaged at offset of the interruption. Further, the extent of attention-related enhancement to the interrupter directly correlated with reduced working memory performance, revealing how neural network dynamics shape cognitive operations in the face of interference.

Interference in Long-Term Memory

Working memory and attention are not the only cognitive domains affected by interference. Wais et al. (2010) demonstrated a negative impact of distractions on long-term memory performance. Participants encoded a study list of items and were later probed regarding recognition of these items. Visual distractors during the recall phase significantly reduced accuracy. Neurally, diminished recollection was associated with the disruption of functional connectivity in a network involving the left inferior frontal gyrus, hippocampus, and visual cortices. The authors concluded that bottom-up influences from visual distractions interfere with the top-down selection of episodic details mediated by a capacity-limited frontal con-trol region, resulting in impaired recollection. Subsequently, our lab showed a similar impact of auditory distractions on long-term memory performance (Wais & Gazzaley, 2011).

Overall, these studies characterize the impact of external interference on cogni-tion in young adults. Other studies in our lab have sought to understand how such processes change as people get older, and converging evidence now supports the idea that older adults have a specific deficit in interference resolution (Gazzaley, 2013). We have shown that older adults experience deficits in the suppression of externally presented distracting information (Clapp et al., 2011) and that these deficits occur at early visual processing stages (Clapp & Gazzaley, 2012; Gazzaley et al., 2005, 2008). Interestingly, we found that these deficits were mediated by a failure to maintain functional connectivity between PFC and visual cortices (Clapp et al., 2011). In a pattern similar to younger adults, older adults also disengage sensory-prefrontal memory maintenance networks when faced with an interrup-tion. Notably, however, these networks in older adults fail to re-engage post-inter-ruption, with prefrontal control regions remaining functionally connected to the interrupter, even though it is no longer relevant. We have also seen prolonged association with distractors that was several hundreds of milliseconds longer in older adults, compared to young adults, leading to a negative impact on the pro-cessing of later relevant inputs (Cashdollar et al., 2013). Finally, our lab has also characterized selective age-related deficits in motor inhibition processes and showed that they seem to be distinct from the sensory inhibition deficits (Anguera & Gazzaley, 2012). A recent placebo-controlled study of a cholinergic enhancer (Donepezil) showed that older adults with mild cognitive impairments regain interference sup-pression function and neural network connectivity with augmented cholinergic activity (Pa et al., 2013), pointing to a potential neurochemical basis for some suppression deficits.

This research on how the brain deals with interruptions, examined in both healthy young and older adults, provides important clues as to the neural mechanism that might explain behavioral patterns observed in high media multitaskers. As mentioned above, heavy media multitaskers were significantly more susceptible to interference from irrelevant stimuli in cognitive tasks and could not filter out interference in work-ing memory, relative to those with a lower degree of media multitasking (Ophir et al., 2009). Our research highlights the importance of efficient communication between top-down control regions and posterior visual processing areas for effectively engag-ing and maintaining attention in a goal-directed manner. Repeated multitasking with multiple forms of media may lead to repeated disengagement and re-engagement of top-down attentional networks, which could introduce neural noise and variability in the system. Further, if heavy media multitaskers do rely more on a breadth-biased form of cognitive control, this may bias them to rely more on bottom-up attention processes, when compared to low media multitaskers (Cain & Mitroff, 2011; Lin, 2009). Studies in non-human primates have shown that top-down and bottom-up attention rely on oscillatory synchrony in frontoparietal networks at different frequency ranges (Buschman & Miller, 2007, 2010). Thus, chronic engagement in heavy media multitasking might lead to an increased reliance on neural rhythms that are attuned to bottom-up stimuli. Finally, our research on older adults points to a specific deficit in the ability to suppress irrelevant inputs, potentially leading to a greater difficulty in older adults' abilities to manage multiple, competing streams of media and making it more challenging for older adults to adapt to a constantly changing tech landscape.

Impact of Technology and Media on Developmental Neuroplasticity

A growing body of literature is beginning to document the long-term effects of media and technology usage by young children. While the bulk of research in this domain has focused on health and societal consequences of TV exposure in early childhood (Cheng et al., 2010; Christakis et al., 2004; Johnson et al., 2004; Lumeng et al., 2006), an increasing number of studies are attempting to examine downstream effects on neuroplasticity. Drawing on evidence from animal studies that showed positive gains in neuroplasticity following environmental enrichment in early pre- and post-natal development (Cancedda et al., 2004; Liu, He, & Yu, 2012; Sale et al., 2007), we have seen an explosion in the availability of commercial products that claim to stimulate infant brains (Garrison & Christakis, 2005). It remains unknown, however, whether these enrichment products have positive effects on brain development (Bavelier, Green, & Dye, 2010), leading one set of investigators to develop a mouse model meant to simulate overstimulation of newborn mice with audio-visual inputs (Christakis, Ramirez, & Ramirez, 2012). After several weeks of being subjected to auditory and visual stimulation just following birth, the mice showed decrements in a number of behavioral domains, when tested as juveniles, including increased risk-taking behaviors, decreased short-term memory, and learning impairments, as compared to control mice. It is important to note, however, that this study employed a passive and unavoidable stimulation paradigm, which likely differs in important ways from the use of commercial cognitive enrichment products, or even TV viewing, which is typically done by choice (Bilimoria, Hensch, & Bavelier, 2012).

Television Exposure and Brain Volumes

In a more ecologically valid study, Takeuchi et al. (2013) used a combined cross-sectional and longitudinal design to track structural brain changes associated with duration of television viewing. This study found a significant positive correlation between the number of hours spent watching TV and gray matter density in frontopolar cortex and the medial PFC, as well as a positive correlation with the ratio of gray-to-white matter density in primary visual cortex (Takeuchi et al., 2013). Perhaps more striking was the finding of a negative correlation between frontopolar/medial PFC gray matter density and subsequent verbal IQ, measured several years later. While Takeuchi et al. (2013) did not examine functional MRI data, and thus did not report functional connectivity measures, it is interesting to note that medial PFC is a key node in the default mode network (Buckner, Andrews-Hanna, & Schacter, 2008). Perhaps an extended amount of TV viewing at an early age reinforces activity in the default mode network, which is associated with idle behavior, mind wandering, and distractibility (Berman et al., 2010; Mason et al., 2007). Indeed, our lab has shown that functional connectivity between visual and default mode network areas was greatest when participants viewed task-irrelevant visual distractions (Chadick & Gazzaley, 2011).

Action Video Games and the Brain

Another area that has received considerable attention is the effect of engagement with action video games for extended periods of time, particularly in later childhood and young adulthood. Much of this interest stems from the finding that young adults who are video game "experts" have been shown to have superior attention capacities (Dye, Green, & Bavelier, 2009; Green & Bavelier, 2003). Interestingly, the neural basis of this superior performance was shown to be enhanced suppression of distracting sensory information compared to neural activity in non-gamers (Mishra, Zinni, Bavelier, & Hillyard, 2011). More research is needed, however, to determine the causal direction of such effects, and video games remain a controversial subject. This controversy stems largely from the perception that most commercial action video games are filled with violent content, leading to popular concern about the negative impact on social affect. Such concern, however, is not solely based on research. In fact, increasing video game play over the last few years has been associated with declining crime rates, speculated to be due to availability of a safe alternate avenue to vent real-life frustration in action game play (Puzzanchera, Adams, & Sickmund, 2011).

In summary, there appears to be real evidence for both positive and negative effects of increasing media and tech usage on developmental neuroplasticity. Research in this area is just beginning to scratch the surface of the issue, and more ecologically valid studies that track both structural and functional brain changes longitudinally will be needed to determine the differential impacts of various types of technologies on developing brains.

Harnessing Technology and Media to Enhance Neurocognition

Given that technology is here to stay, an important question is whether it is possible to harness the power of an ever-growing tech and media industry to somehow enhance our lives by promoting neural and cognitive health. A prime example of such a scenario is in the realm of cognitive neurotherapeutics. Development and scientific evaluation of such interventions, especially in the form of computerized cognitive training that is accessible to many people, is a major research emphasis at the Gazzaley laboratory, and we end this chapter by summarizing recent advances in the effects of cognitive training on the brain.

Enhancing External Interference Resolution

To address the issue of heightened distractibility in aging and in many neuropsychiatric populations, we recently embarked on adaptive distractor training in parallel experiments on older rats and older humans (Mishra, deVillers Sidani, Merzenich, & Gazzaley, 2014). The goal was to train older adults and rats to suppress the neural processing of distracting stimuli via engagement in an environment of progressively increasing distractor challenge. This training required discrimination of relevant informative targets amidst irrelevant distractor non-targets, which resemble the target to a greater and greater extent as performance improves. The degree of distractor challenge is thus adaptively determined by the discrimination performance of the trainee on each trial. At the end of the adaptive distractor training, both rats and humans showed significant improvement in target discrimination amidst distractors. Neurons in the auditory cortices of trained rats showed suppression of distractor responses and tonotopic reorganization that yielded sharper neuronal tuning and reduced spatial receptive field overlap. In humans, we found enhanced target-linked oscillatory activity in the theta band in frontal areas and attenuation of early sensory auditory processing of distractors in trained, compared to untrained individuals. Overall, this study showed how adaptive training can be used to selectively tune deficient neural circuits by focusing the adaptive task challenge on the deficient neurobehavioral process. This critical insight paves the way for the effective development of future cognitive training and neurotherapeutic approaches that are selectively targeted to specific neural dysfunctions.

As described earlier in this chapter, a major concern about the increasing availability of new technologies is the accompanying pressure to engage in multitasking – a behavior that becomes more challenging as we grow older (Anguera et al., 2013). In an attempt to combat age-related declines in multitasking performance and to improve cognitive control abilities more broadly, our lab recently developed a video game designed to target these skills. The video game "NeuroRacer" was developed in the lab in collaboration with professional game designers and was built to assess perceptual discrimination abilities ("Sign" task) with and without concurrent visuomotor tracking ("Drive" task). The "Sign" task required discrimination of a specific colored shape target amidst a rapid sequential stream of eight other colored shapes that either had one or no common features with the target shape. During "Sign and Drive" the "Sign" task had to be performed concurrently with the "Drive" task to maintain a car in the center of a winding road using a joystick. Concurrent "Sign and Drive" performance was compared to "Sign only" performance to generate a multitasking cost index. Multitasking performance was observed to steadily deteriorate in a linear fashion across the lifespan, with an average cost of –26% in the second decade of life declining to –65% in the seventh decade.

Enhancing Cognitive Control Abilities in Older Adults

Anguera et al. (2013) then used "NeuroRacer" to investigate whether multitasking abilities on the game can be improved through training. In a randomized controlled trial design, older adults were assigned to one of three groups: multitasking training (MTT), single task training, active control, or no-contact control. After training at home for four weeks, we found multitasking performance costs on the game were significantly reduced exclusively in the MTT group. Further, these improvements reached levels that were superior to the performance of a 20-year-old cohort that performed a diagnostic version of the game. In addition to multitasking gains, critically, we also found transfer of training benefits in the realms of working memory and sustained attention, which suggested that a common, underlying mechanism of cognitive control was challenged and enhanced in the MTT group.

To assess the neural basis of the performance improvements, Anguera et al. (2013) focused on oscillatory power and frontal-occipital coherence measures in midline frontal theta (4–7Hz) oscillations that are known markers of top-down engagement. Notably midline frontal theta power was enhanced to levels comparable to younger adults selectively in the MTT group. These data clearly demonstrated that selective neuroplastic changes stemmed from the cognitively demanding interference between the "Sign" and "Drive" tasks when participants were motivated to engage in them simultaneously. Coupled with previous findings of increased midline frontal theta on a variety of cognitive control tasks (Mitchell, McNaughton, Flanagan, & Kirk, 2008), our results support a common neural basis for cognitive control processes, which can be enhanced by immersion in an adaptive, high-interference environment.

Overall, we evidence large and sustained reduction in interference costs and generalized benefits on cognitive control in our immersive, neuroscientifically designed video games. Prolonged engagement and training on such technologies may in turn benefit the many clinical populations with deficient cognitive control (e.g., ADHD, depression, dementia).

Conclusion

It is unquestionable that innovations in technology and media will continue at a lightning pace, resulting in new methods for interacting with our worlds and bringing with them new sources of distractions, as well as potential avenues for enhancing our lives. As can be seen from the studies reviewed in this chapter, the question of how such technologies affect our brains acutely and chronically is complicated and often controversial. While a cursory view of the literature seems to paint media multitasking and early life technology exposure in a negative light, a more nuanced exploration shows some profoundly promising aspects of how new technologies might be harnessed to enhance cognition in at-risk populations, leading to better lives. Thus, it is essential that we continue to pursue research in this domain.

References

Anguera, J. A., & Gazzaley, A. (2012). Dissociation of motor and sensory inhibition processes in normal aging. *Clinical Neurophysiology, 123*(4), 730–740.

Anguera, J. A., Boccanfuso, J., Rintoul, J. L., Al-Hashimi, O., Faraji, F., Janowich, J., ... Gazzaley, A. (2013). Video game training enhances cognitive control in older adults. *Nature, 501*(7465), 97–101.

Ball, W., & Holland, S. (2009). The fear of new technology: A naturally occurring phenomenon. *American Journal of Bioethics, 9*(1), 14–16.

Barley, S. R., Meyerson, D. E., & Grodal, S. (2010). E-mail as a source and symbol of stress. *Organization Science, 22*(4), 887–906.

Bavelier, D., Green, C. S., & Dye, M. W. G. (2010). Children, wired: For better and for worse. *Neuron, 67*(5), 692–701.

Berman, M. G., Peltier, S., Nee, D. E., Kross, E., Deldin, P. J., & Jonides, J. (2010). Depression, rumination and the default network. *Social Cognitive and Affective Neuroscience*, 548–555.

Berridge, K. C., & Robinson, T. E. (1998). What is the role of dopamine in reward: Hedonic impact, reward learning, or incentive salience? *Brain Research. Brain Research Reviews, 28*(3), 309–369. Retrieved November 21, 2014, from http://www.ncbi.nlm.nih.gov/pubmed/9858756

Berry, A. S., Zanto, T. P., Rutman, A. M., Clapp, W. C., & Gazzaley, A. (2009). Practice-related improvement in working memory is modulated by changes in processing external interference. *Journal of Neurophysiology*, 1779–1789.

Bickart, K. C., Hollenbeck, M. C., Barrett, L. F., & Dickerson, B. C. (2012). Intrinsic amygdala-cortical functional connectivity predicts social network size in humans. *Journal of Neuroscience, 32*(42), 14729–14741.

Bickart, K. C., Wright, C. I., Dautoff, R. J., Dickerson, B. C., & Barrett, L. F. (2011). Amygdala volume and social network size in humans. *Nature Neuroscience, 14*(2), 163–164.

Bilimoria, P. M., Hensch, T. K., & Bavelier, D. (2012). A mouse model for too much TV? *Trends in Cognitive Sciences, 16*(11), 529–531.

Bollinger, J., Rubens, M. T., Masangkay, E., Kalkstein, J., & Gazzaley, A. (2011). An expectation-based memory deficit in aging. *Neuropsychologia, 49*(6), 1466–1475.

Boomsma, D. I. (1998). Genetic analysis of cognitive failures (CFQ): A study of Dutch adolescent twins and their parents, *European Journal of Personality, 12*(5), 321–330.

Boswell, W. R., & Olson-Buchanan, J. B. (2007). The use of communication technologies after hours: The role of work attitudes and work-life conflict. *Journal of Management, 33*(4), 592–610.

Brass, M., Derrfuss, J., Forstmann, B., & von Cramon, D. Y. (2005). The role of the inferior frontal junction area in cognitive control. *Trends in Cognitive Sciences, 9*(7), 314–316.

Broadbent, D. E., Cooper, P. F., FitzGerald, P., & Parkes, K. R. (1982). The cognitive failures questionnaire (CFQ) and its correlates. *British Journal of Psychology, 21*, 1–16.

Buckner, R. L., Andrews-Hanna, J. R., & Schacter, D. L. (2008). The brain's default network: Anatomy, function, and relevance to disease. *Annals of the New York Academy of Sciences, 1124*, 1–38.

Bunge, S. A. (2004). How we use rules to select actions: A review of evidence from cognitive neuroscience. *Cognitive, Affective, and Behavioral Neuroscience, 4*(4), 564–579. Retrieved November 21, 2014, from http://www.ncbi.nlm.nih.gov/pubmed/15849898

Buschman, T. J., & Miller, E. K. (2007). Top-down versus bottom-up control of attention in the prefrontal and posterior parietal cortices. *Science, 315*(5820), 1860–1862.

Buschman, T. J., & Miller, E. K. (2010). Shifting the spotlight of attention: Evidence for discrete computations in cognition. *Frontiers in Human Neuroscience, 4*, 194.

Cain, M. S., & Mitroff, S. R. (2011). Distractor filtering in media multitaskers. *Perception, 40*(10), 1183–1192.

Cancedda, L., Putignano, E., Sale, A., Viegi, A., Berardi, N., & Maffei, L. (2004). Acceleration of visual system development by environmental enrichment. *Journal of Neuroscience, 24*(20), 4840–4848.

Cashdollar, N., Fukuda, K., Bocklage, A., Aurtenetxe, S., Vogel, E. K., & Gazzaley, A. (2013). Prolonged disengagement from attentional capture in normal aging. *Psychology and Aging, 28*(1), 77–86.

Chadick, J. Z., & Gazzaley, A. (2011). Differential coupling of visual cortex with default or frontal-parietal network based on goals. *Nature Neuroscience, 14*(7), 830–832.

Cheng, S., Maeda, T., Yoichi, S., Yamagata, Z., Tomiwa, K., & Japan Children's Study Group. (2010). Early television exposure and children's behavioral and social outcomes at age 30 months. *Journal of Epidemiology, 20*(Supplement II), S482–S489.

Choudhury, S., & McKinney, K. A. (2013). Digital media, the developing brain and the interpretive plasticity of neuroplasticity. *Transcultural Psychiatry, 50*(2), 192–215.

Christakis, D. A., Ramirez, J. S. B., & Ramirez, J. M. (2012). Overstimulation of newborn mice leads to behavioral differences and deficits in cognitive performance. *Scientific Reports, 2*, 546.

Christakis, D. A., Zimmerman, F. J., DiGiuseppe, D. L., & McCarty, C. A. (2004). Early television exposure and subsequent attentional problems in children. *Pediatrics, 113*(4), 708–713. Retrieved November 21, 2014, from http://www.ncbi.nlm.nih.gov/pubmed/15060216

Clapp, W., & Gazzaley, A. (2010). Distinct mechanisms for the impact of distraction and interruption on working memory in aging. *Neurobiology of Aging, 20*(4), 859–872.

Clapp, W. C., & Gazzaley, A. (2012). Distinct mechanisms for the impact of distraction and interruption on working memory in aging. *Neurobiology of Aging, 33*(1), 134–148.

Clapp, W. C., Rubens, M. T., Sabharwal, J., & Gazzaley, A. (2011). Deficit in switching between functional brain networks underlies the impact of multitasking on working memory in older adults. *Proceedings of the National Academy of Sciences of the United States of America, 108*(17), 7212–7217.

Derbyshire, D. (2009). Social websites harm children's brains: Chilling warning to parents from top neuroscientist. *Daily Mail.* Retrieved November 21, 2014, from http://www.dailymail.co.uk/news/article-1153583/Social-websites-harm-childrens-brains-Chilling-warning-parents-neuroscientist.html

Dye, M. W. G., Green, C. S., & Bavelier, D. (2009). The development of attention skills in action video game players. *Neuropsychologia, 47*(8–9), 1780–1789.

Forster, S., & Lavie, N. (2007). High perceptual load makes everybody equal: Eliminating individual differences in distractibility with load. *Psychological Science, 18*(5), 377–381.

Fowler, J. H., Dawes, C. T., & Christakis, N. A. (2009). Model of genetic variation in human social networks. *Proceedings of the National Academy of Sciences of the United States of America, 106*(6), 1720–1724.

Fowler, J. H., Settle, J. E., & Christakis, N. A. (2011). Correlated genotypes in friendship networks. *Proceedings of the National Academy of Sciences of the United States of America, 108*(5), 1993–1997.

Garrison, M. M., & Christakis, D. A. (2005). *A teacher in the living room? Educational media for babies, toddlers, and preschoolers.* Menlo Park, CA: Henry J. Kaiser Family Foundation.

Gazzaley, A. (2013). Top down modulation deficit in the aging brain: An emerging theory of cognitive aging. In D. T. Stuss & R. T. Knight (Eds.), *Principles of frontal lobe function* (2nd ed.). New York, NY: Oxford University Press.

Gazzaley, A., Clapp, W., Kelley, J., McEvoy, K., Knight, R. T., & D'Esposito, M. (2008). Age-related top-down suppression deficit in the early stages of cortical visual memory processing. *Proceedings of the National Academy of Sciences of the United States of America, 105*(35), 13122–13126.

Gazzaley, A., Cooney, J. W., Rissman, J., & D'Esposito, M. (2005). Top-down suppression deficit underlies working memory impairment in normal aging. *Nature Neuroscience, 8*(10), 1298–1300.

Gazzaley, A., & D'Esposito, M. (2007). Top-down modulation and normal aging. *Annals of the New York Academy of Sciences, 1097,* 67–83.

Gazzaley, A., Rissman, J., & D'Esposito, M. (2004). Functional connectivity during working memory maintenance. *Cognitive, Affective, and Behavioral Neuroscience, 4*(4), 580–599.

Green, C. S., & Bavelier, D. (2003). Action video game modifies visual selective attention. *Nature, 423*(6939), 534–537.

Grobart, S. (2011). Staying in touch with technology. *The New York Times,* p. F1. Retrieved November 21, 2014, from http://www.nytimes.com/2011/03/03/business/retirementspecial/03Tech.html

Hasher, L., Zacks, R. T., & May, C. P. (1999). Inhibitory control, circadian arousal, and age. In D. Gopher & A. Koriat (Eds.), *Attention and performance XVII.* Cambridge, MA: MIT Press.

Healey, M. K., Campbell, K. L., & Hasher, L. (2008). Cognitive aging and increased distractibility: Costs and potential benefits. *Progress in Brain Research, 169,* 353–363.

Hill, E., Hawkins, A., Ferris, M., & Weitzman, M. (2001). Finding an extra day a week: The positive influence of perceived job flexibility on work and family life balance. *Family Relations, 50*(1), 49–58. Retrieved November 21, 2014, from http://onlinelibrary.wiley.com/doi/10.1111/j.1741-3729.2001.00049.x/full

Hofmann, W., Vohs, K. D., & Baumeister, R. F. (2012). What people desire, feel conflicted about, and try to resist in everyday life. *Psychological Science, 23*(6), 582–588.

Johnson, J. G., Cohen, P., Kasen, S., First, M. B., & Brook, J. S. (2004). Association between television viewing and sleep problems during adolescence and early adulthood. *Archives of Pediatrics and Adolescent Medicine, 158*(6), 562–568.

Junco, R., & Cotten, S. R. (2012). No A 4 U: The relationship between multitasking and academic performance. *Computers and Education, 59*(2), 505–514.

Kanai, R., Bahrami, B., Roylance, R., & Rees, G. (2012). Online social network size is reflected in human brain structure. *Proceedings. Biological Sciences/The Royal Society, 279*(1732), 1327–1334.

Kanai, R., Dong, M. Y., Bahrami, B., & Rees, G. (2011). Distractibility in daily life is reflected in the structure and function of human parietal cortex. *Journal of Neuroscience, 31*(18), 6620–6626.

Kessler, S. (2011). 38% of college students can't go 10 minutes without tech. *Mashable Tech.* Retrieved November 21, 2014, from http://mashable.com/2011/05/31/college-tech-device-stats/

Kirschner, P. A., & Karpinski, A. C. (2010). Facebook and academic performance. *Computers in Human Behavior, 26*(6), 1237–1245.

LaRose, R. (2010). The problem of media habits. *Communication Theory, 20*(2), 194–222.

Lin, L. (2009). Breadth-biased versus focused cognitive control in media multitasking behaviors. *Proceedings of the National Academy of Sciences of the United States of America, 106*(37), 15521–15522.

Ling, R. (2004). *The mobile connection: The cell phone's impact on society.* San Francisco, CA: Morgan Kauffmann.

Liu, N., He, S., & Yu, X. (2012). Early natural stimulation through environmental enrichment accelerates neuronal development in the mouse dentate gyrus. *PLOS ONE, 7*(1), e30803.

Lui, K. F. H., & Wong, A. C.-N. (2012). Does media multitasking always hurt? A positive correlation between multitasking and multisensory integration. *Psychonomic Bulletin and Review, 19*(4), 647–653.

Lumeng, J. C., Rahnama, S., Appugliese, D., Kaciroti, N., & Bradley, R. H. (2006). Television exposure and overweight risk in preschoolers. *Archives of Pediatrics and Adolescent Medicine, 160*(4), 417–422.

Mason, M. F., Norton, M. I., Van Horn, J. D., Wegner, D. M., Grafton, S. T., & Macrae, C. N. (2007). Wandering minds: The default network and stimulus-independent thought. *Science, 315*(5810), 393–395.

Minear, M., Brasher, F., McCurdy, M., Lewis, J., & Younggren, A. (2013). Working memory, fluid intelligence, and impulsiveness in heavy media multitaskers. *Psychonomic Bulletin and Review, 20*(6), 1274–1281.

Mishra, J., Anguera, J. A., Ziegler, D. A., & Gazzaley, A. (2013a). A cognitive framework for understanding and improving interference resolution in the brain. *Progress in Brain Research, 207*, 351–377.

Mishra, J., deVillers Sidani, E., Merzenich, M. M., & Gazzaley, A. (2014). Adaptive training diminishes distractibility in aging across species. *Neuron, 84*(5), 1091–1103.

Mishra, J., & Gazzaley, A. (2012). Attention distributed across sensory modalities enhances perceptual performance. *Journal of Neuroscience, 32*, 12294–12302.

Mishra, J., & Gazzaley, A. (2013). Preserved discrimination performance and neural processing during crossmodal attention in aging. *PLOS ONE, 8*(11), e81894.

Mishra, J., Zanto, T., Nilakantan, A., & Gazzaley, A. (2013). Comparable mechanisms of working memory interference by auditory and visual motion in youth and aging. *Neuropsychologia, 51*(10), 1896–1906.

Mishra, J., Zinni, M., Bavelier, D., & Hillyard, S. A. (2011). Neural basis of superior performance of action videogame players in an attention-demanding task. *Journal of Neuroscience, 31*(3), 992–998.

Mitchell, D. J., McNaughton, N., Flanagan, D., & Kirk, I. J. (2008). Frontal-midline theta from the perspective of hippocampal "theta." *Progress in Neurobiology, 86*(3), 156–185.

Ng, B. D., & Wiemer-Hastings, P. (2005). Addiction to the Internet and online gaming. *Cyberpsychology and Behavior, 8*(2), 110–113.

Obel, C., Henriksen, T. B., Dalsgaard, S., Linnet, K., Skajaa, E., Thomsen, P., & Olsen, J. (2004). Does children's watching of television cause attention problems? Retesting the hypothesis in a Danish cohort. *Pediatrics, 114*(5), 1371–1372.

Ophir, E., Nass, C., & Wagner, A. D. (2009). Cognitive control in media multitaskers. *Proceedings of the National Academy of Sciences of the United States of America, 106*(37), 15583–15587.

Pa, J., Berry, A. S., Compagnone, M., Boccanfuso, J., Greenhouse, I., Rubens, M. T., ... Gazzaley, A. (2013). Cholinergic enhancement of functional networks in older adults with mild cognitive impairment. *Annals of Neurology, 73*(6), 762–773.

Puzzanchera, C., Adams, B., & Sickmund, M. (2011). Juvenile Court Statistics 2008. National Center for Juvenile Justice. Retrieved from http://www.ncjj.org/pdf/jcsreports/jcs2008.pdf

Rideout, V. J., Foehr, U. G., & Roberts, D. F. (2010). *Generation M: Media in the lives of 8–18 year-olds.* Menlo Park, CA: Henry J. Kaiser Family Foundation.

Rissman, J., Gazzaley, A., & D'Esposito, M. (2004). Measuring functional connectivity during distinct stages of a cognitive task. *NeuroImage, 23*(2), 752–763.

Rosen, L. D. (2007). *Me, MySpace, and I: Parenting the Net generation.* New York, NY: Palgrave Macmillan.

Rosen, L. D., Carrier, L. M., & Cheever, N. A. (2010). *Rewired: Understanding the iGeneration and the way they learn.* New York, NY: Palgrave Macmillan.

Rosen, L. D., Carrier, L. M., & Cheever, N. A. (2013). Facebook and texting made me do it: Media-induced task-switching while studying. *Computers in Human Behavior, 29*(3), 948–958.

Rutman, A. M., Clapp, W. C., Chadick, J. Z., & Gazzaley, A. (2010). Early top-down control of visual processing predicts working memory performance. *Journal of Cognitive Neuroscience, 22*(6), 1224–1234.

Sale, A., Cenni, M. C., Ciucci, F., Putignano, E., Chierzi, S., & Maffei, L. (2007). Maternal enrichment during pregnancy accelerates retinal development of the fetus. *PLOS ONE, 2*(11), e1160.

Sana, F., Weston, T., & Cepeda, N. J. (2013). Laptop multitasking hinders classroom learning for both users and nearby peers. *Computers and Education, 62*, 24–31.

Sanbonmatsu, D. M., Strayer, D. L., Medeiros-Ward, N., & Watson, J. M. (2013). Who multi-tasks and why? Multi-tasking ability, perceived multi-tasking ability, impulsivity, and sensation seeking. *PLOS ONE, 8*(1), e54402.

Small, G., & Vorgan, G. (2008). *iBrain: Surviving the technological alteration of the modern mind.* New York, NY: HarperCollins.

Song, I., LaRose, R., Eastin, M. S., & Lin, C. A. (2004). Internet gratifications and Internet addiction: On the uses and abuses of new media. *Cyberpsychology and Behavior, 7*(4), 384–394.

Takeuchi, H., Taki, Y., Hashizume, H., Asano, K., Asano, M., Sassa, Y., ... Kawashima, R. (2013). The impact of television viewing on brain structures: Cross-sectional and longitudinal analyses. *Cerebral Cortex*, online first. doi: 10.1093/cercor/bht315

Valcour, P. M., & Hunter, L. W. (2005). Tecnology, organizations, and work-life integration. In E. E. Kossek & S. J. Lambert (Eds.), *Work and life integration: Organizational, cultural, and individual perspectives* (pp. 61–84). Mahwah, NJ: Lawrence Erlbaum Associates.

Wais, P. E., & Gazzaley, A. (2011). The impact of auditory distraction on retrieval of visual memories. *Psychonomic Bulletin and Review, 18*(6), 1090–1097.

Wais, P. E., Rubens, M. T., Boccanfuso, J., & Gazzaley, A. (2010). Neural mechanisms underlying the impact of visual distraction on retrieval of long-term memory. *Journal of Neuroscience, 30*(25), 8541–8550.

Waterston, M. L. (2011). The techno-brain. *Generations, 35*(2), 77–83.

Wood, E., Zivcakova, L., Gentile, P., Archer, K., De Pasquale, D., & Nosko, A. (2012). Examining the impact of off-task multi-tasking with technology on real-time classroom learning. *Computers and Education, 58*(1), 365–374.

Zanto, T. P., Rubens, M. T., Bollinger, J., & Gazzaley, A. (2010). Top-down modulation of visual feature processing: The role of the inferior frontal junction. *NeuroImage, 53*(2), 736–745.

2

Similarities and Differences in Workplace, Personal, and Technology-Related Values, Beliefs, and Attitudes Across Five Generations of Americans

Larry D. Rosen and José M. Lara-Ruiz

California State University, Dominguez Hills

In 1991 William Strauss and Neil Howe published their book entitled *Generations: The History of America's Future, 1584–2069*, which took a long view of how America has seen a series of what they refer to as "generations" or cohorts of people born over a span of approximately 20 years. They broke this down as comprising four phases of life: childhood, young adulthood, midlife, and old age. Strauss and Howe argued that these approximate divisions reflected the similar experiences of a group of people born between a set of years in three major areas: (1) major historical and social trends; (2) a common core of beliefs, attitudes, and behaviors; and (3) a sense that they "belong" in that 20-year-span cohort.

This definition of a 20-year span constituting a generation has persisted and has been somewhat controversial in defining the exact years for a succession of generations. For example, most researchers in this area agree that Baby Boomers, the progeny of the immediately prior generation – variously called the Silent or Traditional Generation – were born following World War II during a period of rapidly increased birth rate and a belief system that involved rejecting the values of their parents while redefining their own values as inherently different from more traditional values. While Strauss and Howe define this generation as extending from 1943 to 1960, the more common definition that has emerged – adopted by the United States Census Bureau – has Baby Boomers being born between 1946 and 1964 (Colby & Ortman, 2014).

In 1964 British journalists Jane Deverson and Charles Hamblett published their treatise on a subculture that they called Generation X. The "X" reflected that this counterculture generation was, at the time, not definable in terms of values and beliefs. Although the generation of teens and young adults that they interviewed was really part of the Baby Boomer generation, this set the stage for later. In 1991, this

The Wiley Handbook of Psychology, Technology, and Society, First Edition. Edited by Larry D. Rosen, Nancy A. Cheever, and L. Mark Carrier.

term was popularized by science fiction writer Douglas Coupland in his book *Generation X: Tales for an Accelerated Culture*, which chronicled young adults in the late 1980s, born in the mid-1960s. With this in mind, definitions of Generation X typically range from 1965 to somewhere in the late 1970s or early 1980s.

In 1997 Donald Tapscott, an American economist, interviewed 300 teens and young adults and, based on those interviews, defined a new generation which he dubbed the "Net Generation." Born between 1977 and 1997 – again using Strauss and Howe's 20-year span as their yardstick – Net Geners, as they were called, emerged as a new cohort who were born into a world of technology and surrounded from birth by high-tech toys, and grew up with high-tech tools and devices as their predominant cultural norm. Sometimes referred to as *digital natives* – distinguishing them from *digital immigrants* who came before (Prensky, 2001) – the Net Generation were variously called Generation Y, Generation Next, Generation M (for media), Generation Me, or Millennials and their span has been widely debated, beginning as early as the late 1970s and ending as late as 2004 (Horvitz, 2012).

In 2010, Rosen, Carrier, and Cheever introduced a new generation, called the iGeneration, in their book *Rewired: Understanding the iGeneration and the Way They Learn*, which was first used in a song of the same title by the American hip-hop artist named MC Lars in 2004. The moniker iGeneration was given to reflect the commonalities in the use of technologies such as iPhones, iTunes, iPods, Wii, and other devices that were individualized and customized to fit the lives of those born prior to the new millennium. This book broke tradition with Strauss and Howe's 20-year designation and defined the Net Generation as being born in the 1980s and the iGeneration being born in the 1990s, based on the ubiquity of technology and the rapid pace of change as well as the introduction of new technologies that vault from inception to societal penetration in a matter of months rather than years or decades. Rosen et al. (2010) pointed out that while radio, the telephone, and television – the province of Baby Boomers – took decades to penetrate society, newer technologies such as the World Wide Web, iPods, and social media websites took less than four years to do the same. With newer technologies such as YouTube taking only one year to rise from inception to 50 million users – the accepted definition of societal penetration (Rangaswamy & Gupta, 2000) – Rosen and colleagues argued that generations were now being truncated into "mini-generations" as media and technologies shaped their lives.

The current research project, discussed later in this chapter, takes the past work and establishes the following definitions of five generations to be studied: Baby Boomers (1946–1964), Generation X (1965–1979), Net Generation (1980–1989), iGeneration (1990–1999), and a new mini-generation, called Generation "C" for connectedness, born following the new millennium. These dates, it should be noted, are somewhat arbitrary but the point of this chapter is to demonstrate how the rapid change in technology and media options can and does change our values, beliefs, and attitudes. No doubt that these generational units will not fit everyone born during the stated years, but the majority of cohorts will exhibit consistent values based on their common historical and social trends and their common use of various technologies and media. For example, while Net Geners grew up immersed in the World Wide Web, their younger siblings grew up with "i" devices and *their* younger siblings are growing up with a constant connection to the world through a multitude of modalities, including "i" devices plus social media and other platforms that encourage electronic connections and public sharing. For a good description of the process of defining generations, see a recent edited book entitled *Generational Diversity at Work: New Research Perspectives*, with particular focus on a chapter by Urwin, Buscha, and Parry (2014) that explores the question of where we should "cut" the generational dates. In addition, several other articles have been written which examine and critique the definitions of various generations (Parry & Urwin, 2011; Trzesniewski & Donnellan, 2010; Twenge, 2010; Twenge, Campbell, Hoffman, & Lance, 2010). In this study we will take the viewpoint that generations are defined by cohort birth years and explore the possibility that the newest generations are actually mini-generations of less than 20 years as shown by cohort differences in values, beliefs, and technology use and attitudes.

Previous Overview Studies of Values and Beliefs

Many recent articles have explored various similarities and differences in work values and beliefs, most comparing two or maybe three generations in specific work domains such as schools, hospitals, and corporate workplaces (Becton, Walker, & Jones-Farmer, 2014; Chi, Maier, & Gursoy, 2013; Edge, 2014; Hernaus & Vokic, 2014; Jobe, 2014; Krahn & Galambos, 2014; Lyons & Kuron, 2014; Malik & Khera, 2014; McCarthy, Cleveland, & Heraty, 2014; Mencl & Lester, 2014; Urwin et al., 2014; Whitney-Gibson, Greenwood, & Murphy, 2011). In addition, fewer studies have investigated generational personal values, each focusing on a subset of values across two or more generations (Campbell & Twenge, 2014; Rajput, Kochhar, & Kesharwani, 2013; Srinivasan, John, & Christine 2014; Urick & Hollensbe, 2014; Whitney-Gibson et al., 2011). Finally, even fewer recent studies have examined technology use across generations (Bolton et al., 2013; Carrier, Cheever, Rosen, Benitez, & Chang, 2009; Leung, 2013; Oh & Reeves, 2014). The current study will present data that examine personal values, work values, and technology-related values across a large sample of five generations of Americans that are not tied to a single profession. A brief summary of relevant research in each of these three areas is presented below. This review is by no means exhaustive but is designed to give the reader a sense of the variation in values and beliefs across generations. However, we present these data with a caveat best expressed by Jean Twenge, Keith Campbell, and their colleagues: "Our society has labeled each generation differently to separate the cohorts from each other, although most research suggests that cohort effects are linear rather than categorical, with steady change over time rather than sudden shifts at birth year cutoffs" (Twenge et al., 2010, p. 1120).

Work Values

Studies have examined a variety of workplace and work-related values both across multiple generations and within a single generation. Table 2.1 captures a subset of the values and those research reports that examined them. As can be seen in this table, researchers have examined myriad values, beliefs, and attitudes that run the gamut from psychological constructs (e.g., extrinsic vs. intrinsic values) to social aspects of work (e.g., collaboration and social responsibility in the workplace) to tangible workplace benefits including salary and working conditions.

Table 2.1   Representative research reports on workplace values, attitudes, and beliefs across and within generations.

Workplace values, beliefs, attitudes	*Research reports*
General work-related attitudes	Cogin, 2012; Costanza et al., 2012; Soni et al., 2011
Respect/trust in authority	Gursoy et al., 2008
Financial aspirations	Taylor & Keeter, 2010
Collaboration	Brack, 2012; Gursoy et al., 2008; Tapscott, 2009
Performance evaluation	Kowske et al., 2010; Tapscott, 2009
Motivation/rewards	Gursoy et al., 2008; Yusoff et al., 2013
Work/play distinction	Cisco, 2011; Cogin, 2012; Gursoy et al., 2008; Tapscott, 2009; Twenge, 2010; Twenge et al., 2010
Leisure value	Twenge et al., 2010
Public vs. private spheres	Tapscott, 2009
Loyalty	Costanza et al., 2012; Gursoy et al., 2008; Soni et al., 2011; Tapscott, 2009
Work ethic	Kramer, 2010; Meriac et al., 2010; Sessa et al., 2007
Job security	Kowske et al., 2010
Extrinsic values/money	Cisco, 2011; Kowske et al., 2010; Krahn & Galambos, 2014; Twenge, 2010; Twenge et al., 2010
Job satisfaction	Costanza et al., 2012; Kowske et al., 2010
Job mobility	Cisco, 2011; Costanza et al., 2012; Tapscott, 2009
Intrinsic values/optimism	Sessa et al., 2007
Delegation of authority	Sessa et al., 2007
Big picture orientation	Sessa et al., 2007
Cultural sensitivity	Sessa et al., 2007
Polychronicity	Brasel & Gips, 2011
Media multitasking	Anguera et al., 2013; Brasel & Gips, 2011; Carrier et al., 2009; David et al., 2013; Helsper & Eynon, 2010; Jacobsen & Forste, 2011; Judd & Kennedy, 2011; Lee et al., 2012; Nicholas et al., 2011; Robb et al., 2011; Terry & Sliwinski, 2012; Voorveld & van der Goot, 2013
Workplace social media use	Cisco, 2011
Job flexibility/flexible schedules	Cisco, 2011
Socially responsible work environment	Strauss, 2013
Entrepreneurial aspirations	Gallup & Operation HOPE, 2013
Interesting/challenging work/opportunity to use skills and make decisions	Brack, 2012; Twenge et al., 2010; Zipcar, 2014

Personal Values

Table 2.2 displays a partial listing of research studies that examined personal values either across two or more generations or within a single generation. Again, as is evident in Table 2.2, studies have examined a wide variety of personal values including psychological issues such as narcissism as well as values toward achievement, politics, religion, trust, and many other areas.

Technology-Related Values

Table 2.3 displays a sample of research reports that examined technology-related values, beliefs, and attitudes, which range from beliefs about the positive or negative aspects of technology to personal use to psychological impacts of technology.

With the information from Tables 2.1, 2.2, and 2.3 the following large-scale study of more than 2,500 Americans across five defined generations and mini-generations was undertaken with the following research questions:

Table 2.2 Representative research reports on personal values, attitudes, and beliefs across and within generations.

Personal values, beliefs, attitudes	Research reports
Education	Taylor & Keeter, 2010
Political affiliation, activism, attitudes	Debevec et al., 2013; Lariscy et al., 2011; Morgan, 2014; Nam, 2012; Robinson & Martin, 2009; Taylor & Keeter, 2010
Family relationships/trust	Nickelodeon, 2013; Robinson & Martin, 2009; Tapscott, 2009; Taylor & Keeter, 2010
General trust	Morgan, 2014
Altruism	Taylor & Keeter, 2010; Twenge, 2010; Twenge et al., 2010
Religiosity	Debevec et al., 2013; Taylor & Keeter, 2010
Attitudes toward marriage	Taylor & Keeter, 2010
Attitudes toward parenting	Taylor & Keeter, 2010
Personal rights and equality	Strauss, 2013; Taylor & Keeter, 2010
Individualism	Twenge, 2010
Assertiveness	Twenge, 2009
Narcissism	Twenge, 2009
Social connections	Robinson & Martin, 2009; Twenge et al., 2010
Entitlement	Cogin, 2012
Independence	Cogin, 2012
Financial attitudes	Debevec et al., 2013
Confidence	Debevec et al., 2013
Sense of self	Nickelodeon, 2013
Status signifiers	Nickelodeon, 2013
Desire for fame	Uhls & Greenfield, 2012
Openness to other points of view	Robinson & Martin, 2009
Sexual attitudes	Robinson & Martin, 2009
Optimism	Robinson & Martin, 2009

Table 2.3 Representative research reports on technology-related values, attitudes, and beliefs across and within generations.

Technology-related values, beliefs, attitudes	Research reports
Prefer different technologies	Bullen et al., 2011; Bunzel, 2012; Commonsense Media, 2011; Commonsense Media, 2013; Helsper & Eynon, 2010; Joiner et al., 2012; Nickelodeon, 2013; Nielsen Company, 2014; Robb et al., 2011; Romero et al., 2013; Takeuchi, 2011; Voorveld & van der Goot, 2013; Zichuhr, 2011
Video use including television	Taylor & Keeter, 2010
Internet skills	Hargittai & Hinnant, 2008
Screen time limits	Commonsense Media, 2011; Commonsense Media, 2013
Connected/communication	Bullen et al., 2011; Jacobsen & Forste, 2011; Joiner et al., 2012; Lester et al., 2012; Taylor & Keeter, 2010
Impact on closeness to family/friends	Nielsen Company, 2014
Positive impact of technology on life	Nielsen Company, 2014; Taylor & Keeter, 2010
Technology and efficiency	Taylor & Keeter, 2010
Social networking	Bunzel, 2012; Joiner et al., 2013; Lester et al., 2012; Romero et al., 2013; Taylor & Keeter, 2010
Technology as a sixth sense	Alexander, 2011
Online safety/privacy	Takeuchi, 2011
General attitudes toward technology	Joiner et al., 2013
Educational technology use	Billings et al., 2005; Kolikant, 2010; Stapleton et al., 2007
Anxiety about technology use	Joiner et al., 2012; Joiner et al., 2013
Internet identification/self-efficacy	Helsper & Eynon, 2010; Joiner et al., 2012; Joiner et al., 2013
Technology engagement	Helsper & Eynon, 2010

- RQ1: What similarities and differences in workplace values, beliefs, and attitudes exist between five generations?
- RQ2: What similarities and differences in personal values, beliefs, and attitudes exist between five generations?
- RQ3: What similarities and differences in technology-related values, beliefs, and attitudes exist between five generations?

Empirical Study of Generational Similarities and Differences in Workplace, Personal, and Technology-Related Values, Beliefs, and Attitudes

In order to assess the generational similarities and differences in personal and work values, as well as technology use, we developed an online, anonymous survey in 2010 that included 88 items that we selected through an exhaustive literature search including all studies in Tables 2.1, 2.2, and 2.3 plus additional sources. With a sample size of 1,451 participants who answered the survey items for themselves and for one of their children under the age of 18, those 88 items – each using a five-point Likert scale from strongly agree to strongly disagree – were factor analyzed to develop 18 subscales, eight dealing with personal values and beliefs, six with work values and beliefs, and four with beliefs surrounding technology usage. In addition, nine items queried daily hours of technology use (plus one item about daily hours of reading for pleasure) – each using an eight-point scale of hours per day that were, when a range was presented, converted to the median hours per day of that option including 0, 1, 2, 3, 4–5 (converted to 4.5 hours per day), 6–8 (converted to 7), 9–10 (converted to 9.5), and more than 10 (converted conservatively to 11). Another three items examined social media usage each on a six-point frequency scale ranging from never, once a month, several times a month, once a week, several times a week, and daily.

The entire final sample ($N = 2,594$) – after removing 308 (10.6%) participants who either did not complete the survey or answered in a pattern suggesting they were not reading the questions – included 168 Baby Boomers, 618 members of Generation X, 470 members of the Net Generation, 654 members of the iGeneration, and 684 members of Generation "C." Two points are worth noting about these samples: (1) data from the younger participants (born after 1992 and being younger than 18 at the time of the survey administration) – including 94% of the iGeneration participants and 100% of the Generation C participants – were supplied by the parents, not the children, and (2) the dates for the youngest two generations – the iGeneration and Generation "C" – are, as discussed in this chapter, established as shorter than previous generations. While we have no way of assessing the validity of the data from the youngest samples, we have used this methodology successfully in prior research (Rosen, Cheever, Cummings, & Felt, 2008). In addition, we took all possible steps to statistically balance the effects of age variations within each generation by using age as a covariate as we will describe in the next section of the chapter.

Factor Analyses to Determine Values and Beliefs

Data from the sample of nearly 2,600 adults and children were used to develop factors or subscales of values and beliefs. Thirty-nine items centered on personal values, beliefs, and attitudes were analyzed separately and produced eight varimax-rotated factors with eigenvalues greater than 1 accounting for 59% of the variance. The 25 items used to assess work values, beliefs, and attitudes produced six factors and accounted for 61% of the variance while the 22 items dealing with technology values, beliefs, and attitudes produced four factors accounting for 65% of the variance. A .50 factor-loading cutoff was used and those items that exceeded that criterion were averaged to produce a subscale score for each factor. Overall, six personal value items and two work value items did not meet the .50 factor-loading criterion and were eliminated. No items loaded on more than one factor. Table 2.4 details the resultant factors with their highest loaded item.

Generational Comparisons on Values, Beliefs, and Attitudes

The five generations were compared on the personal, work, and technology-related values, beliefs, and attitudes subscales using two-way multivariate analyses of covariance (MANCOVAs) with all 18 factors listed in Table 2.4 as dependent variables, with generation and gender as independent variables and median income and birth

Table 2.4 Personal, workplace, and technology-related values, beliefs, and attitudes factors (**bold**) and highest loaded item (*italics*).

Personal	Workplace	Technology-related
1. **Social, confident, secure** *"I enjoy social activities."*	1. **Work perks** *"I like to do work that will make me good money."*	1. **Technology dependence** *"I feel it is important to be able to access the Internet any time I want."*
2. **Family relationships** *"I trust my family."*	2. **Work determination** *"I feel it is important to put lots of thought into a project."*	2. **Technology optimism** *"I think that it is OK to talk about personal problems with people that you only know online."*
3. **Shallowness** *"I know that I am good because everybody keeps telling me so."*	3. **Work depth** *"I am motivated by success rather than by praise from others."*	3. **Technology enthusiasm** *"With technology anything is possible."*
4. **Attention, realism, honesty, optimism** *"I have a good attention span."*	4. **Job preference** *"I prefer a high-status job that people look up to and respect."*	4. **Technology pessimism** *"New technology makes life more complicated."*
5. **Children know more and deserve things** *"I feel that children know more about the world than I did at their age."*	5. **Task-switching preference** *"When doing a number of assignments, I like to switch back and forth between them rather than do one at a time."*	
6. **Asceticism** *"I actually buy only the things I need."*	6. **Preferring group work over individual work** *"I prefer a job where I can work with and help people."*	
7. **Political beliefs** *"I trust our political leaders."*		
8. **Skepticism** *"I am a skeptical person."*		

year as covariates. Gender was used as a second independent variable based on prior research comparing generations that found gender differences in values, attitudes, and beliefs (Krahn & Galambos, 2014; Parry & Urwin, 2011). Median income (derived from census figures for the family home ZIP code) was included to factor out any differences due to family income and birth year was included to factor out any potential age differences within any generational group as recommended by generational comparison research (Krahn & Galambos, 2014; Parry & Urwin, 2011). MANCOVA – using Roy's largest root – indicated that overall there was a significant difference across generations ($F(18, 2263) = 31.78$, $p < .001$) as well as a significant difference across genders ($F(18, 2260) = 2.96$, $p < .001$) and a significant interaction between generation and gender ($F(18, 2263) = 2.36$, $p < .001$). Further univariate tests are presented in Table 2.5 for each of the 18 values and beliefs subscales.

Table 2.5 F-scores for individual values, beliefs, and attitudes subscales.

Values and beliefs subscales	Generations	Gender	Generations × Gender
PERSONAL VALUES, BELIEFS, AND ATTITUDES			
Social, confident, secure	3.03*	9.41**	0.31
Family relationships	6.09***	10.73***	1.57
Shallowness	1.59	9.88**	1.68
Attention, realism, honesty, optimism	2.47*	6.64**	0.51
Children know more and deserve things	2.17	9.10**	1.93
Asceticism	3.81**	5.80*	0.58
Political beliefs	1.30	3.68	0.18
Skepticism	6.92***	2.28	2.28
WORKPLACE VALUES, BELIEFS, AND ATTITUDES			
Work perks	3.34**	4.70*	1.15
Work determination	3.33**	3.41	2.66*
Work depth	15.99***	0.29	1.52
Likes group work	0.21	0.06	0.32
Job preference	24.42***	0.02	1.66
Task-switching preference	7.12***	0.40	1.12
TECHNOLOGY-RELATED VALUES, BELIEFS, AND ATTITUDES			
Technology dependence	106.72***	0.07	0.88
Technology optimism	80.76***	0.65	2.25
Technology enthusiasm	42.82***	1.26	0.16
Technology pessimism	10.91***	3.87*	1.66

$*p < .05$
$**p < .01$
$***p < .001$

The figures that follow show the generation by gender interaction graph for each of the 18 subscales listed in Table 2.4, including the mean scores (and standard error bars) for males and females separately for each of the five generations. Each is discussed in turn in three ways: (1) generational similarities and differences are assessed with a main effect F-test and trend analyses; (2) gender similarities and differences are examined via the main effect F-test; and (3) the interaction of gender and generation is assessed by examining differences in mean scores compared to the standard error within each generation. In comparing generation mean scores, trend analyses were chosen over multiple comparisons as they provide a sense of how generations are changing over time and whether those changes are linearly increasing or decreasing, or whether, perhaps, more complex trends are evident such as one might expect if values skip generations. The inclusion of gender as a second independent variable will show us how values, beliefs, and attitudes vary as a function of gender both within and between generations.

Personal Values and Beliefs

The following charts and discussion highlight the generation and gender comparisons for the eight personal values and beliefs listed in Table 2.4.

Figure 2.1 corroborates the significant gender main effect showing that females across all generations feel more confident and secure than males. Despite the significant main effect of generation, and the appearance of an increase across generations, there were no significant trends, although the linear trend was marginally significant at a more liberal .10 criterion ($p = .098$).

Figure 2.2 shows that as seen in the main effect of gender, females felt more strongly about family relationships than males. The significant effect of generation was manifested by a significant quadratic trend ($p < .001$) as seen in the U-shape in Figure 2.2, with the Net Generation showing the lowest value and belief in family relationships and adjacent generations on either chronological side showing increases, particularly among the younger generations with an increasing trend toward the importance of family relationships. This, of course, makes sense as members of both the iGeneration and Generation C likely live with their parents or family.

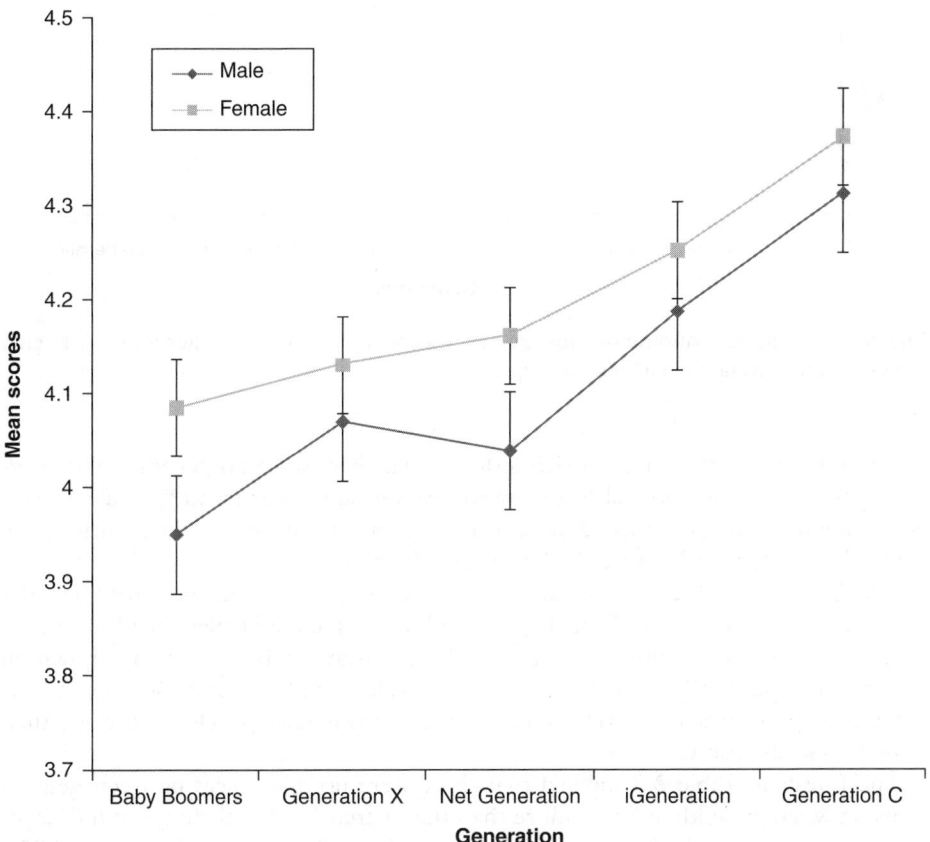

Figure 2.1   Social, confident and secure subscale mean scores by gender across generations. Higher scores indicate being more social, confident, and secure.

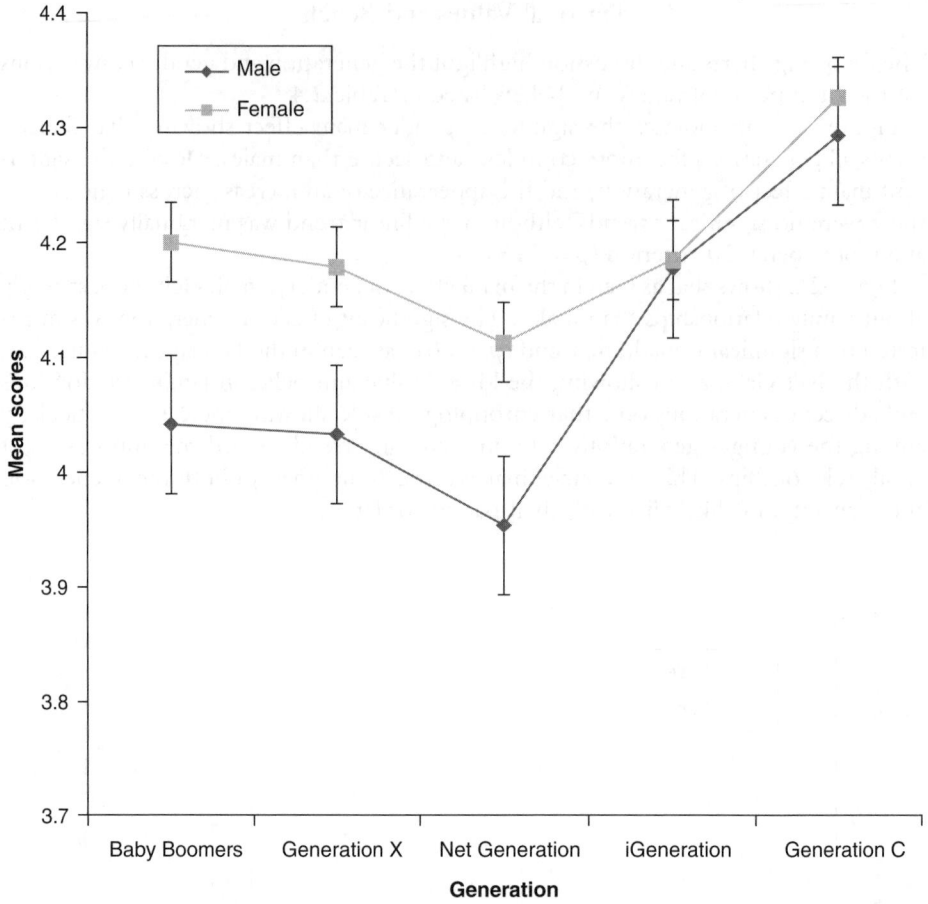

Figure 2.2   Family relationships subscale mean scores by gender across generations. Higher scores indicate stronger family relationships.

The F-tests reported in Table 2.5 indicate that there were no generational differences; however, a polynomial test showed a significant linear trend (p = .039) with increasing shallowness across generations, as seen in Figure 2.3. In addition, the F-test showed that males were shallower than females.

The F-tests in Table 2.5 indicated a significant gender difference, with females shown as more attentive, realistic, honest, and optimistic than males. In addition, the significant generation difference showed a significant cubic trend, as shown in Figure 2.4 – specifically, a rise in this mean subscale score from Baby Boomers to the Net Generation participants followed by a drop to the iGeneration low score and then a rise for Generation C.

The F-tests in Table 2.5 showed that there were no differences between generations on whether children know more than their parents did at their age and deserve more things and yet the linear trend as seen in Figure 2.5 was significant (p = .002), showing that there was evidence of increasing belief in this value from older to younger generations. In addition, with the exception of Generation C, females felt more

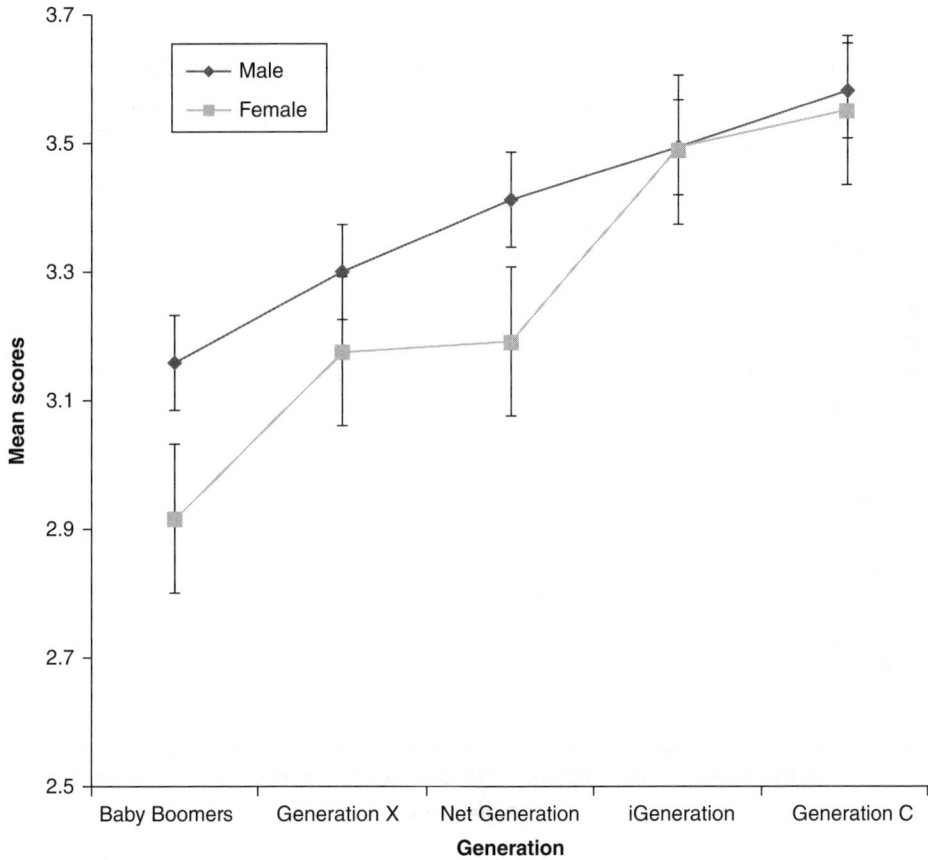

Figure 2.3 Shallowness subscale mean scores by gender across generations. Higher scores indicate more shallowness.

positive about this belief than males, although the main effect of gender did not reach significance, most likely due to the small gender differences in the older generations and the equality of males and females in Generation C.

The trends found in asceticism and displayed in Figure 2.6 – self-discipline and avoidance of indulgences – were complex. First, from the omnibus F-tests, with the scale being reversed and showing higher scores as less ascetic, males were less ascetic than females and there was a significant difference among generations. Trend analyses indicated a significant cubic trend ($p = .016$) and a significant quartic (fourth-order) trend ($p = .012$), which accounts for the pattern of increasing scores – less asceticism – from Baby Boomers to Net Geners, a drop for iGeneration members, and an increase again for Generation C to a level between the iGeneration and the Net Generation.

According to the F-tests in Table 2.5 there were neither gender nor generational differences in political beliefs likely due to the large variability in values within each generation. There were also no significant polynomial trends, as can be seen in Figure 2.7.

According to the omnibus F-tests, there were no gender differences in skepticism as shown in Figure 2.8, but there was a significant difference between generations

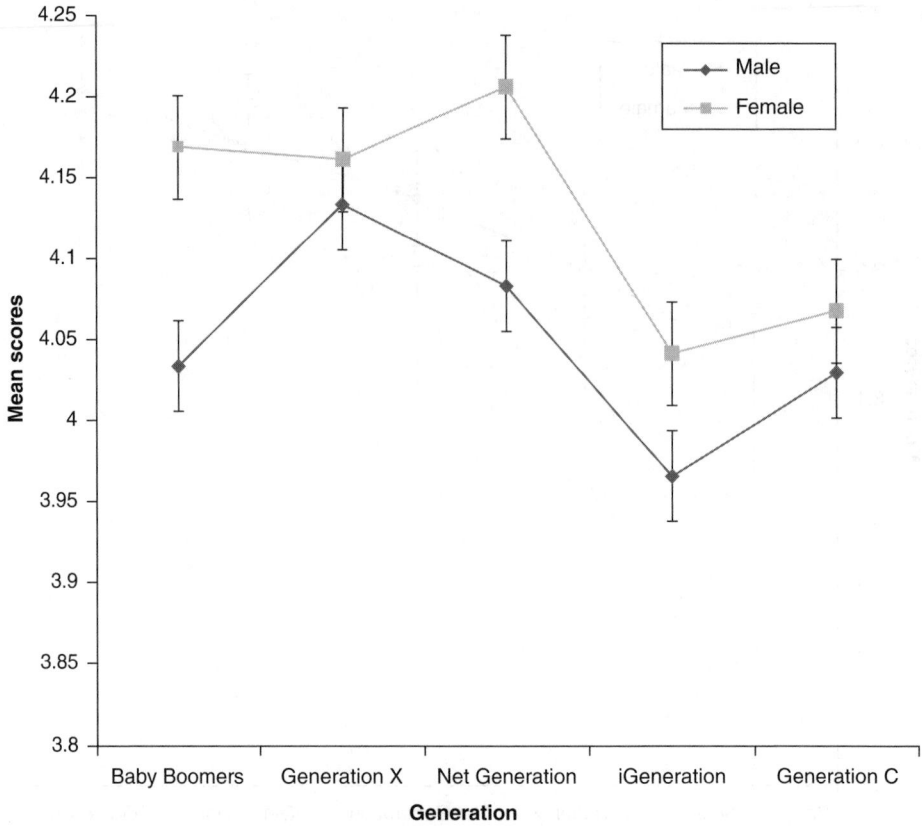

Figure 2.4 Attention, realism, honesty, and optimism subscale mean scores by gender across generations. Higher scores indicate being more attentive, realistic, honest, and optimistic.

that was reflected in the significant quadratic trend ($p < .001$) as well as a significant quartic (fourth-order) trend ($p = .014$). This pattern of a U-shape trend plus a fourth-order trend generated the pattern of increasing skepticism scores from Baby Boomers to the Net Generation followed by a small reduction in the younger two generations.

Work Values and Beliefs

The following figures highlight the generation and gender effects for the six work values listed in Table 2.4. As these are work values and were reported for Generation C and some of the iGeneration teens, the trends may not reflect their values but rather the *presumed* values as seen by their parents. The data from Generation C – and perhaps the iGeneration – should be viewed with caution as they may refer to parental beliefs about values of *schoolwork* rather than traditional adult work.

Figure 2.9 displays the comparisons by gender and generation on work perks (e.g., salary) and the F-tests in Table 2.5 showed that averaged across generations,

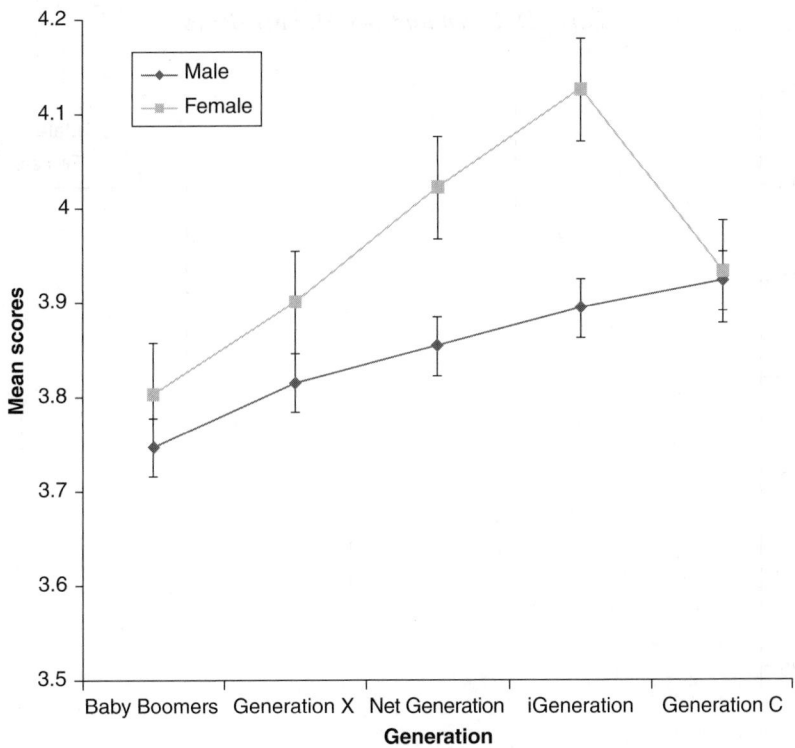

Figure 2.5 Children know more and deserve things subscale mean scores by gender across generations. Scores indicate a belief that children know more than their parents and deserve more things.

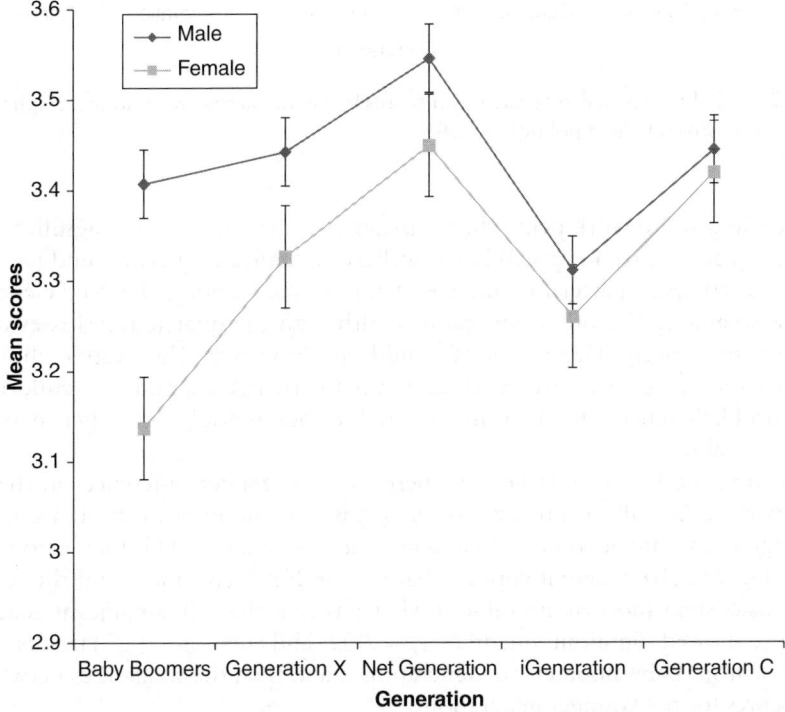

Figure 2.6 Asceticism subscale mean scores by gender across generations. Higher scores indicate less asceticism.

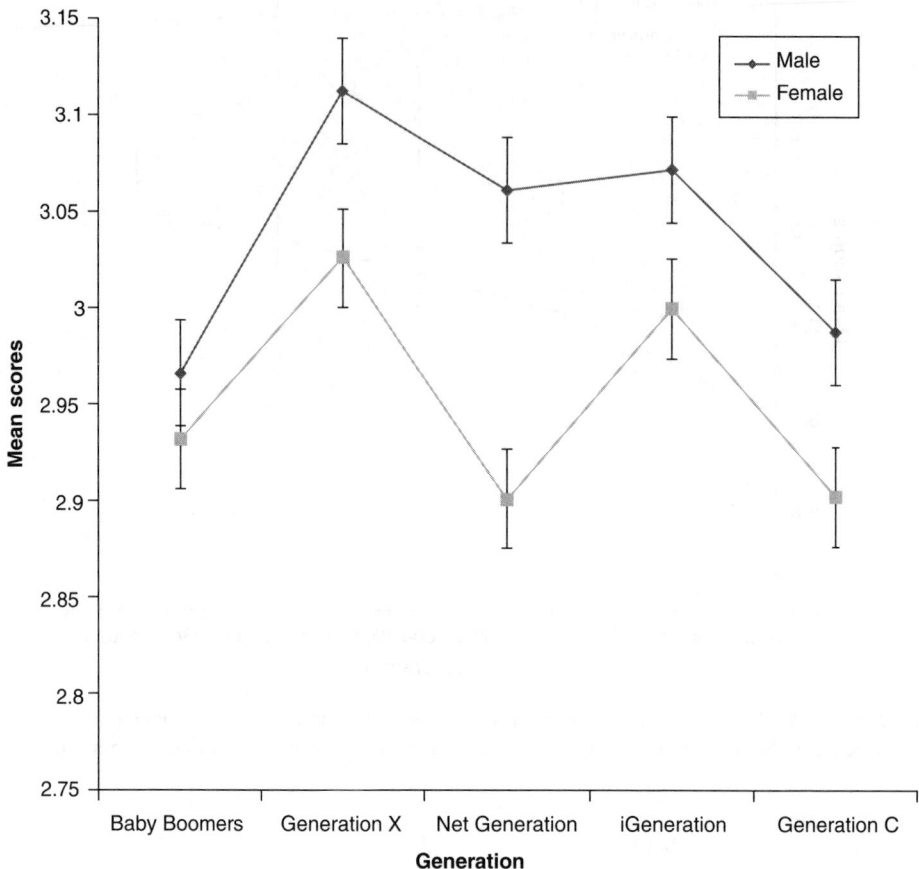

Figure 2.7 Political beliefs subscale mean scores by gender across generations. Higher scores indicate more strongly held political beliefs.

males desired more work perks than females and that there was a significant generational quadratic trend ($p = .021$) as well as a significant quartic trend ($p = .009$) showing a complex pattern of increased importance among the Net Generation and less so among the other generations, although the quartic trend is evident in the upswing among Generation C children. However, the reader should be reminded that parents answered these items for their Generation C children and they most likely reflect "work" values related to their schoolwork rather than future workplace values.

As seen in the F-test in Table 2.5, there were no gender differences in the belief about working carefully on projects but there was a significant main effect of generation and a significant interaction between gender and generation. This interaction can be seen in Figure 2.10, where it appears that for the Net Generation, and the iGeneration, females show more of this value and belief than males. The significant generation difference showed significant quadratic ($p = .002$) and cubic ($p = .027$) trends, as seen in the rise from Baby Boomers to Generation X and then the similarities between the mean scores for the younger generations.

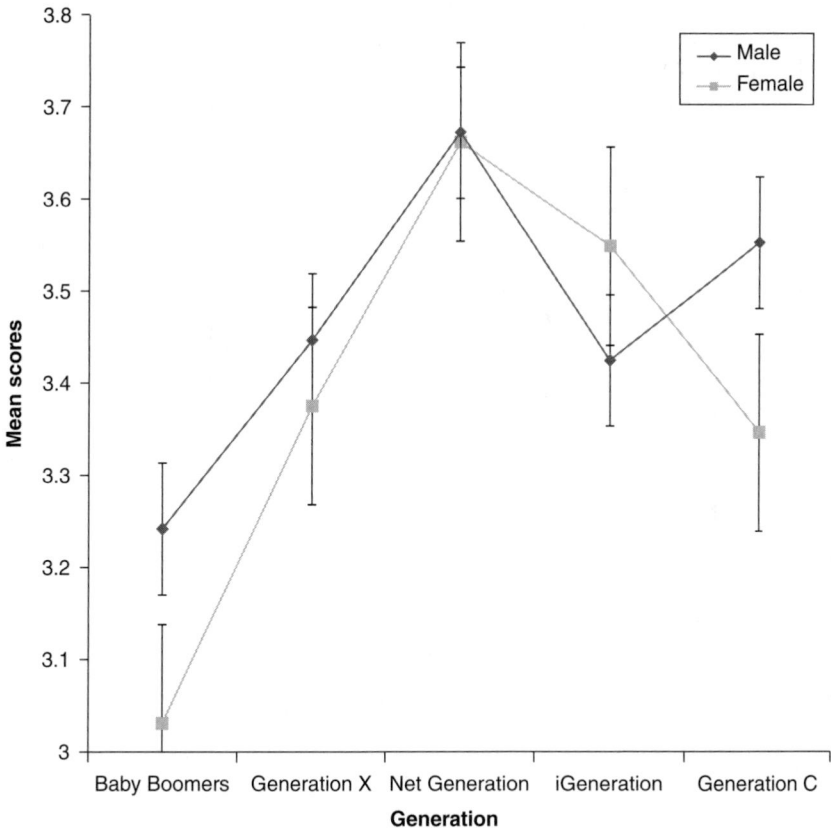

Figure 2.8   Skepticism subscale mean scores by gender across generation. Higher scores indicate more skepticism.

As seen in Table 2.5, only the generation main effect for motivation for success was significant with no apparent gender differences for any generation. This main effect did show a significant quadratic trend ($p < .001$), which is evident in the peak in Figure 2.11 in motivation for success among Net Generation males and females who are most likely new to the workplace and striving for a well-paying position.

As seen in Table 2.5 there were, again, no significant overall gender differences but there were significant generation differences that were apparent in the importance of job status. Trend analysis showed significant quadratic ($p < .001$) and cubic ($p < .001$) trends, which are evident in the pattern seen in Figure 2.12 that peaks at the Net Generation and iGeneration and shows lesser value at the two older generations and the youngest generation, who are not in the workforce and are having those values rated by their parents.

In Table 2.5 task-switching preference demonstrated no difference between genders but a strong significant difference between generations, which is reflected in Figure 2.13 as a significant quadratic trend ($p < .001$) that appears to peak for the

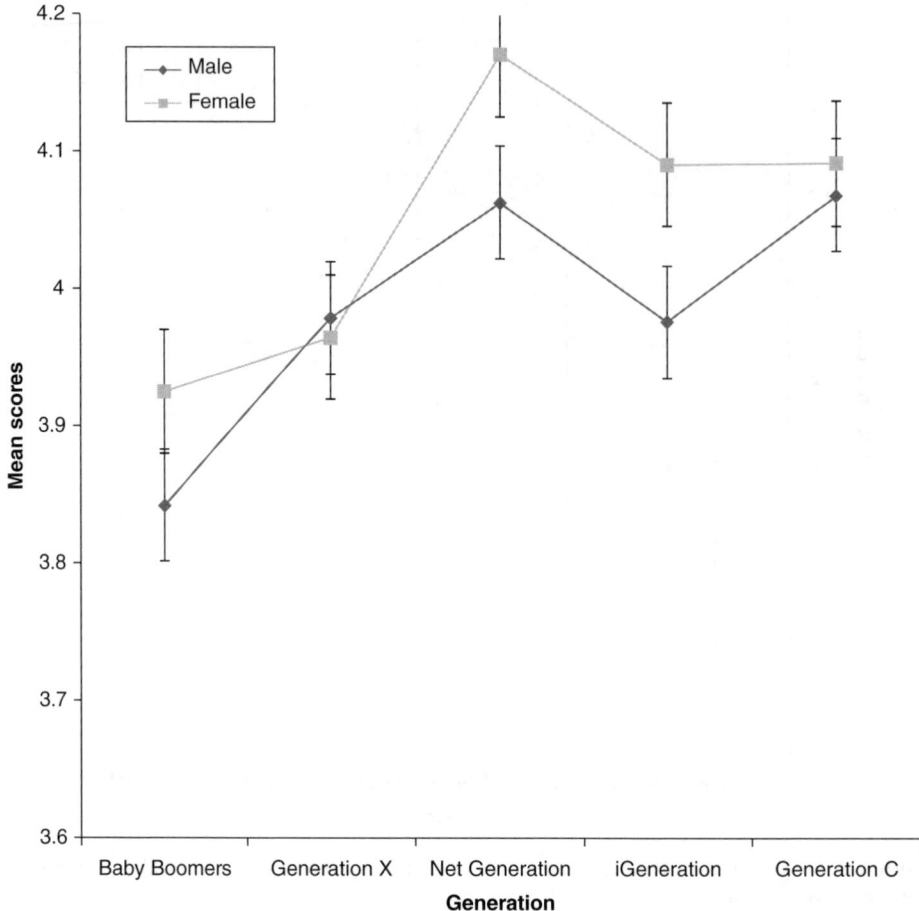

Figure 2.9 Work perks subscale mean scores by gender across generations. Higher scores indicate desiring more work perks.

iGeneration (and perhaps more for female iGeners than male iGeners, as seen by their standard error bars, which do not overlap).

According to Table 2.5, there were no gender differences or generation differences on this value or belief as shown in Figure 2.14. There were no significant trends.

Technology Values and Beliefs

Figure 2.15 displays the results for gender and generations regarding dependence on technology. As can be seen in the figure, there were no gender differences but there was a significant generation main effect, which was reflected in significant quadratic ($p < .001$), cubic ($p < .001$), and quartic ($p = .017$) trends. This can be seen by the slowly increasing dependence from Baby Boomers to the iGeneration – a less steep increase than other figures with only a quadratic trend due to the two additional significant trends (see, for example, Figure 2.13 where there was only a

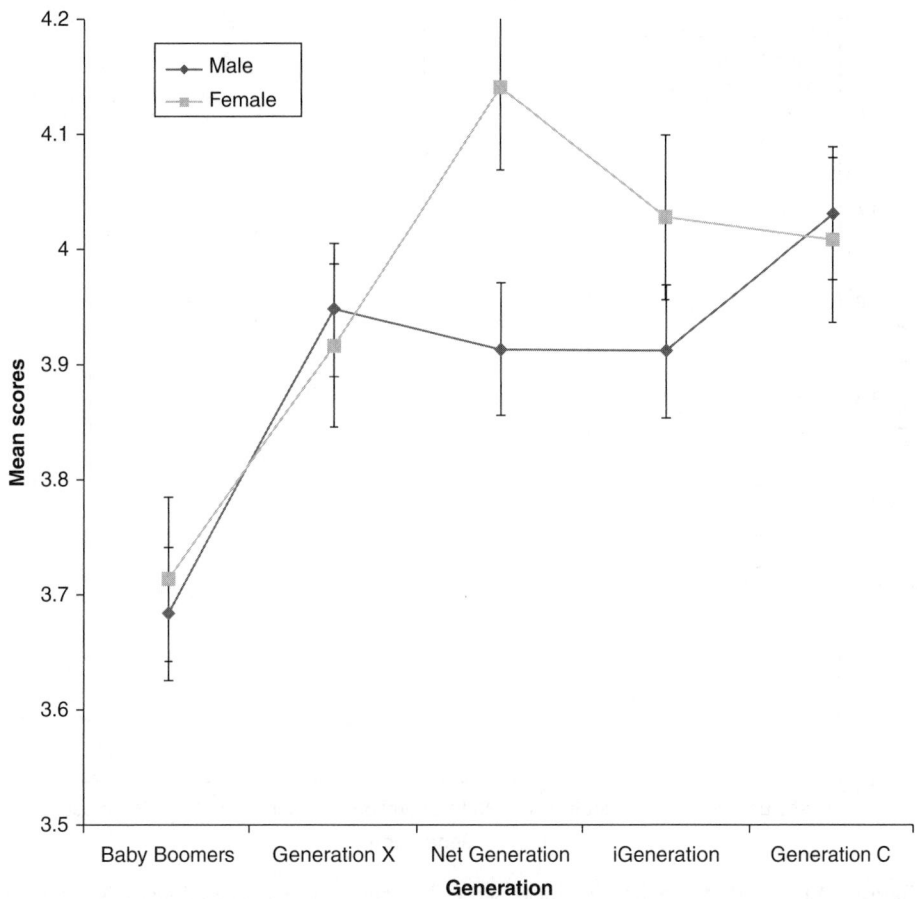

Figure 2.10 Work determination subscale mean scores by gender across generations. Higher scores indicate more work determination.

significant quadratic trend – and then a drop for Generation C children. Again, as parents rated these values, this may reflect their perception of their child's dependence on technology).

Figure 2.16 shows an identical trend to Figure 2.15 with technological optimism showing an increase across generations and a decrease for the young Generation C children. Trend analysis showed significant linear (p = .016), quadratic (p < .001), cubic (p < .001), and even quartic (p < .001) trends, which contributed to the pattern seen in Figure 2.16.

As with the previous two figures, Figure 2.17 shows no gender difference but significant quadratic (p < .001), cubic (p < .001), and quartic generational trends (p = .018) with younger generations up to the iGeneration showing increasing enthusiasm for technology and Generation C parents rating their children as less enthusiastic than iGeneration members.

Finally, Figure 2.18 displays the somewhat complex view that technology is not all good and makes life more complicated. There was a significant gender effect with males overall being more pessimistic, although this is not evident in all generations. In

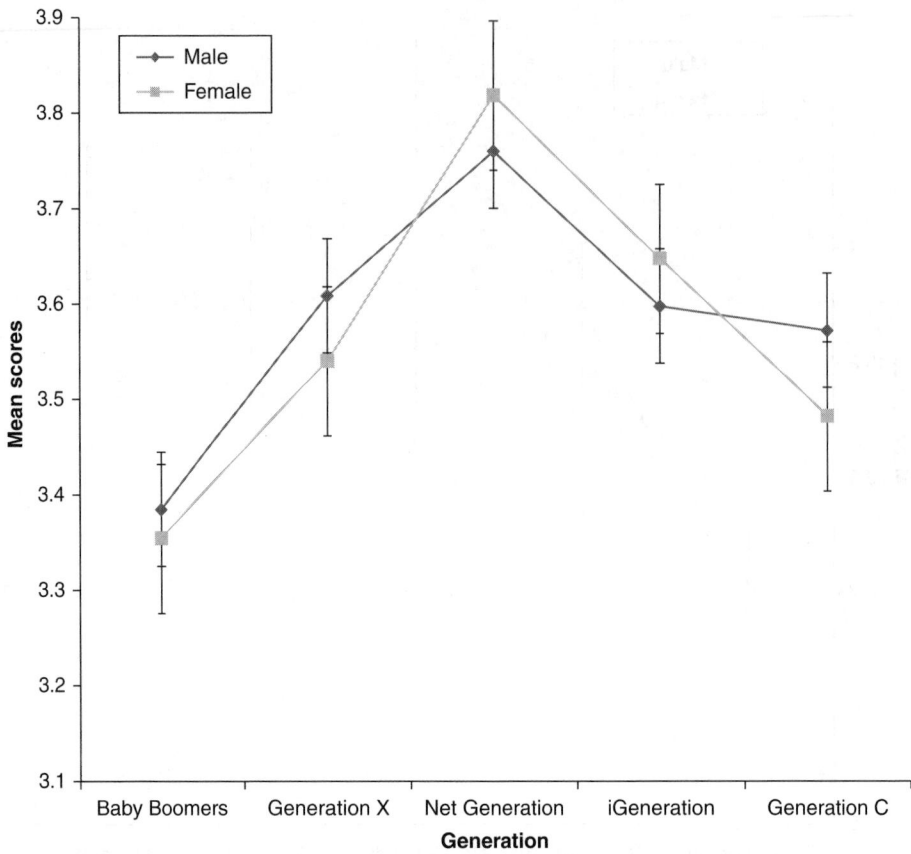

Figure 2.11 Work depth subscale mean scores by gender across generations. Higher scores indicate more work depth.

addition, the significant generation main effect is reflected in significant cubic ($p = .003$) and quartic ($p < .001$) trends, as seen in the up and down pattern with peaks of pessimism among the Boomers, Net Geners, and Generation C and less pessimism among the iGeneration and perhaps Gen X members, although this latter trend is not strong.

Technology Use

As mentioned earlier, the number of hours per day of the use of nine different technologies – going online, using a computer but not online, sending and receiving email, instant messaging or chatting, talking on the telephone, texting, playing video games, listening to music, and watching television – were calculated from the response scale for each participant. These data were subjected to a varimax rotated factor analysis, and a minimum criterion of .50 loading, which indicated that there were two factors with eigenvalues greater than 1, a general technology use factor (online, offline, email, IM/chat, phone, text, and music) and a second factor of two activities that use the television set: playing video games and watching television.

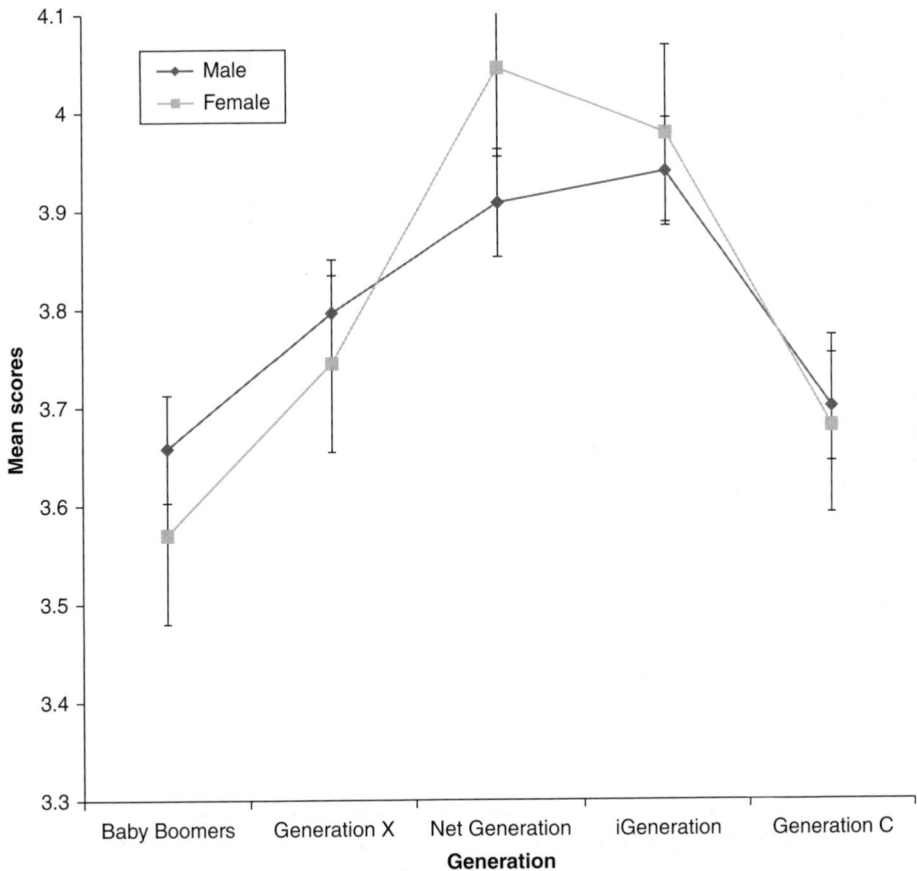

Figure 2.12   Job preference subscale mean scores by gender across generations. Higher scores indicate higher job preference.

The ANCOVA for general technology use – with generation and gender as independent variables and median income and birth year as covariates – indicated that there was a generation difference ($F(4,2297) = 104.94$, $p < .001$) that was reflected in significant quadratic and cubic trends (both $p < .001$). This trend is shown in Figure 2.19. This trend analysis indicates that general technology use increases from Baby Boomers to Gen X to the Net Generation, then slightly increases to the iGeneration, and then decreases for Generation C down to the level of the Baby Boomers. Neither the gender main effect ($F(1,2297) = 1.66$, $p = .198$) nor the generation × gender interaction ($F(4,2297) = 0.36$, $p = .835$) was significant.

The comparisons for television set use showed a different pattern, as seen in Figure 2.20. For this subscale, both gender ($F(1,2297) = 18.47$, $p < .001$) and generations main effects ($F(4,2297) = 9.50$, $p < .001$) were significant as well as their interaction ($F(4,2297) = 3.67$, $p = .005$). The main effect of generation showed significant quadratic ($p = .041$) and cubic ($p < .001$) effects. Figure 2.20 indicates that

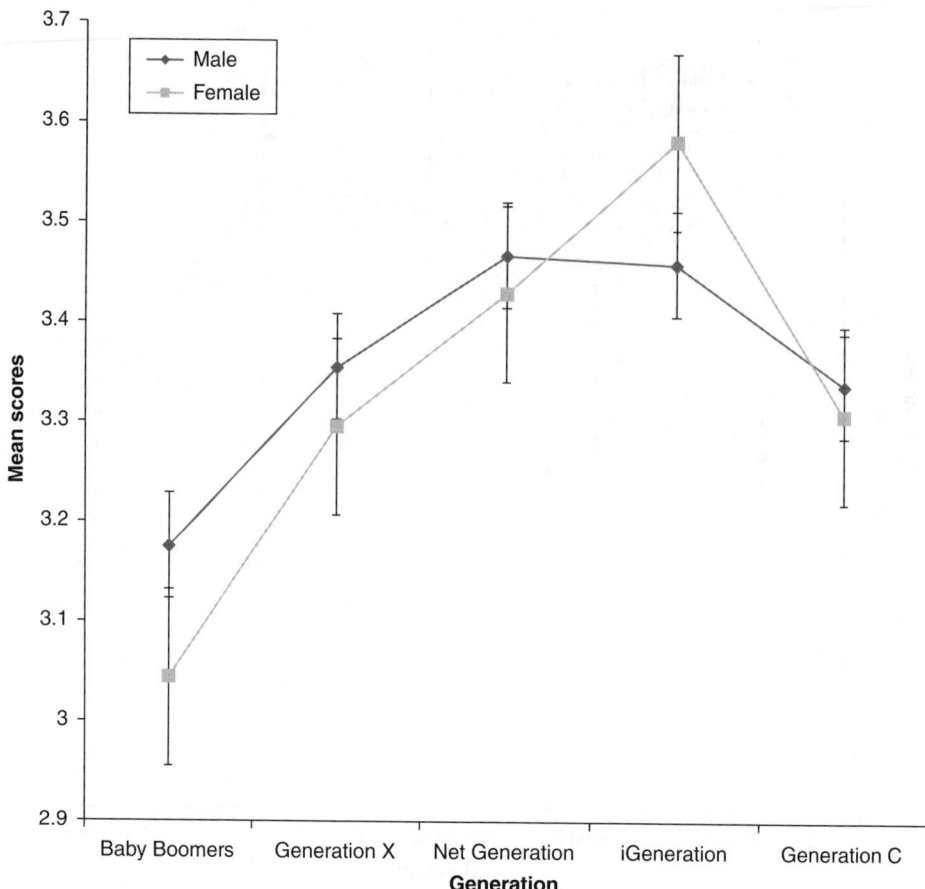

Figure 2.13 Task-switching preference subscale mean scores by gender across generations. Higher scores indicate more preference for task-switching.

use of television and video gaming increases steadily from older to younger generations, with a reduction for Generation C back to the level of the Net Generation. Overall, males used these two technologies more than females.

Participants were asked how often they used Facebook and, if they used it at all, they were asked how often they read postings, post status updates, and post photos on a six-point frequency scale from never to daily. A factor analysis indicated that all three loaded on a single Facebook use factor and a mean score was calculated for each Facebook user. Generation C children who technically were not eligible for using Facebook were eliminated from the analyses and an analysis of covariance indicated that the generation effect was significant ($F(3,1439) = 10.13, p < .001$) and only the linear trend was significant ($p = .009$). As seen in Figure 2.21, there was a steady increase in Facebook use across generations. In addition, the gender main effect was significant ($F(1,1439) = 7.72, p = .006$), with males using Facebook more than females. The interaction was not significant ($F(3,1439) = 0.45, p = .717$).

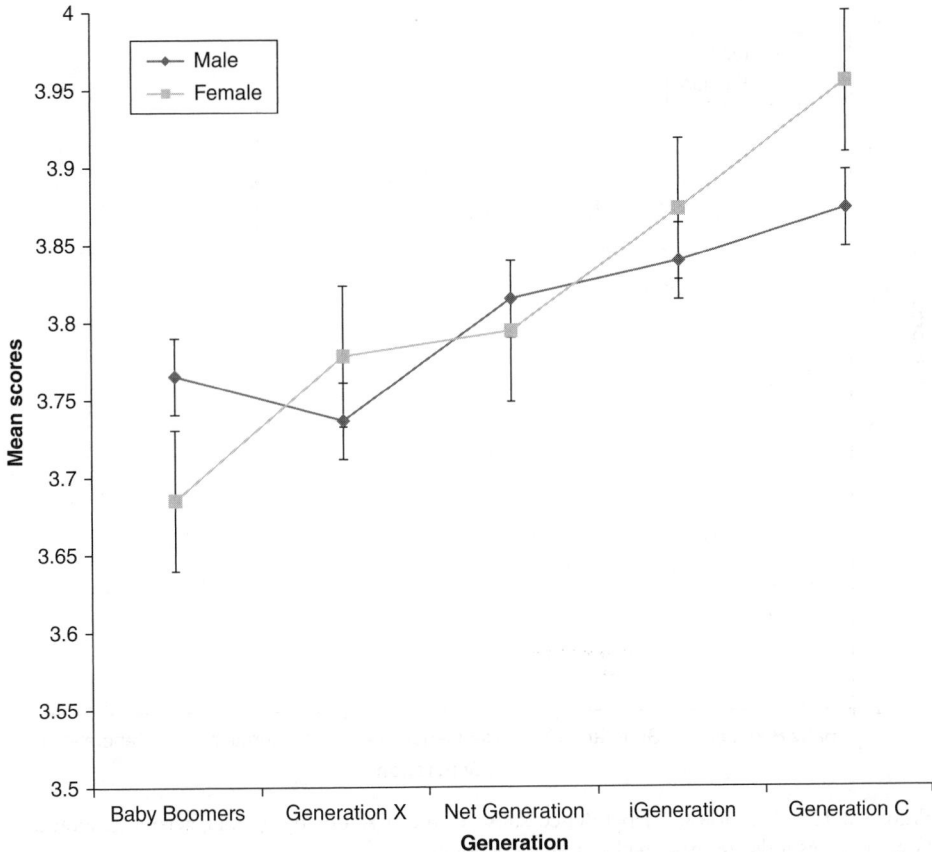

Figure 2.14   Like group work subscale mean scores by gender across generations. Higher scores indicate liking group work more.

Overall Results Summary

Table 2.6 displays a summary of the results of the comparison of gender and generation on all 18 values and beliefs subscales. As seen in the prior results, there are clear differences in all but two values and beliefs – political beliefs and liking group work – among generations, with some showing trends increasing from younger to older generations, some showing that either the Net Generation or the iGeneration held stronger beliefs, and some showing more complex patterns. Gender differences were less frequent, with 10 of the 18 subscales showing no differences between the values and beliefs of males and females, five showing females having stronger values and beliefs, and three showing males holding stronger values and beliefs. This complex picture will be discussed further later in this chapter.

Based on this constellation of results seen in Table 2.6, a post-hoc discriminant function analysis was performed, attempting to separate five generations using the 18 values, beliefs, and attitudes subscales and two of the technology usage scales (Facebook use was eliminated as it only compared four generations and not all five).

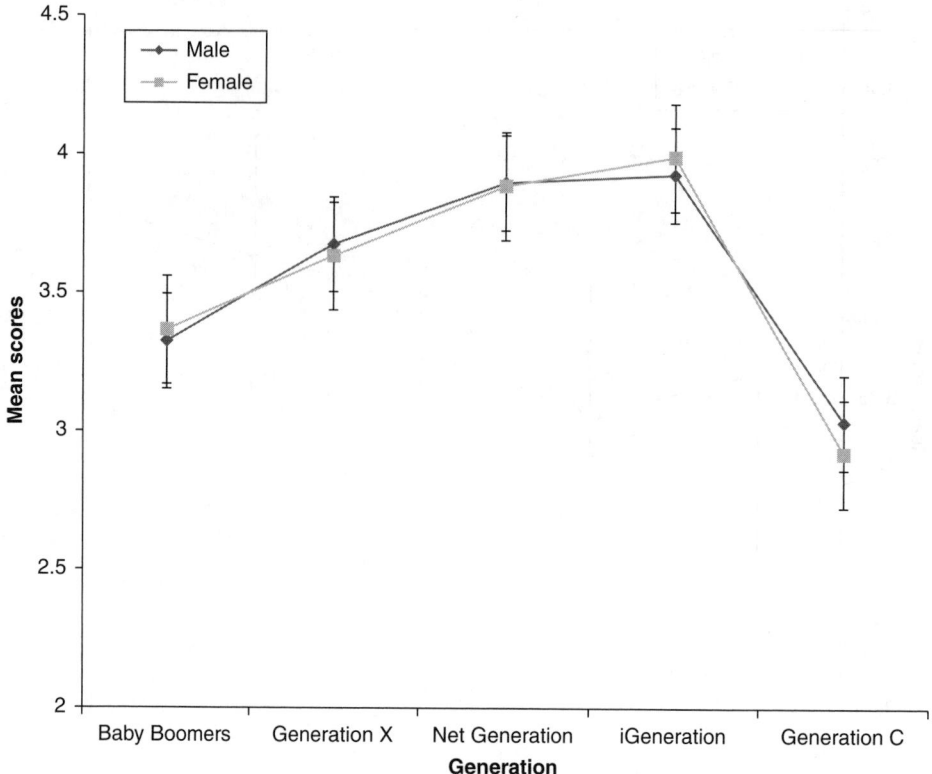

Figure 2.15   Technology dependence subscale mean scores by gender across generations. Higher scores indicate more technology dependence.

The results indicated that while four functions were used to discriminate between the five generations, only the first function (eigenvalue = .706; percent variance accounted for = 69%) and the second function (eigenvalue = .279; percent variance = 27%) were responsible for the majority of the significant discrimination (Function 1: Wilks' lambda $\chi 2$ = 2106.61, $p < .001$; Function 2: Wilks' lambda $\chi 2$ = 740.58, $p < .001$). When the group centroids and standardized canonical discriminant function coefficients were examined, it was evident that Function 1 primarily discriminated between Generation "C" (centroid = −1.26) and the iGeneration (centroid = −.16), while the other three generations were nearly identical (centroids: Baby Boomers = .84, Generation X = .72, and Net Generation = .79). The top discriminating variables were all related to technology: technology dependence (β = .523), technological optimism (β = −.517), and general technology use (β = .500). The second discriminant function appeared to more broadly differentiate between four of the five generations, with Generation C and Generation X similar in location on this function (centroids: Baby Boomers = −.96, Generation C = −.35, Generation X = −.30, Net Generation = .14, iGeneration = .80). Again, the primary discriminators – in fact, the only two with beta weights above .40 – included technological optimism (β = .700) and general technology use (β = .409). No other beta weight for Function 2 was higher than .20, again indicating that technology-related

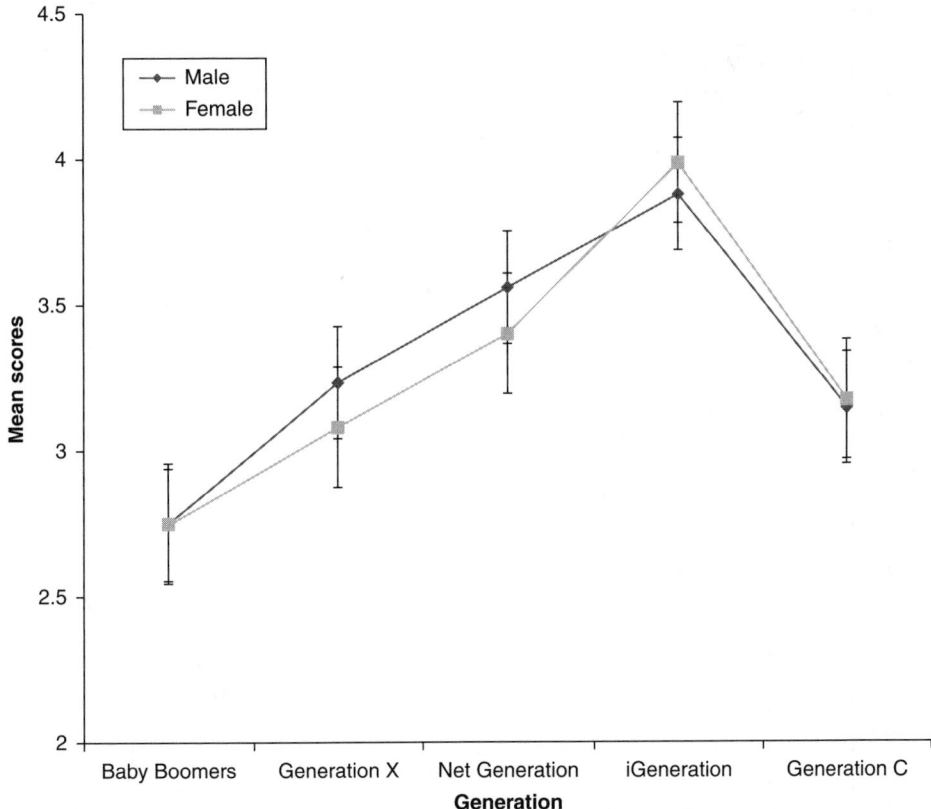

Figure 2.16 Technology optimism subscale mean scores by gender across generations. Higher scores indicate higher technology optimism.

values, beliefs, and attitudes, as well as general technology usage, were the primary ways of discriminating between generations, and particularly between the younger mini-generations.

Discussion

The study of generations is somewhat complex in several areas, including defining the generation cohorts and determining how and when to compare them. Early generational definitions (cf. Strauss & Howe, 1991) chose to define a generation as an approximately 20-year span such that at any given time there would be three active generations. As mentioned earlier in this chapter, this definition has come under scrutiny as social, cultural, and world events have occurred at a rapidly increasing rate and we have all had to react to them, which then further solidifies or alters our values, beliefs, and attitudes. In addition, given the importance of technology in our lives, it has become increasingly clear that the technology and media choices themselves have helped define and alter values, beliefs, and attitudes. With new technologies arriving on the scene and penetrating society in a matter of days instead of years as happened

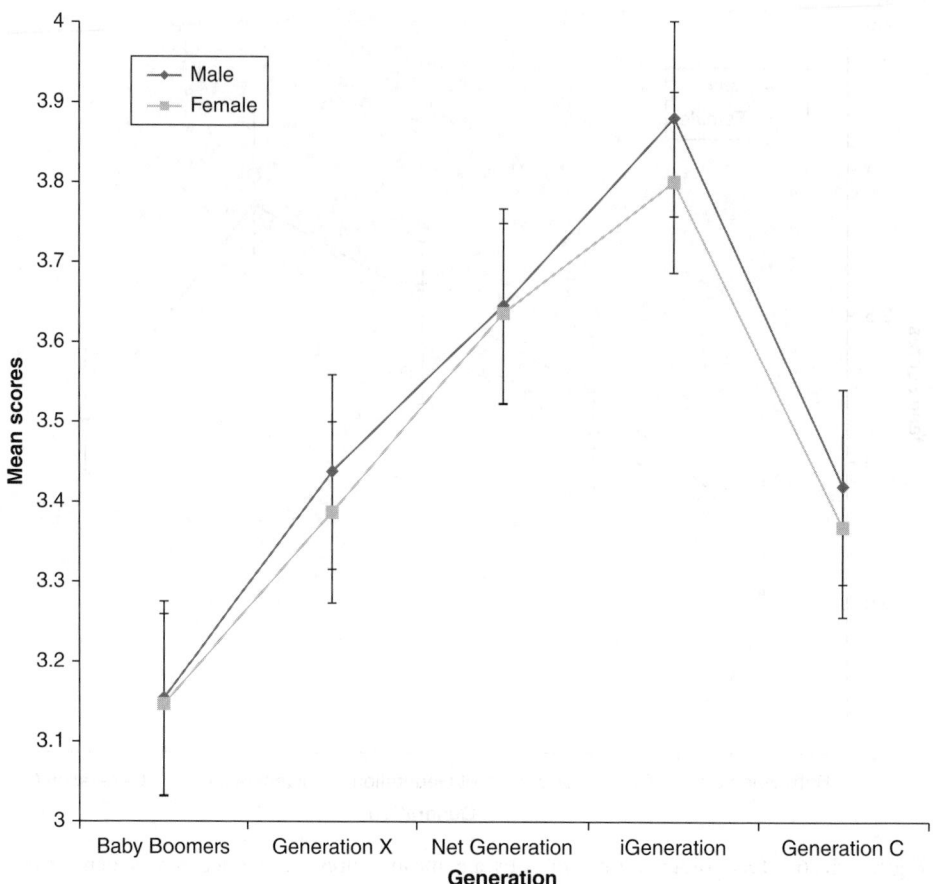

Figure 2.17 Technology enthusiasm subscale mean scores by gender across generations. Higher scores indicate more technology enthusiasm.

during earlier generations, this may provide an impetus for redefining a generational span (Rosen, 2007). This study has taken the approach that rapid increases in the appearance and popularity of new media and technologies may be driving shorter generational spans that we have defined as "mini-generations." Accordingly, this study administered a large number of items concerning values, beliefs, and attitudes to more than 2,500 members of two 20-year generations – Baby Boomers and Generation X – as well as to members of three mini-generations – Net Generation, iGeneration, and Generation "C" – although it should be noted that data for members of the youngest generation were supplied by parents.

The results of this study were mixed. As seen in Table 2.6, in some cases there were clear trends from older to younger generations. For example, younger generations were found to be more social, confident, and secure as well as more shallow, feeling that younger people know more and deserve more "things" and desire stronger family relationships. Other results showed more complex patterns, with the new Generation "C" being different from the iGeneration in most analyses other than skepticism and some work-related values. In terms of technology use, there were clear trends showing

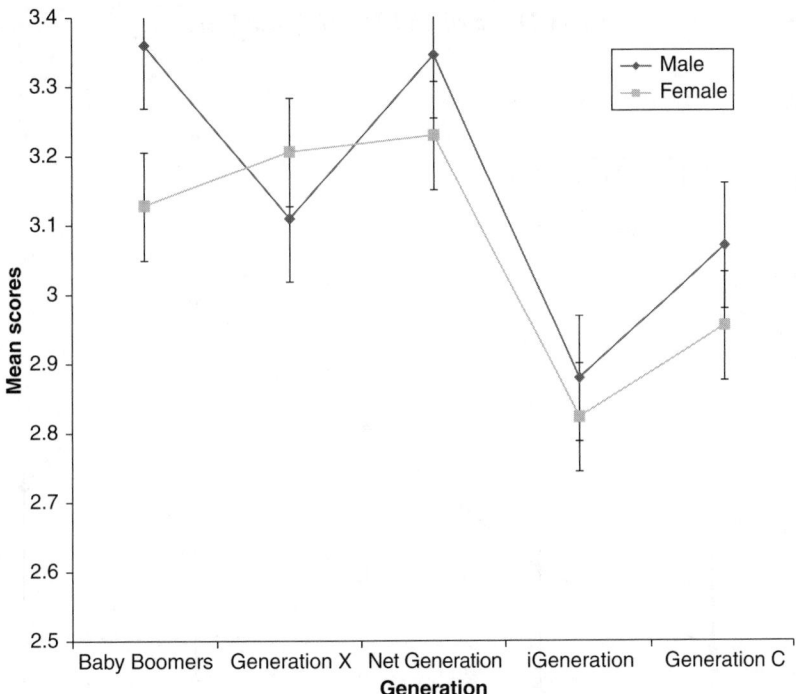

Figure 2.18 Technology pessimism subscale mean scores by gender across generations. Higher scores indicate more technology pessimism.

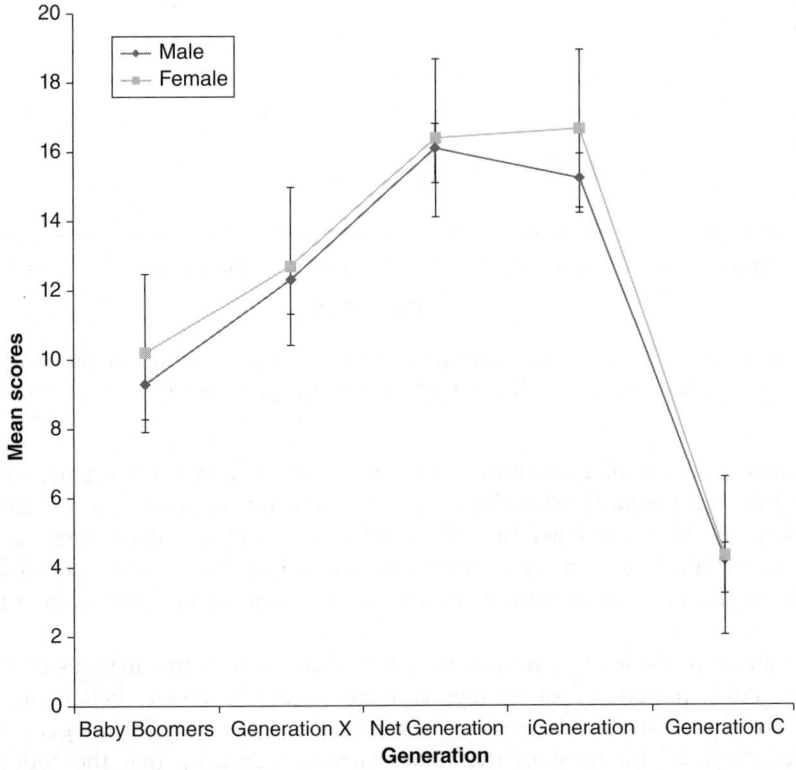

Figure 2.19 General technology use subscale mean score by gender across generations. Higher scores indicate more daily hours using technology.

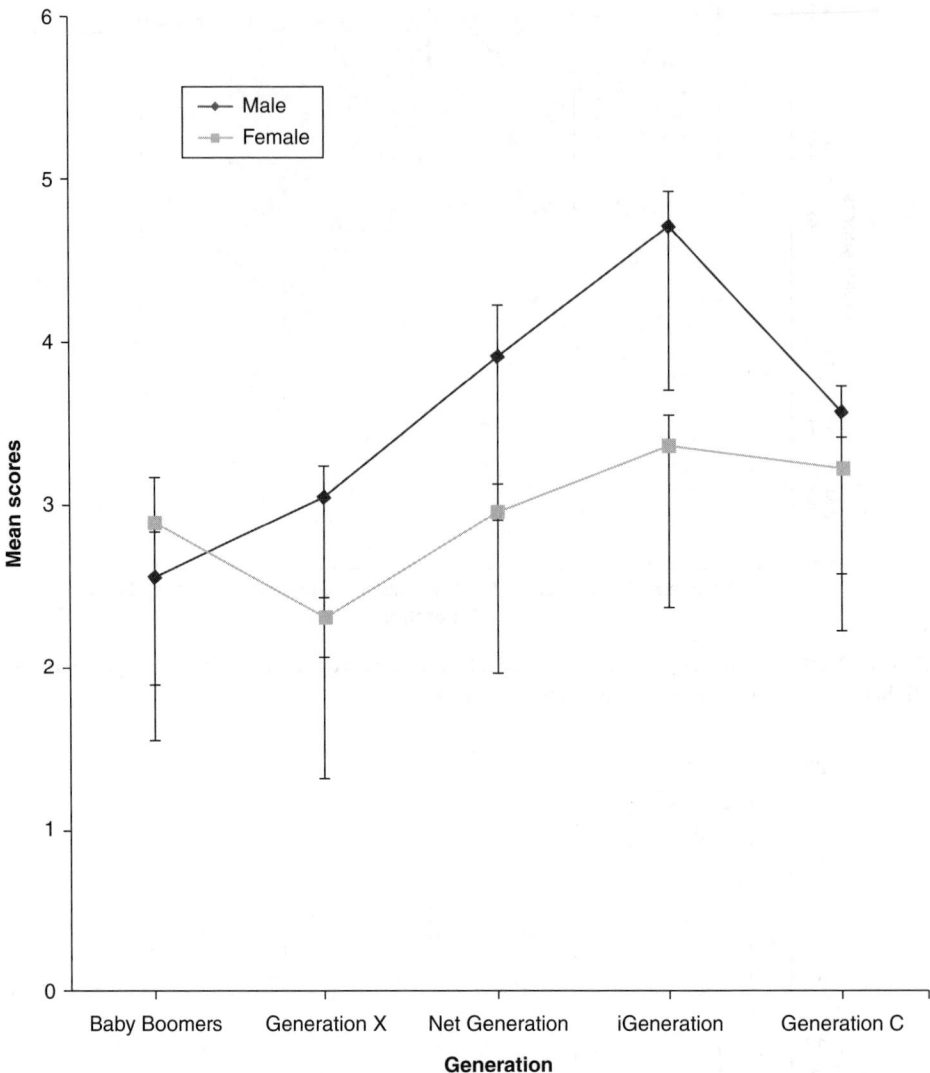

Figure 2.20 TV and video game use subscale mean scores by gender across generations. Higher scores indicate more daily hours watching television and playing video games.

differences between all generations, with the three younger mini-generations all showing the most general technology use, television and video gaming use, and even Facebook use (although Generation "C" children were not included in this analysis as they were technically too young to be on Facebook). In all three factors of technology use, the largest consumers were members of the iGeneration followed by the Net Generation.

In addition to these clear trends, however, there were many analyses showing a more complex pattern of similarities and differences in values, beliefs, and attitudes across generations. Regardless, however, there were significant generational statistical "trends" for most of the values factors, indicating that the addition of

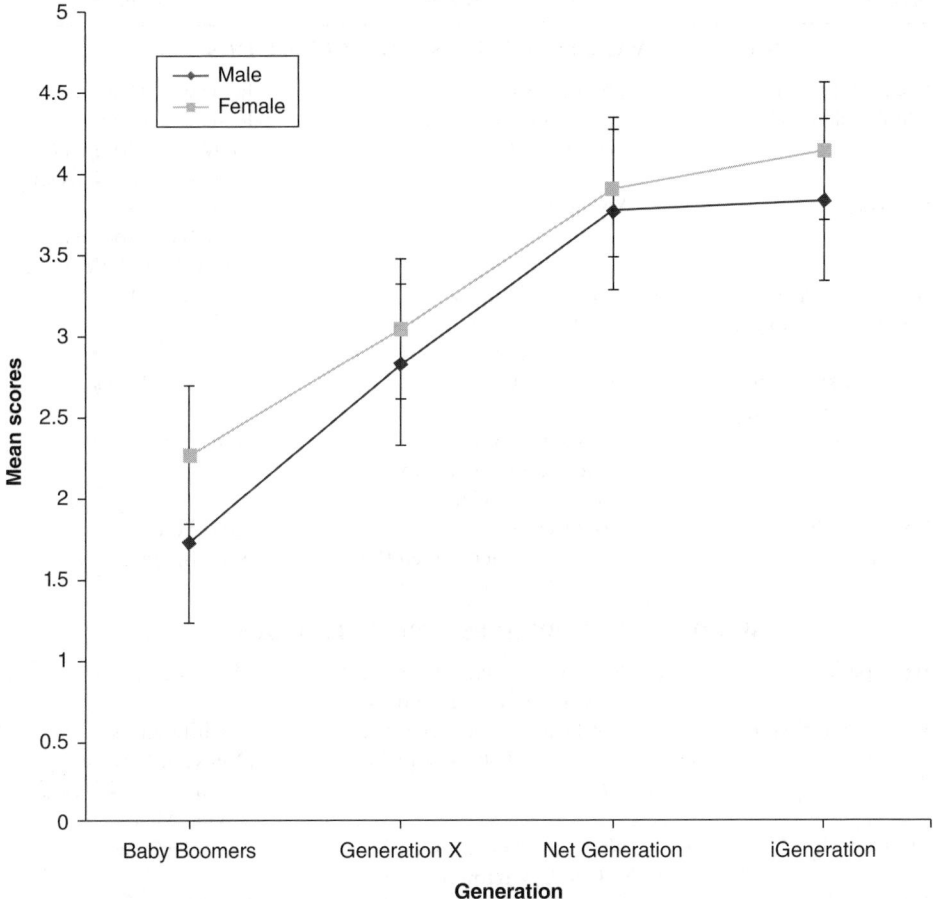

Figure 2.21 Facebook use subscale mean score by gender across generations. Higher scores indicate more Facebook usage.

mini-generations may have some validity and deserves further study. It should be noted that these mini-generations were somewhat arbitrarily defined and future research should consider using specific social, political, or cultural events as benchmarks in defining these new short, mini-generations.

In 2001 Marc Prensky, an American writer and speaker, delineated between younger learners and older educators asserting that from an educational standpoint he was seeing a "really big discontinuity," which he maintained might even be seen as a "singularity, an event which changes things so fundamentally that there is absolutely no going back" (Prensky, 2001, p. 1). This discontinuity or singularity produced what Prensky called a differentiation between "digital natives" – those born in the 1980s and beyond – and "digital immigrants," who were born prior to the 1980s and prior to the cascading impact of technology on our lives. In introducing digital natives, Prensky described them as "native speakers of the digital language of computers, video games and the Internet" (Prensky, 2001, p. 1) and contrasted their elders as "those of us who were not born into the digital world but have, at some

Table 2.6 Summary of personal, work, and technologically related values and beliefs.

Values and beliefs subscales	Generations	Gender
PERSONAL VALUES, BELIEFS, AND ATTITUDES		
Social, confident, secure	Younger > Older	Females > Males
Family relationships	Gen C > iGen > all others Net Gen < Others	Females > Males (only Baby Boomers, Gen X, and Net Gen)
Shallowness	Younger > Older	Males > Females (only Baby Boomers, Gen X, and Net Gen)

Attention, realism,
  honesty, optimism
	Net Gen (Highest) > Gen X >
	  Baby Boomers > Gen C >
	  iGeneration (Lowest)
		Females > Males

Children know more and deserve things	Younger > Older	Females > Males

Asceticism	Net Gen (Highest) >
	  Gen X = iGen > Baby
	  Boomers = Gen C
		Females > Males

Political beliefs	No differences	No differences
Skepticism	Net Gen > iGen = Gen C > Gen X > Baby Boomers	No differences
WORK VALUES, BELIEFS, AND ATTITUDES		
Work perks	Net Gen > iGen = Gen C > Gen X > Baby Boomers	Males > Females

Work determination	Net Gen = iGen = Gen C >
	  Gen X > Baby Boomers
		No differences
		(Net Gen & iGen
		  Females > Net Gen &
		  iGen Males)

Work depth	Net Gen > iGen = Gen X > Gen C > Baby Boomers	No differences
Job preference	Net Gen > iGen = Gen X > Gen C > Baby Boomers	No differences

Task-switching
  preference
	iGen > Net Gen > Gen C =
	  Gen X > Baby Boomers
		No differences
		(iGen Females > iGen
		  Males)

Likes group work	No differences	No differences
TECHNOLOGY-RELATED VALUES, BELIEFS, AND ATTITUDES		
Technology dependence	iGen > Net Gen > Gen X > BB > Gen C	No differences
Technology optimism	iGen > Net Gen = Gen C > Gen X > Baby Boomers	No differences
Technology enthusiasm	iGen > Net Gen > Gen C = Gen X > Baby Boomers	No differences

Technology pessimism	Baby Boomers = Net Gen >
	  Gen X > Gen C > iGen
		Males > Females
		(except Gen X where
		  Females > Males)

TECHNOLOGY USAGE SCALES		
General technology use	iGen > Net Gen > Gen X = Gen C > Baby Boomers	No differences
TV and video gaming	iGen > Net Gen = Gen C > Gen X > Baby Boomers	Males > Females (except Baby Boomers)
Facebook use	Increasing use younger > older	No differences

later point in our lives, become fascinated by and adopted many or most of the new technology" (Prensky, 2001, pp. 1–2).

While Prensky's differentiation made intuitive sense in the early years of the millennium, it has been criticized as being simplistic and over-arching in its labeling of all children (and now teens and young adults) born over a lengthy period of time as similar in their world view due to their shared use of myriad technologies (Bennett, Maton, & Kervin, 2008; Selwyn, 2009), and some have offered that digital natives are not one continuous generation but, rather, a series of smaller ones (Palfrey & Gasser, 2013). This study, with its three mini-generations – Net Generation, iGeneration, and Generation "C" – spanning the digital native era, has demonstrated clear differences in technology use as well as differences in values, beliefs, and attitudes, suggesting that the digital native label may be overly inclusive. In addition, the post-hoc discriminant function analysis discovered that the major discriminating variables, particularly between the three younger mini-generations, were technologically-related values, beliefs, attitudes, and technology usage, further strengthening the link between technology and generational divisions.

In summary, this study makes a fairly strong case for considering that the definition of a generation as spanning approximately 20 years may no longer be valid. Instead, this study demonstrated that even dividing generations using a fairly arbitrary cutoff at the end of each decade resulted in solid differences between mini-generations in workplace, personal, and technology-related values, beliefs, and attitudes. Hopefully these results will spur future studies to further investigate a new way of defining generations as lasting less than 20 years.

Finally, how do these generational differences in values relate to the rapidly changing technological landscape? One glimpse can be seen in comparing generations on their technological usage where we found clear generation-based trends on all three factors – general technology use, television and video gaming, and Facebook use – in spite of the arbitrary decade-ending cutoffs and in spite of factoring out median income and birth year, the latter of which equalized the between-generation comparisons in terms of variability within one generational group. In addition, the set of four technology-related values, beliefs, and attitudes – technology dependence, technology optimism, technology enthusiasm, and technology pessimism – also showed clear generational trends across the larger generations as well as between the mini-generations. Finally, a post-hoc discriminant function analysis demonstrated that those technology values, beliefs, and attitudes, coupled with general technology usage, were primarily responsible for differentiating between the three mini-generations, indicating that the 20-year span may no longer be valid as a generational marker.

Limitations

While this study opted to compare cross-sectional data taken at one point in time, there are other options to examining generational similarities and differences. For example, Twenge (2010) and her colleagues kept age constant while comparing similar data for two sets – mini-generations – of high school seniors separated in time. Others (Jin & Rounds, 2012; Krahn & Galambos, 2014) have instead taken a longitudinal approach and examined attitudes and values for the same set of participants across two time periods to determine the consistency of their beliefs. In addition, while the current study collected data only for Americans, other studies have shown similar value similarities and differences with people from other countries (e.g., Cogin, 2012; Lin, Cheong, Kim, & Jung, 2010; Krahn & Galambos, 2014).

This study has also taken a totally different approach in defining mini-generations as lasting half as many years as the previous definition of a 20-year span. Although their parents supplied data from the youngest age group – called Generation "C" in this study – it is important to note that there were some very clear differences between this younger mini-generation and their older brothers and sisters and parents in the two older mini-generations that fit the patterns of previous generations. The fact that there were differences among the three mini-generations, including the results from the discriminant function analysis implicating technology in the differentiation of mini-generations, suggests that defining mini-generations may have some validity and needs to be considered in future research and in discussions of how our values, beliefs, and attitudes are being constantly challenged and established by our immersion in an ever-changing technological landscape.

Acknowledgments

Mr. Alex Spradlin and Ms. Erika Torres performed the study reported in this chapter under the auspices of the George Marsh Applied Cognition Laboratory at California State University, Dominguez Hills. Their contributions were invaluable to this study and this chapter, as were the contributions of the GMAC Lab mentors, including Dr. L. Mark Carrier and Dr. Nancy Cheever, co-authors of this handbook.

References

Alexander, C. S. (2011). A study of the cognitive determinants of Generation Y's entitlement mentality. *Academy of Educational Leadership, 16*(1), 1.

Anguera, J. A., Boccanfuso, J., Rintoul, J. L., Al-Hashimi, O., Faraji, F., Janowich, J., ... Gazzaley, A. (2013). Video game training enhances cognitive control in older adults. *Nature, 501*(7465), 97–101.

Becton, J. B., Walker, H. J., & Jones-Farmer, A. (2014). Generational differences in workplace behavior. *Journal of Applied Social Psychology, 44*(3), 175–189.

Bennett, S., Maton, K., & Kervin, L. (2008). The "digital natives" debate: A critical review of the evidence. *British Journal of Educational Technology, 39*(5), 775–786.

Billings, D. M., Skiba, D. J., & Connors, H. R. (2005). Best practices in web-based courses: Generational differences across undergraduate and graduate nursing students. *Journal of Professional Nursing, 21*(2), 126–133.

Bolton, R. N., Parasuraman, A., Hoefnagels, A., Migchels, N., Kabadayi, S., Gruber, T., ... Solnet, D. (2013). Understanding Generation Y and their use of social media: A review and research agenda. *Journal of Service Management, 24*(3), 245–267.

Brack, J. (2012). Maximizing Millennials in the workplace. *UNC Executive Development*, 1–14.

Brasel, S. A., & Gips, J. (2011). Media multitasking behavior: Concurrent television and computer usage. *Cyberpsychology, Behavior, and Social Networking, 14*(9), 527–534.

Bullen, M., Morgan, T., & Qayyum, A. (2011). Digital learners in higher education: Generation is not the issue. *Canadian Journal of Learning and Technology/La revue canadienne de l'apprentissage et de la technologie, 37*(1). Retrieved November 21, 2014, from http://www.cjlt.ca/index.php/cjlt

Bunzel, D. (2012). *The digital generation: College students, brands, and engagement with digital media*. Retrieved November 21, 2014, from http://digitalmediaix.com/dmix_report/the-digital-generation/

Campbell, S. M., & Twenge, J. M. (2014). Is it kids today or just the fact that they're kids? In E. Parry (Ed.), *Generational diversity at work: New research perspectives* (pp. 69–80). New York, NY: Routledge.

Carrier, L. M., Cheever, N. A., Rosen, L. D., Benitez, S., & Chang, J. (2009). Multitasking across generations: Multitasking choices and difficulty ratings in three generations of Americans. *Computers in Human Behavior, 25*, 483–489.

Chi, C. G., Maier, T. A., & Gursoy, D. (2013). Employees' perceptions of younger and older managers by generation and job category. *International Journal of Hospitality Management, 34*, 42–50.

Cisco. (2011, November 2). The new workplace currency – it's not just salary anymore: Cisco study highlights new rules for attracting young talent into the workplace. Retrieved November 21, 2014, from http://newsroom.cisco.com/press-release-content?type=webcontent&articleId=532138

Cogin, J. (2012). Are generational differences in work values fact or fiction? Multi-country evidence and implications. *International Journal of Human Resource Management, 23*(11), 2268–2294.

Colby, S. L., & Ortman, J. M. (2014, May). *The baby boom cohort in the United States: 2012 to 2060 population estimates and projections*. U.S. Department of Commerce, Economics and Statistics Administration. Retrieved November 21, 2014, from http://www.census.gov/prod/2014pubs/p25-1141.pdf

Commonsense Media. (2011, October 25). Zero to eight: Children's media use in America. Retrieved November 21, 2014, from https://www.commonsensemedia.org/research/zero-to-eight-childrens-media-use-in-america

Commonsense Media. (2013, October 28). Zero to eight: Children's media use in America 2013. Retrieved November 21, 2014, from https://www.commonsensemedia.org/research/zero-to-eight-childrens-media-use-in-america-2013

Costanza, D. P., Badger, J. M., Fraser, R. L., Severt, J. B., & Gade, P. A. (2012). Generational differences in work-related attitudes: A meta-analysis. *Journal of Business and Psychology, 27*(4), 375–394.

Coupland, D. (1991). *Generation X: Tales for an accelerated culture*. New York, NY: St. Martin's Press.

David, P., Xu, L., Srivastava, J., & Kim, J. H. (2013). Media multitasking between two conversational tasks. *Computers in Human Behavior, 29*(4), 1657–1663.

Debevec, K., Schewe, C. D., Madden, T. J., & Diamond, W. D. (2013). Are today's Millennials splintering into a new generational cohort? Maybe! *Journal of Consumer Behaviour, 12*(1), 20–31.

Deverson, J., & Hamblett, C. (1964). *Generation X: What's behind the rebellious anger of Britain's untamed youth? Here in their own words is how they really feel about drugs, drink, God, sex, class, color and kicks*. Greenwich, CT: Fawcett Crest.

Edge, K. (2014). A review of the empirical generations at work research: Implications for school leaders and future research. *School Leadership and Management, 34*(2), 136–155.

Gallup & Operation HOPE. (2013). 2013 Gallup-HOPE Index report. Retrieved November 21, 2014, from http://www.gallup.com/services/176750/2013-gallup-hope-index-report.aspx

Gursoy, D., Maier, T. A., & Chi, C. G. (2008). Generational differences: An examination of work values and generational gaps in the hospitality workforce. *International Journal of Hospitality Management, 27*(3), 448–458.

Hargittai, E., & Hinnant, A. (2008). Digital inequality differences in young adults' use of the Internet. *Communication Research, 35*(5), 602–621.

Helsper, E. J., & Eynon, R. (2010). Digital natives: Where is the evidence? *British Educational Research Journal, 36*(3), 503–520.

Hernaus, T., & Vokic, N. P. (2014). Work design for different generational cohorts: Determining common and idiosyncratic job characteristics. *Journal of Organizational Change Management, 27*(4), 6–6.

Horvitz, B. (2012, May 4). After Gen X, Millennials, what should next generation be? *USA Today*. Retrieved November 21, 2014, from http://usatoday30.usatoday.com/money/advertising/story/2012-05-03/naming-the-next-generation/54737518/1

Jacobsen, W. C., & Forste, R. (2011). The wired generation: Academic and social outcomes of electronic media use among university students. *Cyberpsychology, Behavior, and Social Networking, 14*(5), 275–280.

Jin, J., & Rounds, J. (2012). Stability and change in work values: A meta-analysis of longitudinal studies. *Journal of Vocational Behavior, 80*(2), 326–339.

Jobe, L. L. (2014). Generational differences in work ethic among 3 generations of registered nurses. *Journal of Nursing Administration, 44*(5), 303–308.

Joiner, R., Gavin, J., Brosnan, M., Cromby, J., Gregory, H., Guiller, J., … Moon, A. (2012). Gender, Internet experience, Internet identification, and Internet anxiety: A ten-year followup. *Cyberpsychology, Behavior, and Social Networking, 15*(7), 370–372.

Joiner, R., Gavin, J., Brosnan, M., Cromby, J., Gregory, H., Guiller, J., … Moon, A. (2013). Comparing first and second generation digital natives' Internet use, Internet anxiety, and Internet identification. *Cyberpsychology, Behavior, and Social Networking, 16*(7), 549–552.

Judd, T., & Kennedy, G. (2011). Measurement and evidence of computer-based task switching and multitasking by "Net Generation" students. *Computers and Education, 56*(3), 625–631.

Kolikant, Y. B. D. (2010). Digital natives, better learners? Students' beliefs about how the Internet influenced their ability to learn. *Computers in Human Behavior, 26*(6), 1384–1391.

Kowske, B. J., Rasch, R., & Wiley, J. (2010). Millennials' (lack of) attitude problem: An empirical examination of generational effects on work attitudes. *Journal of Business and Psychology, 25*(2), 265–279.

Krahn, H. J., & Galambos, N. L. (2014). Work values and beliefs of "Generation X" and "Generation Y." *Journal of Youth Studies, 17*(1), 92–112.

Kramer, L. W. (2010). Generational diversity. *Dimensions of Critical Care Nursing, 29*(3), 125–128.

Lariscy, R. W., Tinkham, S. F., & Sweetser, K. D. (2011). Kids these days: Examining differences in political uses and gratifications, Internet political participation, political information efficacy, and cynicism on the basis of age. *American Behavioral Scientist, 55*(6), 749–764.

Lee, J., Lin, L., & Robertson, T. (2012). The impact of media multitasking on learning. *Learning, Media and Technology, 37*(1), 94–104.

Lester, S. W., Standifer, R. L., Schultz, N. J., & Windsor, J. M. (2012). Actual versus perceived generational differences at work: An empirical examination. *Journal of Leadership and Organizational Studies, 19*(3), 341–354.

Leung, L. (2013). Generational differences in content generation in social media: The roles of the gratifications sought and of narcissism. *Computers in Human Behavior, 29*(3), 997–1006.

Lin, W. Y., Cheong, P. H., Kim, Y. C., & Jung, J. Y. (2010). Becoming citizens: Youths' civic uses of new media in five digital cities in East Asia. *Journal of Adolescent Research, 25*(6), 839–857.

Lyons, S., & Kuron, L. (2014). Generational differences in the workplace: A review of the evidence and directions for future research. *Journal of Organizational Behavior, 35*(S1), S139–S157.

Malik, S., & Khera, S. N. (2014). New generation – great expectations: Exploring the work attributes of Gen Y. *Global Journal of Finance and Management, 6*(5), 433–438.

McCarthy, J., Cleveland, J. N., & Heraty, N. (2014). Beyond generational differences? In E. Parry (Ed.), *Generational diversity at work: New research perspectives* (pp. 164–181). New York, NY: Routledge.

Mencl, J., & Lester, S. W. (2014). More alike than different: What generations value and how the values affect employee workplace perceptions. *Journal of Leadership and Organizational Studies.* Retrieved November 21, 2014, from http://jlo.sagepub.com/content/early/2014/04/15/1548051814529825.abstract

Meriac, J. P., Woehr, D. J., & Banister, C. (2010). Generational differences in work ethic: An examination of measurement equivalence across three cohorts. *Journal of Business Psychology, 25*, 315–324.

Morgan, J. (2014, May 20). *The decline of trust in the United States: A look at the trend and what can be done about it.* Retrieved November 21, 2014, from https://medium.com/@slowerdawn/the-decline-of-trust-in-the-united-states-fb8ab719b82a

Nam, T. (2012). Dual effects of the Internet on political activism: Reinforcing and mobilizing. *Government Information Quarterly, 29*, S90–S97.

Nicholas, D., Rowlands, I., Clark, D., & Williams, P. (2011, January). Google Generation II: Web behaviour experiments with the BBC. *Aslib Proceedings, 63*(1), 28–45.

Nickelodeon. (2013, November 20). Nickelodeon introduces "The story of me" research study, providing inside look at today's emerging generation of kids. Retrieved November 21, 2014, from http://www.prnewswire.com/news-releases/nickelodeon-introduces-the-story-of-me-research-study-providing-inside-look-at-todays-emerging-generation-of-kids-232684201.html

Nielsen Company. (2014, February 26). *Millennials: Technology = social connection.* Retrieved November 21, 2014, from http://www.nielsen.com/content/corporate/us/en/insights/news/2014/millennials-technology-social-connection.html

Oh, E., & Reeves, T. C. (2014). Generational differences and the integration of technology in learning, instruction, and performance. In J. M. Spector, M. D. Merrill, J. Elen, & M. J. Bishop (Eds.), *Handbook of research on educational communications and technology* (pp. 819–828). New York, NY: Springer.

Palfrey, J., & Gasser, U. (2013). *Born digital: Understanding the first generation of digital natives.* New York, NY: Basic Books.

Parry, E., & Urwin, P. (2011). Generational differences in work values: A review of theory and evidence. *International Journal of Management Reviews, 13*(1), 79–96.

Prensky, M. (2001). Digital natives, digital immigrants. *On the Horizon, 9*(5), 1–6.

Rajput, N., Kochhar, R., & Kesharwani, S. (2013). Do motivational strategies and issues differ across generations? An analytical study. *Global Journal of Enterprise Information Systems, 5*(1), 2–10.

Rangaswamy, A., & Gupta, S. (2000). Innovation adoption and diffusion in the digital environment: Some research opportunities. *New Product Diffusion Models*, 75–96.

Robb, M., Takeuchi, L., & Kotler, J. (2011, March). *Always connected: The new digital media habits of young children.* Joan Ganz Cooney Center at Sesame Workshop. Retrieved November 21, 2014, from http://www.joanganzcooneycenter.org/publication/always-connected-the-new-digital-media-habits-of-young-children/

Robinson, J. P., & Martin, S. P. (2009) Social attitude differences between Internet users and non-users: Evidence from the General Social Survey. *Information Communication and Society, 12*(4), 508–524.

Romero, M., Guitert, M., Sangrà, A., & Bullen, M. (2013). Do UOC students fit in the Net Generation profile? An approach to their habits in ICT use. *International Review of Research in Open and Distance Learning, 14*(3), 158–181.

Rosen, L. D. (2007). *Me, MySpace, and I: Parenting the Net generation.* New York, NY: Palgrave Macmillan.

Rosen, L. D., Carrier, L. M., & Cheever, N. A. (2010). *Rewired: Understanding the iGeneration and the way they learn.* New York, NY: Palgrave Macmillan.

Rosen, L. D., Cheever, N. A., Cummings, C., & Felt, J. (2008). The impact of emotionality and self-disclosure on online dating versus traditional dating. *Computers in Human Behavior, 24,* 2124–2157.

Selwyn, N. (2009, July). The digital native: Myth and reality. *Aslib Proceedings, 61*(4), 364–379.

Sessa, V. I., Kabacoff, R. I., Deal, J., & Brown, H. (2007). Generational differences in leader values and leadership behaviors. *Psychologist-Manager Journal, 10*(1), 47–74.

Soni, S., Upadhyaya, M., & Kautish, P. (2011). Generational differences in work commitment of software professionals: Myth or reality? *Abhigyan, 28*(4), 30–42.

Srinivasan, V., John, D. A., & Christine, M. N. (2014). Generational cohorts and personal values. In E. Parry (Ed.), *Generational diversity at work: New research perspectives* (pp. 185–205). New York, NY: Routledge.

Stapleton, J. L., Wen, H. J., Starrett, D., & Kilburn, M. (2007). Generational differences in using online learning systems. *Human Systems Management, 26*(2), 99–109.

Strauss, K. (2013, September 17). Do Millennials think differently about money and career? Retrieved November 21, 2014, from http://www.forbes.com/sites/karstenstrauss/2013/09/17/do-millennials-think-differently-about-money-and-career/

Strauss, W., & Howe, N. (1991). *Generations: The history of America's future, 1584–2069.* New York, NY: Morrow.

Takeuchi, L. M. (2011). *Families matter: Designing media for a digital age.* Joan Ganz Cooney Center at Sesame Workshop. Retrieved November 21, 2014, from http://www.joanganzcooneycenter.org/publication/families-matter-designing-media-for-a-digital-age/

Tapscott, D. (1997). *Growing up digital: The rise of the Net generation.* New York, NY: McGraw-Hill.

Tapscott, D. (2009). *Grown up digital: How the Net generation is changing your world.* New York, NY: McGraw-Hill.

Taylor, P., & Keeter, S. (2010). Millennials: A portrait of Generation Next. Confident. Connected. Open to change. Pew Research Center. Retrieved November 21, 2014, from http://www.pewsocialtrends.org/files/2010/10/millennials-confident-connected-open-to-change.pdf

Terry, C. P., & Sliwinski, M. J. (2012). Aging and random task switching: The role of endogenous versus exogenous task selection. *Experimental Aging Research, 38*(1), 87–109.

Trzesniewski, K. H., & Donnellan, M. B. (2010). Rethinking "Generation Me": A study of cohort effects from 1976–2006. *Perspectives on Psychological Science, 5*(1), 58–75.

Twenge, J. M. (2009). Generational changes and their impact in the classroom: Teaching Generation Me. *Medical Education, 43*(5), 398–405.

Twenge, J. M. (2010). A review of the empirical evidence on generational differences in work attitudes. *Journal of Business and Psychology, 25*(2), 201–210.

Twenge, J. M., Campbell, S. M., Hoffman, B. J., & Lance, C. E. (2010). Generational differences in work values: Leisure and extrinsic values increasing, social and intrinsic values decreasing. *Journal of Management, 36*(5), 1117–1142.

Uhls, Y. T., & Greenfield, P. M. (2012). The value of fame: Preadolescent perceptions of popular media and their relationship to future aspirations. *Developmental Psychology, 48*(2), 315–326.

Urick, M. J., & Hollensbe, E. C. (2014). Toward an identity-based perspective of generations. In E. Parry (Ed.), *Generational diversity at work: New research perspectives* (pp. 114–128). New York, NY: Routledge.

Urwin, P., Buscha, F., & Parry, E. (2014). Back to basics: Is there a significant generational dimension and where does it "cut"? In E. Parry (Ed.), *Generational diversity at work: New research perspectives* (pp. 81–94). New York, NY: Routledge.

Voorveld, H. A., & van der Goot, M. (2013). Age differences in media multitasking: A diary study. *Journal of Broadcasting and Electronic Media, 57*(3), 392–408.

Whitney-Gibson, J., Greenwood, R. A., & Murphy, E. F., Jr. (2011). Generational differences in the workplace: Personal values, behaviors, and popular beliefs. *Journal of Diversity Management, 4*(3), 1–8.

Yusoff, W., Fauziah, W., Tan, S. K., Rajah, S., & Rajah, S. (2013). Employee satisfaction and citizenship performance among generation X and Y. Retrieved November 21, 2014, from http://eprints.uthm.edu.my/4118/1/paper_105.pdf

Zichuhr, K. (2011, February 3). *Generations and their gadgets.* Pew Internet & American Life Project. Retrieved November 21, 2014, from http://www.pewinternet.org/2011/02/03/generations-and-their-gadgets/

Zipcar. (2014, January 27). Zipcar's annual millennial survey shows the kids are all right. Retrieved November 21, 2014, from http://www.zipcar.com/press/releases/fourth-annual-millennial-survey

3

Internet Credibility and Digital Media Literacy

Nancy A. Cheever and Jeffrey Rokkum

California State University, Dominguez Hills

As technological advancements continue to increase online users' access to information, the availability of unverified online material is on the rise. The accuracy of this information varies widely, and policies to verify Internet content are in their infancy. Further, the proliferation of blogging and other forms of writing available on the Internet has changed the way the news and information are presented and consumed. While people seeking information in the past turned to edited print sources such as newspapers, books, and encyclopedias, today's information seekers almost always turn to the Internet (Biddix, Chung, & Park, 2011; Smith, 2014), where they are exposed to millions of information sources that, to them, appear to all have the same level of accuracy. Stories by veteran journalists, bloggers, advertisers, and ordinary citizens share a medium that is reliant on the user to decipher its credibility. This chapter will examine the literature surrounding the credibility, trust, and perception of Internet information, and present some of the issues and programs for Internet and digital media literacy education.

Use of Online Content

Nearly 40% of the world's population uses the Internet to locate information (Internet World Stats, 2014). In the United States, 86% of all adults use the Internet and approximately 72% of the population uses it on a daily basis (Smith, 2014). More than 50% of Americans use the Internet to conduct banking, and 56% access the Internet through mobile devices such as smartphones. The Pew Research Center found that in May 2011, 92% of adults who used the Internet used search engines to find information, while 59% did so on a typical day (Purcell, 2011), making searching the most popular online activity among U.S. adults. Scholars have used a wide range of assessment methods for capturing and tracking a person's Internet usage. However, the Internet's vast reach and myriad ways in which people use the medium make measuring Internet skills and usage difficult (Litt, 2013). While this chapter will not examine the various methods of testing people's Internet search skills, we will examine the research surrounding how people assess the credibility of online information and programs to educate people on how best to utilize the medium.

The Wiley Handbook of Psychology, Technology, and Society, First Edition. Edited by Larry D. Rosen, Nancy A. Cheever, and L. Mark Carrier.
© 2015 John Wiley & Sons, Ltd. Published 2015 by John Wiley & Sons, Ltd.

Research in our media psychology laboratory in the mid-2000s involving a large sample of Southern California residents showed that in general Internet users were not assessing the credibility of online sources before using the information (Cheever, 2007). We found that people were more likely to turn to an Internet source rather than a printed source when searching for information about a topic. For news, almost all respondents (96%) reported it is likely they would turn to an online news website, 89% would turn to the television, and 68% said it is likely they would turn to a newspaper. Fewer people were likely to turn to blogs – written either by reporters or peers – than other news sources. We concluded that people in the mid-2000s did not appear to possess the skills necessary to find the best information on the Internet. Our data showed that most people use only the first five links on a Google search. Just 15% use the first 10 links, 12% use all the links of the first page only, and 20% use links on any of the first three pages. Just 3% use links on more than the first three pages, which some educators say is necessary to find the best and most reliable information.

More recent research by the Pew Research Center found that teacher's assessments of the Internet as a tool for their students reported it was helpful, yet they had reservations about the credibility of the information and their students' understanding of this credibility (Purcell et al., 2012). When asked about the impact of digital technologies and the Internet on their students' research skills, 77% of these teachers said it had been "mostly positive." Almost all (99%) teachers agreed that the Internet provides access to a wider range of resources, and 65% agreed "that the Internet makes today's students more self-sufficient researchers." Three-quarters of the teachers "strongly agreed" that search engines have "conditioned students to expect to be able to find information quickly and easily," and most agreed that the amount of information is overwhelming to most students (83%). They also agreed that current available technologies discourage students from utilizing a "wide range of sources when conducting research" (71%), and 60% agreed that these technologies "make it harder for students to find credible sources of information."

Credibility of Online Material

In 1998 *Lancet* published a paper by British physician Andrew Wakefield and his colleagues about a possible link between autism and measles-mumps-rubella (MMR) vaccinations, which led to a flurry of sensational media reports and subsequent decline in vaccinations in the United States and the United Kingdom (Willingham & Helft, 2014). When investigative journalist Brian Deer discovered the research to be seriously flawed, 10 of 12 of the paper's authors (Wakefield was not one of them) and *Lancet* retracted the main interpretations of the findings. In the years that followed, several papers by leading scientists published in respected journals (among them *Pediatrics*, the *New England Journal of Medicine*, and the *Journal of the American Medical Association*), investigating the link between vaccines and autism – and involving millions of data points – have shown no such association, yet people continue to avoid vaccinating their children. In 2010, *Lancet* retracted the entire paper and Mr. Wakefield's medical license was revoked (Dominus, 2011), yet the vaccination rate in the United States has continued to decline. Why? One of the major contributions is the presentation of false information on websites that appeal to people looking for evidence that vaccines will hurt their children. Also called confirmation bias, people seeking acceptance of their already held beliefs can find a number of Internet sources that exacerbate their fears and attempt to prove something that the scientific world has already shown to be false. When people lack the ability or desire to objectively evaluate Internet sources, the information they find can have profound effects.

Researchers define and measure online credibility in many ways. Greer (2003) defined a credible online source as one that provides correct information without bias, and contains material written by experts who are trustworthy. Flanagin and Metzger (2007) identified the two primary sources of online source credibility as trustworthiness and expertise. They pointed to site-design features, cross-media comparisons, source attributions, and the role of the user's reliance on web information as the primary ways to assess credibility. Secondary features include having the appropriate credentials displayed, a well-known reputation from sponsors, and a lack of commercial content. Other researchers define credibility as believability, since credible information and credible people are believable (Tseng & Fogg, 1999), and others attribute credibility to trustworthiness and competence (Fritch & Cromwell, 2001). Finally, Johnson and Kaye (2010) assessed Internet credibility using a multidimensional construct consisting of accuracy, fairness, believability, and depth of information.

Some researchers apply criteria for general source credibility to the online world, since judgments of Internet sources are often based on the perceptions of the people who create them. Traditional models of credibility that help determine online credibility are author identity, sponsor credibility, author's credentials, and author's affiliations (Warnick, 2004). Tseng and Fogg (1999) identified four main types of credibility: (1) presumed credibility, which refers to how much the perceiver believes someone or something because of general assumptions held about the person or object; (2) reputed credibility, which is how much someone believes a piece of information because of a third party's report; (3) surface credibility, which is how much the perceiver believes someone has credibility based upon a simple inspection of the source; and (4) experienced credibility, which refers to how much a person believes someone or something based on firsthand experience. People with a greater need for information are more likely to accept information provided from technology. More specifically, people in unfamiliar situations, or ones who have failed at a task, perceive computing technology as more credible.

Research has shown that people avoid the laborious task of information evaluation and instead utilize website design and ease of usage (Metzger, Flanagin, & Medders, 2010). Since people do not spend too long on any one website, users are likely to develop heuristics for analyzing webpages quickly. Since one of the most dominant aspects of the webpage is the way it looks, users analyze data based on surface aspects. People are not likely to verify information they found, and instead rely upon these strategies they have developed before to analyze the information. Focus groups comprising the various geographical areas of the United States revealed a strong trend of utilizing social networks that are online and offline to help find and evaluate information that was found on the Internet. Metzger and colleagues (2010) found that information assessment strategies coalesced into four different subgroups: social information pooling, social confirmation of personal opinion, enthusiastic endorsement, and resource sharing via interpersonal exchange. For social information pooling participants were more likely to utilize testimonials, proportion of positive to negative reviews, and the overall feedback system when making their choices. They also reported that the more reviews or testimonials they found on a website the more credible they found it, even though reviews and testimonials do not produce true credibility. Blogs, wikis, and social networking sites were found to be less credible, as they engendered a sense of skepticism among participants, especially among older participants.

In our study back in 2007, when visiting an unfamiliar website, the majority of people reported doing a variety of activities to verify the credibility of the site, including comparing it with other sources, checking the credentials and email address of the author, checking the extension of the website, and checking when the site was updated or created (Cheever, 2007). This indicates that most people were concerned about the credibility of the websites they visited, but the level of concern for the website's credibility varied. Table 3.1 shows the percentage of people in our study who performed a variety of evaluative activities when visiting a website.

Through factor analysis, we determined there are three levels of activity, or what we called "concern," that people have when determining the credibility of a website. The first is *mildly concerned*, with the activities confined to checking material on the website itself (checking email address of author, check the extension, check the purpose of the site, check when it was updated or created). The second factor is *concerned*, with activities moving beyond the website and into other areas, such as checking the credentials of the author both through the site and with outside sources, checking to see whether the site is reviewed by experts, and whether the site is promoting or advocating something. The third level is *extremely concerned* about the credibility of a website, with activities moving outside the website itself and directly addressing credibility issues (emailing the author and checking the accuracy of the site by comparing it to other sources).

More recent studies on how people make online credibility judgments show that factors such as page layout, cross-checkability, and the actual URL drive people's perception of online credibility (Dochterman & Stamp, 2010). Analyzing 629 comments generated by focus groups, Dochterman and Stamp (2010) discovered the most important factors in determining website credibility relate to the website's look and the user's familiarity and interest, and included professionalism, content, page layout,

Table 3.1 Percentage of whether the respondent checks certain information on the websites they are unfamiliar with to verify the credibility of the site.

Variable	Checks	Does not check
Check credentials of author (from website)	60%	40%
Check credentials of author (from other sources)	38%	62%
Email author	7%	93%
Look at email address	50%	50%
Check if site is an advocacy group	33%	67%
Check whether info on site is reviewed by experts	54%	46%
Check when website was created/updated	60%	40%
Check extensions (.com, .edu)	56%	44%
Check accuracy by comparing to other sources	66%	34%
Check whether page is from organization or individual	44%	56%
Check purpose of website	46%	54%

and authority. Westerwick (2013) discovered experimentally that the look of a site did not compensate for low sponsor (the organization, group, or person referenced on top of a website) credibility. However, a higher ranking in search engine results increased sponsor credibility, thus indirectly influencing source credibility. Fogg et al. (2002) found that most people mentioned "design look" of the site most frequently when assessing a website's credibility, with 46% of the participants mentioning that attribute. Other scholars have discovered that online users rely on others to make their credibility assessments, with the use of group-based tools such as online ratings or social networking sites and by invoking cognitive heuristics to evaluate online sources (Metzger et al., 2010). Metzger and colleagues explain that since people do not spend too long on any one website, users are likely to develop heuristics (choices based on previous information) for analyzing webpages. People are not likely to verify information they found, and instead rely upon these strategies they have developed before to analyze the information.

Past studies have shown that source cues – such as online search result placement – can increase the perceived credibility of online information, but websites or weblogs with no established source credibility may struggle to find readers (Greer, 2003). "Information from sources rated as high in expertise leads to the greatest attitude change among those receiving the message; low-expertise sources typically produce no changes in attitude" (p. 13). Wikipedia, for instance, the largest and arguably the most widely used online "encyclopedia," has perceived credibility due to source cues, but may lack real credibility due to the nature of its information, most of which is written and posted by readers rather than experts, and is in varying stages of accuracy.

Blogs

Weblogs, or blogs for short, are a source of online information that is easily accessible yet has varying degrees of credibility. Blogging provides a vehicle for people to voice their opinions and offer information while receiving feedback (Kuhn, 2005). Postings include individuals' opinions and views about various topics; news written by legitimate journalists; political commentary; and marketing, advertising, promotion, customer service, and business and professional issues (Dearstyne, 2005). Their use ranges from youngsters sharing their thoughts and adults sharing their daily minutiae to journalists uncovering truths about governmental cover-ups. Some blogs are so popular they have advertising on their sites; others utilize the distribution tool Rich Site Summary (RSS) to syndicate their content to blog subscribers (Gomez, 2005). As with many websites, advertisements, search engine optimization techniques, and RSS use can give blogs source credibility, making them seem more trustworthy than they may be.

Kaye (2005) found that people use weblogs for the following reasons: (1) to seek information and news; (2) convenience; (3) personal fulfillment; (4) political surveillance; (5) social surveillance; and (6) expression and group affiliation. Kaye found that people who were involved in or interested in politics used weblogs more often than others. While they are an efficient way of disseminating information, many weblogs are not vetted through editors, making much of the content unreliable and unverified. While some bloggers use the same journalistic practices as those in news organizations (reporting and information gathering through a variety of credible and verifiable sources), many bloggers do not. They challenge traditional journalism and create ethical concerns within the journalism field and in research communities because of their power to influence public opinion (Kuhn, 2005). A wide range of opinions exist regarding the importance of bloggers: some believe they are essential watchdogs who keep traditional journalists honest while others say they are merely a vehicle for the narcissistic or discontented and a haven for those fed up with "liberal media" (Kaye, 2005). Some traditional journalists are critical of bloggers, who they believe are "hacks" that need "serious editing," and bloggers are critical of journalists, who they say do not have the freedom to tackle the real issues plaguing the country. Some researchers have proposed a code of ethics that balances freedom and responsibility (Kuhn, 2005; Morozov, 2005); others argue blogging should not be restricted in order for free speech to flourish (Kaye, 2005). In the end, those who do practice legitimate journalism through this medium earn the trust of their readers and gain the largest audiences.

As blogging becomes more mainstream, the distinction between the audience and the media source has been blurring (Mackinnon, 2005). Mackinnon writes that there has been an extreme power shift from the traditional producers and purveyors of media to the people formerly known as the audience. The readers have now been more threaded into the journalistic procedures (known as citizen journalism) due to their newfound ability to produce the stories themselves. This has led to a loss of control by typical media, since others outside the typical media can now be the purveyors of information. Some media organizations engage in "crowd-sourcing," whereby they enlist the expertise of citizens to inform their stories. Blogging has now erupted to examine the ideas that are being spread through the typical media and journalism in order to verify their authenticity. Mackinnon writes that blogging and journalism share a key space in the media; however, readership and how they are utilized will help to decide the future of the media. With anyone being able to provide input, people all over the world who are experts within the subject matter can assist to make the story more credible and legitimate by providing much necessary facts.

Haas (2005) argues that blogs and mainstream media are becoming one and the same, citing many similarities between the two mediums and the practices of political bloggers. Bloggers tend to follow the same topics that mainstream press presents, and rely on information from these media to source their opinions, most of which point to the same conclusions. Hargrove and Stempel (2007) had similar findings when they compared Americans' use of blogs for news and how they compare to traditional news sources. The authors found that "despite the growth in blog use, blogs are still not a major source of news" (p. 100). Just 12% of their sample said they got news from a blog in the past week and just 7% had turned to blogs to get news more than two days in the past two weeks. They concluded that blogs are not a threat to mainstream news sources. Regardless, the perceived credibility of blogs is still a threat to information literacy. Journalists themselves turn to blogs for information exchange, especially those who work for online publications (Chung, Kim, Trammell, & Porter, 2007).

In a study examining politically interested Internet users' perceptions of blog credibility, Kim (2012) asked respondents to report their general Internet use, reliance on blogs for political news and information, and to rate the degree of accuracy, fairness, believability, and in-depthness of blogs. The author also measured political attitudes including the respondents' interest in politics, trust in the government, strength of party affiliation, and their political efficacy. Kim found that politically interested online users who interact more with news content found blogs more credible. Specifically, respondents "perceived political blogs as credible because political blogs provided more in-depth information than fair or accurate information" (p. 429). The study also discovered that online information seekers appreciate the more in-depth commentary or analysis blogs provide – and perceive this to be credible – rather than evaluating its accuracy or fairness, "two fundamental criteria in judging credible news via traditional news media" (p. 429). The author suggests that to rebuild public trust in traditional news, organizations must be the "forum leader" in the process of news production and distribution. Recognizing the power of audiences will lead to a better relationship with audiences in the new media landscape.

Armstrong and McAdams (2009) researched the perceived credibility given to blogs and whether the credibility extended to the blog writers and users. Particularly, the study used an experimental design to examine how gender cues may influence blog credibility. The authors conducted two experiments with three conditions employed (male, female, and no gender). In both studies, respondents read one blog entry. In the first study, all respondents read a blog post about rebuilding homes in New Orleans after Hurricane Katrina and in the second study, respondents were randomly assigned to read a blog post about bottled water or college rankings. Each blog post was approximately 570 words long, each with six external links containing additional information about the blog content. They found that blog posts by men were viewed as more credible than blog posts by women; and the writing style and topic of the blog influenced the perception of the post. The authors did not measure interest in the subject, which may have played a role in the participants' perception of credibility.

Online News Credibility

The credibility of news has declined dramatically over the past 30 years. In the mid-2000s, the Pew Research Center reported that 45% of the U.S. population believed little to nothing of what they read in newspapers, an increase of 30% from 1985 (Thorson, Vraga, & Ekdale, 2010), when newspapers were arguably the most respected form of journalism. Today, the "news" is still presented by more traditional media – television, radio, print – but the majority of information is provided by countless websites with varying degrees of credibility. This section will examine the research surrounding the perceived credibility of online news.

Most websites that deliver "news" include recycled stories from legacy media (traditional news sources). In fact roughly 5% of the content on non-traditional media websites is original (Brooks, Kennedy, Moen, & Ranly, 2014). Flanagin and Metzger (2007) found that details of the font, font size, layout, and graphics played a role in perceived credibility of online news sources. They measured three types of credibility: (1) message credibility, which included aspects of the message such as quality, accuracy, currency, and language intensity; (2) site credibility, which included site features, amount of visuals on site, and the extent of interactivity among site users; and (3) sponsor credibility, which included knowledge of reputation and experience with sponsor. Four genres of websites were used: a news organization, a relevant e-commerce site, a special interest group, and a personal webpage. All sites contained a similar story of possible harmful effects of pregnant women flying in airplanes. Participants could not see the URL, which they were directed to when accessing the study's site. The results showed that both the news organization site and the e-commerce site were perceived to be significantly more credible than the special interest group site and the personal website. The sponsor of the news organization site was rated significantly more credible than the sponsors of all other genres of sites. For message credibility, the message on the news organization site was rated significantly more credible than messages on all other genres of sites. The authors found no significant relationships between Internet/web experience and message credibility, site credibility, or sponsor credibility.

The distinction between various information sources was the focus of a study by Johnson and Kaye (2010), who assessed Internet credibility using a multidimensional construct consisting of believability, fairness, accuracy, and depth of information. Respondents judged the credibility of differing information sources – online cable news, online broadcast news, and online newspapers and blogs – with each of their traditional media counterparts on a 1–5 scale of believability, fairness, accuracy, and depth of each source. Talk radio was equated to online blogs due to the usual ideological bent present in both mediums. The authors found that 36% of participants thought that online newspapers were moderately to very believable in the information that they post, with 35% reporting the same for the depth of the articles. A third reported that blogs are moderately to very believable, 32% reported the same for accuracy, and 57% reported the same for depth, indicating that people believe blogs are much more in depth than any other online news source. However, this did not increase their perceived credibility. Reliance on a certain medium (online or offline) was a strong predictor in whether the medium was viewed as credible. Reliance on blogs for information was a strong positive predictor of belief in their credibility.

Thorson, Vraga, and Ekdale (2010) discovered that the context of news stories affects their credibility by examining uncivil online commentary on legitimate news stories. The authors' goal was to determine how people perceive credibility based on social judgment theory, and to understand the circumstances that may cause readers to "make a cognitive link between evaluations of blog message credibility and evaluations of news story credibility" (p. 303). News stories that were rated more credible were adjacent to blog posts that were uncivil rather than civil, suggesting that people perceive the balance and tone of a mainstream news story to be more credible when placed next to a rude comment.

Other studies on news credibility have found that men and people of higher socio-economic status (SES) believe newspapers are more credible than do other demographics, while women and people of lower SES believe television to be more credible (Greer, 2003). Young people believe newspaper information more than older people, and women find cable news to be more credible than do men. Audiences find online information has varying levels of credibility. People who feel that a source is credible will also believe the information from that source is credible (Greer, 2003).

Cugelman, Thelwall, and Dawes (2008) investigated the similarities and differences of the credibility among traditional and new news media. Using a telephone interview method, the researchers interviewed 536 adults ages 18 and older. Participants were active news consumers across a variety of media: print, television, and the Internet. The survey contained adapted questions from Gaizano and McGrath's credibility scale such as "I'd like to know what you think about online news, television news, or newspapers." Online news was shown highest in credibility, and online users rated online news more positively than television news or newspapers.

The perception of information is important in understanding whether people perceive high or low online news credibility. In their study of Iraq War-related information Choi, Watt, and Lynch (2006) found that opponents of the war believed the Internet sources to be more credible than did pro-war or neutral respondents. The diversity of information was cited most often as why the group perceived high credibility of Internet sources about the war. Johnson and Kaye (2004) found that the adult users' Internet experience did not predict how they perceived Internet credibility, nor did the number of activities they performed online. They found that those who were online for a shorter period of time relied on the Internet more than veteran web users. This may suggest that people who have used the Internet for many years understand its limitations, or perhaps those who have been online longer believe they have more expertise in locating credible information on the Internet.

Social media as a source of news is also on the rise. Roughly two-thirds of the adult U.S. population uses Facebook, and half of those users get their news at least partially from there (Holcomb, Gottfried, & Mitchell, 2013). About half of Facebook and Twitter users report getting their news information from the social media websites (Holcomb, Gottfried, & Mitchell, 2013), which amounts to approximately 30% of the population. Two-thirds of news consumers get news from just one social networking site, and for 85% of those people that single site is Facebook. A quarter get their news information from two websites and 9% get it from at least three sites. Smith, Lee, Ben, and Itai (2014) examined Twitter users' habits and discovered that Twitter followers gather around a specific story from a well-known media outlet, when many people retweet the same message, which demonstrates that the classical media still do hold sway.

Young People's Perception of Online Material

In a study investigating patterns of how students search and utilize information gathered online, Biddix, Chung, and Park (2011) administered a questionnaire that queried participants' Internet usage and behaviors with open-ended responses to the following behaviors: (a) information-seeking processes used for study; (b) usage patterns during a recent project online; (c) academic reasons for using the Internet; (d) perception of reliability for academic sources; and (e) effective usage of the Internet to improve academic performance. Their results found that students used Internet searches more frequently than other sources for searching academic information. However, when having to find information for class projects, students preferred using library resources such as books and articles as these resources have been pre-accepted by being kept in a library. Although finding information on the web was much faster, it was perceived as less credible.

Lackaff and Cheong (2008) investigated how students interpret and understand online credibility – specifically when using Wikipedia – through focus groups and online survey methodology. It was organized in three research levels: the extent to which students attributed credibility to online sites, the process in which students interpreted and evaluated information online, and the way students verified authorship. The questionnaire tested for factors such as personal epistemology (speed of knowledge acquisition and knowledge construction and modification), Internet search skills (individual's confidence in their ability to acquire information), social contexts of technology use (individual's access to social support for computer and Internet problems), and "cues" (questions such as *how will each of the following affect your decision to use the information?*) based on credibility interpretation. The results showed that individuals with social problem-solving resources readily available made more use of Internet information. Self-efficacy was correlated with frequency of searches for online information. In other words, the participants believed that the more frequently they used the Internet to search for information, the more proficient they became in acquiring information from the Internet. Participants perceived sites in which an author was listed as more credible than those without listed authors. Self-efficacy was significantly correlated with the four authorship cues. Speed of knowledge acquisition, knowledge construction, and knowledge modification was significantly correlated with authorship – if a user found an author listed with the site, the user was quicker in deciding whether to use that site for its resources. Students also tended to regard themselves as computer savvy and felt confident in their information-seeking abilities. Also, familiarity was significantly correlated with knowledge acquiring – if the person was previously familiar with the knowledge, then they perceived it as a piece of information credible enough to acquire and use. This research sheds light as to how Wikipedia is utilized for information gathering and the perceived credibility therein – computer literacy plays a great role in acquiring accurate knowledge.

In a study of Canadian youth's online information searches about mental health issues, Rasmussen-Pennington, Richardson, Garinger, and Contursi (2013) used a focus group approach with 21 heavy social media users. Many of the study's participants reported great difficulty with examining a website's credibility, and due to the difficulty in determining credibility they reported not believing the information they found. One theme that resonated with participants was that the most trusted person within the mental health realm would be someone who has had the illness before, since they know what you are going through as well. Poor mental health literacy among the younger members was an issue as well, since they thought of mental illness as those who are developmentally disabled or a person that "others don't want to be around." In order to see a physical person for information about mental health depended upon the type of relationship. Even though social media sites are extremely popular, there was marked ambivalence about how people's Facebook friends would interpret a mental health page, which might lead to youth avoiding those services if they think that their friends would judge it harshly or negatively. The participants also reported feeling a closer bond to people who had gone through similar experiences instead of following the websites with hard data and scientific studies. A major step forward would be to reduce the stigma of mental health thereby increasing mental health literacy, which would enable youth to use plain and clear language to describe what they are going through. The authors suggest using a peer-to-peer environment to allow youths to become advocates for their peers, which would allow for the coordination of many young voices to achieve a much larger goal.

Trust in Online Material

Research has shown that trust is associated with online source use (Li, Browne, & Chau, 2006) and that trust is a key variable for maintaining a successful long-term online relationship with a website (Casalo, Flavian, & Guinaliu, 2007). According to Casalo et al., trust has three main belief components: honesty, benevolence, and competence. Honesty is the belief that one will keep one's word while benevolence "reflects the belief that one of the parties is interested in the well-being of the other" (p. 2). Competence is related to the perceptions of the website contents, specifically whether they are true. Further, to trust a website one must believe in the reliability or strength of that site (Dutton & Shepherd, 2006). Casalo et al. (2007) found that people's levels of trust predicted their commitment level to a website. Therefore, people with more trust in the site had a longer relationship with it.

Dutton and Shepherd (2006) defined Internet trust as confident expectation. They believe that cybertrust (trust in online material) is influenced by several factors, including experience, proximity, and education. Katz and Rice (2002) found that people who are more trusting have more trust in the Internet, and Dutton and Shepherd (2006) discovered that people discontinue using websites because of a perceived risk or lack of trust. Those who perceive a risk involved in using a website will turn to other sites. If people were aware that Wikipedia and weblogs had credibility issues, they may perceive a risk involved with using the information.

Utz, Kerkhof, and van den Bos (2012) conducted two studies that examined the impact that customer reviews had upon consumer trust in online stores. A Pew research poll in 2008 found that more people would shop online if they had more trust within the online environment. Typically, without consumer reviews, the retailer had much more information about the quality of the goods and the services than the buyer did. Additionally, positive reviews on a product helped increase sales while negative reviews decreased them. When items are being compared online, an item with only negative reviews will sell more than an item with no reviews, due to the idea that any review is better than no review. Across both studies there was an effect of perceived trustworthiness of online stores based on customer reviews. Information provided by fellow consumers had a much higher impact upon the perceived trustworthiness of websites than the store's reputation. These results illustrated the newfound power that consumers have as the Internet has now made it possible for consumers to easily express their opinions about a product within an easily accessible open forum.

Metzger and colleagues (2010) found that since people were not able to access as much information as easily, in the past people deferred to experts for information; however, since now anyone can reach any information, people tend to disregard authorities altogether.

In our laboratory research we attempted to discover a relationship between the respondents' levels of general trust and use and trust of unverified online information (Cheever, 2007). After performing regression analysis it was determined trusting and non-trusting individuals were not significantly different in their use of these sources. However, a correlation existed between levels of trust and use and preference of author in Wikipedia articles. It appears that how trusting someone is does not have a bearing on whether they trust unverified online information, but it does correlate with their preference and use of Wikipedia. This contradicted studies that show people who possess more trust have more trust in Internet sites and those who perceive a risk are less likely to use a website (Dutton & Shepherd, 2006; Katz & Rice, 2002), and supported studies that show trust is associated with online source use (Li et al., 2006).

Digital Media Literacy

Digital media literacy has been defined as a person's ability to understand, access, and create content using a digital medium (Park, 2012). Within traditional mass media, media literacy can be interpreted as the ability to read and comprehend messages. In order to accomplish this, a basic understanding of how messages are produced and then conveyed in the media is required. Within the realm of digital media many new skills, as well as an ability to understand the messages, come into play. People must first have the correct type of device to view the information, such as a computer, and know how to use the device. Then being able to find the content comes next, since most digital media is not spread the same way as traditional media, which requires the user to search through and filter through a massive amount of information. At this point the traditional skill of interpreting the mediating message is required. Messages sent out through digital media tend to be unfiltered, and distributed to the people who actively seek them out. The interactive nature of digital media, with the ability to directly contact the authors, greatly differentiates digital media from mass media.

The accessibility of Internet information makes it easy for students to locate information, but there is a concern that they are not using the best information. Several studies have shown that students do not possess optimal Internet skills, both in searching for and evaluating websites (Bond, Fevyer, & Pitt, 2006). In separate studies, researchers found that students had either too much information to wade through, or simply did not take the time to find the best information and use it for academic study. Wood (2004) asserts that students lack the ability to critically analyze Internet information and assume that all the information is truthful and equal. Bond et al. (2006) found that people tend to "self-learn" how to search for information using the Internet, and concluded that this approach did not help them learn basic search skills, nor did it support their problem-solving skills. Several published approaches to this problem include librarian-written manuals helping students become literate in online information, and guides from the International Reading Association that help students identify credible sources from a variety of search engines (Henry, 2006).

New media literacy and classic media literacy share common characteristics, but specialized criteria and definitions are needed for new media literacy (Lin, Li, Deng, & Lee, 2013). New media broadly encompass computer and communication technologies, in addition to the differing types of media production, distribution, and usage. There are four base socio-cultural characteristics of new media: (1) each medium has its own unique language; (2) each message is constructed; (3) the different types of media have embedded values and ideology; and (4) media serve various purposes. New media literacy is a combination of information, conventional literacy, and social skills applied within a digital context. This new definition was proposed due to the general gaps that were created in the literature where technical and socio-cultural characteristics were left out.

Metzger and colleagues (2010) found that because people rely on heuristics to determine online credibility, the capacity for digital media to connect people offers a new potential for determining information credibility. The Internet has enabled a separation between credibility and authority that has never been present before. In their assessment of online credibility using focus groups, the authors suggest the importance of group-based means of credibility assessment, as well as the key role that is played by heuristics for determining credibility online. The prevalence of context clues providing a basis for assessment indicates a context-based approach to credibility assessment.

Programs to Improve Digital and Media Literacy Skills

Programs to teach people how to search for and interpret online material are in their infancy. Most American school districts now have media literacy guidelines in place, but they vary from state to state and district to district. Organizations such as the Center for Media Literacy and the European Media Literacy Forum offer workshops and programs to help improve these skills in primary and secondary schools and beyond, yet no universal guidelines are in place.

In the United States, the National Association for Media Literacy Education (NAMLE) focuses on educating individuals of all ages on how to develop the habits and skills that are required to be an effective critical thinker and communicator in today's world (NAMLE, 2007). In order to engage in effective media analysis multiple steps need to be taken. One is the understanding that all media messages are constructed, and that through each medium there are differing characteristics and strengths with a unique language for each (NAMLE, 2007; Rosen, Carrier, & Cheever, 2010). All messages that are produced are there for a particular purpose, and they each contain certain embedded values and points of view. The creators of the messages embed their own values and beliefs within their messages, and these messages can influence beliefs, values, attitudes, behaviors, and even the democratic process. NAMLE (2007) emphasized that media literacy encompasses both analysis and expression through the media. Media literacy is something that is cultivated over time – it is a set of skills that is continually evolving as people develop their skills and knowledge. Media literacy education is important to assist in developing an informed, reflective, and engaged society, and is essential for correct functioning of a democratic society. NAMLE propagates the idea that when educated properly, students and citizens can become more skeptical instead of cynical about the process, while helping to develop a diverse point of view. Media literacy education focuses more on teaching students how to think critically and to arrive at a conclusion that is in line with their own values, including relating the values to their own lives.

The American Academy of Pediatrics recommends limiting time spent on technology, for children, down to less than two hours per day from the usual seven hours per day that is done currently (AAP, 2014). The AAP recommends offering educational media, newspapers, books, or board games as alternatives to general media consumption. Viewing website content with children can also assist in teaching children about what questionable content is and thereby putting it into context, which will help children to develop media literacy (Rosen, Cheever, & Carrier, 2012). The recommendations provided by the AAP are for parents to establish a screen-free zone within the home by making sure there are no televisions, video games, or computers within their children's bedrooms and by having a family dinner without the television.

Additionally they should spend one or two hours maximum on media content, and it should be high-quality content. In the newly found time children can be developing hobbies, outdoor playing, reading, and utilizing their imaginations. The AAP recommend strongly against any entertainment media for children under the age of 2.

Gross and Latham (2011) surveyed first-year students at a Canadian community college with below-proficient information literacy to determine the best approach to improve their skills. Despite the emphasis on media literacy throughout high school and college, the authors concluded that many students enter college without competence in information literacy. As of 2006 only 13% of 3,800 students who took the ETS Information and Communication Technology test achieved scores that showed they were information literate. To determine whether the researchers would be able to increase the number of people who report improved literacy skills, and to see if they are improved through self-generated and imposed information searching, an educational intervention was initiated. The goal was to determine whether students could have a noticeable change in the skills that were required to find, evaluate, and utilize information, and whether the researchers could identify a change in their conception of those skills. The students who participated stated that they had not considered information skills before participating in the workshop, but afterward they felt information skills were important in today's society. Students who attended the workshop also stated that they felt more confident with their searching skills than they did before the workshops and they stated they had not been given a lot of information on how to find, evaluate, or use information prior to the intervention. The interviews indicated that students did report learning at least one thing from the workshops, and in many cases multiple new skills. However, whether the workshops changed their conception of information skills was mixed. The students stated that they had not considered these as skills before the workshop, which is in line with research that is indicative of the feeling that information literacy is a skill and instead people are considering information seeking as a product rather than a process.

In a follow-up study, Gross, Latham, and Armstrong (2012) introduced the following research goals: "(1) Change conception of the skills required to find, evaluate and use information; (2) Change conception of personal ability to find, evaluate and use information; (3) Teach a minimum of one skill that students can readily use that will improve both self-generated and imposed task outcomes" (p. 106). The first two goals focus more upon changing the perceptions that the learners have, while the third goal is a skill acquisition. In order to test the research goals, 64 students participated in focus groups across six sessions at two community colleges. First-year college students might not see information literacy as a skill that is needed or can be acquired. Since they do not see it as a skill that could be learned, they usually see it as innate, and measureable only if the information is and can be evaluated. In order to combat these beliefs, the three-step ASE (analyze, search, evaluate) process model of information skills was designed to help individuals find the necessary information. The intervention used is unique in that it is guided by theory, research based, and designed so it can be adapted and adopted by professionals.

Scholars have argued that traditional approaches to media literacy do not work in countries with limited access to resources and/or different cultural contexts. Raju (2013) explains that the current information literacy education model in African countries is ineffective. Since the current literacy model is built upon Western models, it cannot be applied blindly in all situations. The risk of utilizing one main definition,

Raju argues, is there is a danger of reducing the complex idea of information literacy to a technical skill that is seen as merely functional. Since some of the current definitions of information literacy are quite reductionist in nature and skills based, they need to be operationalized to include qualitative aspects so that information literacy education can teach individuals to recognize social constructs and the cultural authorities of knowledge. Raju calls for a combination of the Western model of information literacy along with an incorporation of a context-based definition for local African societal development and individual empowerment.

In Croatia, information literacy is poorly defined and delineated (Poler Kovačič, Zgrabljić Rotar, & Erjavec, 2012). The current goals of information literacy in Croatia are, according to Poler Kovačič et al., to teach students to use computers and computer programs. This goal only helps those students who have technical skills. The stated goals show that information literacy education is currently more focused on building a communication infrastructure, since technology is now being perceived as a vehicle that can be utilized to transform Croatia into a competitive member of the European Union (EU) and the global market as a whole. The methodology was in-depth interviews with 25 language professors to get in-depth information about the perceptions, experiences, and feelings of research subjects. All participants reported a high level of faith in the potential of technology to make their society more modernized. All respondents agreed that information literacy is going to be important for the employability of future students. Additionally, the belief permeated that people who are unable to learn and utilize information literacy would be left behind. Some problems that are broached include the seemingly positive-only focus of the information provided about the Internet, and some of the professors interviewed stated that they were concerned about people neglecting to teach students about the negative and problematic sides of the Internet. Currently Croatian information literacy is too narrow as it focuses on preparing students to be competitive within the EU and the global market, instead of teaching true information literacy skills. In order to remedy this situation, the authors suggest integrating the concepts of critical literacy into the current Croatian concepts of information literacy.

Conclusion

Internet use for information seeking continues to grow, with two-thirds of the American population currently utilizing the web on a daily basis. Research on the credibility of Internet information reveals several different conceptual frameworks for defining and measuring online credibility, and that in general people do evaluate the credibility of the information they seek, but their skill levels may be lacking. In general people evaluate an online source's credibility by its authors' attributes, but studies show they rely more on the design, look, peer reviews, and source credibility of online information to inform their credibility assessments rather than understanding whether the material has been edited, verified, or vetted through a formal process. Further, people tend to learn how to seek information through trial and error rather than being taught how to locate the best information for the task at hand. Formal programs to enhance people's digital media literacy can be useful if they teach people that information literacy is a skill to be learned and cultivated over time; unfortunately the general consensus indicates people consider information seeking more as a product than as a process. More aggressive media literacy training is needed to assuage the negative effects of utilizing non-credible online material.

References

American Academy of Pediatrics (AAP). (2014). Media and children. Retrieved June 15, 2014, from http://www.aap.org/en-us/advocacy-and-policy/aap-health-initiatives/Pages/Media-and-Children.aspx

Armstrong, C. L., & McAdams, M. J. (2009). Blogs of information: How gender cues and individual motivations influence perceptions of credibility. *Journal of Computer-Mediated Communication*, 14(3), 435–456.

Biddix, J. P., Chung, C. J., & Park, H. W. (2011). Convenience or credibility? A study of college student online research behaviors. *The Internet and Higher Education*, 14(3), 175–182.

Bond, C. S., Fevyer, D., & Pitt, C. (2006). Learning to use the Internet as a study tool: A review of available resources and exploration of students' priorities. *Health Information and Libraries Journal*, 23, 189–196.

Brooks, B. S., Kennedy, G., Moen, D. R., & Ranly, D. (2014). *News reporting and writing*. Boston, MA: Bedford/St. Martin's.

Casalo, L. V., Flavian, C., & Guinaliu, M. (2007). The influence of satisfaction, perceived reputation and trust on a consumer's commitment to a website. *Journal of Marketing Communications*, 13(1), 1–17.

Cheever, N. A. (2007). Wikipedia and weblogs: Assessing the perceived credibility, trust and use of unverified online information. Unpublished manuscript, Department of Communications, California State University, Dominguez Hills, Carson, CA.

Choi, J. H., Watt, J. H., & Lynch, M. (2006). Perceptions of news credibility about the war in Iraq: Why war opponents perceived the Internet as the most credible medium. *Journal of Computer-Mediated Communication*, 12, 209–229.

Chung, D. S., Kim, E., Trammell, K. D., & Porter, L. V. (2007). Uses and perceptions of blogs: A report on professional journalists and journalism educators. *Journalism and Mass Communication Educator*, 305–322.

Cugelman, B., Thelwall, M., & Dawes, P. (2008). Website credibility, active trust and behavioural intent. In H. Oinas-Kukkonen et al. (Eds.), *Persuasive technology* (pp. 47–57). Berlin and Heidelberg, Germany: Springer.

Dearstyne, B. W. (2005). BLOGS: The new information revolution? *Information Management Journal*, 39(5), 38–44.

Dochterman, M. A., & Stamp, G. H. (2010). Part 1: The determination of web credibility: A thematic analysis of web user's judgments. *Qualitative Research Reports in Communication*, 11(1), 37–43.

Dominus, S. (2011). The crash and burn of an autism guru. *New York Times Magazine*. Retrieved September 5, 2014, from http://www.nytimes.com/2011/04/24/magazine/mag-24Autism-t.html?pagewanted=all&_r=0

Dutton, W. H., & Shepherd, A. (2006). Trust in the Internet as an experience technology. *Information, Communication, and Society*, 9(4), 433–451.

Flanagin, A. J., & Metzger, M. J. (2007). The role of site features, user attributes, and information verification behaviors on the perceived credibility of web-based information. *New Media and Society*, 9(2), 319–342.

Fogg, B. J., Kameda, T., Boyd, J., Marshall, J., Sethi, R., Sockol, M., & Trowbridge, T. (2002). Stanford-Makovsky Web Credibility Study 2002: Investigating what makes web sites credible today. A research report by the Stanford Persuasive Technology Lab in collaboration with Makvosky & Company. Stanford University, Stanford, CA.

Fritch, J. W., & Cromwell, R. L. (2001). Evaluating Internet resources: Identity, affiliation, and cognitive authority in a networked world. *Journal of the American Society for Information Science and Technology, 52*(6), 499–507.

Gomez, J. (2005). Thinking outside the blog: Navigating the literary blogosphere. *Publishing Information and Technology,* 3–11.

Greer, J. D. (2003). Evaluating the credibility of online information: A test of source and advertising influence. *Mass Communication and Society, 6*(1), 11–28.

Gross, M., & Latham, D. (2011). Experiences with and perceptions of information: A phenomenographic study of first-year college students. *The Library Quarterly, 81*(2), 161–186.

Gross, M., Latham, D., & Armstrong, B. (2012). Improving below-proficient information literacy skills: Designing an evidence-based educational intervention. *College Teaching, 60*(3), 104–111.

Haas, T. (2005). From "public journalism" to the "public's journalism"? Rhetoric and reality in the discourse on weblogs. *Journalism Studies, 6*(3), 387–396.

Hargrove, T., & Stempel, G. H. (2007). Use of blogs as a source of news presents little threat to mainline news media. *Newspaper Research Journal, 28*(1), 99–102.

Henry, L. A. (2006). Searching for an answer: The critical role of new literacies while reading on the Internet. *The Reading Teacher, 59*(7), 614–627.

Holcomb, J., Gottfried, J., & Mitchell, A. (2013, November 14). News use across social media platforms. Pew Research Centers Journalism Project. Retrieved June 24, 2014, from http://www.journalism.org/2013/11/14/news-use-across-social-media-platforms/

Internet World Stats. (2014). Retrieved August 15, 2014, from http://www.internetworldstats.com/stats.htm

Johnson, T. J., & Kaye, B. K. (2010). Choosing is believing? How web gratifications and reliance affect Internet credibility among politically interested users. *Atlantic Journal of Communication, 18*(1), 1–21.

Johnson, T. J., & Kaye, B. K. (2004). For whom the web toils: How Internet experience predicts web reliance and credibility. *Atlantic Journal of Communication, 12*(1), 19–45.

Katz, J. E., & Rice, R. E. (2002). *Social consequences of Internet use: Access, involvement, and interaction.* Cambridge, MA: MIT Press.

Kaye, B. K. (2005). It's a blog, blog, blog, blog world. *Atlantic Journal of Communication, 13*(2), 73–95.

Kim, D. (2012). Interacting is believing? Examining bottom-up credibility of blogs among politically interested Internet users. *Journal of Computer-Mediated Communications, 17,* 422–435.

Kuhn, M. (2005). *Interactivity and prioritizing the human: A code of blogging ethics.* Paper presented at the annual convention of the Association for Education in Journalism and Mass Communication, San Antonio, TX.

Lackaff, D., & Cheong, P. H. (2008). Communicating authority online: Perceptions and interpretations of Internet credibility among college students. *Open Communication Journal, 2,* 143–155.

Li, D., Browne, G. J., & Chau, P. Y. K. (2006). An empirical investigation of web site use using a commitment-based model. *Decision Science, 37*(3), 427–444.

Lin, T.-B., Li, J.-Y., Deng, F., & Lee, L. (2013). Understanding new media literacy: An explorative theoretical framework. *Educational Technology and Society, 16*(4), 160–170.

Litt, E. (2013). Measuring users' Internet skills: A review of past assessments and a look toward the future. *New Media and Society, 15*(4), 612–630.

Mackinnon, R. (2005, April 4). Blogging, journalism and credibility. *The Nation.* Retrieved June 12, 2014, from http://www.thenation.com/article/blogging-journalism-and-credibility

Metzger, M. J., Flanagin, A. J., & Medders, R. B. (2010). Social and heuristic approaches to credibility evaluation online. *Journal of Communication, 60*(3), 413–439.

Morozov, A. E. (2005). *Minding the gap: An ethical perspective on the use of weblogs in journalistic practice.* Paper presented at the annual convention of the Association for Education in Journalism and Mass Communication, San Antonio, TX.

National Association for Media Literacy Education (NAMLE). (2007, November). Core principles of media literacy education in the United States. Retrieved June 15, 2014, from http://namle.net/wp-content/uploads/2013/01/CorePrinciples.pdf

Park, S. (2012). Dimensions of digital media literacy and the relationship with social exclusion. *Media International Australia, Incorporating Culture and Policy, 142,* 87.

Poler Kovačič, M., Zgrabljić Rotar, N., & Erjavec, K. (2012). Information literacy in Croatia: An ideological approach. *Journal of Language, Identity and Education, 11*(3), 151–166.

Purcell, K. (2011). Search and email still top the list of most popular online activities. Pew Research Journalism Project. Retrieved August 23, 2014, from http://www.pewinternet. org/2011/08/09/search-and-email-still-top-the-list-of-most-popular-online-activities/

Purcell, K., Rainie, L., Heaps, A., Buchanan, J., Friedrich, L., Jacklin, A., ... Zickuhr, K. (2012). How teens do research in the digital world. Pew Research Internet Project. Retrieved August 27, 2014, from http://www.pewinternet.org/2012/11/01/how-teens-do-research-in-the-digital-world/

Raju, J. (2013). Viewing higher education information literacy through the African context lens. *African Journal of Library, Archives and Information Science, 23*(2), 105–111.

Rasmussen-Pennington, D. M., Richardson, G., Garinger, C., & Contursi, M. L. (2013). "I could be on Facebook by now": Insights from Canadian youth on online mental health information resources. *Canadian Journal of Information and Library Science, 37*(3), 183–200.

Rosen, L. D., Carrier, L. M., & Cheever, N. A. (2010). *Rewired: Understanding the iGeneration and how they learn.* New York, NY: Palgrave Macmillan.

Rosen, L. D., Cheever, N. A., & Carrier, L. M. (2012). *iDisorder: Understanding our obsession with technology and overcoming its hold on us.* New York, NY: Palgrave Macmillan.

Smith, A. (2014, April 3). Older adults and technology use. Pew Internet & American Life Project. Retrieved August 25, 2014, from http://www.pewinternet.org/2014/04/03/older-adults-and-technology-use/

Smith, M., Lee, R., Ben, S., & Itai, H. (2014, February 20). Mapping Twitter topic networks: From polarized crowds to community clusters. Pew Research Internet Project. Retrieved June 16, 2014, from http://www.pewinternet.org/2014/02/20/mapping-twitter-topic-networks-from-polarized-crowds-to-community-clusters/

Thorson, K., Vraga, E., & Ekdale, B. (2010). Credibility in context: How uncivil online commentary affects news credibility. *Mass Communications and Society, 13,* 289–313.

Tseng, S., & Fogg, B. J. (1999). Credibility and computing technology. *Communications of the ACM, 42*(5), 39–44.

Utz, S., Kerkhof, P., & van den Bos, J. (2012). Consumers rule: How consumer reviews influence perceived trustworthiness of online stores. *Electronic Commerce Research and Applications, 11*(1), 49–58.

Warnick, B. (2004). Online ethos source credibility in an "authorless" environment. *American Behavioral Scientist, 48*(2), 256–265.

Westerwick, A. (2013). Effects of sponsorship, website design, and Google ranking on the credibility of online information. *Journal of Computer-Mediated Communication, 18,* 194–211.

Willingham, E., & Helft, L. (2014, September 5). The autism-vaccine myth. NOVA. Retrieved September 5, 2014, from http://www.pbs.org/wgbh/nova/body/autism-vaccine-myth. html

Wood, G. (2004). Academic original sin: Plagiarism, the Internet and librarians. *Journal of Academic Librarianship, 30,* 237–242.

4

Gender Digital Divide

Does it Exist and What are the Explanations?

Richard Joiner, Caroline Stewart, and Chelsey Beaney

University of Bath

We have conducted research on the gender digital divide for more than 10 years and this chapter provides a summary of this work. Throughout this time the disappearance and even reversal of this gender digital divide has been reported, but we hope to show that the proclamation of its disappearance is premature and that it is still very much with us. We will also discuss the consequences, if any, of this gender digital divide. There are several different conceptualizations of the digital divide (for a review see Hargittai & Hsieh, 2013). Atwell (2001) makes a useful distinction between primary and secondary digital divides. The primary digital divide concerns differences in accessing the Internet, whereas the secondary digital divide concerns differences in Internet use. This chapter will focus on gender differences in types of usage and thus on the secondary gender digital divide.

The history of the Internet began in the 1960s with the development of the ARPANET, which led to protocols for networking between networks. Tim Berners-Lee, a software engineer working at CERN, invented the World Wide Web in 1989. He developed the first web browser in 1990 (Berners-Lee & Fischetti, 2000), which was swiftly followed by the development of the NCSA Mosaic, which was an easy-to-install and easy-to-use Internet graphical browser (Andreessen & Bina, 1994). There was then an explosion in popularity in the Internet, with 16 million users in 1995 (ITU, 2013), but by 1999 the number had increased to 248 million and today is estimated to be 2.7 billion, approximately 38% of the world population.

This explosion in popularity of the Internet and the generally held view that those individuals with access to it were going to enjoy significant economic, educational, and political advantages led a number of people to raise concerns about a digital divide. The National Telecommunications and Information Administration's report in 1995 was one of the first to raise concerns about digital inequalities (NTIA, 1995) and reported that different demographic groups had different Internet adoption rates. Further reports showed that there was a gradual increase in the proportion of Americans who had access to the Internet at home and who were going online, but certain groups were much more likely to have access to the Internet than others

The Wiley Handbook of Psychology, Technology, and Society, First Edition. Edited by Larry D. Rosen, Nancy A. Cheever, and L. Mark Carrier.

(NTIA, 1995, 1998, 1999, 2000). Those who were connected tended to be male, younger people, non-Hispanic White, urban residents, the highly educated, and those with higher income (Hoffman & Novak, 1998).

Concerns about a potential gender digital divide were raised when a number of surveys reported males were more likely to have access to the Internet than females. The first survey reported by the Graphical Visualization and Usability Center (GVUC) at Georgia Tech University showed that in 1994, 95% of Internet users were male and 5% were female (GVUC, 1994). Morahan-Martin (1998) reported in her review of the literature that about two-thirds of Internet users were males; they account for 77% of total online time and went online more frequently.

Some people suggested that this gender difference was temporary and that with time it would disappear. This view is supported by the GVUC surveys, which show that there was an increase in the number of females accessing the Internet between 1994 and 1998 (see Figure 4.1). Furthermore, the proportion of new female Internet users is approximately the same as the proportion of new male Internet users. In fact, in the ninth GVUC survey (1998), the proportion of new female Internet users was actually greater than the proportion of new male Internet users (52% female, 48% male). The "early" adopters were mostly male, but they have now been joined by late adopters who are as likely to be female as male. Thus, the Internet was seen to be moving from a predominantly male activity to a more gender-neutral activity.

Others have suggested that these differences are more permanent and are reflections of gender differences in wider society and that, as long as they remain, so will the gender differences in Internet use. Some have explained them in terms of gender difference in socio-economic status (Bimber, 2000). GVUC surveys and other surveys have consistently shown that education, income, and job status have been associated with Internet use, thus more men than women use the Internet because of gender differences in socio-economic status. Still others explain them in terms of gender differences in gender roles. These gender roles provide social expectations which shape males' and females' use of the Internet. Finally, others explain them in terms of gendered perceptions of computer technology. Computer technology was seen as a stereotypically male activity. Initially, the Internet was only accessible via computers and thus was vulnerable to some of the gender stereotypical views associated with computers, which made computers, and by association the Internet, less attractive to women. Furthermore, the online culture that developed in the early days of the Internet was thought to reflect masculine norms of acceptable behavior and language use. The Internet was developed by men for men, as the quote below shows.

> The toy has changed, but it is still a boy's toy that boys and men build and play. The focus has changed from mechanics to electronics, but technology is still a male domain. (Morahan-Martin, 1998, p. 7)

These masculine norms tolerate online hostility (flaming) and harassment, which made the Internet less attractive to women than men. These explanations are not necessarily mutually exclusive and they may explain all or some of the observed gender differences in Internet use.

Thus we decided to conduct a study that investigated whether there were gender differences in types of Internet use in young people.

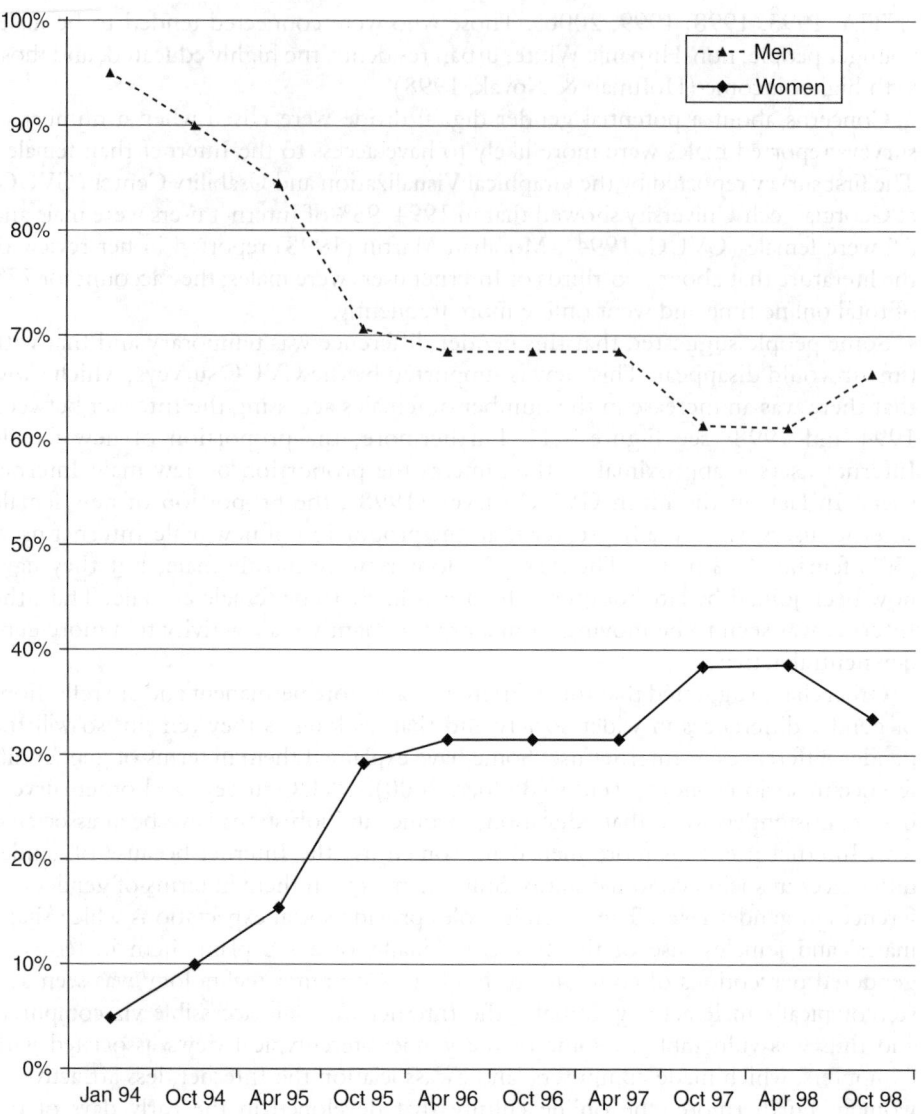

Figure 4.1 Gender differences in Internet adoption, 1994 to 1998.

Study 1

Study 1 was conducted in 2002 and involved 608 first-year psychology undergraduate students from the universities of Bath, Greenwich, Glasgow Caledonian, Kingston, Loughborough, and the West of England (see Joiner et al., 2005, for a full report). There were 490 females and 118 males and the average age was 23 years. We measured students' use of the Internet with the following eight items: (1) email, (2) chat, (3) newsgroups, (4) web games, (5) other specialist websites (e.g., sports websites, TV websites), (6) shopping, (7) downloading or listening to music, and (8) listening to radio stations over the World Wide Web. Students were asked to estimate the number

Table 4.1   Gender differences in the participants' use of the Internet in Study 1.

Internet activities	Male		Female		t
	M	SD	M	SD	
Email	2.9	1.1	2.8	1.1	0.78
Chat (e.g., MSN, ICQ)	2.0	1.3	1.9	1.2	0.48
Newsgroups/discussion groups	1.2	.7	1.1	.5	1.87
Game websites	1.5	.8	1.3	.6	3.45*
Other specialist websites (e.g., sports, TV)	2.3	1.0	1.9	.8	5.17*
Surfing the web with no set purpose	2.2	1.1	2.0	.9	1.93
Shopping	1.5	.7	1.5	.7	0.13
Downloading (e.g., pictures, games, music, videos, animation, text software)	2.4	1.2	1.7	.9	5.98*
Listening to radio stations over the World Wide Web	1.3	.8	1.2	.6	1.68
Total breadth of Internet use	16.0	5.6	1	4.0	4.01*

*$p < 0.05$

of times they used the above items in an average week. Total breadth of use of the Internet was the sum of all the students' use of the specific items above.

We found a number of gender differences in Internet use (see Table 4.1). Males had a greater breadth of Internet use (t (481) = 4.01, $p < 0.05$, $d = 0.36$) and there were gender differences in the type of Internet use. Males were significantly more likely to use game websites (t (545) = 3.45, $p < 0.05$, $d = 0.18$) and other specialist websites (t (567) = 5.17, $p < 0.05$, $d = 0.43$), and to download material from the Internet (t (560) = 5.98, $p < 0.05$, $d = 0.50$). These findings are consistent with research at the time showing that males are more likely to use the Internet for entertainment than females (Jackson, Erwin, Gardner, & Schmitt, 2001; Schweingruber, Brandenburg, & Miller, 2001; Odell, Korgen, Schumacher, & Delucchi, 2000; Sherman et al., 2000). Unlike previous studies we found no gender differences in participants' use of the Internet for communication. So, in sum, in 2002 we found that there were gender differences in Internet use supporting the view that the initial gender differences in Internet use were reflections of wider gender differences in society.

Ten years later the Internet had changed considerably, with the introduction of social network sites (Facebook was launched in 2004) and microblogging (Twitter was created in 2006). These changes have led some people to once more suggest that "there is little reason for concern about sex inequalities in Internet access and usage now" (Ono & Zavodny, 2003, p. 111). Figure 4.2 is a graph of the findings from the surveys conducted by the Pew Internet and American Life Project (2013) from 2000 until 2013 and confirms that the percentage of males and females accessing the Internet has been approximately the same since around 2007. Similarly, surveys conducted by the Oxford Internet Institute from 2003 until 2013 (Dutton & Blank, 2011) also show that in the United Kingdom the percentage of males and females accessing the Internet reached parity by about 2007 (see Figure 4.2). Furthermore, Fallows (2005) reports in her review of the Pew Internet and American Life Project survey in 2005 that the percentage of young women (86%) is greater than the

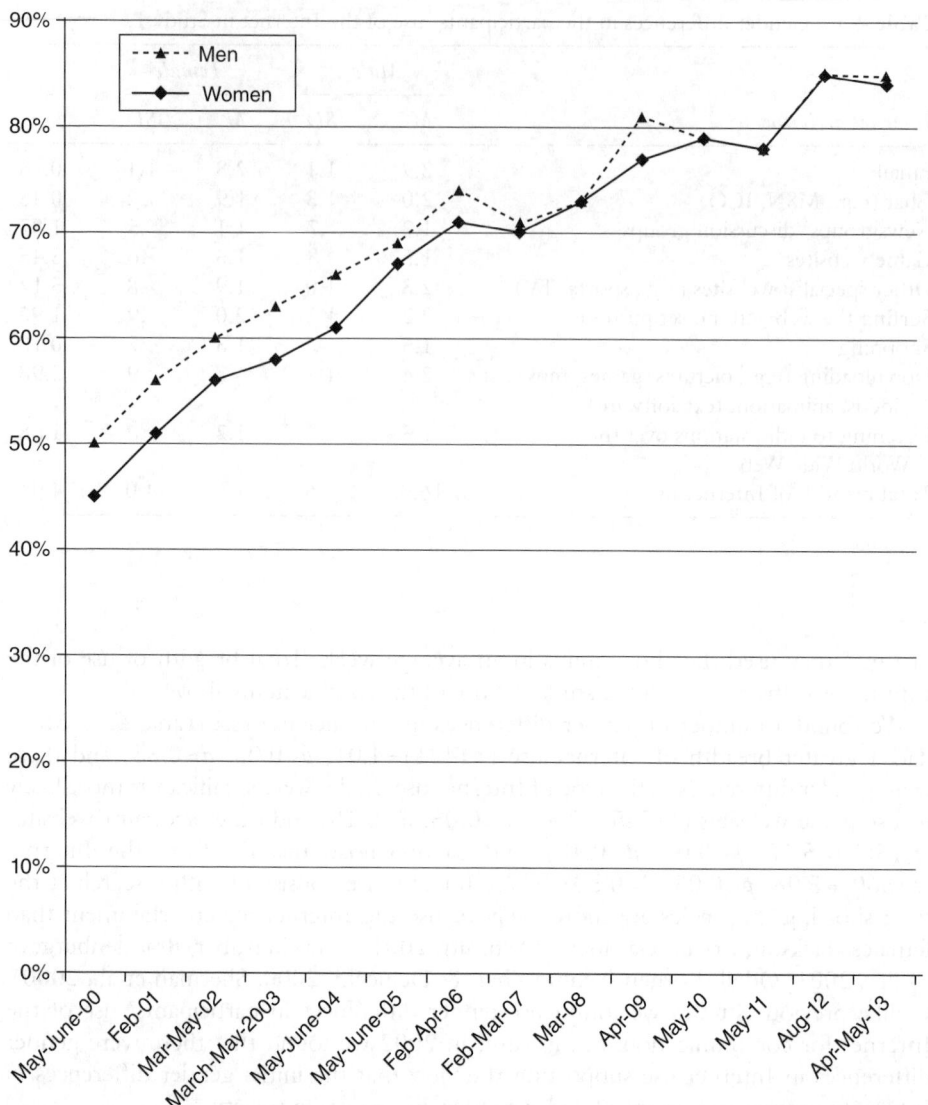

Figure 4.2   Gender differences in Internet adoption in the United States, 2000 to 2013 (Pew Research Internet Project, 2013).

percentage of young men (80%) accessing the Internet and concludes that in future years the percentage of females will surpass the percentage of males as the younger cohort of women ages. Moreover, in purely numerical terms, the number of females has already surpassed the number of males accessing the Internet in both the United Kingdom and the United States, because the number of females is greater than the number of males in both the populations of the UK and the United States, thus supporting the view that the gender divide in terms of access has indeed been reversed in both the UK and United States.

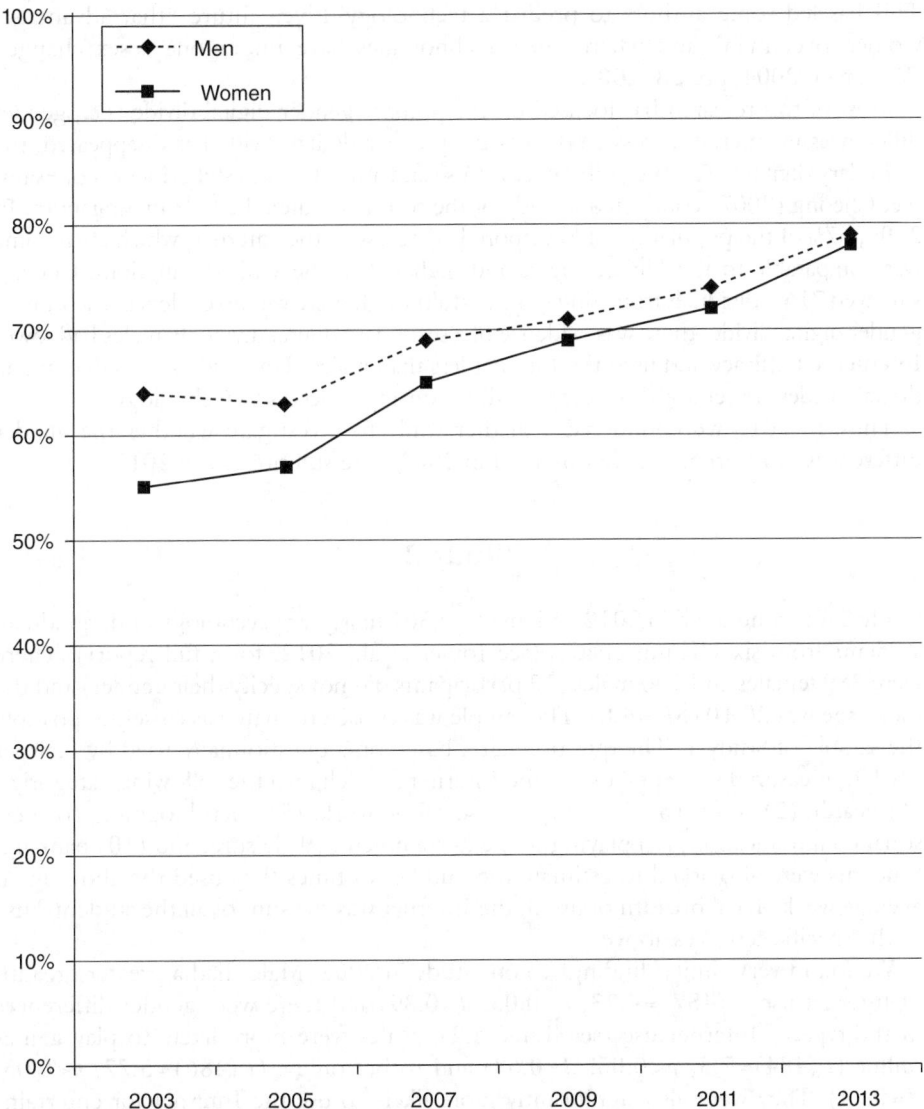

Figure 4.3 Gender differences in Internet adoption in the UK, 2003 to 2013 (Dutton & Blank, 2011).

Schofield (2005) and others argue that this reversal in the gender digital divide is because of developments in digital technology of more "female-oriented" applications:

[Also] there have been moves towards areas that appeal strongly to women such as capturing family memories and communication. In other words, women's interests have not necessarily changed, but digital technology has finally caught up with them. (Schofield, 2005, p. 24)

This has led some authors to predict a technology-driven future "that advantages women over men" and where "new technologies have undergone a sex change" (Wajcman, 2004, pp. 33, 103).

Most of this research has focused on the primary gender digital divide (i.e., gender differences in Internet access). Whereas the primary digital divide has disappeared, the secondary digital divide (i.e., differences in use and attitudes) was still evident. For example, Cheong (2007) conducted a study of the secondary digital divide in Singapore. In 2005, 67% of the population of Singapore had access to the Internet, which at the time was comparable to the United States and higher than the United Kingdom. Cheong surveyed 716 individuals from Singapore and although there was no evidence of a primary gender digital divide, there was evidence of a secondary digital divide. Females had lower Internet self-efficacy and used the Internet less than males. This study shows that not all digital divides are removed by just providing equality of access to technology.

Thus, in 2012 we conducted a further study to investigate whether the gender differences in Internet use we observed in 2002 were still present in 2012.

Study 2

Study 2 was conducted in 2012 and involved 501 first-year psychology undergraduate students from six UK universities (see Joiner et al., 2012, for a full report). There were 389 females and 100 males (12 participants did not specify their gender) and the mean age was 20.10 ($SD=4.8$). The sample was chosen to match as closely as possible the sample of Study 1. The questionnaire, based on a questionnaire used by Helsper (2010), measured students' use of the Internet and fell into the following categories: (1) health, (2) adult, (3) shopping, (4) social network, (5) microblogging, (6) personal communication, (7) playing, (8) entertainment, (9) leisure, and (10) banking. Students were also asked to estimate the number of times they used the above in an average week. Total breadth of use of the Internet was the sum of all the students' use of the specific activities above.

We found very similar findings to our study in 2002. Males had a greater breadth of Internet use ($t(457)=4.23$, $p<0.05$, $d=0.39$) and there were gender differences in the type of Internet use (see Table 4.2). Males were more likely to play games online ($t(484)=7.3$, $p<0.05$, $d=0.68$) and to bet online ($t(486)=5.77$, $p<0.05$, $d=0.54$). They were also significantly more likely to use the Internet for entertainment. Males were significantly more likely to download music ($t(486)=2.46$, $p<0.05$, $d=0.23$), download videos ($t(485)=5.11$, $p<0.05$, $d=0.48$), and listen to music online ($t(486)=2.52$, $p<0.05$, $d=0.22$). Males were more likely to use websites with adult content ($t(483)=13.89$, $p<0.05$, $d=1.27$) and more likely to get information about a product ($t(481)=3.93$, $p<0.05$, $d=0.36$).

Females, on the other hand, were more likely to use the Internet for communication compared to males. They were significantly more likely to use email ($t(484)=2.08$, $p<0.05$, $d=0.19$) and telephone over the web ($t(484)=2.58$, $p<0.05$, $d=0.24$) than males; however, males were more likely than females to use newsgroups ($t(485)=1$, $p<0.05$, $d=0.47$). Females used social network sites significantly more than males ($t(485)=2.18$, $p<0.05$, $d=0.20$). Females were more likely than males to make travel reservations online ($t(484)=2.66$, $p<0.05$, $d=0.25$). There was no gender difference observed in terms of using the Internet for banking activities or health activities.

Table 4.2 Gender differences in the participants' use of the Internet in Study 2.

Internet activities	Male		Female		
	M	SD	M	SD	t
Health information online	0.8	0.8	0.8	0.7	0.00
Sites with adult content	1.9	1.6	0.3	0.8	13.89*
Get information about a product or service	2.5	1.0	2.0	1.0	3.93*
Buying a product or service online	1.8	1.0	1.7	0.9	0.94
Social networking site	4.2	1.3	4.5	1.0	2.18
Microblogging	1.3	1.9	1.1	1.7	1.18
Newsgroups/discussion groups	1.6	1.5	0.9	1.1	1*
Email	4.3	0.8	4.5	0.8	2.08*
Chat	1.8	1.9	1.5	1.7	1.67
Making telephone calls using the Internet	1.7	1.6	2.2	1.7	2.58*
Playing games online	1.6	1.6	0.7	1.0	7.26*
Participating in betting and gambling online	0.5	1.0	0.1	0.4	5.77*
Virtual worlds	0.1	0.6	0.1	0.4	1.26
Downloading music	2.1	1.5	1.8	1.2	2.46*
Downloading videos	1.7	1.6	0.9	1.2	5.11*
Watching television over the World Wide Web	2.5	1.6	2.5	1.4	0.10
Listening to music over the World Wide Web	3.4	1.6	3.0	1.5	2.52*
Making travel reservations/booking	0.8	0.7	1.0	0.7	2.66*
Looking for information about what is on locally	1.2	1.1	1.3	0.9	0.87
Looking for travel information	1.4	1.0	1.5	0.9	0.71
Paying bills online	0.8	0.9	0.7	0.9	0.75
Using online banking services	1.8	1.4	2.0	1.3	1.10
Checking investments	0.3	0.8	0.2	0.7	0.45
Online dating	0.1	0.4	0.1	0.5	0.16
Total breadth of Internet use	40.0	11.9	35.0	9.4	4.23*

*$p < .05$

These findings are very similar to our previous findings of 10 years ago and more recent reported findings. In spite of equality in Internet access, other studies like ours have found large differences in breadth of Internet use (Fallows, 2005; Hargittai, 2010; Helsper, 2010; Ono & Zavodny, 2003; Wasserman & Richmond-Abbott, 2005). There is also research which has shown that males go online more frequently than females (Fallows, 2005). Research has also consistently found gender differences in the types of Internet use. Females tend to use the Internet more for communication, whereas males tend to use the Internet for entertainment (Chen, 2013; Cotten & Jelenewicz, 2006; Kimbrough, Guadagno, Muscanell, & Dill, 2013; Padilla-Walker, Nelson, Carroll, & Jensen, 2010). Thus, even after 10 years the findings support the view that gender differences in Internet use are more resistant to change than some people have argued and are reflecting larger gender differences in wider society.

Another major change in the Internet since 2002 has been the development of smartphones, tablet PCs, e-readers, and the rise of the mobile Internet. We are moving into a "post-PC" era where more and more people are using mobile devices as their default gateway for accessing the Internet (King, 2012). According to a poll of leading technological experts, accessing the Internet via a desktop computer or a laptop is soon going to be an activity of the past (Rainie & Anderson, 2008). The majority of these experts agreed that by 2020 some form of mobile device will be the primary connection tool to the Internet. Smartphones have been defined as any phone that allows for Internet connection (Matthews, Pierce, & Tang, 2009), although in most cases they allow for much greater functionality. These functions include the ability to play audio and media, allow access to emails, voice, and data telecommunications, and download applications, games, and files as well as view websites and surf the Internet (Ofcom Report, 2013). These additional functions have transformed mobile phones from telecommunication devices to mobile computers (Matthews et al., 2009; Walsh, White, Cox, & Young, 2011). In the United States, 56% of adults own a smartphone (Smith, 2013). The figure in the United Kingdom is currently estimated at 22.2 million adult smartphone users (aged 16+), translating to 51% of the adult population, almost double the proportion in 2011 (27%) (Ofcom Report, 2013).

Therefore, we decided to conduct a third study investigating gender differences in the use of the mobile Internet.

Study 3

Study 3 was conducted in 2013 and involved 600 first-year undergraduate students from five UK universities. There were 388 females and 207 males and the mean age was 20.10 (SD=4.8). The questionnaire asked about the students' uses of their mobile phone and had the following questions: (1) making or receiving calls, (2) sending or receiving texts, (3) taking photos, (4) accessing Facebook, (5) accessing Twitter, (6) accessing the Internet, (7) video calls, (8) downloading an app, (9) checking bank account, (10) listening to music, and (11) watching a video. Students were asked to estimate the number of times they used the above in an average week. Total breadth of use of their mobile phone was the sum of all the students' uses of the specific activities above.

Table 4.3   Gender differences in the participants' use of the Internet in Study 3.

	Male		Female		
Internet activities	M	SD	M	SD	t
Making or receiving calls	3.6	1.1		1.0	4.08*
Sending or receiving texts	4.7	0.7	4.9	0.4	3.26*
Taking a picture	2.6	1.4	3.1	1.4	4.40*
Email	3.8	1.7	3.8	1.6	0.18
Playing a game	2.6	1.7	1.8	1.6	5.56*
Accessing Facebook	4.2	1.6	4.4	1.4	1.44
Accessing Twitter	1.9	2.3	2.2	2.3	1.83
Accessing the Internet	4.3	1.4	4.5	1.3	0.95
Video calls	1.3	1.4	1.1	1.5	1.80
Downloading an app	1.8	1.2	1.7	1.3	0.92
Checking bank account	1.6	1.5	1.3	1.5	2.14*
Listening to music	3.3	1.9	3.2	1.9	0.43
Watching a video	2.8	1.8	2.1	1.6	4.89*
Total	35.0	12.1	34.0	10.7	0.92

*p<.05

We found gender differences in how students used their mobile phone that were very similar to the gender differences we found for the Internet in 2002 and 2012. Females tended to use their mobile phones for communication. They made and received more calls than males (t (591) = 4.08, $p < 0.05$, $d = 0.33$). They sent and received more text messages (t (590) = 3.26, $p < 0.05$, $d = 0.27$) and took more pictures (t (592) = 4.40, $p < 0.05$, $d = 0.36$). Males, on the other hand, used their mobile phone more for entertainment. They were more likely to play games than females (t (586) = 5.56, $p < 0.05$, $d = 0.46$) and watch videos on their mobile phones than females (t (587) = 4.89, $p < 0.05$, d = 0.40). They were also more likely to check their bank accounts on their mobile phones (t (591) = 2.14, $p < 0.05$, $d = 0.17$).

Discussion

In sum, in this chapter we have reported a series of studies that we conducted over the last 10 years which have examined gender differences in the use of the Internet. Study 1 was conducted in 2002 and found that males had a greater breadth of Internet use than females; they used the Internet more for games and entertainment than females. Study 2 was conducted in 2012 and, as in our previous study, we found that males had a greater breadth of Internet use than females and they used the Internet more for games and entertainment than females. The differentiation between males and females was more distinct in Study 2 than in Study 1, because in Study 2 we found gender differences in communication and that females were using social network sites more than males. Study 3 was conducted in 2013 to investigate gender differences in mobile Internet and we obtained similar findings to our previous studies. Males used the mobile Internet for playing games and entertainment, whereas females used it more for communication. Thus over time and across different technologies, gender differences in Internet use still persist.

The finding that females use the Internet for communication more than males and that males use the Internet more for entertainment than females has been found consistently. It was originally reported by a number of papers more than 10 years ago (Jackson et al., 2001; Sherman et al., 2000), but has also been reported more recently (Chen, 2013; Cotten & Jelenewicz, 2006; Kimbrough et al., 2013; Padilla-Walker et al., 2010). So what can explain these gender differences in Internet use? One possible explanation was that it would be just a matter of time before these gender differences would disappear. Initially males adopted the Internet, but over time more and more females adopted it and the suggestion was that, given more time, the gender difference in Internet use would disappear. The time explanation certainly was one reason for the disappearance of the primary digital divide. As we reported above, in the United Kingdom and the United States the primary gender digital divide has virtually disappeared (Dutton & Blank, 2011; Pew Research Internet Project, 2013); in fact, there is even evidence that it has reversed in both numerical and percentage terms (Chen, 2013). Some people argue that "the long-reported sex and ethnic differences in Internet engagement over the 1990s and 2000s are proving to be transitory phenomena, perhaps related to initial generational differences in Internet socialization that are now diminishing in significance" (White & Selwyn, 2013, p. 13). However, the time explanation cannot account for the persistence of the secondary gender digital divide over time and over different technologies, which we and others have reported (Joiner et al., 2005, 2012). These findings suggest that the secondary digital divide will not disappear with time.

Gender differences in socio-economic status are another possible explanation for the gender differences in Internet use. Socio-economic differences certainly were a major factor in explaining the primary gender digital divide. In an early study, Bimber (2000) reported that when socio-economic status was controlled for, the primary digital divide disappeared but, interestingly, the secondary digital divide did not. Thus, gender differences in socio-economic status are unlikely to explain gender differences in Internet use.

Another explanation for the gender differences in Internet use concerns the nature of online culture. Some authors suggested that the online culture that developed in the early days of the Internet reflected masculine norms of acceptable behavior and language use, where online hostility (flaming) and harassment were tolerated, and this culture made the Internet less attractive to females. Certainly, the almost universal adoption of the Internet by females would suggest that these masculine norms are not commonplace on the Internet today and are not putting off females from using the Internet. However, there still remain areas of the Internet where the online culture is not supportive of female participation. For example, a survey conducted by the United Nations in 2010 reported that 13% of contributors to Wikipedia were female (Glott, Schmidt, & Ghosh, 2010). Collier and Bear (2012) conducted a full-scale user survey of Wikipedia to establish the reasons for this gender difference in contributions. They found that the gender differences in contributions to Wikipedia could be explained by a number of factors. First, there can be a high level of conflict in Wikipedia, where different editors engage in "edit wars" and try to cancel out each other's contributions. Research has shown that women tend to avoid conflict more than men and thus this high level of conflict within Wikipedia may lead to a gender contribution gap. Second, gender difference in confidence may also partly explain the gender differences in Wikipedia contributions. Collier and Bear (2012) found that even after controlling for other factors, 43% of females were reluctant to contribute because they did not feel they had enough knowledge and expertise to warrant a contribution. Finally, 34% of females were less likely to contribute because they were not comfortable editing other people's work.

A further explanation may lie in the gendered perception of computer technology. In the 1980s and 1990s there was a concern that computers were perceived as a male-dominated activity. Numerous studies in these decades reported that males had much more positive attitudes toward computers and were more likely to use computers than females (for review see Whitley, 1997). The Internet was initially only accessible via the computer and thus it was thought to be susceptible to the same gendered perceptions, which were making it less attractive to females. Early research investigating gender differences in the Internet did report that males had more positive attitudes to the Internet than females (Durndell & Haag, 2002; Jackson et al., 2001; Schumacher & Morahan-Martin, 2001; Torkzadeh & Van Dyke, 2002; Wu & Tsai, 2006). Today, the Internet is accessible via numerous devices and thus not so strongly associated with the negative stereotypes connected with computers. Thus, we may expect that these gender differences in attitudes toward the Internet may be disappearing, but contrary to this expectation recent research has found that males have more positive attitudes toward the Internet than females (Cheong, 2007; Ertl & Helling, 2011; Hargittai, 2010; Koch, Muller, & Sieverding, 2008; Meelissen & Drent, 2008; Sáinz & Eccles, 2012; Sáinz & López-Sáez, 2010). Selwyn (2007) reported a very interesting study on a survey of students conducted to examine whether different aspects of ICT use continue to be seen in particularly gendered terms by young adults. He found that gender continued to be important in how young people perceived ICT in society. Many of the generalizations of gender and ICT identified in the 1980s and 1990s were still evident in Selwyn's sample in 2007. He found that females preferred the softer aspects of ICT and preferred functionality over form. Furthermore, high levels of ICT use and expertise were associated with increased gender stereotyping of computers as masculine. Thus, these studies demonstrate the robustness of gender stereotypes and how they influence the way people use the Internet. It possibly explains why we have consistently found that males have a greater breadth of use of the Internet compared to females.

A further and related explanation to the above is that it is not just gendered perceptions of technology that shape how individuals use the Internet but the social expectations based on individuals' gender roles. Kennedy, Wellman, and Klement (2003) discussed how women are the communicators and networkers in the family. They spend more time than men emailing and using social networking sites to communicate with family and friends. Women's Internet use is shaped by the expectations society has of their roles as childcare providers, kin keepers, and networkers. In contrast, males' use of the Internet is less social and they spend more time searching for information and using it for recreational purposes. This explanation may account for the differential use of the Internet by males and females. Females use it more for communicating and males use it more for entertainment.

Conclusion

In conclusion, the chapter started with the question of whether the gender digital divide has disappeared over the last 20 years. Although the primary digital divide (i.e., in terms of access to the Internet) has disappeared and even reversed in that time, the secondary gender digital divide in Internet use appears to have persisted over time and across different technologies. We suggest that this secondary digital divide is best explained by a combination of negative gendered stereotypes concerning technology and social expectations based on individuals' gender roles. Thus, gender differences in the use of the Internet are more a reflection of gender differences in wider society and thus more resistant to change than some people have suggested.

Acknowledgments

This chapter would not have been possible without the support and help of a number of colleagues over the years. The authors would particularly like to thank Mark Brosnan, John Cromby, Charles Crook, Jill Duffield, Helen Gregory, Jane Guiller, Pam Maras, Amy Moon, and Adrian Scott.

References

Andreessen, M., & Bina, E. (1994). NCSA Mosaic: A global hypermedia system. *Internet Research*, 4(1), 7–17.

Atwell, P. (2001). The first and the second digital divide. *Sociology of Education, 74*(3), 171–191.

Berners-Lee, T., & Fischetti, M. (2000). *Weaving the web: The original design and ultimate destiny of the World Wide Web by its inventor.* New York, NY: HarperInformation.

Bimber, B. (2000). Measuring the gender gap on the Internet. *Social Science Quarterly, 81*(3), 868–876.

Chen, W. (2013). The implications of social capital for the digital divides in America. *The Information Society, 29*(1), 13–25.

Cheong, P. H. (2007). Gender and perceived Internet efficacy: Examining secondary digital divide issues in Singapore. *Women's Studies in Communication, 30*(2), 205–228.

Collier, B., & Bear, J. (2012, February). Conflict, criticism, or confidence: An empirical examination of the gender gap in Wikipedia contributions. In *Proceedings of the ACM 2012 Conference on Computer Supported Cooperative Work* (pp. 383–392). New York, NY: ACM.

Cotten, S. R., & Jelenewicz, S. M. (2006). A disappearing digital divide among college students? *Social Sciences Computer Review, 24*(4), 497–506.

Durndell, A., & Haag, Z. (2002). Computer self-efficacy, computer anxiety, attitudes towards the Internet and reported experience with the Internet, by gender, in an East European sample. *Computers in Human Behavior, 18*(5), 521–535.

Dutton, W., & Blank, G. (2011). *Next generation users: The Internet in Britain.* Oxford Internet Survey 2011. Oxford Internet Institute Report. Retrieved October 1, 2013, from www.oii.ox.ac.uk/publications/oxis2011_report.pdf

Ertl, B., & Helling, K. (2011). Promoting gender equality in digital literacy. *Journal of Educational Computing Research, 45*(4), 477–503.

Fallows, D. (2005). How women and men use the Internet. Pew Research Internet Project. Retrieved October 1, 2013, from http://www.pewinternet.org/Reports/2005/How-Women-and-Men-Use-the-Internet.aspx

Glott, R., Schmidt, P., & Ghosh, R. (2010). *Wikipedia survey: Overview of results.* Tokyo, Japan: United Nations University, Collaborative Creativity Group.

Graphical Visualization and Usability Center (GVUC). (1994). GVU's 1st WWW user surveys. Retrieved November 23, 2014, from http://www.cc.gatech.edu/gvu/user_surveys/survey-01-1994/

Hargittai, E. (2010). Digital na(t)ives? Variation in Internet skills and uses among members of the "Net Generation." *Sociological Inquiry, 80*(1), 92–113.

Hargittai, E., & Hsieh, Y. P. (2013). *Digital inequality.* In W. H. Dutton (Ed.), *Oxford handbook of Internet studies* (pp. 129–150). New York, NY: Oxford University Press.

Helsper, E. J. (2010). Gendered Internet use across generations and life stages. *Communication Research, 37*(3), 352–374.

Hoffman, D. L., & Novak, T. P. (1998). Bridging the racial divide on the Internet. *Science, 280*(5362), 390–391.

ITU. (2013). ICT facts and figures. Retrieved November 23, 2014, from http://www.itu.int/en/ITU-D/Statistics/Pages/facts/default.aspx

Jackson, L. A., Ervin, K. S., Gardner, P. D., & Schmitt, N. (2001). Gender and the Internet: Women communicating and men searching. *Sex Roles, 44*(5–6), 363–379.

Joiner, R., Gavin, J., Brosnan, M., Cromby, J., Gregory, H., Guiller, J., ... Moon, A. (2012). Gender, Internet experience, Internet identification, and Internet anxiety: A ten-year follow-up. *Cyberpsychology, Behavior, and Social Networking, 15*(7), 370–372.

Joiner, R., Gavin, J., Duffield, J., Brosnan, M., Crook, C., Durndell, A., ... Lovatt, P. (2005). Gender, Internet identification, and Internet anxiety: Correlates of Internet use. *CyberPsychology and Behavior, 8*(4), 371–378.

Kennedy, T., Wellman, B., & Klement, K. (2003). Gendering the digital divide. *IT and Society, 1*(5), 72–96.

Kimbrough, A. M., Guadagno, R. E., Muscanell, N. L., & Dill, J. (2013). Gender differences in mediated communication: Women connect more than do men. *Computers in Human Behavior, 29*(3), 896–900.

King, R. (2012, October 29). IDC: We're in the midst of the "Great PC exodus on the Internet." *ZDNet.* Retrieved October 1, 2013, from http://www.zdnet.com/idcwere-in-the-midst-of-the-great-pc-exodus-on-the-internet-7000006532/

Koch, S. C., Muller, S. M., & Sieverding, M. (2008). Women and computers: Effects of stereotype threat on attribution of failure. *Computers and Education, 51*(4), 1795–1803.

Matthews, T., Pierce, J., & Tang, J. (2009). No smart phone is an island: The impact of places, situations, and other devices on smart phone use. IBM Research Report RJ10452. Retrieved October 1, 2013, from http://domino.research.ibm.com/library/cyberdig.nsf/1e4115aea78b6e7c85256b360066f0d4/f5fd878b5b062aca85257635004ec3f5

Meelissen, M. R. M., & Drent, M. (2008). Gender differences in computer attitudes: Does the school matter? *Computers in Human Behavior, 24*(3), 969–985.

Morahan-Martin, J. (1998). Males, females and the Internet. In J. Gackenbach (Ed.), *Psychology and the Internet* (pp. 169–197). San Diego, CA: Academic Press.

National Telecommunications and Information Administration (NTIA). (1995). *Falling through the Net: A survey of the "Have Nots" in rural and urban America.* Washington, DC: U.S. Department of Commerce.

National Telecommunications and Information Administration (NTIA). (1998). *Falling through the Net II: New data on the digital divide.* Washington, DC: U.S. Department of Commerce.

National Telecommunications and Information Administration (NTIA). (1999). *Falling through the Net: Defining the digital divide.* Washington, DC: U.S. Department of Commerce.

National Telecommunications and Information Administration (NTIA). (2000). *Falling through the Net: Toward digital inclusion.* Washington, DC: U.S. Department of Commerce.

Odell, P. M., Korgen, K. O., Schumacher, P., & Delucchi, M. (2000). Internet use among female and male college students. *CyberPsychology and Behavior, 3*(5), 855–862.

Ofcom Report. (2013). *Adults' media use and attitudes report 2013.* Retrieved November 23, 2014, from http://stakeholders.ofcom.org.uk/market-data-research/other/media-literacy/media-lit-research/adults-2013/

Ono, H., & Zavodny, M. (2003). Gender and the Internet. *Social Science Quarterly, 84*(1), 111–121.

Padilla-Walker, L. M., Nelson, L. J., Carroll, J. S., & Jensen, A. C. (2010). More than just a game: Video game and Internet use during emerging adulthood. *Journal of Youth and Adolescence, 39*(2), 103–113.

Pew Research Internet Project. (2013). *Trend data (adults).* Pew Internet & American Life Project. Retrieved October 1, 2013, from http://www.pewinternet.org/Trend-Data-(Adults).aspx

Rainie, L., & Anderson, J. (2008). *The future of the Internet III.* Pew Internet & American Life Project. Retrieved October 1, 2013, from http://www.pewinternet.org/Reports/2008/The-Future-of-the-Internet-III.aspx

Sáinz, M., & Eccles, J. (2012). Self-concept of computer and math ability: Gender implications across time and within ICT studies. *Journal of Vocational Behavior, 80*(2), 486–499.

Sáinz, M., & López-Sáez, M. (2010). Gender differences in computer attitudes and the choice of technology-related occupations in a sample of secondary students in Spain. *Computers and Education, 54*(2), 578–587.

Schofield, J. (2005, February 10). Toys for boys and girls. *Guardian.* Retrieved October 1, 2013, from http://www.theguardian.com/technology/2005/feb/10/gadgets.gadgets

Schumacher, P., & Morahan-Martin, J. (2001). Gender, Internet and computer attitudes and experiences. *Computers in Human Behavior, 17*(1), 95–110.

Schweingruber, H., Brandenburg, C. L., & Miller, L. M. (2001). Middle school students' technology practices and preferences: Re-examining gender differences. *Journal of Educational Multimedia and Hypermedia, 10*(2), 125–140.

Selwyn, N. (2007). Hi-tech = guy-tech? An exploration of undergraduate students' gendered perceptions of information and communication technologies. *Sex Roles, 56*(7–8), 525–536.

Sherman, R. C., End, C., Kraan, E., Cole, A., Campbell, J., Birchmeier, Z., & Klausner, J. (2000). The Internet gender gap among college students: Forgotten but not gone? *CyberPsychology and Behavior, 3*(5), 885–894.

Smith, A. (2013). *Smartphone ownership – 2013 update*. Pew Internet & American Life Project. Retrieved October 1, 2013, from http://pewinternet.org/Reports/2013/Smartphone-Ownership-2013.aspx

Torkzadeh, G., & Van Dyke, T. P. (2002). Effects of training on Internet self-efficacy and computer user attitudes. *Computers in Human Behavior, 18*(5), 479–494.

Wajcman, J. (2004). *TechnoFeminism*. Cambridge, UK: Polity Press.

Walsh, S. P., White, K. M., Cox, S., & Young, R. M. (2011). Keeping in constant touch: The predictors of young Australians' mobile phone involvement. *Computers in Human Behavior, 27*(1), 333–342.

Wasserman, I. M., & Richmond-Abbott, M. (2005). Gender and the Internet: Causes of variation in access, level, and scope of use. *Social Science Quarterly, 86*(1), 252–270.

White, P., & Selwyn, N. (2013). Moving on-line? An analysis of patterns of adult Internet use in the UK, 2002–2010. *Information, Communication and Society, 16*(1), 1–27.

Whitley, B. E. (1997). Gender differences in computer-related attitudes and behavior: A meta-analysis. *Computers in Human Behavior, 13*(1), 1–22.

Wu, Y. T., & Tsai, C. C. (2006). University students' Internet attitudes and Internet self-efficacy: A study at three universities in Taiwan. *CyberPsychology and Behavior, 9*(4), 441–450.

5

Access and Attitudes to Digital Technologies Across the Adult Lifespan

Evidence from Distance Education

John T. E. Richardson and Anne Jelfs

The Open University

A good deal has been written about attitudes to digital technologies among students in higher education. Much of this literature has focused upon the idea that today's young adults constitute a distinct generation, a "Net Generation" of "digital natives" who think and learn in qualitatively different ways from older people. However, testing this idea in the context of higher education is difficult because the majority of students are young people who have entered college or university within a few years of leaving secondary education. In this chapter, we describe the results of a survey carried out with students in distance education, who are often older and more representative of the adult population. By using a large sample of students, stratified by age, we are able to present a distinctive set of data concerning access to digital technology, attitudes to digital technologies, and approaches to studying across the adult lifespan.

Digital Technologies in Higher Education

Around the world, the twenty-first century has seen the wholesale introduction of a variety of digital technologies in higher education. Nowadays, institutions routinely employ learning management systems (virtual learning environments) and web-based applications to deliver both curriculum content and student support. Lang and Arroway (2013) surveyed the use of digital technologies at institutions in the United States, and Walker, Voce, and Ahmed (2012) provided a similar picture for institutions in the United Kingdom. These developments have been matched by changes in the use of digital technologies on the part of students themselves.

In the United States, for instance, Smith and Caruso (2010, pp. 41–42) found that 98% of undergraduate students owned their own computers, and 63% also owned an Internet-capable handheld device such as an iPhone. Students were sometimes asked to use digital tools by their teachers, but more often they adapted

The Wiley Handbook of Psychology, Technology, and Society, First Edition. Edited by Larry D. Rosen, Nancy A. Cheever, and L. Mark Carrier.

the tools that they used in their personal lives to fit their academic context. However, students' preferences are definitely in favor of portable devices: Dahlstrom (2012, pp. 13–15) found that 86% of all undergraduate students in the United States owned a laptop computer, but only 33% owned a desktop; similarly, 62% owned a smartphone, but fewer than 40% owned a feature (conventional) cellular phone. The situation in the United Kingdom is broadly similar (National Union of Students, 2010).

Digital Natives and Digital Immigrants

The increased use of digital technologies among young adults in general has led some writers to argue that they constitute a distinct population who think and learn in qualitatively different ways from older people (see Jones & Shao, 2011, for a review of this debate and a discussion in the light of evidence from countries around the world). This idea originated in research by Strauss and Howe (1991), who analyzed American history in terms of a series of generations. They coined the term "Millennial Generation" to refer to children born between 1982 and 2000. They developed this idea in subsequent writings that explicitly identified the "Millennials" with students entering higher education from 2000 onwards (Howe & Strauss, 2000, 2003). In the meantime, Tapscott (1998) used the term "Net Generation" on the grounds that the most significant characteristic about this group was their exposure to computers, the Internet, and other digital media. Oblinger (2003) similarly argued that what was distinctive about Strauss and Howe's Millennials was their access to technology and especially the Internet. Indeed, she later argued that exposure to technology was more important in defining this group of individuals than age *per se* (Oblinger & Oblinger, 2005).

Prensky (2001a, 2001b) coined the term "digital natives" to describe this group on the basis that they were "native speakers" of the digital language of computers, video games, and the Internet. He argued that the emergence of this group had led to significant changes:

> A really big discontinuity has taken place. One might even call it a "singularity" – an event which changes things so fundamentally that there is absolutely no going back. This so-called "singularity" is the arrival and rapid dissemination of digital technology in the last decades of the twentieth century. (Prensky, 2001a, p. 1)

Another term used to characterize this group was "Generation Y" (to differentiate them from the previous Generation X). This term was first used in an editorial in *Advertising Age* magazine (Viewpoint, 1993) to denote a generation characterized by their purchasing power (Markiewicz, 2003; Wolburg & Pokrywczynski, 2001). More recently, however, it has been used to refer to their familiarity with digital technologies (e.g., Halse & Mallinson, 2009; Jorgensen, 2003).

All these commentators argue that because of exposure to technology in people born since the early 1980s, there is a mismatch between their expectations of higher education and the teaching practices that they find on their admission (e.g., Oblinger, 2003). Indeed, some argue that young adults' exposure to digital technologies has led to changes in the structure and function of their brains (Prensky,

2001b; Tapscott, 2009). Having originally dismissed older people (and especially older teachers) as "digital immigrants" who had to try to adapt to using digital technologies, Prensky (2009) more recently acknowledged that they might aspire to achieving "digital wisdom," which he defined as "wisdom arising *from* the use of digital technology to access cognitive power beyond our innate capacity" and "wisdom *in* the prudent use of technology to enhance our capabilities" (p. 1), and he claimed that this too would lead to changes in their brains' organization and structure.

The same commentators have argued in turn that these developments have important implications for teaching and course design in higher education (Howe & Strauss, 2003; Prensky, 2010; Tapscott & Williams, 2010). Even so, the whole idea of a Net Generation and of digital natives has been called into question. Bennett, Maton, and Kervin (2008) reviewed the relevant literature, and they concluded: "There is no evidence of widespread and universal disaffection, or of a distinctly different learning style the like of which has never been seen before" (p. 783). Selwyn (2009) similarly cast doubt on the view that "current generations of children and young people are innate, talented users of digital technologies" (p. 364). Like Selwyn, Jones (2011, 2012) argued that the Net Generation and digital natives viewpoint rested on a misplaced technological and biological determinism. Schulmeister (2010) argued that large surveys of children and young people in various countries had failed to support the latter view.

In particular, Pedró (2009) conducted a meta-analysis of research from countries in the Organization for Economic Cooperation and Development (OECD) and found that there was insufficient evidence that students' use of digital technologies had influenced the way that they learned, their preferences and perceptions regarding teaching and learning in higher education, or their general intellectual development. On the contrary, surveys from Australia, the United Kingdom, and the United States indicate that students are broadly content with the digital technologies that their universities provide and with the level of competence shown by their teachers (Dahlstrom, 2012; Jones, Ramanau, Cross, & Healing, 2010; Jones & Shao, 2011; Kennedy, Judd, Churchward, Gray, & Krause, 2008; Smith & Caruso, 2010). In short, the Net Generation and digital natives hypotheses are essentially speculations for which there is little or no direct evidence.

One reason for researchers to be interested in the attitudes of students in higher education to the use of digital technologies is that they appear to be related to how they go about studying. Goodyear, Asensio, Jones, Hodgson, and Steeples (2003) surveyed students at four universities in the United Kingdom who were taking courses delivered by networked learning (see also Goodyear, Jones, Asensio, Hodgson, & Steeples, 2005). They found that students who had more positive attitudes to digital technologies were more likely to adopt a "deep" approach to studying (aimed at understanding the course content), were more likely to adopt a "strategic" approach to studying (aimed at achieving the highest grades), and were less likely to adopt a "surface" approach to studying (aimed at being able to reproduce the course materials for the purposes of assessment). Similar results were obtained by Foster and Lin (2007) at one UK university and by Chen, Lambert, and Guidry (2010) using data from a survey of students at 45 institutions across the United States.

Access and Attitudes to Digital Technologies
in Older Students

A major difficulty in evaluating the Net Generation and digital natives hypotheses is that most research into students' use of and attitudes toward technologies has been carried out with young people who have gone straight from secondary school (high school) to university. Older students have tended to be marginalized or ignored completely in this literature. Even so, there exists a complementary stereotype that people in the oldest age groups make less use of digital technology than do younger adults. Older people are often assumed to have poorer access to technology, less motivation to make use of technology, and fewer digital skills than younger adults (Peacock & Künemund, 2007; Wagner, Hassanein, & Head, 2010). In both the United States (Zickuhr, 2013) and the United Kingdom (Office for National Statistics, 2012), it is true that older adults are less likely than younger adults to access the Internet. Even so, this may well not apply to older students in the technology-rich environment of higher education.

One exception to the marginalization of older students in higher education is a survey that was carried out by Jones et al. (2010) with students at five different English universities (see also Jones & Hosein, 2010). They found clear age-related differences in the students' use of digital technologies. For instance, the younger students were more likely than the older students to use laptops or handheld devices rather than desktop computers, and they were more likely to use new forms of technology such as wikis, blogs, or virtual worlds. They also found clear age-related differences in the students' attitudes to technologies, such that the older students reported having less confidence in their use of digital tools than did the younger students. Nevertheless, Jones et al. found that neither the older students nor the younger students constituted a single homogeneous group in their use of digital technologies. Moreover, there was no evidence for any discontinuity in technology use around the age of 30, as would have been predicted by the Net Generation and digital natives hypotheses. Indeed, other factors (most especially gender) were as important in influencing the students' use of digital technologies. This is consistent with research in the United States that found even among younger college students, technological expertise varied with gender, class, and race, mainly as a consequence of unequal opportunities in K-12 education (Goode, 2010). One recent study found that the same factors were responsible for variations in the diversity of activities in which students engaged on the social networking site Facebook (Junco, 2013).

One basic problem with the survey carried out by Jones et al. (2010), however, was that nearly all of the older students were taking courses by distance learning with the UK Open University (where the average age of students is around 40), whereas most of the younger students were enrolled at campus-based institutions. In other words, Jones et al. had confounded variations in age with differences in the mode of course delivery. This led us to carry out our own survey involving a large sample of Open University students, stratified by age. For reasons of space, we only report selected findings here; for a more detailed account, please see our published report (Jelfs & Richardson, 2013).

Methodology: A Survey of Distance Learning Students

Given the total numbers of students available to be surveyed under the Open University's normal procedures (which among other things preclude any student being asked to participate in more than two research projects in any year), we decided to draw 2,000 students at random from those aged 60–69 and 1,000 students at random from those aged 70 and over. Further random samples of 1,000 students were drawn from those aged 21–29, 30–39, 40–49, and 50–59. In short, this study involved a total sample of 7,000 students, stratified by age. It should be noted that the university makes widespread use of computer-based support, including DVDs, subject-support websites, and networking sites. Indeed, for most of its courses, the university expects students to have access both to a computer and to the Internet. Nevertheless, only the students in the youngest of our six age groups would represent Millennials, the Net Generation, or digital natives, whereas students in the remaining age groups would constitute digital immigrants.

The survey questionnaire was compiled on the basis of previous studies and in particular the instruments described by Jones et al. (2010) and Jones and Hosein (2010). We describe the major sections of the survey questionnaire below. It concluded with the question: "Do you have any other comments you would like to add about using ICT [information and communication technologies]?" The students' comments served to illuminate and elaborate some of the results that we obtained using closed questions and rating scales.

The questionnaire was prepared both as an online survey and as a postal survey. In June 2010, all the students were contacted by email and invited to participate in the online survey through a secure dedicated website. However, they were also told that, if they preferred to respond using a paper version of the questionnaire, they would receive one shortly. After two weeks, any students who had not responded online were sent a reminder letter through the regular mail, together with a paper version of the questionnaire and a prepaid return envelope. The reminder letter invited them to participate either by completing the paper version of the questionnaire or by completing the online alternative.

Completed questionnaires were returned by 4,066 (or 58.1%) of the students. The response rate increased monotonically from 31% for students aged 21–29 to 81% for those aged 70 and over. Of all the respondents, 60% had responded online, whereas 40% had completed the paper questionnaire. The preference for online responding is not surprising, given that the participants were provided with the online survey two weeks before the paper survey and also given that they were expected to be familiar with the online environment in their academic studies. The percentage of respondents who had responded online increased monotonically from 46% for students aged 21–29 to 66% in those aged 60–69 and then declined slightly to 60.5% in students aged 70 and over. In other words, when they are given a choice between responding on paper or online, and when they have similar access to relevant forms of technology, older students were more likely to respond to questionnaire surveys online than are younger students.

Table 5.1   Percentage of students with access to different technologies by age.

Technology	21–29	30–39	40–49	50–59	60–69	70 and over
Desktop computer	43.2	54.8	66.4	70.6	68.5	70.0
Laptop computer	86.0	81.7	77.2	74.6	66.8	52.3
Personal digital assistant	3.9	7.0	6.8	7.9	4.9	2.7
Mobile phone	74.4	65.1	70.7	70.1	68.3	56.3
Portable digital music player	46.5	42.8	37.1	34.3	28.7	16.9
USB memory stick	76.3	68.9	72.4	74.3	67.2	46.3
Handheld games player	13.0	10.7	10.2	6.8	3.9	1.6
Console games player	25.0	18.8	15.8	7.0	3.4	1.5

Source: From Jelfs & Richardson (2013), p. 343. Copyright 2012 by the British Educational Research Association.

Survey Results: Access to Digital Technologies in Distance Learning Students

Table 5.1 shows the percentage of respondents in each age group who reported that they had access to different technologies for study purposes. (The technologies are listed in the order in which they were presented in the questionnaire.) As required by their courses, nearly all students had access to a computer; indeed, the results imply that some had access to two computers or more.[1] Because of the large number of tests of statistical significance in the analysis of the survey data, the threshold probability level (α) was set at .01 to avoid spuriously significant results (i.e., Type I errors).

The students in the older age groups were more likely than the students in the younger age groups to have access to a desktop computer, $\chi^2(5, N = 4066) = 107.35, p < .001$, whereas the students in the younger age groups were more likely than the students in the older age groups to have access to a laptop computer, $\chi^2(5, N = 4066) = 203.34, p < .001$. These results are consistent with those that were obtained by Jones et al. (2010), and they are also consistent with what we know about the use of technologies among young adults studying at campus-based institutions (Dahlstrom, 2012).

The students in the younger age groups were also more likely than the students in the older age groups to have access to a mobile phone, $\chi^2(5, N = 4066) = 56.16, p < .001$, a portable digital music player, $\chi^2(5, N = 4066) = 146.46, p < .001$, a hand-held game player, $\chi^2(5, N = 4066) = 97.88, p < .001$, or a console game player, $\chi^2(5, N = 4066) = 301.29, p < .001$. A qualitative study carried out in Australia found that distance learners make use of mobile devices of this sort to support their learning in varied locations and for a range of learning activities (Andrews, Tynan, & James, 2011). The middle-aged students were more likely than those in the other age groups to have access to a personal digital assistant or palmtop computer, $\chi^2(5, N = 4066) = 25.00, p < .001$. (For younger readers: These devices were popular toward the end of the twentieth century, but nowadays their functionality has been superseded by that of smartphones.) The students aged 70 and over were less likely than those in the other age groups to have access to a USB memory stick or flash drive, $\chi^2(5, N = 4066) = 191.90, p < .001$, presumably because they had less need to transfer files from one computer to another.

We did not ask students about their access to the latest forms of technology such as tablet computers. (The Apple iPad was launched in April 2010, just two months

Table 5.2   Percentage of students with access to the Internet at different locations by age.

Location	21–29	30–39	40–49	50–59	60–69	70 and over
Home	91.2	93.2	93.6	94.4	95.6	93.0
Library or other public facility	11.7	9.4	8.5	7.4	8.2	5.0
Work	42.2	50.1	44.6	41.2	14.5	1.7
Internet café	4.5	3.1	2.1	1.4	2.1	0.7
Home of friend or family member	14.6	6.3	3.5	3.9	3.3	3.0
Anywhere (e.g., via mobile phone)	21.1	21.4	18.7	13.0	10.1	3.8

Source: From Jelfs & Richardson (2013), p. 344. Copyright 2012 by the British Educational Research Association.

before our survey.) Even so, an internal Open University survey carried out in 2012 found that the take-up of such devices for study purposes was still relatively low: only 12% of the students surveyed reported that they used an iPad in connection with their Open University studies (Moore, 2012). The situation may have changed since then, of course. We believe that instructors and course designers in both campus-based and distance education need to exploit the opportunities that are offered by tablet computers and e-book readers, because they may be more accessible for all students than older forms of technology.

Again as required by their courses, nearly all of the respondents (99%) had access to the Internet. This proportion varied with age from 100% in respondents aged 21–29 to 98% in respondents aged 70 and over, $\chi^2(5, N = 4066) = 22.81, p < .001$. Nearly all the respondents with Internet access (97%) used broadband, and this proportion did not vary significantly with age. Table 5.2 shows the percentage of respondents in each age group who reported that they had access to the Internet in different locations. The students in the younger age groups were more likely than the students in the older age groups to have Internet access in a library or other public facility, $\chi^2(5, N = 4066) = 17.06, p = .004$, at work, $\chi^2(5, N = 4066) = 684.31, p < .001$, at an Internet café, $\chi^2(5, N = 4066) = 20.28, p = .001$, at the home of a friend or family member, $\chi^2(5, N = 4066) = 87.57, p < .001$, or anywhere (i.e., via a mobile phone or other portable device), $\chi^2(5, N = 4066) = 132.43, p < .001$. However, there was no significant variation with age in the proportion of respondents who had Internet access at home. Rønning and Grepperud (2006) similarly found that nearly 95% of distance learning students in Norway had access to the Internet in their own homes.

Confidence in Using Digital Technologies in Distance Learning Students

We asked the respondents to say how confident they felt undertaking 13 computing tasks using response alternatives labeled "very confident," "fairly confident," "not really confident," "not at all confident," and "never used." However, it proved difficult to analyze these responses because 3,277 (or 81%) of the respondents reported that they had never carried out one or more of the 13 tasks. Table 5.3 shows the

Table 5.3 Percentage of students who have never carried out different tasks by age.

Task	21–29	30–39	40–49	50–59	60–69	70 and over
Word processing	0.3	1.1	1.3	1.6	1.8	5.1
Email	0.0	0.0	0.2	0.9	0.8	2.8
Spreadsheets	3.0	4.3	8.1	7.7	12.0	21.1
Web searching tools	0.0	0.3	0.6	0.4	0.8	3.0
Internet for shopping	1.4	1.9	2.3	4.1	8.1	17.8
Internet for studying	0.3	0.3	1.3	0.5	2.7	7.5
Internet for online communication	16.9	27.4	34.4	33.7	43.4	52.6
Social networks	9.5	22.0	33.0	44.3	58.1	68.1
Sharing with others	28.4	34.0	47.7	49.2	58.1	67.2
Wikis	8.1	7.6	14.3	16.0	20.1	30.3
Wikis as part of studies	29.7	32.3	40.6	37.6	46.3	51.2
Personal blog	60.1	63.6	67.2	68.7	76.9	79.8
Blog as part of studies	50.8	50.0	58.3	55.8	60.8	64.3

Source: From Jelfs & Richardson (2013), p. 345. Copyright 2012 by the British Educational Research Association.

percentage of respondents in each age group who reported that they had never carried out each task. The students in the older age groups were more likely than the students in the younger age groups to report that they had never carried out each of the tasks, $\chi^2(5, N = 4066) \geq 33.37$, $p < .001$, in each case.

Even so, confidence in using digital technologies was a common theme in the students' concluding comments. Those whose work involved digital technologies were, not surprisingly, confident about using them in their studies:

> I am an IT tutor myself and therefore am confident in the use of IT as a learning strategy. I am also responsible for Moodle in my workplace, so am very comfortable with the OU [Open University] VLE [virtual learning environment]. (36-year-old female student)

For other students (including some older students), their lack of confidence was the main issue:

> Lack of confidence with regard to some aspects of ICT probably relates to my age as, although I do use a computer, I am not keeping up to date with more recent uses and use mine in a more basic form. (64-year-old male student)

> Because of my age (80+) I don't have complete confidence with the computer. (80-year-old male student)

Nevertheless, some described the increased confidence that they achieved with the help of family members, tutors, or other students:

> When I first started studying with the OU, I was very uncertain of my ability to cope, but as things were explained and with the help of other students I am quite confident and able to take part. When I saw other people make mistakes too, I gained more confidence. (83-year-old male student)

Students with Disabilities in Distance Education

The Open University has a long-standing commitment to promoting equal opportunities in education, including equal opportunities for people with disabilities. Conversely, many people with disabilities turn to distance education to avoid the problems of access that are often posed by campus-based institutions of higher education. Indeed, for many people who have severe disabilities or chronic illness, distance learning may be the only practical means of access to higher education (Newell & Debenham, 2009). At the time when we carried out our survey, there were nearly 11,000 students (or 6% of the total student population) taking courses with the Open University who had declared themselves as having one or more disabilities. We did not target students with disabilities in our survey, but many disabilities are more common in older people, and it is not surprising that they are more common in older students (Richardson, 2010).

We asked the students in our survey whether they used various assistive technologies (such as screen reading software or speech recognition software). None of the technologies that we mentioned was used by more than 5% of the respondents, and there was no significant variation with age in their use of any of the technologies. Nevertheless, some of the respondents referred to their disabilities and the role of digital technologies in their concluding comments:

> Because I am well into my eighties and am very deaf I prefer Internet and e-mail communication as face-to-face or on phone I have difficulties. I have a voice recorder to record tutorials in an effort to interpret later what has been said. (84-year-old male student)

> ICT is so very useful, but I should try to use the Internet more for information and to boost my confidence. Having a computer is a godsend as I am disabled in many ways and find the assistive technology very helpful especially Dragon [speech recognition software]. I could not do without my digital recorder. (73-year-old female student)

> I find it useful but quite like to just sit with my study books in a comfy chair and think more than do things on the computer. Even so, I have found my Dragon software invaluable due to a lot of pain at time. (52-year-old female student)

Attitudes to Digital Technologies in Distance Learning Students

We presented the students with nine statements about their attitudes toward digital technology. In each case, they were asked to indicate the extent of their agreement or disagreement with the relevant statement using a five-point scale. The response alternatives were labeled "totally agree" (scored 5), "somewhat agree" (scored 4), "not sure" (scored 3), "somewhat disagree" (scored 2), and "totally disagree" (scored 1). A factor analysis of their responses suggested that six of these statements could be taken to constitute a single scale representing their attitudes to technology:

- I have access to all the ICT necessary to study with the OU.
- I am not clear about how the use of ICT can improve my learning.
- I enjoy using ICT in my studies.
- I think the importance of using ICT in education is overstated.
- I am excited by the use of ICT at the OU.
- I am reluctant to use ICT in my OU studies.

It should be noted that three of the items are positively worded, whereas the other three are negatively worded and therefore were reverse coded (so that 1 is coded as 5, whereas 5 is coded as 1). The students were assigned scores on this scale by taking the mean of their responses to the six items after the negatively worded items had been coded in reverse. Of the 4,066 respondents, 3,812 had responded to all six items in this scale. An analysis of variance was carried out on these students' scores using the independent variables of age group, gender, and response mode.

Table 5.4 shows the mean scores obtained by the online and postal respondents in each age group, adjusted for any possible effect of gender. The students in the younger age groups had more positive attitudes to technology than did the students in the older age groups, $F(5, 3788) = 40.79$, $p < .001$. The overall effect of response mode was not statistically significant, but there was a significant interaction between the effects of age group and response mode, $F(5, 3788) = 3.17$, $p = .007$. Table 5.4 shows that the online respondents tended to have more positive attitudes to technology than did the postal respondents, but this was significant only in the students aged 60–69, $F(1, 3788) = 14.45$, $p < .001$, and in the students aged 70 and over, $F(1, 3788) = 11.94$, $p < .001$. For students in the younger age groups, there was essentially no difference between the online respondents and the postal respondents in their attitudes to technology. Finally, there was a significant main effect of gender, $F(1, 3788) = 10.33$, $p = .001$, such that the men ($M = 3.87$) tended to have somewhat more positive attitudes than the women ($M = 3.76$).

Table 5.4 shows that in each age group the mean score was above the midpoint of the response scale (3), indicating that all of the students held broadly positive attitudes to technology regardless of their ages. Nevertheless, in their concluding comments, some of the older students were clearly ambivalent about having to use digital technologies in their courses:

> I am in the age group that finds using a computer quite frustrating at times – they never seem to do what I think they should! Unfortunately though I do not want to spend a lot of time studying how to use a computer so tend to learn by trial and error – usually more error than anything. (62-year-old male student)

> As a freelance non-fiction author, I use my PC as a clever typewriter, but I do not value its wide-ranging scope for research (including shopping for relevant textbooks). I'm the age and background, however, that still prefers handwritten notes and leafing through the pages of books. (73-year-old male student)

> As I am fast approaching my 80s I am afraid that I hate using online studying and cannot be bothered to communicate on forums, although I do read everything that is posted. I do, however, Google quite a lot to confirm or find different approaches to anything mentioned in the course materials. (77-year-old female student)

Table 5.4　Mean scores on attitudes to technology by age and response mode.

Response mode	21–30	30–39	40–49	50–59	60–69	70 and over
Online	4.01	4.05	3.89	3.86	3.77	3.50
Postal	4.18	3.92	3.95	3.77	3.59	3.27

Note. Scores are on a scale from 1 (low) to 5 (high).
Source: From Jelfs & Richardson (2013), p. 347. Copyright 2012 by the British Educational Research Association.

I started learning to use computers when I started OU courses – admittedly at an advanced age and am still largely on a learning curve. (80-year-old male student)

Attitudes to Digital Technologies and Approaches to Learning and Studying

Finally, we also asked the students about the approaches to studying that they adopted on their courses, because previous research had shown that older students were more likely to adopt a deep approach to studying and less likely to adopt a surface approach to studying than younger students (see Baeten, Kyndt, Struyven, & Dochy, 2010, for a review). We used an Approaches to Learning and Studying Inventory that had been developed by Entwistle, McCune, and Hounsell (2003). This measures the use of a deep approach (six items), a surface approach (four items), and two aspects of a strategic approach (monitoring studying and organized studying, four items each). Sample items for the four scales are shown in Table 5.5.[2] Once again, for each of the 18 items, the students were asked to indicate the extent of their agreement or disagreement with the relevant statement using a five-point scale. They were assigned scores on each of the four scales as the mean of their responses to the relevant items.

There were 3,773 respondents with usable data on both attitudes to technology and approaches to studying. A multivariate analysis of variance was carried out on the students' scale scores using age group, gender, and response mode as independent variables and attitudes to technology as a covariate. There was a significant multivariate effect of attitudes to technology, $F(4, 3745) = 69.51$, $p < .001$. The students with more positive attitudes to technology tended to have higher scores on deep approach, $B = +.14$, monitoring studying, $B = +.13$, and organized studying, $B = +.13$, and they tended to have lower scores on surface approach, $B = -.18$, than did the students with less positive attitudes. These results are consistent with the findings by Chen et al. (2010), by Foster and Lin (2007), and by Goodyear et al. (2003, 2005) that were obtained in the context of campus-based education. They imply that students with more positive attitudes to technology are more likely to adopt desirable approaches to studying and are less likely to adopt undesirable approaches to studying.

There was a significant multivariate effect of age group, $F(20, 12422) = 6.57, < .001$. The students in the older age groups tended to have higher scores on deep approach, monitoring studying, and organized studying, but they tended to have lower scores on surface approach than did the students in the younger age groups. These results are consistent with those reviewed by Baeten et al. (2010) (for further discussion of

Table 5.5   Sample items in the Approaches to Learning and Studying Inventory.

Scale	Sample item
Deep approach	I look at evidence carefully to reach my own conclusion about what I'm studying.
Surface approach	Much of what I learn seems no more than lots of unrelated bits and pieces in my mind.
Monitoring studying	I go over the work I've done to check my reasoning and see that it all makes sense.
Organized studying	I organize my study time carefully to make the best use of it.

these results, see Richardson, 2013). They imply that older students are more likely to adopt desirable approaches to studying and less likely to adopt undesirable approaches to studying. The explanation for this that is most commonly suggested is that older students are more likely than younger students to be studying out of intrinsic interest or for their own personal development (e.g., Gow & Kember, 1990; Richardson, 1994; Watkins, 1982).

There was also a significant multivariate effect of gender, $F(4, 3745) = 16.72, p < .001$. The women had significantly higher scores on organized studying than did the men. There was, however, no significant gender difference in their scores on deep approach, surface approach, or monitoring studying. Finally, there was a significant multivariate effect of response mode, $F(4, 3745) = 5.87, p < .001$. The online respondents had significantly higher scores on monitoring studying but significantly lower scores on organized studying than did the postal respondents. There was, however, no significant effect of response mode on their scores on either deep approach or surface approach.

Conclusions

Our survey provided a number of findings relevant to the Net Generation and digital natives hypotheses. Our first result was that, when given a choice between responding on paper or online and with similar access to relevant forms of technology, older people are more likely to respond to questionnaire surveys online than are younger students, at least in the case of those taking courses with the Open University. As we concluded in the full report of this survey, this in itself suggests that researchers, practitioners, and policymakers need to beware of accepting stereotypes regarding the abilities and motivation of older people when using digital technologies (Jelfs & Richardson, 2013).

In our survey, the students in the younger age groups did report more positive attitudes to digital technologies than did the students in the older age groups, and we did find evidence that some older students were ambivalent about using digital technologies in their courses. However, our second result of relevance to the Net Generation and digital natives hypotheses was that in every age group the mean score on students' attitudes to digital technologies was above the midpoint of the response scale, which we take to indicate broadly positive attitudes across the adult lifespan. It certainly should not be assumed that older people as a group are resistant or incapable of making use of digital technologies in their studies.

It would, of course, be foolish to seek to deny that there are age-related variations in students' access and attitudes to technology across the adult lifespan. Our findings show clear patterns for younger students to have access to a wider range of digital technologies (Table 5.1) in a wider range of locations (Table 5.2), to have used digital technologies to carry out a wider range of tasks (Table 5.3), and to hold more positive attitudes to the use of digital technologies in their studies (Table 5.4). Nevertheless, in every case, these are monotonic trends extending across most or all of the adult lifespan. Consistent with the results obtained by Jones et al. (2010), we found no evidence for any discontinuity in technology use around the age of 30, as would be predicted by the Net Generation and digital natives hypotheses. In short, these hypotheses do not help us to understand the nature of age-related variations in students' access and attitudes to technology.

Finally, we are able to disentangle the relationship between students' age, their attitudes to digital technologies, and their approaches to studying. Their age is negatively associated with their attitudes to digital technologies; their age is positively associated with their use of desirable approaches to studying; and their attitudes to digital technologies are also positively associated with their use of desirable approaches to studying. We conclude that students' ages and their attitudes to digital technologies are distinct predictors of their approaches to studying in both campus-based and distance education. This in turn leads us to infer that, in both kinds of setting and whatever their age, today's students regard the use of digital technologies as an integral part of their experience of higher education.

Acknowledgments

Parts of this chapter are based on material contained in the article by Jelfs and Richardson (2013). We are grateful to Chetz Colwell for her assistance in the design and execution of the survey and for analyzing the students' open-ended comments. We are also grateful to the staff of the Open University's Survey Office for designing, distributing, and processing the survey, to Stephanie Lay for identifying the student samples, and to Chris Jones and Binhui Shao for many helpful discussions.

Notes

1   Having said that, the most common complaint in the students' concluding comments related to the Open University's lack of support for students using Apple Macintosh computers. The University's current policy is stated as follows: "The Apple Macintosh ('Mac') is a popular alternative but the OU can offer only limited technical support for Apple computers. Much of the OU course software delivered on CD or DVD is intended primarily for use with Microsoft Windows" (The Open University, 2011, p. 13). This may not be a sensible policy in the future because, according to at least one commentator, global sales of PCs are now in decline and yet Microsoft has failed to make a significant impact on the market for smartphones and tablet computers (Arthur, 2013).

2   The complete questionnaire can be found at http://www.etl.tla.ed.ac.uk/ questionnaires/ETLQ.pdf (accessed November 2014).

References

Andrews, T., Tynan, B., & James, R. (2011). The lived experience of learners' use of new media in distance teaching and learning. *On the Horizon, 19*, 321–330.

Arthur, C. (2013, August 27). Steve Ballmer heads for retirement, but where now for Microsoft? *Guardian*. Retrieved November 24, 2014, from http://www.theguardian.com/business/2013/aug/27/microsoft-ballmer-retirement

Baeten, M., Kyndt, E., Struyven, K., & Dochy, F. (2010). Using student-centered learning environments to stimulate deep approaches to learning: Factors encouraging or discouraging their effectiveness. *Educational Research Review, 5*, 243–260.

Bennett, S., Maton, K., & Kervin, L. (2008). The "digital natives" debate: A critical review of the evidence. *British Journal of Educational Technology, 39*, 775–786.

Chen, P.-S. D., Lambert, A. D., & Guidry, K. R. (2010). Engaging online learners: The impact of web-based learning technology on college student engagement. *Computers and Education, 54*, 1222–1232.

Dahlstrom, E. (2012). *ECAR study of undergraduate students and information technology, 2012.* Boulder, CO: EDUCAUSE Center for Applied Research. Retrieved November 24, 2014, from http://net.educause.edu/ir/library/pdf/ERS1208/ERS1208.pdf

Entwistle, N., McCune, V., & Hounsell, J. (2003). Investigating ways of enhancing university teaching–learning environments: Measuring students' approaches to studying and perceptions of teaching. In E. De Corte, L. Verschaffel, N. Entwistle, & J. van Merriënboer (Eds.), *Powerful learning environments: Unravelling basic components and dimensions* (pp. 89–107). Oxford, UK: Pergamon.

Foster, J., & Lin, A. (2007). Approaches to studying and students' use of a computer-supported learning environment. *Education for Information, 25,* 155–168.

Goode, J. (2010). Mind the gap: The digital dimension of college access. *Journal of Higher Education, 81,* 583–618.

Goodyear, P., Asensio, M., Jones, C., Hodgson, V., & Steeples, C. (2003). Relationships between conceptions of learning, approaches to study and students' judgements about the value of their experiences of networked learning. *ALT-J, 11*(1), 17–27.

Goodyear, P., Jones, C., Asensio, M., Hodgson, V., & Steeples, C. (2005). Networked learning in higher education: Students' expectations and experiences. *Higher Education, 50,* 473–508.

Gow, L., & Kember, D. (1990). Does higher education promote independent learning? *Higher Education, 19,* 307–322. Retrieved November 24, 2014, from http://www.jstor.org/stable/3447188

Halse, M. L., & Mallinson, B. J. (2009). Investigating popular Internet applications as supporting e-learning technologies for teaching and learning with Generation Y. *International Journal of Education and Development Using Information and Communication Technology, 5*(5), 58–71. Retrieved November 24, 2014, from http://ijedict.dec.uwi.edu/include/getdoc.php?id=4673&article=861&mode=pdf

Howe, N., & Strauss, W. (2000). *Millenials rising: The next great generation.* New York, NY: Vintage Books.

Howe, N., & Strauss, W. (2003). *Millennials go to college: Strategies for a new generation on campus. Recruiting and admissions, campus life, and the classroom.* Washington, DC: American Association of Collegiate Registrars and Admissions Officers.

Jelfs, A., & Richardson, J. T. E. (2013). The use of digital technologies across the adult life span in distance education. *British Journal of Educational Technology, 44,* 338–351.

Jones, C. (2011). Students, the Net Generation, and digital natives: Accounting for educational change. In M. Thomas (Ed.), *Deconstructing digital natives: Young people, technology and the new literacies* (pp. 30–45). New York, NY: Routledge.

Jones, C. (2012). Networked learning, stepping beyond the Net Generation and digital natives. In L. Dirckinck-Holmfeld, V. Hodgson, & D. McConnell (Eds.), *Exploring the theory, pedagogy and practice of networked learning* (pp. 27–41). New York, NY: Springer.

Jones, C., & Hosein, A. (2010). Profiling university students' use of technology: Where is the Net Generation divide? *International Journal of Technology, Knowledge, and Society, 6*(3), 43–58.

Jones, C., Ramanau, R., Cross, S., & Healing, G. (2010). Net Generation or digital natives: Is there a distinct new generation entering university? *Computers and Education, 54,* 722–732.

Jones, C., & Shao, B. (2011). *The Net Generation and digital natives: Implications for higher education.* York, UK: Higher Education Academy. Retrieved November 24, 2014, from https://www.heacademy.ac.uk/node/4011

Jorgensen, B. (2003). Baby Boomers, Generation X and Generation Y? Policy implications for defence forces in the modern era. *Foresight, 5*(4), 41–49.

Junco, R. (2013). Inequalities in Facebook use. *Computers in Human Behavior, 29,* 2328–2336.

Kennedy, G. E., Judd, T. S., Churchward, A., Gray, K., & Krause, K.-L. (2008). First-year students' experiences with technology: Are they really digital natives? *Australasian Journal of Educational Technology, 24,* 108–122. Retrieved November 24, 2014, from http://www.ascilite.org.au/ajet/ajet24/kennedy.pdf

Lang, L., & Arroway, P. (2013). *2012 CDS executive summary report*. Boulder, CO: EDUCAUSE Core Data Service. Retrieved November 24, 2014, from http://net.educause.edu/ir/library/pdf/PUB8009.pdf

Markiewicz, P. (2003). Who's filling Generation Y's shoes? Retrieved November 24, 2014, from http://www.brandchannel.com/features_effect.asp?pf_id=156

Moore, R. (2012). *Student ICT ownership survey 2012: Final report*. Milton Keynes, UK: The Open University, Learning and Teaching Solutions.

National Union of Students. (2010). *Student perspectives on technology: Demand, perceptions and training needs*. Bristol, UK: Higher Education Funding Council for England. Retrieved November 24, 2014, from http://www.hefce.ac.uk/data/year/2010/studentperspectivesontechnologydemandperceptionsandtrainingneeds/

Newell, C., & Debenham, M. (2009). Disability, chronic illness and distance education. In P. Rogers, G. Berg, J. Boettcher, C. Howard, L. Justice, & K. Schenk (Eds.), *Encyclopedia of distance learning* (2nd ed., Vol. 2, pp. 646–654). Hershey, PA: Information Science Reference.

Oblinger, D. (2003). Boomers, Gen-Xers, and Millennials: Understanding the new students. *EDUCAUSE Review*, *38*(4), 37–47. Retrieved November 24, 2014, from http://net.educause.edu/ir/library/pdf/ERM0342.pdf

Oblinger, D., & Oblinger, J. (2005). Is it age or IT: First steps toward understanding the Net Generation. In D. G. Oblinger & J. L. Oblinger (Eds.), *Educating the Net Generation* (pp. 12–31). Boulder, CO: EDUCAUSE. Retrieved November 24, 2014, from http://net.educause.edu/ir/library/pdf/pub7101.pdf

Office for National Statistics. (2012). *Internet access – households and individuals, 2012 part 2*. London, UK: Author. Retrieved November 24, 2014, from http://www.ons.gov.uk/ons/dcp171778_301822.pdf

The Open University. (2011). *Using a computer to support your study*. Milton Keynes, UK: Author. Retrieved November 24, 2014, from http://www2.open.ac.uk/students/skillsforstudy/doc/using-a-computer-to-support-your-study.pdf

Peacock, S. E., & Künemund, H. (2007). Senior citizens and Internet technology: Reasons and correlates of access versus non-access in a European comparative perspective. *European Journal of Ageing*, *4*, 191–200.

Pedró, F. (2009). *New millennium learners in higher education: Evidence and policy implications*. Paris, France: Organization for Economic Cooperation and Development, Centre for Educational Research and Innovation. Retrieved November 24, 2014, from http://www.pgce.soton.ac.uk/ict/NewPGCE/PDFs10/NML-in-Higher-Education.pdf

Prensky, M. (2001a). Digital natives, digital immigrants, Part 1. *On the Horizon*, *9*(5), 1–6.

Prensky, M. (2001b). Digital natives, digital immigrants, Part 2: Do they really think differently? *On the Horizon*, *9*(6), 1–6.

Prensky, M. (2009). H. sapiens digital: From digital immigrants and digital natives to digital wisdom. *Innovate*, *5*(3). Retrieved November 24, 2014, from http://www.wisdompage.com/Prensky01.html

Prensky, M. (2010). *Teaching digital natives: Partnering for real learning*. Thousand Oaks, CA: Corwin Press.

Richardson, J. T. E. (1994). Mature students in higher education: I. A literature survey on approaches to studying. *Studies in Higher Education*, *19*, 309–325.

Richardson, J. T. E. (2010). Course completion and attainment in disabled students taking courses with the Open University UK. *Open Learning*, *25*, 81–94.

Richardson, J. T. E. (2013). Approaches to studying across the adult life span: Evidence from distance education. *Learning and Individual Differences*, *26*, 74–80.

Rønning, W. M., & Grepperud, G. (2006). The everyday use of ICT in Norwegian flexible education. *Seminar.net*, *2*(1). Retrieved November 24, 2014, from http://seminar.net/files/vol2-1/TheEverydayUseofICT-Seminar-vol2-1.pdf

Schulmeister, R. (2010). Deconstructing the Net Generation thesis. *QWERTY*, *5*(2), 26–60.

Selwyn, N. (2009). The digital native: Myth and reality. *Aslib Proceedings*, *61*, 364–379.

Smith, S. D., & Caruso, J. B. (2010). *ECAR study of undergraduate students and information technology, 2010* (ECAR report No. 6). Boulder, CO: EDUCAUSE Center for Applied Research. Retrieved November 24, 2014, from http://net.educause.edu/ir/library/pdf/ERS1006/RS/ERS1006W.pdf

Strauss, W., & Howe, N. (1991). *Generations: The history of America's future, 1584 to 2069.* New York, NY: Quill.

Tapscott, D. (1998). *Growing up digital: The rise of the Net Generation.* New York, NY: McGraw-Hill.

Tapscott, D. (2009). *Grown up digital: How the Net Generation is changing your world.* New York, NY: McGraw-Hill.

Tapscott, D., & Williams, A. D. (2010). Innovating the 21st-century university: It's time! *EDUCAUSE Review, 45*(1), 16–25. Retrieved November 24, 2014, from http://net.educause.edu/ir/library/pdf/ERM1010.pdf

Viewpoint: Generation Y. (1993, August 30). Editorial. *Advertising Age*, p. 16.

Wagner, N., Hassanein, K., & Head, M. (2010). Computer use by older adults: A multi-disciplinary review. *Computers in Human Behavior, 26*, 870–882.

Walker, R., Voce, J., & Ahmed, J. (2012). *2012 survey of technology enhanced learning for higher education in the UK.* Oxford, UK: Universities and Colleges Information Systems Association. Retrieved November 24, 2014, from http://www.ucisa.ac.uk/~/media/groups/ssg/surveys/TEL_survey_2012_final_ex_apps

Watkins, D. (1982). Identifying the study process dimensions of Australian university students. *Australian Journal of Education, 26*, 76–85.

Wolburg, J. M., & Pokrywczynski, J. (2001). A psychographic analysis of Generation Y college students. *Journal of Advertising Research, 41*(5), 31–52. Retrieved November 24, 2014, from http://www.jar.warc.com/ArticleCenter/default.asp?ID=71848&Type=Article&Med=PDF

Zickuhr, K. (2013). *Who's not online and why.* Washington, DC: Pew Research Center, Internet & American Life Project. Retrieved November 24, 2014, from http://www.pewinternet.org/2013/09/25/whos-not-online-and-why/

6

Navigating Psychological Ethics in Shared Multi-User Online Environments

Jeff Gavin[1] and Karen Rodham[2]

[1] *University of Bath*
[2] *Staffordshire University*

"Sorry – coming into this late – but
Noooooooooooooooooooooooooooooooooooooooooooooooooooooooo!!!"

This was a response to a lengthy email exchange between us and two other similarly experienced psychology researchers, as we negotiated an ethical dilemma instigated by our research into online support. What could possibly have prompted this *cri de coeur*?

The Changing Ethical Landscape of Online Research

Over the last decade, we have built up a body of research utilizing the Internet as a means of collecting data (e.g., Adams, Rodham, & Gavin, 2005; Gavin, Rodham, & Poyer, 2008; Rodham, Gavin, & Miles, 2007; Rodham, Gavin, Lewis, St. Denis, & Bandalli, 2013). Our research program has moved from using static self-contained message boards to multimedia photo and video sharing sites, and most recently to the multi-authored collaborative environment of wiki-technology. Each technological shift has raised different ontological, epistemological, and ethical questions which have prompted us to write think-pieces exploring these questions.

In our first paper (Rodham & Gavin, 2006) we focused specifically on issues of consent and anonymity as they applied to online data collection, both interactive (e.g., online surveys and focus groups) and observational (i.e., textual analyses of message boards). We concluded that the ethical issues raised when planning and implementing online data collection (such as gaining consent and maintaining anonymity or confidentiality of participants) were no different to those raised by more traditional approaches to data collection. Our follow-up paper (Rodham & Gavin, 2011) focused on more dynamic forms of naturally occurring data, such as online forums, blogs, and profiles. However, by this time the online landscape had changed considerably; the boundaries between what was considered public and private had

The Wiley Handbook of Psychology, Technology, and Society, First Edition. Edited by Larry D. Rosen, Nancy A. Cheever, and L. Mark Carrier.
© 2015 John Wiley & Sons, Ltd. Published 2015 by John Wiley & Sons, Ltd.

become harder to distinguish. As the Internet evolved, self-presentation and expression online became decentered and dispersed across multiple users and domains. Researchers were thus compelled to engage with this increasingly interactive, participatory, and multi-authored environment. Social networking sites such as Facebook, MySpace, and YouTube, microblogging platforms such as Twitter, and collaborative sites such as Wikipedia were challenging the notions of the single author and autonomous self-presentation occurring in a clearly delineated space. The ethical issues surrounding these types of environments were less clear-cut, and our critical discussion of them highlighted many of the ethical ambiguities encountered when researching twenty-first-century online social practices.

We concluded our 2011 paper with the observation that traditional ethical approaches to research were in many ways incommensurate with recent developments in the ways that humans communicate and interact on the Internet, and with transformations to the Internet itself. Several questions remained unanswered: How do researchers deal with new Internet platforms and changing trends in Internet use? How can decisions about public and private spaces, informed consent, or anonymity be addressed in online environments containing several layers of text, image, and audio-visual input from multiple sources across multiple, linked sites? There was a need, we suggested, to produce a set of more flexible guidelines; ones that paid greater attention to the context and intentions of Internet users. It was important to update not only the guidelines themselves, but also the language used to frame them. We argued there was a need to do away with terms such as "anonymity," "consent," and "privacy," and start thinking in terms of "open" or "closed" networks, public and private "target audiences," and "implied consent."

Since then, the pace of change has steadily increased: we have seen smartphones come to dominate the mobile phone market (Guglielmo, 2013), thus vastly expanding the ease and range of communication options available; Facebook has undergone innumerable tweaks, one complete overhaul, and the incorporation of further social networking technologies. In addition, wearable, ubiquitous, and desktop technologies are synched to each other and to those of users' immediate and distal social networks, in ways that ethics committees a decade ago could not have envisaged. Indeed, as we have gained further experience with the increasingly sophisticated and fluid online environment, the disconnect between traditional ethical guidelines and the online research environment has become more apparent and our position has shifted. Hence the opening *cri de coeur*: as online researchers, the ethical dilemmas we encounter are increasingly opaque. As the rules of online and offline behavior diverge, traditional ethics, as they apply to face-to-face research, no longer provide clear-cut answers.

This chapter affords us the opportunity to draw from our experience as researchers of online identities, support, and coping to explore how decisions about public and private spaces, informed consent, and anonymity are addressed in online environments containing several layers of text, image, and audio-visual input from multiple sources across multiple, linked sites. We consider the nature of online data itself: Is it text-based or person-based? This has a direct bearing on a more ethically focused question: Is online data public or private? These questions lie at the nexus of three (often contradictory) sets of interests: those of the websites, those of the researched, and those of the researchers. Finally, in light of these considerations we ask: How can online researchers protect the anonymity and confidentiality of the researched?

To begin, however, we ask a seemingly more basic question: What do the relevant professional bodies have to say about the ethics of online research?

What do the Formal Ethical Guidelines Say?

Over the past 15 years, relevant professional bodies have struggled to produce guidelines that keep abreast of the fast-paced changing nature of the online world. In our earlier paper (Rodham & Gavin, 2011) we noted that professional bodies were late to respond to developments in online research and, when they did, took one of two approaches. Some, such as the British Sociological Association (2002) and the American Psychological Association (2002), did not produce any guidelines *per se* but instead put the onus on researchers to keep abreast of developments in online research. To date, their position remains the same:

> Members should *take special care* when carrying out research via the Internet. Ethical standards for Internet research are *not well developed* as yet ... Members who carry out research online should ensure that they are *familiar with ongoing debates* on the ethics of Internet research. (British Sociological Association, 2002)

Other professional bodies, such as the British Psychological Society (BPS, 2007), wrote specific guidelines for Internet research which were already out of date by the time they were released. However, since then, the BPS (2013) has altered its ethical stance and has published "Ethics Guidelines for Internet-Mediated Research" (IMR), which they consider to be supplemental and subordinate to their overarching Code of Ethics and Conduct for Psychologists. Unlike the earlier version, it is made clear that these guidelines are not intended to be used as a rulebook, but instead as a set of guiding principles. Furthermore, it is explicitly stated that the BPS recognizes that the online environment is one which undergoes regular and rapid change and that over time, "new considerations are likely to become salient." Consequently, the BPS calls for a "return to 'first principles' and an informed application of general ethical principles to the new situation" (BPS, 2013, p. 5).

Four key principles are thus outlined by the BPS. *Respect for autonomy and the dignity of persons* concerns issues such as consent, confidentiality, anonymity, and privacy of research participants. *Social responsibility* involves maintaining respect for and avoiding disruption to social structures, and a consideration of the consequences and outcomes of research. The remaining two principles, *scientific value* and *maximizing benefit and minimizing harm*, concern the scientific quality of the research balanced against the well-being of the researched. The way in which online researchers grapple with these issues, however, is contingent on how they conceptualize online data.

Is Online Data Text or People?

According to the BPS (2013), key considerations related to the autonomy and dignity of persons involved in Internet research are: rights for privacy, confidentiality, and anonymity; valid consent; withdrawal; and fair treatment. Central to this principle are two critical questions: What is considered public and what is considered private on the

Internet? And subsequently, do Internet researchers need to seek consent? To answer these questions, however, Internet researchers must first ask themselves a more fundamental question: What is the nature of Internet data? Is it text-based or person-based? McKee and Porter (2009) argue that the answer to this question is inextricably bound with a researcher's epistemological position with regard to whether the Internet is considered a space or a place. They note that the bulk of online data is text-based, but is frequently complicated by the often real-time, conversational nature of much of online communication. This prompts them to ask: "Should researchers treat the material in online spaces such as discussion forums, chats, or virtual worlds as published work by authors – and thus available to be quoted following fair use and copyright guidelines governing the public domain?" – or "should such online material be treated as communications among persons, and thus the researcher is not so much a reader but an observer, studying the real-time or archived interactions of persons to which different use ethics apply?" (p. 74).

These distinctions are shown in Table 6.1. An understanding of the Internet as a *space* emphasizes texts. From this point of view the Internet is a medium through which public texts circulate and any dialogue taking place in this space is rendered as published textual data (Bassett & O'Riordan, 2002). Aside from copyright considerations, these texts should be available for reproduction and study. An understanding of the Internet as a *place*, on the other hand, puts the emphasis on people. The Internet is a place made up of different communities of people having conversations. The dialogue is between people in this place, who should be considered "human subjects" and afforded appropriate rights and considerations in relation to ethical research with humans (McKee & Porter, 2009).

In contrast we suggest that it is in fact the research question that positions the data as either *person*-based or *text*-based, thus clarifying the place/space question. This fluidity is illustrated through a program of studies we have conducted of a photo sharing forum for people who self-harm. Indeed, this forum was considered to be both a *space* to exchange texts in one study (Bandalli, Gavin, & Rodham, 2010) and a *place* for people to converse in another (Rodham et al., 2013). In the former study we performed a textual analysis of the words carved into forum members' bodies, as displayed in their uploaded photos. Here the data consisted of 224 photos, and the study was considered *text-based*. In the latter study, we performed thematic analysis on the description of and comments about these photos, in order to explore forum users' motivations for participating in this forum. Here the focus was on *people* and the data consisted of conversations between people in a community. However, despite treating this study as person-based, it did not automatically follow that we sought consent. Indeed, we did not. This decision was based on our reflections on the nature of this place: Was it public or private?

Table 6.1 Two views of the Internet.

View of Internet	Space	Place
Location	Medium	Community, culture, world
Object of study	Publication (public, published)	People
Ethical rights	Author rights (copyright); researcher rights (public access)	Person rights, community norms

Source: Adapted from McKee & Porter (2009), p. 82.

Is Online Content Public or Private?

The distinction between public and private Internet content and communities is a well-trodden area that we have discussed in our previous ethics publications. At the heart of this matter is consent. On the surface, the simple argument is that if a website or chat room is public, consent is not required; if a website or chat room is private, consent should be sought from the site administrator or users themselves. Of course, in reality, the issue is not so straightforward. For example, on many social networking sites (such as Facebook or Instagram) users can choose the extent to which their content (either all or in part) is private or public; thus the user rather than the nature of the websites determines whether content is public or private. It is too simplistic, therefore, to base the public/private distinction on generalized considerations about the site alone. Moreover, it is no longer feasible to make this simple binary distinction between public and private. Furthermore, online data need to be judged in terms of both how much information a person reveals about their identity and how widely accessible the content is. Recognition should be given to the fact that in online settings data can be "publicly private" or "privately public" (Lange, 2008). For example, an online message board can be public in the sense that participants reveal identifying information, but private in the sense that it is password protected or accessible by invitation only (that is, publicly private). On the other hand, an online forum might contain little identifying information about its members but be accessible by all Internet users (that is, privately public).

However, not all online data can be easily classified as privately public or publicly private. For example, those who research online *networks* need to consider *whose privacy* is being considered. For example, a typical sequence of events might play out as follows: a YouTube member uploads a video. Others comment on this video, which is subsequently discovered by other Internet users through social aggregators and search services. These people add comments to the original video entry (which they might link to from their own YouTube, Facebook, or Twitter accounts via "liking" or "sharing" the video or "following" the original poster), view the video, and add further comments on YouTube, thus intensifying and contributing further to a networked discussion across multiple sites, with multiple authors, and text, hypertext, and audio-visual content. If a researcher were to study this discussion, whose consent would be sought? Whose right to anonymity needs protecting? If only one link in this network of sites is considered "private," does that render the whole exchange private? Or does a "private" user linking and contributing to this multi-site discussion render his or her contributions public?

If we cannot rely on the nature of the website or chat room to determine the level of privacy ascribed to online data, where do we turn? The answer to the question of whether online content is public or private depends on who is asking the question. Often the researcher and researched will give different answers. Some researchers have argued that if information is publicly available on the web, then it should be treated as any other publicly available text, such as a newspaper, and be considered available for study (e.g., Walther, 2002). As McKee and Porter rhetorically ask:

> If as members of the surfing public we can access Sarah's page, then why shouldn't we as researchers be allowed to use the information as well, especially since Sarah has made this information fully and publicly available to anyone who has access to the Web? (2009, p. 2)

Accessing Web Content: Website Policies and Legal Considerations

In practice, however, it does not automatically follow that because web content *can* be accessed by researchers it *should* be accessed by researchers. The debate around the privacy of online content is more complex than a simple consideration of accessibility. It involves a consideration of three components: the chosen privacy settings and expectation of website users (i.e., the researched), the website or chat room privacy policies, and legal considerations with regard to the access and publication of online data (Moreno, Goniu, Moreno, & Diekema, 2013). Unfortunately for online researchers, these three components are often incompatible. Indeed, in the case of both website and user expectations, they are often self-contradictory.

In terms of website and chat room privacy policies, although the issue of privacy is explicitly addressed, its stance is not always apparent, especially with regard to researchers. When users first sign up to a social networking site, for example, they must first agree to the site's privacy policy. Two of the most popular sites (and therefore two common sources of online data) are Facebook and Twitter. They each state that unless users explicitly make their content private (by applying the privacy options provided by the site), they should expect their content to be publicly available. For example, as of 2013, Twitter's privacy policy states that:

> Our services are primarily designed to help you share information with the world ... Our default is almost always to make the information you provide public but we generally give you settings to make the information more private if you want. Your public information is broadly and instantly disseminated.

Similarly, Facebook's data use policy currently places the onus on the user to determine his or her own level of privacy:

> If you're comfortable making something you share open to anyone, choose Public from the audience selector before you post. Something that is Public can be seen by people who are not your friends, people off of Facebook, and people who view content through different media (new and old alike) such as print, broadcast (television, etc.) and other sites on the Internet. When you comment on other people's Public posts, your comment is Public as well. (Facebook Data Use Policy, 2014)

However, once again we come up against the complexities of a networked community; the level of a user's privacy is not an individual decision but is dispersed throughout the user's network of friends, and may change long after the content is posted. Indeed, Facebook warns users to be aware of this possibility:

> When you comment on or "like" someone else's story, or write on their timeline, that person gets to select the audience. For example, if a friend posts a Public story and you comment on it, your comment will be Public. Often, you can see the audience someone selected for their story before you post a comment; however, the person who posted the story may later change their audience. So, if you comment on a story, and the story's audience changes, the new audience can see your comment. (Facebook Data Use Policy, 2014)

The implication of both Facebook's and Twitter's privacy policies is that if users set their privacy settings to "public" then they should not have a reasonable expectation of privacy, and that this content can be disseminated beyond the membership of the site ("Choosing to make your information public is exactly what it sounds like: anyone, including people off Facebook, will be able to see it," Facebook Data Use Policy, 2014). Presumably this includes researchers. However, Facebook's Statement of Rights and Responsibilities implies otherwise:

> If you collect information from users, you will: obtain their consent, make it clear you (and not Facebook) are the one collecting their information, and post a privacy policy explaining what information you collect and how you will use it.

Federal courts in the United States seem to give more credence to the privacy policy than to the rights and responsibilities of users, at least when it comes to Facebook. Recent court rulings have ruled that social media users should not have a "reasonable" expectation of privacy with regard to their posted content (Moreno et al., 2013), in part on the basis that sharing information widely with others is the *raison d'être* of social media such as Facebook. Such rulings are important to online researchers as institutional review boards (IRBs) often turn to privacy-related court cases to guide decisions regarding potential privacy violations in the research context (Moreno et al., 2013).

But what are users' actual expectations, and how might this "authorized" distribution of users' content impact their rights to anonymity and confidentiality? As Bromseth (2003) notes: "Defining a space from the 'outside,' based on access, and from the 'inside,' based on participants' experience of the social activities taking place are ... two different positions that do not necessarily correspond" (p. 73). How do users feel about researchers accessing their online content? Using an experimental approach, Hudson and Bruckman (2004) demonstrated that participants' expectations of privacy conflict with the actual accessibility of these public chatrooms and have the potential to impede research in online settings. They did this by investigating how users of public online chatrooms respond to (a) an awareness of the presence of a researcher and (b) to a variety of consent options. When given the option to opt *in* to the study, only half a percent chose to do so. Conversely, when given the option to opt *out*, again, only half a percent chose to do so. Therefore, Hudson and Bruckman concluded that whether opt in or opt out, attempting to seek consent to study interactions in public online forums is not viable when conducting research.

In contrast, online researchers interviewed by McKee and Porter (2009) suggested that truly belonging and engaging with an online community was a critical requirement for studying it, asserting that instead of simply requesting consent, researchers should put time into the group and become participants themselves. In our view, this is unrealistic, and implies that all Internet research, at least as it applies to the study of online communities, must utilize a participant-observer methodology. Indeed, Hudson and Bruckman (2004) suggest that simply seeking consent from public online chatrooms alerts potential participants as well as moderators to the presence of the researcher; not only might this alter the dynamics of the group, but they also found that it was likely to lead to the researchers themselves being ejected from the forums.

Deciding whether it is appropriate to announce one's presence as a researcher and/ or seek consent to study a publicly available online community therefore should involve a consideration of the possible implications, such as altering the dynamics of the group and possible negative reactions from some members of the community. The two authors of this chapter study, among other things, issues of support and identity in online communities for young people who engage in various forms of self-harm, as well as forums for people recovering from or trying to maintain eating disordered behavior. As forty-something researchers who neither self-harm, nor have an eating disorder, it is unrealistic (from a moral, ethical, and practical standpoint) for us to participate in these groups. Indeed, it may be unethical to even announce our presence as observers.

How Online Researchers Can Protect the Anonymity and Confidentiality of the Researched

Whether one considers online content as public or private, and regardless of the website's privacy policies and the reasonable expectations of users, it behoves online researchers to safeguard the anonymity and confidentiality of the researched (i.e., the users whose content forms the basis of the data). Indeed, this is one of the central tenets of all professional ethics guidelines.

In research using data gathered from online sources, it is not enough to simply anonymize the published data, however. This was clearly demonstrated in the cautionary example of the "Taste, Ties, and Time" study conducted by an experienced research team in 2008 (Lewis, Kaufman, Gonzalez, Wimmer, & Christakis, 2008; see Zimmer, 2010 for review). With the permission of Facebook and the university in question, these researchers analyzed and publicly released data derived from the Facebook profiles of 1,700 Facebook users, the entire cohort of students at a U.S. university (Lewis et al., 2008). In an attempt to protect the anonymity and privacy of the researched, identifying information such as student names and identification numbers were removed from the published data set. However, the unique combination of demographic and university characteristics (such as ethnic background of students and combination of degrees offered) enabled the university, and potentially individual students whose data were harvested, to be identified. This study has subsequently become a case study for the issues faced by researchers when studying data derived from such sites. Zimmer (2010), for example, states that this incident "reveals the fragility of the perceived privacy of the subjects under study" and that the study itself highlights the numerous conceptual gaps in researchers' understandings of the privacy risks associated with online research. These include rethinking traditional notions of anonymity, consent, the relative expertise of institutional review boards, and identifying and respecting expectations of privacy on social network sites.

For example, even though all identifying information was removed, each user's gender, race, ethnicity, hometown state, and major were identified in the publicly available data set. As Zimmer points out, once the university is identified, a student with a unique set of characteristics (such as the only female Bulgarian law major, to take a hypothetical example) could be personally identified.

It should be noted that this research had received ethics approval from the relevant IRBs, and the researchers did attempt to protect the privacy of the researched. At the time, however, the researchers did not fully grasp the complexities of social networking (Zimmer, 2010). Just as the researchers had an insufficient understanding of the array of privacy concerns around social networking, perhaps IRB panels are similarly lacking. As we have said, the relevant professional bodies are slowly responding to the unique set of ethical concerns related to online research, but to what extent do IRB panels understand them? For example, the BPS highlights "social responsibility" as a key ethical principle to be upheld in online research, but without an understanding of the types of information contained in a typical profile or the interconnectedness of social media (such as one's Twitter account being linked to one's Facebook and Instagram account), is a typical IRB member in a position to determine whether a study has adequately addressed this ethical principle? From experience, we can attest that many members of IRBs have little if any experience or knowledge of contemporary social networking sites or practices. Given the proliferation of online research, perhaps the standard membership of IRB panels needs to be broadened to include online researchers as a matter of course, and even invite social network users themselves when relevant.

Social Responsibility

The principle of social responsibility implies that it is not just individuals whose identity needs to be protected, but also communities. Members of often researched but socially derided online communities, such as those supporting self-harm or pro-anorexia, can find their online communities shut down by their host site, usually following a flurry of short-term media attention. Researchers must therefore ask themselves what role dissemination of their findings might play in this process. Could their research lead to unwanted publicity, thereby leading to the demise of the community being investigated? So, questions of dissemination are intertwined with issues of anonymity, confidentiality, and to some extent consent.

When writing up Internet research for publication, it is important to think about whether the individuals and groups involved are identifiable. Are the published data searchable? That is, if extracts are put into a search engine, can the original post be found? This could render both the poster and the site identifiable. How can published data be made unsearchable? One way is to alter the data sufficiently for it not to be picked up by search engines. However, altering data is ethically questionable in any form of research, but especially when language or self-presentation is central to the analysis. The problem of identification becomes more vexed when considering visual data.

Since online users are increasingly investing in visual representations of themselves (McKee & Porter, 2009), researchers are also engaging with multimedia data, including photos, videos, and screenshots. How can such data be anonymized or de-identified? A solution used by one of the authors in disseminating his research on online dating is to illustrate his arguments with screenshots of his own (mock) online dating profile (Gavin & Griffin, 2012). However, for our research on "self-pics" of self-harm it would not be appropriate to use "mock" screenshots; therefore in disseminating this research we used only photos of injuries that included no identifying images such as faces or distinctive backgrounds (i.e., they are privately public), or we published content analysis of the images without any accompanying photographs. In this way we were mindful of three of the tenets outlined by the BPS: we avoided disrupting social structures (i.e., we are socially responsible), we maintained confidentiality and anonymity (thereby respecting the autonomy and dignity of persons), and we protected participants from any adverse effect arising from our research (thereby maximizing benefits and minimizing harm).

This final point, however, poses some unique challenges to online researchers. Unlike most psychological research, in the online environment the researcher and the researched are rarely co-located in time or space. In the majority of Internet research, not only is there no face-to-face contact between researcher and participant, often the participant is unidentifiable to the researcher, who will only have a pseudonym or screen name for his or her participants. How then is a researcher to know if a participant is being harmed, or is in distress, during the research process? How is a researcher to know if a participant has stopped responding because of some aspect of the research, or whether he or she has simply withdrawn from the study by logging off? If the researcher determines that there is potential harm, what should and could be done? In this respect, the problems faced by online researchers are no different to those faced by traditional researchers.

Our research on identity construction in pro-anorexia ("pro-ana") online support forums (Gavin et al., 2008) confronted us with this very issue. One of the regular contributors to the forum suddenly stopped posting. She had been steadily (and deliberately) losing weight to the point of multiple hospitalizations when she stopped posting. The other forum members expressed concern for her safety, and distress that they had no way of contacting her outside of the forum. Despite being an important part of the group, no one in the forum knew her real name or real-world contact details. Had we been conducting the study in "real time," this would have compelled us as researchers to question whether and how we should respond. In this example, however, the question was moot: we had conducted a risk analysis prior to engaging in the research and identified this as a potential problem. Since we had no way of knowing who members really were in the offline world, our ability to intervene would have been limited. We therefore made the decision to analyze data gathered retrospectively. As such, the disappearance of this forum member had occurred approximately 18 months prior to us reading the unfolding events in the forum.

But what about research conducted in real time? As part of a recent study of online support, we established an online community for people living with complex regional pain syndrome (Rodham et al., 2013). This is a little understood condition that has wide-ranging and long-term health repercussions. The community consisted of both a traditional online forum and a wiki. Our aims were twofold: (1) to provide a place where support could grow, and (2) to test whether a collaborative writing task facilitated support in ways that a traditional forum does not. This was a private community and the site was password protected, with members registered by us (we therefore had access to participants' real-world email contact details supplied by them when they registered). Before registering for the site, members were provided with information about the study and required to provide consent for their posts to be analyzed. Several months into the study, a member of the research team (Researcher 1) noticed that a member of the forum had posted a comment about not coping. Although the post suggested that this individual was very depressed and potentially suicidal, none of the other members of the community had responded. Another member of the research team (Researcher 2) outlined a number of options in an email to the rest of the team, and concluded with the following suggestion:

"So what to do? It seems a real shame that there is no reply to this message. Our laissez-faire philosophy suggests that it is a community matter and we should do nothing. A bit like natural selection, members who can't hack it wither away leaving only those who can thrive in this environment. But this isn't natural selection. It is an attempt to foster the development of a supportive community. So I think it sets a poor precedent. [...] If we do intervene, it could be with a post under our existing identities or we could ask [computer technician] to create a fake account so it doesn't look as though we are descending from upon high. [...] I shall ask [computer technician] to create an androgynous dummy account called "Alex" that we could use for this purpose. So what do you think?"

Researcher 1 responds positively to this suggestion. This triggers Researcher 3 to write:

"Sorry – coming into this late – but
Nooooooooooooooooooooooooooooooooooooooooooooooooooooooooooo!!!
   We cannot deceive people and let them think someone real is helping them – that's completely unethical and I cannot be party to it. It is the sort of thing that could completely explode in our faces."

This example brings together many of the issues we have explored in this chapter, not least whether a researcher should respond or intervene, and if so, when and how. Researchers need to balance several conflicting interests; the objectivity of scientific research, their effect on the dynamics of the group, ensuring safety in the context of the study, while also recognizing the limitations and boundaries of their levels of expertise and ability to intervene and support.

Conclusion

Given that so much of our social, civic, and private lives are now conducted online, it would be remiss (some might say unethical) to eschew the opportunity of researching publicly available online communities on the basis of users' expectations of privacy. Indeed, as the Internet has become more complex, so too have the ethical dilemmas facing online researchers. We do not claim to have all the answers, but reflecting on our own research has highlighted important and novel questions that researchers must ask if they are to ethically conduct online research in the current digital age.

References

Adams, J., Rodham, K., & Gavin, J. (2005). Investigating the "self" in deliberate self-harm. *Qualitative Health Research*, 15(10), 1293–1309.

American Psychological Association (APA). (2002). The ethical principles of psychologists and code of conduct. Retrieved November 28, 2008, from http://www.apa.org/ethics/code2002.html

Bandalli, P., Gavin, J., & Rodham, K. (2010). A content analysis of the words engraved onto the skin during self-injury. International Society for the Study of Self Injury, June 26–27, Northwestern University Feinberg School of Medicine, Chicago, IL.

Bassett, E. H., & O'Riordan, K. (2002). Ethics of Internet research: Contesting the human subjects research model. *Ethics and Information Technology, 4*, 243–247.

British Psychological Society (BPS). (2007). Report of the working party on conducting research on the Internet: Guidelines for ethical practice in psychological research online. Retrieved October 7, 2013, from http://www.bps.org.uk/publications/policy-and-guidelines/research-guidelines-policy-documents/

British Psychological Society (BPS). (2013). Ethics guidelines for Internet-mediated research. Retrieved November 29, 2013, from http://www.bps.org.uk/system/files/Public%20files/inf206–guidelines-for-internet-mediated-research.pdf

British Sociological Association. (2002). Statement of ethical practice for the British Sociological Association. Retrieved November 25, 2014, from http://www.britsoc.co.uk/about/equality/statement-of-ethical-practice.aspx

Bromseth, J. (2003). Ethical and methodological challenges in research on net-mediated communication in a Norwegian research context. In M. Thorseth (Ed.), *Applied ethics in Internet research* (pp. 67–85). Trondheim, Norway: NTNU University Press.

Gavin, J., & Griffin, C. (2012). The technological affordances of online dating sites: A comparative study. 10th Asia Pacific Conference on Computer Human Interaction (APCHI2012), August 28–31, Matsue, Japan.

Gavin, J., Rodham, K., & Poyer, H. (2008). The presentation of "pro-anorexia" in online group interactions. *Qualitative Health Research, 18*(3), 325–333.

Guglielmo, C. (2013). Smartphones dominate mobile phone sales in Q3, Lenovo joins Samsung, Apple in top three. Retrieved November 25, 2014, from http://www.forbes.com/sites/connieguglielmo/2013/11/14/smartphones-dominate-mobile-phone-sales-in-q3-lenovo-joins-samsung-apple-in-top-three/

Hudson, J. M., & Bruckman, A. (2004). "Go away": Participant objections to being studied and the ethics of chatroom research. *The Information Society, 20*, 127–139.

Lange, P.G. (2008). Publicly private and privately public: Social networking on YouTube. *Journal of Computer-Mediated Communication, 13*(1), 361–380.

Lewis, K., Kaufman, J., Gonzalez, M., Wimmer, A., & Christakis, N. (2008). Tastes, ties, and time: A new social network dataset using Facebook.com. *Social Networks, 30*(4), 330–342.

McKee, H. A., & Porter, J. E. (2009). *The ethics of Internet research: A rhetorical, case-based process.* New York, NY: Peter Lang.

Moreno, M. A., Goniu, N., Moreno, P. S., & Diekema, D. (2013). Ethics of social media research: Common concerns and practical considerations. *Cyberpsychology, Behavior and Social Networking, 16*(9), 708–713.

Rodham, K., & Gavin, J. (2006). The ethics of using the Internet to collect qualitative research data. *Research Ethics Review, 2*(3), 83–116.

Rodham, K., & Gavin, J. (2011). The ethics of online research: The new challenges of new media. In D. Vegros & J. Sáenz (Eds.), *Peer-to-peer networks and Internet policies.* New York, NY: Nova.

Rodham, K., Gavin, J., & Miles, M. (2007). I hear, I listen and I care: A qualitative investigation into the function of a self-harm message board. *Suicide and Life Threatening Behaviour, 37*(4), 422–430.

Rodham, K., Gavin, J., Lewis, S., St. Denis, J. M., & Bandalli, P. (2013). An investigation of the motivations driving the online representation of self-injury. *Archives of Suicide Research, 17*(3), 173–183.

Walther, J. B. (2002). Research ethics in Internet enabled research: Human subjects issues and methodological myopia. *Ethics and Information Technology, 4*, 205–216.

Zimmer, M. (2010). "But the data is already public": On the ethics of research in Facebook. *Ethics and Information Technology, 12*, 313–325.

Part II

Children, Teens, and Technology

7

Executive Function in Risky Online Behaviors by Adolescents and Young Adults

L. Mark Carrier, Vanessa Black, Ludivina Vasquez, Aimee D. Miller, and Larry D. Rosen

California State University, Dominguez Hills

Going online can be dangerous for adolescents and young adults where they are vulnerable to exposure to online verbal abuse (e.g., "flaming" or impulsive or assertive behavior that does not consider the recipients' feelings; see Orengo Castellá, Zornoza Abad, Prieto Alonso, & Peiró Silla, 2000; Siegel, Dubrovsky, Kiesler, & McGuire, 1986), pornography, threatening messages, gruesome pictures, racist content, and suicide content. Other potential negative outcomes are being embarrassed, being harassed, engaging in sexual exchanges, receiving unwanted sexual solicitations, and receiving spam. Being cyberbullied is a serious negative outcome that is associated with emotional distress, delinquent behavior, social anxiety, and reduced self-esteem (Floros, Siomos, Fisoun, Dafouli, & Geroukalis, 2013; Hinduja & Patchin, 2007; Kowalski, Limber, & Agatston, 2008; Mishna, Cook, Gadalla, Daciuk, & Solomon, 2010; Ybarra, Mitchell, Wolak, & Finkelhor, 2006). Another serious negative outcome is an online meeting turning into an offline sexual encounter, possibly leading to child abuse. Statistics show that negative outcomes related to online behaviors are occurring at a significant rate. For example, 13% of American female teenagers and 24% of female teenagers in New Zealand had met a stranger offline that they originally met online (Berson & Berson, 2005). In the United States, 20% of a national sample of 10- to 17-year-olds reported being victimized online either through an unwanted sexual solicitation or online harassment (Ybarra, Mitchell, Finkelhor, & Wolak, 2007). Approximately 15% of American high school kids were electronically bullied in 2013 (Kann et al., 2014). After partitioning Dutch adolescents aged 12 to 18 years old into groups based on their problematic risk behavior, 6.1% showed a high-risk developmental pathway for online sexual risk behaviors (Baumgartner, Sumter, Peter, & Valkenburg, 2012).

Youths engage in risky online behaviors that raise the chances of these negative outcomes. One category of risky behaviors is online disclosure of information such as personal or private information, relationship information, addresses, and personal

The Wiley Handbook of Psychology, Technology, and Society, First Edition. Edited by Larry D. Rosen, Nancy A. Cheever, and L. Mark Carrier.

views (Al-Saggaf & Nielsen, 2014; Baumgartner, Valkenburg, & Peter, 2010; Berson, 2003a; Christofides, Muise, & Desmarais, 2012; Dombrowski, LeMasney, Ahia, & Dickson, 2004; Valkenburg & Peter, 2009; Valkenburg, Sumter, & Peter, 2011). Another category is meeting strangers online (Berson, 2003a; Berson & Berson, 2005; Dombrowski et al., 2004; Hong, Li, Mao, & Stanton, 2007; Liau, Khoo, & Ang, 2005; Livingstone & Helsper, 2007; Whittle, Hamilton-Giachritsis, Beech, & Collings, 2013a; Whittle, Hamilton-Giachritsis, Beech, & Collings, 2013b). Using file-sharing programs (Berson & Berson, 2005; Wolak, Mitchell, & Finkelhor, 2007), visiting inappropriate websites (Liau et al., 2005), and failing to use privacy settings (Christofides et al., 2012) also are categories of risky online behaviors.

Numerous variables have been considered to be contributors to risky online behavior in youths. Table 7.1 shows an incomplete but large listing of such factors gleaned from a small subset of the studies that have been published, organized into groupings by the present authors. The groupings include developmental factors, demographic factors, environmental factors, social/cultural factors, Internet use factors, parental factors, abuse/victimization factors, educational factors, situational factors, personality factors, and cognitive factors. Some factors are not under the control of youths or their parents, such as the demographic factor of gender or developmental factors due to age. Similarly, the online world itself might play a role in risky online behaviors (ROB). The social/cultural factor related to the online "culture" that promotes sharing on social networking websites is a good example. Another example is the structure of websites that leads to sharing and disclosure of personal information (i.e., the websites "afford" sharing). Other factors are malleable, such as family-related factors of parental monitoring and the use of parental software.

Executive Function

Executive function (EF) is a concept that could underlie several of the specific factors in the groupings in Table 7.1. Three main dimensions of EF have been identified (National Scientific Council on the Developing Child & National Forum on Early Childhood Policy and Programs, 2011). The first dimension is working memory that allows for temporary information storage necessary to perform tasks (Kandel, Schwartz, Jessell, Siegelbaum, & Hudspeth, 2013). The second dimension is inhibitory control, which provides a filter for thoughts and impulses that allows youths to resist distractions and temptations. In other words, it allows youths to think before they act. Also, it contributes to being able to focus on important tasks and to control emotions. The third dimension is mental flexibility. Mental flexibility leads to self-control, the avoidance of rigidity, and the application of different responses to different settings as appropriate. These basic EF processes are used to achieve higher-level processing that includes planning, organizing, multitasking, and problem solving (Baddeley & Hitch, 1974; Barkley, 2001; Bierman, Nix, Greenberg, Blair, & Domitrovich, 2008; Blair, 2002, 2006; Cockburn, 1995; Diamond, 2002; Diamond & Lee, 2011; Duckworth, Akerman, MacGregor, Salter, & Vorhaus, 2009; Erickson et al., 2007; Hale, Myerson, Rhee, Weiss, & Abrams, 1996; Hughes, 2002; Kliegel, Mackinlay, & Jäger, 2008; Rogers & Monsell, 1995). With respect to the factors that might influence risky online behaviors in adolescents and young adults, executive function could play a role in online disinhibition, impulsiveness, bad judgment, and others (see Table 7.1).

Table 7.1 Groupings of factors that could influence risky online behaviors by youths.

Grouping	Specific factors	Sample studies
Developmental	Maturity/puberty	Valkenburg et al., 2011
	Ego development	Valkenburg et al., 2011
	Pushing boundaries	Whittle et al., 2013b
	Identity development	Baumgartner et al., 2010; Christofides et al., 2012; Livingstone, 2008
	Personality development	Christofides et al., 2012
	Sexual interest	Baumgartner et al., 2010
Demographic	Gender	Baumgartner et al., 2010; Mishna et al., 2010; Valkenburg et al., 2011; Vandoninck et al., 2010
Environmental	Comfort online	Valkenburg et al., 2011
	Lack of visual cues	Berson, 2003a; Berson & Berson, 2005
	Online disinhibition	Berson, 2003a; Whittle et al., 2013a
	Website affordances	Livingstone, 2008
Social/cultural	Encouragement of sharing	Christofides et al., 2012
	Friend relationships	Valkenburg et al., 2011; Valkenburg & Peter, 2009
	Online culture	Berson & Berson, 2005
	Peer norms	Sasson & Mesch, 2014
Internet use	Internet addiction	Kim et al., 2010
	Online experience	Livingstone & Helsper, 2007; Vandoninck et al., 2010
	Specific use of Internet	Baumgartner et al., 2010; Liau et al., 2005
Parental	Parental engagement	Byrne et al., 2014; Kim et al., 2010; Whittle et al., 2013b
	Parental relationship	Livingstone & Helsper, 2007; Vandoninck et al., 2010; Whittle et al., 2013b; Ybarra et al., 2007
	Use of software	Wolak et al., 2007
	Parental monitoring	Baumgartner et al., 2010
	Parental rules	Liau et al., 2005; Sasson & Mesch, 2014
	Family difficulties	Whittle et al., 2013b
Abuse/ victimization	Victimizing others	Ybarra et al., 2007
	Prior abuse	Ybarra et al., 2007
	Prior victimization	Wolak et al., 2007; Ybarra et al., 2007
Educational	Prior counseling	Berson & Berson, 2005; Liau et al., 2005; Wolak et al., 2007
	Lack of knowledge	Berson, 2003a
Situational	Life satisfaction	Livingstone & Helsper, 2007; Whittle et al., 2013b
	Vulnerability	Whittle et al., 2013b
	Mental health	Mitchell et al., 2001; Wolak et al., 2007
	Appeals to emotion	Dombrowski et al., 2004; Whittle et al., 2013a
	Troubled	Liau et al., 2005; Mitchell et al., 2001
Personality	Impulsiveness	Wolak et al., 2007
	Sensation seeking	Livingstone & Helsper, 2007
	Self-confidence	Vandoninck et al., 2010
	Extraversion	Baumgartner et al., 2010
	Curiosity	Baumgartner et al., 2010
Cognitive	Bad judgment	Wolak et al., 2007

Biological Bases

Biological bases of executive functions also tie them together. Complex goal-oriented tasks, problem solving, planning, and behavior regulation are performed in the frontal lobe (Duncan, 1986; Kimberg & Farah, 1993; Payne, Duggan, & Neth, 2007; Rubinstein, Meyer, & Evans, 2001; Shallice, 1994; Stuss & Benson, 1986), and more specifically in the prefrontal cortex (Aron, Robbins, & Poldrack, 2004; Badre, 2008; Bavelier, Green, Pouget, & Schrater, 2012; Botvinick, 2008; Garrett, 2011; Johnson, 2008; Koechlin, 2008; Luria, 1976; Sakai, 2008). There are finer roles posited for specific parts of the prefrontal areas, such as mediation of empathic and socially appropriate behavior in a lateral orbitofrontal circuit and organization of complex behavioral responses in a dorsolateral prefrontal circuit (Kandel et al., 2013). Damage to prefrontal areas leads to poor decision-making and choices, as well as harmful behavior (Garrett, 2011). In addition, transcranial direct current stimulation over the dorsolateral prefrontal cortex can transiently improve cognitive functions like working memory and planning (Dockery, Hueckel-Weng, Birbaumer, & Plewnia, 2009; Fregni et al., 2005; Marshall, Mölle, Hartwig, Siebner, & Born, 2005; Peña-Gómez et al., 2012; Zaehle, Sandmann, Thorne, Jäncke, & Herrmann, 2011).

Influence of EF on Risky Online Behaviors by Youths

The studies considered in this chapter investigated variables that influence ROB and that might be linked to executive function. Reviewing the small set of studies revealed three ways that ROB by adolescents and young adults might be influenced by EF. First, executive function skills associated with individual differences between youths could have an effect on risky online behaviors (trait EF). Second, executive function skills could be temporarily altered or suspended when an adolescent or young adult goes online due to inherent characteristics of the online world (online EF effects). Third, the undeveloped brains of youths could lead to problems with EF and thus increase ROB (age-related EF).

Trait Executive Function

According to the idea that trait EF is a factor in ROB, individual differences in the quality of executive function processing could affect the chances of engaging in risky behaviors. In other words, youths at the same age level would differ in EF skills due to various factors. Along these lines, there is some evidence for the role of impulsivity in ROB by youths. Floros et al. (2013) linked trait impulsiveness to perpetrating cyberbullying and to being a victim of cyberbullying in Greek high school students. They examined the epidemiology of cyberbullying in Greece to determine the impact of related psychosocial factors. The authors conducted a cross-sectional survey of 2,017 Greek students and their parents regarding being the victim of cyberbullying, perpetrating cyberbullying, parental practices, and factors related to problematic Internet use. Floros et al. (2013) showed that Internet cyberbullying rose in the same population over two years, that security practices by parents influenced the chances of being a victim, and that impulsive Internet use predicted both being a victim and victimizing others. Another study linked impulsivity to sexting in teens. Temple and colleagues (2014) investigated whether sexting adolescents have more psychosocial health problems than those who did not sext. A sample of 937 high school students in Texas completed measures of sexting, impulsivity, substance use, depression, and anxiety. Sexting was related only to impulsivity and substance abuse after adjusting for other factors. The authors, interpreting the connection between teen sexting and substance abuse, said that the behaviors could be linked by impulsivity.

In another case, impulsiveness and compromised judgment were used as explanatory factors in understanding the results of risky online behavior. Wolak et al. (2007) looked at youths' unwanted exposure to pornography on the Internet. Their national telephone survey of a sample of United States youth Internet users (ages 10–17) found that there were large amounts of unwanted exposure to pornography online from youth, generally irrespective of age, sex, and other factors (i.e., involving typical Internet use). Some groups were more likely to experience unwanted exposure, including those who use file-sharing programs (i.e., downloading music or images posted online by other people), older teens, those with offline interpersonal victimization, and those with borderline or clinically significant depression. Some factors reduced exposure, including using filtering software and attending an online safety presentation for youth organized by law enforcement agencies. The authors speculated that the connection between online exposure and offline victimization might be explained by a third factor such as impulsiveness or compromised judgment.

EF Altered by Going Online

When individuals go online, they might sense that their actions will be lost in the hundreds or thousands of other actions being taken simultaneously by other Internet users. This sense of deindividuation could lead to the loss of self-regulation and to impulsive behavior (Diener, 1980; McKenna & Bargh, 2000; Zimbardo, 1970).

In the context of risky online interactions with strangers, Berson (2003b) logically linked the lack of self-regulation in youths to this risky behavior. She argued that the loss or lowering of self-regulation when online could increase the chances of self-disclosing private information. In turn, this online disinhibition eventually might increase the chances of a youth being "groomed" by an online predator, referring to the process through which such predators make friends with and gain the confidence of young victims online. In a qualitative study of open-ended questionnaire responses from teenage girls in the United States and New Zealand, Berson and Berson (2005) examined girls' offline encounters with people they met online, age differences in behaviors, and time spent online. The authors gained the insights from the participants' comments that the lack of visual cues online, the perceived security of being online, and the perceived anonymity online contributed to the girls' potentially risky behaviors that went part and parcel with Internet-based explorations of their self-identities. Further, the researchers suggested that the reduced fear of others online and a sense of remoteness from harm could have led to poor decision-making and to a disregard of social rules.

EF Development

The parts of the brain used for internal control, multitasking, planning, self-awareness, and social cognitive skills begin to form shortly after birth, undergo the most change during adolescence, grow through early adulthood, and decline later in life at about 30 years old (Blakemore, 2010; Weintraub et al., 2013). In a process known as "pruning," neural connections primarily in the prefrontal cortex are whittled down in order to fine-tune the neural circuits responsible for impulse control and planning, and the same pruning process is evident in the limbic system that involves emotional processing (Spear, 2000; Wade & Tavris, 2012). Myelination – providing a fatty sheath of insulation for cells – helps to connect the limbic system to the prefrontal cortex and might continue from the late teen years to the mid-20s. These developmental changes have been linked to impulsive behaviors in the adolescent years, with strong emotions overwhelming rational decision-making (Feist & Rosenberg, 2010; Steinberg, 2007; Wade & Tavris, 2012) and possibly resulting in ROB in youths (Berson, 2003b).

Two Studies on Risky Online Behaviors and EF

In summary, there are at least three logical ways that executive function could impact risky online behaviors by adolescents and young adults. Within a particular age group, individual differences in executive function-based task performance could be a factor. Specifically, youths with relatively poor EF would be more likely to engage in ROB than youths with relatively good EF. Or, it is possible that going online could alter executive function performance in youths regardless of their baseline EF skills. Finally, diminished EF due to a young age could influence ROB. This could happen either because executive function skills are not being used at all or because EF skills are utilized but not very good. If this assertion is true, we would expect to see increased ROB at young, compromised ages, low rates of ROB at ages where EF areas of the brain are fully developed, and then possibly increased ROB again when EF performance begins to decline with age. Because the logical argument for the role of executive function is compelling, and because there are not many studies that have looked at EF factors in ROB, two studies were conducted that attempted to assess whether executive function is an important factor in risky online behavior by adolescents and young adults.

Two cross-sectional studies were conducted involving Internet users from the Southern California area in the age ranges 13 years and above. In both cases, EF was measured with the Webexec, an online questionnaire that measures ongoing EF performance (Buchanan et al., 2010). The Webexec includes six items that ask people to rate the extent to which they have problems in certain areas, including (1) maintaining focus, (2) concentrating, (3) multitasking, (4) maintaining a train of thought, (5) finishing tasks, and (6) acting on impulse. Their data showed that the Webexec scores were associated in the expected directions with other measures of executive function and that the scores were associated with cannabis use and reports of memory problems in a drug questionnaire. The Webexec also showed good internal consistency in both of the present studies. Inter-item reliability in the first study (risky behavior frequency study) was .861 (Cronbach's alpha) ($N=871$) with a mean score of 11.4 ($SD=3.8$); inter-item reliability in the second study (vignette study) was .906 ($N=465$) with a mean score of 11.4 ($SD=3.9$). These means were similar in absolute size to the means found with normal non-clinical samples of adults by Buchanan et al. (2010). The authors concluded that the Webexec measures executive functions in normal populations.

Self-Report Study

The first study was a correlational study examining participants' engagement in a variety of offline and online risky behaviors. Participants answered items in an online questionnaire asking about the frequency with which they engage in such behaviors. The questionnaires were administered to 871 adolescents, young adults, and adults from the Los Angeles area on two occasions in 2011. The questionnaires assessed sharing private information and expressing one's views and feelings, both offline and online. Examples of sharing one's views and feelings are arguing with someone in public (offline) or in an electronic social network (online). Expressing one's views and feelings can be a very healthy behavior, but online, public sharing of personal feelings has been linked to online victimization. Examples of sharing one's private information are letting one's address be printed in a newspaper (offline) or posting one's address on a social network (online).

To reduce the number of dependent variables in the analyses, the set of risky online behaviors was subjected to an exploratory factor analysis using Varimax rotation. After removing items that did not substantially correlate with other items, as well as items that did not contribute to the factor solution, two factors emerged. Based on the content of the items loading above .50 on each factor, the two factors were labeled Risky Disclosure/Interaction and Unsecure Practices. Risky Disclosure/Interaction included sharing one's religious views online, posting photos of one's creative work online, expressing one's intimate feelings online, arguing with somebody online, and starting an online conversation with a stranger. Unsecure Practices included posting one's home address online, submitting private information without reading a privacy policy, posting one's hometown or other private information online, and downloading pirated material. Two subscales were formed by taking the mean response for the subset of items included in each factor. The inter-item reliability for the Risky Disclosure/Interaction subscale was good, with a Cronbach's alpha of 0.77 (5 items); the inter-item reliability for Unsecure Practices was below the conventional level of acceptability (Cronbach's alpha = 0.62; 4 items) but the subscale was retained out of theoretical interest.

Vignette Study

The second study was a quasi-experimental study that investigated participants' reactions to realistic online messages from strangers. Messages were created that were similar to those sent by online predators hoping to groom and lure young respondents into potentially dangerous online relationships. A control set of messages were created that did not contain predatory content; rather, these control messages were similar in content to spam messages or advertisements. There were two conditions in the study. In an uninstructed (i.e., naturalistic) condition, the respondents were not given any instructions about how to behave when responding to the messages. In a "safety" condition, the respondents were told to behave in a way that would be considered safe. The study was conducted online, recruiting participants from the Los Angeles area in 2012. The 465 study participants, including teenagers and adults of both sexes and varied ethnic backgrounds, were required to evaluate the message senders in terms of their personal characteristics (e.g., honesty). Also, participants estimated how they would behave in response to the message (e.g., meet the message sender offline). There were five "behavioral" responses to the messages that were measured. In each case, participants rated the likelihood that they would respond in a particular way. The five responses were becoming "friends" with the message sender, replying to the message, becoming friends on a social networking site, meeting the person face to face, and telling someone else that you received the message. The response scale was 1 = "not at all," 2 = "somewhat," 3 = "very," and 4 = "completely." A subscale was formed by taking the mean of the five items. This scale was shown to be highly reliable ($\alpha = .91$, $M = 8.84$, $SD = 2.81$).

Both studies also measured demographic information (age, sex, and ethnicity), as well as other respondent characteristics that might be relevant to ROB, including depression (Beck's Depression Inventory-II; Beck, Steer, & Brown, 1996), hours spent online (Daily Media Usage Scale; Carrier, Cheever, Rosen, Benitez, & Chang, 2009), life satisfaction (Satisfaction with Life Scale; Diener, Emmons, Larsen, & Griffin, 1985), and general trust (General Trust Scale; Yamagishi & Yamagishi, 1994). The self-report study additionally measured shyness (Revised Cheek and Buss Shyness Scale; Crozier, 2005) and the vignette study additionally measured self-esteem (Rosenberg Self-Esteem Scale; Rosenberg, 1979) and family satisfaction (Family Satisfaction Scale; Olson & Wilson, 1982).

The goal of the studies was to examine trait EF (i.e., individual differences) and EF development (age-related changes) in risky online behaviors. The analysis plan was to use hierarchical linear regression to ascertain specific patterns in the correlational data. To assess the effect of individual differences in EF upon ROB, the effect of EF after factoring out age and other potentially confounding variables was examined. The hypotheses were:

Hypothesis 1:   EF problems (i.e., Webexec scores) would predict increased likelihood of problematic behaviors or responses online.

Hypothesis 2:   Age-related changes in EF would influence risky online behaviors.

The indirect effect of age through executive function was examined. To look at this effect of age-related EF, the effect of age was examined before and after adding EF to the hierarchical regression. Changes in the effect of age were attributed to age-related EF. It was expected that ROB would decrease as age increased and lowered the number of EF problems.

Results

Only the participants in the age groups directly of interest to the chapter were included in the analyses: early teens (13 to 16 years old), late teens (17 to 19 years old), early 20s (20 to 25 years old), and late 20s (26 to 30 years old). Based on the earlier description of executive function development, EF was expected to be underdeveloped in the first three groups and to peak in the final group of participants in their late 20s. Therefore, EF problems (i.e., Webexec scores) were expected to be highest in the youngest group and to decline steadily as age increased. Examination of the distributions of the key variables in both studies revealed that five participants in the self-report study had especially high depression scores (> 3.5 SDs above the mean); therefore, these five participants were excluded from the analyses. The demographics of the two samples are shown in Table 7.2, revealing a predominantly Hispanic ethnic composition that reflects the Los Angeles metropolitan area where the samples were recruited (U.S. Census Bureau, 2014). Table 7.3 shows the samples' scores by developmental age group on several measures, including a key variable of depression that was presumed to influence executive function processes through known links between depression and attention, memory, and self-regulation via prefrontal cortex (Kandel et al., 2013). Inspection of this table reveals that the two samples had generally normal or average levels of depression, general trust, life satisfaction, and time spent online on a typical day.

Figure 7.1 shows Webexec scores as a function of developmental age group. Examination of the graph suggests general linear decreases in EF problems as age increases, as expected from the prior discussion of developmental changes in EF. However, the trend did not appear to be entirely linear as problems increased from early to late teens in the behavior frequency study and stayed constant between those two age groups in the vignette study. Further, EF problems increased in the late 20s in the behavior frequency study. Because the analysis plan was to use multiple regression to test the hypothesis, it was decided to investigate the linear and polynomial relationships between developmental age group and ROB prior to running the multiple regressions (Cohen, Cohen, West, & Aiken, 2003). Investigation of the linear, quadratic, and cubic components of the changes in ROB scores with respect to raw age scores revealed that: (1) the quadratic and cubic components significantly contributed to risky disclosures/interactions; (2) the cubic component significantly contributed to unsecure practices; and (3) the cubic component significantly contributed to sensitivity to predatory vignettes. Based on these results, it was decided to include all three components of age into the regression analyses.

Table 7.2 Demographics by developmental age group in two studies of risky online behaviors.

Characteristics	Age group			
	Early teens	Late teens	Early 20s	Late 20s
Self-report study (N=705)				
Sample size	163	125	312	105
Mean age (SD)	14.9 (1.1)	17.6 (.8)	22.3 (1.6)	27.3 (1.3)
Female n (%)	95 (58.3)	75 (60.0)	184 (59.0)	54 (51.4)
Asian n (%)	25 (15.3)	19 (15.2)	40 (12.8)	20 (19.0)
Black n (%)	27 (16.6)	32 (25.6)	57 (18.3)	16 (15.2)
Hispanic n (%)	83 (50.9)	53 (42.4)	148 (47.4)	41 (39.0)
White n (%)	28 (17.2)	21 (16.8)	67 (21.5)	28 (26.7)
Vignette study (N=383)				
Sample size	80	66	192	45
Mean age (SD)	14.9 (.9)	17.9 (.9)	22.0 (1.7)	27.8 (1.5)
Female n (%)	46 (57.5)	36 (54.5)	102 (53.1)	23 (51.1)
Asian n (%)	10 (12.5)	6 (9.1)	29 (15.1)	6 (13.3)
Black n (%)	18 (22.5)	4 (6.1)	25 (13.0)	7 (15.6)
Hispanic n (%)	43 (53.8)	51 (77.3)	122 (63.5)	27 (60.0)
White n (%)	9 (11.3)	5 (7.6)	16 (8.3)	5 (11.1)

Table 7.3 Other relevant characteristics by developmental age group in two studies of ROB.

Characteristics	Age group			
	Early teens	*Late teens*	*Early 20s*	*Late 20s*
Self-report study (*N*=705)				
Depression (*SD*)[a]	8.9 (8.6)	9.0 (8.3)	8.7 (7.9)	9.0 (8.4)
Hours online (*SD*)	10.7 (9.9)	11.0 (10.3)	8.7 (8.3)	10.3 (9.0)
Life satisfaction (*SD*)[b]	22.0 (7.4)	22.7 (7.0)	22.1 (7.0)	20.8 (8.0)
Trust (*SD*)[c]	3.2 (1.0)	3.1 (1.0)	2.9 (.9)	2.8 (1.0)
Vignette study (*N*=383)				
Depression (*SD*)[a]	9.7 (9.8)	11.8 (11.5)	10.9 (10.2)	10.5 (10.5)
Hours online (*SD*)	19.3 (18.9)	20.0 (17.1)	17.5 (15.0)	15.8 (14.1)
Life satisfaction (*SD*)[b]	22.4 (6.8)	22.7 (7.0)	22.5 (6.4)	22.9 (7.4)
Trust (*SD*)[c]	3.7 (1.3)	3.5 (1.2)	3.4 (1.2)	3.5 (1.2)

[a] BDI-II scores are interpreted as 0–10 (normal), 11–16 (mild disturbance), 17–20 (borderline clinical), 21–30 (moderate), 31–40 (severe), and over 40 (extreme) (Beck et al., 1996).
[b] Satisfaction With Life scores are interpreted as 5–9 (extremely dissatisfied), 10–14 (dissatisfied), 15–19 (slightly below average), 20–24 (average), 25–29 (high), 30–35 (very high) (Diener et al., 1985).
[c] Higher scores on the seven-point scale indicate more general trust (Yamagishi & Yamagishi, 1994).

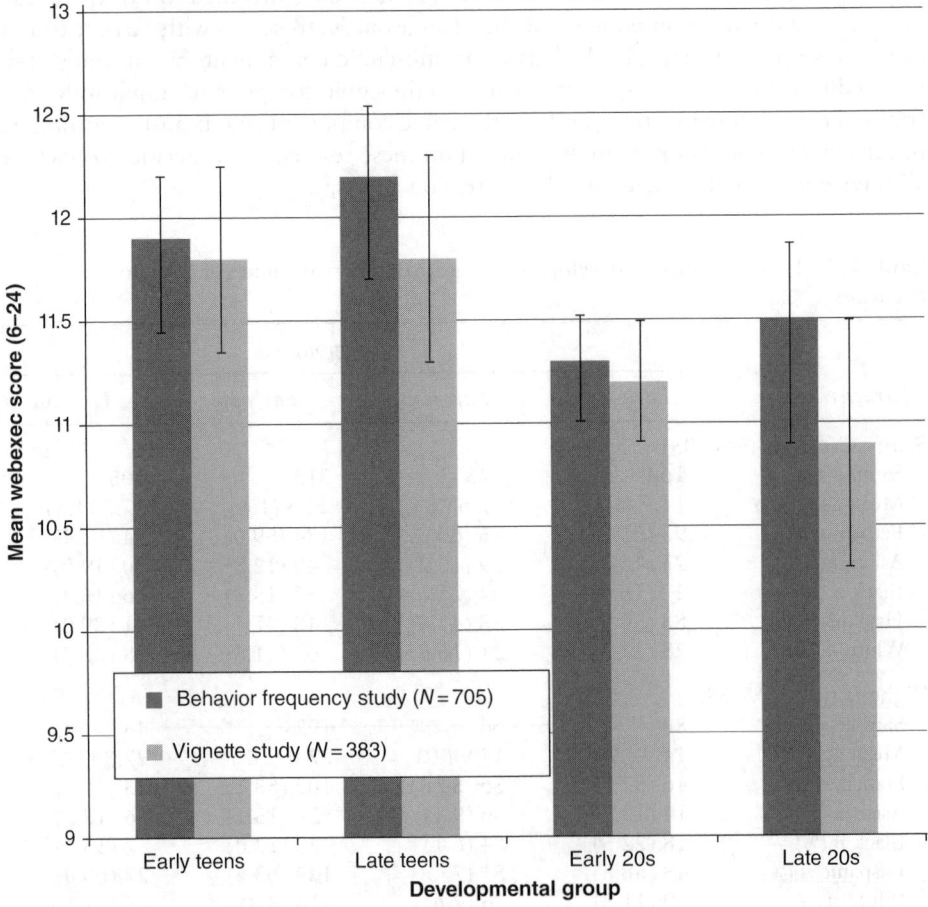

Figure 7.1 Executive function problems with respect to developmental age group in two studies of ROB.

Risky Disclosure/Interaction

Four steps were used in the hierarchical linear regression. Sex, ethnicity, and age were entered together in the first equation on the basis that these were fixed characteristics of each participant. Depression was entered into the second equation on the basis that it could be directly influenced by each of the first-level variables and that it could be a causal factor in executive function problems. Executive function problems (i.e., Webexec scores) were entered into the third equation. Finally, the fourth equation contained other variables that were expected to influence ROB, possibly be influenced by EF, but not be causes of changes in EF. These variables were shyness, hours spent online, life satisfaction, and trust.

The results of the analysis are shown in Table 7.4. Regarding individual differences in EF, the results demonstrated that EF problems significantly impacted engaging in risky online disclosures and interactions after factoring out age, sex, and ethnicity (equation 3). Those with higher Webexec scores – indicating more executive functioning problems – showed increased Risky Disclosure/Interaction scores. Further, adding additional factors to the analysis produced only a slight change in the impact of EF problems on ROB, and EF problems remained a significant predictor even after adding those other factors (equation 4). This showed that most of the impact of EF problems on risky behaviors is not via shyness, hours spent online, life satisfaction, or trust. Regarding age-related changes in EF, there was no significant age-related EF effect through the linear component of age; the beta weight for linear age changed only slightly when adding EF problems to the model (equations 2 and 3). Further, although the results showed indirect effects of quadratic and cubic age on ROB via EF problems, these effects were relatively small. Comparing equation 2 to equation 3 revealed that the beta weight for the cubic component decreased from .55 to .50

Table 7.4 Beta weights from hierarchical regression analyses for variables predicting risky disclosure/interaction ($N = 705$).

Variable	Equation 1	Equation 2	Equation 3	Equation 4
Age[a]				
Linear	−.22**	−.23**	−.21**	−.21**
Quadratic	.36	.37*	.32	.18
Cubic	.54**	.55**	.50**	.38*
Depression		.07*	.01	.00
EF problems			.15***	.13**
Shyness				−.08*
Hours online				.33***
Life satisfaction				−.02
Trust				.10**
R^2	.04	.05	.06	.19
F for change in R^2	4.10***	3.90*	12.88***	26.80***

Note. Standardized beta weights are shown. Control variables of sex and ethnicity were included in the analysis but are not shown.
[a] Age was represented as three components to capture non-linear effects.
*$p < .05$
**$p < .01$
***$p < .001$

Table 7.5 Summary of hierarchical regression analysis for variables predicting unsecure practices ($N = 705$).

Variable	Equation 1	Equation 2	Equation 3	Equation 4
Age[a]				
Linear	−.08	−.08	−.07	−.07
Quadratic	.26	.27	.23	.15
Cubic	.36*	.38*	.33	.27
Depression		.16***	.08*	.07
EF problems			.16***	.14***
Shyness				−.01
Hours online				.17***
Life satisfaction				−.01
Trust				.06
R^2	.04	.07	.09	.12
F for change in R^2	4.43***	17.86***	14.87***	5.90***

Note. Standardized beta weights are shown. Control variables of sex and ethnicity were included in the analysis but are not shown.

[a] Age was represented as three components to capture non-linear effects.

*$p < .05$

**$p < .01$

***$p < .001$

when adding EF problems to the model, showing an indirect effect of age via EF problems of .05. The indirect effect through the quadratic component also was .05. These indirect effect sizes were smaller than the direct effects of age-quadratic and age-cubic upon risky behaviors and smaller than the indirect effects through the other variables.

Other notable effects were that the significant impact of depression – leading to increased ROB – was mediated almost entirely through EF problems (equations 2 and 3), that shyness significantly decreased risky disclosure and interaction (equation 4), that time spent online significantly increased ROB (equation 4), that age had a significant impact on ROB – both decreasing it and increasing it through the different components – after taking into account all of the other variables (equation 4), and that general trust in people significantly raised ROB scores (equation 4).

Unsecure Practices

The second outcome variable from the self-report study was Unsecure Practices. To investigate Unsecure Practices, the same model as for Risky Disclosure/Interaction was used to conduct the hierarchical regression analysis. The results are shown in Table 7.5. Individual differences leading to increased EF problems significantly raised the chances of engaging in unsecure practices regardless of age, sex, or ethnicity (equation 3). Further, the beta weight for EF problems changed very little after adding other potentially relevant variables (equations 3 and 4), which showed that this effect largely was independent of the effects of shyness, hours online, life satisfaction, and trust. The effects of the three components of age were assessed before and after adding EF problems to the model (equations 2 and 3) to investigate the impact of age-related EF. The linear component of age barely was affected; there was an indirect effect of linear age via EF problems of –.01. Adding EF problems to the model reduced the impacts of the quadratic and cubic components of age only slightly more. The indirect effect of quadratic age upon unsecure practices via executive function was .03 and the indirect effect of cubic age was .03 (equations 2 and 3). Other interesting effects were that shyness did not impact unsecure practices (equation 4), that age did not impact ROB after factoring out EF problems and other factors (equation 4), and that time spent online significantly increased the engagement in ROB (equation 4).

Reactions to Predatory Messages from Strangers

Nearly the same model was used to test the impact of EF upon reactions to predatory messages from strangers. Instructional condition (act naturally vs. act safely) was added to the second equation along with depression. It was added prior to adding EF problems to the model because of the possibility that the instructions might lead to changes in how much participants engage their executive function during the task. Also, a fifth equation was added. The fifth equation included reactions to the non-predatory, control vignettes. This variable was meant to represent general reactions to messages from strangers.

The results of the analysis are shown in Table 7.6. Individual differences in EF significantly impacted reactions to the predatory vignettes after factoring out age, sex, and ethnicity (equation 3). Persons with relatively higher Webexec scores – indicating more executive functioning problems – were more likely to say that they would react to the messages using risky behaviors. Even after removing the effects of the other variables, including reactions to the control vignettes, EF problems remained a significant predictor of reactions to the predatory vignettes (equation 5). EF had little indirect effect via the control reactions as shown by the small reduction in beta weight for EF problems when control reactions were added to the model (equations 4 and 5). A large part of the total effect of EF problems was due to its indirect effect through the other variables of self-esteem, hours online, and trust. This can be seen by the reduction in the beta weight for EF problems when those variables were added to the model (equations 3 and 4). The beta weights in Table 7.6 suggest that part of the effect of individual differences in EF is that those people with more executive functioning problems show reduced self-esteem, increased general trust in people, and increased hours spent online. There were significant positive and negative influences of age upon reactions to predatory messages, indicated by the significant quadratic and cubic components of age in the original equation (equation 1). However, these effects of age did not appear to occur through age's influence on EF: adding EF problems to the model resulted in only small changes in the beta weights associated with age (equations 2 and 3).

The regression analysis produced several other results to highlight. First, the positive and negative effects of age appeared to operate indirectly through other variables. For example, the beta weight for the quadratic component of age decreased by .05 when adding the other relevant variables to the model and again by .06 when adding control reactions to the model (equations 3, 4, and 5). Thus, increasing age resulted in poor reactions to the predatory vignettes through its effect on the other variables (mostly, self-esteem, hours online, and trust) and through its effect on reactions to the harmless vignettes. Second, depression significantly increased the poor reactions to the predatory

vignettes and this effect was due primarily to the combined effects through EF problems (equations 2 and 3) and through the other relevant variables (equations 3 and 4).
Third, self-esteem significantly reduced negative reactions to predatory vignettes, and
part of its effect was indirect via changes in reactions to the control messages (equations 4 and 5). Fourth, the number of hours spent online and general trust significantly
impacted how participants reacted to predatory messages, but almost entirely because
of an indirect effect via control message reactions (equations 4 and 5). In both cases,
increasing values of the variables led to increasingly poor reactions to the control
vignettes that also resulted in poor reactions to the predatory vignettes.

Discussion

There were two original hypotheses for these studies:

Hypothesis 1:   Individual differences in EF would impact ROB, with persons
                having relatively poor EF skills showing relatively high levels of
                ROB, and
Hypothesis 2:   Age-related changes in EF would impact ROB, with persons hav-
                ing relatively undeveloped EF showing greater ROB. More spe-
                cifically, EF problems would be greatest in the youngest group and
                steadily decline through the oldest group, with concomitant
                reductions in ROB.

The results of both studies supported Hypothesis 1. In the self-report study, EF
problems significantly predicted risky behaviors – both Risky Disclosure/Interaction
and Unsecure Practices – after factoring out age and other demographic variables,
depression, shyness, online hours, life satisfaction, and trust. In other words, participants who self-reported more problems with planning, organizing, and maintaining
focus were more likely than other persons to also engage in those risky online behaviors. Further, although depression significantly contributed to both types of risky
behaviors, the effect of depression involved EF problems. With risky disclosures/inter-
actions, depression almost entirely operated through its effect on EF problems; with
unsecure practices, a significant proportion of the effect of depression was through EF
problems. In the vignette study, people's risky reactions to predatory messages were
predicted by self-reported EF problems. As with the self-report study, the effect of EF
problems was significant after factoring out age and other demographic variables. In
that study, a large part of the effect of EF problems was through other variables such
as self-esteem (EF problems lowered self-esteem), general trust in others (EF problems
increased general trust), and hours spent online (EF problems increased hours online).

In contrast to the first hypothesis, the second hypothesis mostly was not supported
by the results. For risky disclosure/interaction, unsecure practices, and reactions to the
vignettes, none of the components of age effects upon ROB showed much change
when adding EF problems to the linear regression models. So, any effects of age upon
ROB mostly were independent of EF problems. Nonetheless, other age effects were
apparent and occurred simultaneously in the two studies. When looking at risky disclo-
sures/interactions, linearly increasing age was significantly associated with less ROB,
and this effect showed very little indirect influence through the other variables in the

Table 7.6 Summary of hierarchical regression analysis for variables predicting reactions to predatory messages (N = 383).

Variable	Equation 1	Equation 2	Equation 3	Equation 4	Equation 5
Age[a]					
Linear	.16	.13	.13	.13	.07
Quadratic	.21**	.21**	.20**	.15*	.09*
Cubic	−.26*	−.23	−.20	−.12	−.10
Depression		.24***	.13*	.04	.09*
Instructions[b]		.04	.06	.10*	.11**
EF problems			.25***	.12*	.10**
Self-esteem				−.34***	−.15**
Hours online				.12**	.03
Life satisfaction				.00	.05
Trust				.25***	.09*
Family satisfaction				.06	.00
Control reactions					.63***
R^2	.08	.14	.19	.36	.64
F for change in R^2	4.68***	11.86***	23.63***	19.34***	321.62***

Note. Standardized beta weights are shown. Sex and ethnicity are not shown.
[a] Age was represented as three components to capture non-linear effects.
[b] Instructions were coded as 1 = act safely and 2 = act naturally.
*$p < .05$
**$p < .01$
***$p < .001$

study (Table 7.4). One possible explanation of this effect is that people may learn to be less risky through their experiences online and that the number of these experiences increases with advancing age. Linear age had smaller, non-significant effects upon the other risky outcomes (Tables 7.5 and 7.6). Since risky disclosure/interaction involves posting of information of the type that might occur on a routine – even daily – basis, negative experiences related to this kind of ROB could be occurring more frequently for people, leading to experience-related reductions in ROB. In contrast, negative outcomes that lead to behavior change might be occurring relatively infrequently when it comes to unsecure practices (e.g., making accounts on websites) and to reacting to predatory messages (since predatory messages might arrive only occasionally).

With respect to the quadratic component of age, the results showed that there was a positive effect upon ROB with all three outcomes. However, the quadratic component did not make a statistically significant impact upon unsecure practices. The positive beta weight for this component indicates that ROB was relatively high in the youngest groups and also in the oldest groups. Inspection of the results reveals that the largest portion of the total effect of quadratic age is direct and not via other variables in the studies. One possible variable that would explain this effect is that younger adolescents and older young adults are under relatively less parental control, monitoring, and home rules. In younger adolescents, this could be because parents are not fully aware of what their young teens are doing online and are underestimating the time their children spend online (Byrne, Katz, Lee, Linz, & McIlrath, 2014). In young adults, this could be because they are either no longer living with their parents or that they are given more independence by their parents due to their age.

The cubic component of age was positive and statistically significant in the analyses of risky disclosure/interaction and unsecure practices (Tables 7.4 and 7.5). Cubic age indicates that young ages show relatively extreme low values of ROB, the older ages show relatively extreme high values of ROB, and the middle ages show ROB values in between the two other age brackets. The majority of this effect is direct – not occurring through the other measured variables in the self-report study. This component in the self-report study could reflect age-related psychological factors other than EF (e.g., changes in sexual interest) that might be expected to be relatively absent in the youngest groups and relatively extreme in the oldest groups. The cubic component of age produced a negative effect on reactions to predatory vignettes in the vignette study (Table 7.6). Most of this effect was indirect, via other variables measured in the study; the largest indirect effect was through self-esteem, hours online, and trust. As age increased, increasing self-esteem lowered the chances of reacting poorly to the predatory vignettes. In contrast, the time spent online and general trust both increased non-linearly with age, and these two variables increased the chances of poor reactions.

The effects of the personality variables – shyness, trust, and self-esteem – largely matched the expectations that would come about from prior research on youth ROB. Prior research suggests that extreme shyness is associated with Internet addiction (Caplan & High, 2011; Chen & Peng, 2008; Lam, Peng, Mai, & Jing, 2009; Morahan-Martin & Schumacher, 2000; Yang & Tung, 2007; see also Vondráčková & Šmahel, Chapter 27 in this volume). Further, Internet addiction has been linked to risky online behavior by youths (Table 7.1). Therefore, it might be expected that high levels of shyness would be linked to ROB. However, in the present self-report study, increasing shyness had the opposite effect upon risky disclosure/interaction, significantly reducing the likelihood of it occurring. Additionally, shyness did not significantly affect unsecure practices online. Logically speaking, it makes sense that being shy would reduce one's online interactions with others, leading to less ROB. Also, since interacting with others is not a part of unsecure practices, it is reasonable that shyness would not affect this behavior.

Trust in others is important in building relationships. A component of establishing this trust is personal information disclosure (Archer, Christofides, Nosko, & Wood, 2014; Laurenceau, Feldman Barrett, & Pietromonaco, 1998; Rubin, 1975). Online, trust is associated with decreased information control (e.g., using privacy settings) (Christofides et al., 2012). Thus, trust is expected to be positively associated with risky disclosure/interaction, unsecure practices, and responding to messages from strangers. Indeed, the present results showed that being more trusting in others was associated with increased risky disclosure/interaction (Table 7.4) and with poor reactions to predatory messages (Table 7.6). There was no meaningful effect of trust upon unsecure practices, possibly because the present measure of unsecure practices did not include behaviors involving other individuals online; rather, it measured behaviors involving interactions with websites or computer systems (e.g., opening accounts on websites).

One would expect self-esteem to affect ROB in youth because prior research has shown that persons with relatively high self-esteem have less negative self-disclosure on social networking sites than persons with relatively low self-esteem (Feinstein, Bhatia, Latack, & Davila, 2014; Forest & Wood, 2012) and that Internet addiction – one of the factors that might lead to ROB (Table 7.1) – is linked to low self-esteem (Caplan & High, 2011; Chen & Peng, 2008; Yang & Tung, 2007; see also

Vondráčková & Šmahel, Chapter 27 this volume). Also, across the lifespan, self-esteem rises and this rise has been linked to information control measures taken by Internet users (Christofides et al., 2012). In a review of factors affecting kids' ROB, Livingstone and Smith (2014) identified low self-esteem as a characteristic that leads to vulnerability. Not surprisingly, then, in the present vignette study, self-esteem significantly reduced the chances of poor reactions to predatory messages. A little more than one-half of this effect was through reactions to the control messages, suggesting that self-esteem reduces the chances of responding to any messages from strangers, not just predatory ones.

Predictions about the effects of the situational variables of family and life satisfaction are not clear-cut. While one study found that life satisfaction was positively associated with Facebook usage in college students in the United States (Valkenburg, Peter, & Schouten, 2006), a study of young people in Europe found that those young children and teens not satisfied with life might use the Internet to compensate with their offline difficulties (Livingstone & Helsper, 2007). The latter could possibly lead to being groomed online by predators (Whittle et al., 2013b). The present studies did not find any evidence to support the idea that family or life satisfaction significantly impacts ROB by youth. One possibility is that the participants in the present studies did not show severe enough dissatisfaction for there to be such an effect. Examination of the data distributions for both studies revealed that there were 111 cases of persons who were either extremely dissatisfied or dissatisfied with life (15.7%) in the self-report study and 45 such cases in the vignette study (11.7%). Therefore, there seem to have been enough persons who were dissatisfied with life to find an effect. So, another possibility is that the inclusion of the other variables in the studies, such as depression, eliminated the impact of satisfaction.

Adolescents are spending a lot of time online and playing video games; 41.3% of adolescents in the United States use the computer for non-school reasons or play video games three or more hours per day on a typical day (Kann et al., 2014). High-frequency video game playing has been found to be a risk factor for gaming addiction (Gentile, 2009; Spekman, Konijn, Roelofsma, & Griffiths, 2013; see also Groves et al., Chapter 29 this volume). Since Internet addiction has been associated with risky online behavior, it might be expected that the amount of time spent online could indirectly lead to ROB in youths. Further, spending time on Facebook has been linked to posting personal information (Christofides et al., 2012) and time online has been linked to meeting online strangers offline (Berson & Berson, 2005). Therefore, time spent online was expected to predict ROB in the present studies. The results confirmed the expectations, with time spent online significantly increasing the chances of risky disclosure/interaction, unsecure practices, and poor reactions to predatory vignettes in all age groups. The latter effect almost entirely operated through reactions to the control vignettes, suggesting that poor reactions to the predatory vignettes was due to a reduction in response threshold for reacting to the messages from strangers.

Theoretical and Practical Implications

Based on the limited prior research and on the results of the new data presented here, it is clear that executive function is relevant to considering the causes of risky online behaviors by adolescents and young adults. However, more research is needed in order to examine the possibility that the act of going online itself leads to changes in EF. It would seem that investigating this particular role of EF requires a measure of EF that is sensitive to momentary changes. Also, more information is required to understand the details of how individual differences in EF affect risky online behaviors. Practically speaking, the possibility of age-related effects on executive function, although not supported here, suggests that parents should be aware of young people's limitations in executive functions. Acknowledging developmental differences in executive function can help to improve prevention work in adolescents and young adults by building on their existing EF skills (Berson, 2003a, 2003b; Berson & Berson, 2005). Specific instruction in impulse control while going online might be necessary (Floros et al., 2013). Also, children, adolescents, and perhaps even young adults must continue to be monitored when online while their EF skills are underdeveloped (Berson, 2003b). Software and website designers should put safeguards into programs and online environments where possible and allow for parental controls.

Acknowledgments

The authors thank Nancy A. Cheever, Alex O. Spradlin, Angelina Prodromides, and Kelly Whaling for research assistance. Portions of this work were funded by the National Institutes of Health (NIH/MBRS RISE R25 GM62252) and were previously presented at the Annual Convention of the American Psychological Association, August 2012, and at the Association for Psychological Science Convention, May 2014.

References

Al-Saggaf, Y., & Nielsen, S. (2014). Self-disclosure on Facebook among female users and its relationship to feelings of loneliness. *Computers in Human Behavior*, *36*, 460–468.

Archer, K., Christofides, E., Nosko, A., & Wood, E. (2014). Exploring disclosure and privacy in a digital age: Risks and benefits. Manuscript submitted for publication.

Aron, A. R., Robbins, T. W., & Poldrack, R. A. (2004). Inhibition and the right inferior frontal cortex. *Trends in Cognitive Science*, *8*(4), 170–177.

Baddeley, A. D., & Hitch, G. (1974). Working memory. In G. H. Bower (Ed.), *Psychology of learning and motivation* (Vol. *8*, pp. 47–89). New York, NY: Academic Press.

Badre, D. (2008). Cognitive control, hierarchy, and the rostro-caudal organization of the frontal lobes. *Trends in Cognitive Science*, *12*(5), 193–200.

Barkley, R. A. (2001). The executive functions and self-regulation: An evolutionary neuropsychological perspective. *Neuropsychology Review*, *11*(1), 1–29.

Baumgartner, S. E., Sumter, S. R., Peter, J., & Valkenburg, P. M. (2012). Identifying teens at risk: Developmental pathways of online and offline sexual risk behavior. *Pediatrics*, *130*(6), e1489–e1496.

Baumgartner, S. E., Valkenburg, P. M., & Peter, J. (2010). Unwanted online sexual solicitation and risky sexual online behavior across the lifespan. *Journal of Applied Developmental Psychology*, *31*(6), 439–447.

Bavelier, D., Green, C. S., Pouget, A., & Schrater, P. (2012). Brain plasticity through the life span: Learning to learn and action video games. *Annual Review of Neuroscience*, *35*, 391–416.

Beck, A. T., Steer, R. A., & Brown, G. K. (1996). *Manual for the Beck Depression Inventory-II*. San Antonio, TX: Psychological Corporation.

Berson, I. R. (2003a). Grooming cybervictims: The psychosocial effects of online exploitation for youth. *Journal of School Violence, 2*(1), 5–18.

Berson, I. R. (2003b). Making the connection between brain processing and cyberawareness: A developmental reality. In *Proceedings of the NetSafe II Conference*. Auckland, NZ: The Internet Safety Group of New Zealand.

Berson, I. R., & Berson, M. J. (2005). Challenging online behaviors of youth: Findings from a comparative analysis of young people in the United States and New Zealand. *Social Science Computer Review, 23*(1), 29–38.

Bierman, K. L., Nix, R. L., Greenberg, M. T., Blair, C., & Domitrovich, C. E. (2008). Executive functions and school readiness intervention: Impact, moderation, and mediation in the Head Start REDI program. *Development and Psychopathology, 20*(3), 821–843.

Blair, C. (2002). School readiness: Integrating cognition and emotion in a neurobiological conceptualization of children's functioning at school entry. *American Psychologist, 57*(2), 111–127.

Blair, C. (2006). How similar are fluid cognition and general intelligence? A developmental neuroscience perspective on fluid cognition as an aspect of human cognitive ability. *Behavioral and Brain Sciences, 29*(2), 109–160.

Blakemore, S.-J. (2010). The developing social brain: Implications for education. *Neuron, 65*(6), 744–747.

Botvinick, M. M. (2008). Hierarchical models of behavior and prefrontal function. *Trends in Cognitive Science, 12*(5), 201–208.

Buchanan, T., Heffernan, T. M., Parrott, A. C., Ling, J., Rodgers, J., & Scholey, A. B. (2010). A short self-report measure of problems with executive function suitable for administration via the Internet. *Behavior Research Methods, 42*(3), 709–714.

Byrne, S., Katz, S. J., Lee, T., Linz, D., & McIlrath, M. (2014). Peers, predators, and porn: Predicting parental underestimation of children's risky online experiences. *Journal of Computer-Mediated Communication, 19*, 215–231.

Caplan, S. E., & High, A. C. (2011). Online social interaction, psychosocial well-being, and problematic Internet use. In K. S. Young & C. Nabuco de Abreu (Eds.), *Internet addiction: A handbook and guide to evaluation and treatment* (pp. 35–53). Hoboken, NJ: John Wiley & Sons.

Carrier, L. M., Cheever, N. A., Rosen, L. D., Benitez, S., & Chang, J. (2009). Multitasking across generations: Multitasking choices and difficulty ratings in three generations of Americans. *Computers in Human Behavior, 25*(2), 483–489.

Chen, Y.-F., & Peng, S. S. (2008). University students' Internet use and its relationship with academic performance, interpersonal relationships, psychosocial adjustment, and self-evaluation. *CyberPsychology and Behavior, 11*(4), 467–469.

Christofides, E., Muise, A., & Desmarais, S. (2012). Hey mom, what's on your Facebook? Comparing Facebook disclosure and privacy in adolescents and adults. *Social Psychological and Personality Science, 3*(1), 48–54.

Cockburn, J. (1995). Task interruption in prospective memory: A frontal lobe function. *Cortex, 31*(1), 87–97.

Cohen, J., Cohen, P., West, S. G., & Aiken, L. S. (2003). *Applied multiple regression/correlation analysis for the behavioral sciences* (3rd ed.). New York, NY: Routledge.

Crozier, W. R. (2005). Measuring shyness. *Personality and Individual Differences, 38*(8), 1947–1956.

Diamond, A. (2002). Normal development of prefrontal cortex from birth to young adulthood: Cognitive functions, anatomy, and biochemistry. In D. T. Stuss & R. T. Knight (Eds.), *The frontal lobes* (pp. 466–503). Oxford, UK: Oxford University Press.

Diamond, A., & Lee, K. (2011). Interventions shown to aid executive function development in children 4 to 12 years old. *Science, 333*(6045), 959–964.

Diener, E. (1980). Deindividuation: The absence of self-awareness and self-regulation in group members. In P. Paulus (Ed.), *The psychology of group influence* (pp. 1160–1171). Hillsdale, NJ: Lawrence Erlbaum Associates.

Diener, E. D., Emmons, R. A., Larsen, R. J., & Griffin, S. (1985). The satisfaction with life scale. *Journal of Personality Assessment, 49*(1), 71–75.

Dockery, C. A., Hueckel-Weng, R., Birbaumer, N., & Plewnia, C. (2009). Enhancement of planning ability by transcranial direct current stimulation. *Journal of Neuroscience, 29*(22), 7271–7277.

Dombrowski, S. C., LeMasney, J. W., Ahia, C. E., & Dickson, S. A. (2004). Protecting children from online sexual predators: Technological, psychoeducational, and legal considerations. *Professional Psychology: Research and Practice, 35*(1), 65–73.

Duckworth, K., Akerman, R., MacGregor, A., Salter, E., & Vorhaus, J. (2009). *Self-regulated learning: A literature review.* London, UK: Centre for Research on the Wider Benefits of Learning, Institute of Education.

Duncan, J. (1986). Disorganization of behaviour after frontal-lobe damage. *Cognitive Neuropsychology, 3*(3), 271–290.

Erickson, K. I., Colcombe, S. J., Wadhwa, R., Bherer, L., Peterson, M. S., & Scalf, P. E. (2007). Training-induced plasticity in older adults: Effects of training on hemispheric asymmetry. *Neurobiology of Aging, 28*(2), 272–283.

Feinstein, B. A., Bhatia, V., Latack, J. A., & Davila, J. (2014). Social networking and depression. Manuscript submitted for publication.

Feist, G. J., & Rosenberg, E. L. (2010). *Psychology: Perspectives and connections* (2nd ed.). New York, NY: McGraw-Hill.

Floros, G. D., Siomos, K. E., Fisoun, V., Dafouli, E., & Geroukalis, D. (2013). Adolescent online cyberbullying in Greece: The impact of parental online security practices, bonding, and online impulsiveness. *Journal of School Health, 83*(6), 445–453.

Forest, A. L., & Wood, J. V. (2012). When social networking is not working: Individuals with low self-esteem recognize but do not reap the benefits of self-disclosure on Facebook. *Psychological Science, 23*(3), 295–302.

Fregni, F., Boggio, P. S., Nitsche, M., Bermpohl, F., Antal, A., Feredoes, E., … Pascual-Leone, A. (2005). Anodal transcranial direct current stimulation of prefrontal cortex enhances working memory. *Experimental Brain Research, 166*, 23–30.

Garrett, B. (2011). *Brain and behavior: An introduction to biological psychology.* Los Angeles, CA: Sage.

Gentile, D. A. (2009). Pathological video game use among youth 8 to 18: A national study. *Psychological Science, 20*(5), 594–602.

Hale, S., Myerson, J., Rhee, S. H., Weiss, C. S., & Abrams, R. A. (1996). Selective interference with the maintenance of location information in working memory. *Neuropsychology, 10*(2), 228–240.

Hinduja, S., & Patchin, J. W. (2007). Offline consequences of online victimization. *Journal of School Violence, 6*(3), 89–112.

Hong, Y., Li, X., Mao, R., & Stanton, B. (2007). Internet use among Chinese college students: Implications for sex education and HIV prevention. *CyberPsychology and Behavior, 10*(2), 161–169.

Hughes, C. (2002). Executive functions and development: Why the interest? *Infant and Child Development, 11*(2), 69–71.

Johnson, G. M. (2008). Cognitive processing differences between frequent and infrequent Internet users. *Computers in Human Behavior, 24*, 2094–2106.

Kandel, E. R., Schwartz, J. H., Jessell, T. M., Siegelbaum, S. A., & Hudspeth, A. J. (Eds.) (2013). *Principles of neural science* (5th ed.). San Francisco, CA: McGraw-Hill.

Kann, L., Kinchen, S., Shanklin, S. L., Flint, K. H., Hawkins, J., Harris, W. A., … Zaza, S. (2014). *Youth risk behavior surveillance – United States, 2013.* Atlanta, GA: Center for Surveillance, Epidemiology, and Laboratory Services, Centers for Disease Control and Prevention (CDC), U.S. Department of Health and Human Services.

Kim, J. H., Lau, C. H., Cheuk, K.-K., Kan, P., Hui, H. L. C., & Griffiths, S. M. (2010). Brief report: Predictors of heavy Internet use and associations with health-promoting and health risk behaviors among Hong Kong university students. *Journal of Adolescence, 33*(1), 215–220.

Kimberg, D. Y., & Farah, M. J. (1993). A unified account of cognitive impairments following frontal lobe damage: The role of working memory in complex organized behavior. *Journal of Experimental Psychology: General, 122*(4), 411–428.

Kliegel, M., Mackinlay, R., & Jäger, T. (2008). Complex prospective memory: Development across the lifespan and the role of task interruption. *Developmental Psychology, 44*(2), 612–617.

Koechlin, E. (2008). The cognitive architecture of the human lateral prefrontal cortex. In P. Haggard, Y. Rosetti, & M. Kawato (Eds.), *Attention and performance* (pp. 483–509). New York, NY: Oxford University Press.

Kowalski, R. M., Limber, S., & Agatston, P. W. (2008). *Cyber bullying: Bullying in the digital age*. Oxford, UK: Wiley Blackwell.

Lam, L. T., Peng, Z. W., Mai, J. C., & Jing, J. (2009). Factors associated with Internet addiction among adolescents. *CyberPsychology and Behavior, 12*(5), 551–555.

Laurenceau, J.-P., Feldman Barrett, L. A., & Pietromonaco, P. R. (1998). Intimacy as an interpersonal process: The importance of self-disclosure and perceived partner responsiveness in interpersonal exchanges. *Journal of Personality and Social Psychology, 74*(5), 1238–1251.

Liau, A. K., Khoo, A., & Ang, P. H. (2005). Factors influencing adolescents' engagement in risky Internet behavior. *CyberPsychology and Behavior, 8*(6), 513–520.

Livingstone, S. (2008). Taking risky opportunities in youthful content creation: Teenagers' use of social networking sites for intimacy, privacy and self-expression. *New Media and Society, 10*(3), 393–411.

Livingstone, S., & Helsper, E. (2007). Taking risks when communicating on the Internet: The role of offline social-psychological factors in young people's vulnerability to online risks. *Information, Communication and Society, 10*(5), 619–643.

Livingstone, S., & Smith, P. K. (2014). Harms experienced by child users of line and mobile technologies: The nature, prevalence and management of sexual and aggressive risks in the digital age. *Journal of Child Psychology and Psychiatry, 55*(6), 635–654.

Luria, A. R. (1976). *Cognitive development: Its cultural and social foundations.* Cambridge, MA: Harvard University Press.

Marshall, L., Mölle, M., Hartwig, R., Siebner, H., & Born, J. (2005). Bifrontal transcranial direct current stimulation slows reaction time in a working memory task. *BMC Neuroscience, 6*, 23.

McKenna, K. Y. A., & Bargh, J. A. (2000). Plan 9 from cyberspace: The implications of the Internet for personality and social psychology. *Personality and Social Psychology Review, 4*(1), 57–75.

Mishna, F., Cook, C., Gadalla, T., Daciuk, J., & Solomon, S. (2010). Cyber bullying behaviors among middle and high school students. *American Journal of Orthopsychiatry, 80*(3), 362–374.

Mitchell, K. J., Finkelhor, D., & Wolak, J. (2001, June 20). Risk factors for and impact of online sexual solicitation of youth. *Journal of the American Medical Association, 285*(23), 3011–3014.

Morahan-Martin, J., & Schumacher, P. (2000). Incidence and correlates of pathological Internet use among college students. *Computers in Human Behavior, 16*(1), 13–29.

National Scientific Council on the Developing Child & National Forum on Early Childhood Policy and Programs. (2011, February). *Building the brain's "air traffic control" system: How early experiences shape the development of executive function.* Boston, MA: Center on the Developing Child at Harvard University.

Olson, D. H., & Wilson, M. (1982). Family satisfaction. Family inventories: Inventories used in a national survey of families across the family life cycle. In D. H. Olson, H. I. McCubbin, H. Barnes, A. Larson, M. Muxen, & M. Wilson (Eds.), *Family social science* (pp. 25–31). St. Paul, MN: University of Minnesota Press.

Orengo Castellá, V., Zornoza Abad, A. M., Prieto Alonso, F., & Peiró Silla, J. M. (2000). The influence of familiarity among group members, group atmosphere and assertiveness on uninhibited behavior through three different communication media. *Computers in Human Behavior, 16*, 151–159.

Payne, S. J., Duggan, G. B., & Neth, H. (2007). Discretionary task interleaving: Heuristics for time allocation in cognitive foraging. *Journal of Experimental Psychology: General, 136*(3), 370–388.

Peña-Gómez, C., Sala-Lonch, R., Junqué, C., Clemente, I. C., Vidal, D., Bargalló, N., ... Bartés-Faz, D. (2012). Modulation of large-scale brain networks by transcranial direct current stimulation evidenced by resting-state functional MRI. *Brain Stimulation, 5*(3), 252–263.

Rogers, R., & Monsell, S. (1995). The costs of a predictable switch between simple cognitive tasks. *Journal of Experimental Psychology: General, 124*(2), 207–231.

Rosenberg, M. (1979). *Conceiving the self.* New York, NY: Basic Books.

Rubin, Z. (1975). Disclosing oneself to a stranger: Reciprocity and its limits. *Journal of Experimental and Social Psychology, 11*(3), 233–260.

Rubinstein, J. S., Meyer, D. E., & Evans, J. E. (2001). Executive control of cognitive processes in task switching. *Journal of Experimental Psychology: Human Perception and Performance, 27*(4), 763–797.

Sakai, K. (2008). Task set and prefrontal cortex. *Annual Review of Neuroscience, 31*, 219–245.

Sasson, H., & Mesch, G. (2014). Parental mediation, peer norms and risky online behavior among adolescents. *Computers in Human Behavior, 33*, 32–38.

Shallice, T. (1994). Multiple levels of control processes. In C. Umilta & M. Moscovitch (Eds.), *Attention and performance XV: Conscious and nonconscious information processing* (pp. 395–420). Cambridge, MA: MIT Press.

Siegel, J., Dubrovsky, V., Kiesler, S., & McGuire, T. W. (1986). Group processes and computer-mediated communication. *Organizational Behavior and Human Decision Processes, 37*(2), 157–187.

Spear, L. P. (2000). The adolescent brain and age-related behavioral manifestations. *Neuroscience and Biobehavioral Reviews, 24*(4), 417–463.

Spekman, M. L. C., Konijn, E. A., Roelofsma, P. H. M.P. , & Griffiths, M. D. (2013). Gaming addiction, definition and measurement: A large-scale empirical study. *Computers in Human Behavior, 29*, 2150–2155.

Steinberg, L. (2007). Risk taking in adolescence: New perspectives from brain and behavioral science. *Current Directions in Psychological Science, 16*(2), 55–59.

Stuss, D. T., & Benson, D. F. (1986). *The frontal lobes.* New York, NY: Raven Press.

Temple, J. R., Le, V. D., van den Berg, P., Ling, Y., Paul, J. A., & Temple, B. W. (2014). Brief report: Teen sexting and psychosocial health. *Journal of Adolescence, 37*(1), 33–36.

U.S. Census Bureau. (2014). *State and county QuickFacts.* Retrieved November 25, 2014, from http://quickfacts.census.gov/qfd/index.html#

Valkenburg, P. M., & Peter, J. (2009). Social consequences of the Internet for adolescents: A decade of research. *Current Directions in Psychological Science, 18*(1), 1–5.

Valkenburg, P. M., Peter, J., & Schouten, A. P. (2006). Friend networking sites and their relationship to adolescents' well-being and social self-esteem. *CyberPsychology and Behavior, 9*(5), 584–590.

Valkenburg, P. M., Sumter, S. R., & Peter, J. (2011). Gender differences in online and offline self-disclosure in pre-adolescence and adolescence. *British Journal of Developmental Psychology, 29*(2), 253–269.

Vandoninck, S., d'Haenens, L., & Donoso, V. (2010). Digital literacy of Flemish youth: How do they handle online content risks? *Communications*, 35(4), 397–416.

Wade, C., & Tavris, C. (2012). *Invitation to psychology* (5th ed.). Boston, MA: Pearson.

Weintraub, S., Dikmen, S. S., Heaton, R. K., Tulsky, D. S., Zelazo, P. D., Bauer, P. J., ... Gerson, R. C. (2013). Cognition assessment using the NIH Toolbox. *Neurology*, 80(11 Suppl. 3), S54–64.

Whittle, H., Hamilton-Giachritsis, C., Beech, A., & Collings, G. (2013a). A review of online grooming: Characteristics and concerns. *Aggression and Violent Behavior*, 18(1), 62–70.

Whittle, H., Hamilton-Giachritsis, C., Beech, A., & Collings, G. (2013b). A review of young people's vulnerabilities to online grooming. *Aggression and Violent Behavior*, 18(1), 135–146.

Wolak, J., Mitchell, K., & Finkelhor, D. (2007). Unwanted and wanted exposure to online pornography in a national sample of youth Internet users. *Pediatrics*, 119(2), 247–257.

Yamagishi, T., & Yamagishi, M. (1994). Trust and commitment in the United States and Japan. *Motivation and Emotion*, 18(2), 129–166.

Yang, S. C., & Tung, C. J. (2007). Comparison of Internet addicts and non-addicts in Taiwanese high school. *Computers in Human Behavior*, 23(1), 79–96.

Ybarra, M. L., Mitchell, K. J., Finkelhor, D., & Wolak, J. (2007). Internet prevention messages: Targeting the right online behaviors. *Archives of Pediatric Adolescent Medicine*, 161(2), 138–145.

Ybarra, M. L., Mitchell, K. J., Wolak, J., & Finkelhor, D. (2006). Examining characteristics and associated distress related to Internet harassment: Findings from the Second Youth Internet Safety Survey. *Pediatrics*, 118(4), e1169–e1177.

Zaehle, T., Sandmann, P., Thorne, J. D., Jäncke, L., & Herrmann, C. S. (2011). Transcranial direct current stimulation of the prefrontal cortex modulates working memory performance: Combined behavioural and electrophysiological evidence. *BMC Neuroscience*, 6(12), 2.

Zimbardo, P. (1970). The human choice: Individuation, reason, and order versus deindividuation, impulse, and chaos. In W. J. Arnold & D. Levine (Eds.), *Nebraska symposium on motivation* (Vol. 17, pp. 237–307). Lincoln, NE: University of Nebraska Press.

8

Cyberbullying
Prevalence, Causes, and Consequences
Robin M. Kowalski and Elizabeth Whittaker
Clemson University

Rehtaeh Parsons. Audrie Pott. Gabrielle Molina. Tyler Clementi. Megan Meier. Ryan Halligan. Marcus Bielenberg. Amanda Todd. The list of names of young people whose lives have been devastated by cyberbullying is long. Both Rehtaeh and Audrie hung themselves in 2013 at the age of 15 after photos of them being sexually assaulted while vomiting or passed out from excessive alcohol use circulated over social media. Although the alleged assaults were captured in the photos, the girls, like many others, found themselves ostracized by their friends, leading to feelings of depression, anxiety, suicidal ideation, and, ultimately, suicide. Although the number of instances of cyberbullying that culminate in suicide are relatively infrequent, a multitude of negative consequences follow cyberbullying for victims, perpetrators, and bystanders, a point we will return to below. The purpose of this chapter is to provide an overview of cyberbullying. We will begin with an examination of the wired culture in which youth today are being raised. Then, after defining cyberbullying, we will examine prevalence rates of cyberbullying, similarities and differences between cyberbullying and traditional bullying, and characteristics of victims and perpetrators of cyberbullying, followed by a discussion of the effects of cyberbullying for all of those involved.

Internet Use Among Adolescents

The Internet and related communication technologies have revolutionized the way in which people communicate with one another and gain access to information. As a communication tool, the Internet allows for rapid textual, voice, and video communication from one person to countless others and allows for users to access an immense array of information across a wide variety of dimensions, improving education, employment, and civic engagement (Akman & Mishra, 2010). If anyone doubts people's dependence on technology, deprive them of access to email or wireless technologies for a few hours, and they will soon realize how tied we all are to technology. Adolescents, in particular, seem forever tethered to their technology, leading Canadian cyberbullying researcher Bill Belsey to refer to today's youth as the "always on" generation (Belsey, n.d.). Most of these children and young adults have never experienced a world without

The Wiley Handbook of Psychology, Technology, and Society, First Edition. Edited by Larry D. Rosen, Nancy A. Cheever, and L. Mark Carrier.

technology at their disposal, leading to a digital divide between their parents (i.e., digital immigrants) and themselves (i.e., digital natives) (Zickuhr & Smith, 2012).

Internet usage has become increasingly widespread in recent years, particularly among adolescents. Almost all youth (95%) between the ages of 12 and 17 use the Internet, and 68% of school students use the Internet while at school (Hitlin & Rainie, 2005; Lenhart, 2010; Madden, Lenhart, & Duggan, 2013). Ninety-three percent of adolescents report that they have a computer or the availability of one at their home. However, young people are becoming less and less likely to use these computers to access the Internet. According to the Pew report examining teens and the Internet (Madden et al., 2013), adolescents are just as likely to say they have a smartphone as to say they own a personal computer. Thirty-seven percent of adolescents say that they have a smartphone, an increase of 14% in just two years. Twenty-five percent of teens are most likely to access the Internet using their smartphone, compared to only 15% of adults (Madden et al., 2013). This change in how young people are accessing the Internet has implications for cyberbullying as young people now have at their ready disposal the technological means to perpetrate cyberbullying.

The ways in which youth use the Internet and other communication technologies change rapidly. Just a few years ago, instant messaging via AOL was the venue of choice. Today, youth communicate through a variety of electronic media including Twitter, Facebook, YouTube, chatrooms, and texting. Some of the most popular venues frequented by young people on the Internet (and some of the leading venues for cyberbullying) are social networking sites (Katzer, Fetchenhauer, & Belschak, 2009). Social media sites, defined as "any Web site that allows social interaction" (O'Keeffe & Clarke-Pearson, 2011), are very popular among adolescents, and include social networking sites (e.g., Facebook, MySpace, LinkedIn), video sites (e.g., YouTube), gaming sites and virtual worlds (e.g., Second Life), and blogs (Kowalski & Giumetti, 2014; O-Keeffe & Clarke-Pearson, 2011). Facebook has emerged as the current predominant social networking site, with 73% of those who use social networking sites having a Facebook profile (Lenhart, Purcell, Smith, & Zickuhr, 2010). Facebook has a total of more than one billion active users (users who have logged onto the site at least one time in the past month), and 22% of teens surveyed check their profile more than 10 times a day, with 51% checking more than once a day (Commonsense Media, 2009; Fowler, 2012). The availability of smartphones has made access to social media just a button away.

Social networking sites are useful in allowing people to communicate with friends or acquaintances, and to share news or personal events with these friends and acquaintances (Kowalski & Giumetti, 2014; Reich, Subrahmanyam, & Espinoza, 2012). Additionally, social networking sites allow users to share local or world news with friends, and to comment on it. However, social networking sites and related technologies also present the potential for an individual to be victimized through them. In a study conducted by Jones, Mitchell, and Finkelhor (2013), which explored online activities of adolescents ages 10 to 17, 82% of those who were cyberbullied in 2010 had first been cyberbullied through Facebook. Additionally, our ability to provide feedback through comments and posts, while sometimes useful, can also provide a forum within which people can cyberbully one another.

In a recent study, Kowalski and Whittaker (2013) examined the type of cyber aggression used on several social networking sites, including Facebook, YouTube, as well as other forums. They used Radian6, a Salesforce product that allows users to search a large variety of social networking sites for posts that include select key words. The authors searched for posts containing words related to cyber aggression, then used Pyżalski's (2012) taxonomy to sort and classify the posts. Although the research is still ongoing, initial analyses highlight the rampant presence of cyber incivility online via social media.

Defining Cyberbullying

There is a general consensus among those who research cyberbullying that, broadly speaking, electronic bullying involves the use of electronic communication technologies to bully others (Kowalski, Limber, & Agatston, 2012). However, identifying the more specific features of cyberbullying has proven more difficult (Langos, 2012; Ybarra, Boyd, Korchmaros, & Oppenheim, 2012). Whereas some researchers take a more global perspective in defining cyberbullying (e.g., "Have you ever been bullied via the Internet"), others are much more specific in identifying the particular technologies (e.g., email, instant messaging, social network sites) that must be involved for cyberbullying to occur. How cyberbullying is defined is important because it has implications for how the construct is measured in research studies. Slightly different conceptualizations of cyberbullying lead to slightly different measurements of the construct, which, naturally, lead to different prevalence rates of the behavior, outcomes, and so on. As more research is conducted on the topic, the hope is that researchers will begin to move toward more of a consensus in terms of both how cyberbullying should best be defined and how cyberbullying should best be measured. For a more complete discussion of measurement issues related to cyberbullying, the reader is referred to Kowalski, Giumetti, Schroeder, and Lattanner (2014).

Typologies of Cyberbullying

In an effort to further explicate cyberbullying, some investigators have developed cyberbullying taxonomies. Willard (2007) created a taxonomy based on features of the cyberbullying behavior itself. This taxonomy includes flaming (i.e., an online fight), harassment (i.e., repetitive, offensive messages sent to a victim), outing and trickery (i.e., sharing personal information, which was often obtained through trickery, without the consent of the individual), exclusion (i.e., blocking the person from friend lists/ contact lists), impersonation (i.e., posing as the victim online and sending negative or inappropriate information to others as if it were being sent from the victim), cyberstalking (i.e., using electronic communications to stalk another person by sending repetitive threatening communications), and sexting (i.e., distributing negative, sexual pictures of another without that person's consent).

More recently, Pyżalski (2012) developed a classification that is more focused on the victim and the victim's relationship to the perpetrator. It includes electronic aggression against the vulnerable (i.e., the victims are "weaker" people, such as the homeless, alcoholics, etc., who are typically unaware of the victimization, and the aggression frequently has some visual material depicting the victims in embarrassing situations), random electronic aggression (i.e., the victim is anonymous to the perpetrator and the act is usually an impulsive act such as an attack on an unknown person in a chat room), electronic aggression against groups (i.e., the victim is a group of people, such as an ethnic or religious group), and electronic aggression against celebrities (i.e., the victims are well-known people, such as celebrities) (Pyżalski, 2012). This taxonomy may be useful when the perpetrator and victim do not know each other, which is often the case with cyberbullying, as some researchers have found that 35% of the adolescents sampled had been victimized while using chat rooms, which are often anonymous or pseudonymous (Katzer et al., 2009).

Of these two taxonomies, Willard's (2007) may be subsumed within Pyżalski's (2012). People may use any of the different tactics suggested by Willard to perpetrate cyberbullying via the different venues suggested by Pyżalski. Given the diverse ways in which cyberbullying can occur and the myriad venues by which perpetrators can engage in cyberbullying, these taxonomies are useful for allowing researchers to begin to come to terms with who does what to whom under what circumstances.

How Cyberbullying Differs from Traditional Bullying

Given the extensive literature on traditional bullying, a logical question that emerges with cyberbullying is the extent to which cyberbullying is similar to and different from traditional bullying, and the extent to which we can learn about cyberbullying by drawing upon our knowledge of traditional bullying. Both traditional bullying and cyberbullying share in common three primary features: they are both acts of aggression; they typically occur among individuals between whom there is a power imbalance; and the behaviors are often repeated (Kowalski & Limber, 2007; Kowalski, Limber, & Agatston, 2012; Olweus, 1993, 2013). Two important qualifiers are noteworthy. First, the source of power imbalance may differ between cyberbullying and traditional bullying. Although the power differential with cyberbullying may be social, relational, or physical, as with traditional bullying, it may also reflect differences between the victim and perpetrator in technological expertise (Dooley, Pyżalski, & Cross, 2009; Monks & Smith, 2006). In addition, perceived anonymity may lead perpetrators to perceive they have a power advantage over targets. A second qualifier involves the repetitive nature of cyberbullying. A single inflammatory email sent to hundreds or thousands of individuals has a repetitive quality, as does a single degrading post on a website read repeatedly by the target.

However, there are key ways in which cyberbullying and traditional bullying differ from one another. One of the key differences involves the anonymity or *perceived* anonymity that often surrounds cyberbullying. Research by Kowalski and Limber (2007) showed that just under 50% of victims of cyberbullying did not know the identity of the individual who cyberbullied them. Research on deindividuation suggests that people will say and do things anonymously that they would never consider saying in their everyday, face-to-face interactions (Diener, 1980; Postmes & Spears, 1998). This means that there may be significantly more people who would be willing to perpetrate cyberbullying than traditional bullying, and, as previously mentioned, this anonymity can play into the imbalance of power between the victim and the perpetrator. Additionally, anonymity also prevents perpetrators from witnessing the negative effects of their behavior on the victim, making it less likely that they will feel empathy and remorse for their actions (Sourander et al., 2010).

The accessibility of the victim is also different in traditional bullying and cyberbullying situations. Traditional bullying most often occurs at school during the school day (Nansel et al., 2001), while cyberbullying can occur 24 hours a day, seven days a week. Even if a victim chooses not to view aggressive posts left on a website about him or her, that does not negate the fact that others may be viewing those posts at any time of the day or night. Also, because of the nature of the venues through which this takes place, cyberbullying has a much larger potential audience than traditional bullying, as thousands may see the cruel posts, instead of just a few people at school. As noted earlier, even if the insulting posts or comments are only posted once by a particular person, there is still some feeling of repetition as these posts remain directly accessible to the victim for far longer than any harsh verbal taunts, so the victim may be repeatedly exposed to the bullying post or comment.

While victims of both cyberbullying and traditional bullying are hesitant to report the bullying, the reasons behind this reticence vary. Victims of traditional bullying often cite fear of retribution from the perpetrators as the reason they do not report the bullying, whereas victims of cyberbullying do not report the situation because they are afraid that parents or other adults will remove the technology through which they have been cyberbullied in order to protect them (Kowalski, Limber, & Agatston, 2012).

Because of how the technology used to cyberbully functions, those who cyberbully cannot immediately see the effects of their actions on the victim as they can in traditional bullying (Vannucci, Nocentini, Mazzoni, & Menesini, 2012; see also Dooley et al., 2009). The victim's response is delayed until the victim becomes aware of the cyberbullying by checking the text or the website, which suggests that there may be different motives behind cyberbullying behavior than behind traditional bullying behavior. Parry Aftab (2011) has attempted to explicate the possible motives behind cyberbullying, and has hypothesized that there may be four types of cyberbullying perpetrators. Her typology includes "vengeful angels," who are retaliating for past wrongs, including being bullied at school; the "power-hungry cyber bully," who seeks to exert his or her power over others (this is the most similar category to the traditional bully); "mean girls," who cyberbully out of boredom (although this type of bully certainly does not have to be female); and the "inadvertent" cyberbully, who replies to a cyberbullying perpetrator in a way similar to how the perpetrator approached them. While this list may be helpful in discussing possible motives for perpetrators of cyberbullying, it remains to be supported empirically.

In addition to these conceptual differences, several researchers have empirically tested the relationship between traditional bullying and cyberbullying. A common degree of overlap that has been observed is between victims of cyberbullying and victims of traditional bullying as well as between perpetrators of cyberbullying and perpetrators of traditional bullying (e.g., Fanti, 2012; Gradinger, Strohmeier, & Spiel, 2009; Hinduja & Patchin, 2008; Kowalski, Morgan, & Limber, 2012; Schneider, O'Donnell, Stueve, & Coulter, 2012; Smith et al., 2008). Alternatively, other researchers have observed only weak relationships between cyberbullying and traditional bullying. Varjas, Henrich, and Meyers (2009), for example, while finding strong correlations between cyberbullying victimization and perpetration, observed weak relationships between involvement in cyberbullying as victim or perpetrator and involvement in traditional bullying. A meta-analysis conducted by Kowalski et al. (2014) found strong relationships between cybervictimization and traditional victimization; however, the strength of this relationship was moderated by other variables such as grade level, country of origin, and measurement issues. In addition, perpetration of traditional bullying was strongly related to perpetration of cyberbullying.

It may be that any overlap observed between traditional bullying and cyberbullying may be related to the venue through which the cyberbullying occurs (Kowalski et al., 2014). Those who traditionally bully may be more likely to perpetrate certain types of cyberbullying, for example in chat rooms, thinking that they may be anonymous, and be more likely to be targets of cyberbullying via social networking sites, although further research is needed to investigate this relationship.

The relationship between traditional bullying and cyberbullying may also stem, in part, from the fact that cyberbullying may be perpetrated as retaliation for traditional bullying victimization. Prior research has supported a relationship between traditional bullying victimization and cyberbullying perpetration. This suggests that some individuals may be motivated to engage in cyberbullying as a means of retaliating for prior victimization (Holfeld & Grabe, 2012). In keeping with this, Gradinger, Strohmeier, and Spiel (2012) found that the most common motive for cyberbullying was anger. People who are angry may be more inclined to invoke a hostile attribution bias perceiving hostile intent on the part of another, whether or not that was really the intent.

Prevalence Rates of Cyberbullying

The prevalence of cyberbullying has fluctuated from study to study, varying with the definition provided (or not) to participants, the time frame used to inquire about cyberbullying (e.g., one month, six months, one year, lifetime), the stringency of the criteria used to determine whether cyberbullying occurred (e.g., at least one vs. three times or more a month), and the age of the participants sampled, which are only a few of the many variables that differ from study to study. Whether or not the rates of cyberbullying are remaining more or less constant (Olweus, 2013), or increasing with time and ever-changing technologies (Slonje & Smith, 2008) has been vigorously debated as well, and the differing variables in each study make this particularly difficult to determine.

Typically, prevalence rates for cyberbullying victimization are estimated to be between approximately 10 and 40% (e.g., Lenhart, 2010; O'Brennan, Bradshaw, & Sawyer, 2009; Pontzer, 2010). However, three studies have found much higher prevalence rates. Juvonen and Gross (2008) found that 72% of their respondents reported being victimized online, but they did not use the term cyberbullying, asking instead how often they had experienced "mean things," which were defined as "anything that someone else does that upsets or offends someone" (p. 499). Aftab (2011) found that, among adolescents aged 12–13, approximately 53% reported being victims of cyberbullying (see also Raskauskas & Stoltz, 2007). In a more recent study, 65% of participants reported experiencing cyberbullying at least once in their lifetime (Gomez-Garibello, Shariff, McConnell, & Talwar, 2012). Importantly, however, the more liberal criterion used of cyberbullying occurring "at least once" can lead to higher prevalence rates observed in some studies compared to those obtained when a more conservative criterion of "2 to 3 times a month or more" is used.

Prevalence rates vary across studies in part because of the different venues used to assess cyberbullying. These measurement issues, in turn, often reflect what is trending in technology at the time data are collected. Indeed, the most common venues by which cyberbullying occurs are reflective of the most popular types of technology at a particular point in time. The Youth Internet Safety Surveys (Jones et al., 2013) reveal some interesting trends in where this cyberbullying takes place. In the 2000 and 2004 surveys, participants reported that instant messaging was the most common venue through which cyberbullying first began (34% and 47%, respectively), while in 2010, 82% of the cyberbullying experienced by participants was initiated on social networking sites (Jones et al., 2013). Juvonen and Gross (2008) found that the most prevalent venues through which cyberbullying occurred among American students ages 12 to 17 were message boards (26%) and instant messaging (20%); Kowalski and Limber (2007) found that instant messaging (67%) was the most frequently used venue for cyberbullying, whereas Kwan and Skoric (2013) found that slightly under 60% of 13- to 17-year-old Singaporean youth who were users of Facebook had been targets of cyberbullying on Facebook, and 57% indicated that they had cyberbullied others on Facebook. Given how popular social networking sites have become in recent years, though, it is no surprise that cyberbullying appears to have shifted to these venues. Ultimately, however, while estimates of prevalence and the venues through which it occurs may vary, cyberbullying is still a problem experienced by many youth and adults. The fact that prevalence rates change with technology only highlights the fact that educators and parents need to be aware of the changing trends and keep up with the changes as quickly as our youth are.

Prevalence rates also vary across studies as a function of demographic characteristics of the samples, such as age, gender, and race. With regards to age, cyberbullying has often been thought to be a problem of middle school children and, indeed, a number of youth in middle school have experienced cyberbullying as victims and/or perpetrators. The Fight Crime survey with preteens found that children 6 to 8 years of age were significantly *less* likely than children 9 to 11 years of age to have been cyberbullied within the previous year (13% and 21%, respectively), supporting the idea that cyberbullying emerges during the middle school years (Fight Crime sponsored studies: Opinion research corporation, 2014). However, the 2007 National Crime Victimization Survey (Robers, Zhang, Truman, & Snyder, 2010) found that 10th and 11th graders experienced higher rates of cyberbullying than students in grades six through nine. Even among middle-schoolers, variations in rates of cyberbullying have been observed. In one study, significant differences by grade in the frequency with which youth had cyberbullied others were found, with sixth graders being significantly less likely to be involved with cyberbullying as either bullies or bully/victims than seventh or eighth graders, and somewhat less likely to be targets of cyberbullying (Kowalski & Limber, 2007; see also Hinduja & Patchin, 2008; Williams & Guerra, 2007; Wolak, Mitchell, & Finkelhor, 2007). Grade differences were also seen in the venue through which cyberbullying occurred. Eighth graders reported being victimized more through instant messaging and text messaging than either sixth or seventh graders. Sixth graders used text messaging and instant messaging to perpetrate cyberbullying less frequently than seventh or eighth graders (Kowalski & Limber, 2007). However, it should be noted that these venues may have changed in recent years, as use of social networking sites has increased greatly since 2007. Our belief is that age differences in the experience of youth with cyberbullying will diminish as younger and younger children gain experience with technology.

Importantly, recent work with college students suggests that cyberbullying is not just a "middle school problem" but that cyberbullying occurs among older populations, most notably among college students (Kowalski, Giumetti, Schroeder, & Reese,

2012). In fact, in a recent study by Kowalski et al. (2012), 35% of a sample of college students said that their first occurrence of cyberbullying was in college. Of those who had been cyberbullied, 44% said that the majority of the cyberbullying occurred in college, 30% in high school, and 26% in middle school, although this may change as younger and younger people have access to more and more technology. Schenk and Fremouw (2012) similarly found that 9% of a sample of college students were cyber-victims. With websites such as juicycampus.com and collegeacb, college students experiencing cyberbullying is hardly surprising.

Gender differences in cyberbullying perpetration and victimization have also been found in some studies, although not in others. Research over the past few years has shown that males are more likely to engage in more direct forms of aggression, whereas females are more likely to engage in indirect aggression (Bjorkqvist, Lagerspetz, & Osterman, 1992; Kowalski, Limber, & Agatson, 2012). Given that cyberbullying is a type of indirect aggression, it is not surprising that some studies have found that girls are more likely than boys to engage in cyberbullying (Kowalski & Limber, 2007; Robers et al., 2010; Smith et al., 2008; Tokunaga, 2010). In the Kowalski and Limber (2007) survey, 25% of the girls and 11% of the boys said that they had experienced cyberbullying at least once in the previous two months; 13% of girls and 9% of boys reported perpetrating cyberbullying at least once in the past two months. Alternatively, some studies have found no significant gender differences in experiencing cyberbullying (e.g., Hinduja & Patchin, 2008; Mishna, Cook, Gadalla, Daciuk, & Solomon, 2010; Slonje & Smith, 2008; Williams & Guerra, 2007; Ybarra & Mitchell, 2004). Yet other studies have found no gender differences in participants' overall experience with cyberbullying, but did find gender differences in the venues through which the cyberbullying was perpetrated. For example, Hinduja and Patchin (2008) found that females were more likely than boys to be targeted by email, and Alonzo and Aiken (2004) found that males were more likely to engage in flaming than females.

Still other research has found that males are more likely to perpetrate cyberbullying whereas females are more likely to be victims of cyberbullying (Sourander et al., 2010). Given that individual studies have slightly different conceptualizations of cyberbullying and, thus, different measurements of the construct (for a more detailed discussion of this issue see Kowalski et al., 2014), we believe that researchers should be cautious in being too quick to draw conclusions regarding the relationship between gender and cyberbullying.

The influence of race and ethnicity on the prevalence rates of cyberbullying behavior has been vastly understudied relative to other demographic variables. Hinduja and Patchin (2008) and Ybarra and her colleagues (2007) found no evidence for racial differences in people's experiences with cyberbullying. Shapka and Law (2013), on the other hand, found cultural differences in cyberbullying experiences when they compared East Asian adolescents and those of European descent. Specifically, adolescents of European descent reported a higher rate of involvement with cyberbullying than East Asian adolescents. Importantly, however, race and ethnicity are not features immediately observable in the virtual world. Therefore, one would not necessarily expect that they would be related to cyberbullying behavior, at least from a victimization perspective, particularly given that a sizable percentage of cyberbullying occurs under the umbrella of anonymity (Kowalski, Limber, & Agatston, 2012).

Characteristics of Victims and Perpetrators

Beyond demographic variables, a host of person and situational variables are related to involvement in cyberbullying for both victims and perpetrators. Among victims, social intelligence (Hunt, Peters, & Rapee, 2012) is inversely related to cyberbullying, and hyperactivity (Dooley, Shaw, & Cross, 2012) positively correlated with cyberbullying. Relative to those not involved with cyberbullying, victims of cyberbullying tend to engage in riskier online behavior, such as disclosing very personal information online (Bauman, 2010; Görzig, & Ólafsson, 2013), and have a higher level of exposure to violent video games (Lam, Cheng, & Liu, 2013).

Targets of cyberbullying have also shown higher levels of depression, anxiety, and suicidal ideation, and lower levels of self-esteem, perhaps linked in part to observations that they have fewer friends compared to those individuals not involved with cyberbullying (Hinduja & Patchin, 2008; Kowalski et al., 2014; Kowalski & Limber, 2013; Ybarra & Mitchell, 2004). Caution should be used, however, when examining these psychological variables as predictors of cyberbullying. It is equally plausible that they are consequences of prior traditional or cyberbullying victimization that sets them up as targets for further victimization. Additional longitudinal research is needed in this area to tease apart these effects.

Relative to individuals not involved with cyberbullying, perpetrators of cyberbullying display lower levels of empathy, particularly cognitive empathy (Ang & Goh, 2010), and higher levels of narcissism (Ang, Tan, & Mansor, 2011; Fanti, Demetriou, & Hawa, 2012). Similar to victims of cyberbullying, perpetrators also report higher levels of depression and anxiety and lower levels of self-esteem (Didden et al., 2009; Ybarra & Mitchell, 2004). Unlike targets, however, perpetrators do not report a reduced number of friendships but rather a higher number relative to persons uninvolved in bullying. Like targets, perpetrators are also more likely to spend a disproportionate amount of time online relative to those not involved with cyberbullying (Hinduja & Patchin, 2008; Ybarra & Mitchell, 2004). This time spent online is likely correlated with a level of technological expertise observed among perpetrators (Walrave & Heirman, 2011).

Perpetrators also display a number of other maladaptive behaviors, relative to those uninvolved with cyberbullying. They show higher rates of alcohol and drug use, more run-ins with law enforcement, and a higher rate of physical altercations (Kowalski et al., 2014; Ybarra & Mitchell, 2004). Some of these maladaptive behaviors may originate in the values and attitudes of cyberbullying perpetrators. Research suggests that perpetrators of cyberbullying display a different set of attitudes and values relative to victims and those not involved with cyberbullying. Williams and Guerra (2007) found that perpetrators report moral approval of bullying (see also Bartlett & Gentile, 2012). Other researchers have noted that perpetrators of cyberbullying morally disengage or minimize the negative impact of their behavior on the victim (Bandura, 1999; Bauman, 2010; Pornari & Wood, 2010; Walrave & Heirman, 2011).

Both victimization and perpetration have been associated with academic difficulties including disliking school, poor performance in school, higher absenteeism, and problems with concentration (Beran & Li, 2007; Kowalski et al., 2014; Kowalski & Limber, 2013; Ybarra & Mitchell, 2004).

Cyberbullying victimization and perpetration are also inversely related to support from friends, parents, and a positive school climate. Supportive friends represent a protective factor for cyberbullying victimization and perpetration (Fanti et al., 2012). Cyberbullying victimization is higher among youth whose parents provide little parental monitoring of online activities (Aoyama, Utsumi, & Hasewaga, 2012) or who fail to communicate with their children about online safety (Wade & Beran, 2011). Youth who report poor relationships with their parents and low parental support display higher levels of cyberbullying perpetration (Wang, Iannotti, & Nansel, 2009; Ybarra & Mitchell, 2004). Students who find an inviting, warm school environment report lower rates of victimization and perpetration (Williams & Guerra, 2007).

Consequences of Cyberbullying

This chapter began recounting names and stories of young people who committed suicide *in part* as a result of cyberbullying. While no one would suggest that any suicide is singly determined and while statistics would indicate that the number of individuals who resort to suicide following a history of cyberbullying is relatively small, the fact that we discuss it at all in connection with cyberbullying highlights the serious effects that can follow from this behavior. Indeed, in 2010, the Centers for Disease Control convened a panel of experts to examine the relationship between involvement of youth in bullying and suicide-related behaviors. Out of this panel discussion came a series of articles published in the *Journal of Adolescent Health* highlighting the link between bullying and suicide and what public health strategies can be brought to bear on this problem (for an overview of these articles see Hertz, Donato, & Wright, 2013).

A host of other negative consequences accrue to victims, perpetrators, and bystanders of cyberbullying. Being a victim of cyberbullying is related to a number of physical and psychological problems including suicidal ideation, depression, low self-esteem, anxiety, loneliness, somatic symptoms, school absences, poor school performance, and drug and alcohol use (e.g., Hinduja & Patchin, 2007; Kowalski et al., 2014; Kowalski & Limber, 2013). Being a perpetrator of cyberbullying is associated with drug and alcohol use, anxiety, depression, low self-esteem, and poor academic achievement, as well as higher levels of loneliness (Kowalski et al., 2014).

The degree to which people, particularly victims, experience the negative effects of cyberbullying is not uniform, but rather depends upon an appraisal process. According to Lazarus and Folkman (1984), people's appraisals occur in two stages. In the primary appraisal stage, they evaluate the demands imposed by a particular situation, specifically the harm, threat, and challenge presented by that situation. In the secondary appraisal stage, they evaluate the degree to which they have the resources to deal with this situation. Thus, two individuals could be victimized in the same way but evaluate the cyberbullying very differently. Person and situational variables influence both the primary and secondary appraisal processes. For example, an individual who has a history of victimization via traditional bullying or cyberbullying is likely to perceive more harm, threat, and challenge in a new situation and may evaluate his or her coping abilities as weaker than someone who has not had prior experience with any type of bullying. In support of this, research by Staude-Müller, Hansen, and Voss (2012) showed that individuals with higher levels of neuroticism who had a prior history of victimization had more adverse reactions to their victimization. Similarly, individuals with autism spectrum disorders would be expected to appraise situations involving traditional bullying or cyberbullying differently than neurotypical individuals

(Kowalski & Fedina, 2011). Much more research is needed, however, regarding exactly how cyberbullying situations and coping abilities are appraised by targets.

The method of the cyberbullying also affects how serious the bullying is perceived to be. For example, one study indicated that college students perceived cyberbullying via the distribution of inappropriate pictures and video clips on social media sites to be more upsetting than other types of cybervictimization (Slonje & Smith, 2008). Certain social media may be appraised as more harmful or threatening in terms of a person's social image or as exceeding an individual's ability to cope, perhaps because the circulation of the image or text via that particular medium is so wide.

An important qualifier is in order when discussing the effects of cyberbullying. Given that many youth who are involved with cyberbullying are also involved with traditional bullying, it is difficult to disentangle the extent to which the negative effects that are discussed as resulting from involvement in cyberbullying are due exclusively to cyberbullying or to traditional bullying or both (Olweus, 2013; see, however, Bonanno & Hymel, 2013). As Olweus (2013) stated well, "to find out about the possible negative effects of cybervictimization is a complex and challenging research task." We would like to suggest, however, that there are many youth who are involved in either type of bullying independently of the other who experience a host of negative outcomes, including, in some instances, suicide. Additionally, we want to highlight that the pattern of effects that emerges with traditional bullying and with cyberbullying varies according to other individual difference measures, such as gender, highlighting the need to examine the effects of both traditional bullying and cyberbullying (Bauman, Toomey, & Walker, 2013).

The Future of Cyberbullying Research

Because research in the area of cyberbullying is only about a decade old, much remains to be learned. Among the most pressing issues is for researchers to reach a consensus on how best to define and measure cyberbullying. This will aid in resolving disparities that currently characterize the field. Additionally, more longitudinal research is needed that will allow researchers to explicate more clearly antecedents and consequences of cyberbullying. This research should also help in identifying the effects of cyberbullying independent of those resulting from traditional bullying. In addition, relatively recent research is investigating cyberbullying in intimate relationships, with a particular focus on the role that the absence of bystanders may play in exacerbating the adverse effects of cyberbullying (e.g., Alvarez, 2012). This represents an important new direction for cyberbullying research. The hope is that all of this research that is to come will inform prevention and intervention efforts. The process will be an ongoing one, however, with technology ever changing.

References

Aftab, P. (2011). Cyberbullying/stalking & harassment. Retrieved November 26, 2014, from https://www.wiredsafety.org/subjects/cyberbullying.php

Akman, I., & Mishra, A. (2010). Gender, age and income differences in Internet usage among employees in organizations. *Computers in Human Behavior*, 26(3), 482–490.

Alonzo, M., & Aiken, M. (2004). Flaming in electronic communication. *Decision Support Systems, 36*(3), 205–213.

Alvarez, A. R. (2012). "IH8U": Confronting cyberbullying and exploring the use of cybertools in teen dating relationships. *Journal of Clinical Psychology, 68,* 1205–1215.

Ang, R. P., & Goh, D. H. (2010). Cyberbullying among adolescents: The role of affective and cognitive empathy, and gender. *Child Psychiatry and Human Development, 41,* 387–397.

Ang, R. P., Tan, K., & Mansor, T. A. (2011). Normative beliefs about aggression as a mediator of narcissistic exploitativeness and cyberbullying. *Journal of Interpersonal Violence, 26*(13), 2619–2634.

Aoyama, I., Utsumi, S., & Hasegawa, M. (2012). Cyberbullying in Japan: Cases, government reports, adolescent relational aggression, and parental monitoring roles. In Q. Li, D. Cross, & P. K. Smith (Eds.), *Cyberbullying in the global playground: Research from international perspectives* (pp. 183–201). Oxford, UK: Blackwell.

Bandura, A. (1999). Moral disengagement in the perpetration of inhumanities. *Personality and Social Psychology Review, 3,* 193–209.

Bartlett, C. P., & Gentile, D. A. (2012). Attacking others online: The formation of cyberbullying in late adolescence. *Psychology of Popular Media Culture, 1,* 123–135.

Bauman, S. (2010). Cyberbullying in a rural intermediate school: An exploratory study. *Journal of Early Adolescence, 30*(6), 803–833.

Bauman, S., Toomey, R. B., & Walker, J. L. (2013). Associations among bullying, cyberbullying, and suicide in high school students. *Journal of Adolescence, 36,* 341–350.

Belsey, B. (n.d.). Cyberbullying: An emerging threat to the "always on" generation. Retrieved November 26, 2014, from http://www.cyberbullying.ca/pdf/Cyberbullying_Article_by_Bill_Belsey.pdf

Beran, T., & Li, Q. (2007). The relationship between cyberbullying and school bullying. *Journal of Student Wellbeing, 1*(2), 15–33. Retrieved November 26, 2014, from http://www.ojs.unisa.edu.au/index.php/JSW/article/viewFile/172/139

Bjorkqvist, K., Lagerspetz, K. M. J., & Osterman, K. (1992). The development of direct and indirect aggressive strategies in males and females. In K. Bjorkqvist & P. Nimela (Eds.), *Of mice and women: Aspects of female aggression* (pp. 51–64). San Diego, CA: Academic Press.

Bonanno, R. A., & Hymel, S. (2013). Cyber bullying and internalizing difficulties: Above and beyond the impact of traditional forms of bullying. *Journal of Youth and Adolescence, 42,* 685–697.

Commonsense Media. (2009, August 10). Is social networking changing childhood? Retrieved November 26, 2014, from https://www.commonsensemedia.org/about-us/news/press-releases/is-social-networking-changing-childhood

Didden, R., Scholte, R. H. J., Korzilius, H., de Moor, J. M. H., Vermeulen, A., O'Reilly, M., … Lancioni, G. E. (2009). Cyberbullying among students with intellectual and developmental disability in special education settings. *Developmental Neurorehabilitation, 12,* 146–151.

Diener, E. (1980). *The psychology of group influence.* New York, NY: Lawrence Erlbaum Associates.

Dooley, J. J., Pyżalski, J., & Cross, D. (2009). Cyberbullying versus face-to-face bullying: A theoretical and conceptual review. *Zeitschrift für Psychologie/Journal of Psychology, 217,* 182–188.

Dooley, J. J., Shaw, T., & Cross, D. (2012). The association between the mental health and behavioural problems of students and their reactions to cyber-victimization. *European Journal of Developmental Psychology, 9*(2), 275–289.

Fanti, K. A. (2012). A longitudinal study of cyberbullying: Examining risk and protective factors. *European Journal of Developmental Psychology, 9,* 168–181.

Fanti, K. A., Demetriou, A. G., & Hawa, V. V. (2012). A longitudinal study of cyberbullying: Examining risk and protective factors. *European Journal of Developmental Psychology, 9*(2), 168–181.

Fight Crime sponsored studies: Opinion research corporation. (2006). *Cyberbullying teen*. Retrieved November 26, 2014, from http://www.fightcrime.org/cyberbullying/cyberbullyingteen.pdf

Fowler, G. A. (2012, October 4). Facebook: One billion and counting. *The Wall Street Journal*. Retrieved November 26, 2014, from http://online.wsj.com/articles/SB10000872396390443635404578036164027386112

Gomez-Garibello, C., Shariff, S., McConnell, M., & Talwar, V. (2012). Adolescents' evaluation of cyberbullying events. *Alberta Journal of Educational Research, 58*. Retrieved November 26, 2014, from http://ajer.synergiesprairies.ca/ajer/index.php/ajer/article/view/1060

Görzig, A., & Ólafsson, K. (2013). What makes a bully a cyberbully? Unravelling the characteristics of cyberbullies across twenty-five European countries. *Journal of Children and Media, 7*(1), 9–27.

Gradinger, P., Strohmeier, D., & Spiel, C. (2009). Traditional bullying and cyberbullying: Identification of risk groups for adjustment problems. *Zeitschrift für Psychologie/Journal of Psychology, 217*(4), 205–213.

Gradinger, P., Strohmeier, D., & Spiel, C. (2012). Motives for bullying others in cyberspace: A study on bullies and bully-victims in Austria. In Q. Li, D. Cross, & P. K. Smith (Eds.), *Cyberbullying in the global playground: Research from international perspectives* (pp. 263–284). Oxford, UK: Wiley Blackwell.

Hertz, M. F., Donato, I., & Wright, J. (2013). Bullying and suicide: A public health approach. *Journal of Adolescent Health, 53* (Suppl.), A1–A10.

Hinduja, S., & Patchin, J. W. (2007). Offline consequences of online victimization: School violence and delinquency. *Journal of School Violence, 6*, 89–112.

Hinduja, S., & Patchin, J. W. (2008). Cyberbullying: An exploratory analysis of factors related to offending and victimization. *Deviant Behavior, 29*, 129–156.

Hitlin, P., & Rainie, L. (2005). *Teens, technology, and school* (data memo). Washington, DC: Pew Internet & American Life Project. Retrieved November 26, 2014, from http://www.pewinternet.org/files/old-media/Files/Reports/2005/PIP_Internet_and_schools_05.pdf.pdf

Holfeld, B., & Grabe, M. (2012). An examination of the history, prevalence, characteristics, and reporting of cyberbullying in the United States. In Q. Li, D. Cross, & P. K. Smith (Eds.), *Cyberbullying in the global playground: Research from international perspectives* (pp. 117–142). Oxford, UK: Wiley Blackwell.

Hunt, C., Peters, L., & Rapee, R. M. (2012). Development of a measure of the experience of being bullied in youth. *Psychological Assessment, 24*(1), 156–165.

Jones, L. M., Mitchell, K. J., & Finkelhor, D. (2013). Online harassment in context: Trends from three youth Internet safety surveys (2000, 2005, 2010). *Psychology of Violence, 3*, 53–69.

Juvonen, J., & Gross, E. F. (2008). Extending the school grounds? Bullying experiences in cyberspace. *Journal of School Health, 78*, 496–505.

Katzer, C., Fetchenhauer, D., & Belschak, F. (2009). Cyberbullying: Who are the victims? A comparison of victimization in Internet chatrooms and victimization in school. *Journal of Media Psychology, 21*, 25–36.

Kowalski, R. M., & Fedina, C. (2011). Cyber bullying in ADHD and Asperger Syndrome populations. *Research in Autism Spectrum Disorders, 5*(3), 1201–1208.

Kowalski, R. M., & Giumetti, G. (2014). Wall posts and tweets and blogs, oh my! A look at cyber bullying via social media. In C. Marcum & G. Higgins (Eds.), *Social networking as a criminal enterprise* (pp. 91–110). New York, NY: CRC Press.

Kowalski, R. M., Giumetti, G., Schroeder, A., & Lattanner, M. (2014). Bullying in the digital age: A critical review and meta-analysis of cyberbullying research among youth. *Psychological Bulletin, 140*, 1073–1137.

Kowalski, R. M., Giumetti, G., Schroeder, A., & Reese, H. (2012). Cyberbullying among college students: Evidence from multiple domains of college life. In C. Wankel & L. Wankel (Eds.), *Misbehavior online in higher education* (pp. 293–321). Bingley, UK: Emerald Publishing Group.

Kowalski, R. M., & Limber, S. E. (2007). Electronic bullying among middle school students. *Journal of Adolescent Health, 41*(6), S22–S30.

Kowalski, R. M., & Limber, S. (2013). Psychological, physical, and academic correlates of cyberbullying and traditional bullying. *Journal of Adolescent Health, 53,* S13–S20.

Kowalski, R. M., Limber, S. E., & Agatston, P. W. (2012). *Cyberbullying: Bullying in the digital age* (2nd ed.). Oxford, UK: Wiley Blackwell.

Kowalski, R. M., Morgan, C. A., & Limber, S. E. (2012). Traditional bullying as a potential warning sign of cyberbullying. *School Psychology International, 33,* 505–519.

Kowalski, R. M., & Whittaker, E. (2013). Cyber aggression on social networking sites. Unpublished manuscript, Clemson University.

Kwan, G., & Skoric, M. M. (2013). Facebook bullying: An extension of battles in school. *Computers in Human Behavior, 29*(1), 16–25.

Lam, L. T., Cheng, Z., & Liu, X. (2013). Violent online games exposure and cyberbullying/victimization among adolescents. *Cyberpsychology, Behavior, and Social Networking, 16,* 159–165.

Langos, C. (2012). Cyberbullying: The challenge to define. *Cyberpsychology, Behavior, and Social Networking, 15,* 285–289.

Lazarus, R. S., & Folkman, S. (1984). *Stress, appraisal, and coping.* New York, NY: Springer.

Lenhart, A. (2010, May 6). Cyberbullying: What the research is telling us. Retrieved November 26, 2014, from http://www.pewinternet.org/Presentations/2010/May/Cyberbullying-2010.aspx

Lenhart, A., Purcell, K., Smith, A., & Zickuhr, K. (2010). Social media and mobile Internet use among teens and young adults. Retrieved November 26, 2014, from http://www.pewinternet.org/files/old-media/Files/Reports/2010/PIP_Social_Media_and_Young_Adults_Report_Final_with_toplines.pdf

Madden, M., Lenhart, A., & Duggan, M. (2013). Teens and technology, 2013. Retrieved November 26, 2014, from http://www.pewinternet.org/Reports/2013/Teens-and-Tech.aspx

Mishna, F., Cook, C., Gadalla, T., Daciuk, J., & Solomon, S. (2010). Cyber bullying behaviors among middle and high school students. *American Journal of Orthopsychiatry, 80*(3), 362–374.

Monks, C. P., & Smith, P. K. (2006). Definitions of bullying: Age differences in understanding of the term, and the role of experience. *British Journal of Developmental Psychology, 24*(4), 801–821.

Nansel, T., Overpeck, M., Pilla, R., Ruan, W., Simons-Morton, B., & Scheidt, P. (2001). Bullying behaviors among U.S. youth: Prevalence and association with psychosocial adjustment. *Journal of the American Medical Association, 285,* 2094–2100.

O'Brennan, L. M., Bradshaw, C. P., & Sawyer, A. L. (2009). Examining developmental differences in the social-emotional problems among frequent bullies, victims, and bully/victims. *Psychology in Schools, 46,* 100–115.

O'Keeffe, G. S., & Clarke-Pearson, K. (2011). The impact of social media on children, adolescents, and families. *Pediatrics, 127,* 800–804.

Olweus, D. (1993). *Bullying at school: What we know and what we can do.* Oxford, UK: Blackwell.

Olweus, D. (2013). School bullying: Development and some important challenges. *Annual Review of Clinical Psychology, 9,* 1–14.

Pontzer, D. (2010). A theoretical test of bullying behavior: Parenting, personality, and the bully/victim relationship. *Journal of Family Violence, 25,* 259–273.

Pornari, C. D., & Wood, J. (2010). Peer and cyber aggression in secondary school students: The role of moral disengagement, hostile attribution bias, and outcome expectancies. *Aggressive Behavior, 36,* 81–94.

Postmes, T., & Spears, R. (1998). Deindividuation and antinormative behavior: A meta-analysis. *Psychological Bulletin, 123,* 238–259.

Pyżalski, J. (2012). From cyberbullying to electronic aggression: Typology of the phenomenon. *Emotional and Behavioural Difficulties, 17*(3–4), 305–317.

Raskauskas, J., & Stoltz, A. D. (2007). Involvement in traditional and electronic bullying among adolescents. *Developmental Psychology, 43*, 564–575.

Reich, S. M., Subrahmanyam, K., & Espinoza, G. (2012). Friending, IMing, and hanging out face-to-face: Overlap in adolescents' online and offline social networks. *Developmental Psychology, 48*(2), 356–368.

Robers, S., Zhang, J., Truman, J., & Snyder, T. D. (2010). Indicators of school crime and safety: 2010 (NCES 2011-002/NCJ230812). U.S. Department of Education, U.S. Department of Justice Office of Justice Programs. Retrieved November 26, 2014, from http://nces.ed.gov/pubs2011/2011002.pdf

Schenk, A. M., & Fremouw, W. J. (2012). Prevalence, psychological impact, and coping of cyberbully victims among college students. *Journal of School Violence, 11*, 21–37.

Schneider, S., O'Donnell, L., Stueve, A., & Coulter, R. S. (2012). Cyberbullying, school bullying, and psychological distress: A regional census of high school students. *American Journal of Public Health, 102*, 171–177.

Shapka, J. D., & Law, D. M. (2013). Does one size fit all? Ethnic differences in parenting behaviors and motivations for adolescent engagement in cyberbullying. *Journal of Youth and Adolescence, 42*(5), 723–738.

Slonje, R., & Smith P. K. (2008). Cyberbullying: Another main type of bullying? *Scandanavian Journal of Psychology, 49*, 147–154.

Smith, P. K., Mahdavi, J., Carvalho, M., Fisher, S., Russell, S., & Tippett, N. (2008). Cyberbullying: Its nature and impact in secondary school pupils. *Journal of Child Psychology and Psychiatry, 49*(4), 376–385.

Sourander, A., Klomek, A. B., Ikonen, M., Lindroos, J., Luntamo, T., Koskelainen, M., … Henenius, H. (2010). Psychosocial risk factors associated with cyberbullying among adolescents. *Archives of General Psychiatry, 67*, 720–728.

Staude-Müller, F., Hansen, B., & Voss, M. (2012). How stressful is online victimization? Effects of victim's personality and properties of the incident. *European Journal of Developmental Psychology, 9*, 260–274.

Tokunaga, R. S. (2010). Following you home from school: A critical review and synthesis of research on cyber bullying victimization. *Computers in Human Behavior, 26*, 277–287.

Vannucci, M., Nocentini, A., Mazzoni, G., & Menesini, E. (2012). Recalling unpresented hostile words: False memories predictors of traditional and cyberbullying. *European Journal of Developmental Psychology, 9*, 182–194.

Varjas, K., Henrich, C. C., & Meyers, J. (2009). Urban middle school students' perceptions of bullying, cyberbullying, and school safety. *Journal of School Violence, 8*, 159–176.

Wade, A., & Beran, T. (2011). Cyberbullying: The new era of bullying. *Canadian Journal of School Psychology, 26*(1), 44–61.

Walrave, M., & Heirman, W. (2011). Cyberbullying: Predicting victimization and perpetration. *Children and Society, 25*, 59–72.

Wang, J., Iannotti, R. J., & Nansel, T. R. (2009). School bullying among adolescents in the United States: Physical, verbal, relational, and cyber. *Journal of Adolescent Health, 45*, 368–375.

Willard, N. E. (2007). *Cyberbullying and cyberthreats: Responding to the challenge of online social aggression, threats, and distress.* Champaign, IL: Research Press.

Williams, K. R., & Guerra, N. G. (2007). Prevalence and predictors of Internet bullying. *Journal of Adolescent Health, 41*, 14–21.

Wolak, J., Mitchell, K., & Finkelhor, D. (2007). Does online harassment constitute bullying? An exploration of online harassment by known peers and online-only contacts. *Journal of Adolescent Health, 41*(6), S51–S58.

Ybarra, M. L., Boyd, D., Korchmaros, J. D., & Oppenheim, J. (2012). Defining and measuring cyberbullying within the larger context of bullying victimization. *Journal of Adolescent Health, 51,* 53–58.

Ybarra, M. L., Diener-West, M., & Leaf, P. J. (2007). Examining the overlap in Internet harassment and school bullying: Implications for school intervention. *Journal of Adolescent Health, 41,* 42–50.

Ybarra, M. L., & Mitchell, K. J. (2004). Online aggressor/targets, aggressors, and targets: A comparison of associated youth characteristics. *Journal of Child Psychology and Psychiatry, 45,* 1308–1316.

Zickuhr, K., & Smith, A. (2012, April 13). Digital differences. Retrieved November 26, 2014, from http://pewinternet.org/Reports/2012/Digital-differences/Overview.aspx

9

A Step Toward Understanding Cross-National and Cross-Cultural Variances in Cyberbullying

Fatih Bayraktar

Masaryk University and Eastern Mediterranean University

World Internet Usage and Population Statistics (2012) indicate that 34% of the world's population uses the Internet regularly. When the continents are compared, the lowest penetration rate is in Africa (16%) and the highest penetration rate is in North America (79%) followed by Australia/Oceania (68%) and Europe (63%). Although these rates show a kind of digital divide or digital inequality among nations and cultures living in different regions of the world, the Internet (when used) may equalize its users. According to d'Haenens, Koeman, and Saeys (2007), information communication technologies (ICT) have the capacity to counteract social inequalities and resolve cultural differences. Moreover, empirical evidence has shown that spending time on the Internet is related to increased digital literacy and digital skills, which bring with them the potential to access a greater range of opportunities (Kalmus, Runnel, & Siibak, 2009; Livingstone & Haddon, 2009; Livingstone & Helsper, 2007). However, time on the Internet may also be associated with some online risks (Kirwil & Lauris, 2012; Stald & Ólafsson, 2012; van der Hof & Koops, 2012). One of these risks is cyberbullying, a new form of aggressive behavior using modern ICT. The research on cyberbullying started in the early 2000s in Australia, Europe, and North America (Nocentini et al., 2010) in accordance with the higher Internet penetration rates mentioned above, and has currently spread to Asia (see Aoyama, Utsumi, & Hasegawa, 2012; Tippett & Kwak, 2012) and Africa (see Burton & Mutongwizo, 2009; Moodley, 2012). However, the main portion of the research conducted on cyberbullying still comes from Anglophone countries, and there is lack of information about cross-national/cross-cultural variances of cyberbullying. This bias in the international research on cyberbullying can be the result of the common use of English for communication in academia; reports or articles in other languages will not become known if they are not translated into English. Also, the varying labeling and definitions of cyberbullying in the studies conducted in different countries make the results difficult to compare. For example, Mora-Merchán, Del Rey, and Jäger (2010) stressed that there was a lack of common terminology used for labeling cyberbullying, especially in non-English-speaking countries. They also mentioned that even English-speaking countries do not share a common terminology. For example, in

The Wiley Handbook of Psychology, Technology, and Society, First Edition. Edited by Larry D. Rosen, Nancy A. Cheever, and L. Mark Carrier.
© 2015 John Wiley & Sons, Ltd. Published 2015 by John Wiley & Sons, Ltd.

the United States and English-speaking Canada, the terms *Internet harassment* and *cyber-harassment* are frequently used instead of *cyberbullying* (Beran & Li, 2005; Mora-Merchán et al., 2010). Despite these disadvantages, the main focus of this chapter is to look at cyberbullying phenomena from an international perspective and try to capture the national/cultural differences. The first section deals with cross-national differences in cyberbullying prevalence rates. The second section deals with variances in the definitions and perceptions of cyberbullying across nations/cultures. In the third section, the roles of independent/interdependent self-construal and femininity/masculinity as potential indicators of cultural variance and their associations with cyberbullying/cybervictimization are discussed along with empirical findings.

Prevalence Rates of Cyberbullying in Cross-National/Cross-Cultural Studies

A small number of studies, using the same methodology to evaluate cyberbullying, indicated varying prevalence rates across nations and cultures for cyberbullying/cybervictimization. For example, Li (2008) compared Chinese and Canadian adolescents. She found that 16% of Canadian adolescents and 17% of Chinese adolescents had been victimized online. The rates were different for participation in cyberbullying: 10% and 4% among Canadian and Chinese adolescents, respectively. Further statistical analysis indicated that Canadian adolescents reported significantly more participation in bullying behaviors online than their Chinese counterparts. However, the author discussed this finding not as a result of cultural difference but of better access to various ICT for Canadian adolescents after the findings of other researchers (e.g., Hasebrink, Livingstone, Haddon, & Ólafsson, 2009; Smith et al., 2008), who noted that greater penetration of mobile and Internet infrastructure could increase the risk of cyberbullying. In another study, Aoyama and colleagues (2012) compared the prevalence rates of cyberbullying/cybervictimization among Japanese and U.S. students. They showed that Japanese participants reported significantly less cyberbullying and cybervictimization than their counterparts in the United States. The authors discussed this difference as a result of the varied mean age level in the two samples (the mean age of the Japanese students was about two years older than in the U.S. sample). Similarly, Shapka and Law (2013) compared East Asian (mainly Chinese) and European students living in Canada. Their results were in line with previous findings, showing that East Asians reported less cyberbullying than their European counterparts. The authors explained this difference in prevalence as a result of the collectivist nature and Confucian/Taoist religious traditions of East Asians, which focus on social harmony that is accomplished with non-aggressive social interactions.

There are a few international projects that focused on cyberbullying phenomena. For example, the DAPHNE II program, titled "An investigation into forms of peer–peer bullying at school in preadolescent and adolescent groups: New instruments and preventing strategies," compared Italy, England, and Spain for cyberbullying and cybervictimization. Genta et al. (2012) differentiated between mobile and Internet bullying/victimization and classified cases as occasional or severe. The adolescents in Italy reported high levels of bullying/victimization across all categories. The Spanish adolescents reported predominantly occasional Internet victimization and reported the lowest rates of severe bullying/victimization. Adolescents from England reported the lowest rates of occasional victimization (both mobile and Internet). The authors stressed the correlation between owning a mobile phone and getting involved in cyberbullying/cybervictimization, although they added that cultural differences can also influence the differences in prevalence.

Another European-centered project (i.e., EU Kids Online) indicated that the percentage of respondents reporting some form of bullying or harassment online ranges between 10% and 52% (Hasebrink et al., 2009) across 25 European countries. EU Kids Online II (the follow-up project) indicated that 7% of 9- to 16-year-olds reported experiencing cyberbullying in the previous 12 months (Livingstone, Haddon, Görzig, & Ólafsson, 2011); 6% were victims of cyberbullying, 2% were perpetrators, and 1% both experienced and participated in cyberbullying. The incidence of both cyberbullying and cybervictimization was highest in Estonia, Romania, and Sweden. The lowest rates were in Portugal, Italy, and Turkey (Lampert & Donoso, 2012).

A recent study, using the same data, showed that 3.3% of the variation in cyberbullying was attributable to between-country differences (Görzig & Ólafsson, 2012). According to further results, the risk of participating in cyberbullying was lowest in Greece and highest in Estonia. It must be stressed that the risk rates were different for all countries. Also, the cross-country differences in cyberbullying were not significantly explained by broadband (i.e., Internet) penetration but partially by mobile phone penetration. The authors discussed individual-level variables, but not country-level variables, to explain cyberbullying.

With different methodology, the prevalence rates can differ dramatically from country to country. For example, in one of the widest cross-national reports on cyberbullying, which included countries from Central Europe, Eastern Europe, the Benelux region, the Mediterranean region, France, Germany, Ireland, Britain, Australia, Japan, and the United States, prevalences of cyberbullying and cybervictimization varied from 0.4% to 52.5% and 0.4% to 61.9%, respectively (Mora-Merchán et al., 2010). The lowest rates for cyberbullying and cybervictimization were found in Scandinavian countries (i.e., Finland and Norway), and the highest rates were found in Belgium. Another European-centered project (COST – Cooperation of Science and Technology Action IS0801: "Cyberbullying: Coping with negative and enhancing positive uses of new technologies in relationships in educational settings"), which involved 28 European countries, also indicated very different prevalence and incidence rates of cyberbullying. These large differences may arise from the use of various methodological approaches. Ybarra (2009) distinguishes between two methods for the evaluation of cyberbullying: (1) using definition-based scales/questionnaires to identify involvement in cyberbullying and (2) using a set of items related to cyberbullying and asking participants to choose from these items. The author showed that studies applying the second method tend to have significantly higher prevalence rates of cyberbullying. Another possible explanation for the variation in prevalence rates is the use of different frequencies and/ or different time periods of cyberbullying in survey questions (Campbell, 2010).

Various Definitions and Perceptions of Cyberbullying Across Nations/Cultures

Cyberbullying is often described as the online part of a continuum of traditional bullying (Gradinger, Strohmeier, & Spiel, 2009; Hinduja & Patchin, 2008; Olweus, 2012). Therefore, traditional bullying and cyberbullying share a lot of common features. Both behaviors are aggressive/hostile; there is a power imbalance between bully and victim; and bullying both offline and online is intentional and repetitive (Dooley, Pyżalski, & Cross, 2009; Li, 2007; Slonje & Smith, 2008). On the other hand, in the case of cyberbullying a degree of technological expertise is required; cyberbullies are much more invisible or anonymous compared to traditional bullies, and the act of bullying in cyberspace typically happens when the bully and victim are physically distant (Cowie, 2009; Li, Smith, & Cross, 2012). Although these fundamental aspects are widely used as the main features of cyberbullying, still there is not a universally accepted definition of this phenomenon (Slonje, Smith, & Frisén, 2013).

When traditional bullying is taken into account, it is well known that the term bullying is not universal and used in different words/meanings from language to language (Smith, Cowie, Ólafsson, & Liefooghe, 2002). This can also change the basic aspects of bullying across nations/cultures (Smith & Brain, 2000). Nabuzoka (2003) mentioned that bullying can take various forms and the significance of bullying behaviors may vary from one culture to another. Accordingly, culture may shape bullying (Li, 2008). For example *Ijime* (a Japanese word used for bullying) mainly applies to emotional harm to others, such as ostracizing/excluding or systematically ignoring individuals in the peer group, and thus it is primarily identified as a group behavior (Morita, Soeda, Soeda, & Taki, 1999). *Wang-Ta* and *Jun-Ta* (Korean equivalents of bullying) imply only social exclusion by classmates and by the school respectively (Smith, 2004). It seems that the aspects of cyberbullying may also vary across cultures. For example, Cowie (2009) compared cyberbullying in Japan and the United Kingdom and wrote about a case in Japan in which the victim was bullied by a group of schoolmates via mobile phones. Victims in the United Kingdom, in contrast with Japan, were more often bullied by friends. Bearing in mind that *Ijime* is a group behavior, it can be suggested that the features of traditional bullying apply to cyberbullying in Japan.

Cross-national variations in the labeling and cultural perception of cyberbullying can also be observed within the same continent. Nocentini and colleagues (2010) mention some variations in the usage and perception of cyberbullying among the adolescents from three European countries (Germany, Spain, and Italy). For example, German adolescents created a unique term, *photing*, by mixing *mobbing* (the term used for bullying in German) and *photos* to capture the concept of bullying with photos. These adolescents also used a similar word, *cyber-mobbing*, for cyberbullying. Italian adolescents used the term *virtual bullying* and Spanish adolescents used *harassment via Internet* to refer to cyberbullying. In parallel with the differences in terminology, the perception of the seriousness of cyberbullying behaviors varied across the three countries. For example, German adolescents stressed the publicity of cyberbullying (because mobbing is mainly a public behavior), while Spanish adolescents focused on the harassment.

A study from Finland (Salmivalli & Pöyhönen, 2012) indicated that there are two different labels for cyberbullying: bullying on the Internet (*nettikiusaaminen*) and bullying via mobile phones (*kännykkäkiusaaminen*). Similarly, Tippett and Kwak (2012) noted that two terms are used instead of cyberbullying in South Korea: cyber-violence (*cyber-pokyruk*) and malicious comments (*ak-peul*). The authors explained that these behaviors generally occur during online game bullying, which seems to be unique to South Korea. In other words, the perception of cyberbullying in South Korea might be mainly related to bullying in online games.

The definition and perception of cyberbullying can differ according to the tools/means used to harass others. For example, a relatively recent report from South Africa

(Burton & Mutongwizo, 2009) showed that mobile phones, but not the Internet, were the main tools used in cyber aggression among South African adolescents, in contrast with Europe (Välimäki et al., 2012) and the United States (Juvonen & Gross, 2008), where the Internet is the main medium of cyberbullying. These adolescents reported that cyber aggression was frequently experienced through voice calls, text messaging, and instant messaging. Therefore, it can be suggested that the perception of cyberbullying among South African adolescents mainly includes bullying via mobile phones. In sum, the studies showed that cyberbullying can be labeled, defined, and perceived differently across countries.

Tackling Culture-Related Psychological Variables in Cyberbullying Phenomena: Associations Between Self-Construals, Masculinity–Femininity, and Cyberbullying/Cybervictimization

Although some researchers stress that culture does not play a critical role in cyber-bullying (Görzig & Ólafsson, 2012; Ybarra, Mitchell, & Lenhart, 2010), others point out that the perception and definition of cyberbullying varies according to cultural factors that affect online relationships (Calmaestra, Ortega, Maldonado, & Mora-Merchán, 2010; Menesini, 2012). Varying prevalence rates can also be explained by cultural differences (Genta et al., 2012; Mora-Merchán & Ortega-Ruiz, 2007; Shapka & Law, 2013). However, it is still not clear how culture explains the variances in cyberbullying. It is also almost impossible to measure the culture as a high-level sociological construct in any empirical way (Gross & Rayner, 1985). At this point, though it is impossible to quantify the culture itself, lower-level, culture-related psychological constructs can be associated with cyberbullying. The need for this kind of research has already been acknowledged (e.g., Cross, Li, Smith, & Monks, 2012; Walrave & Heirman, 2010), but to the best of our knowledge, it has not yet been conducted.

After the seminal study by Markus and Kitayama (1991), culture and self have started to be described as two interrelated constructs. For example, Gudykunst et al. (1996) stated that "members of individualistic cultures are socialized to rely predominantly on their independent self-construal, and members of collectivistic cultures are socialized to rely predominantly on their interdependent self-construals" (p. 516). Yoshihisa and colleagues (1995) also pointed out that anyone who has individualistic tendencies in any society may have an independent self-construal. Accordingly, many researchers (e.g., Gardner, Gabriel, & Lee, 1999; Lu & Gilmour, 2007; Singelis, 1994) measured independent vs. interdependent self-construals as the abstractions of individualism vs. collectivism. Similarly, masculinity and femininity (M-F) can be seen as cultural-level variables (Hofstede, 1984; Spector, Cooper, & Sparks, 2001) but at the same time can be measured as individual-level variables (e.g., Bem, 1981; Gini & Pozzoli, 2006; Ross, 1983).

The independent/interdependent self-construal model focuses on the relationship between individuals and the group with which they are identified (Singelis, 1994). Markus and Kitayama (1991) defined independent self-construal as an independent view of the self (e.g., being unique, autonomous, separate from the social context).

Interdependent self-construal, on the other hand, was defined as an interdependent image of the self (e.g., conforming to group norms, others' expectations, and group-related goals). Masculinity and femininity are concepts describing characteristics that are considered typical for males and females. Masculinity is characterized by instrumental personality traits such as self-affirmation, social dominance, independence, and aggressiveness; femininity is characterized by expressive traits such as warmth, sensitivity, nurturing, and interdependence (Maccoby, 1998; Young & Sweeting, 2004). The aforementioned characteristics of M-F might indicate the link between independent–interdependent self-construals and gender role orientations. Empirical evidence has shown that people with independent self-construals are more prone to having masculine features, and on the other hand, people with interdependent self-construals are more prone to having feminine features (Cross & Madson, 1997a, 1997b; Kim, 1994; Nyman, 1997; Oetzel, 1998).

The link between individual self-construals and cyberbullying is mostly unknown. Thus far, only one study, to our knowledge, has examined the link between independent vs. interdependent self-construal and cyberbullying/cybervictimization directly (i.e., Cetin, Eroglu, Peker, Akbaba, & Pepsoy, 2012). This study found a negative correlation between relational interdependent self-construal and cyberbullying. Relational interdependent self-construal is defined as constructing self in relation to close interpersonal relationships, but not in relation to a group or society (Cross, Bacon, & Morris, 2000). It is important to mention that relational interdependent self-construal is more common in individualistic cultures and at this point may coexist with independent self-construal (Cross et al., 2000; Cross & Madson, 1997a, 1997b; Kashima et al., 1995).

However, we can hypothesize some associations between these traits and cyberbullying by summing up some of the findings on a cultural level. Taking into account the close connection between bullying and cyberbullying, we review the literature on traditional as well as cyberbullying. For example, Craig et al. (2009) found cross-national differences in traditional bullying between children in 40 countries; specifically, adolescents in Baltic countries reported higher rates of bullying and victimization, whereas northern European countries reported the lowest rates. Nansel, Craig, Overpeck, Saluja, and Ruan (2004) found similar results from samples in 25 European countries indicating that students in Lithuania (one of the Baltic countries) reported more bullying and victimization; on the other hand, Sweden had the lowest self-reported prevalence of bullying and victimization.

In the EU Kids Online project, 14% of Estonian children aged 9–16 reported being cyberbullied, while only 2% of Italian children had had the same experience (Livingstone et al., 2011). Estonia is characterized as a collectivistic country (Realo, 1998; Suh, Diener, Oishi, & Triandis, 1998), whereas Italy is an individualistic country (Green, Deschamps, & Paez, 2005; Suh et al., 1998), suggesting that children in more individualistic societies are less involved in cybervictimization. Similarly, in a recent study, d'Haenens (2012) clustered the same 25 European countries using Hofstede's (1984) cultural values and found that children and adolescents living in more individualistic countries showed lower levels of online risk, including for cyberbullying and cybervictimization. Although these findings include cross-national comparisons, we suggest that people with more independent self-construals would be less prone to cyberbullying/cybervictimization, in accordance with the aforementioned link between self and culture (Gudykunst et al., 1996; Markus & Kitayama, 1991; Singelis, 1994; Yoshihisa et al., 1995).

In the existing cyberbullying research, we found mostly results explaining the link with gender, but not with M-F as a spectrum of personality traits. Moreover, findings related to gender differences in cyberbullying/cybervictimization were contradictory. Some studies showed that males tend to be more involved in cyberbullying, while females to be cybervictimized (Aricak et al., 2008; Dilmac, 2009; Li, 2007; Slonje & Smith, 2008), other studies indicate the reverse (Bauman, 2012; Kowalski & Limber, 2007), and yet other research found no difference (Ortega, Calmaestra, & Mora-Merchán, 2008; Smith et al., 2008; Wolak, Mitchell, & Finkelhor, 2007). These mixed results can suggest that it may not be "femaleness" or "maleness," but M-F, that is related to cyberbullying/cybervictimization. But considering the trouble with varying definitions of cyberbullying in the aforementioned studies (Tokunaga, 2010), we also assessed this link in traditional bullying. The literature indicates that overt bullying, which involves the intent to harm others directly (physically or emotionally), was found to be related to masculinity. By contrast, relational bullying, which intends to harm an individual's social relations or status, was related to femininity (see Card, Stucky, Sawalani, & Little, 2008 for a wide literature review). Moreover, in a recent longitudinal study, social exclusion – a subtype of relational victimization – was found to be positively related with femininity (Lee & Troop-Gordon, 2011). Studies examining bullying more generally (i.e., total scores instead of bullying subtypes) found that more masculine people tended to bully others (Craig & Peppler, 1995; Gini & Pozzoli, 2006; Phillips, 2007; Salmivalli, Lagerspetz, Bjorkqvist, Osterman, & Kaukianien, 1996). In contrast, more feminine people tended to be bullied (Breslau, Chilcoat, Kessler, Peterson, & Lucia, 1999; Genta et al., 2012; Gini & Pozzoli, 2006). It seems that independence, self-affirmation, social dominance, aggressiveness, and other masculine features may increase the risk of being involved in bullying; on the other side, warmth, sensitivity, interdependence, and other feminine features may increase the risk of being victimized. Therefore, following the literature on traditional bullying and victimization, we may suggest that cybervictimization is positively correlated with femininity and cyberbullying is positively correlated with masculinity.

Associating Independent Self-Construal, Masculinity–Femininity, and Cyberbullying/Cybervictimization: Mediation and Moderation Effects

The literature review indicated that independent self-construal might be negatively correlated with cyberbullying/cybervictimization; on the other hand, feminine tendencies might increase the likelihood of being bullied, while masculine tendencies might increase the likelihood of bullying others in cyberspace. In other words, independent self-construal might be a protective factor against cyberbullying, masculinity might be a risk factor for engaging in cyberbullying, and femininity might be a risk factor for experiencing cybervictimization. Following Masten (2001), variable-focused studies of resilience (i.e., *indirect model of risk and resilience and interaction model*) can be used as two models to examine the protective role of independent self-construal and M-F as risk factors. There are ample empirical data supporting these models and their application to the risk and protective factors of specific variables such as family economic hardship and adolescent academic performance, stress and competence, and

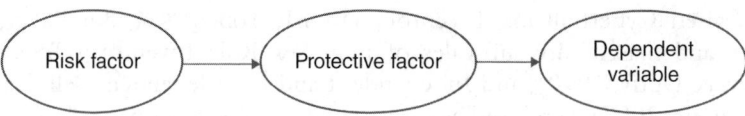

Figure 9.1 The indirect model of risk and resilience (inspired by Masten, 2001).

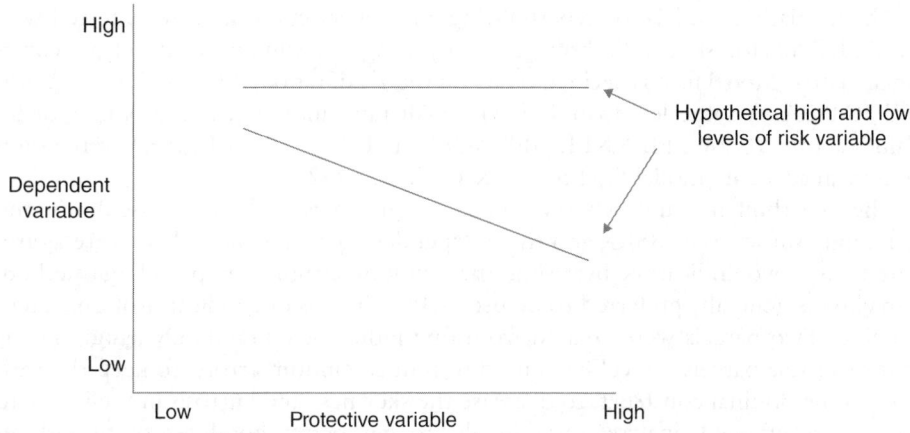

Figure 9.2 Interaction model of risk and resilience (inspired by Masten, 2001).

marital transitions and adjustment (Conger, Conger, & Elder, 1997; Garmezy, Masten, & Tellegen, 1984; Hetherington, Bridges, & Glendessa, 1998; Masten & Coatsworth, 1995). Luthar, Cicchetti, and Becker (2000) also recommended these models and their application to the study of risks in their review article. The indirect model of risk and resilience has suggested a protective variable mediating the relationship between a risk factor and a dependent variable (see Figure 9.1).

The interaction model of risk and resilience has suggested a protective variable which acts as a moderator between a risk factor and a dependent variable (see Figure 9.2).

As seen in the literature review, culture-related psychological constructs can be associated with cyberbullying/cybervictimization. Following Cross and colleagues (2012), also Walrave and Heirman (2010), who acknowledged the need for empirical evidence to support this association, we conducted research in three universities from the main regions of North Cyprus. We used indirect and interaction models of risk and resilience, which were described above. In the *indirect model*, independent self-construal was expected to mediate the association between M-F (as risk factors) and cyberbullying/cybervictimization (as dependent variables) in a negative direction. In the *interaction model* it was hypothesized that higher independent self-construal scores as the protective variable would have a moderator role in the relationship between M-F (as risk factors) and cyberbullying/cybervictimization (as dependent variables).

A total of 393 university students (56% females) between the ages of 19 and 35 ($M = 24.25$, $SD = 2.51$) were selected for the study. The participants were from various national and cultural backgrounds (40% Cypriot, 39% Turkish, 21% African, 6% European, and 4% Asian).

The Revised Cyberbullying Inventory (RCBI; Topçu & Erdur-Baker, 2010), femininity and masculinity subscales of Bem Sex Role Inventory (BSRI; Wong, McCreary, & Duffy, 1990), and Independent and Interdependent Self Scale (IISS; Lu & Gilmour, 2007) were used as measurement tools. Cronbach alphas were .81 and .79 for cyberbullying and cybervictimization forms of RCBI, .82 and .78 for masculinity and femininity subscales of the BSRI, and .89 for the independent self subscale of the IISS.

The mediation models for cyberbullying and cybervictimization were tested with LISREL 8.80 (Jöreskog & Sörbom, 1993) by using a maximum likelihood and covariance matrix. Model fit was decided based on the χ^2/df ratio, CFI, NNFI, GFI, AGFI, and RMSEA. A value less than 1/5 for χ^2/df ratio indicated the goodness of fit. Values above .90 for CFI, NNFI, GFI, AGFI and below .10 for RMSEA were evaluated as an adequate model fit (Browne & Cudeck, 1992).

The cyberbullying and cybervictimization subscales of RCBI, masculinity and femininity subscales of BSRI, and the independent self subscale of IISS were aggregated into two indicators by using the random assignment parceling method. Parceling is generally preferred to be used when there is one indicator of one latent variable. Two parcels were created from one indicator by randomly assigning the items to these parcels. Parceling is used to reduce random errors, to keep the variance of the original construct, to decrease the skewness and kurtosis in the items, to have more efficient analyses, and finally, to get better goodness of fit indexes (Bandalos, 2002; Bandalos & Finney, 2001; Gribbons & Hocevar, 1998; Little, Cunningham, Shahar, & Widaman, 2002; Takahashi & Nasser, 1996; Thompson & Melancon, 1996).

The mediation (indirect effect) was provided by the LISREL results, and also by using the Sobel test, which indicated whether the decrease in the power of association between two variables was significant or not (z-value between 1.96 and 2.50 indicated that the decrease is significant at the level of $p = .05$, and a z-value above 2.51 indicated that the decrease is significant at the level of $p = .01$).

Multiple regression analysis was conducted to measure the moderator role of independent self-construal between M-F and cyberbullying/cybervictimization. Centered scores were entered into the analysis in the first step, and two-way interactions in the second step, following Aiken and West (1991). The moderator effect of a variable is confirmed when interactions are significant.

The Incidence of Cyberbullying and Cybervictimization among University Students

The results revealed that 6% of our sample engaged in cyberbullying behaviors at least once in the last 6 months and 8% were being subject to cybervictimization at least once in the same time gap. According to the self-reports, the highest frequency among cyberbullying items was for "*Teasing about information or comments written on a forum site*" and the highest frequency among cybervictimization items was for "*Taking information from a personal computer (documents, photos, messenger conversations ... etc.) without permission.*" There was no significant difference among national groups in terms of cyberbullying and cybervictimization.

Mediator Role of Independent Self-Construal between M-F and Cyberbullying/Cybervictimization

The model which tested the mediator role of independent self-construal between masculinity and cyberbullying did not show a good model fit even after revisions depending on modification indexes (χ^2 (8, $N = 393$) = 92.34, $p < .001$, $RMSEA = .12$, $GFI = .89$, $AGFI = .88$, $CFI = .76$, $NNFI = .81$). On the other hand, the goodness of fit indexes of the mediation model which tested the mediator role of independent self-construal between femininity and cybervictimization were adequate ($\chi^2(6$, $N = 393$) = 7.37, $p = .28$, $RMSEA = .03$, $GFI = .99$, $AGFI = .98$, $CFI = 1.00$, $NNFI = .99$). LISREL results showed that independent self-construal significantly mediated between femininity and cybervictimization (standardized coefficient for indirect effect = .06, $p < .01$). The results of the Sobel test also indicated that the decrease in the power of association between femininity and cybervictimization was significant when independent self-construal mediated the association ($z = 2.43$, $p = .02$). It should be noted that the association between femininity and cybervictimization was in a positive direction (standardized coefficient: .37) before mediation analysis. Figure 9.3 shows the standardized coefficients in the model.

Moderator Role of Independent Self-Construal between Male/Female and Cyberbullying/Cybervictimization

The moderator model of independent self-construal between masculinity and cyberbullying did not reveal significant results. On the other hand, independent self-construal moderated the association between femininity and cybervictimization ($F = 3.91$, $p < .001$, $R^2 = .04$; $\beta = -.14$, $t = -2.43$, $p < .01$). The interaction showed that participants with the highest scores on independent self-construal and lowest scores on femininity had the lowest cybervictimization scores, while those with the lowest scores on independent self-construal and highest scores on femininity had the highest cybervictimization scores (see Figure 9.4).

Discussion

Existing cross-cultural studies in the cyberbullying literature (e.g., Aoyama et al., 2012; Li, 2008) generally have not been able to succeed in explaining which cultural features account for the variance in cyberbullying between samples from different cultural backgrounds. The authors frequently explained the differences as the result of demographic variables (e.g., Aoyama et al., 2012) or variances in Internet and mobile

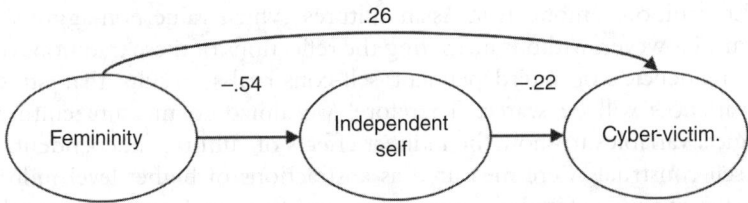

Figure 9.3 The mediator role of independent self-construal between femininity and cybervictimization. *Note*: All standardized coefficients were significant ($p < .01$).

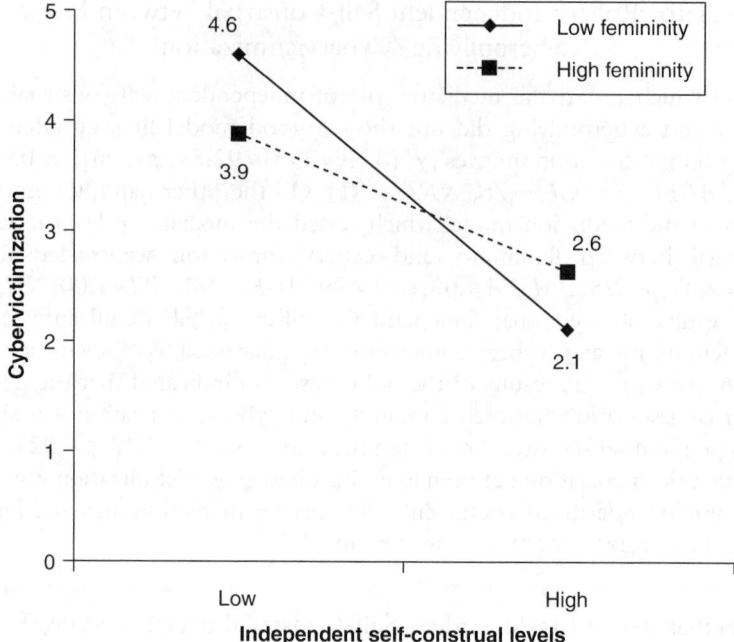

Figure 9.4 The moderator role of independent self-construal between femininity and cybervictimization.

phone penetration (e.g., Li, 2008). Although these explanations are not false, it was interesting that these authors did not try to explain the differences from a cross-cultural perspective. To the best of our knowledge, only one study (i.e., Shapka & Law, 2013; see above) explained the differences of prevalence in cyberbullying between East Asian and European adolescents by taking culture into account. However, the interpretations were indirect because the authors did not measure culture-related variables (e.g., individualistic/collectivistic tendencies) among the participants. Also, all participants were living in the same region (Lower Mainland of British Columbia) and the role of acculturation was not assessed.

Despite the aforementioned limitations of cross-cultural studies in cyberbullying literature, it is critical to note that East Asian samples in all of the studies mentioned above showed less cyberbullying than their Western counterparts. In fact, these results parallel findings in the literature on general aggression, where it has been shown that East Asian adolescents exhibit a lower level of aggressive behavior than European ones (Kornadt, 2000). Kornadt (2002) explains these differences as the result of Confucian and Taoist traditions among East Asian cultures, which value non-aggressive social interactions. However, without measuring the reflections of these traditions (e.g., collectivistic tendencies or interdependent self-construals), results that stress cross-cultural variances will be scarce. Therefore, we aimed to measure culture-related psychological variables to show the indirect effects of culture. Independent, interdependent self-construals were measured as abstractions of higher-level individualism and collectivism values. Similarly, masculinity and femininity were measured as individual-level abstractions of cultural-level constructs. In contrast with existing findings, we hypothesized that independent self-construal as the individual-level reflection of individualistic cultures would be related with less cyberbullying and cybervictimization, by following the literature. Another individual-level reflection of culture (i.e., masculinity–femininity) was hypothesized to be associated with cyberbullying (masculinity) and cybervictimization (femininity).

The results revealed that the mediating/moderating role of independent self-construal between masculinity and cyberbullying was not significant. This result can arise from the link between independent self-construal and masculinity (Cross & Madson, 1997a; Kim, 1994; Nyman, 1997). In other words, independent self-construal was not found to be a protective factor between masculinity and cyberbullying because the association between the protective factor (i.e., independent self-construal) and the risk factor (i.e., masculinity) was positive.

On the other hand, independent self-construal had a significant mediator and moderator role between femininity and cybervictimization. In other words, people with stronger independent self-construals were cyberbullied less, even when they had feminine tendencies. As mentioned before, independent self-construal is the independent view of self as being unique, autonomous, and separate from the social context (Markus & Kitayama, 1991). On the other hand, femininity is characterized by warmth, sensitivity, nurturing, and interdependence (Maccoby, 1998; Young & Sweeting, 2004). Considering these traits in individuals, according to our results, it seems that independent self-construal can be a protective factor, while femininity is a risk factor for cybervictimization.

This study did not focus on the mediator–moderator role of interdependent self-construal and the associations between masculinity and cybervictimization and femininity and cyberbullying simply for practical reasons. Femininity and cyberbullying, in particular, can be associated via the well-known connection between relational bullying and femininity (Card et al., 2008) and the conceptualization of cyberbullying as a specific form of indirect bullying (Hemphill et al., 2012; Li et al., 2012). Future studies must examine these untested models to enrich the literature.

The findings can be used as a basis for cross-cultural and cross-national studies by bearing the strong associations between individual- and cultural-level variables in mind. Therefore our study can be evaluated as a step toward understanding cross-cultural and cross-national variances in cyberbullying phenomena.

Acknowledgments

The author acknowledges the support of the project VITOVIN (CZ.1.07/2.3.00/20.0184) and Employment of Newly Graduated Doctors of Science for Scientific Excellence (CZ.1.07/2.3.00/30.0009), which are co-financed by the European Social Fund and the state budget of the Czech Republic.

References

Aiken, L. S., & West, S. G. (1991). *Multiple regression: Testing and interpreting interactions.* Newbury Park, CA: Sage.

Aoyama, I., Utsumi, S., & Hasegawa, M. (2012). Cyberbullying in Japan: Cases, government reports, adolescent relational aggression, and parental monitoring roles. In Q. Li,

D. Cross, & P. K. Smith (Eds.), *Cyberbullying in the global playground: Research from international perspectives.* Oxford, UK: Wiley Blackwell.

Aricak, T., Siyahnan, S., Uzunhasanoglu, A., Saribeyoglu, S., Ciplak, S., & Yilmaz, N. (2008). Cyberbullying among Turkish adolescents. *CyberPsychology and Behavior, 11,* 253–261.

Bandalos, D. L. (2002). The effects of item parceling on goodness-of-fit and parameter estimate bias in structural equation modeling. *Structural Equation Modeling, 9*(1), 78–102.

Bandalos, D. L., & Finney, S. J. (2001). Item parceling issues in structural equation modeling. In G. A. Marcoulides & R. E. Schumacker (Eds.), *New developments and techniques in structural equation modeling* (pp. 269–296). Mahwah, NJ: Lawrence Erlbaum Associates.

Bauman, S. (2012). Cyberbullying in the United States. In Q. Li, D. Cross, & P. K. Smith (Eds.), *Cyberbullying in the global playground: Research from international perspectives.* Oxford, UK: Wiley Blackwell.

Bem, S. L. (1981). *Bem Sex Role Inventory: Professional manual.* Palo Alto, CA: Consulting Psychologists Press.

Beran, T., & Li, Q. (2005). Cyber-harassment: A new method for an old behavior. *Journal of Educational Computing Research, 32,* 265–277.

Breslau, N., Chilcoat, H. D., Kessler, R. C., Peterson, E. L., & Lucia, V. C. (1999). Vulnerability to assaultive violence: Further speculation of the sex difference in post-traumatic stress disorder. *Psychological Medicine, 29,* 813–821.

Browne, M. W., & Cudeck, R. (1992). Alternative ways of assessing model fit. *Sociological Methods and Research, 21,* 230–258.

Burton, P., & Mutongwizo, T. (2009). Inescapable violence: Cyberbullying and electronic violence against young people in South Africa. *Center for Justice and Crime Prevention Issue Paper, 8,* 1–12.

Calmaestra, J., Ortega, R., Maldonado, A., & Mora-Merchán, J. A. (2010). Exploring cyber-bullying in Spain. In J. A. Mora-Merchán, A. Joaquín, & T. Jäger (Eds.), *Cyberbullying: A cross national comparison* (pp. 146–162). Landau, Germany: Verlag Empirische Pädagogik.

Campbell, M. (2010). Editorial: Research on cyberbullying. *Australian Journal of Guidance and Counselling, 20,* iii–iv.

Card, N. A., Stucky, B. D., Sawalani, G. M., & Little, T. D. (2008). Direct and indirect aggression during childhood and adolescence: A meta-analytic review of intercorrelations, gender differences, and relations to maladjustment. *Child Development, 79,* 1185–1229.

Cetin, B., Eroglu, Y., Peker, A., Akbaba, S., & Pepsoy, S. (2012). The investigation of relationship among relational-interdependent self-construal, cyberbullying, and psychological disharmony in adolescents: An investigation of structural equation modeling. *Educational Sciences: Theory and Practice, 12,* 646–653.

Conger, R. D., Conger, K. J., & Elder, G. H. (1997). Family economic hardship and adolescent academic performance: Mediating and moderating processes. In G. Duncan & J. Brooks-Gunn (Eds.), *Consequences of growing up poor* (pp. 228–310). New York, NY: Russell Sage Foundation.

Cowie, H. (2009). Tackling cyberbullying: A cross-cultural comparison. *International Journal of Emotional Education, 1,* 3–13.

Craig, W., Harel-Fisch, Y., Fogel-Grinvald, H., Dostaler, S., Hetland, J., Simons-Morton, B., … HBSC Bullying Writing Group. (2009). A cross-national profile of bullying and victimization among adolescents in 40 countries. *International Journal of Public Health, 54,* S216–S224.

Craig, W. M., & Peppler, D. J. (1995). Peer processes in bullying and victimization on the playground. *Canadian Journal of School Psychology, 2,* 41–60.

Cross, D., Li, Q., Smith, P. K., & Monks, H. (2012). Understanding and preventing cyberbullying. In Q. Li, D. Cross, & P. K. Smith (Eds.), *Cyberbullying in the global playground: Research from international perspectives.* Oxford, UK: Wiley Blackwell.

Cross, S. E., Bacon, P. L., & Morris, M. L. (2000). The relational interdependent self-construal and relationships. *Journal of Personality and Social Psychology, 78,* 791–808.

Cross, S. E., & Madson, L. (1997a). Models of the self: Self-construals and gender. *Psychological Bulletin, 122,* 5–37.

Cross, S. E., & Madson, L. (1997b). Elaboration of models of the self: Reply to Baumeister and Sommer (1997) and Martin and Ruble (1997). *Psychological Bulletin, 122,* 51–55.

d'Haenens, L. (2012, November). *Vulnerability and on-line resilience among children across Europe.* Paper presented at Cyberspace 2012, Brno, Czech Republic.

d'Haenens, L., Koeman, J., & Saeys, F. (2007). Digital citizenship among ethnic minority youths in the Netherlands and Flanders. *New Media and Society, 9,* 278–299.

Dilmac, B. (2009). Psychological needs as a predictor of cyberbullying: A preliminary report on college students. *Educational Sciences: Theory and Practice, 9,* 1307–1325.

Dooley, J. J., Pyżalski, J., & Cross, D. (2009). Cyberbullying vs. face-to-face bullying. *Zeitschrift für Psychologie/Journal of Psychology, 217,* 182–188.

Gardner, W. L., Gabriel, S., & Lee, A. Y. (1999). "I" value freedom, but "We" value relationships: Self-construal priming mirrors cultural differences in judgment. *Psychological Science, 10,* 321–326.

Garmezy, N., Masten, A. S., & Tellegen, A. (1984). The study of stress and competence in children: A building block for developmental psychopathology. *Child Development, 55,* 97–111.

Genta, M. L., Smith, P. K., Ortega, R., Brighi, A., Guarini, A., Thompson, F., … Calmaestra, J. (2012). Comparative aspects of cyberbullying in Italy, England, and Spain. In Q. Li, D. Cross, & P. K. Smith (Eds.), *Cyberbullying in the global playground: Research from international perspectives.* Oxford, UK: Wiley Blackwell.

Gini, G., & Pozzoli, T. (2006). The role of masculinity in children's bullying. *Sex Roles, 54,* 585–588.

Görzig, A., & Ólafsson, K. (2012). What makes a bully a cyberbully? Unravelling the characteristics of cyberbullies across twenty-five European countries. *Journal of Children and Media, 7*(1), 9–27.

Gradinger, P., Strohmeier, D., & Spiel, C. (2009). Traditional bullying and cyberbullying: Identification of risk groups for adjustment problems. *Zeitschrift für Psychologie/Journal of Psychology, 217,* 205–213.

Green, E. G. T., Deschamps, J. C., & Paez, D. (2005). Variation of individualism and collectivism within and between 20 countries. *Journal of Cross-Cultural Psychology, 36,* 321–339.

Gribbons, B. C., & Hocevar, D. (1998). Levels of aggregation in higher level confirmatory factor analysis: Application for self-concept. *Structural Equation Modeling, 5,* 377–390.

Gross, J. L., & Rayner, S. (1985). *Measuring culture: A paradigm for the analysis of social organization.* New York, NY: Columbia University Press.

Gudykunst, W. B., Matsumoto, Y., Ting-Toomey, S., Nishida, T., Kim, K., & Heyman, S. (1996). The influence of cultural individualism–collectivism, self construals, and individual values on communication styles across cultures. *Human Communication Research, 22,* 510–413.

Hasebrink, U., Livingstone, S., Haddon, L., & Ólafsson, K. (2009). *Comparing children's online opportunities and risks across Europe: Cross-national comparisons for EU Kids Online* (2nd ed.). LSE, London, UK: EU Kids Online.

Hemphill, S. A., Kotevski, A., Tollit, M., Smith, R., Herrenkohl, T. I., Toumbourou, J. W., & Catalano, R. F. (2012). Longitudinal predictors of cyber and traditional bullying perpetration in Australian secondary school students. *Journal of Adolescent Health, 51,* 59–65.

Hetherington, E. M., Bridges, M., & Glendessa, M. I. (1998). What matters? What does not? Five perspectives on the association between marital transitions and children's adjustment. *American Psychologist, 53,* 167–184.

Hinduja, S., & Patchin, J. W. (2008). Cyberbullying: An exploratory analysis of factors related to offending and victimization. *Deviant Behaviour, 29,* 129–156.

Hofstede, G. (1984). *Culture's consequences* (abridged ed.). Thousand Oaks, CA: Sage.

Jöreskog, K. G., & Sörbom, D. (1993). *LISREL 8: Structural equation modeling with Simplis command language.* Hillsdale, NJ: Lawrence Erlbaum Associates.

Juvonen, J., & Gross, E. F. (2008). Extending the school grounds? Bullying experiences in cyberspace. *Journal of School Health, 78*, 496–505.

Kalmus, V., Runnel, P., & Siibak, A. (2009). Opportunities and benefits online. In S. Livingstone & L. Haddon (Eds.), *Kids online* (pp. 71–82). Bristol, UK: Policy Press.

Kashima, Y., Yamaguchi, S., Kim, U., Choi, S. C., Gelfand, M. J., & Yuki, M. (1995). Culture, gender, and self: A perspective from individualism-collectivism research. *Journal of Personality and Social Psychology, 69*, 925–937.

Kim, M. S. (1994). Cross-cultural comparisons of the perceived importance of conversational constraints. *Human Communication Research, 21*, 128–151.

Kirwil, L., & Lauris, Y. (2012). Experimenting with the self online: A risky opportunity. In S. Livingstone, L. Haddon, & A. Gorzig (Eds.), *Children, risk and safety on the Internet: Research and policy challenges in comparative perspective* (pp. 113–126). Bristol, UK: Policy Press.

Kornadt, H. J. (2000). Biology, culture and childrearing: The development of social motives. In H. Keller, Y. H. Poortinga, & A. Schälmerich (Eds.), *Between biology and culture: Perspectives on ontogenetic development* (pp. 191–211). Cambridge, UK: Cambridge University Press.

Kornadt, H. J. (2002). Social motives and their development in cultural context. *Online Readings in Psychology and Culture, 5*(3). http://dx.doi.org/10.9707/2307-0919.1048

Kowalski, R., & Limber, S. (2007). Electronic bullying among middle-school students. *Journal of Adolescent Health, 41*, S22–S30.

Lampert, C., & Donoso, V. (2012). Bullying. In S. Livingstone, L. Haddon, & A. Görzig (Eds.), *Children, risk and safety on the Internet: Research and policy challenges in comparative perspective* (pp. 141–149). Bristol, UK: Policy Press.

Lee, E. A. E., & Troop-Gordon, W. (2011). Peer socialization of masculinity and femininity: Differential effects of overt and relational forms of peer victimization. *British Journal of Developmental Psychology, 29*, 197–213.

Li, Q. (2007). New bottle but old wine: A research of cyberbullying in schools. *Computers in Human Behavior, 23*, 1777–1791.

Li, Q. (2008). A cross-cultural comparison of adolescents' experience related to cyberbullying. *Educational Research, 50*, 223–234.

Li, Q., Smith, P. K., & Cross, D. (2012). Research into cyberbullying context. In Q. Li, D. Cross, & P. K. Smith (Eds.), *Cyberbullying in the global playground: Research from international perspectives* (pp. 3–12). Oxford, UK: Wiley Blackwell.

Little, T. D., Cunningham, W. A., Shahar, G., & Widaman, K. F. (2002). To parcel or not to parcel: Exploring the question, weighing the merits. *Structural Equation Modeling, 9*, 151–173.

Livingstone, S., & Haddon, L. (2009). *EU Kids Online: Final report.* LSE, London, UK: EU Kids Online.

Livingstone, S., Haddon, L., Görzig, A., & Ólafsson, K. (2011). *Risks and safety on the Internet. The perspective of European children. Full findings.* London, UK: London School of Economics and Political Science.

Livingstone, S., & Helsper, E. (2007). Gradation in digital inclusion: Children, young people and the digital divide. *New Media and Society, 9*, 671–696.

Lu, L., & Gilmour, R. (2007). Developing a new measure of independent and interdependent views of the self. *Journal of Research in Personality, 41*, 249–257.

Luthar, S. S., Cicchetti, D., & Becker, B. (2000). The construct of resilience: A critical evaluation and guidelines for future work. *Child Development, 71*, 543–562.

Maccoby, E. E. (1998). *The two sexes: Growing up apart, coming together.* Cambridge, MA: Belknap Press/Harvard University Press.

Markus, H. R., & Kitayama, S. (1991). Culture and the self: Implication for cognition, emotion, and motivation. *Psychological Review, 98,* 224–253.

Masten, A. (2001). Ordinary magic: Resilience processes in development. *American Psychologist, 56,* 227–238.

Masten, A. S., & Coatsworth, J. D. (1995). Competence, resilience, and psychopathology. In D. Cicchetti & D. Cohen (Eds.), *Developmental psychopathology. Vol. 2: Risk, disorder, and adaptation* (pp. 715–752). New York, NY: John Wiley & Sons.

Menesini, E. (2012). *Report of Working Group 1 of COST Action IS0801.* Joint Conference of Bullying and Cyberbullying: The Interface Between Science and Practice, Vienna, Austria.

Moodley, I. (2012). Cyberbullying: A legal framework for South African educators. *SA Publiekreg-SA Public Law, 27,* 539–558.

Mora-Merchán, J. A., Del Rey, R., & Jäger, T. (2010). Cyberbullying: Review of an emergent issue. In J. A. Mora-Merchán, A. Joaquín, & T. Jäger (Eds.), *Cyberbullying: A cross national comparison* (pp. 271–281). Landau, Germany: Verlag Empirische Pädagogik.

Mora-Merchán, J. A., & Ortega-Ruiz, R. (2007). The new forms of school bullying and violence. In R. Ortega, J. A. Mora-Merchán, & T. Jäger (Eds.), *Acting against school bullying and violence: The role of media, local authorities and the Internet* (pp. 7–34). Retrieved November 26, 2014, from http://iamnotscared.pixel-online.org/data/database/publications/618_Acting_against_school_bullying_and_violence.pdf

Morita, Y., Soeda, H., Soeda, K., & Taki, M. (1999). Japan. In P. K. Smith, Y. Morita, J. Junger-Tas, D. Olweus, R. Catalano, & P. Slee (Eds.), *The nature of school bullying: A cross-national perspective* (pp. 309–323). London, UK: Routledge.

Nabuzoka, D. (2003). Experiences of bullying-related behaviours by English and Zambian pupils: A comparative study. *Educational Research, 45,* 95–109.

Nansel, T. R., Craig, W., Overpeck, M. D., Saluja, G., & Ruan, J. (2004). Cross-national consistency in the relationship between bullying behaviors and psychosocial adjustment. *Archives of Pediatric Adolescent Medicine, 158,* 730–736.

Nocentini, A., Calmaestra, J., Schultze-Krumbholz, A., Scheithauer, H., Ortega, R., & Menesini, E. (2010). Cyberbullying: Labels, behaviours and definition in three European countries. *Australian Journal of Guidance and Counselling, 20,* 129–142.

Nyman, J. (1997). *Men alone: Masculinity, individualism, and hard-boiled fiction.* Amsterdam, the Netherlands: Editions Rodopi B.V.

Oetzel, J. G. (1998). Explaining individual communication processes in homogeneous and heterogeneous groups through individualism–collectivism and self-construal. *Human Communication Research, 25,* 202–224.

Olweus, D. (2012). Cyberbullying: An overrated phenomenon? *European Journal of Developmental Psychology, 9*(5), 520–538.

Ortega, R., Calmaestra, J., & Mora-Merchán, J. A. (2008). *Cuestionario cyberbullying.* Cordoba, Spain: Universidad de Córdoba.

Phillips, D. A. (2007). Punking and bullying: Strategies in middle school, high school and beyond. *Journal of Interpersonal Violence, 22,* 158–178.

Realo, A. (1998). Collectivism in an individualist culture: The case of Estonia. *Trames, 2,* 19–39.

Ross, M. W. (1983). Femininity, masculinity and sexual orientation: Some cross-cultural comparison. *Journal of Homosexuality, 9,* 27–36.

Salmivalli, C., & Pöyhönen, V. (2012). Cyberbullying in Finland. In Q. Li, D. Cross, & P. K. Smith (Eds.), *Cyberbullying in the global playground: Research from international perspectives* (pp. 57–72). Oxford, UK: Wiley Blackwell.

Salmivalli, C., Lagerspetz, K., Bjorkqvist, K., Osterman, K., & Kaukianien, A. (1996). Bullying as a group process: Participant roles and their relations to social status within the group. *Aggressive Behavior, 22,* 1–15.

Shapka, J. D., & Law, D. M. (2013). Does one size fit all? Ethnic differences in parenting behaviors and motivations for adolescent engagement in cyberbullying. *Journal of Youth and Adolescence, 42*, 723–738.

Singelis, T. M. (1994). The measurement of independent and interdependent self-construals. *Personality and Social Psychology Bulletin, 20*, 580–591.

Slonje, R., & Smith, P. K. (2008). Cyberbullying: Another main type of bullying? *Scandinavian Journal of Psychology, 49*, 147–154.

Slonje, R., Smith, P. K., & Frisén, A. (2013). The nature of cyberbullying, and strategies for prevention. *Computers in Human Behavior, 29*(1), 26–32.

Smith, P. (2004). Bullying: Recent developments. *Child and Adolescent Mental Health, 9*, 98–103.

Smith, P., & Brain, P. (2000). Bullying in schools: Lessons from two decades of research. *Aggressive Behavior, 26*, 1–9.

Smith, P. K., Cowie, H., Ólafsson, R. F., & Liefooghe, A. P. D. (2002). Definitions of bullying: A comparison of terms used, and age and gender differences, in a fourteen-country international comparison. *Child Development, 73*(4), 1119–1133.

Smith, P. K., Mahdavi, J., Carvalho, M., Fisher, S., Russell, S., & Tippett, N. (2008). Cyberbullying: Its nature and impact in secondary school pupils. *Journal of Child Psychology and Psychiatry, 49*(4), 376–385.

Spector, P. E., Cooper, C. L., & Sparks, K. (2001). An international study of the psychometric properties of the Hofstede Values Survey Module 1994: A comparison of individual and country/province level results. *Applied Psychology: An International Review, 50*, 269–281.

Stald, G., & Ólaffson, K. (2012). Mobile access: Different users, different risks, different consequences? In S. Livingstone, L. Haddon, & A. Gorzig (Eds.), *Children, risk and safety on the Internet: Research and policy challenges in comparative perspective* (pp. 285–296). Bristol, UK: Policy Press.

Suh, E., Diener, E., Oishi, S., & Triandis, H. C. (1998). The shifting basis of life satisfaction judgments across cultures: Emotions versus norms. *Journal of Personality and Social Psychology, 74*, 482–493.

Takahashi, T., & Nasser, F. (1996). The impact of using item parcels on ad hoc goodness of fit indices in confirmatory factor analysis: An empirical example. *American Educational Research Association*, April 1996, New York, NY.

Thompson, B., & Melancon, J. G. (1996). *Using item "Testlest"/"Parcels" in confirmatory factor analysis: An example using the PPSDQ-78*. (ERIC Document No. ED 404349).

Tippett, N., & Kwak, K. (2012). Cyberbullying in South Korea. In Q. Li, D. Cross, & P. K. Smith (Eds.), *Cyberbullying in the global playground: Research from international perspectives*. Oxford, UK: Wiley Blackwell.

Tokunaga, R. S. (2010). Following you home from school: A critical review and synthesis of research on cyberbullying victimization. *Computers in Human Behavior, 26*, 277–287.

Topçu, Ç., & Erdur-Baker, Ö. (2010). The Revised Cyberbullying Inventory (RCBI): Validity and reliability studies. *Procedia: Social and Behavioral Sciences, 5*, 660–664.

Välimäki, M., Almeida, A., Cross, D., O'Moore, M., Berne, S., Deboutte, G., … Sygkollitou, E. (2012). *Guidelines for preventing cyber-bullying in the school environment: A review and recommendations*. Booklet of Working Group 3 of COST Action IS0801 addressing Cyber-bullying. Retrieved November 26, 2014, from https://sites.google.com/site/costis0801/guideline

van der Hof, S., & Koops, B. J. (2012). Adolescents and cybercrime: Navigating between freedom and control. *Policy and Internet, 3*, 1–28.

Walrave, M., & Heirman, W. (2010). Towards understanding the potential triggering features of technology. In S. Shariff & A. H. Churchill (Eds.), *Truths and myths of cyber-bullying: International perspectives on stakeholder responsibility and children's safety*. New York, NY: Peter Lang.

Wolak, J., Mitchell, K. J., & Finkelhor, D. (2007). Does online harassment constitute bullying? An exploration of online harassment by known peers and online-only contacts. *Journal of Adolescent Health, 41*, 851–858.

Wong, F. Y., McCreary, D., & Duffy, K. G. (1990). A further validation of the Bem Sex Role Inventory: A multi-trait multi-method study. *Sex Roles, 22*, 249–259.

World Internet Usage and Population Statistics. (2012). Retrieved November 26, 2014, from http://www.internetworldstats.com/stats.htm

Ybarra, M. (2009). *Cyberbullying: Definition and measurement issues.* Paper presented at the COST Action IS0801, Vilnius, Lithuania.

Ybarra, M., Mitchell, K. J., & Lenhart, A. (2010). Cyberbullying research in the United States. In J. A. Mora-Merchán, A. Joaquín, & T. Jäger (Eds.), *Cyberbullying: A cross national comparison* (pp. 255–268). Landau, Germany: Verlag Empirische Pädagogik.

Yoshihisa, K., Susumu, Y., Uichol, K., Sang-Chin, C., Michele, G. J., & Masaki, Y. (1995). Culture, gender, and self: A perspective from individualism–collectivism research. *Journal of Personality and Social Psychology, 69*, 925–937.

Young, R., & Sweeting, H. (2004). Adolescent bullying, relationships, psychological well-being, and gender-atypical behavior: A gender diagnosticity approach. *Sex Roles, 50*, 525–537.

10

Sexual Communication in the Digital Age

Michelle Drouin

Indiana University–Purdue University

Not long ago, written correspondence was time-delayed. Messages were carried by pigeon, horse, ship, truck, or plane, finally landing into the hands of a person who may have been waiting anxiously for days, weeks, or even months. Some of these messages were romantic or sexual in nature, and a quick Internet search will yield countless examples of classic love letters written by famous writers such as Cicero, Oscar Wilde, and Ernest Hemingway. Romantics among us might reflect fondly on those times – when love letters were laden with anticipation and gratification came only after some delay.

Today, most love messages bear little resemblance to the love letters of yore. Communicating love or lust for another might take as little as a few seconds (counting the time from when one one begins to compose a message to the time it lands in the recipient's inbox), poetic musings have been supplanted by sentiments such as "Show me ur bra," and pigeons and horses have been replaced by text messages, Facebook, Twitter, Snapchat, instant messaging, and email. In the wake of this phenomenon, a growing body of empirical work has emerged focused on sexting, or the transmission of sexually explicit material via text or Internet messages. These studies have examined the prevalence of sexting and the personality and relationship characteristics and risk factors that are associated with this behavior. This chapter will summarize the research findings to date and will also highlight some of the exciting new directions in sexting research.

Sexual Communication via Modern-day Technologies

In the current landscape of interpersonal communication, text messaging and social networking platforms prevail, especially among teens and young adults (e.g., Lenhart, 2012; Lenhart, Ling, Campbell, & Purdell, 2010; Smith, 2012; Smith, 2014). Approximately 80% of Americans send text messages (Duggan & Rainie, 2012), and they send or receive an average of 41.5 text messages per day (Smith, 2012). Meanwhile, Facebook and Twitter are the most popular social networks worldwide, with 1.15 billion and 500 million users, respectively (Smith, 2012). Not surprisingly,

The Wiley Handbook of Psychology, Technology, and Society, First Edition. Edited by Larry D. Rosen, Nancy A. Cheever, and L. Mark Carrier.

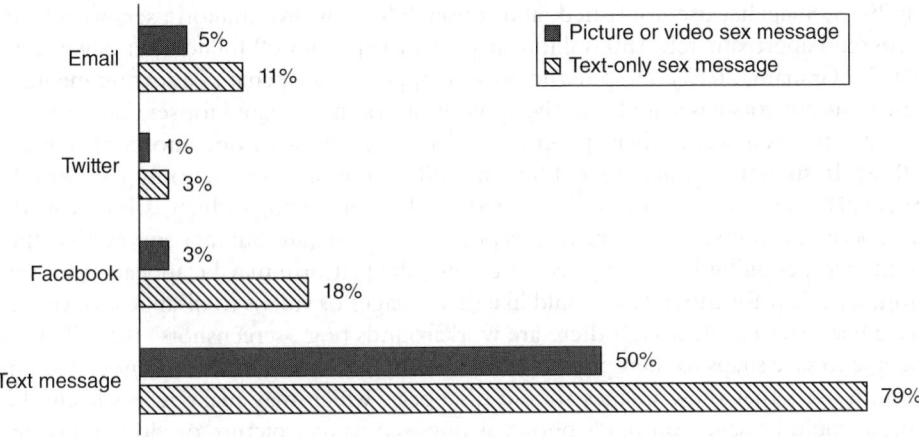

Figure 10.1 Percentage of those who had ever sent sex text-only or sex pictures or videos to committed partners via email, Twitter, Facebook, or text message.

considering their prominent role in interpersonal communication, each of these mediums (text messaging, Facebook, and Twitter) has been cited for its role in sexual communication. For example, several years ago, media sources brought attention to Facebook and Twitter as mediums for sexual communication when a U.S. congressman tweeted a picture of himself in his underwear (e.g., Canning & Hopper, 2011). Notably, despite this media attention, Facebook and Twitter do not appear to be the most popular mediums for sexual communication in the United States. Instead, the medium of choice appears to be text messaging, at least among young adults. In a recent study of 253 undergraduates, we found that most participants who sent sexually explicit text or picture or video messages to their relationship partners did so through text message, rather than Facebook, Twitter, or email (Drouin, Vogel, Surbey, & Stills, 2013). Figure 10.1 shows the frequency of use of the different mediums to send sexting messages to committed partners; these distributions are similar to what was found with other types of romantic relationships (i.e., casual sex partners and cheating partners) (Drouin et al., 2013).

Although text messaging was the primary medium for exchanging sexual messages among the young adults in the Drouin et al. (2013) study, clearly, other mediums were also used. Therefore, studies that limit their sexting questions to only messages sent via cell phones may not be capturing the full scope of sexting behaviors. Moreover, researchers studying sexting (as well as parents and educators) should also be aware that new applications have surfaced that might be particularly suited for this type of communication.

Imagine that you could send a sexual text or picture message and then have it disappear after a few seconds. This might be especially appealing to those who want to ensure that their messages are not forwarded beyond the original recipient or kept indefinitely on someone's phone or computer. Luckily for these people, such technology now exists in the form of the instant messaging application Snapchat. Pictures or short videos sent through Snapchat disappear within seconds; the actual disappearance time depends on the sender, who sets a vanishing timer of up to 10 seconds.

In 2013, Snapchat use flourished, and it now has about five million users worldwide who send approximately 150 million snaps daily (up from 60 million per day in early 2013) (Graham, 2013). Despite the obvious appeal of Snapchat as a sexting medium, one of its creators has stated that the application was not created for sexting; rather, it was created as a space where people could just be silly with one another (Graham, 2013). In support of this, a recent Survata (2013) poll showed that only 13.1% of the Snapchat users they surveyed ($N = 715$) used it for sexting, which is less than the 26.5% of text messaging users who reported in a separate Survata survey that they used text messaging for sexting. Nevertheless, the platform may be appealing for sexting, especially for those who would like their images or videos to disappear once they have been viewed. Although there are workarounds (e.g., screenshots) that allow for people to save snaps to their phones (Graham, 2013), there may be an understanding among users that these images should disappear, which may make it less likely that snaps would be saved on one's phone as opposed to text picture or video messages. As Snapchat and other applications with privacy features become more prevalent, it will be worthwhile for researchers to explore the ways in which people interact sexually on these platforms.

Prevalence of Sexting

Early research into the sexting phenomenon focused mainly on the prevalence of sexting (e.g., Associated Press & MTV, 2009; Lenhart, 2009; National Campaign to Prevent Teen and Unplanned Pregnancy, 2008). More recent studies have focused mostly on the correlates of sexting (e.g., psychological and relationship characteristics, and risk factors); however, nearly all sexting research provides some information about its prevalence. As shown in Table 10.1, there is some variability in the prevalence of sexting across studies, but there is also a consistent pattern: more young adults than preteens and teens have reported that they have engaged in sexting. These results are not surprising when one considers the sharp rise in overall sexual activity that happens during the teenage years. For example, only about 6% of teenagers have had sex by the age of 15, but this number rises to 71% by the time a person reaches 19 (Guttmacher Institute, 2013). As sexting appears to be part of the repertoire of sexual experience (Drouin & Tobin, 2014), it would be expected that sexting activity would rise as sexual experience rises. However, we have little data on the sexting experiences of older and/or married adults, as most studies have focused on youth and unmarried young adults. Therefore, it would be useful to examine sexting behaviors and motivations among older and/or married individuals; this is a promising direction for future research.

Despite the consistent pattern of young adults engaging in more sexting than preteens and teens, there is some variability on the reported prevalence of sexting within each age group (see Table 10.1). This is likely due to variance in the descriptions of sexting and methodologies across studies (Drouin et al., 2013; Lounsbury, Mitchell, & Finkelhor, 2011; Mitchell, Finkelhor, Jones, & Wolak, 2012). To increase comparability across studies, recent researchers have emphasized the need for more detail within sexting studies, focusing on the different types of content contained in sexting messages as well as the relationship contexts in which these messages are sent (Drouin et al., 2013; Mitchell et al., 2012).

Table 10.1 Summary of findings for sexting prevalence statistics in youth/teen and adult samples.

Study	Sample	Prevalence	Other correlates or findings
Associated Press & MTV (2009)	1,247 teens and young adults from an online panel (aged 14–24)	24% of 14- to 17-year-olds and 33% of 18- to 24-year-olds had been involved in naked sexting. 29% reported receiving messages "with sexual words or images."	Sexual activity in last week and being sexually active related to sexting; 17% had forwarded images they received and 55% of this group forwarded images to more than one person.
Cox Communications (2009)	655 teens (aged 13–18) recruited online	19% of teens had engaged in (sent, received, or forwarded) sexting involving nude or nearly nude images; 12% of girls and 6% of boys had sent a sext message.	Most sext messages were sent to boyfriends or girlfriends in response to requests or to have fun. Approximately 1 in 10 had sent sext messages to a person they "don't know."
Dake et al. (2012)	6th to 12th graders in the Midwest (aged 12–18)	17% had engaged in sexting, ranging from 3% of 12-year-olds to 32% of 18-year-olds.	Significant relationships with sexual behaviors, substance abuse, poorer emotional health, and time texting.
Fleschler Peskin et al. (2013)	1,034 minority 10th graders (43% Black, 57% Hispanic) from an urban Texas school	21.2% had sent a nude or semi-nude picture/video to someone; 31% had received a nude or semi-nude picture.	Images do get shared: 8.8% shared a nude or semi-nude image with someone it was not intended for; 18.2% had such an image shared with them.
Lenhart (2009)	800 teens aged 12–17	4% had sent a nude or semi-nude suggestive image of themselves; 15% had received such an image; 8% of 17-year-olds sent a sexually suggestive image via text vs. 4% of 12-year-olds.	Sexting more frequent among older teens. No gender differences in frequency of sending a sexually suggestive picture. Sexting more frequent between couples or between friends or those who want to be romantically involved. Sexts can be forwarded.
National Campaign to Prevent Teen and Unplanned Pregnancy (2008)	1,280 teens aged 13–19	20% had sent or posted nude or semi-nude pictures or videos.	Sexting more frequent between couples or between those who want to be romantically involved. 15–25% sent sext messages to someone they only knew online.

(continued on pg. 180)

Table 10.1 (Continued)

Study	Sample	Prevalence	Other correlates or findings
Benotsch et al. (2013)	763 young adult undergraduates (aged 18–25)in the mid-Atlantic	44% reported having engaged in sexting. Of sexters, 62% received and sent at least one image, 32% received only, and 6% had sent a sexual image only.	Significant relationships with sexual and substance abuse risk factors as well as overall texting.
Delevi & Weisskirch (2013)	304 undergraduates (aged 18–30) on the West Coast	75.7% sent a text-only sext message; 67.4% sent sexual propositions; 45.7% sent a photo sext message; 43.7% sent a photo in underwear, and 28.9% sent a nude photo of themselves.	Men engage in more sexting of various types than women. Extraversion, neuroticism, low agreeableness, and problematic phone use associated with sexting.
Dir, Coskunpinar, et al. (2013)	278 undergraduates (aged 18–43) in the Midwest	67.4% had sent sext text messages, and 46.6% had sent sext pictures.	Sexting expectancies (positive and negative) influence sexting behavior. Gender, race, sexual identity, and relationship status influence sexting expectancies and behaviors.
Drouin & Landgraff (2012)	744 undergraduates (aged 18–36) in the Midwest who had been in a committed relationship	67% had sent sexually explicit word-only texts, and 54% had sent sexually explicit pictures or videos to relationship partners.	Anxious attachment associated with sending sex word-only texts; avoidant attachment associated with sending sex pictures or videos, especially among men.
Drouin et al. (2013)	253 young adult undergraduates (aged 18–26) in the Midwest	55–78% of individuals had sent sex texts and 37–49% had sent sex pictures or videos, depending on relationship type.	Motivations for sending sext pictures or videos were flirtation, partner request, and desire to initiate sex. Less explicit content (e.g., partially nude) was more common. 26% to 52% feared image would be forwarded, 3% to 21% did forward, depending on relationship type.
Gordon-Messer et al. (2013)	3,447 young adults (aged 18–24) in the U.S. recruited via respondent-driven sampling	28.2% both sent (of themselves) and received (of someone else) sexually suggestive nude or nearly nude photo or videos on their cell phones; 12.6% were receivers only, and 2% were senders only.	Lifetime sexual activity related to sexting. Recent sexual activity was associated with sexting, but for those who had been active in last 30 days, there was no relationship between sexting activity and number of partners or proportion of unprotected anal or vaginal sex partners. Sexting often reciprocal.

Content of Sext Messages

The descriptions of sexting behavior have varied somewhat across studies. Researchers have used terms such as "sexually suggestive," "nude or nearly/partially nude" (e.g., Gordon-Messer et al., 2013; Lenhart, 2009; National Campaign to Prevent Teen and Unplanned Pregnancy, 2008; Weisskirch & Delevi, 2011), "naked" (AP & MTV, 2009), "erotic or nude" (Ferguson, 2011), and "sexually explicit" (Drouin & Landgraff, 2012; Rice et al., 2012). Meanwhile, in their 11-item Sexual Behaviors Scale (Dir, Coskunpinar, Steiner, & Cyders, 2013; Dir, Steiner, Coskunpinar, & Cyders, 2013), Dir and colleagues use the term "sexually provocative" to describe the sext texts and pictures people send and receive via mobile phone or Internet social networking sites. Other researchers have not provided a definition, instead just referring to the behavior as sexting (e.g., Dake, Price, Maziarz, & Ward, 2012). Therefore, a recent goal of sexting research has been to distinguish between different types of content contained in sext messages.

One of the first studies with this goal focused on a sample of youth aged 10–17 (Mitchell et al., 2012). Of the 2.5% of youth who had sent a sexual image in the past year that they appeared in or created, 54% had sent images that featured someone's breasts, genitals, or bottom, and 26% sent images that were completely nude (Mitchell et al., 2012). Meanwhile, of the 7.1% of the youth who had *received* a sexual message in the past year, 84% indicated that the images featured someone's breasts, genitals, or bottom, and 53% indicated that they featured someone completely nude (Mitchell et al., 2012). For both categories of messages (sent and received) the top three categories of content were naked breasts, genitals, and completely nude.

More recently, Drouin et al. (2013) explored the content of sexting messages within a sample of young adult undergraduates. We focused on five types of content: sexually suggestive but clothed, nearly nude, nude, solo sex act (e.g., masturbation), and sex with another person. For those who had ever sent a sexual picture or video to any type of relationship partner (i.e., committed, casual sex, or cheating partner), 49% had sent a sexually suggestive but clothed picture or video, 65% had sent a nearly nude picture or video, 37% had sent a nude picture or video, and 19% sent a picture or video of themselves involved in a solo sex act (Drouin et al., 2013). Among all types of relationship partners, pictures or videos of sex with another person were sent very rarely (Drouin et al., 2013). Thus, overall, individuals were more likely to send less explicit sexual content via sext messaging. In their sample of undergraduates, Weisskirch and Delevi (2011) and Delevi and Weisskirch (2013) found a similar trend: individuals were more likely to send milder content (e.g., pictures in underwear) than more explicit content (e.g., fully nude).

At present, the trends in content are relatively similar in teens and young adults, with more individuals opting to send less explicit content over more explicit content. However, as new technologies emerge and sexuality norms and the role of technology in sexuality evolve, researchers will need to be cognizant of the factors that may influence the content that individuals exchange via the Internet and mobile phone.

Motivations for Engaging in Sexting

In terms of the motivations associated with sexting, researchers have primarily focused on attachment characteristics, personality factors, or other types of personal motivations (e.g., fun or partner request) for sexting behaviors. In two of the first studies to examine sexting and its correlates, Weisskirch and Delevi (2011) and Drouin and Landgraff (2012) explored the relationships between attachment style and sexting behaviors. Weisskirch and Delevi (2011) found that those high in attachment anxiety were more likely to solicit sexual activity via text message, but only when they were in the context of a relationship. Those high in attachment anxiety were also more likely to regard sexting in a positive way (e.g., believe that sexting would enhance the relationship and believe that their partners would expect sexting). As those who are anxiously attached have intense desires to be close to their partners and are likely to fear that their partners might leave them, the fact that they are using sexting as a means to engage their partners and enhance their relationships is unsurprising and corresponds to research suggesting that anxiously attached individuals use sex to gain reassurance from their partners (Davis, Shaver, & Vernon, 2004). Meanwhile, Drouin and Landgraff (2012) found that both anxious and avoidant attachment predicted the frequency of sending sexually explicit text-only messages within committed relationships, but only avoidant attachment was related to the frequency of sending sexually explicit pictures or videos. These relationships were significant among both men and women; however, avoidant men were more likely to send sexually explicit messages of both types than avoidant women (Drouin & Landgraff, 2012). Those high in avoidant attachment are more likely to fear intimacy, dependence, and self-disclosure and try to keep themselves independent from their partners. Therefore, for these individuals, sexting may provide a means of meeting sexual needs (their own and their partner's) without investing too much emotional energy.

With regard to the personality characteristics that are associated with sexting, Delevi and Weisskirch (2013) found that those high in extraversion and neuroticism and those low in agreeableness were more likely to engage in a variety of sexting behaviors, including sending sexually suggestive or nude photos or photos in underwear. Meanwhile, in their study of undergraduates, Dir, Cyders, and Coskunpinar (2013) found that sensation seeking and negative urgency (or an individual's tendency to act rashly when experiencing negative emotions) were related to sexting. In turn, sexting was related to engaging in real-world sexual hookups (i.e., unplanned, casual sexual encounters). Taken together, these studies suggest that those who are more outgoing and engage in more risk-taking behaviors are more likely to engage in sexting, which is somewhat unsurprising considering the inherent risks of sexting (e.g., forwarding, cyberbullying).

In terms of other motivations toward sexting, Weisskirch and Delevi (2011) and Dir, Coskunpinar, et al. (2013) examined attitudes toward sexting as a predictor of sexting behavior. Weisskirch and Delevi (2011) found that those with fun and carefree attitudes toward sexting were more likely to send sexual text messages of all types (e.g., in underwear, nude, etc.) whereas those who perceived more risk in the act were less likely, but not significantly so, to send sexual text messages (Weisskirch & Delevi, 2011). Additionally, those with higher relational expectations regarding sexting, including beliefs that a partner expects sexting messages and that it improves relationships, were more likely to send sexually suggestive word-only or photo messages, nude photos, and texts soliciting sexual activity (Weisskirch & Delevi, 2011). Dir, Coskunpinar, et al. (2013) had similar findings; those with high positive expectancies about sending and receiving sext messages (e.g., sexting or receiving makes one feel excited, adventurous, or sexy) were more likely to engage in sexting. In contrast, those with high negative expectancies about sending and receiving sext messages (e.g., sexting or receiving makes one feel guilty, dirty, or embarrassed) were significantly less likely to engage in sexting (Dir, Coskunpinar, et al., 2013).

Other researchers have used more direct questions about motivations toward sexting. In their youth sample, Mitchell et al. (2012) found that most of their respondents (51%) sent sexual text messages because it was a part of the romantic aspect of their relationship, and some others (23%) sent these messages as a prank or joke. Interestingly, despite the media reports of cyberbullying, none of the respondents reported sending sexual messages out of revenge, conflict, or bullying/harassment. Although these findings are encouraging, it is quite possible that the social desirability bias influenced responses on this measure. Nevertheless, Mitchell et al.'s (2012) study built upon previous research that showed that motivations for sending sext messages were usually for fun or flirtation, as a joke, or as a sexy present for a relationship partner (AP & MTV, 2009). Meanwhile, in a more recent study of adults aged 18–53, Parker, Blackburn, Perry, and Hawks (2013) found that among couples who engaged in sexting, the sexual motives of hedonism and intimacy were strongly related to sexting frequency with their relationship.

Overall, the motivations for sexting cannot be characterized as wholly positive or negative; instead it seems that there are some motivations for sexting that are associated with relationship or psychological health (e.g., because a person wants to have fun or engage a partner sexually) and some motivations that are associated with relationship weakness (e.g., because a person is neurotic or does not have a secure attachment to their partner). As this is an emerging field, more work on the topic is necessary in order to gain a better understanding of the reasons for which preteens, teens, and adults engage in sexting behavior. Moreover, because technological changes happen quickly and these changes may affect the ways in which people communicate sexually, it will be important to continually examine these issues for as long as sexting remains part of the sexual landscape.

Risk Factors Associated with Sexting

On its own, sexting poses a risk to those who engage in it. First, there are legal issues surrounding sexting, especially if the sexual images involve minors. The website of the National Conference of State Legislatures (http://www.ncsl.org/research/telecommunications-and-information-technology/2013-sexting-legislation.aspx) provides a summary of each state's sexting bills and legislature as of the end of 2013. Although few states have approved sexting legislation, a growing number of states have sexting bills that are at some point in the legislative process. These bills are aimed predominantly at minors and some include conditions for cyberbullying and sexting that occurs within schools. Sacco, Argudin, Maguire, and Tallon (2010) provide an overview of the constitutional and statutory frameworks that are relevant to sexting, focusing on child pornography and obscenity.

Related to this, another risk of sexting is the psychological harm and cyberbullying that might ensue if sexting images are circulated beyond the original recipient. Cases of cyberbullying have been highlighted in the media, and teenage girls have even killed themselves after they had been bullied about their sexting images (Meyer, 2009). Moreover, survey studies have shown that images often do get shared or forwarded beyond the original recipient (AP & MTV, 2009; Drouin et al., 2013; Fleschler Peskin et al., 2013). Even if they are sent within the context of committed relationships, sexually explicit pictures and videos are sometimes forwarded, but they are more likely to be forwarded in casual sexual and cheating relationships (Drouin et al., 2013).

In response to these direct risks, programs to curb sexting behavior, especially among teens, have been initiated in the United States and abroad. For example, in 2011, the Australian government created a Cybersmart program to educate Australian youth about the dangers of sexting, and there have also been several websites set up with the same agenda (Fisher, Sauter, Slobodniuk, & Young 2012). However, Fisher et al. (2012) suggested that in order to be effective the material in the programs needs to be more interesting and programs need to target younger audiences. Meanwhile, in a more recent initiative in the United Kingdom, teachers were given sexting advice guides that give information on how to deal with sexting cases within the schools (Press Association, 2013). This is in line with Ringrose, Gill, Livingstone, and Harvey's (2012) recommendation that teachers be given lesson plans to address sexting issues. Ringrose et al. (2012) also recommended that students be given resources so that they can address sexting issues with their peers and parents have access to web-based education resources. All of these recommendations were based on a review of the literature and on their interviews with a small group of 8- to 10-year-olds in inner-city London schools (Ringrose et al., 2012). In the United States, many sexting programs have emerged in the past few years; a recent Google search for "sexting prevention" returned almost 500,000 hits. These sexting prevention efforts are usually organized by state or local governments or foundations concerned with child and teen welfare. According to Meyer (2009), schools may also play a big role in prevention, as students could be prosecuted under the sexual harassment criteria of Title IX. However, despite the growing number of sexting prevention programs in the United States and abroad, there is no known empirical evidence about whether teachers, parents, or students are benefiting from these initiatives. This is certainly an area where more empirical research is needed.

Apart from the risks of forwarding and bullying that are associated with sexting, one primary concern of researchers and educators is that sexting could be a gateway for engaging in other risky behaviors. There are several risk factors that are associated with participating in sexting. The known studies on the topic and the risk factors associated with sexting (sexual, substance abuse, and emotional/psychological/interpersonal) are displayed in Table 10.2. As shown, sexting is associated with a number of risk factors. Most of these research studies have suggested that those who engage in sexting are more likely to engage in risky sexual behavior and substance abuse, with the exception of Gordon-Messer et al. (2013) who found almost no significant associations between sexting behaviors and sexual or psychological risk factors. As Table 10.2 summarizes, most studies have shown that they are also likely to have a number of emotional or interpersonal issues such as sadness and attempted suicide, histrionic personality traits, and negative urgency. As these findings are based solely on cross-sectional studies, the direction of influence has not been explored, and it is

Table 10.2 Risk factors associated with sexting in recent research.

Study	Sexual	Substance abuse	Psychological/interpersonal
Benotsch et al. (2013)	Unprotected sex, sex with multiple partners, and sex after drinking or drugs in last 3 months; history of STI; lifetime sexual partners	Use of alcohol, marijuana, ecstasy, or cocaine in last 3 months	Texting frequency
Dake et al. (2012)	Anal sex, having 4 or more sexual partners, not using contraception during last intercourse, oral sex, ever having sexual intercourse, forced into sexual intercourse	Marijuana use, smoking cigarettes, binge drinking or alcohol consumption in the past 30 days	Attempted or contemplated suicide in past year; sad or hopeless feelings for at least two continuous weeks in last year
Dir, Cyders, et al. (2013)	Sexual hookups	Problematic alcohol use	Sensation seeking; negative urgency
Ferguson (2011)	Unprotected sex with no desire for children; not related to number of partners or unprotected sex with a new partner		Histrionic personality traits; positive attitudes toward sexting
Gordon-Messer et al. (2013)	Lifetime sexual activity, recent sexual activity (past 30 days). Of those who had been sexually active in past 30 days, no significant association with number of partners or proportion of unprotected vaginal or anal sex partners		No significant differences between sexters and non-sexters in depression, anxiety, or self-esteem

unclear whether sexting precedes these other risks or whether these other risks precede sexting. This is a promising direction for future research.

New Directions: Sexting Compliance and Coercion

For more than a decade, researchers have been studying sexual compliance or unwanted but consensual sexual activity, or sexual activity that individuals engage in even though they do not want to (e.g., Bay-Cheng & Eliseo-Arras, 2008; Impett &

Peplau, 2002, 2003; O'Sullivan & Allgeier, 1998; Sprecher, Hatfield, Cortese, Potapova, & Levitskaya, 1994). Studies have shown that unwanted but consensual sexual activity is quite common. For example, approximately one-third to one-half of the individuals in O'Sullivan and Allgeier's (1998) and Sprecher et al.'s (1994) samples indicated that they had engaged in unwanted but consensual sexual activity. In a recent study (Drouin & Tobin, 2014), we examined whether or not this type of sexual compliance had extended into the virtual world in the form of *unwanted but consensual sexting*.

In line with the AP and MTV (2009) study that reported that almost two-thirds (61%) of teens and young adults (14–24) who had sent a naked picture or video of themselves had been pressured at least once to do so, we expected the prevalence of unwanted but consensual sexting to be high in our sample of undergraduates. This is indeed what we found. In our sample, approximately half (48% of men and 55% of women) had engaged in unwanted but consensual sexting with a committed relationship partner (Drouin & Tobin, 2014). They mostly did so for flirtation, foreplay, fostering intimacy, and fulfilling a partner's needs. However, some consented to unwanted sexting to avoid conflict in their relationship, and this was particularly common among those with anxious or avoidant attachments to their partners. Anxious attachment was also significantly related to the frequency of unwanted but consensual sexting, but the motive to avoid an argument was a mediator in this relationship. Overall, our results are similar to what has been found in previous work examining unwanted but consensual (face-to-face) sexual activity (Impett & Peplau, 2002, 2003; O'Sullivan & Allgeier, 1998); therefore, we suggested that unwanted but consensual sexting is now part of the sexual repertoire of young adults. Moreover, because of the relations between unwanted sexting, anxious attachment, and motive to avoid an argument, we suggested that interventions aimed at curbing compliant sexting behavior might focus on conflict resolution and sexual negotiation or assertiveness strategies with romantic relationships. That said, we acknowledge, as do Walker, Sanci, and Temple-Smith (2011), that a survey of youth might be helpful to gather feedback about what elements should be included in a developmentally appropriate intervention.

We also examined whether sexual compliance online was related to other risk factors, such as drug and alcohol use or previous physical abuse by a partner (Drouin & Tobin, 2013, 2014). With regard to substance use, 40% of respondents indicated that they had consented to unwanted sexting because they had been drinking, and 16% indicated that they had consented because they were taking drugs (Drouin & Tobin, 2014). Meanwhile, 79% of those who had ever been physically abused by a romantic partner had participated in unwanted but consensual sexting, as opposed to only 40% of those who had never been abused by a romantic partner (Drouin & Tobin, 2013). An independent samples *t*-test showed that there was a significant difference in the frequency of consenting to unwanted sexting between those who had and had not been abused. As co-victimization, or physical and sexual victimization (broadly defined) that occurs within the same time period (Smith, White, & Holland, 2003), has been a focus of the recent relationship literature, we suggested that researchers and educators: (1) examine the ways in which sexual victimization may be extended into the virtual world, and (2) be aware that unwanted sexting may be an indicator of other types of physical and sexual abuse.

New Directions: Computer-Mediated Sexual Communication and Couples

Before the Internet, people wanting to make romantic or sexual connections usually did so with people who lived in close geographic proximity. Telephones and letters could be used to form and sustain long-distance relationships; however, connections would often be made first in a face-to-face context before long-distance relationships ensued. All of this changed with the advent of the Internet. Online dating sites (e.g., Match.com, Eharmony.com, Plentyoffish.com, OkCupid.com) allow for people to make connections with others all over the world, and potential romantic partners can have instantaneous conversations via instant messaging or even live video conversations via platforms like Skype and Facetime. Even those who are already in committed relationships have the ability to make connections with others anonymously through websites like AshleyMadison.com, a discreet dating website created for married people who want to have affairs. As of August 2013, AshleyMadison.com had more than 21.5 million members, which secured its rank as "the world's leading married dating service for discreet encounters" (www.ashleymadison.com).

Not surprisingly, considering the purpose of the website, a study by Wysocki and Childers (2011) found that a large number of the 5,000 AshleyMadison.com users they surveyed had engaged in sexting. Approximately one-third (29%) had had "sex via texting" (p. 230), and one-half (51.1%) had sent nude photos of themselves either via their mobile phones or email (Wysocki & Childers, 2011). Additionally, infidelity was also common: while in a serious relationship, two-thirds (63.7%) of respondents had "cheated online" and three-fourths (73.7%) had cheated in real life. Notably, not all of the respondents were married; some were unmarried, presumably looking for "uncomplicated" sexual relationships (Wysocki & Childers, 2011). These results suggest that those seeking sexual relationships online are likely to engage in both online and offline sexual relationships with others; however, again the direction of influence here is unclear.

Even if people are not looking for discreet affairs, they might be tempted to look through their online dating alternatives when they are in mediocre relationships or when their relationships hit a rough patch (Slater, 2013). Therefore, media sources are beginning to suggest that online dating sites might be a threat to monogamy (e.g., Roiphe, 2013; Slater, 2013). Despite the recent media attention, this practice – evaluating alternative relationship situations – is far from uncommon, and it is an integral part of well-established interpersonal relationship theories, such as the interdependence theory (Kelley & Thibault, 1978) and the investment model of developing relationships (Rusbult, 1980). However, because of the prevalence and ease of use of modern technologies, people have more opportunities than ever to forge and sustain relationships with those with whom they have romantic or sexual desires.

In our recent studies (Dibble & Drouin, 2014; Dibble, Drouin, Aune, & Boller, in press), we have focused on computer-mediated communication with relationship alternatives with a particular focus on *back burners*, or those with whom we forge or maintain contact in order to establish a future romantic or sexual relationship. In our samples of undergraduates, most participants (66%) reported that they had at least one contact in the communication channel they used most frequently (e.g., Facebook, text messaging, Twitter) that they considered a back burner (Dibble et al., in press). Additionally, a staggering 92% indicated that they had at least one contact in their most frequently used channel with whom they would like to be romantically or sexually involved if single (Dibble et al., in press). On average, people communicated with their back burners or other romantic/sexual desirables about once a week (Dibble et al., in press). Meanwhile, single people and those who rated the quality of their alternatives higher had more back burners than those in committed relationships and those who rated the quality of their alternatives lower, respectively (Dibble & Drouin, 2014). Moreover, those who rated the quality of their alternatives high had more back burners with whom they communicated platonically *and* back burners with whom they communicated romantically/sexually (Dibble & Drouin, 2014). Considering the high prevalence of communication with relationship alternatives via modern communication channels and the significant relationships between number of alternatives and relationship factors, we will continue to examine the role of technology in the formation and maintenance of romantic and sexual relationships.

Thus far, computer-mediated communication and sexting have been presented only as potential threats to existing relationships or a means to establish new ones; however, Parker et al.'s (2013) study showed that sexting could also be an indicator of relationship health within existing relationships. Parker et al. (2013) found that couples who had higher consensus scores (a dimension of relationship satisfaction) were also more likely to engage in sexting. The authors go on to suggest that sexting might be used in couples' therapy in order to increase intimacy between partners. Although a small number of previous studies have mentioned positive relational motivations for sexting, such as flirting and having fun (e.g., Cox Communications, 2009; Drouin et al., 2013), most focus on risks and harms. To date, this is the only known study to explicitly examine the relational benefits of sexting. As research in this field continues, it will be important to investigate the ways in which computer-mediated sexual communication may be used in positive ways, for example, to help people establish their sexual identities, engage in sexual negotiations, or improve their romantic relationships.

Summary

This is an exciting time for research related to technology; technology is changing quickly, and new innovations are spurring new social and psychological phenomena. One such phenomenon – sexting – has evoked moral panic among parents, educators, and legislators worldwide, as the distribution of sexual content, especially among minors, may have significant legal and psychological repercussions. Based on a comprehensive review of the teen and adult sexting literature, it is clear that sexting does occur among minors; however, the rate of sexting (especially involving nude pictures) is still relatively low among young teens. That said, the prevalence of sexting increases substantially from the pre-teenage years to young adulthood, and one-third to one-half of young adults, especially those in committed, romantic relationships, have engaged in sexting involving pictures. Because research has shown that sexting is associated with a variety of sexual and substance abuse risk factors, insecure attachments, negative psychological characteristics (e.g., depression, neuroticism, and histrionic personality traits), and sexual compliance, more research should be directed toward sexting education and intervention. However, more research examining the potential benefits of sexting is also needed. Over the last two decades, most researchers have been reporting the negative impacts of technology on sexuality (Döring, 2009); a shift in this research will present a more balanced view of the ways in which technology is intersecting with sexuality in today's society.

References

Associated Press (AP) & MTV. (2009, September 23). AP-MTV Digital abuse study, executive summary. Retrieved November 26, 2014, from http://www.athinline.org/MTV-AP_Digital_Abuse_Study_Executive_Summary.pdf

Bay-Cheng, L. Y., & Eliseo-Arras, R. K. (2008). The making of unwanted sex: Gendered and neoliberal norms in college women's unwanted sexual experiences. *Journal of Sex Research*, *45*, 386–397.

Benotsch, E. G., Snipes, D. J., Martin, A. M., & Bull, S. S. (2013). Sexting, substance use, and sexual risk behavior in young adults. *Journal of Adolescent Health*, *52*, 307–313.

Canning, A., & Hopper, J. (2011, June 6). Rep. Anthony Weiner's sexting scandal: Why did he do it? *ABC News*. Retrieved November 26, 2014, from http://abcnews.go.com/US/sexting-scandal-rep-anthony-weiner-tweet-facebook-photos/story?id=13770641

Cox Communications. (2009, May). *Teen online and wireless safety survey: Cyberbullying, sexting, and parental controls*. Atlanta, GA: Cox Communications, National Center for Missing & Exploited Children. Retrieved November 26, 2014, from http://www.cox.com/wcm/en/aboutus/datasheet/takecharge/2009-teen-survey.pdf

Dake, J. A., Price, J. H., Maziarz, L., & Ward, B. (2012). Prevalence and correlates of sexting behavior in adolescents. *American Journal of Sexuality Education*, *7*, 1–15.

Davis, D., Shaver, P. R., & Vernon, M. L. (2004). Attachment style and subjective motivations for sex. *Personality and Social Psychology Bulletin*, *30*, 1076–1090.

Delevi, R., & Weisskirch, R. S. (2013). Personality factors as predictors of sexting. *Computers in Human Behavior*, *29*(6), 2589–2594.

Dibble, J. L., & Drouin, M. (2014). Using modern technology to keep in touch with back burners: An investment model analysis. *Computers in Human Behavior*, *34*, 96–100.

Dibble, J. L., Drouin, M., Aune, K. S., & Boller, R. R. (in press). Simmering on the back burner: Communication with and disclosure of relationship alternatives. *Communication Quarterly*.

Dir, A. L., Coskunpinar, A., Steiner, J. L., & Cyders, M. A. (2013). Understanding differences in sexting behaviors across gender, relationship status, and sexual identity, and the role of expectancies in sexting. *Cyberpsychology, Behavior, and Social Networking*, *16*, 568–574.

Dir, A. L., Cyders, M. A., & Coskunpinar, A. (2013). From the bar to the bed via mobile phone: A first test of the role of problematic alcohol use, sexting, and impulsivity-related traits in sexual hookups. *Computers in Human Behavior*, *29*, 1664–1670.

Dir, A. L., Steiner, J. L., Coskunpinar, A., & Cyders, M. A. (2013). Sexting Behaviors Scale. Unpublished technical report.

Döring, N. M. (2009). The Internet's impact of sexuality: A critical review of 15 years of research. *Computers in Human Behavior*, *25*, 1089–1101.

Drouin, M., & Landgraff, C. (2012). Texting, sexting, attachment, and intimacy in college students' romantic relationships. *Computers in Human Behavior*, *28*, 444–449.

Drouin, M., & Tobin, E. (2013). Compliant sexting and physical abuse. Unpublished manuscript.

Drouin, M., & Tobin, E. (2014). Unwanted but consensual sexting among young adults: Relations with attachment and sexual motivations. *Computers in Human Behavior*, *31*, 412–418.

Drouin, M., Vogel, K. N., Surbey, A., & Stills, J. R. (2013). Let's talk about sexting, baby: Computer-mediated sexual behaviors among young adults. *Computers in Human Behavior, 29*, A25–A30.

Duggan, M., & Rainie, L. (2012, November 25). Cell phone activities 2012. Pew Internet & American Life Project. Retrieved November 26, 2014, from http://www.pewInternet. org/Reports/2012/Cell-Activities.aspx

Ferguson, C. J. (2011). Sexting behaviors among young Hispanic women: Incidence and association with other high-risk sexual behaviors. *Psychiatric Quarterly, 82*, 239–243.

Fisher, S., Sauter, A., Slobodniuk, L., & Young, C. (2012). Sexting in Australia: The legal and social ramifications. Parliament of Victoria Law Reform Committee Sexting Inquiry. Retrieved November 26, 2014, from http://www.parliament.vic.gov.au/images/stories/ committees/lawrefrom/isexting/subs/S07_-_Salvation_Army_Oasis_Hunter.pdf

Fleschler Peskin, M., Markham, C. M., Addy, R. C., Shegog, R., Thiel, M., & Tortolero, S. R. (2013). Prevalence and patterns of sexting among ethnic minority urban high school students. *Cyberpsychology, Behavior and Social Networking, 16*, 454–459.

Gordon-Messer, D., Bauermeister, J., Grodzinski, A., & Zimmerman, M. (2013). Sexting among young adults. *Journal of Adolescent Health, 52*(3), 301–306.

Graham, J. (2013, June 5). Snapchat's young audience fuels a growth streak. *USA Today.* Retrieved November 26, 2014, from http://www.usatoday.com/story/tech/columnist/ talkingtech/2013/06/05/snapchat-growth-streak/2359129/

Guttmacher Institute. (2013, June). Fact sheet: American teens' sexual and reproductive health. New York, NY: AGI. Retrieved November 26, 2014, from http://www.guttmacher. org/pubs/FB-ATSRH.pdf

Impett, E. A., & Peplau, L. A. (2002). Why some women consent to unwanted sex with a dating partner: Insights from attachment theory. *Psychology of Women Quarterly, 26*, 360–370.

Impett, E. A., & Peplau, L. A. (2003). Sexual compliance: Gender, motivational, and relationship perspectives. *Journal of Sex Research, 40*, 87–100.

Kelley, H. H., & Thibault, J. E. (1978). *Interpersonal relations: A theory of interdependence.* New York, NY: John Wiley & Sons.

Lenhart, A. (2009, December 15). Teens and sexting. Pew Internet & American Life Project. Retrieved November 26, 2014, from http://www.ncdsv.org/images/ pewinternet_teensandsexting_12-2009.pdf

Lenhart, A. (2012, March 19). Teens, smartphones, and texting. Pew Internet & American Life Project. Retrieved November 26, 2014, from http://www.pewinternet.org/files/ old-media/Files/Reports/2012/PIP_Teens_Smartphones_and_Texting.pdf

Lenhart, A., Ling, R., Campbell, S., & Purdell, K. (2010, April 20). Teens and mobile phones. Pew Internet & American Life Project. Retrieved November 26, 2014, from http:// pewInternet.org/Reports/2010/Teens-and-Mobile-Phones.aspx

Lounsbury, K., Mitchell, K. J., & Finkelhor, D. (2011). The true prevalence of sexting. *Crimes Against Children Research Center,* 1–4. Retrieved November 26, 2014, from http://unh. edu/ccrc/pdf/Sexting%20Fact%20Sheet%204_29_11.pdf

Meyer, E. J. (2009, December 16). Gender and Schooling. Ending bullying and harassment, and promoting sexual diversity in schools. *Psychology Today.* Retrieved, November 26, 2014, from http://www.psychologytoday.com/blog/gender-and-schooling/200912/ sexting-and-suicide

Mitchell, K. J., Finkelhor, D., Jones, L. M., & Wolak, J. (2012). Prevalence and characteristics of youth sexting: A national study. *Pediatrics, 129*, 13–20.

National Campaign to Prevent Teen and Unplanned Pregnancy. (2008). Sex and tech: Results from a survey of teens and young adults. Retrieved November 26, 2014, from http:// thenationalcampaign.org/resource/sex-and-tech

O'Sullivan, L. F., & Allgeier, E. R. (1998). Feigning sexual desire: Consenting to unwanted sexual activity in heterosexual dating relationships. *Journal of Sex Research, 35*, 234–243.

Parker, T. S., Blackburn, K. M., Perry, M. S., & Hawks, J. M. (2013). Sexting as an intervention: Relationship satisfaction and motivation considerations. *American Journal of Family Therapy, 41,* 1–12.

Press Association. (2013, March 19). Teachers to be given "sexting" curb guide. *The Huffington Post,* United Kingdom. Retrieved November 26, 2014, from http://www.huffingtonpost.co.uk/2013/03/19/teachers-to-be-given-sexting-guide_n_2910151.html

Rice, E., Rhoades, H., Winetrobe, H., Sanchez, M., Montoya, J., Plant, A., & Kordic, T. (2012). Sexually explicit cell phone messaging associated with sexual risk among adolescents. *Pediatrics, 130,* 667–673.

Ringrose, J., Gill, R., Livingstone, S., & Harvey, L. (2012). *A qualitative study of children, young people and "sexting": A report prepared for the NSPCC.* London, UK: NSPCC.

Roiphe, K. (2013, February 1). I love you. Now text me: How online relationships are more real than real ones. *Slate.* Retrieved November 26, 2014, from http://www.slate.com/articles/life/roiphe/2013/02/online_dating_is_it_more_real.html

Rusbult, C. E. (1980). Commitment and satisfaction in romantic associations: A test of the investment model. *Journal of Experimental Social Psychology, 16,* 172–186.

Sacco, D., Argudin, R., Maguire, J., & Tallon, K. (2010). *Sexting: Youth practices and legal implications* (Publication No. 2010-8). Harvard University, The Berkman Center for Internet & Society. Retrieved November 26, 2014, from https://cyber.law.harvard.edu/publications/2010/Sexting_Youth_Practices_Legal_Implications

Slater, D. (2013, January 2). A million first dates: How online romance is threatening monogamy. *The Atlantic.* Retrieved November 26, 2014, from http://www.theatlantic.com/magazine/archive/2013/01/a-million-first-dates/309195/

Smith, A. (2012, November 30). The best (and worst) of mobile connectivity. Pew Internet & American Life Project. Retrieved November 26, 2014, from http://pewInternet.org/Reports/2012/Best-Worst-Mobile.aspx

Smith, C. (2014, November 25). How many people use 700 of the top social media, apps, and digital services? *Digital Marketing Ramblings.* Retrieved November 26, 2014, from http://expandedramblings.com/index.php/resource-how-many-people-use-the-top-social-media/

Smith, P. H., White, J. W., & Holland, L. J. (2003). A longitudinal perspective on dating violence among adolescent and college-aged women. *American Journal of Public Health, 93,* 1104–1109.

Sprecher, S., Hatfield, E., Cortese, A., Potapova, E., & Levitskaya, A. (1994). Token resistance to sexual intercourse and consent to unwanted sexual intercourse: College students' dating experiences in three countries. *Journal of Sex Research, 31,* 125–132.

Survata. (2013, February 7). Is Snapchat only used for sexting? We asked 5,000 people to find out. Survata Blog. Retrieved November 26, 2014, from http://survata.com/blog/is-snapchat-only-used-for-sexting-we-asked-5000-people-to-find-out/

Walker, S., Sanci, L., & Temple-Smith, M. (2011). Sexting and young people: Experts' views. *Youth Studies Australia, 30*(4), 8–16.

Weisskirch, R. S., & Delevi, R. (2011). "Sexting" and adult romantic attachment. *Computers in Human Behavior, 27,* 1697–1701.

Wysocki, D., & Childers, C. (2011). "Let my fingers do the talking": Sexting and infidelity in cyberspace. *Sexuality and Culture, 15,* 217–239.

11

Mobile Phone Dependency

What's All the Buzz About?

Michelle Drouin, Daren Kaiser, and Daniel A. Miller

Indiana University–Purdue University

Two weeks ago, I (MD) checked my phone three times when I thought I had heard a message notification but I really had not. Twice I thought I heard a *ding* while my phone was sitting on the kitchen counter, a few feet from where I stood, and once I thought I felt it vibrate while I was carrying it in my bag. Each time that I checked my phone but saw no notifications of a new call or message, I was somewhat perplexed. I have heard many tales of *phantom vibration syndrome* (PVS), and I have even studied it, but until then I had never really experienced it. As our recent work (Drouin, Kaiser, & Miller, 2012) has shown that the experience of phantom vibrations is related to cell phone dependency, I started to wonder what these phantom vibrations really meant. Was I addicted to my cell phone? I do sleep with it beside my bed; however, it is turned off. Most days it is near me (within a few feet), but sometimes I do not even know where it is until I have to leave the house. I try to return text messages immediately, but sometimes it takes days. Is this an addiction? Am I going to experience PVS all of the time?

I thought … I pondered … I wondered … for about 30 seconds. (Because we do live in a fast-paced society, and I do not have time to dwell.) Then, as most psychologists would probably do, I thought about my recent circumstances – a new phone with Internet and new mobile applications (e.g., WhatsApp) that had an array of different sounds for their notifications (novelty) and a sister backpacking in Panama with me as her only contact (stress). I rationalized that my experience of PVS was circumstantial – an ephemeral anomaly – that would be gone as quickly as it came. And I was correct: I have not experienced phantom vibrations since.

Although I have determined that I have neither mobile phone addiction nor (at present) any of its symptoms, there are many people worldwide who do. In this chapter, we will present recent statistics on mobile phone use and then discuss a variety of topics related to problematic mobile phone use.

The Wiley Handbook of Psychology, Technology, and Society, First Edition. Edited by Larry D. Rosen, Nancy A. Cheever, and L. Mark Carrier.

The Mobile Phone Era

In 2009, a panel of eight judges from the Wharton School was asked to judge the top innovations in the past 30 years (Korkki, 2009) – mobile phones were considered the third most important innovation, behind the Internet and computers. Like the Internet and computers, mobile phones are now ubiquitous, and their use has skyrocketed in the last decade. According to a report by the International Telecommunication Union (ITU, 2013), mobile phone subscriptions rose from about 2 billion worldwide in 2005 to about 6.8 billion estimated worldwide in 2013. Considering the world's population is about 7 billion people (United States Census Bureau, 2013), this means that if each subscription belonged to a single subscriber, about 96% of the world's population would have a mobile phone. Therefore, we are approaching a 100% penetration rate for mobile phone use worldwide (ITU, 2013). Notably, the penetration rate has already surpassed this mark in developed countries, where penetration is currently 128% (ITU, 2013). Because of the already high penetration rate, mobile phone subscription growth over the last decade has been lower in developed countries than in developing countries; however, worldwide, the increase in subscriptions is still impressive: approximately 1.4 billion subscriptions have been added in the past three years alone (ITU, 2013).

These statistics are somewhat unsurprising if one considers the sophistication of modern mobile phones. Although the first cell phones were capable of voice calls only, that all changed about 20 years ago, when the first text message was sent. Since that time, text messaging has become a mainstay of the mobile communication movement, and its use continues to rise. According to recent statistics, there were 5.9 trillion text messages sent in 2011, and this number is expected to reach 9.4 trillion by 2016 (Clark-Dickson, 2012). However, cell phone technology has evolved considerably in the last decade, and cell phones have progressed beyond text message technology so that most, if not all, of a person's communication can be conducted via a cell phone. People can now easily access email and connect to others on social networking sites via integrated applications on their small, mobile handsets. Moreover, smartphones can record high-quality videos, play favorite music, and download almost anything from the web (albeit often at a slower rate than a desktop computer). Thus, mobile phones are a sort of one-stop shop for mobile communication, and as the following research will show, many people are very devoted to their one-stop shops.

Problematic Mobile Phone Use

As mobile phone use gained popularity, researchers began to study the ways in which individuals used this technology to interact with others, and it quickly became obvious that people were becoming reliant on their mobile phones. Therefore, in the last decade, a growing body of research has centered on mobile phone dependency or problematic mobile phone use. Problematic mobile phone use can be defined as mobile phone use that causes problems in a user's life (e.g., sleeping, financial, compulsive, or dependence problems). It is often considered a subcategory of a larger issue known as technology (or cyber) addiction, and it has become so prevalent that some have advocated for it to be included as a diagnostic category of addiction in the *Diagnostic and Statistical Manual of Mental Disorders* (e.g., Chóliz, 2010).

Mobile phone addiction shares some of the properties of other types of behavioral and cyber addiction (Billieux, 2012). For example, psychological traits such as self-esteem and impulsivity are shared risk factors for different types of cyber addiction (Billieux, 2012). Because of these shared traits, Billieux (2012) suggested that mobile phone addiction should be evaluated as a subtype of cyber addictions. However, there are also specific risk factors that do not necessarily transfer across the various types of cyber addiction (e.g., illusions of control or social competence). Consequently, Billieux (2012) suggested that researchers and clinicians should focus on the online *activity* that a person is addicted to rather than the technology or specific website/application. This is a very important distinction considering the sophistication of modern phones. Although one person might use their mobile phone often and primarily to make voice calls, another person might spend the majority of their phone time on social networking sites. Thus, as modern mobile technologies and even websites (e.g., Facebook) become even more multifunctional, researchers of mobile phone or cyber addiction must begin to focus on specific activities people are over-engaged in (e.g., voice calls or social networking) rather than which technology or website they are using (Griffiths, 2012).

One of the first studies to examine mobile phone addiction was conducted in Australia by Bianchi and Phillips (2005). Bianchi and Phillips (2005) created a scale to measure problematic phone use (Mobile Phone Problem Use Scale or MPPUS) and also examined the correlates of this behavior. In their study, younger participants who were extraverts and had high self-esteem were more likely to have higher scores on the MPPUS scale. Since this time, many other researchers have studied problematic phone use with different populations (e.g., youth, teens, and adults) across the world. A summary of these studies, including their measure of problematic mobile phone use and the characteristics associated with problematic phone use, are listed in Table 11.1.

As shown in Table 11.1, even across cultures there appears to be some consistency in the correlates of problematic mobile phone use. For example, there is some consistency across studies that women (Beranuy, Oberst, Carbonell, & Chamarro, 2009; Jenaro, Flores, Gómez-Vela, González-Gil, & Caballo, 2007; Takao, Takahashi, & Kitamura, 2009) and extraverts (e.g., Ezoe et al., 2009; Hong, Chiu, & Huang, 2012) are more likely to report problematic mobile phone use. However, there are also some inconsistencies across studies for characteristics such as depression (Billieux, Van der Linden, D'Acremont, Ceschi, & Zermatten, 2007; Güzeller & Coşguner, 2012; Ha, Chin, Park, Ryu, & Yu, 2008; Jenaro et al., 2007), loneliness (Güzeller & Coşguner, 2012; Takao et al., 2009), and self-esteem (Bianchi & Phillips, 2005; Ha et al., 2008; Hong et al., 2012), with some studies reporting positive relationships and some reporting null or negative relationships between these characteristics and problematic mobile phone use.

These disparate findings could be attributable to a number of socio-cultural, historical, or methodological factors. It is quite possible, for example, that the Turkish high school students in Güzeller and Coşguner's (2012) study are different from the Japanese university students in Takao et al.'s (2009) study because of differences in the socio-cultural context of mobile phone use in Turkey versus Japan, or in high school versus university. These socio-cultural differences could have contributed to the finding that loneliness was related to problematic mobile phone use in Güzeller and Coşguner's (2012) sample but not in Takao et al.'s (2009) sample. It is also

Table 11.1 Summary of known studies examining problematic mobile phone use.

Study	Sample	Measure of problematic mobile phone use	Correlates of problematic mobile phone use/dependency
Beranuy et al. (2009)	365 Spanish university students (M age = 21.37)	CERM – Cuestionario de Experiencias Relacionadas con el Móvil	Female gender, psychological distress, and some aspects of emotional intelligence
Bianchi & Phillips (2005)	195 Australian adults (aged 18–35, M = 36.07) recruited via various methods	The Mobile Phone Problem Use Scale (MPPUS)	Young age, extraversion, and high self-esteem
Billieux et al. (2007)	108 Swiss undergraduate women psychology students (aged 19 to 48, M = 24.17)	Single-item measure of perceived dependence on mobile phone	Urgency, lack of perseverance, impulsivity. Anxiety and depression were not predictors
Billieux et al. (2008)	339 Swiss participants from the community (aged 20–35, M = 25.80)	Problematic Mobile Phone Use Questionnaire (PMPUQ)	Urgency
Chung (2011)	188 high school girls (aged 16–19) in South Korea	Problematic Mobile Phone Use Questionnaire (PMPUQ; National Information Society Agency, 2006)	Interpersonal solidarity
Ehrenberg et al. (2008)	200 Australian university students (M age = 19.06)	Three item measure of salience, loss of control, and withdrawal	Neuroticism
Ezoe et al. (2009)	132 Japanese women nursing students (aged 18–49, M = 24.5)	Mobile Phone Dependence Questionnaire (MPDQ; Toda et al., 2004)	Extraversion, neuroticism, and unhealthy personal health practices
Güzeller & Coşguner (2012)	770 Turkish high school students (M age ≈ 16)	Problematic Mobile Phone Use Scale (PMPUS)	Depression and loneliness
Ha et al. (2008)	595 Korean technical school students (M age = 15.9)	Excessive Cellular Phone Use Survey (EC-PUS)	Depression, anxiety, difficulty in emotional expression, low self-esteem, and Internet addiction
Hong et al. (2012)	269 Taiwanese women undergraduates	Mobile Phone Addiction Scale (MPAS); revised from Young's (1998) Internet Addiction Scale	Extraversion, anxiety, low self-esteem, mobile phone usage behavior

(continued on pg. 196)

Table 11.1 (*Continued*)

Study	Sample	Measure of problematic mobile phone use	Correlates of problematic mobile phone use/dependency
Jenaro et al. (2007)	337 Spanish college students (aged 18 to 32, $M = 21.6$)	Cell-Phone Over-Use Scale (COS)	Female gender, somatic complaints, insomnia, social dysfunction, anxiety, and depression. No significant relations with substance abuse, pathological gambling, or health behaviors (e.g., sleep and exercise)
Kwon et al. (2013)	197 South Koreans from two companies and two universities (aged 18 to 53 years, $M = 26.06$)	Smartphone Addiction Scale	Lower education level, university students, higher self-reported smartphone addiction
Takao et al. (2009)	444 Japanese university students (aged 18 to 39, $M = 20.77$)	MPPUS; Bianchi & Phillips (2005)	Female gender, self-monitoring, and approval motivation. No significant relations with loneliness
Thomée et al. (2011)	4,156 Swedish young adults (aged 20–24)	Mobile phone use measure including frequency of calls and SMS messages	Stress, sleep disturbances, depression, and mental health outcomes one year later
Walsh et al. (2011)	292 Australian youth (aged 16 to 24, $M = 20.22$)	Mobile Phone Involvement Questionnaire (MPIQ; Walsh et al., 2010)	Female gender, younger age, self-identity, and in-group norm. No significant relations with self-esteem and need to belong
Yen et al. (2009)	10,191 Taiwanese junior and senior high school students (aged 12–19, $M = 14.6$)	Problematic Cellular Phone Use Questionnaire (PCPU-Q)	Functional impairments (e.g., poor academic performance and financial problems) and depression

Note. Measures without references were developed by the author(s).

possible that differences could have emerged because of the changes in mobile phone use that have occurred over the last five years. Perhaps, four or five years ago when mobile phone use was on the rise but not yet at 100% penetration rate, many people were using their phones excessively because of the relative novelty of the mobile phone; however, now that mobile phones have lost their novelty effect, perhaps they are used excessively primarily by those who are lonely. Alternatively, it could be that excessive mobile phone use is causing loneliness, but it took time for this effect to emerge. Either of these historical explanations, or even other alternative explanations, could have influenced the results of these studies. Finally, methodological differences between the two studies could have contributed to conflicting findings. Güzeller and Coşguner (2012) created a scale (PMPUS) with three constructs: negative effect, compulsion-persistence, and withdrawal-tolerance, whereas Takao et al. (2009) used the unidimensional MPPUS (Bianchi & Phillips, 2005). Additionally, there were differences in the way these researchers treated their data. While Takao et al. (2009) used regression analyses to determine whether loneliness made unique contributions to problematic mobile phone behavior, Güzeller and Coşguner (2012) used only zero-order correlations to evaluate the relationship between the PMPUS and loneliness. The correlation between loneliness and problematic mobile phone behavior was low in Güzeller and Coşguner's (2012) study, and the authors acknowledged that significant findings may have emerged because of the very large sample size.

In sum, although there are some consistencies across studies in the correlates of problematic mobile phone use, there are also some disparate findings, which are likely attributable to a number of factors. As researchers continue to do work on this topic, they should be cognizant of the ways in which methodological incongruities can be minimized. Billieux (2012) addressed one of these incongruities by advocating for some consistency in scale use across studies. Billieux (2012) provided an overview of the validated measures that existed at the time, which included the basis for each measure (e.g., substance abuse literature or existing studies) as well as its functional properties (i.e., number of items and factors). According to Billieux (2012), the MPPUS (Bianchi & Phillips, 2005) has been used widely as a unidimensional scale; however, newer multidimensional scales that delineate different types of problematic phone use (e.g., PMPUQ; Billieux, Van der Linden, & Rochat, 2008) might be more appropriate considering the many functions of mobile phones (Griffiths, 2012). Moreover, as mobile phone technology changes so quickly, researchers should be aware of mobile phone innovations so that the scales they use reflect the mobile phone capabilities of the time. As an example, Kwon et al. (2013) developed the multidimensional Smartphone Addiction Scale (SAS), which addresses most of the newest capabilities of modern mobile technologies. However, the SAS includes items like "My fully charged battery does not last for one whole day" (p. 4), which may not be relevant as technology changes. Therefore, the development and validation of problematic mobile phone use scales should remain an active area of research in the coming years.

Mobile Phone Use: The Case of Text Messaging

Recent media headlines have suggested that text messaging is on the decline (e.g., Halper, 2013); however, the actual story is that the popularity of platforms for sending mobile phone messages has shifted slightly from traditional text messaging to chat applications (e.g., WhatsApp) and comments on social networking sites (e.g., Facebook and Twitter). Text messaging still remains one of the most popular communication methods, especially among teens and young adults (e.g., Lenhart, 2012; Smith, 2012). Recent Pew reports showed that among those who text, 18- to 24-year-old Americans sent or received an average of 109.5 text messages per day (Smith, 2012), and teens (12–17) sent or received an average of 167 texts per day (Lenhart, 2012). In contrast, real-time voice communication is on the decline in these age groups. For example, in Lenhart's (2012) sample of teens, the prevalence of daily voice calls with friends went down from 38% to 26% in two years (from 2009 to 2011).

Although a shift from voice to text communication may not seem problematic in itself – texters, after all, are engaged in the process of writing, which is arguably a good skill to hone – some have become concerned that these virtual technologies are inhibiting our ability to really connect with others (e.g., Gorry, 2009; Sigman, 2009; Turkle, 2011). Turkle (2011) has even suggested that adolescents' development might be affected in a profound way, as they are both tethered to their communication technologies through constant contact with others and leveraging these technologies to keep emotional distance. As an example, a person need not ask another to go on a date face to face or even via a voice conversation any more; instead, dating is often done informally through a string of text and Facebook messages (Williams, 2013). Therefore, people no longer have to plan dates, nor do they have to work up the courage to propose formal dates (Williams, 2013). This relatively small change may affect the way we approach other planning activities in our lives and our confidence in initiating face-to-face or voice interactions. Moreover, it is just one example of the many ways in which modern technology, specifically text messaging or instant messaging technology, may be affecting human interaction and development.

Even if one accepts that these global effects are part of the evolution of humans, some of the more specific, proximal effects of text messaging have attracted media and empirical attention. A few years ago, a *New York Times* headline suggested that "Texting may be taking a toll" on the mental and even physical health (e.g., texting thumb) of American teens and young adults (Hafner, 2009). Psychologists and researchers suggested that text messaging was influencing development, and the need for constant communication was promoting anxiety and dependence (Hafner, 2009). Although no known studies have examined the causal relationships between text messaging and declines in mental and physical health, there are a number of studies that have examined the correlational relationships between these variables. For example, Igarashi, Motoyoshi, Takai, and Yoshida (2008) found that among Japanese high school students, text message dependency was positively related to neuroticism, which is associated with negative emotional states including moodiness and anxiety. Text message dependency was also positively related to extraversion in their sample (Igarashi et al., 2008). These findings are similar to what was found in Australian samples during the same time period; Butt and Phillips (2008) and Ehrenberg, Juckes, White, and Walsh (2008) found that text message use was related to neuroticism and extraversion. Additionally, in Butt and Phillips' (2008) sample, text message use was also negatively related to conscientiousness. Meanwhile, in their more recent study of Japanese adults, Lu et al. (2011) found that text messaging dependency was positively related to depression; however, mobile phone addiction was negatively related to anxiety. Considered together, these studies suggest that text messaging dependency is associated with a variety of psychological traits, some considered positive (e.g., extraversion) and some considered negative (e.g., neuroticism and depression).

Text messaging dependency has also been linked to auditory and tactile hallucinations in the form of *phantom vibration syndrome* (Drouin et al., 2012). Phantom vibrations are vibrations that a person feels or hears even when their phone is not really vibrating or ringing (Drouin et al., 2012). Laramie (2007) was the first to examine this phenomenon empirically. He found that "phantom ring" was common in his general population sample (approximately two-thirds had experienced it), and it was significantly related to impulsivity, mobile phone use, mobile phone problem use, and use of the mobile phone to modulate affect. Subsequently, Rothberg et al. (2010) examined phantom vibration among medical staff and found that a similar percentage (68%) had experienced phantom vibrations but few (7%) found the vibrations bothersome. Although the samples were different, Rothberg et al.'s (2010) findings were somewhat similar to our recent findings (Drouin et al., 2012). Most of the undergraduates in our sample (89%) had experienced phantom vibrations, but only a few (9%) found them bothersome or tried to stop them (14%). More importantly, we found that text message dependency, specifically the emotional reaction aspect of dependency as measured by Igarashi et al.'s (2008) text message dependency scale, was a predictor of the bothersomeness of phantom vibrations. Meanwhile, neuroticism, extraversion, and conscientiousness were all predictive of some aspect of text message dependency (Drouin et al., 2012). Overall, these studies show that those who are more dependent on their mobile phones and text messaging, and especially those who are sensitive in their reactions to their text messages, are more likely to experience auditory or tactile hallucinations associated with their mobile phones.

A recent study by Lin, Lin, Li, Huang, and Chen (2013) has also provided some evidence that phantom vibrations are related to stress. Lin et al. (2013) examined phantom vibration syndrome in samples of medical students and found that the percentage of students who experienced phantom vibrations or phantom ringing (differentiated in this study) varied from 50.0% to 95.9% (phantom vibrations) and 27.4% to 87.7% (phantom ringing) depending on which phase the students were in their internship process. The lowest prevalence rates for both phantom vibrations and phantom ringing were found during the two-week period after the internship ended and before the internship started, respectively. Meanwhile, the highest prevalence rate for phantom vibrations/ringing occurred at some time during the course of the internship. Interestingly, although anxiety and depression scores increased and then decreased in a similar pattern, there were no significant correlations between the experience of these phantom perceptions and anxiety or depression. Because they were independent of anxiety and depression, Lin et al. (2013) concluded that these hallucinations were likely aggravated by stress, which provides support for models of stress-induced psychosis.

As mobile phone and text messaging dependency have both been linked with stress and anxiety in both the media and empirical studies (Cheever, Rosen, Carrier, & Chavez, 2014), a goal of future research should be to further examine the relationships between these variables. If, as Lin et al. (2013) suggest, phantom vibrations/ringing are aggravated by stress, it is also possible that mobile phone and text messaging addictions are aggravated by stress. Consequently, interventions or treatments designed to combat these addictions might target circumstantial factors rather than enduring psychological traits.

New Directions: Recognition and Treatment of Problematic Mobile Phone Use

One interesting line of research examines individuals' recognition and understanding of their own addictive mobile phone behaviors. More than six years ago, Australian youth in Walsh, White, and Young's (2008) sample were already expressing concerns that they were addicted to their mobile phones. They cited compulsive checking behaviors as well as limiting their travel or activities so that they could be in constant contact with others. At about the same time period, almost half (48.9%) of the adolescents in Yen et al.'s (2009) Taiwanese sample indicated that they had experienced at least one symptom of problematic cell phone use in the last year, and 16.7% indicated that they had four or more symptoms. Prevalence of these symptoms, especially a reduction in time for social, academic, or recreational activities because of mobile phone use, was associated with functional impairments such as financial trouble, poor academic performance, and poor relationships with friends and family members (Yen et al., 2009). More recent studies in the United States (e.g., Smith, 2012) have found that a fair number of American mobile phone users (11%) worry that they spend too much time on their mobile device, and this number is higher among those with iPhones (15%) and young adults 18–24 (21%). A need for constant contact and compulsive checking behaviors are still prevalent in these samples: almost two-thirds of Americans age 18–34 sleep next to their cell phones so that they do not miss anything or wake up in the night to answer text messages, and more than three-fourths of them check for messages or missed calls even when they have not heard their phone ringing (Smith, 2012).

Addictive behaviors related to mobile phone use could be considered part of the broader construct of nomophobia. Nomophobia has been defined as the fear of being without mobile technology, such as phones or mobile computers, and if recent media reports and polls are accurate, it afflicts millions of people worldwide (e.g., Michael & Sheppard, 2013). Empirical research on nomophobia is just beginning to emerge. For example, Dixit et al. (2010) examined nomophobia among medical students in India and found that almost one in five (18.5%) were nomophobes. Meanwhile, King et al. (2013) conducted a case study and treatment protocol with a single man with nomophobia. In their study, King et al. (2013) developed a successful treatment protocol for the patient's nomophobia, using medication and cognitive behavioral therapy to shift some of the man's interactions from online to face to face.

Although these two seminal studies on nomophobia have added to our knowledge of the disorder, they did not use validated instruments or accepted clinical criteria for classifying nomophobes. Dixit et al. (2010) based their classifications on their survey of mobile phone dependence, which was adapted from a now-defunct website that described nomophobia. Meanwhile, because there was no existing *Diagnostic and Statistical Manual of Mental Disorders* (DSM-IV; APA, 2000) entry for nomophobia, King et al. (2013) made their diagnosis based on the patient's symptoms, referencing the definition provided by Wikipedia and media sources. Despite its growing popularity as a term to describe this aspect of mobile addiction (a Google search returned 137,000 results), no known validated measures or clinical criteria exist for the diagnosis of nomophobia. As media reports are suggesting that many people are experiencing nomophobia (e.g., Michael & Sheppard, 2013), it would be prudent for researchers to develop a validated scale for this aspect of mobile addiction and conduct further empirical studies to substantiate these claims. Although an individual scale or diagnostic category for nomophobia would be ideal, it might also be useful to include nomophobia as a subscale of an existing problematic mobile phone use scale, especially considering the shared traits in mobile addiction (Billieux, 2012). Insofar as existing scales are concerned, Kwon et al.'s (2013) SAS subscale of withdrawal includes several items that may be considered symptoms of nomophobia, such as "Won't be able to stand not having a smartphone" and "Feeling impatient and fretful when I am not holding my smartphone." Therefore, it might be fruitful to revise or expand the construct of withdrawal in future mobile phone dependency scales so that it accommodates nomophobia.

Finally, one of the most significant contributions of King et al.'s (2013) study was the authors' suggestion that nomophobia should be examined with relation to other, possible comorbid mental disorders. King et al. (2013) made this recommendation based on the fact that their patient also had a social phobia disorder, as classified by the DSM-IV (APA, 2000). This suggestion aligns well with the recent findings of Rosen, Whaling, Rab, Carrier, and Cheever (2013), who found that technology-related anxieties and attitudes were predictive of the clinical symptoms of several mental disorders including narcissistic, antisocial, paranoid, obsessive, and histrionic personality disorders. Moreover, even after these technology-related attitudes and anxieties were controlled for, online behaviors, especially Facebook behaviors, were predictive of mood and personality disorders (Rosen et al., 2013). That said, cell phone use was associated with decreased depressive symptoms in Rosen et al.'s (2013) sample, which suggests that these technology-related anxieties, attitudes, and behaviors may be associated with some types of mental illness and not others. Considered together, King et al. (2013) and Rosen et al. (2013) established that comorbidity exists between cyber addictions/dependency behaviors and certain types of mental disorders (i.e., anxiety and personality disorders). Future research should explore whether these cyber addictions are simply manifestations of other mental illnesses or causal agents in the development of other mental illnesses.

New Directions: Mobile Phones as Mechanisms for Behavior Change

Although most of this review has highlighted the ways in which mobile phone use is problematic, a promising line of research examines the ways in which mobile phones, specifically text messages, can be used for behavior change through health-related interventions. Text messages have been used to deliver information and interventions related to a variety of health concerns, including smoking, HIV, weight loss and nutrition, immunizations, pre- and postnatal health, and substance abuse (e.g., Irvine et al., 2012; Kerr et al., 2012; Siedner, Haberer, Bosco Bwana, Ware, & Bangsberg, 2012; Snuggs et al., 2012; Stockwell et al., 2012; Whittaker et al., 2012; Ybarra et al., 2013). As an example, Irvine et al. (2012) engaged a group of disadvantaged men in Scotland in an interactive alcohol intervention using text messages. The uptake of their intervention was good: of the 34 participants, 88% answered questions posed to them about their drinking, and at least one person responded to every general text message sent, even though those messages did not request a reply. Therefore, Irvine et al. (2012) suggested that text messages could be a low-cost unobtrusive method to engage hard-to-reach populations in interventions and collect real-time data on these populations.

Due to the success of these programs, behavior change initiatives using text messages are constantly in development, and much recent research has focused on developing tailored interventions based on feedback from targeted groups (e.g., Muench, Weiss, Kuerbis, & Morgenstern, 2013; Owens et al., 2011; Wright, Fortune, Juzang, & Bull, 2011). For example, Owens et al. (2011) sought feedback from service users and clinicians on how to develop a successful text message intervention to decrease the repetition of self-harm, and Wright et al. (2011) gathered information from the target group themselves about how to effectively deliver HIV information to young Black men. Meanwhile, in a study focused on addiction, Muench et al. (2013) surveyed those who were in an outpatient substance abuse treatment program to determine whether they might be receptive to text message follow-up care and what types of content they felt might be most useful. Of those surveyed, 98% indicated they might be interested in using text messages during and after treatment, and most indicated that benefit-driven messages would be preferred over consequence-driven messages. A significant number would also want to use text messaging to alert a counselor (78%) or friend (96%) that they were at risk for relapse (Muench et al., 2013). The results from focus group studies have been largely encouraging, and most participants believe that text-messaging interventions could be used as behavior change mechanisms.

In sum, the addictive properties of phones might be harnessed in positive ways, to affect other health behaviors and addictions. This type of research is encouraging, as it shifts the focus from the negative aspects of cell phone dependency to the positive ones and provides a promising line of future research.

Summary

Overall, problematic mobile phone use appears to be widespread and (across many studies) associated with a variety of negative psychological characteristics, such as anxiety, depression, neuroticism, poor sleep, and stress. Recent studies have also suggested that problematic mobile phone behaviors may be comorbid with other mental disorders, such as anxiety, mood, and personality disorders (King et al., 2013; Rosen et al., 2013). Therefore, the media furor may not be entirely unfounded – nomophobia, mobile phone addiction, and text message addiction, whether they are considered independently or part of the same construct, are real problems within modern society. Moreover, people are becoming aware of their addictions, and in coming years, it is likely that many people will seek treatment for their addictions. Fortunately for these people, help appears to be abundant: a Google search for "mobile phone addiction treatment" returned more than 26 million hits.

Perhaps future research should explore more directly whether these addictions are just symptoms of more general mental disorders (e.g., anxiety or mood disorders) or whether they can even be considered addictions at all. In a series of studies, Atchley and Warden (2012) showed that information has short-lived value among college students, which makes immediate texts or calls appealing. However, they also showed that college students make intentional choices about how quickly they share information, depending on social distance. Therefore, whether or not a person responds immediately to a text or phone call appears to be an intentional choice, not one driven purely by addiction.

The fact that people are making intentional choices about their mobile phone use also means that the positive aspect of mobile phone dependency may not be so positive: behavior change interventions via text messaging may have limited success. People have the choice to read and respond to messages on their phones, and they may be less inclined to do so when they receive messages from people with whom they share no social intimacy. That said, it is worthwhile to do what we can, while we can, to leverage existing technology to increase individuals' access to information and interventions. With new, game-changing technologies on the horizon (e.g., Google Glass), it is likely that the problems associated with mobile phones (e.g., phantom vibrations and nomophobia) will be ephemeral anomalies for everyone – until the next set of addictive behaviors and symptoms emerges.

References

American Psychiatric Association (APA). (2000). *Diagnostic and statistical manual of mental disorders* (4th ed.) (DSM-IV). Washington, DC: Author.

Atchley, P., & Warden, A. C. (2012). The need of young adults to text now: Using delay discounting to assess informational choice. *Journal of Applied Research in Memory and Cognition, 1,* 229–234.

Beranuy, M., Oberst, U., Carbonell, X., & Chamarro, A. (2009). Problematic Internet and mobile phone use and clinical symptoms in college students: The role of emotional intelligence. *Computers in Human Behavior, 25,* 1182–1187.

Bianchi, A., & Phillips, J. G. (2005). Psychological predictors of problem mobile phone use. *Cyberpsychology and Behavior, 8,* 39–51.

Billieux, J. (2012). Problematic use of the mobile phone: A literature review and a pathways model. *Current Psychiatry Reviews, 8,* 299–307.

Billieux, J., Van der Linden, M., D'Acremont, M., Ceschi, G., & Zermatten, A. (2007). Does impulsivity relate to perceived dependence on and actual use of the mobile phone? *Applied Cognitive Psychology, 21,* 527–537.

Billieux, J., Van der Linden, M., & Rochat, L. (2008). The role of impulsivity in actual and problematic use of the mobile phone. *Applied Cognitive Psychology, 22,* 1195–1210.

Butt, S., & Phillips, J. G. (2008). Personality and self reported mobile phone use. *Computers in Human Behavior, 24,* 346–360.

Cheever, N., Rosen, L. R., Carrier, L. M., & Chavez, A. (2014). Out of sight is not out of mind: The impact of restricting wireless mobile device use on anxiety among low, moderate and high users. *Computers in Human Behavior, 37,* 290–297.

Chóliz, M. (2010). Mobile phone addiction: A point of issue. *Addiction, 105,* 373–374.

Chung, N. (2011). Korean adolescent girls' addictive use of mobile phones to maintain interpersonal solidarity. *Social Behavior and Personality, 39,* 1349–1358.

Clark-Dickson, P. (2012, May 29). Press release: SMS will remain more popular than mobile messaging apps over next five years. Informa Telecoms & Media. Retrieved November 26, 2014, from http://blogs.informatandm.com/4971/press-release-sms-will-remain-more-popular-than-mobile-messaging-apps-over-next-five-years/

Dixit, S., Shukla, H., Bhagwat, A. K., Bindal, A., Goyal, A., Zaidi, A. K., & Shrivastava, A. (2010). A study to evaluate mobile phone dependence among students of a medical college and associated hospital of central India. *Indian Journal of Community Medicine, 35,* 339–341.

Drouin, M., Kaiser, D., & Miller, D. (2012). Phantom vibrations in young adults: Prevalence and underlying psychological characteristics. *Computers in Human Behavior, 28,* 1490–1496.

Ehrenberg, A., Juckes, S., White, K. M., & Walsh, S. P. (2008). Personality and self-esteem as predictors of young people's technology use. *Cyberpsychology and Behavior, 11,* 739–741. doi: 10.1089/cpb.2008.0030

Ezoe, S., Toda, M., Yoshimura, K., Naritomi, A., Rei, D., & Morimoto, K. (2009). Relationships of personality and lifestyle with mobile phone dependence among female nursing students. *Social Behavior and Personality: An International Journal, 37,* 231–238.

Gorry, G. (2009). Empathy in the virtual world. *Chronicle of Higher Education, 56*(2), B10–B12.

Griffiths, M. D. (2012). Facebook addiction: Concerns, criticism, and recommendations – A response to Andreassen and colleagues. *Psychological Reports, 110,* 518–520.

Güzeller, C. O., & Coşguner, T. (2012). Development of a problematic mobile phone use scale for Turkish adolescents. *Cyberpsychology, Behavior, and Social Networking, 15,* 205–211.

Ha, J., Chin, B., Park, D., Ryu, S., & Yu, J. (2008). Characteristics of excessive cellular phone use in Korean adolescents. *Cyberpsychology and Behavior, 11,* 783–784. doi: 10.1089/cpb.2008.0096

Hafner, K. (2009, May 25). Texting may be taking a toll. *The New York Times.* Retrieved November 27, 2014, from http://www.nytimes.com/2009/05/26/health/26teen.html?hpw&_r=0

Halper, M. (2013, April 29). The rise and $23 billion fall of text messaging. *SmartPlanet.* Retrieved November 27, 2014, from http://www.smartplanet.com/blog/bulletin/the-rise-and-23-billion-fall-of-text-messaging/18525

Hong, F., Chiu, S. I., & Huang, D. (2012). A model of the relationship between psychological characteristics, mobile phone addiction and use of mobile phones by Taiwanese university female students. *Computers in Human Behavior, 28,* 2152–2159.

Igarashi, T., Motoyoshi, T., Takai, J., & Yoshida, T. (2008). No mobile, no life: Self-perception and text-message dependency among Japanese high school students. *Computers in Human Behavior, 24,* 2311–2324.

International Telecommunication Union (ITU). (2013, February). ICT facts and figures. *ITU Telecommunication Development Sector.* Retrieved November 27, 2014, from http://www.itu.int/en/ITU-D/Statistics/Documents/facts/ICTFactsFigures2013.pdf

Irvine, L., Falconer, D. W., Jones, C., Ricketts, I. W., Williams, B., & Crombie, I. K. (2012). Can text messages reach the parts other process measures cannot reach? An evaluation of a behavior change intervention delivered by mobile phone. *PLOS ONE, 7*(12), 1–7. doi: 10.1371/journal.pone.0052621

Jenaro, C., Flores, N., Gómez-Vela, M., González-Gil, F., & Caballo, C. (2007). Problematic Internet and cell-phone use: Psychological, behavioral, and health correlates. *Addiction Research and Theory, 15,* 309–320.

Kerr, D. A., Pollard, C. M., Howat, P., Delp, E. J., Pickering, M., Kerr, K. R., … Boushey, C. J. (2012). Connecting Health and Technology (CHAT): Protocol of a randomized controlled trial to improve nutrition behaviours using mobile devices and tailored text messaging in young adults. *BMC Public Health, 12,* 477–486.

King, A. S., Valença, A. M., Silva, A. O., Baczynski, T. T., Carvalho, M. R., & Nardi, A. E. (2013). Nomophobia: Dependency on virtual environments or social phobia? *Computers in Human Behavior, 29,* 140–144.

Korkki, P. (2009, March 7). Internet, mobile phones named most important inventions. *The New York Times.* Retrieved November 27, 2014, from http://www.nytimes.com/2009/03/08/business/08count.html?_r=0

Kwon, M., Lee, J.-Y., Won, W.-Y., Park, J.-W., Min, J.-A., Hahn C, … Kim, D. J. (2013). Development and validation of a smartphone addiction scale (SAS). *PLOS ONE, 8*(2), 1–7.

Laramie, D. (2007). *Emotional and behavioral aspects of mobile phone use.* [PhD thesis]. Alliant International University, San Diego, CA.

Lenhart, A. (2012, March 19). Teens, smartphones, and texting. Pew Internet & American Life Project. Retrieved November 27, 2014, from http://www.pewinternet.org/~/media/Files/Reports/2012/PIP_Teens_Smartphones_and_Texting.pdf

Lin, Y., Lin, S., Li, P., Huang, W., & Chen, C. (2013). Prevalent hallucinations during medical internships: Phantom vibration and ringing syndromes. *PLOS ONE, 8*(6), 1–6.

Lu, X., Watanabe, J., Liu, Q., Uji, M., Shono, M., & Kitamura, T. (2011). Internet and mobile phone text-messaging dependency: Factor structure and correlation with dysphoric mood among Japanese adults. *Computers in Human Behavior, 27,* 1702–1709. doi: 10.1016/j.chb.2011.02.009

Michael, P., & Sheppard, F. (2013, June 2). Nomophobia, the fear of not having a mobile phone, hits record numbers. *News.com.au.* Retrieved November 27, 2014, from http://www.news.com.au/technology/nomophobia-the-fear-of-not-having-a-mobile-phone-hits-record-numbers/story-e6frfro0-1226655033189#ixzz2ckLUIFRW

Muench, F., Weiss, R. A., Kuerbis, A., & Morgenstern, J. (2013). Developing a theory driven text messaging intervention for addiction care with user driven content. *Psychology of Addictive Behaviors, 27,* 315–321.

National Information Society Agency (NIA). (2006). An analysis of the causes of mobile phone addiction. Retrieved November 27, 2014, from http://www.nia.or.kr

Owens, C., Farrand, P., Darvill, R., Emmens, T., Hewis, E., & Aitken, P. (2011). Involving service users in intervention design: A participatory approach to developing a text-messaging intervention to reduce repetition of self-harm. *Health Expectations, 14,* 285–295.

Rosen, L. D., Whaling, K., Rab, S., Carrier, L. M., & Cheever, N. A. (2013). Is Facebook creating "iDisorders"? The link between clinical symptoms. *Computers in Human Behavior, 29,* 1243–1254.

Rothberg, M. B., Arora, A., Hermann, J., Kleppel, R., St. Marie, P., & Visintainer, P. (2010). Phantom vibration syndrome among medical staff: A cross sectional survey. *BMJ, 341,* c6914.

Siedner, M. J., Haberer, J. E., Bosco Bwana, M., Ware, N. C., & Bangsberg, D. R. (2012). High acceptability for cell phone text messages to improve communication of laboratory results with HIV-infected patients in rural Uganda: A cross-sectional survey study. *BMC Medical Informatics and Decision Making, 12,* 56–62.

Sigman, A. (2009). Well connected? *Biologist, 56,* 14–20.

Smith, A. (2012). The best (and worst) of mobile connectivity. Pew Internet & American Life Project. Retrieved November 27, 2014, from http://pewinternet.org/Reports/2012/Best-Worst-Mobile.aspx

Snuggs, S., Mcrobbie, H., Myers, K., Schmocker, F., Goddard, J., & Hajek, P. (2012). Using text messaging to prevent relapse to smoking: Intervention development, practicability and client reactions. *Addiction, 107*(2), 39–44.

Stockwell, M. S., Kharbanda, E., Martinez, R., Lara, M., Vawdrey, D., Natarajan, K., & Rickert, V. I. (2012). Text4Health: Impact of text message reminder-recalls for pediatric and adolescent immunizations. *American Journal of Public Health, 102*(2), e15–e21.

Takao, M., Takahashi, S., & Kitamura, M. (2009). Addictive personality and problematic mobile phone use. *Cyberpsychology and Behavior, 12,* 501–507. doi: 10.1089/cpb.2009.0022

Thomée, S., Harenstam, A., & Hagberg, M. (2011). Mobile phone use and stress, sleep disturbances and symptoms of depression among young adults: A prospective cohort study. *BMC Public Health, 11*(66), 66–76. Retrieved November 27, 2014, from http://www.biomedcentral.com/content/pdf/1471-2458-11-66.pdf

Toda, M., Monden, K., Kubo, K., & Morimoto, K. (2004). Cellular phone dependence tendency of female university students. *Japanese Journal of Hygiene, 59,* 383–386.

Turkle, S. (2011). *Alone together: Why we expect more from technology and less from each other.* New York, NY: Basic Books.

United States Census Bureau. (2013, July 31). U.S. and world population clock. Retrieved from http://www.census.gov/popclock/

Walsh, S. P., White, K. M., Cox, S., & Young, R. M. (2011). Keeping in constant touch: The predictors of young Australians' mobile phone involvement. *Computers in Human Behavior, 27,* 333–342.

Walsh, S. P., White, K. M., & Young, R. M. (2008). Over-connected? A qualitative exploration of the relationship between Australian youth and their mobile phones. *Journal of Adolescence, 31,* 77–92.

Walsh, S. P., White, K. M., & Young, R. M. (2010). Needing to connect: The impact of self and others on young people's involvement with their mobile phone. *Australian Journal of Psychology, 62,* 194–203.

Whittaker, R., Matoff-Stepp, S., Meehan, J., Kendrick, J., Jordan, E., Stange, P., ... Rhee, K. (2012). Text4baby: Development and implementation of a national text messaging health information service. *American Journal of Public Health, 102,* 2207–2213.

Williams, A. (2013, January 11). The end of courtship? *The New York Times.* Retrieved November 27, 2014, from http://www.nytimes.com/2013/01/13/fashion/the-end-of-courtship.html?pagewanted=all

Wright, E., Fortune, T., Juzang, I., & Bull, S. (2011). Text messaging for HIV prevention with young Black men: Formative research and campaign development. *AIDS Care, 23,* 534–541.

Ybarra, M. L., Holtrop, J. S., Bağci Bosi, A., Bilir, N., Korchmaros, J. D., & Salih Emri, A. K. (2013). Feasibility and acceptability of a text messaging-based smoking cessation program in Ankara, Turkey. *Journal of Health Communication, 18,* 960–973.

Yen, C., Tang, T., Yen, J., Lin, H., Huang, C., Liu, S., & Ko, C. (2009). Symptoms of problematic cellular phone use, functional impairment and its association with depression among adolescents in Southern Taiwan. *Journal of Adolescence, 32,* 863–873.

Young, K. S. (1998). Internet addiction: The emergence of a new clinical disorder. *Cyberpsychology and Behavior, 1,* 237–244.

12

Assessing the Written Language of Text Messages

Abbie Grace and Nenagh Kemp

University of Tasmania

Mobile phones have become a part of everyday life, following a phenomenal growth in sales since the invention of the first handheld model in 1973 (Cooper et al., 1975; De Souza e Silva, 2006). By 2011, mobile phone subscriptions outnumbered people in 105 countries, with a total of nearly six billion subscriptions globally, averaging 86 subscriptions per hundred people worldwide (International Telecommunication Union, 2012). The 20th anniversary of the first text message was celebrated in December 2012, and according to statistics released by Portio Research (2012), a trillion text messages were sent globally in one year for the first time in 2005, and 8.5 trillion messages were sent in 2012. The subsequent development of a text messaging "language" during this rapid growth has afforded a unique opportunity to observe a rapidly forming and changing style of communication and to investigate the factors that influence its development.

The language used by texters (the senders of text messages) on their mobile phones has been referred to by a variety of terms, including "text speak" (Drouin & Davis, 2009), "textish" (Faulkner & Culwin, 2005), "teen-talk" (Thurlow & Brown, 2003), and "textese" (e.g., Drouin & Driver, 2014; Kemp, 2010; Verheijen, 2013), the term chosen for use in this chapter. The specific respellings, contractions, and additions to conventional English contained in text messages (e.g., *awsum* for *awesome*, *ppl* for *people*, and emoticons such as *:-p*) are referred to here as "textisms" (see Rosen, Chang, Erwin, Carrier, & Cheever, 2010; Wood, Jackson, Hart, Plester, & Wilde, 2011). Textism use may be motivated by various factors, including efficiency in character use, social capital, and communicative enhancement of messages, as explained below. The unique technological and social contexts in which text messaging occurs may affect the type and extent of textism use. Research on texting has mainly examined how texters use language on their phones, and the relationship between texting and other literacy skills, with varying results. Studies of textism use and the factors that affect this use have varied greatly in methodology, and in the factors examined in the research design. It is therefore crucial to examine these questions to help inform the interpretation of results already obtained, and to design future research. In this chapter, we consider the methodologies and factors examined in previous studies of textism use in text messages and

The Wiley Handbook of Psychology, Technology, and Society, First Edition. Edited by Larry D. Rosen, Nancy A. Cheever, and L. Mark Carrier.

discuss what their results can reveal about the nature of textisms and their importance in text-based communication.

The Technological Context of Texting

The unique context of computer-mediated communication (CMC) has driven the development of language features such as textisms and quick-fire phrasing (Crystal, 2001; Freiermuth, 2002; Greenfield & Subrahmanyam, 2003). CMC encompasses formats that predated mobile phones, such as email and online chat, but when texting first became popular, it was the only one of these technologies that was entirely mobile. Although they share many features with other forms of CMC, text messages are unique in several ways. The synchronicity of text messages falls between the immediacy of an online chat conversation and the convenience of an email, for which an immediate response may not be expected. Unlike online chat conversations, text messages are stored on recipients' phones, but unlike email messages, which are often used in a formal office/work context, text messages frequently involve conversations between friends and family.

The creation of early text messages was restricted by the constraints of small mobile phone keypads, whereas online chat and emails were constructed via full QWERTY keyboards. Text entry on early mobile phones was completed via alpha-numeric keypads on which characters were selected via multiple key presses. Messages were limited to 160 characters per message, and together with the financial cost of charges per message, provided an incentive for texters to minimize character use (Crystal, 2008; Hillebrand, 2010). It is plausible that all of these factors combined to shape uniquely the text messaging language that developed among texters. The resulting language norms provide an opportunity to investigate the characteristics of this rapidly changing mode of communication, and the motivations associated with its use.

Recently, there has been a blurring of the lines that once separated text messaging from other forms of computer-mediated communication. Advances in mobile phone technology have included the addition of predictive software programs to phones, overcoming the need for multiple key presses to select any character. Full keyboards and/or touchscreens now represent the most typical interface on more recent mobile phone models. More recently, the invention of smartphones capable of Internet connectivity (e.g., via mobile broadband) has allowed alternative forms of communication such as email to occur via mobile phones. The iPhone, first released in the United States in 2007, included all of these new technologies, and by mid-2012, ownership of these and other smartphones was linked to approximately one billion mobile broadband subscriptions globally (ITU, 2012). Other technological advances include Over the Top (OTT) services (such as WhatsApp and BBM, BlackBerry Messenger) where instant messages are sent from mobile phones and costs are covered in the user's Internet fees.

The Social Context of Texting

The development of textese may also have been affected by the demographic characteristics of its dominant users; that is, by adolescents and young adults (e.g., Ling & Baron, 2007; Shortis, 2007; Thurlow & Brown, 2003). Large-scale reports, such as

Pew Internet surveys in the United States, have confirmed that the most frequent users of text messages are young people aged 14 to 24 years (100 to 200 messages a day; Lenhart, 2012; Smith, 2011) and that most of these messages were to friends (Lenhart, Ling, Campbell, & Purcell, 2010). Similar results have been found in Norway (Ling, Bertel, & Sundsøy, 2012) and Australia (ACMA, 2012). Ling and colleagues calculated that senders and recipients in this age group accounted for 60 times as many messages as would be expected if texting were spread evenly across all age groups. Participation in texting and textism use has been ascribed social value as a marker of group identity among young people (Reid & Reid, 2004), and representations of youth accents (e.g., *gunna* for *going to*, *laterz* for *see you later*, and *bin* for *been*) have been observed as an important feature of textese (Thurlow & Brown, 2003; Shortis, 2007).

The Nature and Study of Textese

The rapid uptake of new communication technologies by young people has led to an increasing range of empirical research of the resultant language forms and conclusions regarding the nature of textese. In 2001, Crystal referred to the "Netspeak" of computer-mediated communication as a "development of millennial significance," noting that a "new medium of linguistic communication does not arrive very often, in the history of the race" (pp. 238–239). Rather than representing a new language as such, textese has been described as a hybrid of written and spoken language (Baron, 2008; Crystal, 2008; Freiermuth, 2002, Greenfield & Subrahmanyam, 2003; McWhorter, 2013), whose communicative power lies in the creative additions that can be made to messages, such as exclamatory spellings (e.g., *awww my darling*) and novel words (e.g., the kiss *mmmwwahh*) (e.g., Crystal, 2008; Frehner, 2008; Thurlow & Brown, 2003).

In the early days of text messaging, many journalists in the popular press were less charitable about the appearance of textese, raising strongly worded concerns about the dangers to conventional English it apparently presents. Thurlow (2006) reviewed more than 100 media reports from around the world regarding computer-mediated communication and found that reports were largely negative and alarmist. He concluded that the use of derogatory descriptions such as "cyber-slang" and "technobabble" reflected long-standing cultural fears of both new technology and youth culture. In light of these types of concerns, a number of researchers began to investigate two important issues: firstly, the nature of textism use in messages (e.g., Drouin & Driver, 2014; Frehner, 2008), and secondly, the relationship between textism use and conventional literacy skills (e.g., Kemp & Bushnell, 2011; Plester, Lerkkanen, Linjama, Rasku-Puttonen, & Littleton, 2011). Secondary to these questions are details about how the outcomes of research into both of these issues vary with gender and technology. These studies are considered in more detail below.

Methodological Issues in Text Language Research

As text messaging research is a relatively new area of study, methodological options for message collection and textism categorization are still being explored. Published studies of text messaging language began to appear in the early 2000s (e.g., Androutsopoulos &

Schmidt, 2002; Brown, 2002; Grinter & Eldridge, 2003). Since then, a number of methodologies have emerged, several of which involve the direct collection of text messages from those who have sent them, such as by copying messages from phones, as discussed in detail in this chapter. Other researchers have studied textism use by accessing large, anonymous corpora of text messages (e.g., Beasley, 2009; Choudhury et al., 2007; Herring & Zelenkauskaite, 2008, 2009). Furthermore, some have gathered estimates of textism use through survey questions (e.g., Drouin, 2011; Massengill Shaw, Carlson, & Waxman, 2007), a method which may limit the validity of participants' responses.

Methodological Variation in Message Collection

In studies involving the active collection of text messages from individual participants, researchers have used several different methodologies. One experimental method is to ask participants to "translate" a set of words or messages from Standard English into textese (e.g., Drouin & Davis, 2009; Neville, 2003), with some researchers designing messages to include words that appear frequently in messages written by similar participant groups (e.g., De Jonge & Kemp, 2012; Kemp, 2010). There are two advantages of translation-based methods: the increased comparability of messages between participants (as the range of possible textisms is limited), and the fact that words of particular interest can be targeted. However, the proportion of textisms contained in these messages compared to all words may be inflated due to the intentional inclusion of high numbers of words that are easily abbreviated. Further, the instructions given may encourage participants to use more textisms than they normally would. For example, Drouin and Davis (2009, p. 53) instructed their participants to "translate the following sentence from Standard English into text speak (e.g., from 'better' to 'btr')" and Kemp (2010, p. 58) said to "write using text-messaging abbreviations such as *u* for *you* and *2* for *to*."

Another text message collection method has been to ask participants to write a message in response to a specified situation. This scenario-based message elicitation method was employed by Plester, Wood, and Joshi (2009) because children were not permitted to use their phones at school. This technique avoids the potential ethical and financial issues involved in asking children to send messages to a researcher's phone. However, as with message translation, message elicitation tasks may inadvertently encourage participants to try to think of textisms to match as many words as possible, rather than to attempt an accurate representation of their overall textism use. This method thus may also lead to overestimates of people's textism use.

To overcome the difficulties of collecting realistic messages from experimental tasks, naturalistic collection methods have also been used. In some cases, participants have been asked to copy messages sent (and sometimes received) from their phones (e.g., Bodomo, 2010; Drouin & Driver, 2014; Ling & Baron, 2007). However, variation exists even in studies involving messages copied from phones. In one study, participants filled out text messaging diaries for two weeks (Faulkner & Culwin, 2005), and in another, messages were collected from participants' iPhones over a period of six months via an installed data-collection software application (Tossell et al., 2012). Where naturalistic messages are collected after participation in a text language study has been agreed, it is possible that messages might start to show higher rates of textisms than in messages sent prior to the research beginning, if participants believe that textism use is expected by the researcher. Even experimental methods may lead participants to over-represent their textism use. In separate studies of 10- to 12-year-olds' text messages, the density of textisms compared to total words was found to be 57–59% in translated messages (Plester, Wood, & Bell, 2008) and only 34% in scenario-based messages (Plester et al., 2009). Grace, Kemp, Martin, and Parrila (2012) compared the text messages of Australian undergraduates who each created messages under two experimental conditions: translation of a message written in conventional English, and in response to a scenario (e.g., "Write down what you would text to a friend to tell them you are going to be five minutes late to meet them."). Each participant also copied previously sent messages from their phone. It was found that translated messages contained significantly higher densities of textisms (27%) than the scenario-based messages (22%), and in turn than in the naturalistic messages (19%). Therefore it is recommended that investigations of textism use be based on naturalistic text messages wherever possible, and where it is not possible, it should be acknowledged that textism densities may be overestimated.

Methodological Variation in Textism Categorization and Counting

Once messages have been collected, message length can be calculated and textisms categorized. As with message collection, categorization and counting methods have been inconsistent across studies. Questions have arisen over which words are counted as textisms, the names and definitions of categories, and the categories in which specific textisms belong.

Textisms are similar to word-forms that predate mobile phones, and are accepted beyond the context of text messages. This adds complexity to decisions about which words to count as textisms in texting research. For example, some words commonly considered as textisms in current research first appeared in literature more than one hundred years ago (e.g., *wiv* for *with*, *gonna* for *going to*; see Crystal, 2008; Shortis, 2007). The shortening of words certainly existed long before the advent of text messaging. As well as the long use of such common abbreviations as *Mon* for *Monday*, there are many conventional shortened forms of English names in historical records (e.g., *Wm* for *William*; *Xpr* for *Christopher*), and abbreviated words of Latin are seen engraved on the ruins of the temples of ancient Rome. Even the seemingly recent initialism *OMG* appeared in a letter from Lord Fisher to Sir Winston Churchill in 1917, glossed as "Oh! My God!" (Locker, 2012, p. 1). Both *OMG* and *LOL* (laugh out loud) have recently been added to the Oxford English Dictionary (OED, 2011), and anecdotal reports suggest that some written textisms have even crossed into spoken language (e.g., "lols" and "sad face!", the verbal equivalent of the graphic textism ☹; heard in personal conversations with university students). This transfer of written textisms into spoken language, in addition to the better-known representation of spoken forms in written messages (such as *hafta* for *have to* or *pleeeaaaaase* for an emphasized *please*), demonstrates that the lines between whole words and textisms, in written and spoken language, are becoming more blurred.

Another methodological issue to consider is the wide variation shown in the way that researchers have categorized the textisms that they have observed in their studies. For example, some researchers have counted traditional acronyms (e.g., *UK* for *United Kingdom*; Plester et al., 2009) and spelling errors as textisms (e.g., *excelent* for *excellent*; Thurlow & Brown, 2003), whereas others have not. Category names for words such as *gonna* for *going to* include "accent stylization" (Thurlow & Brown,

2003), "accent simulation" (Shortis, 2007), and "youth code" (Plester et al., 2008). Varying category definitions have resulted in the textism *u* for *you* being categorized within "abbreviations" (Ling & Baron, 2007), "shortenings" (Rosen et al., 2010), and "letter/number homophones" (Thurlow & Brown, 2003). The categorization schemes presented in key studies of text messages from English-speaking countries are summarized in Table 12.1 to provide a full comparison of categorization options for future researchers. Categories are sorted into the broader textism types "contractive," "expressive," and "other" textisms as employed by Grace et al. (2012). Contractive textisms involve character deletions (e.g., the homophone *r* for *are*), while expressive textisms involve the addition of extra characters (e.g., *hooooome* for *home*). "Other" textism types include spelling errors, typos, and textism categories in which at least some of the words do not change in length (e.g., unconventional spelling such as *thankx* for thanks) or exist in any other form (e.g., the youth stylizations *gah* to express frustration and *whoop whoop* to express joy).

Most of the categorization schemes shown in Table 12.1 include references to shortenings, contractions, homophones, and youth stylizations, although variations in names and category definitions clearly exist. Several key studies of textism use are not included in Table 12.1 as textism categorization was either not performed, or was not clear from the published articles. For example, Massengill Shaw et al. (2007) referred to textisms overall as "abbreviations," but analyzed each textism individually without categorizing types. Tagg (2009) included several detailed linguistic analyses organized by transformation (e.g., final syllable omission), by spelling variation function (e.g., regiolectal respelling, such as *summort* for *something*), and by spelling variation form (e.g., colloquial respelling, such as the *dd* in *liddle* for *little*). Wood, Jackson, et al. (2011) reported only that they used those categories specified in Plester et al. (2009). Drouin (2011), Kemp and Bushnell (2011), and Wood, Meachem, et al. (2011) did not report textism analyses by category, and Tossell et al. (2012) only analyzed emoticon use in messages. Shortis (2007) proposed categories similar to those above, as well as several further categories: color/movement/pictorial imagery, stage directions (e.g., *Monsieur [said in a French accent]*), and special effects such as writing in *webdings* font (so that message is only understood when converted to an alphabetic font).

Estimates of textism density (the number of textisms as a proportion of total words in messages) may be affected by some, but not all, of the variations in which categories are included or how categories are defined. For example, the varied categorization of *u* for *you* as a letter homophone (e.g., Neville, 2003), an abbreviation (Ling & Baron, 2007), or an omission of non-essential letters (Cingel & Sundar, 2012) does not affect the calculation of overall textism density, because this spelling is still counted as only one textism. However, the inclusion of textism categories such as spelling errors, traditional acronyms, and omitted capitalization would lead to inflated estimates of textism use compared to studies that exclude these transformation types from textism counts. Furthermore, some textisms contain changes from more than one category (e.g., *im* for *I'm*, in which both capitalization and an apostrophe have been omitted). Such textisms have been counted in more than one category by some researchers (e.g., De Jonge & Kemp, 2012; Varnhagen et al., 2009), but in only one by others, on the basis of their first transformation only (e.g., just the omitted capital in *im* for *I'm*; Plester et al., 2009), leading to lower textism densities than if all transformations had been counted,

Table 12.1 Categories and textism examples listed in selected studies of language in text messages (all studies were of text messages written in English).

	Grinter & Eldridge, 2003	Thurlow & Brown, 2003	Neville, 2003	Bieswanger, 2007
Categories for contractive textism types	Abbreviations: Ad hoc (*spose: suppose*) Abbreviations: Known (*mins*) Dropping single letter (*ritten: written*) Sounds: Letters (*fone: phone*) Sounds: Symbols (*th@s: that's*) Sounds: Numbers (*gr8: great*) Acronyms: Separate words (*PWB: please write back*) Acronyms: Single word (*w: with*) Acronyms: compound word (*gf: girlfriend*) Foreign short forms (*bs: besos*)	Shortenings (*Uni: University*) Contractions (*nt: night*) g-clippings (*goin: going*) Other clippings (*hav: have*) Acronyms (*DI: Detective Inspector*) Initialisms (*V: Very*) Letter/number homophones (*B: be*) Non-conventional spellings (*fone: phone*) Accent stylization (*de: the*)	Letter and number homophones (*u: you*) Abbreviations (*ppl: people*) Spoken slang shortenings (*soz: sorry*) Dropped vowels (*hppn: happen*) Phonetic abbreviation (*sed: said*) Downward converging accent feature simulation (*wanna: want to*) Substitution of hard "th" sounds: "d"s (*dat: that*) Symbols (*congr@ulate: congratulate*) Initialisms (*SYL: see you later*)	Initialisms (*NY: New York*) Clippings (*bday: birthday*) Contractions (*don't: do not*) Letter/number homophones (*b: be*) Phonetic spellings (*bin: been*) Word-value characters (*x: kiss*)
Categories for expressive textism types		Typographic symbols (*!!*) Emoticons (*:->*)		
Categories for other and mixed textism types	Hybrid: Using two or more of the above (*b4: before*) Foreign letters (*ii: :-)*)	Misspellings and typos (*excelent: excellent*)	Misspellings	

(continued on pg. 214)

Table 12.1 *(Continued)*

	Ling & Baron, 2007	Frehner, 2008	Plester et al., 2008	Dronin & Davis, 2009
Categories for contractive textism types	Acronyms (*lol: laughing out loud*) Abbreviations (*U: you*) Vowel deletions (*b: be*) Miscellaneous lexical shortenings (*Sun: Sunday*) Contractions (*can't: cannot*)	Letter and number homophones (*r: are*) Clippings (*jus: just*) Consonant spelling (*mst: must*) Apostrophes (*evans: Evan's*) Phonological approximation and other non-standard shortenings (*dis: this*)	Rebus, or letter/number homophones (*C U L8R: see you later*) Other phonological reductions (*nite: night*) Symbols (*&: and*) Acronyms (*WUU2: what you up to*) Youth code (*hafta: have to*)	Initialisms (*tryl: talk to you later*) Letter/number homophones (*c: see*) Shortenings (*ur: you're*)
Categories for expressive textism types	Emoticons (*smileys*)	Emulated prosody and onomatopoeic exclamatory spelling (*looove: love*) Emoticons (**8−)) [analyzed separately]*		
Categories for other and mixed textism types		Misspellings [*analyzed separately*] Capitalization [*analyzed separately*] Punctuation [*analyzed separately*]		

	Plester et al., 2009	Kemp, 2010	Rosen et al., 2010	Bushnell et al., 2011
Categories for contractive textism types	Shortenings (*tues*) Contractions (*hmwrk*) g-clippings (*swimmin*) Other clippings (*hav*) Omitted apostrophes (*dads*) Acronyms (*BBC*) Initialisms (*lol*) Symbols (*@*) Letter/number homophones (*2moro*)	Initialisms (*brt: be right there*) Letter homophones (*BN: being*) Contractions (*tim: time*) Number homophones (*aQr8: accurate*) Phonological spelling (*parz: parents*) Capitalization drop (*i: I*)	Linguistic textisms: Acronyms (*LOL, L8R*) Lowercase "i" in place of uppercase I as a personal pronoun Removing apostrophes from contractions (*dont: don't*) Shortening words (*tht: that*)	Letter/number homophones (*l8: late*) Contractions (*bday: birthday*) Omitted apostrophes (*cant: can't*)

	Coe & Oakhill, 2011	Durkin et al., 2011	Holtgraves, 2011	Veater et al., 2011
Categories for expressive textism types	(Symbols also included emoticons (:-o))	*[the examples listed here were taken from a table that did not necessarily include all categories used]*	Contextual textisms: Inserting emoticons or smilies (☺) Using special characters to denote emotional states (.:hug::) Using all capital letters to denote strong emotions (*I AM ANGRY*)	
Categories for other and mixed textism types	Non-conventional spellings (*fone*) Accent stylization (*anuva*) Misspellings (*comming*)	Accent stylization (*d: the*) Slang abbreviation (*parz: parents*)		Accent stylizations (*people: peeps*) Non-conventional spellings (*skool: school*)

	Coe & Oakhill, 2011	Durkin et al., 2011	Holtgraves, 2011	Veater et al., 2011
Categories for contractive textism types	Letter/number homophones *g*-clippings Other clippings Shortenings Contractions Symbol Initialisms *[Textism examples were not included, but categories were based on those in Thurlow & Brown, 2003]*	Non-traditional abbreviations Homophones Letter drop Acronyms *[Textism examples were not included, but categories were based on those in Grinter & Eldridge, 2003, and Plester et al., 2009]*	Slang (*dunno*) Acronym (*LOL*) G drop (*doin*) Number for sound (*L8*) Letter omission (*R: are*) Abbreviations (*x: kiss*) Combined words (*nevermind*)	Shortenings Contractions *g*-clippings Other clippings Symbols Initialisms Homophones Missing apostrophe *[Textism examples were not included, but categories were based on those in Plester et al., 2009]*
Categories for expressive textism types			Expansions (*bitchhhhhhhhh*) Emoticons	
Categories for other and mixed textism types	Accent stylizations Non-conventional spellings	Youth code		Non-conventional spellings Accent stylization

(continued on pg. 216)

Table 12.1 (Continued)

	Cingel & Sundar, 2012	De Jonge & Kemp, 2012	Drouin & Driver, 2014	Grace et al., 2012*
Categories for contractive textism types	Word adaptations: abbreviations or initialisms (*lol, btw*) Omission of non-essential letters (*wud, u*) Substitution of homophones (*be4*)	Shortening/other clipping (*xcellent*) Contraction (*tmrw*) *g*-clipping (*studyin*) Omitted apostrophe (*Kates*) Initialism (*btw*) Combined letter/number homophone (*w8*) Single letter/number homophone (*u, 2*)	Shortening/other clipping (*def*) Contraction (*sry*) *g*-clipping (*talkin*) Omitted apostrophe (*cant*) Initialism (*ttyl*) Combined letter/number homophone (*ur*) Single letter/number homophone (*y, u*)	Single homophones (*u, 2*) Combined homophones (*2nite*) Shortenings (*mon*) Contractions (*msg*) Omitted apostrophes (*cant*) *g*-clippings (*goin*) Initialisms (*btw*) Expressive symbols (*xxx, :D*) Other SYMBOLS (*@, &*) Spelling errors (*rekon*) Other textisms (*abit*)
Categories for expressive textism types	Structural adaptations: Punctuation adaptations Capitalization adaptations	Symbol (:), x)	Symbol (:))	Extra punctuation (*?!*) Extra letters (*pleeease*) Extra words (*cool cool*)
Categories for other and mixed textism types		Spelling error (*ansxer*) Non-standard spelling (*neva*) Accent stylization (*arvo*) Omitted capitalization (*i, oliver*)	Spelling error (*btat's*) Non-standard spelling (*xcitd*) Accent stylization (*didja*) Omitted capitalization (*i, facebook*)	Non-standard spelling (*cos*) Accent stylization (*gonna*) Omitted capitals (*i, sarah*) Extra capitals (*HAPPY BIRTHDAY*)

*Grace et al. (2013a) used the same scheme, but with homophones combined, symbols combined, and the deletion of spelling errors.

both overall and for specific proportions of the different textism types used. Grace et al. (2012) conducted a direct comparison of these two counting methods. They found that although the difference in the textism density calculated from the two counting methods was slight (.18 for counting by first transformation cf. .19 for counting all transformations), that difference represented 660 textisms, or .08 of all transformations categorized. Finally, small differences in textism density data may also result from comparing textisms averaged across the full sample (total textisms divided by total words) with textism densities calculated for individual messages or participants before averaging a second time across the full sample. For example, Drouin and Driver (2014) tested these calculation options and found an overall textism density of .24 for the group, but of .28 when average textism use was calculated for individual participants before being averaged for the group. Therefore researchers need to take into account variations in both textism counting and texting categorization when interpreting their own and others' results.

Textism Categorization of Non-English Textisms

Researchers have studied the types of textisms used in text messages across a range of languages (see Thurlow & Poff, 2012, for a review). Although Table 12.1 refers only to studies of messages written in English, textism types are constructed in similar ways across various languages. For example, Herring and Zelenkauskaite (2009) observed unconventional spellings and abbreviations in Italian text messages such as *t* for *ti*, *ke* for *che*, and *nn* for *non*, similar to textisms observed by Yvon (2010) in French text messages such as *c* for *c'est*, *kon* for *qu'on*, and *pr* for *pour*, and the English textisms *b* for *be*, *sum* for *some*, and *cn* for *can*. Similarly, textism respellings of conventional Spanish include *sl2* for *saludos* (Alonso & Perea, 2008) and in French, *2* for *de* (Anis, 2007), mirroring the phonetic equivalent of *two* in each language, as in the English *2day*. Other languages include textism variations inherent to the language themselves. For example, as noted by Tseliga (2007), non-English letters in Greek may be represented by Roman letters or numbers such as *A8hva* for *Aθηνα* (Athens). Plester and colleagues (2011) note that conventional written Finnish contains contractions that spoken Finnish does not, so that these are seen as more expected and acceptable than contractions in written English. These examples are drawn from European languages, but similar examples can be seen in languages across the world. Categorization schemes should be adjusted as required to recognize the unique characteristics of textism use across varying languages, although it is important to take categorization differences into account when comparing overall textism use between studies.

Broader Categorization of Textism Types

Fine-grained categorizations such as the schemes in Table 12.1 allow for comparisons between specific textism types and literacy scores or participant demographics, but it is also useful to consider larger-grained categorizations of textism types. Broader categorizations of textisms have grouped together textism types in different ways, including "deletions" versus "insertions" based on a comparison between the number of characters in the textism compare to conventional spelling (Herring & Zelenkauskaite, 2009) and "linguistic" versus "contextual" textisms, where contextual textisms are those that add emotional content to the message (e.g., ::*hug*::; Rosen et al., 2010). Similar divisions into "contractive," "expressive," and "other" textism types such as is seen in Table 12.1 have also proven useful. For example, Grace et al. (2012) showed that the differences in messages that were seen across message collection methodologies included differences in the prevalence of these broader textism types. Overall, there were significantly higher textism densities in translated messages than in scenario-based messages than in naturalistic messages, as specified above, and this pattern was also true of contractive textisms. However, the opposite pattern was seen for expressive textisms, in that there were significantly lower densities in translated than scenario-based than naturalistic messages. It may be that students who created messages under experimental conditions were drawing on ideas about their own textism use, or of researcher expectations linked to earlier views of highly abbreviated messages that do not accurately reflect current norms. These possibilities would have been overlooked if the researchers had examined only total textism use, rather than both contractive and expressive types being considered as well.

Other researchers have further analyzed text language in terms of the use of conventional punctuation (Frehner, 2008; Ling & Baron, 2007) and the grammar of textese (Cingel & Sundar, 2012; Wood, Kemp, Waldron, & Hart, 2014). More detailed analyses of textisms include the ways in which phonemes are typically respelled in textism transformations (Frehner, 2008; Tagg, 2009). An awareness of the methodological differences between studies is therefore of benefit to both readers and designers of future research.

Factors Associated with Variations in Textism Use

Whereas methodological differences make comparisons between studies difficult, even studies utilizing similar collection methods have produced varied results. For example, when Australian and British 10- to 12-year-olds translated messages into textese, the resulting messages contained from 24% to 59% textisms (Kemp & Bushnell, 2011; Plester et al., 2008). These kinds of discrepancies between studies suggest that textism use may be influenced by factors beyond methodological concerns, including country and year of data collection, and the analysis of limited combinations of factors. Table 12.2 summarizes key studies of text messages written in English in terms of the demographics of participants and factors included for consideration in each.

The studies summarized in Table 12.2 demonstrate the variety of approaches and factors reported across papers. However, it should be noted that some publications were excluded as they did not analyze textisms in participants' messages. One excluded study was by Faulkner and Culwin (2005), which reported analyses of the message length and purpose of each message in the texting diaries of 21 female and 3 male undergraduates in the United Kingdom (as well as survey responses from a larger group of undergraduates). In another excluded study, by Baron and Ling (2010), two samples of UK undergraduates contributed data on length of phone ownership, length of texting experience, message frequency, and phone technology. Hofferth and Moon (2012) compared the reading proficiency and texting frequency of 1,147 U.S. children of ages 10 to 18 years. These papers report on a variety of other questions, such as the nature of decorations and ringtones on phones, as well as the reason for sending messages and for texting rather than calling (Baron & Ling, 2010).

Table 12.2 Summary of participant details, study design, and factors reported in key studies of text messaging language in texts written in English.

	Grinter & Eldridge, 2003	Thurlow & Brown, 2003	Neville, 2003	Bieswanger, 2007	Ling & Baron, 2007	Massengill Shaw et al., 2007	Frehner, 2008	Plester et al., 2008	Drouin & Davis, 2009
Country	UK	UK	UK	UK	U.S.	U.S.	UK	UK	U.S.
Total participants	10	135	45	–	22	86	568	65; 35[a]	80
Age (in years)	15–16	(undergrads)	11–16	(adults)	(undergrads)	(undergrads)	17–27[b]	10–12	18–48 (undergrads)
Sex ratio (% females)	50%	75%	100%	–	100%	–	52%	–; 74%	70%
Message/textism collection	Diary (sent/received messages), discussion groups	Sent/received messages from phones	Dictation tasks	Messages from a website	Diary (sent messages)	Survey question re. textisms used	Received messages from phones	Translation into text language and vice versa	Translation into text language and vice versa, textism use survey item
Message length	Yes	Yes	–	Yes	Yes	–	Yes	–	–
Textism density	Yes	Yes	Yes*	Yes	Yes	–	Yes	Yes	–
Attitude to textisms	–	–	–	–	–	–	–	–	Yes
Length of phone ownership	–	–	Yes	–	–	–	–	–	–
Length of texting experience	–	–	–	–	–	–	–	–	–
Messaging frequency	–	–	Yes	–	–	Yes	–	Yes	–
Phone technology	–	Yes	Yes	–	–	–	–	Yes	–
Language tasks	–	–	Yes	–	–	Yes	–	Yes	Yes

*Reported as a percentage of participants that used each type.
[a] Data from multiple samples are separated by a semi-colon.
[b] University students.

(continued on pg. 220)

Table 12.2 *(Continued)*

	Plester et al., 2009	Tagg, 2009	Kemp, 2010	Rosen et al., 2010	Bushnell et al., 2011	Coe & Oakhill, 2011	Drouin, 2011	Durkin et al., 2011	Holtgraves, 2011
Country	UK	UK	Australia	U.S.	Australia	UK	U.S.	UK	U.S.
Total participants	88	16	61	335; 383[a]	227	41	152	94	224
Age (in years)	10–12	19–68	(undergrads)	18–25	10–12	10–11	(undergrads)	17	18–41 (undergrads)
Sex ratio (% females)	63%	62%	82%	62%; 57%	66%	–	65%	26%	54%
Message/textism collection	Messages written for scenarios	Sent/received messages from friends (as above) and an online website	Textism use survey item, dictation and translation tasks	Textism use survey item, writing tasks	A list of 30 individual words translated into textese	Message written for a scenario; 16 individual words translated into textisms	Textism use survey item	Message sent in response to a message from the researcher	Sent messages copied from phones
Message length	–	Yes	–	–	–	Yes	–	Yes	Yes
Textism density	Yes	–	Yes	Yes	Yes	Yes	–	Yes	Yes
Attitude to textism use	–	–	–	–	–	–	–	–	–
Length of phone ownership	Yes	–	Yes	–	Yes	Yes	–	–	–

	Plester et al., 2009	Tagg, 2009	Kemp, 2010	Rosen et al., 2010	Bushnell et al., 2011	Coe & Oakhill, 2011	Drouin, 2011	Durkin et al., 2011	Holtgraves, 2011
Length of texting experience	–	–	–	–	Yes	–	–	–	–
Messaging frequency	–	Yes	Yes	Yes	Yes	Yes	Yes	Yes	–
Phone technology	Yes	Yes	Yes	–	Yes	Yes	–	–	–
Language tasks	Yes	–	Yes	Yes	Yes	Yes	Yes	Yes	–

[a]Data from multiple samples are separated by a semi-colon.

	Kemp & Bushnell, 2011	Veater et al., 2011	Wood, Jackson et al., 2011a	Wood, Meachem et al., 2011b	Cingel & Sundar, 2012	De Jonge & Kemp, 2012	Drouin & Driver, 2014	Grace et al., 2012	Tossell et al., 2012	Grace et al., 2013a
Country	Australia	UK	UK	UK	U.S.	Australia	U.S.	Canada; Australia	U.S.	Canada; Australia
Total participants	86	65	114	119	228	53; 52[a]	183	170; 97[a]	21	150; 86[a]
Age (in years)	10–12	10–13	9–10	8–12	10–14	18–24 (undergrads); 13–15	(undergrads)	(undergrads)	(undergrads)	(undergrads)
Sex ratio (% females)	70%	52%	–	59%	61%	72%; 38%	72%	78%; 72%	48%	77%; 73%

(continued on pg. 222)

Table 12.2 (Continued)

	Kemp & Bushnell, 2011	Veater et al., 2011	Wood, Jackson et al., 2011a	Wood, Meachem et al., 2011b	Cingel & Sundar, 2012	De Jonge & Kemp, 2012	Drouin & Driver, 2014	Grace et al., 2012	Tossell et al., 2012	Grace et al., 2013a
Message/textism collection	Dictation tasks	Sent messages copied from phones	Sent messages copied from phones	Sent messages copied from phones	Textism use survey item	Translation into text language	Sent messages copied from phones	Translation / scenario-based/ copied sent messages	Sent/received messages accessed directly from phones	Sent messages copied from phones
Message length	–	–	–	–	–	Yes	Yes	Yes	Yes	–
Textism density	Yes	Yes	Yes	Yes	Yes	Yes	Yes	Yes	Yes[b]	Yes
Attitude to textism use	–	–	–	–	–	–	–	Yes	–	Yes
Length of phone ownership	–	Yes	–	Yes	–	Yes	Yes	Yes	–	Yes
Length of texting experience	–	–	–	–	–	Yes	Yes	–	–	–
Messaging frequency	–	–	Yes	–	Yes	Yes	Yes	Yes	Yes	Yes
Phone technology	Yes	Yes	–	–	–	Yes	Yes	Yes	–	–
Language tasks	Yes	Yes	Yes	Yes	Yes	Yes	Yes	–	–	Yes

[a]Data from multiple samples are separated by a semi-colon.
[b]Only emoticons were analyzed.

Language, Location, and Accent

The inconsistency of factors included in previous studies, as seen in Table 12.2, may be related to the fact that it was not immediately apparent, in this relatively new field of research, which factors would prove to be important. To understand the nature of textisms and their use, we need to understand why texters choose the textisms they do. One likely reason for the varied textism densities seen in different studies is that messages have been collected from participants in various countries. In an investigation of text messaging by undergraduates in five countries, for example, Baron (2010) found that 44% of Korean participants had sent and received more than 30 texts in the previous day, followed by 17% of Italian, 16% of Japanese, 11% of American, and only 1% of Swedish participants. Few studies have analyzed messages in more than one language, but it has been shown that compared to naturalistic messages written in German, naturalistic messages written in English contained higher proportions of abbreviated textisms such as shortenings, contractions, and homophones and fewer initialisms and emoticons (Bieswanger, 2007; Frehner, 2008).

Differences in textism use may occur even between messages written in the same language, but in different countries. For example, Grace et al. (2012) found that Australian undergraduates produced significantly higher densities of textisms than Canadian undergraduates. Furthermore, Shaw (2008) found differences between English-language social networking homepages created in Ireland, England, and the United States. Accent-specific variations were evident in the spelling of both consonants (e.g., *thing* was respelled the most often as *fing* in England and as *ting* in Ireland) and vowels (e.g., *what* and *because* were respelled the most often as *wut* and *cuz/cus* in the U.S., and as *wot* and *coz/cos* in England). The development of textese within a local texting culture might be interrelated with the availability and use of phone technology, as well as attitudes of individuals toward texting and textism use. The pace at which texting culture and language develops is also likely to be affected by the volume of text messages circulated on a local level (Baron & Ling, 2010).

Time and Technology

Differences in textism densities in messages might also be related to the year in which the messages were collected, particularly as phone technology advances and as uptake varies across countries (Baron & Ling, 2010). For example, Kemp and Bushnell (2011) showed that Australian children who used multi-press text entry (where multiple key presses are required to select the correct letter on an alphanumeric keypad) used higher proportions of textisms in their messages than those who used predictive software (where the phone provides word suggestions based on single key presses). As access to updated hardware (such as full keyboards and touchscreens) and software options (such as improved predictive software) continues to increase, textism use may diminish further. Most previous studies regarding change over time have not extended beyond a year (Tossell et al., 2012; Wood, Meachem, et al., 2011). However, in a recent study of four cohorts of first-year university students, Grace and Kemp (2014) found that textism use in messages, particularly contractive textism use (e.g., *wht* for *what*), is decreasing over time, and that expressive textism use (e.g., *WHAAAT??!* for *what*) may be increasing. This is predictable in light of changes in technology that relieve pressure on texters to minimize character use, through the introduction of predictive software and the introduction of full keyboards and touchscreens on phones. The further examination of changes to textism use over time is vital to understanding how textism use is developing in a continually changing technological context.

Social Attitudes

Attitudes toward the appropriateness of using textisms may also affect the types and densities of textisms observed in messages. Grace, Kemp, Martin, and Parrila (2013b) found that university students' use of textisms was positively related to their ratings of the appropriateness of textism use, and that students' attitudes toward textism use differed significantly between formal and informal situations (e.g., a text message to an older family member versus a friend). Drouin and Davis (2009) also observed that participants deemed textism use as appropriate in informal situations but not in formal situations, and the same participants used significantly more textisms in an email to a friend than to a professor in an experimental setting. However, attitudes toward textism use have been shown not to differ significantly between Australian and Canadian undergraduates (Grace et al., 2012), nor between four successive cohorts of Australian undergraduates (Grace & Kemp, 2014). Therefore, although attitudes to textism use are associated with differences in individuals' messages, differences in attitudes do not seem to be able to explain variations in textism use between countries or across time.

Sex and Age

Two further factors that may affect the use of text messaging language are texters' sex and age. Some studies have included consideration of the influence of participant sex, for example, on texting volumes, message length, and textism use. A survey by Baron and Campbell (2010) showed a higher percentage of females than males had sent and received more than 30 text messages in the previous day across five different countries and a higher percentage of males than females in each country had sent/received fewer than five text messages. Tossell and colleagues (2012) reported both higher average message sending rates, and more words per message, for female than male undergraduates. Furthermore, in scenario-based messages, female preteens used more textisms than males (Plester et al., 2009) and in naturalistic messages, women not only sent, but also received, approximately twice as many emoticons in text messages than men (Tossell et al., 2012). In a study involving young adults, Rosen et al. (2010) also found that females both reported sending significantly more text messages and estimated higher textism use for each textism type than males. Grace and Kemp (2014) confirmed that females used more total textisms than males in their naturalistic messages, and in particular, that females used more expressive textisms than males. Overall, then, it seems that females use more textisms and send more messages than males, which may reflect general differences in language use and expression that are manifested in their text messaging behavior. As seen in Table 12.2, ratios of females to males have varied greatly in previous studies of text language, from 12.5% females (Faulkner & Culwin, 2005) to 100% females (Ling & Baron, 2007), and so it is important that the ratio of females to males be reported in future studies.

Another potential effect on textism use that has received little experimental attention is that of participant age. As cited above, texting remains most popular in teenagers and young adults (Faulkner & Culwin, 2005; Lenhart, 2012; Smith, 2011). In studies involving more than one age group, textism use has been found not to differ significantly between adolescents and young adults (De Jonge & Kemp, 2012), but to vary across year levels in 8- to 12-year-olds (Wood, Meachem, et al., 2011). Adults have generally been shown to use more textisms than children in studies using translated messages (e.g., 43–57% textisms for undergraduates [Kemp, 2010], versus 57–59% for children [Plester et al., 2008]), and naturalistic messages (e.g., adults' messages have contained mean textism densities of 5% [Ling & Baron, 2007] to 24–28% [Drouin & Driver, 2014], all considerably lower than the peak of 49% observed in children's naturalistic messages [Wood, Meachem, et al., 2011]). Higher textism use in children compared to older adults may reflect differences in attitudes as individuals develop, such as textism use being viewed as a novelty in young texters.

Empirical studies are informed by the research questions under investigation, but they are also limited by the availability of participants, which may mean that some studies may continue to include a preponderance of females (see Table 12.2), or of younger rather than older adults, as is common in research carried out with undergraduate samples. Nevertheless, the studies reviewed above suggest that the factors of participant sex and age should be taken into account in future work on text messaging, as it appears that both can influence the use of textisms observed.

Combinations of Factors

As summarized above, methodological factors (message collection and textism categorization and counting), group factors (country, time, attitudes toward textisms, texting experience, and developments in phone technology) and individual factors (the sex and age of participants) might affect textism use in messages. How these factors interact is not clear. For example, if attitudes toward the appropriateness of textism use are related to naturalistic textism use, it would be useful to measure differences in attitudes between males and females, and between older and younger participants, to inform any differences in textism use between groups. Similarly, if phone technology affects textism use, then differences in phone technology use between males and females, and between older and younger participants, may also be informative. Attempts to differentiate these effects have produced mixed results. For example, some studies have shown that more females use predictive technology than males (Baron & Ling, 2010; Kemp & Bushnell, 2011), but other studies have reported no significant sex differences in technology use (De Jonge & Kemp, 2012; Drouin & Davis, 2009; Grace & Kemp, 2014). Now that this field of research has developed to the point of identifying key factors that may be associated with textism use, the opportunity exists to differentiate how these factors interact so that we can better understand textism use and how it relates to differences between participants.

Literacy Skills and Textism Use

A further factor that may be associated with textism variations is the literacy skill of message writers. Of the 28 studies of textism use summarized in Table 12.2, 19 also examined participants' language skills. As highlighted earlier, popular media reports have included strong criticism of texting and textism use and its potential negative effect on literacy skills (e.g., Henry, 2008; Humphrys, 2007; Llewthor, 2010), and some educationalists have expressed similar concerns (e.g., Broadhurst, 2008; Geertsema, Hyman, & van Deventer, 2011; Ross, 2007). Contrary to these concerns, however, positive links between literacy and textism use have been found in studies of children's texting (e.g., Coe & Oakhill, 2011; Neville, 2003; Plester et al., 2009), although results for links between textism use and literacy scores for adults have been negative (De Jonge & Kemp, 2012), non-significant (Drouin & Davis, 2009; Kemp, 2010; Massengill Shaw et al., 2007), and a mixture of positive and negative (Grace, Kemp, Martin, & Parrila, 2013a; Rosen et al., 2010; Verheijen, 2013; Wood, Kemp, & Plester, 2014). Verheijen (2013) summarized 18 studies of text messaging and/or online chat. There were positive relationships between textese use and conventional literacy skill in seven studies, negative relationships in two studies, mixed results in seven studies, and no significant correlations in two studies. Further testing is clearly required to understand the reasons for these variations.

However, since the concerns expressed above include the idea that textism use is harming, or even "creeping" into formal writing, another approach is to check for negative effects of text language in educational assessments. Studies involving formal writing samples have produced little evidence that participants are unable or unwilling to avoid textism use in formal situations (Drouin & Davis, 2009; Rosen et al., 2010). In a more direct study, Grace et al. (2013b) checked 303 formal university exam papers for intrusions of textese, but found only a negligible proportion of textisms (an average of less than 1 per 4,500 words). This lack of textism intrusions does not provide direct evidence that students' literacy skills have not been affected by textism use. However, it does show that students' spelling of conventional words has not been overwritten by textism spellings, and that students are able to recognize formal writing as a situation in which textism use is inappropriate. In contrast to anecdotal concerns, then, research-based evidence reviewed above suggests that textism use is *not* having a negative effect on students' conventional literacy skills.

Conclusion

Text messaging research has been conducted to check for any damaging effects of text messaging in some cases, and to track the use of textisms in messages and the factors associated with variations in textism use in others. Early concerns about textism use were based on possible effects related to the highly abbreviated nature of textism use, an adaptation associated in part with older phone technology on which messages were created (Crystal, 2008; Hillebrand, 2010). However, throughout the story of research into text language, there have been signs that textisms carry important communicative value that in fact add to, rather than subtract from, communication, beyond that of merely saving characters for the sake of efficiency. Several researchers have referred to the playful aspects of language used in all forms of CMC (e.g., Baron, 2003; Danet, 2001; Soffer, 2010). Research findings suggest that students employ technology and/ or textisms to further their goals of saving characters and message-writing time, as well as creative enhancements in the form of expressive textism use. Messages often contain representations of facial expression (e.g., ☺, :D, :-p), tone of voice (e.g., *hellllooooo*), enthusiasm (e.g., *whoop whoop!!*), and affection (e.g., *xxoo*). These adaptations display one's abilities to manipulate language to suit the social and situational needs of the communication at hand and sometimes rely on shared meaning between texting partners. Rather than detracting from conventional English, text messaging appears to represent an opportunistic style of communication that enables users to experiment with words and enhance their communication. Some texters do write in conventional English, but many others use inventive spelling and character additions to capture aspects of speech otherwise unavailable in the silence of a written message.

Overall, text messaging research has shown that a number of factors are associated with variations in textism use, such as methodological differences between studies, the age and sex of participants, and the technology on their phones. The ability of texters to participate in textism-rich conversations and to further develop text messaging language style can be seen as an addition to, not a deletion from, their overall set of literacy skills. As new developments in technology continue to arise, this adaptive tendency, both purposeful and incidental, will no doubt continue as users capture the potential of technological advances to enhance their communication. With ongoing changes in technology, it is becoming easier to move freely between text messaging, email, and social media on a single device. It is important for researchers to track the possible homogenizing effects of changing technology on textism use across modes of technology-based communication.

In conclusion, as textese continues to develop over time, it is essential for researchers to develop a strong understanding of the methodological and other factors to consider in future work. To date, textism use has been shown to have little or no negative effect on conventional literacy skills. Instead, the use of textisms seems to have communicative value unique to the informal social and technological environment in which it is situated.

References

Alonso, E., & Perea, M. (2008). SMS: Impacto social y cognitivo (SMS: Social and cognitive impact). *Escritos de Psicología*, 2, 24–31. Retrieved November 28, 2014, from www.escritosdepsicologia.es/descargas/revistas/vol2_1/escritospsicologia_v2_1_2sms.pdf

Androutsopoulos, J., & Schmidt, G. (2002). SMS-Kommunikation: Ethnografische Gattungsanalyze am Beispiel einer Kleingruppe. *Zeitschrift für Angewandte Linguistik, 36*, 49–80.

Anis, J. (2007). Neography: Unconventional spelling in French SMS text messages. In B. Danet & S. C. Herring (Eds.), *The multilingual Internet: Language, culture, and communication online* (pp. 87–115). New York, NY: Oxford University Press.

Australian Communications and Media Authority (ACMA). (2012). *Communications report, 2011–2012*. Retrieved November 28, 2014, from www.acma.gov.au/communicationsreport

Baron, N. S. (2003).Why email looks like speech: Proofreading, pedagogy, and public face. In J. Aitchison & D. M. Lewis (Eds.), *New media language* (pp. 102–113.) New York, NY: Routledge.

Baron, N. S. (2008). *Always on: Language in an online and mobile world*. Oxford, UK: Oxford University Press.

Baron, N. S. (2010). *The dark side of mobile phones*. Retrieved March 15, 2013, from http://www.american.edu/cas/lfs/faculty-docs/upload/The-Dark-Side-of-Mobile-Phones.pdf

Baron, N. S., & Campbell, E. M. (2010, October). *Talking takes too long: Gender and cultural patterns in mobile telephony*. Paper for the conference of the Association of Internet Researchers. Göteborg, Sweden. Retrieved May 29, 2012, from https://www.american.edu/cas/lfs/faculty-docs/upload/Talking-Takes-Too-Long.pdf

Baron, N., & Ling, R. (2010). *Emerging patterns of American mobile phone use: Electronically mediated communication in transition*. Retrieved May 11, 2010, from http://www.ritla.org.br/index.php?option=com_docman&task=doc_download&gid=434

Beasley, R. E. (2009). Short message service (SMS) texting symbols: A functional analysis of 10,000 cellular phone text messages. *The Reading Matrix, 9*, 88–89.

Bieswanger, M. (2007). 2 abbrevi8 or not 2 abbrevi8: A contrastive analysis of different space- and time-saving strategies in English and German text messages. *Texas Linguistics Forum, 50*. Retrieved May 11, 2012, from http://studentorgs.utexas.edu/salsa/proceedings/2006/Bieswanger.pdf

Bodomo, A. B. (2010). *Computer-mediated communication for linguistics and literacy: Technology and natural language education*. Hershey, NY: Information Science Reference.

Broadhurst, C. (2008, February 14). Teachers in a tizz: Is texting destroying the English language? *Howick Times, NZ*. Retrieved January 14, 2012, from http://www.times.co.nz/education/teachers-in-a-tizz-is-texting-destroying-the-english-language.html

Brown, A. (2002). *The language and communication of SMS: An exploratory study of young adults' text-messaging*. [Unpublished BA thesis]. Cardiff University, Wales.

Bushnell, C., Kemp, N., & Martin, F. H. (2011). Text-messaging practices and links to general spelling skill: A study of Australian children. *Australian Journal of Educational and Developmental Psychology, 11*, 27–38.

Choudhury, M., Saraf, R., Jain, V., Mukherjee, A., Sarkar, S., & Basu, A. (2007). Investigation and modeling of the structure of texting language. *International Journal on Document Analysis and Recognition, 10*, 157–174.

Cingel, D. P., & Sundar, S. S. (2012). Texting, techspeak, and tweens: The relationship between text messaging and English grammar skills. *New Media and Society, 14*, 1304–1320.

Coe, J. E. L., & Oakhill, J. V. (2011). "txtN is ez f u no h2 rd": The relation between reading ability and text-messaging behaviour. *Journal of Computer Assisted Learning, 27*, 4–17.

Cooper, M., Dronsuth, R. W., Mikulski, A. J., Lynk, C. N., Jr., Mikulski, J. J., Mitchell, J. F., … Sangster, J. H. (1975). *Radio telephone system*. US Patent number 3,906,166. Filing date: October 17, 1973. Issue date: September 1975. Assignee Motorola. Retrieved February 23, 2013, from http://patft.uspto.gov/netacgi/nph-Parser?Sect2=PTO1&Sect2=HITOFF&p=1&u=/netahtml/PTO/search-bool.html&r=1&f=G&l=50&d=PALL&RefSrch=yes&Query=PN/3906166

Crystal, D. (2001). *Language and the Internet*. Cambridge, UK: Cambridge University Press.

Crystal, D. (2008). *Txtng: The gr8 db8*. Oxford, UK: Oxford University Press.

Danet, B. (2001). *Cyberpl@y: Communicating online*. Oxford, UK: Berg.

De Jonge, S., & Kemp, N. (2012). Text-message abbreviations and language skills in high school and university students. *Journal of Research in Reading, 35*, 49–68.

De Souza e Silva, A. (2006). Interfaces of hybrid spaces. In A. P. Kavoori & N. Arceneaux (Eds.), *The cell phone reader: Essays in social transformation* (Vol. 34 of Digital Formations). New York, NY: Peter Lang.

Drouin, M. A. (2011). College students' text messaging, use of textese and literacy skills. *Journal of Computer Assisted Learning, 27*, 67–75.

Drouin, M., & Davis, C. (2009). R u txting? Is the use of text speak hurting your literacy? *Journal of Literacy Research, 41*, 46–67.

Drouin, M., & Driver, B. (2014). Texting, textese and literacy abilities: A naturalistic study. *Journal of Research in Reading, 37*(3), 250–267.

Durkin, K., Conti-Ramsden, G., & Walker, A. J. (2011). Txt lang: Texting, textism use and literacy abilities in adolescents with and without specific language impairment. *Journal of Computer Assisted Learning, 27*, 49–57.

Faulkner, X., & Culwin, F. (2005). When fingers do the talking: A study of text messaging. *Interacting with Computers, 17*, 167–185.

Frehner, C. (2008). *Email – SMS – MMS: The linguistic creativity of asynchronous discourse in the new media age*. New York, NY: Peter Lang.

Freiermuth, M. R. (2002). *Features of electronic synchronous communication: A comparative analysis of online chat, spoken and written texts*. [PhD dissertation]. Oklahoma State University.

Geertsema, S., Hyman, C., & van Deventer, C. (2011). Short message service (SMS) language and written language skills: Educators' perspectives. *South African Journal of Education*, *31*, 475–487.

Grace, A., & Kemp, N. (2014). Text messaging language: A comparison of undergraduates' naturalistic textism use in four consecutive cohorts. *Writing Systems Research*. doi: 10.1080/17586801.2014.898575

Grace, A., Kemp, N., Martin, F. H., & Parrila, R. (2012). Undergraduates' use of text messaging language: Effects of country and collection method. *Writing Systems Research*, *4*, 167–184.

Grace, A., Kemp, N., Martin, F. H., & Parrila, R. (2013a). Undergraduates' attitudes to text messaging language use and intrusions of textisms into formal writing. *New Media and Society*. doi: 10.1177/1461444813516832

Grace, A., Kemp, N., Martin, F. H., & Parrila, R. (2013b). Undergraduates' text messaging language and literacy skills. *Reading and Writing*, *27*, 855–873.

Greenfield, P. M., & Subrahmanyam, K. (2003). Online discourse in a teen chatroom: New codes and new modes of coherence in a visual medium. *Journal of Applied Behavioural Psychology*, *24*, 713–738.

Grinter, R. E., & Eldridge, M. (2003). Wan2tlk? Everyday text messaging. In *Proceedings of ACM Conference on Human Factors in Computing System (CHI 2003)* (pp. 441–448). Fort Lauderdale, Florida, April 5–10. Retrieved March 7, 2013, from http://www.cc.gatech.edu/~beki/c24.pdf

Henry, J. (2008, August 23). Text message language in A-levels slammed by examiners. *The Telegraph*. Retrieved August 8, 2012, from http://www.telegraph.co.uk/news/uknews/2609506/Text-message-language-in-A-levels-slammed-by-examiners.html

Herring, S. C., & Zelenkauskaite, A. (2008). Gendered typography: Abbreviation and insertion in Italian iTV SMS. In J. F. Siegel, T. C. Nagel, A. Laurente-Lapole, & J. Auger (Eds.), *IUWPL7: Gender in language: Classic questions, new contexts* (pp. 73–92). Bloomington, IN: IULC Publications.

Herring, S. C., & Zelenkauskaite, A. (2009). Symbolic capital in a virtual heterosexual market: Abbreviation and insertion in Italian iTV SMS. *Written Communication*, *26*, 5–31.

Hillebrand, F. (2010). *Short message service*. Chichester, UK: John Wiley & Sons.

Hofferth, S. L., & Moon, U. J. (2012). Cell phone use and child and adolescent reading proficiency. *Psychology of Popular Media Culture*, *1*, 108–122.

Holtgraves, T. (2011). Text messaging, personality, and the social context. *Journal of Research in Personality*, *45*, 92–99.

Humphrys, J. (2007, September 24). I h8 txt msgs: How texting is wrecking our language. *Daily Mail*. Retrieved March 26, 2010, from http://www.dailymail.co.uk/news/article-483511/I-h8-txtmsgs-How-texting-wrecking-language.html

International Telecommunication Union (ITU). (2012). *Key statistical highlights: ITU data release June 2012*. Retrieved August 11, 2012, from http://www.itu.int/ITU-D/ict/statistics/material/pdf/2011%20Statistical%20highlights_June_2012.pdf

Kemp, N. (2010). Texting vs. txting: Reading and writing text messages, and links with other linguistic skills. *Writing Systems Research*, *2*, 53–71.

Kemp, N., & Bushnell, C. (2011). Children's text messaging: Abbreviations, input methods and links with literacy. *Journal of Computer Assisted Learning*, *27*, 18–27.

Lenhart, A. (2012). *Teens, smartphones & texting*. Retrieved February 25, 2013, from http://pewinternet.org/Reports/2012/Teens-and-smartphones.aspx

Lenhart, A., Ling, R., Campbell, S., & Purcell, K. (2010). *Teens and mobile phones.* Retrieved February 24, 2013, from http://www.pewinternet.org/~/media//Files/Reports/2010/PIP-Teens-and-Mobile-2010-with-topline.pdf

Ling, R., & Baron, N. S. (2007). Text messaging and IM: Linguistic comparison of American college data. *Journal of Language and Social Psychology, 26,* 291–298.

Ling, R., Bertel, T. F., & Sundsøy, P. R. (2012). The socio-demographics of texting: An analysis of traffic data. *New Media and Society, 14,* 281–298.

Llewthor, J. K. (2010, December 12). *Text messaging: Bad spelling or destroying the English language?* Retrieved January 14, 2012, from http://www.brighthub.com/education/languages/articles/98524.aspx

Locker, M. (2012, November 29). OMG! First use of abbreviation found in a 1917 letter to Winston Churchill. *Time Magazine.* Retrieved April 26, 2013, from http://newsfeed.time.com/2012/11/29/omg-first-use-of-abbreviation-found-in-a-letter-to-winston-churchill/?iid=obinsite

Massengill Shaw, D., Carlson, C., & Waxman, M. (2007). An exploratory investigation into the relationship between text messaging and spelling. *New England Reading Association Journal, 43,* 57–62.

McWhorter, J. (2013, April 25). Is texting killing the English language? *Time Magazine.* Retrieved April 28, 2013, from http://ideas.time.com/2013/04/25/is-texting-killing-the-english-language/?iid=gs-main-mostpop2

Neville, L. (2003). *Cn U rEd dis? The causes and consequences of a "text message language" in young teenagers.* [Unpublished undergraduate dissertation]. University of Oxford, Oxford, UK.

Oxford English Dictionary (OED). (2011). *March 2011 update.* Retrieved March 7, 2013, from http://public.oed.com/the-oed-today/recent-updates-to-the-oed/previous-updates/march-2011-update/

Plester, B., Lerkkanen, M.-K., Linjama, L. J., Rasku-Puttonen, H., & Littleton, K. (2011). Finnish and UK English pre-teen children's text message language and its relationship with their literacy skills. *Journal of Computer Assisted Learning, 27,* 37–48.

Plester, B., Wood, C., & Bell, V. (2008). Txt msg n school literacy: Does texting and knowledge of text abbreviations adversely affect children's literacy attainment? *Literacy, 42,* 137–144.

Plester, B., Wood, C., & Joshi, P. (2009). Exploring the relationship between children's knowledge of text message abbreviations and school literacy outcomes. *British Journal of Developmental Psychology, 27,* 145–161.

Portio Research. (2012). *Happy birthday SMS!* Retrieved February 24, 2013, from http://www.portioresearch.com/blog/2012/12/happy-birthday-sms!.aspx

Reid, D., & Reid, F. (2004). *Insights into the social and psychological effects of SMS text messaging.* Retrieved February 24, 2012, from http://www.160characters.org/documents/SocialEffectsOfTextMessaging.pdf

Rosen, L. D., Chang, J., Erwin, L., Carrier, L. M., & Cheever, N. A. (2010). The relationship between "textisms" and formal and informal writing among young adults. *Communication Research, 37,* 420–440.

Ross, K. (2007). Teachers say text messages r ruining kids' riting skills. *American Teacher, 92*(3), 4.

Shaw, P. (2008). Spelling, accent and identity in computer-mediated communication. *English Today, 24,* 42–49.

Shortis, T. (2007). Gr8 Txtpectations: The creativity of text spelling. *English Drama Media Journal, 8,* 21–26.

Smith, A. (2011, September 19). *Americans and text messaging.* Retrieved February 25, 2013, from http://pewinternet.org/Reports/2011/Cell-Phone-Texting-2011.aspx

Soffer, O. (2010). "Silent orality": Toward a conceptualization of the digital oral features in CMC and SMS texts. *Communication Theory, 20,* 387–404.

Tagg, C. (2009). *A corpus linguistics study of text messaging.* [PhD thesis]. University of Birmingham.

Thurlow, C. (2006). From statistical panic to moral panic: The metadiscursive construction and popular exaggeration of new media language in the print media. *Journal of Computer-Mediated Communication, 11*, 667–701.

Thurlow, C., & Brown, A. (2003). Generation Txt? The sociolinguistics of young people's text-messaging. *Discourse Analysis Online*. Retrieved February 10, 2010, from http://extra.shu.ac.uk/daol/articles/v1/n1/a3/thurlow2002003.html

Thurlow, C., & Poff, M. (2012). Text messaging. In S. C. Herring, D. Stein, & T. Virtanen (Eds.), *Handbook of the pragmatics of CMC*. New York, NY: Mouton de Gruyter.

Tossell, C. C., Kortum, P., Shepard, C., Barg-Walkow, L. H., Rahmati, A., & Zhong, L. (2012). A longitudinal study of emoticon use in text messaging from smartphones. *Computers in Human Behavior, 28*, 659–663.

Tseliga, T. (2007). "It's all Greeklish to me!" Linguistic and sociocultural perspectives on Roman-alphabeted Greek in asynchronous computer-mediated communication. In B. Danet & S. C. Herring (Eds.), *The multilingual Internet: Language, culture, and communication online* (pp. 116–141). New York, NY: Oxford University Press.

Varnhagen, C. K., McFall, G. P., Pugh, N., Routledge, L., Sumida-MacDonald, H., & Kwong, T. E. (2009). lol: New language and spelling in instant messaging. *Reading and Writing, 23*, 719–733.

Veater, H. M., Plester, B., & Wood, C. (2011). Use of text message abbreviations and literacy skills in children with dyslexia. *Dyslexia, 17*, 65–71.

Verheijen, L. (2013). The effects of text messaging and instant messaging on literacy. *English Studies, 94*, 582–602.

Wood, C., Jackson, E., Hart, L., Plester, B., & Wilde, L. (2011). The effect of text messaging on 9- and 10-year-old children's reading, spelling and phonological processing skills. *Journal of Computer Assisted Learning, 27*, 28–36.

Wood, C., Kemp, N., & Plester, B. (2014). *Text messaging and literacy: The evidence*. Abingdon, UK: Routledge.

Wood, C., Kemp, N., Waldron, S., & Hart, L. (2014). Grammatical understanding, literacy and text messaging in school children and undergraduate students: A concurrent analysis. *Computers and Education, 70*, 281–290.

Wood, C., Meachem, S., Bowyer, S., Jackson, E., Tarczynski-Bowles, M. L., & Plester, B. (2011). A longitudinal study of the relationship between children's text messaging and literacy development. *British Journal of Psychology, 102*, 431–442.

Yvon, F. (2010). Rewriting the orthography of SMS messages. *Natural Language Engineering, 16*, 133–159.

13

Texting Behavior and Language Skills in Children and Adults

Sam Waldron,[1] Nenagh Kemp,[2] Beverly Plester,[1] and Clare Wood[1]

[1] Coventry University
[2] University of Tasmania

The prevalence of text messaging continues to increase in countries across the world (Baron, 2010; Lenhart, Ling, Campbell, & Purcell, 2010; Lexander, 2011; Ofcom, 2012), and a growing body of research is focusing on this form of digital communication and its links with more conventional language skills. This chapter provides an overview of the current research on the use of text messaging and its relation to specific academic abilities, including spelling, reading, phonology, grammar, and general literacy skills. The chapter discusses adult and child cohorts separately because of the striking differences that have been found between the two groups (with further division between child and adolescent samples where necessary), and some suggestions are provided as to why these differences might exist.

What is Textese?

"Textese" is a term used to describe the abbreviated or slang format that many people use while texting (e.g., De Jonge & Kemp, 2012; Drouin, 2011; Thurlow, 2003). Words written in this way have been referred to as "textisms" (Durkin, Conti-Ramsden, & Walker, 2011; Plester, Wood, & Joshi, 2009; Thurlow, 2003). In order to examine textisms in a comprehensive way, a variety of coding schemes have been employed (e.g., Cingel & Sundar, 2012; Powell & Dixon, 2011). A particularly popular scheme is one developed by Thurlow (2003, based on Shortis, 2001), which has been adopted, with some variations, in numerous studies (e.g., Drouin, 2011; Grace, Kemp, Martin, & Parrila, 2012; Plester et al., 2009). A summary of Thurlow's original coding scheme is shown in Table 13.1.

Textese became popular early on to save on time and space when writing text messages (Taylor & Vincent, 2005). This was at a time when texting was still relatively new and expensive, often incurring costs per message. Nowadays people tend to subscribe to monthly packages where texting is unlimited, and to own phones with QWERTY keyboards, rather than the original alphanumeric layout. These changes

The Wiley Handbook of Psychology, Technology, and Society, First Edition. Edited by Larry D. Rosen, Nancy A. Cheever, and L. Mark Carrier.
© 2015 John Wiley & Sons, Ltd. Published 2015 by John Wiley & Sons, Ltd.

Table 13.1 Thurlow's (2003) textism coding scheme.

Type of textism	Explanation	Example
Shortenings	Removing word endings	*bro, mon*
Contractions	Removing letters from the middle of words, usually vowels	*ltr, msg*
g-clippings	Removing the "g" from -*ing* endings	*borin, tryin*
Other clippings	Removing other letters from word endings	*hav, wil*
Initialisms	Using the first letter from every word in a phrase	*lol, brb*
Acronyms	As for initialisms, but constitute official abbreviations	*BBC, UK*
Letter/number homophones	Using the sound of a letter or number to spell part or all of a word	*l8r, 2moro, c, u*
Non-conventional spellings	Spelling phonetically	*fone, luv*
Misspellings/typos	Misspelling words non-phonetically	*comming, rember*
Accent stylization	Representing casual spoken language	*innit, gonna*

mean that cost and time are no longer as big an issue as they once were. Nevertheless, both children and adults continue to use textisms in their messages (e.g., Drouin & Driver, 2012; Grace et al., 2012; Wood, Kemp, Waldron, & Hart, 2014). One important reason is that textisms can show belonging to a social group (Green, 2003; Thurlow, 2003) and can help to maintain social relationships (Ling, 2004; Ling & Yttri, 2002).

Thus, the use of textisms remains an important aspect of communicating by text message. However, this new form of writing has brought with it strong concerns from the popular media, as well as from some educators, that the use of textisms will damage conventional standards of reading and writing, especially in young people (see Thurlow, 2006, for a review). There appear to be two main types of concern. The first is that textisms will start to intrude into formal writing because people will fail to recognize the situations in which textisms are inappropriate. The second, more serious concern is that people's conventional orthographic representations will begin to be overwritten by their textese versions (see Grace, Kemp, Martin, & Parrila, 2013).

Other authors have noted the potential positive influence that textism use could have on writing, especially for children (e.g., Crystal, 2008). Many textisms use unconventional orthography but keep phonological representations intact (e.g., *rite* for *right*), and thus regular exposure to textese could provide writers with practice with phonics. This could, in turn, help to improve reading abilities in children (e.g., Bradley & Bryant, 1983; Hulslander, Olson, Willcutt, & Wadsworth, 2010), who are still developing their knowledge of phonology and orthography. Adults, who have already established their phonological and orthographic skills, may not benefit from any additional phonological practice.

Texting is often seen by children as a fun and playful activity (e.g., Plester et al., 2009), which can encourage children to learn in a way in which they feel comfortable, in contrast to school-based writing, where correctness is important and mistakes are criticized (Crystal, 2008). The enjoyment that children seem to gain from texting can also increase the time that they spend reading and writing text messages, and thus lead to an overall increase in exposure to print (Wood, Meachem, et al., 2011). It should be noted that studies of children's textism use (e.g., Plester, Wood, & Bell, 2008; Plester et al., 2009) suggest that a relatively small range of popular textisms are used extensively (e.g., *c* for *see*, *u* for *you*, *2* for *to*). The more creative textisms often discussed in the popular press (e.g., initialisms such as *brb* for *be right back* and number-based homophones such as *42n8ly* for *fortunately*, used by Powell & Dixon, 2011) are not used so widely. Thus, texting may provide less opportunity for language "play" and learning than sometimes suggested.

In methodological terms, the researchers who have studied the use of texting and textisms have used a variety of task types. These include self-report (participants estimate the use of textisms in the messages they send), translation studies (participants are given sentences to rewrite as they would in a text message), scenario studies (participants compose a text message in response to a scenario), and naturalistic studies (textism use is obtained directly from messages recorded from the participants' phones). The studies detailed in this chapter have also considered both the frequency of messages sent and the density of textisms used in those messages. However, estimating the number of messages sent or received per day does not reflect exposure to textisms as clearly as estimating the proportion of textisms in those messages, and thus textism density is the most meaningful measure to consider in terms of its links to literacy skill.

Reading Ability

As noted above, many textisms rely on phonological decoding, which in turn is robustly related to reading skill (e.g., Melby-Lervåg, Lyster, & Hulme, 2012). Individuals who are strong in the component skills of reading might therefore be expected to be good at creating and deciphering textisms. Alternatively, as suggested in the popular press, frequent exposure to unconventional spellings in text messages could interfere with one's memory for standard spellings, and thus with one's general reading scores. As can be seen from Table 13.2, a variety of aspects of reading ability have been investigated in terms of their link with a range of measures of texting behavior.

Child Cohorts

Plester et al. (2009) examined the textism density of messages elicited from 10- to 12-year-old British children. Controlling for age, short-term memory, phonological awareness, vocabulary, and years of phone ownership, there was still a significant positive relationship between textism density and word reading. Coe and Oakhill (2011), in their sample of British 10- to 11-year-olds, found that although the better and the poorer readers in the sample engaged in the same frequency of texting, the better readers used more textisms than the poorer readers. Johnson (2012) reported a

Table 13.2 Overview of links between texting behavior and reading.

Cohort	Texting measure	Task type	Reading variable	Direction of correlation	Authors
Child	Textism density	Scenario	Real-word reading	Positive	Plester et al. (2009)
	Textism density	Naturalistic	Real-word reading	Positive	Coe & Oakhill (2011)
	Translate textisms to Std English	Translation	Reading fluency	Positive	Johnson (2012)
	Translate textisms to Std English	Translation	Comprehension	Positive	Johnson (2012)
	Textism density	Translation	Real-word reading	Neutral	Kemp & Bushnell (2011)
	Textism density	Translation	Non-word reading	Neutral	Kemp & Bushnell (2011)
Adolescent	Textism density	Translation	Non-word reading	Negative	De Jonge & Kemp (2012)
Adult	Texting frequency	Self-report	Reading fluency	Positive	Drouin (2011)
	Textism density	Translation	Real-word reading	Neutral	Drouin & Davis (2009)
	Textism density	Translation	Read-word reading	Neutral	Kemp (2010)
	Textism density	Naturalistic	Real-word reading (Australia)	Neutral	Grace et al. (2013)
	Textism density	Naturalistic	Non-word reading (Canada)	Neutral	Grace et al. (2013)
	Textism density	Naturalistic	Non-word reading (Australia)	Negative	Grace et al. (2013)
	Textism density	Translation	Non-word reading	Negative	De Jonge & Kemp (2012)
	Textism density	Naturalistic	Reading fluency	Neutral	Drouin & Driver (2012)
	Textism density	Naturalistic	Real-word reading	Negative	Drouin & Driver (2012)

positive correlation in a small study looking at Canadian children's scores on two reading measures and their ability to define five textisms (four of which were initialisms). Kemp and Bushnell (2011), in contrast, found no significant association between 10- to 12-year-old Australian children's reading scores and their use of textisms in a message dictation task. The fact that children had to type these messages onto a phone provided by the experimenter, while being timed, may make these results hard to compare with those from the other untimed, pen-and-paper tasks.

De Jonge and Kemp (2012) reported negative correlations between textism use and literacy skills (reading, non-word reading, spelling, and morphological awareness) in a sample of 13- to 15-year-olds. Some of these participants may have already entered the peak time of texting seen during the older teenage years and the early 20s (described by Lenhart et al., 2010) so that their texting behavior no longer mirrored that of their younger counterparts. This suggests that results from participants in their teenage years should not be analyzed together with those of younger children.

Adult Cohorts

As seen in Table 13.2, adult samples show a much more mixed set of findings in terms of the relationships seen between texting behavior and literacy skills. Drouin (2011) found a positive relationship between self-reported texting frequency and reading fluency in adults. However, such self-report measures are not necessarily accurate, and as noted above, the frequency of sending text messages does not represent the frequency of use of textisms. In translation tasks, there have been few clear links between textism use and literacy. Drouin and Davis (2009) saw no significant associations between undergraduates' use of textisms in a translation task and their scores on tasks of reading fluency and word recognition. They also found no significant difference in either type of reading skill between the group of students who reported that they used textisms in their messages and the group who reported that they did not.

Further neutral evidence comes from Kemp (2010), who found that textism density in translated messages had no significant correlations with real-word reading scores. Grace et al. (2013) saw inconsistent results for the naturalistic textism use of similar cohorts of Canadian and Australian undergraduates. For Canadian students, texting density had no association with non-word reading, but for Australian students, texting density was negatively associated with non-word reading, but not significantly associated with real-word reading. These differences between even very similar cultures, with the same language, suggest that results from different countries must be compared with caution.

Both De Jonge and Kemp (2012), using a translation task, and Drouin and Driver (2012), looking at naturalistic text messages, found negative correlations between adults' textism densities and reading scores, although Drouin and Driver found no correlation between textism use and reading fluency. Drouin and Driver point out the need to consider specific types of textisms produced. These authors distinguish between textisms which reflect the "lazy" omission of characters (such as capital letters and punctuation marks) and textisms which are more creative (such as phonetic respellings and abbreviations). Drouin and Driver did not in fact find overall patterns of textisms of omission being associated with poorer literacy skills and more creative textisms being associated with better literacy skills. However, they did find some individual associations in this direction. For example, among adults who never used predictive text entry, word reading scores were negatively related to omitted apostrophes, and reading fluency scores were positively related to the use of letter/number homophone textisms. This result may help to explain some of the conflicting results between adult studies. Data collected from different samples may have included different proportions of various textism types, which would also vary with the technology of the time of the research. Current mobile phones are more likely to correct errors of punctuation and capitalization than previous models, which might lead to different recorded patterns of textism use at different times.

Overall, then, it seems that the relationship between texting density and various measures of reading skill are generally positive for children, but more often neutral or even negative for older teenagers and adults. We suggest that one reason for these differences is because these children and adults began to use textisms at different stages in terms of learning to read, and thus at different stages of developing their phonological awareness. Children are still acquiring phonological skills and are therefore more likely to benefit from phonological practice through texting. In contrast, the adults in these studies had already developed their phonological knowledge and thus were not likely to benefit from practice with phonology. This could explain the neutral results in the adult category. More specific investigation of different textism types will be necessary to understand the negative links seen with some types of literacy in adults, but it may be that adults who are poorer readers also find it more difficult to create or decipher new, non-phonological textisms.

Spelling Ability

To an even greater extent than reading, spelling has been portrayed in the media as an academic skill that is vulnerable to the (perceived) excessive exposure to textisms (see Crystal, 2008, and Thurlow, 2006, for reviews). Numerous studies have examined the potential links between texting behavior and spelling, as summarized in Table 13.3.

Child Cohorts

Almost all of the child studies presented in Table 13.3 show a positive correlation between textism density and spelling ability. Plester et al. (2008) asked British children aged 11 to 12 years to translate Standard English sentences into text messages. Those children who used more textisms performed better on tasks of spelling ability. Similarly, Bushnell, Kemp, and Martin (2011) found that among 10- to 12-year-old Australian children who were asked to rewrite 30 individual words "as they would in a text message," those who created more textism-like spellings performed better on a standardized spelling test. Kemp and Bushnell (2011) saw no significant links between children's spelling scores and textisms use, but as noted above, the nature of the task (a timed message translation task on the experimenter-provided phone) may have made it difficult to compare with others.

De Jonge and Kemp (2012) reported a negative relationship between textism use in a translation task and spelling score. However, as suggested earlier, this is likely to be due to the 13- to 15-year-old participants being older than the child participants in the other studies, and showing more adult-like texting behavior (Lenhart et al., 2010) and links with literacy.

Table 13.3 Overview of links between texting behavior and spelling.

Cohort	Texting measure	Task type	Spelling variable	Direction of correlation	Authors
Child	Textism density	Translation	Spelling	Positive	Plester et al. (2008)
	Textism density	Translation	Spelling	Positive	Bushnell et al. (2011)
	Textism density	Translation	Spelling	Neutral	Kemp & Bushnell (2011)
	Textism density	Naturalistic	Spelling development	Positive	Wood, Meachem, et al. (2011)
	Textism density	Naturalistic	Spelling development	Positive	Wood, Jackson, et al. (2011)
Adolescent	Textism density	Translation	Spelling	Negative	De Jonge & Kemp (2012)
Adult	Texting frequency	Self-report	Spelling	Neutral	Massengill Shaw et al. (2007)
	Texting frequency	Self-report	Spelling	Positive	Drouin (2011)
	Textism density	Translation	Spelling	Neutral	Drouin & Davis (2009)
	Textism density	Translation	Spelling	Neutral	Kemp (2010)
	Textism density	Translation	Spelling	Negative	De Jonge & Kemp (2012)
	Textism density	Naturalistic	Spelling	Negative	Drouin & Driver (2012)
	Textism density	Naturalistic	Spelling (Canada)	Negative	Grace et al. (2013)
	Textism density	Naturalistic	Spelling (Australia)	Neutral	Grace et al. (2013)

Cross-sectional studies like these do not explain whether practice with textisms encourages better spelling, whether better spelling makes it easier to use textisms, or whether some more general skill underlies both. Longitudinal data, however, can help to determine the direction of causality. Wood, Meachem, et al. (2011) used a longitudinal design with British children between 8 and 12 years of age to examine if texting could increase spelling ability. Spelling ability at the end of the academic year was predicted by textism use at the start of the year, even after controlling for initial verbal IQ, phonological awareness, and spelling ability. However, this relationship was unidirectional, in that improved spelling ability did not significantly influence textism use. Wood, Jackson, Hart, Plester, and Wilde (2011) conducted a randomized intervention control trial to investigate the potential effect on spelling abilities of providing phone access to children who had never had a mobile phone before. For a 10-week period, children aged 9 and 10 years were given access to mobile phones during weekends and a one-week school break. The spelling skills of this group did not improve significantly more than those of a control group over the testing period. However, the use of textisms by children in the phone group accounted for a significant amount of variance in their post-test spelling scores, even after controlling for IQ and pre-test spelling scores. These children's access to the phones was restricted because of the school's ethical concerns, and further changes may have been seen if children were exposed to text messaging throughout the 10-week period, as they would under truly naturalistic circumstances. This is a question for future research.

Adult Cohorts

The findings with adult cohorts are once again less clear than with child cohorts. Massengill Shaw, Carlson, and Waxman (2007) and Drouin (2011) found positive associations with spelling and self-reported texting frequency. However, as mentioned earlier, it is more important to consider the proportion of textisms used. Drouin and Davis (2009) found no significant differences between individuals who reported they were textism users or non-users, on spelling skill or textism fluency (ability and speed in translating from Standard English to textese and vice versa). Within the group who did report using textisms, there was no significant correlation between textism fluency in the experimental tasks and spelling scores.

Studies that have used more direct measures than self-report, however, have seen no evidence of positive relationships with spelling. In a study with Australian undergraduates, Kemp (2010) found no significant correlations between spelling scores and the use of textisms in a translation task. In contrast, negative correlations between spelling scores and textism density were observed in both Standard English messages translated into text messages by another group of Australian undergraduates (De Jonge & Kemp, 2012) and in the naturalistic messages of U.S. undergraduates (Drouin & Driver, 2012). Drouin and Driver also looked at correlations between spelling scores and individual textism types. Although the overall pattern was negative, they saw a positive correlation between spelling scores and the use of accent stylization, but only in those who always used the predictive text entry function. This finding serves as a reminder that both textism type and phone technology should be considered when making generalized conclusions from correlational data.

Grace et al. (2013) found that spelling scores were not significantly related to the textisms used in the naturalistic messages of Australian students, but that they were negatively related for Canadian students. As noted earlier, this difference could be due to cultural differences in the uptake of mobile technology, and/or to differences in types of textisms favored in different countries, which might interact differently with spelling skill.

The importance of considering different categories of textism is emphasized by the results of an experimental study by Powell and Dixon (2011). These authors examined the effect of exposure to 30 different words spelled in different ways, on the pre- and post-test spelling of those words by 94 undergraduates. Participants saw the words spelled either correctly (e.g., *tonight*), misspelled phonologically (e.g., *tonite*), or as a textism (primarily letter/number homophones, e.g., *2nite*). Participants' pre- to post-test spelling of the target words was significantly better after exposure to both correct spellings and textisms, but significantly worse after exposure to misspellings. These findings suggest that greater exposure to letter/number homophones might facilitate spelling abilities. Although both the misspellings and the textisms present in this study were heavily based on phonology, the misspellings were orthographically more similar to the real words, and may thus have created more interference with stored orthographic representations (Katz & Frost, 2001).

The research reviewed here thus suggests that certain types of textisms (e.g., non-conventional spellings) may negatively affect adults' spelling, whereas other types (e.g., letter/number homophones) may affect it more positively. The use of various categories of textism seems to vary between samples, and might help to explain the mixed set of correlations seen in adult research. Somewhere in the teenage years it appears that children start to behave more like adults in terms of texting, as negative relationships start to appear between spelling and textism density. In child cohorts, however, there appears to be a positive link between textism use and spelling, regardless of textism category. We suggest that exposure to textisms can help children to reflect on and reinforce their own phonological representations of words. Children are also less affected by exposure to incorrect orthography than adults (Dixon & Kaminska, 2007; Katz & Frost, 2001), which could help to explain some of the negative relationships seen in adult samples.

Phonology

Phonological awareness is the ability to recognize and manipulate sounds that map on to letters and words, a skill that underpins reading and spelling ability (e.g., Furnes & Samuelsson, 2011). As has been noted, the phonological nature of many textisms means that phonological awareness could play an important role in the ability to create and decipher textisms (Plester et al., 2009). Table 13.4 summarizes the studies which have investigated links between texting behavior and awareness of phonology.

Plester et al. (2009) and Wood, Meachem, et al. (2011) controlled for children's phonology (measured by tasks of Spoonerisms and rapid automatized naming – RAN) and found that textism use still made a unique contribution to word reading and spelling. This contribution fell just short of statistical significance when RAN was controlled for (Plester et al., 2009), which suggests that phonology mediates the relationship between texting and spelling.

Table 13.4 Overview of links between texting behavior and phonological awareness.

Cohort	Texting measure	Task type	PA variable	Direction of correlation	Authors
Child	Textism density	Scenario	Phonological awareness	Positive	Plester et al. (2009)
	Textism density	Naturalistic	Phonological awareness	Positive	Wood, Meachem, et al. (2011)
Child (dyslexic)	Textism density	Naturalistic	Phonological awareness	Neutral	Veater et al. (2011)
Adult	Textism density	Translation	Phonological awareness	Neutral	Kemp (2010)
	Textism density	Naturalistic	Phonological awareness	Neutral	Grace et al. (2013)

The links between textism use and phonological skill have also been examined in children with dyslexia. Veater, Plester, and Wood (2011) found no significant differences in texting density between children who were typical readers and 10- to 13-year-old children who were dyslexic readers. However, the dyslexic children tended to use fewer phonology-based textisms than their peers, probably because children with dyslexia often have problems with phonological decoding (e.g., Gooch, Snowling, & Hulme, 2010). If they use and experiment with phonological textisms less often than their typically developing peers, then children with dyslexia are likely to gain even less practice with phonology, which could lead to further differences between the groups.

Kemp (2010) assessed sensitivity to phonological structure by asking Australian undergraduates to identify the sounds (rather than the letters) in a sentence. Scores on this task did not correlate significantly with textism density use in a translation task. Grace et al. (2013) gave Australian undergraduates a Spoonerisms task of phonological manipulation, but also found no significant association with naturalistic textism use. It may be that adults' phonological awareness is sufficiently developed that they receive no added benefit from practicing phonology through exposure to textisms. Future researchers could consider how the use of phonological textisms by dyslexic adults links with language skills. Further, it will be important to study the use and understanding of phonological and other types of textisms by children and adults who are deaf, and thus have limited, or no, phonological awareness.

Grammatical Ability

Grammar concerns the system and structure of a language, and includes the systems of syntax (the order in which words and phrases are arranged) and morphology (the structure of meaning) (Templeton, 2012). Morphemes, the smallest units of meaning in a language, include suffixes such as *-ed* and *-s*, prefixes such as *un-* and *pre-*, as well as whole words such as *cow*, which can stand on their own or join others to form compounds such as *cowboy*. Morphological awareness underpins the creation of grammatical words (e.g., Nunes, Bryant, & Bindman, 1997) and sentences in conventional writing. It may also be important for reading and writing textisms, which often involve shortening individual morphemes within whole words. For example, the suffix *-ing* is often abbreviated to *N* or *in*, so that *coming* could be written as *comin* or *comN*. Whole-word morphemes can also be preserved by abbreviating them to their initials, so that *girlfriend* becomes *gf* (Kemp, 2010). Some studies have considered the relationship of texting behavior to skills in morphology, or more broadly, in grammar, as shown in Table 13.5.

Kemp (2010) asked Australian university students to complete a task of morphological awareness in which they had to pick out the odd word from triplets such as *honest, meanest, smartest. Honest* is the odd word out because it consists of a single morpheme, whereas *meanest* and *smartest* are both made up of two morphemes: the base word plus the ending *-est*. Kemp found no significant relationship between participants' scores on this task and their use of textisms in a translation task. De Jonge and Kemp (2012) gave the same task to Australian high school and university students and found that scores correlated negatively with their use of textisms in a translation task, but only when texting frequency was taken into account. The skills needed to actively distinguish mono- versus multi-morphemic words might be more complex than the skills needed to find shorter ways to write the morphemes within multi-morphemic words such as *coming* and *girlfriend*. Thus, it is perhaps not surprising that consistently significant relationships have not been found between scores on this morphological awareness task and textism use overall.

Potential links between textism use and grammatical abilities have also been assessed at a more general level. There are various ways in which text messages can transgress the grammatical conventions of written English. One concerns punctuation, which in text messages is often omitted, or replaced by another marker, such as *x* (for a kiss) in place of a conventional full stop. Text messages may also include spellings of word combinations which mimic casual spoken language (e.g., *wanna* for *want to* or *woulda* for *would have*). Adults may forget, or children may fail to learn, the correct versions of these spellings in formal English, especially with cases such as *woulda*, sometimes incorrectly written in full as *would of* (for *would have*). Finally, textism versions are common for individual words whose spelling is usually determined by grammar, such as *to, too,* and *two* (often all written as *2*) or past-tense verbs such as *missed*, whose final *-ed* signals their grammatical status (but which could easily be rewritten phonetically as *mist*). Thus, excessive exposure to textism versions of such grammatical words could lead to ignoring or forgetting the appropriate spelling.

Some researchers have examined the grammatical issue of the punctuation used in text messages. For instance, Rosen, Chang, Erwin, Carrier, and Cheever (2010) asked adults about their use of lower case *i* for pronominal *I* and missing apostrophes in their text messages, and Drouin and Driver (2012) and De Jonge and Kemp (2012) examined omitted apostrophes and capitalization in naturalistic and translated messages, respectively. Only Drouin and Driver compared these categories directly to literacy skills, and they found that only omitted apostrophes were negatively related to word reading (but not to other literacy measures). With the advent of more sophisticated technology, it is important to distinguish whether participants' phones were correcting such grammatical errors, as it is otherwise difficult to draw meaningful conclusions about these aspects of grammatical correctness in text messages.

Table 13.5 Overview of links between texting behavior and grammatical skill.

Cohort	Texting measure	Task type	Variable	Direction of correlation	Authors
Child	Textism density	Self-report	Grammar	Negative	Cingel & Sundar (2012)
	Grammatical errors	Naturalistic	Grammar, orthographic processing	Neutral	Wood, Kemp, Waldron, et al. (2014)
Adolescent	Textism density	Translated	Morphological awareness	Negative	De Jonge & Kemp (2012)
	Grammatical errors	Naturalistic	Grammar, orthographic processing	Neutral	Wood, Kemp, Waldron, et al. (2014)
Adult	Textism density	Translation	Morphological awareness	Neutral	Kemp (2010)
	Textism density	Translation	Morphological awareness	Negative	De Jonge & Kemp (2012)
	Omitted apostrophes	Naturalistic	Reading	Negative	Drouin & Driver (2012)
	Omitted apostrophes	Naturalistic	Spelling, reading fluency	Neutral	Drouin & Driver (2012)
	Omitted capitals	Naturalistic	Reading, reading fluency, spelling	Neutral	Drouin & Driver (2012)
	Grammatical errors	Naturalistic	Grammar (oral, receptive), orthographic processing	Neutral	Wood, Kemp, Waldron, et al. (2014)
	Punctuation and capitalization errors	Naturalistic	Grammar (written)	Negative	Wood, Kemp, Waldron, et al. (2014)

Cingel and Sundar (2012) took a broader view of grammatical skill in their study of 10- to 14-year-olds' texting. These authors asked participants to identify the textisms in three of their own recently sent messages. This method is more reliable than a self-report study asking children to estimate their own textism use, but there is still much room for error. The authors found negative relationships between self-scored textism use and scores on these grammatical tasks. This suggests that those who used more textisms performed more poorly on grammatical tasks. However, the children with the poorer grammatical skills may also have found it harder to reliably identify and classify the textisms that they had used in their own messages. Thus, these results are interesting, but should be interpreted with caution.

Further research is providing a more detailed picture of how texting relates to grammar. Wood, Kemp, Waldron, et al. (2014) developed a coding system that identified all the textisms that violated grammatical conventions. The categories included unconventional orthographic forms (e.g., smiley faces for punctuation), capitalization and punctuation errors (e.g., *im* for *I'm*), word reduction textisms (e.g., *hafta*, *wanna*), word omission (e.g., *Coming too?*), the incorrect use of grammatical homonyms (e.g., *there* for *their*), and the use of ungrammatical word forms (e.g., *is you going?* for *are you going?*). These "errors" are not necessarily mistakes; some may have been written deliberately, to save time or to introduce more expression to a message.

Wood, Kemp, Waldron, et al. (2014) collected examples of naturalistic sent text messages from primary school, secondary school, and adult cohorts at the start of a one-year period. When the data collected at the start of the study were analyzed, it was found that the proportion of grammatical errors in children's sent text messages was not significantly related to their performance on two tasks of grammatical skill, although it was negatively correlated with scores on one of the tasks in adults. This relationship remained even after controlling for individual differences in IQ and spelling ability within the sample. Overall, this suggests that ungrammatical texting behavior in children and adolescents is not related to grammatical understanding; however, in young adults, some negative relationships are apparent. All of these participants are being followed up one year later, to assess the patterns of development across age groups, and to examine whether change in literacy skills over time can be accounted for differently depending on whether the textisms produced are stable (their use was similar between the two time points), or unstable (their use varied between the time points).

Thus far, these findings suggest that in adults, some of the grammatical errors made in texting may be related to poorer literacy skills, but in children and adolescents, there is no such relationship. The longitudinal data will reveal whether change over time in literacy task performance is explained by the incidence of stable or unstable textisms, and whether these patterns differ with age group. For now, we suggest that the violations of conventional grammar that are common in children's and teenagers' messages represent a phase of "play" with language. It seems that children and teenagers may move away from this phase once they have become bored with "playing" with language in this way. Alternatively, the common grammatical violations seen during this phase may reflect inconsistent linguistic self-monitoring during texting. In future, it will also be important to find ways of distinguishing textisms that represent intentional and accidental violations of conventional grammar.

General Writing

The higher-order ability of general writing skill has not been much studied in terms of its relationship to textism use. Nevertheless, it is an important aspect to consider, as it is a conglomerate of the previous skills reviewed; it relies on spelling, grammar, and the ability to reflect on one's own writing. In the one study on this question, Rosen et al. (2010) asked adults to self-report their frequency of sending text messages as well as to write a formal letter to a company and an informal piece on (un)happiness. These pieces were marked using a university graded writing scale. Participants who reported that they texted more frequently performed more poorly on the formal writing task than those who texted less frequently. The converse was true for the informal writing task. This pattern of results could be taken to suggest that frequent texting negatively influences formal writing ability. However, the most common textisms reported by the sample were the use of *i* in place of *I* and the omission of apostrophes, both of which reflect violations of conventional grammar. Thus, rather than the use of textisms themselves being related to poorer formal writing, the production of these grammatical errors in text messages and poorer scores on the formal writing task may be underlain by poorer grammatical skills in general. Participants with no college education were more likely to report using textisms than those with a college education. This suggests that educational background should be considered in mixed samples, especially when, as in this study, the marking scheme for the writing task was based on university exam criteria, with which the student participants would be more experienced. Given that textism use is related to spelling, and spelling contributes to general writing ability, future researchers could consider the links between texting and general writing skill in more detail, and extend this work to child participants as well.

Methodological Issues

Throughout the chapter we have discussed methodological limitations posed by factors such as the lack of reliability and validity from self-report measures (see also Wood, Kemp, & Plester, 2014). One specific finding illustrates the potential discrepancy between people's perceived and actual use of textisms. Grace et al. (2012) found that undergraduates who reported using textisms "none of the time" actually used an average of 13% textisms in their naturalistic messages, whereas those who reported using textisms "some" or "most of the time" used an average of 20%. This result serves as a reminder that even adults' estimates of their own textism use may not be accurate.

The way that textism use is measured can also have a significant effect on the conclusions drawn. Grace et al. (2012) compared textism densities across the three main textism collection methods: translation, elicitation, and the collection of naturalistic data. The highest textism densities were observed in translated messages, followed by scenario-based elicited messages, and the lowest in naturalistic messages. This discrepancy may be due to demand characteristics, where individuals use more textisms in experimental procedures because they want to appear more knowledgeable or fluent in this form of writing, or simply because knowing that the study is about texting makes them overestimate their textism use. Even when participants are asked to write down their messages directly from their phones, they may not do so entirely accurately. Inaccurate transcription may occur through carelessness, or more deliberately: self-presentation motives may lead to biased reporting, which may result in under- or overestimations of textism use. Individuals may also choose text messages which reflect what they want others to think about the way they text, rather than more representative messages. Future researchers should consider the method of Underwood, Rosen, More, Ehrenreich, and Gentsch (2012), who provided participants with communication devices that automatically sent copies of all their sent messages to a secure server searchable by the researchers. However, this method would be too costly for many research groups, and now that most people have their own phones, switching to an unfamiliar research phone could in itself influence the data obtained.

Grace et al. (2012) found differences between undergraduate students at similar universities in Australia and Canada in terms of texting frequency, texting density, and uptake of new technology. This suggests that care must be taken when comparing studies across the world, even with similar participant samples who speak the same language. The use of textisms in different languages will obviously differ even more (Crystal, 2008), and although this chapter focuses on texting in English, the types of abbreviations will depend on the nature of the language of communication.

We must also be cautious about generalizing and comparing studies across time, because mobile phone technology is developing rapidly. Participants in most of the earlier studies reported here had phones with alphanumeric keypads, but in more recent studies, participants have used a mix of QWERTY, alphabetic, and alphanumeric keypads. It is likely that alphanumeric keypads will soon be completely superseded, and the quicker and easier typing associated with QWERTY keyboards could lead to further changes in textism use.

Conclusions

Table 13.6 summarizes the results discussed in this chapter, and leads to the conclusion that texting behavior is related to different abilities in different age groups. In primary school children, textism use is linked consistently positively with measures of spelling, reading, and phonological awareness, while the relationship with grammar is more mixed, with no links, or a negative link, between textism use and grammatical task performance. By secondary school there is quite a different profile, with adolescents showing largely negative relationships between textism use and performance on language tasks. Adults show a more varied set of results, with a mix of neutral and negative correlations between texting behavior and language task scores.

Overall it seems that adult, child, and even adolescent samples cannot be considered together, as the links between texting behavior and literacy skills are so different in the three groups. These differences may stem from a variety of reasons, including the fact that these cohorts have had different experiences of technology, including access to different types of phones, keyboards, and predictive text, as well having had varying numbers of years to experience all of these factors. Perhaps more importantly, at the time of these studies, adult and some adolescent participants had largely consolidated their literacy skills before owning their first mobile phone, whereas many children may have been exposed to textisms while still improving their reading and writing abilities. Children can still benefit from playing and practicing with written language, but adults may not, although it is not yet clear whether adults' use of

Table 13.6 Overview of the relationship between texting behavior and literacy abilities across age groups.

Ability	Children	Adolescents	Adults
Reading	Positive	Negative	Neutral/Negative
Spelling	Positive	Negative	Neutral/Negative
Phonology	Positive	N/A	Neutral
Grammar	Neutral/Negative	Mixed	Neutral/Negative
Morphological Awareness	N/A	Negative	Neutral/Negative
General writing	N/A	N/A	Neutral/Negative

unconventional spelling in text messages could be a cause or a result of poorer linguistic skills. At least some of the variation in adults' textisms use probably comes not from their literacy skills, but from other sources instead, including differences in phone technology, conscientiousness (rather than knowledge) about spelling, and social norms about composing messages in their particular friendship groups. In sum, it appears that the use of textisms is not actively harming, and may even help to promote, children's language skills. For adolescents and adults, the picture is less clear, and continuing research will be necessary to draw out the reasons for some of the negative relationships seen between textism use and performance on measures of language skills.

References

Baron, N. S. (2010). Attitudes toward mobile phones: A cross-cultural comparison. In H. Greif, L. Hjorth, A. Lasen, & C. Lobet (Eds.), *Cultures of participation* (pp. 77–94). Frankfurt, Germany: Peter Lang.

Bradley, L., & Bryant, P. E. (1983). Categorizing sounds and learning to read: A causal connection. *Nature, 30*, 419–421.

Bushnell, C., Kemp, N., & Martin, F. H. (2011). Text messaging practices and links to general spelling ability: A study of Australian children. *Australian Journal of Educational and Developmental Psychology, 11*, 27–38.

Cingel, D., & Sundar, S. (2012). Texting, techspeak, and tweens: The relationship between text messaging and English grammar skills. *New Media and Society*, 1–17.

Coe, J. E. L., & Oakhill, J. V. (2011). "txtN is ez f u no h2 rd": The relation between reading ability and text-messaging behavior. *Journal of Computer Assisted Learning, 27*, 4–17.

Crystal, D. (2008). *Txting: The gr8 db8.* Oxford, UK: Oxford University Press.

De Jonge, S., & Kemp, N. (2012). Text-message abbreviations and language skills in high school and university students. *Journal of Research in Reading, 35*, 49–68.

Dixon, M., & Kaminska, Z. (2007). Does exposure to orthography affect children's spelling accuracy? *Journal of Research in Reading, 30*, 184–197.

Drouin, M. (2011). College students' text messaging, use of textese and literacy skills. *Journal of Computer Assisted Learning, 27*, 67–75.

Drouin, M., & Davis, C. (2009). R u txting? Is the use of text speak hurting your literacy? *Journal of Literacy Research, 41*, 46–67.

Drouin, M., & Driver, B. (2012). Texting, textese and literacy abilities: A naturalistic study. *Journal of Research in Reading*. doi: 10.1111/j.1467-9817.2012.01532.x

Durkin, K., Conti-Ramsden, G., & Walker, A. J. (2011). Txt lang: Texting, textism use and literacy abilities in adolescents with and without specific language impairment. *Journal of Computer Assisted Learning, 27,* 49–57.

Furnes, B., & Samuelsson, S. (2011). Phonological awareness and rapid automatized naming predicting early development in reading and spelling: Results from a cross-linguistic longitudinal study. *Learning and Individual Differences, 21*(1), 85–95.

Gooch, D., Snowling, M., & Hulme, C. (2010). Time perception, phonological skills and executive function in children with dyslexia and/or ADHD symptoms. *Journal of Child Psychology and Psychiatry, 52,* 195–203.

Grace, A., Kemp, N., Martin, F. H., & Parrila, R. (2012). Undergraduates' use of text messaging language: Effects of country and collection method. *Writing Systems Research, 4,* 167–184.

Grace, A., Kemp, N., Martin, F. H., & Parrila, R. (2013). Undergraduates' text messaging language and literacy skills. *Reading and Writing, 27,* 855–873.

Green, N. (2003). Outwardly mobile: Young people and mobile technologies. In J. Katz (Eds.), *Machines that become us: The social context of personal communication technology.* New Brunswick, NJ: Transaction Publishers.

Hulslander, J., Olson, R., Willcutt, E., & Wadsworth, S. (2010). Longitudinal stability of reading-related skills and their prediction of reading development. *Scientific Studies of Reading, 14,* 111–136.

Johnson, M. (2012). Comprehension of Standard English text and digital textism during childhood. *International Journal of Language, Culture and Society, 35,* 1–6.

Katz, L., & Frost, S. J. (2001). Phonology constrains the mental orthographic representation. *Reading and Writing, 14,* 297–332.

Kemp, N. (2010). Texting versus txting: Reading and writing text messages, and links with other linguistic skills. *Writing Systems Research, 2,* 53–71.

Kemp, N., & Bushnell, C. (2011). Children's text messaging: Abbreviations, input methods and links with literacy. *Journal of Computer Assisted Learning, 27,* 18–27.

Lenhart, A., Ling, R., Campbell, S., & Purcell, K. (2010, April 20). Teens and mobile phones. Pew Internet & American Life Project. Retrieved November 28, 2014, from http://pewinternet.org/Reports/2010/Teens-and-Mobile-Phones.aspx

Lexander, K. (2011). Texting and African language literacy. *New Media and Society, 13,* 427–443.

Ling, R. (2004). *The mobile connection: The cell phone's impact on society.* San Francisco, CA: Morgan Kaufmann.

Ling, R., & Yttri, B. (2002). Hyper-coordination via mobile phones in Norway. In J. Katz & M. Aakhus (Eds.), *Perpetual contact: Mobile communication, private talk, public performance* (pp. 139–169). Cambridge, UK: Cambridge University Press.

Massengill Shaw, D., Carlson, C., & Waxman, M. (2007). An exploratory investigation into the relationship between text messaging and spelling. *New England Reading Association Journal, 43,* 57–62.

Melby-Lervåg, M., Lyster, S. H., & Hulme, C. (2012). Phonological skills and their role in learning to read: A meta-analytic review. *Psychological Bulletin, 138,* 322–352.

Nunes, T., Bryant, P., & Bindman, M. (1997). Morphological spelling strategies: Developmental stages and processes. *Developmental Psychology, 33,* 637–649.

Ofcom. (2012). *UK children and parents: Media use and attitudes report.* Retrieved November 28, 2014, from http://stakeholders.ofcom.org.uk/binaries/research/media-literacy/oct2012/main.pdf

Plester, B., Wood, C., & Bell, V. (2008). Txt msg n school literacy: Does texting and knowledge of text abbreviations adversely affect children's literacy attainment? *Literacy, 42,* 137–144.

Plester, B., Wood, C., & Joshi, P. (2009). Exploring the relationship between children's knowledge of text message abbreviations and school literary outcomes. *British Journal of Developmental Psychology, 27,* 145–161.

Powell, D., & Dixon, M. (2011). Does SMS text messaging help or harm adults' knowledge of standard spelling? *Journal of Computer Assisted Learning, 27,* 58–66.

Rosen, L. D., Chang, J., Erwin, L., Carrier, M., & Cheever, N. A. (2010). The relationship between "textisms" and formal and informal writing among young adults. *Communication Research, 37,* 420–440.

Shortis, T. (2001). *The language of ICT: Information and communication technology.* London, UK: Routledge.

Taylor, A., & Vincent, J. (2005). An SMS history. In L. Hamill & A. Lasen (Eds.), *Mobile world: Past, present and future* (pp. 75–91). New York, NY: Springer.

Templeton, S. (2012). Teaching and learning morphology: A reflection on generative vocabulary instruction. *Journal of Education, 192,* 101–107.

Thurlow, C. (2003). Generation txt? The sociolinguistics of young people's text-messaging. *Discourse Analysis Online.* Retrieved November 28, 2014, from http://extra.shu.ac.uk/daol/articles/v1/n1/a3/thurlow2002003.html

Thurlow, C. (2006). From statistical panic to moral panic: The metadiscursive construction and popular exaggeration of new media language in the print media. *Journal of Computer-Mediated Communication, 11,* 667–701.

Underwood, M. K., Rosen, L. H., More, D., Ehrenreich, S. E., & Gentsch, J. K. (2012). The BlackBerry Project: Capturing the content of adolescents' text messaging. *Developmental Psychology, 48,* 295–302.

Veater, H. M., Plester, B., & Wood, C. (2011). Use of text message abbreviations and literacy skills in children with dyslexia. *Dyslexia,* 65–71.

Wood, C., Jackson, E., Hart, L., Plester, B., & Wilde, L. (2011). The effect of text messaging on 9- and 10-year-old children's reading, spelling and phonological processing skills. *Journal of Computer Assisted Learning, 27,* 28–36.

Wood, C., Kemp, N., & Plester, B. (2014). *Text messaging and literacy: The evidence.* London, UK: Routledge.

Wood, C., Kemp, N., Waldron, S., & Hart, L. (2014). Grammatical understanding, literacy and text messaging in school children and undergraduate students: A concurrent analysis. *Computers and Education, 70,* 281–290.

Wood, C., Meachem, S., Bowyer, S., Jackson, E., Tarczynski-Bowles, M. L., & Plester, B. (2011). A longitudinal study of the relationship between children's text messaging and literacy development. *British Journal of Psychology, 102,* 431–442.

14

Are "Friends" Electric?
Why Those with an Autism Spectrum Disorder (ASD) Thrive in Online Cultures but Suffer in Offline Cultures

Mark Brosnan and Jeff Gavin

University of Bath

"The Internet is an essential means for autistic people to improve their lives, because it is often the only way they can communicate effectively."

(Blume, 1997)

"I never knew I could talk so much!! Normally I don't speak much ... but with the computer I can be quite articulate. But I know if I met people I chat to on here – I wouldn't be able to speak as I do on the computer."

A post from a Facebook user with ASD (2013)

What is Autism Spectrum Disorder (ASD)?

Autism spectrum disorder (ASD) is defined by the American Psychiatric Association as a persistent deficit in social communication and social interaction across multiple contexts combined with restricted, repetitive patterns of behavior, interests, or activities (DSM-5; APA, 2013). ASD is identified in around 1% of the population, affecting around four times as many males as females. ASD is a lifelong condition and includes individuals who are low functioning (classic autism) and high functioning (Asperger's syndrome). One prominent theory of ASD proposes that the social communication and interaction difficulties in ASD are a result of a deficit in "empathizing" and restricted and repetitive interests are related to preserved or enhanced "systemizing" (Baron-Cohen, 2002, 2003, 2009).

Empathizing

Baron-Cohen defines empathizing as the drive to identify a person's thoughts and feelings and to respond to these with an appropriate emotion. Empathizing can be assessed through self-report questionnaires, such as the Empathy Quotient

The Wiley Handbook of Psychology, Technology, and Society, First Edition. Edited by Larry D. Rosen, Nancy A. Cheever, and L. Mark Carrier.

(Baron-Cohen & Wheelwright, 2004). The Empathy Quotient asks participants to agree or disagree with statements such as "I can tell if someone is masking their true emotion" and "I tend to get emotionally involved with a friend's problems." Behaviorally, empathizing can be assessed by the Reading the Mind in the Eyes Test (RMET; Baron-Cohen, Wheelwright, Hill, Raste, & Plumb, 2001). The RMET requires individuals to look at the eyes (the rest of the face is not seen) of a series of images and decide which of four words best describes the thoughts or feelings of the person. Whether assessing empathizing by questionnaire or a behavioral measure, a consistent pattern of results is typically found. First, females outperform males and second, males outperform those with ASD (whether male or female). Deficits in empathizing are argued to underpin the deficits in social communication and interaction found in ASD. A great deal of socially relevant information is expressed through the face during face-to-face interaction and difficulties in processing this information impact upon effective social communication and interaction. An emotional expression typically indicates how someone is feeling (e.g., feeling happy if you are smiling – though there are exceptions). Difficulties in processing the emotions of others result in a deficit in understanding their state of mind, that is, their thoughts and feelings (termed "theory of mind").

Systemizing

Whereas empathizing is defined in terms of the social world, systemizing is defined in terms of the non-social world. Systemizing is defined as the drive to analyze or construct a system. Systems can be broadly defined (technological systems, mechanical systems, natural systems, abstract systems) but tend to be highly predictable and follow rules (unlike people). Systemizing can be assessed by self-report questionnaire (Systemizing Quotient; Baron-Cohen, Richler, Bisarya, Gurunathan, & Wheelwright, 2003). The Systemizing Quotient asks participants to agree or disagree with statements such as "If I were buying a car, I would want to obtain specific information about its engine capacity" and "If there was a problem with the electrical wiring in my home, I'd be able to fix it myself." Behaviorally, systemizing can be assessed by tasks such as the Intuitive Physics Test (Lawson, Baron-Cohen, & Wheelwright, 2004), which asks 20 problem-solving questions based around physics/engineering principles. Systemizing is the drive to understand such predictable, rule-based systems and has been found to be high in those studying computer science, mathematics, and physics (Baron-Cohen et al., 1998). Those with ASD can have preserved or enhanced levels of systemizing. Again, a consistent pattern of results has been found when studying systemizing skills. First, males tend to outperform females, and second, those with ASD (whether male or female) tend to outperform males. A focus upon technology as a restricted and repetitive interest in ASD has been reported, and high systemizing skills are argued to underpin competence with technology (as well as other predictable systems). Much anecdotal evidence suggests that those with ASD have a drive to use technology, which can be seen as an aspect of strong systemizing (Moore & Calvert, 2000; Stromer, Kimball, Kinney, & Taylor, 2006). It has also been argued that the methodical orientation and attention to detail aspects of systemizing make people with ASD ideal to work within IT environments (Saran, 2008). Indeed, a famous author with ASD argues that she thinks much like a computer thinks: "My mind is similar to an Internet search engine that searches for photographs. I use language to narrate the photo-realistic pictures that pop up in my imagination" (Grandin, 2000, p. 14).

ASD and Social Media

We therefore have a pattern of social (empathizing) and non-social (systemizing) abilities which indicates:

- Empathizing is greater in females than in males, who, in turn, are better at empathizing than those with ASD (females > males > ASD).
- Systemizing is greater in ASD than in males, who, in turn, are better at systemizing than females (ASD > males > females).

Those with ASD are characterized as having a deficit in social communication and interaction combined with a strength in using systems, such as technological systems. One of the greatest advances of the twenty-first century has been the development of the Internet for the vast majority of the population within the industrial world. The modulation of communication via the Internet has spawned a wealth of research. Of particular interest to this chapter, the Internet has allowed for communication between people who are not physically present, that is, not face to face. Of course, writing letters and the telegram allowed for this centuries ago; however, the Internet affords far greater accessibility and immediacy for non-face-to-face communication. Internet-based communications are also used far more frequently, on many occasions being the most frequent way people communicate with each other. The telephone, too, allows for non-face-to-face communication, although there is still a vocal presence. The Internet has allowed for mass communication to occur without the need for a face-to-face social-emotional presence, a phenomenon termed social media. Social media refers to any Internet site that allows social interaction, including social networking sites such as Facebook (O'Keeffe & Clarke-Pearson, 2011). Given that those with ASD have difficulties in social-emotional processing and strengths in using technological systems, how those with ASD use social media is an important question. Within social media communication, can systemizing strengths compensate for empathizing weaknesses?

Social media has long been argued to be "affect-limited" (Picard, 1998), that is, lacking in ability to express or recognize emotion. Historically the vast majority of online communication has been typed from one person to another. This removes the social-emotional cues, such as facial expression, that those with ASD can have difficulty processing. Thus the affect-limited nature of social media can level the playing field for those with ASD to communicate. Clearly, when communicating solely through typing online, you cannot process someone else's facial emotion whether you have ASD or not. Shore (2001) also argues that computers are often particularly well suited for those with ASD as they provide interactive consistency. A computer has the same response for a given input, so there is no body language or tone of voice messages that need to be decoded. Thus, the interactive consistency could play to systemizing strengths and the affect-limited nature of the communication could ameliorate the empathizing deficits in ASD.

Social Media and Social Capital

This is significant and there is evidence within the general population that social experiences are increasingly occurring online (Livingstone, 2008). What is more, failure to master social media may lead to social exclusion. For many teenagers, having a social network presence is essential to having a social life. As one social networker put it several years ago, "if you're not on MySpace, you don't exist" (boyd, 2007). Facebook in particular can expand and strengthen social networks, and enables members to maintain older friendships that would otherwise have faded away (Young, 2011). For example, if you are not on Facebook and everyone is arranging a social activity through Facebook, you are more likely to be excluded. As a consequence, Facebook use has been found to predict "social capital" (Donath, 2007; Ellison, Steinfield, & Lampe, 2007). Social capital broadly refers to the resources accumulated through the relationships among people. At least two types of social capital have been identified: "bridging social capital," sometimes referred to as "weak ties," consists of diffuse networks of relationships from which people could potentially draw resources (distribution lists, photo directories); and "bonding social capital," sometimes referred to as "strong ties," consists of family and close friends, who might be in a position to provide emotional support (see Steinfield, Ellison, Lampe, & Vitak, 2012, for an overview). Importantly, online social capital extends to the offline world (Ellison et al., 2007; Ellison, Lampe, Steinfield, & Vitak, 2011). This raises the intriguing possibility that mastery of social media could reduce the ASD deficits seen in empathizing in an offline context. The epigraph at the beginning of this chapter indicates that those with ASD can use social media effectively; however, this does not extend to face-to-face communication. The remainder of the chapter will explore this contention.

Who Uses Social Media?

Google executive Eric Schmidt has proclaimed that the entire Earth will be online by 2020 (Gonzales, 2013; Schmidt, 2013). Clearly he may have a vested interest in making such predictions, but the data suggest that around 80% of North Americans are already online, as are two-thirds of Europeans and Australians. South America and the Middle East have around 40% Internet penetration and Africa and Asia around 20–25% (Internet World Stats, 2013). So not the entire Earth yet, but the year-on-year increases in the proportions of population coming online suggest most people on Earth will soon be online. Either way, there are literally billions of people online. So what are they doing? In a major survey of worldwide Internet use, ComScore (2014) report four key findings:

1 Social networking is the most popular online activity worldwide (85% of people who are online report some level of social networking).
2 The importance of Facebook cannot be overstated (75% of social networking).
3 It is not just young people using social networking anymore – it is all age groups.
4 Mobile devices are fueling this "social addiction."

In May 2013, Facebook statistics reported that there were more than a billion active Facebook users, a figure which increased to 1.3 billion in March 2014 (Geekwire, 2013; Statisticsbrain, 2014), including more than half of the population of the United States (Internet World Stats, 2013). The statistics highlighted that in the United States, there were slightly more female than male Facebook users, and 25–34 was the most popular age range (Socialbakers, 2014). Gender is argued to be an important variable when examining computer usage (Brosnan, 1997, 1998), with some research indicating that females are more likely to use the Internet for communication, while males are more likely to use the Internet for information-seeking (Jackson, Ervin, Gardner, & Schmitt, 2001). This may be pertinent as around four times as many males as females are diagnosed with ASD (APA, 2013). Facebook groups based around specific interests exist as forums for communication, and in research conducted on undergraduates from seven United Kingdom universities, we have found that males belong to 19 Facebook groups on average, and females belong to 15 Facebook groups on average (Joiner et al., 2006; Joiner, Brosnan, Duffield, Gavin, & Maras, 2007; Joiner et al., 2012, 2013).

Friends can be identified within Facebook, and Facebook supports 150 billion friend connections. Facebook is clearly a prolific resource for supporting social communication and interaction within an online context. As an aside, Robin Dunbar argues that the human brain has evolved to maintain around 150 social relationships effectively ("Dunbar's number"; Dunbar, 2010). These social relationships are personalized relationships that are reciprocal and based around general obligations of trust and reciprocity, akin to bonding social capital. Dividing the number of Facebook friends by the number of Facebook users gives an average number of Facebook friends per Facebook user of 141.5, which is fairly close to Dunbar's number. Numbers of reported Facebook friends can be much higher than 150 (e.g., Edison, 2014); however, Dunbar's number refers to "bridging social capital" or "strong ties." Interested readers are referred to Dunbar's (2010) book, *How Many Friends Does One Person Need?*.

Do People with ASD use Social Media?

Since the 1990s, people with ASD have been communicating via chatrooms, email lists, and online bulletin boards (Biever, 2007). Those with ASD have been early adopters of online communication forums. Early analyses of the impact of online communication for those with a social communication deficit were startling in how beneficial online communication was found to be. For example, Singer (1999) argued that "the impact of the Internet on autistics may one day be compared to the spread of sign language among the deaf" (p. 69). Blume (1997), too, argued that "for many autistics the Internet is Braille." Both of these analogies highlight how those with impaired communication skills are enabled to communicate online. Blume continues: "autistic communication could be comparable to written communication," to suggest that the written style of communication afforded by Internet-based communication is preferable for those with ASD. Another famous author with ASD writes: "When I need to explain something at a level of complexity for which spoken words evade me, I still run off to the computer and let my fingers talk" (Williams, 2005, p. 252). Thus, on some occasions at least, the writing format supported by social media proves beneficial to those with ASD.

A second key aspect of written communication is the inherent delay, when compared to face-to-face communication. Internet-based communication allows for a delay in response that is almost never allowed in real life. Darius (2002) writes: "there is no such thing as adequate delayed social reactions. One is either quick enough to keep up, or one is weird and socially disabled" (p. 25). Again, a great deal of research has been undertaken on comparing synchronous and non-synchronous communication (Walther & Parks, 2002). It would seem that this is particularly pertinent for those with ASD. The reason that "autistic communication could be comparable to written communication" may be the additional time that is available to reflect upon what is being communicated. The removal of the immediate time pressure to respond may allow those with ASD to communicate more effectively.

Thus, the Internet allows communication between group members for whom social aspects to communication have historically been a hindrance (Dekker, 2006, cited in Davidson, 2008). An interesting issue to emerge from this is that those with ASD can communicate with each other. The Internet has facilitated the formation of a group identity (amongst those typically described as having communication difficulties). Singer (1999) argues that "the Internet has promoted the emergence of new ways of self-identification for autistics" (p. 64). The Internet provides a means to develop and maintain relationships for people with ASD (Jones & Meldal, 2001). This facilitation of online social interaction accords with Singer's (1999) claim that the Internet is the ideal social environment for those with ASD. Singer (1999) argues that those with ASD now have their own country, "a cybercountry – and it's perfect" (p. 65).

The affect-limited nature of online communication is therefore "ASD-compatible," providing a "level playing field" for communication. This, in turn, allows for a "neurological pluralism," that is, equal access for all, irrespective of any neurological differences (Blume, 1997; Brownlow & O'Dell, 2002), as well as the formation of a group identity. The Internet has therefore begun to challenge stereotypes surrounding the competence of people with ASD to communicate effectively. Dekker (2006) notes that "autistic people often report they have few problems communicating with and understanding people 'of their own kind'" (cited in Davidson, 2008). The question then arises as to whether those with ASD can access and use social networking sites, such as Facebook, to communicate with those who do not have ASD.

Do People with ASD use Facebook?

How those with ASD use Facebook forms the basis of the remainder of this chapter and our initial empirical work in this area. Autism-related charities tend to have a Facebook presence. The number of Facebook users who have indicated they "like" these Facebook groups provides an index of usage and interaction with the group. For example, as of March 2014, Autism Awareness (USA) had 859,000 likes and 255,000 interactions/week; Autism Speaks (USA) had 1.1 million likes and 22,000 interactions/week; and the National Autistic Society (UK) had 43,000 likes and 2,000 interactions/week. So there is some evidence that those with an interest in ASD are using Facebook. In addition there is a huge range of user-run Facebook groups based around ASD.

Also, anecdotally, a mother of a young man with ASD emailed us as follows (with permission to reproduce the email):

> I sometimes send my 14 yr old son a message on facebook to say thank you when he has helped me with something around the house, usually after much persuasion from me and complaining from him! He seems to respond positively [to Facebook comments] (last response was "you know normal conversation isnt too bad!") and then when I see him next he is more open to a hug. However if I'd say to him verbally, he rarely responds as is already thinking about something else. I think its because its more permanent when written down and there for longer. If verbal its over quickly and im never sure I have his full attention. I can also send him reminders on facebook e.g. homework, music practice, feed pet, write birthday card. This avoids an angry response as we are not interrupting him, I only need to do once as I know he's seen it ... I have heard from other families of teenage boys with aspergers that they too use email, text and messaging with their child in the same house as they get a better response.

Thus, Facebook can be used on occasion in preference to face-to-face conversations in families who are in the same house together. This quote reflects the comparisons above between autistic communication and written communication. Based on this, our aim was to explore how those with ASD used the primary social networking site, Facebook, and to explore the extent to which empathizing was evident in this online environment, when it has been found to be deficient in the offline environment. To do this we explored open message boards within Facebook. As this is the first time this type of research has been undertaken, some methodological issues need to be addressed.

Ethics

We carefully considered the ethical implications of our studies and conformed to the guidelines produced by the British Psychological Society (BPS, 2009). Facebook sites included open access message boards. Open access message boards are generally perceived and acknowledged by users and members as being in the public domain, freely available to anyone with access to the Internet (Paccagnella, 1997). In posting a message there is "implied license to read or even archive the information it contains" (Mann & Stewart, 2000, p. 46). As such, it was not considered necessary to seek consent from the website manager or the individuals posting and responding to messages on the board (see Rodham & Gavin, 2006; Gavin & Rodham, Chapter 6 in this volume). In accordance with the BPS Ethical Code of Conduct (2009), we ensured that the anonymity of the site and the individuals who posted and/or responded to messages was maintained. We did this by removing any references to names (of the group or community or posters) and places in the quotes we have presented. We also typed the quotes we have presented below into Google to establish that they were not searchable. We also sought and received approval from our department ethics committee.

Research Strategy

The research focuses upon Facebook users who self-identify as having ASD. This research is preliminary and we have no way of confirming the diagnosis. In addition we do not know whether those with ASD who use Facebook are representative of the

ASD population. We will refer to those who self-identify as having ASD as the ASD group. However, these important provisos need to be borne in mind when considering these pilot data.

Is Online Communication Preferable to Offline Communication for Those with ASD?

The literature above suggests that those with ASD may exhibit a preference for online communication. Our first analysis sought to identify if this was the case and, if so, what those with ASD thought the reasons for this were. We therefore analyzed the posts from an ASD Facebook group (community). This group asked for responses to a specific question: *How has your ASD changed since having the freedom to talk to people online instead of face to face?*

There were 46 respondents to this question who self-identified as having ASD. Analysis of these posts revealed five categories of response, illustrated in Figure 14.1.

The most popular response (26/46 = 57%) was that online communication was easier than offline communication, or face to face). Examples from this category include:

> Although I've learned to talk to people face-to-face, it's still ten times easier and more comfortable to talk on-line.

> I normally can talk to people on facebook but don't face to face most of the time...

> Its easier online as no 1 gets to see your nervousness in action.

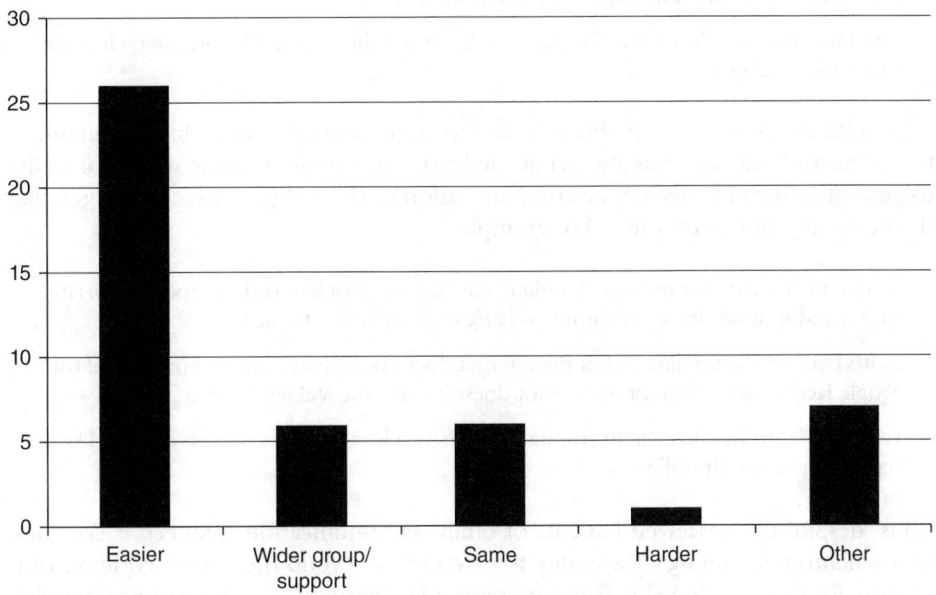

Figure 14.1 Responses to online versus face-to-face communication.

Within these responses the limited affect of reduced cues was frequently cited as a reason why online communication was easier. For example:

> When talking online I feel so much more ease and a lot less pressure to understand social cues.

> It is easier to talk behind a screen, because I don't have to read any gestures, just smileys. :-)

This last point is important. We have found that simple stylized smileys are recognized better by people with ASD compared to controls (Brosnan, Chapman, Johnson, Grawemeyer, & Benton, 2013). These very clear expressions of the basic emotions are recognized and used by those with ASD. It is the more subtle and complex emotions that can be problematic to recognize by those with ASD. Also, one respondent reported that they missed social cues during online communication:

> However ... online it frustrates me when I don't know what's going on with the other person ... no tone, no facial expression, and also being disconnected all the time.

Thus, while the affect-limited nature of the reduced social cues was beneficial in leveling the playing field for many with ASD, there was at least one person with ASD who felt they benefited from the face-to-face social cues.

The second major theme that emerged was the benefit of not having to respond immediately. Having the time to reflect upon communication was frequently seen as beneficial. For example:

> On-line is better for the same reason why I don't use a telephone. I need time to think through my replies before typing or talking. On-line gives me the freedom to do that.

> I like the online stuff because I have the freedom to take the time I need to respond, I can read better than I listen, so I misunderstand less ...

> I find it easier to reflect inwardly and see what it is I think or feel before I type into the Facebook posting.

Despite the perceived benefits of online communication over offline communication, a major limitation was also acknowledged. An emergent theme was the inability to generalize the effective online communication to the offline world (see epigraph at the beginning of this chapter). For example:

> ... It's much easier for me to talk online, email, text. Problem is, I get too comfortable with it and it makes it harder for me to [*talk to*] people face to face.

> ... it's better to talk online ... but the internet does not help in learning how to deal with people face to face – and for me at least doesn't make me feel less lonely.

> Yes it's easier to socialize online, though I still have a lot of trouble in everyday life, I keep very much to myself offline ...

Thus, despite the perceived benefits of online communication (reduced social cues, non-synchronous timing), the ability to extend this beyond the online world remains an issue for those with ASD. This represents a fascinating forum for future research – how do we extend the benefits for communication in those with ASD from the online world to the offline world? Anecdotal evidence suggests it can be done (Schultz & Jacobs, 2012), and communicating via Facebook or avatars through to communicating face to face via Skype represent interesting variants on the degree of a physical/digital presence to the online communication.

Also important to note are the other categories represented in Figure 14.1. Six additional respondents preferred the online communication environment to the offline world. This was not because they found communicating online easier but because it facilitated access to similar people (others with ASD). This is an important function of many online environments, and is a separate advantage to easier online communication. This also highlights a crucial point. The posts from this analysis emanated from a group within which everyone self-identified as having ASD. Future research needs to clarify that perceived benefits in online social-emotional communication are appreciated by the recipients of the communications – including both recipients with and without ASD. In addition, six participants also reported that they found online and offline communication comparable and one respondent found online communication harder than offline communication. (The "other" category included responses such as "good question"). It is important to remember that the ASD group are a diverse group with differing strengths and weaknesses. For the majority, however, the online context does provide an environment which enables communication that is hindered within the offline world. Having established a preference for online communication in those with ASD, our second question concerned the social-emotional content of the communication.

The Expression of Basic Emotions on Facebook by Those with ASD

This second study sought to explore whether those with ASD expressed emotional content in an online context in a manner that was comparable to those without ASD. The literature above highlights that in the offline world, ASD is characterized as deficits in social-emotional communication. However, in the online world, anecdotal evidence (see the epigraph at the head of the chapter) and our first study (above) suggest those with ASD may be able to communicate effectively. So the question arises as to the social-emotional content of the online communication of those with ASD. It could be that in the online context, communication is indistinguishable from communication with those without ASD, that is, communication contains comparable levels of social-emotional content. Conversely, it could be that the online context allows those with ASD to communicate effectively but without the social-emotional content, consistent with the deficits in empathizing described in the offline world.

Our second study therefore looked at the posts of those within an ASD Facebook group. We wanted to explore the use of emotionally laden language in the posts of those who self-identify as having ASD (we were unable to confirm a clinical diagnosis). For this study we focused upon the six basic emotions that have been found to be consistent across time and cultures, namely, happiness, surprise, fear (being afraid), anger, disgust, and sadness (Ekman & Friesen, 1969). These basic expressions of emotion are communicated facially and we are extending this to written communication.

There is a personality construct called "alexithymia," which is characterized by the subclinical inability to identify and describe emotions in the self in any modality, including text. Studies of alexithymia have attempted to identify whether there is a general cross-modality alexithymia in ASD as opposed to a specific deficit in processing facial emotions. Bird et al. (2010), for example, argue that it is alexithymia within those within ASD that underpins the deficit in empathizing. Thus, the deficit is in the inability to identify and describe emotion in the self, not simply a facial emotion recognition deficit in the offline world. We would therefore predict a lack of emotionally laden words within the posts of those with ASD if the online world is consistent with the offline world.

An analysis of all the emotionally laden words in English has been undertaken. Baron-Cohen, Golan, Wheelwright, Granader, and Hill (2010; see also http://www.jkp.com/mindreading/) identified all the emotionally laden words from the English electronic thesaurus in Microsoft Word and clustered them into emotional categories. The six basic emotions are listed in Figure 14.2. "Comfortable," "calm," "amused," etc. were therefore all counted as an expression of the "happy" emotion. The levels refer to when these words typically enter the vocabulary, that is, Level 1 represents the first words typically used. Typically, 4- to 6-year-olds have around 40 emotional words they use consistently and correctly (Level 1); this doubles to around 80 in 7- to 8-year-olds (Level 2), doubles again to around 160 in 9- to 10-year-olds (Level 3), and almost doubles again to just over 300 in 11- to 12-year-olds (Level 4), after which there are minor increases in 13- to 14-year-olds (Level 5) and 15- to 16-year-olds (Level 6). Thus, particularly for the basic emotions, the vast majority of the emotion words in English are used and understood by 12 years of age. There is good evidence that children with ASD also understand the words for basic emotions by the age of 12; for example, they can reliably pair the word "happy" with a picture of a smiling face (Grossman, Klin, Carter, & Volkmar, 2003). We extended this analysis to account for a unique feature of textual representations of emotions found in Facebook and other online communication, namely emoticons. Emoticons provide a visual representation of emotion using keystrokes, almost exclusively based upon stylized facial expressions, for example :) as happy and : (as sad. Although those with ASD can have deficits in recognizing facial emotions (compared to control groups), we have found that those with ASD are better at recognizing emoticons than control groups (Brosnan et al., 2013).

We then identified a comparison group that had a similar number of members, post activity, and age (teenagers) and sex profile (equal numbers of males and females). We identified a group that formed around a physical condition, which was a cancer group, to compare with our ASD group. The ASD group had 45 active members and we analyzed the most recent 108 posts, of which 48% contained emotion words. The cancer group had 41 active members and we analyzed the most recent 102 posts, 49% of which contained emotion words. The presence of emotion words was judged by two independent judges and any disagreements were resolved through discussion. As the methodology was quite explicit, there were very few disagreements as to whether one of the words listed in Figure 14.2 was present or not. Also of interest was whether the emotion words were being used appropriately. Both groups used the emotion words appropriately. Indeed, judges felt they could not distinguish whether the posts were from the ASD or cancer group, unless reference was made explicitly to the condition.

Emotion	Level 1	Level 2	Level 3	Level 4	Level 5	Level 6
Happy	Comfortable	Calm	Amused	Carefree	Jubilant	Exhilarated
	Glad	Cheeky	Content	Casual		
	Happy	Cheered	Easy-going	Sociable		
	Joking	Delighted	Mischievous	Triumphant		
	Lucky	Enjoying	Positive	Unconcerned		
	Merry	Fine	Relieved			
	Safe	Grateful				
	Teasing	Overjoyed				
		Playful				
		Pleasure				
		Proud				
		Relaxed				
Surprised	Surprised	Shocked	Dazed	Appalled	Scandalized	
			Horrified			
			Startled			
			Wonder			
Afraid	Afraid	Desperate	Cowardly	Daunted		Consternation
	Worried	Nervous	Dreading	Disturbed		Cowed
		Threatened	Frantic	Intimidated		Discomforted
			Jumpy	Shaken		
			Panicked	Uneasy		
			Terrified	Vulnerable		
			Watchful			
Angry	Angry	Annoyed	Displeased	Bitter	Miffed	
	Grumpy	Complaining	Explosive	Discontented	Needled	
	Moaning	Furious	Frustrated	Exasperated		
	Moody	Wild		Heated		
				Indignant		

Figure 14.2   Emotion words for each basic emotion.

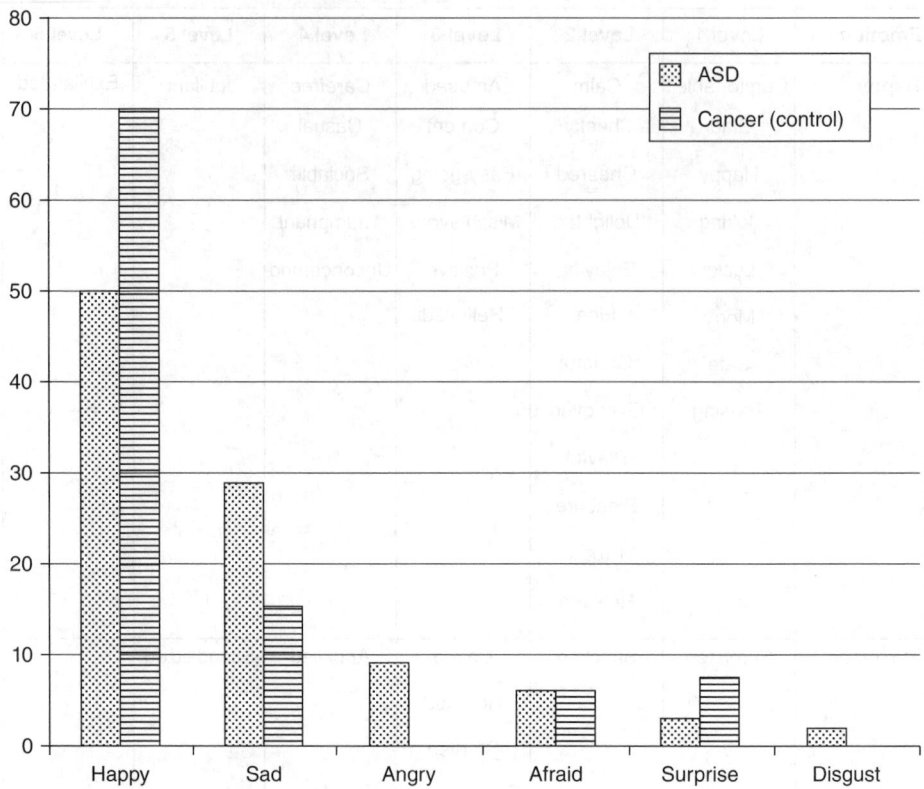

Figure 14.3   Proportions of basic emotions expressed in Facebook posts from ASD and cancer (control) groups.

Having identified that both groups used emotion words appropriately in almost half of their posts, we then analyzed *which* emotion words were used by each group. The percentages of each basic emotion expressed are highlighted in Figure 14.3. For both the ASD and cancer (control) groups, happiness was the most frequently expressed emotion, followed by sadness. The other four basic emotions were expressed relatively rarely (anger, fear, surprise, disgust; note there are fewer words within the disgust category, which may have affected these findings). There were many similarities between these two groups in terms of the amount and content of emotional expression within Facebook posts. However, there was also a trend for those within the ASD group to express less happy and more sad emotions than the cancer (control) group.

While it may seem unusual that those discussing cancer are expressing more happiness than those with ASD, there is research to suggest that the aim of support groups such as these is to provide *positive* support (Rodham, Gavin, Lewis, St. Denis, & Bandalli, 2013). We therefore ran a third study to compare an ASD Facebook group with a control group that did not have a clinical or medical condition. Again we identified a group based upon having a similar number of active members with a similar age and sex demographic profile. The best match was a church-based group of young people who were all located in the same city in the United Kingdom. The same

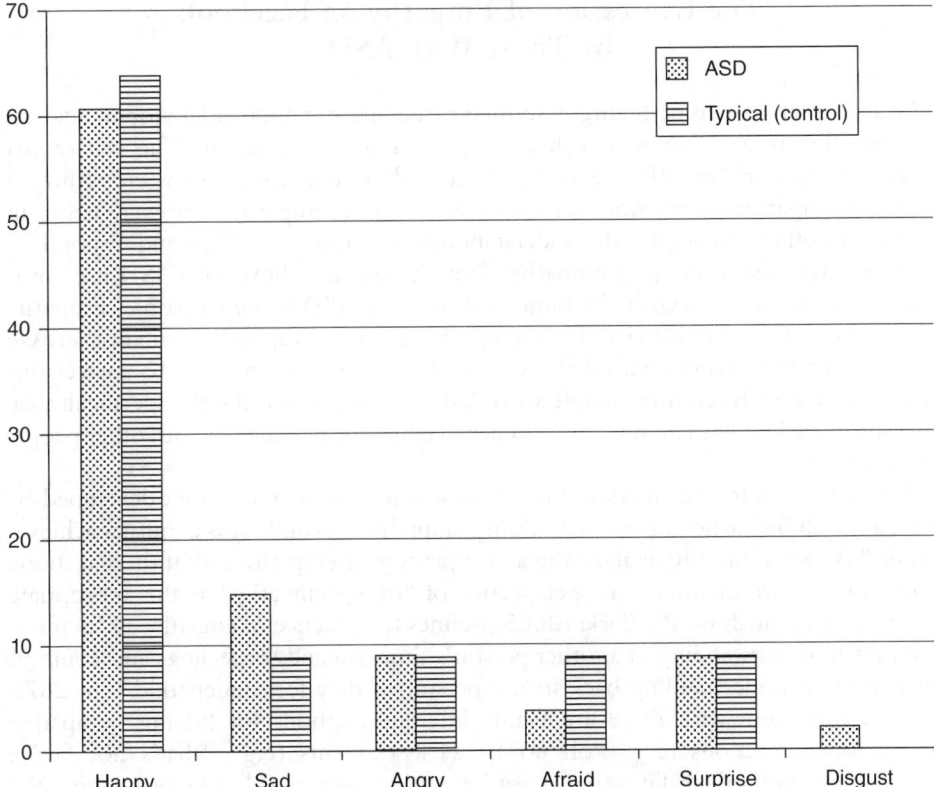

Figure 14.4 Proportions of emotions expressed in Facebook posts of ASD and typically developing (control) groups.

analysis as described above was conducted for the last 100 posts of 2012 for the ASD and control group. In addition we analyzed the structure of the posts, which averaged two to three responses per post, suggesting that both groups were comparably interactive in their Facebook posts. In these posts, the ASD group used emotion words in 35% of their posts, considerably more than the control group, which used emotion words in 12% of their Facebook posts. As with the first study, we examined which emotion words were being used (noting the small numbers for the control group). Again "happy" was the dominant emotion being expressed by both groups. The other five basic emotions were all expressed fairly comparably and to a far lesser degree. The overriding sense of the data is how similar the proportions of emotions used are by both groups, as illustrated in Figure 14.4.

In summary, those with ASD used basic emotion words appropriately when they were online. Moreover they expressed the same pattern of emotions as the control groups (e.g., typical teenagers). In addition, those with ASD expressed emotion comparably to those with other conditions (cancer) and more frequently than those from the typically developing control group. This quantitative analysis indicated that emotion was being used within online communication by those with ASD. Our next study explored qualitatively whether there were examples of empathy being displayed appropriately in online communication by those with ASD.

The Expression of Empathy on Facebook
by Those With ASD

The assessments of empathizing described earlier are not appropriate for an analysis of empathic interaction with others in an online environment. The self-report questionnaires and emotion recognition tasks described above assess empathizing without empathic interaction with another person. Empathy, however, exists in relation to other people. It is the understanding of emotions in others and responding appropriately that underpins empathy. The finding that those with ASD use emotion words is not necessarily the same as those with ASD being empathic. Empathy is an inherently social activity. To *be* empathic involves responding to another. We wanted to ask: Do those with ASD respond to others empathically? To answer this question, we analyzed how people with ASD interact on Facebook. Specifically, we investigated whether there was any evidence of empathic interactions with other people on Facebook.

Our approach to the analysis of empathy was to use the framework developed by Pudlinski (2005), who argued that "doing empathy or sympathy is a mutual achievement." As we wanted to analyze the active process of empathy within the Facebook environment, we identified the perspective of "doing empathy" as the appropriate framework for analysis. Pudlinski (2005) defines the practice of empathy as "demonstrating an understanding of another person's situation and/or feelings and communicating that understanding back to the person so they feel understood" (p. 267). Within this framework there are eight different methods for "doing" empathy: (1) emotive reactions (e.g., "oh no"); (2) assessments (e.g., "that's not fair"); (3) naming another's feelings (e.g., "you're getting clobbered"); (4) formulating the gist of another's troubles (e.g., providing a short summary of their feelings); (5) using an idiom (e.g., "just take each day as it comes"); (6) expressing one's own feelings about another's troubles (e.g., "sorry to hear that"); (7) reporting one's own reactions (e.g., "I'd be pretty angry about that too"); and (8) sharing an experience of similar feelings (e.g., "I feel that way too sometimes").

These eight methods differ along four dimensions:

A   Depth of understanding of the other's trouble.
B   Depth of understanding of the other's feelings.
C   Ability to normalize the other's feelings.
D   Amount of shared similarity of feelings.

Identification of the empathy practice (i.e., 1–8 above) informs an understanding of the dimensions of empathy (i.e., A–D above). For example, the practice of emotive reactions (1 above) indicates a minimal practice of dimension A, or the practice of sharing an experience of similar feelings (8 above) indicates all four dimensions of empathy are being practiced. Our fourth study looked at an ASD Facebook group (a "Facebook community") to explore if there was evidence of the practice of empathy in this online context. We analyzed the most recent 100 threads of 37 active users. The results showed that 89% posted between one and five times, 5.4% 6 to 10 posts, and 5.4% 11+ posts. Of the 37 people, 14 were male and 23 were female. Twenty-two from the 37 (59%) active posters with ASD displayed empathy under Pudlinski's framework. Below are some selected posts from those with ASD.

In response to a post about being anxious about a test:

just relax and try to keep ur mind focused and clear ... which i know is difficult ... when i did my test ill let you into a little secret ... i was in auto mode and i had songs running through my head and it made me relax ... i had Mcfly Party Girl on a loop in my head and it worked ... and i passed my test first time!

In response to concern about getting frustrated over every minute detail:

Don't worry. It's normal. Trust me, I cry if I miss the bus.

In response to a post about being bullied at school:

It is wrong that people treat you that way. I know it doesn't seem like it now but it will get better.

I know how you feel man. Except for being spat on, all those things you have mentioned have happened to me too ...

I wish there was a way I can help!!

Sharing an experience of similar feelings is most evident in these examples, in addition to an example of an assessment (first response to being bullied post). The final example highlights that an empathic offering of help does not fit neatly into the framework. Thus, this framework provides a useful way to analyze empathic interactions within Facebook, though minor amendments (such as offers of support) need to be incorporated. In summary, there is evidence that the four dimensions of empathy identified by Pudlinski are being practiced by those with ASD in an online context. Future research will explore how frequently this occurs with reference to control groups. Importantly, we do not know about these individuals' offline behavior or their behavior in other online contexts. Assessments of empathizing have, to date, not explored the practice of empathy. Future research will compare expression of emotion and empathy between online and offline contexts. This will include the extent to which those with ASD practice empathy in both online and offline settings.

There is a wealth of research to suggest that people who only communicate through online environments can have strong social bonds; for example, between those in online relationships who never actually meet (Whitty & Gavin, 2001). Thus, having strong bonds within online environments is not specific to ASD. The extent to which effective communication within online contexts supports strong social bonds and bonding social capital in those with ASD in online and offline contexts is a fascinating question for future research. There seems initial support for the hypothesis that the deficits identified in the offline word in empathizing in ASD are not present in the online world (i.e., Facebook-based communication). Within the studies described above, the social-emotional communication and interaction within an online context have been comparable for those with and without ASD – that is, "normal."

What is "Normal"?

This raises an interesting question as to whether the affect-limited nature of online communication makes those without ASD communicate in a more ASD-like manner. Again, this is where comparisons between online and offline behavior for future

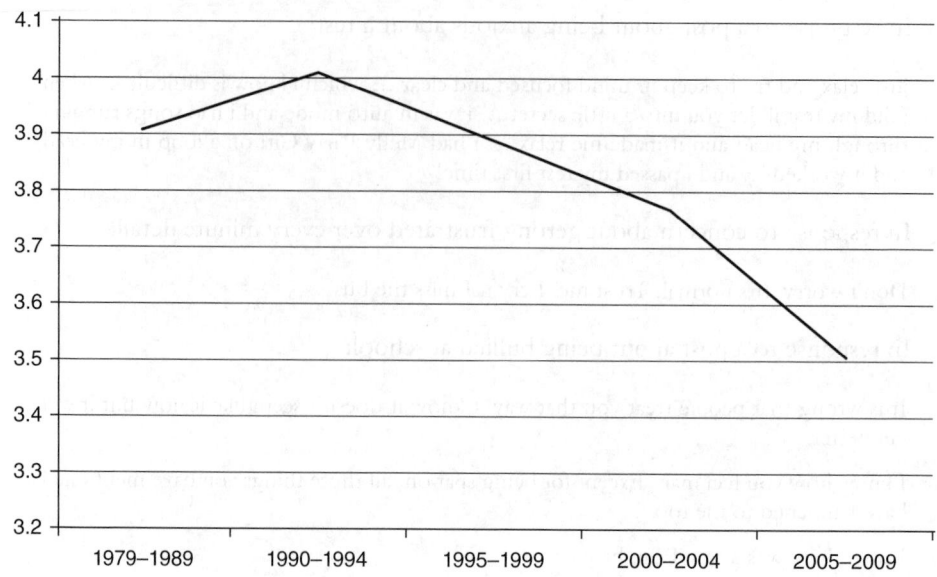

Figure 14.5   College students self-reported empathy from 1979 to 2009.

research will be invaluable. There has also been a suggestion that the preponderance of online communication is reducing empathy within the general population. Konrath, O'Brien, and Hsing (2011) conducted a meta-analysis of the self-reported empathy levels of 13,737 American students over a 30-year period from 1979 to 2009. Figure 14.5 highlights a general trend of declining empathy levels from 1990 to the present day. One of the authors, Ed O'Brien, argued that "It's harder for today's college student to empathize with others because so much of their social lives is done through a computer and not through real life interaction" (Nicholson, 2010). This causality needs to be confirmed; however, it does raise an interesting question as to what is the "normal" level of empathizing, and how consistent is this over time. It's a fascinating possibility that the dominance of online communication could bring about comparable empathizing skills in those with and without autism. However, this is far from being established and any causal relationship between autism and Internet use has been the focus of heated academic debate (see McVeigh, 2011).

What is ASD? Revisited

To return to the first question of this chapter, the DSM-5 criteria suggest that for a diagnosis of ASD, the social communication and interaction deficits should persist across all contexts (and not accounted for by general developmental delay). For a diagnosis, the following criteria must be met: *Problems reciprocating social or emotional interaction, including difficulty establishing or maintaining back-and-forth conversations and interactions, inability to initiate an interaction, and problems with shared attention or sharing of emotions and interests with others.*

Our studies above are provisional; however, in the online context, some of those with ASD do not fully meet these criteria. This could either challenge whether a diagnosis of ASD is appropriate if one has effective social communication interaction online, or lead to the perplexing outcome of people having ASD offline but not online. Alternatively, the online context could be rejected as a social context; however, much of the literature above would make this position hard to justify. We must bear in mind the "caseness" of those with ASD discussed above (i.e., people who self-identify as ASD; we were unable to confirm a clinical diagnosis), but the potential that ASD does not exist online in some individuals who have a diagnosis offline has interesting implications. The affect-limited, time-delayed nature of online communication may ameliorate the deficits in empathizing (offline), allowing for those with ASD to "engage in the practice of empathy" (online). The emotional support indicative of bonding social capital is evident in online contexts, which may contribute to making the "cybercountry perfect" (Singer, 1999, p. 65) for those with "offline ASD." How to generalize the benefits of the online context to the offline world is a paramount question for future research. It is also interesting to note the high proportion of females with ASD who are using social media, when ASD is typically diagnosed more commonly in males (APA, 2013). Finally, the chapter started with a Facebook post from someone with ASD and it seems appropriate to finish in the same way:

> ... thanks to facebook I have known parts of the human being I had never experienced before, I've fallen in love and I've seen the world with different eyes, both the real and the virtual one! So encourage your ASD friends to use facebook, because it can really, really help A LOT.

Acknowledgments

Shradha Suri collected some of the data reported above for her master's thesis. Milo Brosnan helped code some of the data.

References

American Psychiatric Association (APA). (2013). *Diagnostic and statistical manual of mental disorders* (5th ed.) (DSM-5). Arlington, VA: Author.

Baron-Cohen, S. (2002). The extreme male brain theory of autism. *Trends in Cognitive Science, 6*, 248–254.

Baron-Cohen, S. (2003). *The essential difference: Men, women and the extreme male brain.* London, UK: Penguin.

Baron-Cohen, S. (2009). Autism: The empathizing-systemizing (E-S) theory. *Annals of the New York Academy of Science, 1156*, 68–80.

Baron-Cohen, S., Bolton, P., Wheelwright, S., Scahill, V., Short, L., Mead, G., & Smith, A. (1998). Autism occurs more often in families of physicists, engineers, and mathematicians. *Autism, 2*, 296–301.

Baron-Cohen, S., Golan, O., Wheelwright, S., Granader, Y., & Hill, J. (2010). Emotion word comprehension from 4 to 16 years old: A developmental survey. *Frontiers Evolutionary Neuroscience, 2*, 109.

Baron-Cohen, S., Richler, J., Bisarya, D., Gurunathan, N., & Wheelwright, S. (2003). The Systemizing Quotient: An investigation of adults with Asperger syndrome or high-functioning autism, and normal sex differences. *Philosophical Transactions of the Royal Society of London B: Biological Science, 358*, 361–374.

Baron-Cohen, S., & Wheelwright, S. (2004). The empathy quotient: An investigation of adults with Asperger syndrome or high-functioning autism, and normal sex differences. *Journal of Autism and Developmental Disorders, 34*, 163–175.

Baron-Cohen, S., Wheelwright, S., Hill, J., Raste, Y., & Plumb, I. (2001). The "Reading the Mind in the Eyes" test revised version: A study with normal adults, and adults with Asperger syndrome or high-functioning autism. *Journal of Child Psychology and Psychiatry, 42*, 241–251.

Biever, C. (2007, June 27). Web removes social barriers for those with autism. *New Scientist, 2610.*

Bird, G., Silani, G., Brindley, R., White, S., Frith, U., & Singer, T. (2010). Empathic brain responses in insula are modulated by levels of alexithymia but not autism. *Brain, 133*, 1515–1525.

Blume, H. (1997, June 30). Autistics, freed from face-to-face encounters, are communicating in cyberspace. *The New York Times.* Retrieved November 29, 2014, from http://www.nytimes.com/1997/06/30/business/autistics-freed-from-face-to-face-encounters-are-communicating-in-cyberspace.html

boyd, d. (2007). Why youth (heart) social network sites: The role of networked publics in teenage social life. In D. Buckingham (Ed.), *MacArthur Foundation Series on Digital Learning: Youth, identity, and digital media* (pp. 119–142). Cambridge, MA: MIT Press.

British Psychological Society (BPS). (2009). *Code of ethics and conduct.* Retrieved November 29, 2014, from http://www.bps.org.uk/system/files/documents/code_of_ethics_and_conduct.pdf

Brosnan, M. (1997). The fourth "R": Are teachers hindering computer literacy in school children? *Education Section Review, 21*, 29–37.

Brosnan, M. (1998). The implications for academic attainment of perceived gender-appropriateness upon spatial task performance. *British Journal of Educational Psychology, 68*, 203–215.

Brosnan, M., Chapman, E., Johnson, H., Grawemeyer, B., & Benton, L. (2013). When are adolescents with autism spectrum disorder better at emotion recognition than their peers? In *IMFAR, 2013*, San Sebastian, Spain.

Brownlow, C., & O'Dell, L. (2002). Ethical issues in qualitative research in online communities. *Disability and Society, 17*, 685–694.

ComScore. (2014). Worldwide Internet use. Retrieved March 20, 2014, from http://www.comscoredatamine.com/

Darius. (2002). "Darius." In D. Prince-Hughes (Ed.), *Aquamarine blue 5: Personal stories of college students with autism* (pp. 9–42). Athens, OH: Swallow Press.

Davidson, J. (2008). Autistic culture online: Virtual communication and cultural expression on the spectrum. *Social and Cultural Geography, 9*, 791–806.

Dekker, M. (2006). On our own terms: Emerging autistic culture. http://autisticculture.com

Donath, J. (2007). Signals in social supernets. *Journal of Computer-Mediated Communication, 13*, 231–251.

Dunbar, R. (2010). *How many friends does one person need? Dunbar's number and other evolutionary quirks.* London, UK: Faber & Faber.

Edison. (2014). The infinite dial 2014. Retrieved November 29, 2014, from http://www.edisonresearch.com/wp-content/uploads/2014/03/The-Infinite-Dial-2014-from-Edison-Research-and-Triton-Digital.pdf

Ekman, P., & Friesen, W. (1969). The repertoire of non-verbal behavior: Categories, origins, usage, and coding. *Semiotica, 1*, 49–98.

Ellison, N., Lampe, C., Steinfield, C., & Vitak, J. (2011). With a little help from my friends: How social network sites affect social capital processes. In Z. Papacharissi (Ed.), *A networked self: Identity, community, and culture on social network sites.* New York, NY: Routledge.

Ellison, N. B., Steinfield, C., & Lampe, C. (2007). The benefits of Facebook "friends": Social capital and college students' use of online social network sites. *Journal of Computer-Mediated Communication, 12,* 1143–1168.

Geekwire. (2013, May 1). Facebook tops 1.1 billion users, fueled by global adoption and mobile growth. Retrieved November 29, 2014, from http://www.geekwire.com/2013/facebook-tops-11–billion-users-fueled-global-adoption-mobile-growth/

Gonzales, D. (2013, April 15). Google exec Eric Schmidt proclaims entire Earth will be online by 2020, but what will it take? Retrieved November 29, 2014, from http://www.androidauthority.com/eric-schmidt-predicts-internet-future-190416/

Grandin, T. (2000). My mind is a web browser: How people with autism think. *Cerebrum, 2,* 14–22. Retrieved November 29, 2014, from http://www.grandin.com/inc/mind.web.browser.html

Grossman, J. B., Klin, A., Carter, A. S., & Volkmar, F. R. (2003). Verbal bias in recognition of facial emotions in children with Asperger syndrome. *Journal of Child Psychology and Psychiatry, 4,* 369–379.

Internet World Stats. (2013). Internet usage data. Retrieved March 20, 2014, from http://www.internetworldstats.com/america.htm

Jackson, L. A., Ervin, K. S., Gardner, P. D., & Schmitt, N. (2001). Gender and the Internet: Women communicating and men searching. *Sex Roles, 44,* 363–380.

Joiner, R., Brosnan, M., Duffield, J., Gavin, J., & Maras, P. (2007). The relationship between Internet identification, Internet anxiety and Internet use. *Computers in Human Behavior, 23,* 1408–1420.

Joiner, R., Gavin, J., Brosnan, M., Cromby, J., Gregory, H., Guiller, J., … Moon, A. (2012). Gender, Internet experience, Internet identification and Internet anxiety: A ten year follow-up. *Cyberpsychology, Behavior, and Social Networking, 15,* 370–372.

Joiner, R., Gavin, J., Brosnan, M., Cromby, J., Gregory, H., Guiller, J., … Moon, A. (2013). Comparing first and second generation digital natives' Internet use, Internet anxiety, and Internet identification. *Cyberpsychology, Behavior, and Social Networking, 16,* 549–552.

Joiner, R., Gavin, J., Brosnan, M., Crook, C., Duffield, J., Durndell, A., … Scott, A. J. (2006). Internet identification and future Internet use. *Cyberpsychology and Behavior, 9,* 410–414.

Jones, R. S. P., & Meldal, T. O. (2001). Social relationships and Asperger's syndrome: A qualitative analysis of first-hand accounts. *Journal of Intellectual Disabilities, 5,* 35–41.

Konrath, S. H., O'Brien, E. H., & Hsing, C. (2011). Changes in dispositional empathy in American college students over time: A meta-analysis. *Personality and Social Psychology Review, 15,* 180–198.

Lawson, J., Baron-Cohen, S., & Wheelwright, S. (2004). Empathising and systemizing in adults with and without Asperger syndrome. *Journal of Autism and Developmental Disorders, 34,* 301–310.

Livingstone, S. (2008). Taking risky opportunities in youthful content creation: Teenagers' use of social networking site for intimacy, privacy and self-expression. *New Media and Society, 10,* 393–411.

Mann, C., & Stewart, F. (2000). *Internet communication and qualitative research: A handbook of researching online.* London, UK: Sage.

McVeigh, T. (2011, August 6). Research linking autism to Internet use is criticised. *The Guardian.* Retrieved November 29, 2014, from http://www.theguardian.com/society/2011/aug/06/research-autism-internet-susan-greenfield

Moore, M., & Calvert, S. (2000). Brief report: Vocabulary acquisition for children with autism: Teacher or computer instruction. *Journal of Autism and Developmental Disorders, 30,* 359–362.

Nicholson, C. (2010, May 29). College students are less empathic than generations past. Retrieved November 29, 2014, from http://www.scientificamerican.com/podcast/episode.cfm?id=college-students-are-less-empathic-10-05-29

O'Keeffe, G. S., & Clarke-Pearson, K. (2011). The impact of social media on children, adolescents, and families. *Pediatrics, 127*, 800–804.

Paccagnella, L. (1997). Getting the seats of your pants dirty: Strategies for ethnographic research on virtual communities. *Journal of Computer-Mediated Communication, 3*. doi: 10.1111/j.1083-6101.1997.tb00065.x

Picard, R. (1998). *Affective computing.* Cambridge, MA: MIT Press.

Pudlinski, C. (2005). Doing empathy and sympathy: Caring responses to troubles tellings on a peer support line. *Discourse Studies, 7*, 267–288.

Rodham, K., & Gavin, J. (2006). The ethics of using the Internet to gather qualitative research data. *Research Ethics Review, 2*, 92–97.

Rodham, K., Gavin, J., Lewis, S. P., St. Denis, J., & Bandalli, P. (2013). An investigation of the motivations driving the online representation of self-injury: A thematic analysis. *Archives of Suicide Research, 17*, 173–183.

Saran, C. (2008, February 8). Specialisterne finds a place in workforce for people with autism. *Computer Weekly.* Retrieved November 29, 2014, from http://www.computerweekly.com/news/2240084941/Specialisterne-finds-a-place-in-workforce-for-people-with-autism

Schmidt, E. (2013). Retrieved March 20, 2014, from https://plus.google.com/u/0/+EricSchmidt/posts

Schultz, S. M., & Jacobs, G. E. (2012). The social magic of Facebook for adults on the spectrum. *Autism Asperger's Digest.* Retrieved April 29, 2014, from http://autismdigest.com/the-social-magic-of-facebook-for-adults-on-the-spectrum/

Shore, S. (2001). *Beyond the wall: Personal experiences with autism and Asperger syndrome* (2nd ed.). Shawnee Mission, KS: Autism Asperger Publishing Company.

Singer, J. (1999). "Why can't you be normal for once in your life?" From a "problem with no name" to the emergence of a new category of difference. In M. Corker & S. French (Eds.), *Disability discourse* (pp. 59–67). Buckingham, UK: Open University Press.

Socialbakers. (2014). Facebook statistics. Retrieved March 20, 2014, from http://www.socialbakers.com/facebook-statistics/

Statisticsbrain. (2014). Facebook statistics. Retrieved March 21, 2014, from http://www.statisticbrain.com/facebook-statistics/

Steinfield, C., Ellison, N., Lampe, C., & Vitak, J. (2012). Online social network sites and the concept of social capital. In F. L. Lee, L. Leung, J. S. Qiu, & D. Chu (Eds.), *Frontiers in new media research* (pp. 115–131). New York, NY: Routledge.

Stromer, R., Kimball, J. W., Kinney, E. M., & Taylor, B. A. (2006). Activity schedules, computer technology, and teaching children with autism spectrum disorders. *Focus on Autism and Other Developmental Disabilities, 21*, 14–24.

Walther, J. B., & Parks, M. R. (2002). Cues filtered out, cues filtered in: Computer-mediated communication and relationships. In M. L. Knapp & J. A. Daly (Eds.), *Handbook of interpersonal communication* (3rd ed., pp. 529–563). Thousand Oaks, CA: Sage.

Whitty, M., & Gavin, J. (2001). Age/sex/location: Uncovering the social cues in the development of on-line relationships. *Cyberpsychology and Behavior, 4*, 623–630.

Williams, D. (2005). *Autism: An inside-out approach: An innovative look at the mechanics of autism and its developmental cousins.* Philadelphia, PA: Jessica Kingsley.

Young, K. (2011). Social ties, social networks and the Facebook experience. *International Journal of Emerging Technologies and Society, 1*, 20–34.

Part III
Social Media

15

Social Networking and Depression

Brian A. Feinstein, Vickie Bhatia, Jessica A. Latack, and Joanne Davila

Stony Brook University

Advances in technology have expanded the ways in which people can communicate with one another. Social networking sites (SNSs) such as Facebook and MySpace have become particularly popular venues for online social interaction. While SNSs vary in their features and functions, they generally refer to web-based services that allow individuals to create profiles that display personal information, pictures, and lists of friends who also use the services, and provide mechanisms for users to communicate with one another (boyd & Ellison, 2007). Additionally, SNSs tend to provide individuals with opportunities to meet new people, although research suggests that they are primarily used to support pre-existing social relationships (boyd & Ellison, 2007).

In a nationally representative survey of adults in the United States ($N=2,260$) conducted in 2010, 64% of adult Internet users reported using at least one SNS (Hampton, Goulet, Rainie, & Purcell, 2011). This is nearly double the rate of adult Internet users who reported using at least one SNS in 2008 (Hampton, Goulet, Her, & Rainie, 2009), suggesting a dramatic increase in the rate of SNS use among adults. Facebook was by far the most popular SNS that adult SNS users reported using (92%), compared to MySpace (29%), LinkedIn (18%), and Twitter (13%; Hampton et al., 2011). There were several demographic differences in SNS use among adults, including SNS use being greater among women compared to men, younger adults compared to older adults, and individuals living in urban areas compared to rural areas (Duggan & Brenner, 2013). The finding that SNS use was greater among younger adults compared to older adults is consistent with data that more than 70% of youth and young adult (ages 12–29) Internet users reported using SNSs (Lenhart, Purcell, Smith, & Zickuhr, 2010).

To date, most research on SNS use has focused on impression management, friendship networks, online/offline connections, and privacy issues (for a review see boyd & Ellison, 2007). To a lesser extent, researchers have begun to examine the potential impact of SNS use on mental health, particularly depressive symptoms (e.g., sad mood, anhedonia, worthlessness, hopelessness). A recent report has even raised alarms about "Facebook depression," or depression that results from spending too much

The Wiley Handbook of Psychology, Technology, and Society, First Edition. Edited by Larry D. Rosen, Nancy A. Cheever, and L. Mark Carrier.
© 2015 John Wiley & Sons, Ltd. Published 2015 by John Wiley & Sons, Ltd.

time on SNSs (O'Keeffe & Clarke-Pearson, 2011). Although no research supports the claim that simply spending too much time on SNSs can cause depression (see Davila, 2011; Magid, 2011), there are data to suggest that aspects of SNS use may be associated with depressive symptoms. In this chapter, we review the theoretical basis for a potential association between SNS use and depression as well as the empirical literature on this association and its underlying mechanisms. Additionally, we discuss the implications of this research and provide suggestions for future research to expand our understanding of the impact of SNS use on mental health.

Frequency of Social Networking and Depression

Initially, research in this area focused on the potential negative consequences of Internet use in general rather than SNS use in particular. Kraut and colleagues were the first to propose that Internet use could lead to depression (Kraut et al., 1998). They found that the average number of hours spent online per week predicted increases in depressive symptoms one year later among adolescents and adults (Kraut et al., 1998), but this effect disappeared at a two-year follow-up (Kraut et al., 2002). Since then, attempts to replicate this finding have been mixed, with some studies finding significant associations between the amount of Internet use and depressive symptoms (Selfhout, Branje, Delsing, ter Bogt, & Meeus, 2009; van den Eijnden, Meerkerk, Vermulst, Spijkerman, & Engels, 2008) and others failing to find this association (Campbell, Cumming, & Hughes, 2006; Jelenchick, Eickhoff, & Moreno, 2013). A meta-analysis of 43 studies ($N=21{,}258$) found mean correlations between $-.04$ and $-.05$ for the association between Internet use and psychological well-being (Huang, 2010), suggesting that frequency of Internet use alone is unlikely to be related to depression.

Consistent with the stress exposure model of depression (for a review see Tennant, 2002), there is some evidence to suggest that there are negative mental health consequences when Internet use causes impairments in one's offline life. For instance, excessive Internet use has been linked to the neglect of academic and domestic responsibilities, social isolation, and disruption of relationships among adolescents and adults (Griffiths, 2000; McKenna & Bargh, 2000) as well as reduced time spent with family and friends, smaller social circles, and greater loneliness among adults (Nie, Hillygus, & Erbring, 2002). In turn, when Internet use causes impairments in one's offline life, then it appears to be associated with depression. For example, among college-age young adults, Bhatia and Davila (2015) found that offline impairment as a result of Internet use was linked to increases in depressive symptoms over a three-week period. Other studies have found that numerous types of offline impairments are associated with depressive symptoms, such as impairment in work, school, or significant relationships (Kim, LaRose, & Peng, 2009) and impairment in daily functioning and/or failure to fulfill major responsibilities at work, school, or home among college-age young adults (Fortson, Scotti, Chen, Malone, & Del Ben, 2007). Of note, given rapid changes in technology and Internet use, research from 10 years ago may not be representative of current trends. For instance, Nie and colleagues (2002) defined excessive Internet use as five hours per week, which is likely to be more commonplace today than a decade ago. Therefore, further research is needed to examine these associations as the socio-cultural context of Internet use changes.

Subsequent research in this area focused on specific online activities rather than Internet use in general, finding that the social context of Internet use may be particularly important. However, these findings have been mixed as well, with some studies finding that using the Internet for social purposes is associated with higher depressive symptoms and other studies finding it is associated with lower depressive symptoms. For instance, Fortson and colleagues (2007) found that frequent use of chat rooms and using the Internet to meet people were associated with higher depressive symptoms among college-age young adults, while total time spent online was not. Similarly, van den Eijnden and colleagues (2008) found that instant messaging (IMing) with friends predicted increases in depressive symptoms among adolescents, but less social online activities (e.g., information seeking, downloading) did not. In addition, Rosen, Whaling, Rab, Carrier, and Cheever (2013) found that adults who spent more time online and those who performed more impression management on Facebook (e.g., updating one's profile) were more likely to report depressive symptoms. Recent research has attempted to examine the association between how much young adults use Facebook and their mood in real time using experience sampling methodology. Kross and colleagues (2013) asked people questions about their Facebook use and mood five times a day over the course of 14 days, finding that more Facebook use was associated with declines in mood over time. Further, they found that this association was significant for those who reported moderate or high levels of direct social contact, but not for those who reported low levels of direct social contact. The authors speculated that social comparison might be a mechanism through which Facebook use contributes to decreases in mood and that those who experience moderate or high levels of direct social contact as well encounter additional opportunities to engage in social comparison throughout their day.

In contrast to the aforementioned findings, other studies have demonstrated that using the Internet for communication purposes (e.g., social networking, emailing, IMing) is associated with decreases in depressive symptoms, whereas using the Internet for non-communication purposes (e.g., gaming, pornography) is associated with increases in depressive symptoms among adolescents (Selfhout et al., 2009) and adults (Morgan & Cotten, 2003). Rosen and colleagues (2013) also demonstrated benefits to using the Internet for social purposes, finding that having more friends on Facebook was associated with lower depressive symptoms among adults, suggesting that having a larger social network, either online or offline, may serve as a protective factor. Additionally, in a mostly adult sample, Bessière, Pressman, Kiesler, and Kraut (2010) found that increasing the frequency of Internet use to communicate with friends and family from three to five days a week to once a day was associated with small, but significant, decreases in depressive symptoms over an 18-month period.

Several potential explanations for these mixed findings warrant attention. First, it is possible that certain people benefit from using the Internet for social purposes, while others do not. This possibility is consistent with the finding that using the Internet for email and related purposes was associated with a 20–28% reduction in the likelihood of receiving a depression diagnosis among older retired adults, a population for whom social contact may be particularly important (Cotten, Ford, Ford, & Hale, 2012). Similarly, for adolescents who reported having lower-quality friendships, using the Internet for communication purposes (e.g., IMing) was associated with reductions in depressive symptoms over time, whereas using the Internet for non-communication purposes (e.g., surfing) was associated with increases in depressive symptoms (Selfhout et al., 2009). Thus, for those who perceive themselves as having poor-quality friend-ships, using the Internet for social purposes may increase social support and social connectedness. Indeed, adult Internet users tend to report having more friends than non-users (Wang & Wellman, 2010) and both adolescent and adult Internet users tend to report more frequent face-to-face contact with friends than non-users (Brandtzaeg, 2012). Further, for college-age young adults who reported low self-esteem, greater Facebook use was related to building social ties, potentially because online communi-cation mitigated fears of rejection (Steinfield, Ellison, & Lampe, 2008).

Quality of Social Networking Experiences and Depression

Another potential explanation for mixed findings regarding the use of the Internet for social purposes and depressive symptoms is that most research has failed to consider the quality of the social experiences people were having on SNSs. Consistent with evidence that the quality of people's interpersonal experiences is related to depression (e.g., Davila, Stroud, & Starr, 2009; LaGreca, Davila, & Siegel, 2008), it is likely that what happens in the social context of Internet use is also related to depression. Our research group proposed a depression-relevant model of social networking, suggest-ing that the quality of experiences on SNSs, rather than the amount of time spent using them, may be associated with depression (Davila et al., 2012). While there is a strong theoretical basis to expect that the quality of SNS experiences would be related to depression, there is less reason to expect that frequency of SNS use on its own would lead people to feel more depressed.

Consistent with our proposed depression-relevant model of social networking, studies that examine both the frequency and the quality of SNS experiences have found that it is the quality, rather than the simple frequency, that influences depressive symptoms. For instance, our research group found that the amount of time spent on SNSs was not associated with increases in depressive symptoms over a three-week period for college-age young adults. In contrast, those who reported having more negative and less positive interactions on SNSs also reported increases in depressive symptoms (Davila et al., 2012). Additionally, in an adult sample, Bevan, Pfyl, and Barclay (2012) found that being unfriended on Facebook was associated with a nega-tive emotional response and rumination (defined as the tendency to repetitively and passively focus on the causes and consequences of one's distress; Nolen-Hoeksema, Wisco, & Lyubomirsky, 2008). Being unfriended was particularly likely to result in a negative emotional response and rumination for those who were more involved in Facebook, those who were unfriended by a close contact (compared to a distant contact), and those who were unfriended by someone with whom they had initiated the friend request (compared to someone with whom they had not initiated the friend request). Locatelli, Kluwe, and Bryant (2012) also found that negative status updates on Facebook were associated with greater depressive symptoms for college-age young adults. Together, these findings suggest that the quality of one's experiences on SNSs (e.g., negative interactions, being unfriended, posting negative status updates) is in fact related to one's mental health.

In sum, it appears that negative experiences on SNSs as well as using the Internet to the point of experiencing negative consequences in one's offline life are both associated with depressive symptoms. Although research has identified that negative interactions on SNSs contribute to depressive symptoms, it remains unclear what specifically is happening in these interactions that is pathogenic. The variety of features and functions of SNSs provide people with opportunities to engage in different behaviors, such as learning about others (e.g., looking at people's profiles), interacting with others in a delayed time frame (e.g., posting a message on someone's profile, which they may respond to at a later time), and interacting with others in real time (e.g., IMing). Thus, it is important to identify the specific behaviors and processes that take place on SNSs that contribute to depression in order to understand the mechanisms underlying the association between negative experiences on SNSs and depression.

Mechanisms Underlying Social Networking–Depression Link

A few studies have examined the specific behaviors that people engage in on SNSs that contribute to depression. Our research group was among the first to attempt to delineate what specifically people are doing on SNSs that leads them to feel depressed (Feinstein et al., 2013). We proposed that SNSs provide people with ample opportunities to compare themselves to others, which has the potential to contribute to depression. For instance, if a person sees that many of her/his friends are getting jobs and s/he is unemployed and having a difficult time getting a job, then s/he might feel inadequate in that domain. When comparing oneself to others, perceiving oneself as inferior (referred to as negative social comparison) can maintain and exacerbate negative self-appraisals, and lead to increases in negative affect (for a review, see Ahrens & Alloy, 1997).

Although social comparison has received little attention in the literature on SNS use, a qualitative study found that college-age MySpace users reported engaging in social comparison on the site and experiencing negative self-views afterward (Manago, Graham, Greenfield, & Salimkhan, 2008). Research has also found that college-age young adults who spent more time on Facebook were more likely to agree that others were "happier" and "had better lives" (Chou & Edge, 2012), and college-age young adults who looked at profile pictures of attractive members of the same sex reported less positive affect than those who looked at non-attractive members of the same sex (Haferkamp & Krämer, 2011). This emerging body of research provides preliminary support for SNSs providing a context for engaging in negative social comparison, which may then be associated with negative consequences such as depression. Consistent with our hypothesis, we found support for an association between negative social comparison on Facebook and depressive symptoms among college-age young adults (Feinstein et al., 2013). Thus, SNSs can provide novel opportunities for people to compare themselves to others, and these comparisons can have negative influences on well-being.

We were also interested in understanding the mechanism underlying the association between negative social comparison on Facebook and depressive symptoms. One previous study had demonstrated that negative social comparison was associated with greater rumination among college-age young adults (Cheung, Gilbert, & Irons, 2004), which has consistently been implicated in depression (for a meta-analytic review, see Aldao, Nolen-Hoeksema, & Schweizer, 2010). Thus, we proposed that people might ruminate on their perceived inferiority in response to comparing themselves to others on Facebook, which could then contribute to depression. Consistent with our hypotheses, we found that negatively comparing oneself to others while using Facebook predicted increases in rumination, which in turn was associated with increases in depressive symptoms (Feinstein et al., 2013). This is consistent with evidence that rumination maintains and exacerbates depression, which has been suggested to be due to rumination's association with reduced interpersonal problem solving, reduced willingness to engage in pleasant activities, and more pessimistic views about positive events in the future (e.g., Nolen-Hoeksema et al., 2008). The finding that rumination mediated the association between negative social comparison on Facebook and depressive symptoms is also consistent with a recent finding that rumination mediated the association between negative status updates on Facebook and depressive symptoms (Locatelli et al., 2012), suggesting that rumination may play a mechanistic role in the associations between negative experiences on SNSs and depressive symptoms.

Another specific behavior that can occur on SNSs and contribute to depression is being harassed or threatened. Victimization that occurs via technological modalities, such as the Internet and cell phones, is referred to as cybervictimization. Data on the prevalence of cybervictimization suggest that 40–50% of youth (Mishna, Cook, Gadalla, Daciuk, & Solomon, 2010; Mitchell, Finkelhor, Wolak, Ybarra, & Turner, 2011) and 10–43% of college-age young adults (Finn, 2004; Lindsay & Krysik, 2012) endorse such victimization, depending on the sample, time frame, and measure. There is some evidence that cybervictimization is more common among women than men (Feinstein, Bhatia, & Davila, 2014; Kowalski & Limber, 2007), but other research suggests that gender differences depend on the type of cybervictimization (e.g., Mishna et al., 2010). Similar to in-person victimization, cybervictimization is associated with depressive symptoms in cross-sectional studies of adolescents (e.g., Mitchell, Ybarra, & Finkelhor, 2007; Wang, Tonja, & Iannoti, 2011; Ybarra, 2004) and a prospective study of college-age young adults (Feinstein et al., 2014). Our research group also found that the association between cybervictimization and depressive symptoms was mediated by rumination for women. This suggests that women who ruminate about their experiences of cybervictimization may be at particular risk of maintaining and exacerbating their distress.

Risk Factors for Problematic Social Networking Experiences

Although most studies in this area have focused on the extent to which Internet use influences well-being, there is theoretical reason to believe that the association may also function in the opposite direction. Several theories implicate depression in the emergence and maintenance of problematic Internet use. For instance, Davis (2001) proposed that problematic cognitions (e.g., a depressogenic cognitive style, feelings of self-consciousness, social anxiety) coupled with behaviors that maintain or intensify maladaptive thoughts might lead to problematic Internet use. As such, the Internet may function as a venue for people to enact pre-existing psychopathologies. This possibility is consistent with research that has demonstrated that depression is associated with maladaptive interpersonal consequences (e.g., Davila et al., 2009; LaGreca et al., 2008). For instance, interpersonal stress generation theories (e.g., Coyne, 1976; Hammen, 1991, 2006; Joiner & Coyne, 1999) propose that people who are depressed tend to create problems in their relationships, which can then maintain and exacerbate their symptoms. Further, people who are depressed also tend to engage in specific interpersonal behaviors that lead to rejection, such as excessive reassurance seeking (e.g., Joiner,

Metalsky, Katz, & Beach, 1999). Thus, it may be that SNSs serve as an additional venue to engage in these dysfunctional interpersonal behaviors for dysphoric individuals.

Consistent with the aforementioned theoretical rationale, accumulating evidence suggests that certain individuals may in fact be at greater risk for problematic experiences on SNSs than others. For instance, Feinstein, Bhatia, Hershenberg, and Davila (2012) found that depressive symptoms were associated with increases in negative interactions with close friends and romantic partners on SNSs as well as increases in negative affect following such interactions among college-age young adults over a three-week period. In contrast, global and social anxiety symptoms were not associated with increases in problematic experiences on SNSs. These findings suggest that depressed individuals may be more likely than their non-depressed counterparts to engage in behavior on SNSs that leads to negative interactions. Alternatively, it is also possible that depressed individuals may perceive their interactions on SNSs as more negative than non-depressed individuals regardless of the actual content of the interactions. It will be important for future research to examine the actual content of depressed people's interactions on SNSs in order to test this possibility. Additionally, Davila and colleagues (2012) found that rumination and co-rumination (defined as excessive discussion of problems within friendships; Rose, 2002) were both associated with more negative interactions on SNSs and negative affect following such interactions among college-age young adults, suggesting that those who engage in these types of maladaptive emotion regulation strategies may be at increased risk for problematic experiences on SNSs. They also found some support for the hypothesis that the association between negative experiences on SNSs and depressive symptoms would be stronger for those who engaged in more rumination. Although not directly related to depression, Forest and Wood (2012) found that the association between self-esteem and being liked by others was mediated by the valence of self-disclosures on SNSs among college-age young adults. Specifically, those who reported lower self-esteem tended to post less positive and more negative self-disclosures, which then led to others not liking them as much. Together, these findings suggest that poorer mental health and maladaptive emotion regulation may be risk factors for having negative experiences on SNSs, which could then maintain and exacerbate one's depression.

Research has also begun to examine individual differences other than mental health that may put particular people at risk for having negative social networking experiences. For instance, compared to college-age males, college-age females were more likely to report spending more time on Facebook than intended, feeling addicted to Facebook, experiencing decreased sleep due to Facebook use, and feeling closer to online contacts than in-person contacts (Thompson & Lougheed, 2012). Further, females were also more likely than males to report that Facebook use sometimes causes stress and that they experience poorer body image after viewing images of others on Facebook (Thompson & Lougheed, 2012). Additionally, Szwedo, Mikami, and Allen (2010) found that youth whose mothers' behavior undermined their autonomy and relatedness at age 13 had an increased preference for online communication over face-to-face communication, an increased likelihood of forming a friendship with someone they met online, and poorer observed friendship quality in SNS interactions at age 20. This suggests that problematic experiences in one type of relationship may extend to similar experiences in other relationships.

Finally, although most research on risk factors for problematic social networking experiences has focused on contact with people in general (i.e., not making a distinction between close friends, romantic partners, and acquaintances), there is some research that has identified problems that occur on SNSs that are specific to romantic relationships. SNSs provide people with greater access to information about what their romantic partners are doing on a daily basis, which has the potential to promote jealousy and surveillance of one's partner (Muise, Christofides, & Desmarais, 2009). Research that focuses on relationship-specific problems on SNSs could provide clues to other mechanisms linking SNS use to depression, particularly given the well-documented associations between relationship behaviors and depression. For instance, one study found that certain people were more likely than others to monitor their partner's online behavior. Specifically, adults who held more favorable attitudes toward monitoring and those who felt more pressure to monitor were more likely to report engaging in monitoring (Darvell, Walsh, & White, 2011). Further, they found that lower trust in one's partner was associated with higher intention to monitor and monitoring behavior. Additionally, one study found that higher attachment anxiety (e.g., preoccupation with abandonment concerns, doubts about being worthy of love) was associated with higher jealousy and surveillance of one's partner on Facebook, whereas higher avoidant attachment (e.g., discomfort with closeness, difficulty trusting in and depending on others) was associated with less jealousy and surveillance of one's partner on Facebook among adults (Marshall, Bejanyan, Di Castro, & Lee, 2013). They found that the association between attachment anxiety and jealousy was partially mediated by trust, suggesting that individuals who were more anxious about abandonment were also less trusting of their partners, which was then associated with engaging in more jealous behavior on Facebook. Although these studies did not assess depression, it is possible that surveillance of one's partner on Facebook is associated with negative consequences, such as depression. This hypothesis is consistent with evidence that surveillance of one's ex-partner on Facebook was associated with greater distress over the breakup, more negative feelings, sexual desire, and longing for the ex-partner, and less personal growth among a mostly adult sample (Marshall, 2012).

This relatively new area of research suggests that certain individuals may be particularly likely to have negative experiences on SNSs as well as poorer relationships with those who they connect with online. Further, the specific problems that someone experiences on SNSs may differ depending on his/her relationship with the person he/she is interacting with. It will be important for future research to continue to examine risk factors for problematic social networking experiences and the extent to which the associations between SNS use and depression apply to interactions with different types of relationship partners (e.g., acquaintances, friends, romantic partners). Increasing the specificity of these associations has the potential to contribute to more refined theories of social networking and depression and target prevention and intervention efforts at those who need them most.

Implications of Social Networking and Depression Research

Research on SNS use and mental health has important implications for SNS users themselves as well as those who interact with SNS users (e.g., parents, teachers, mental health professionals). Now that SNS use is nearly universal, it is necessary to understand whether aspects of such use can have negative consequences. In contrast to early claims that simply using Facebook too much could lead to depression, our existing knowledge in this area suggests that SNSs provide another venue for people to have social experiences, some of which may be positive and others negative. For those who are having negative experiences on SNSs, these experiences do appear to be related to depression. Parents are encouraged to consider the types of experiences their children are having on SNSs, similar to how they would consider their children's experiences in other social contexts. It is important for parents and teachers to help children develop healthy relationships and the necessary skills to cope with interpersonal stressors. Similarly, mental health professionals are encouraged to assess the types of experiences their clients – particularly their younger clients – are having on SNSs. Clinical interventions designed to enhance adaptive emotion regulation (see Kring & Sloan, 2010) may be particularly useful for individuals, given findings that rumination may be a mechanism through which negative experiences on SNSs influence depressive symptoms (Feinstein et al., 2013, 2014; Locatelli et al., 2012) and that those who engage in more rumination may be at particular risk for negative social networking experiences and negative affect subsequent to such interactions (Davila et al., 2012). It is important to tailor clinical interventions to situations that are going to be relevant to particular clients. As such, clinicians are encouraged to do their best to remain aware of changes in technology that may be relevant to mental health.

Future Directions for Social Networking and Depression Research

Finally, although research on SNS use and depression has made great strides over the past decade, this literature is still in its infancy. As such, there are numerous promising directions for future research. First, there has been a lack of attention to developing and applying theoretical models to SNS use and it will be important for scholars to continue to refine theoretical models to explain the ways in which SNS use influences depression. The research reviewed in this chapter fits well within the broader literature on co-occurring depression and problematic interpersonal functioning, suggesting that these theories are likely to be helpful when considering hypotheses about the potential consequences on SNS use. Second, most research on SNS use and depression has relied on cross-sectional and self-report data. It is critical that we broaden the methodological approaches used in this field in an effort to refine our understanding of these associations. For instance, some studies have examined the actual content of people's interactions on SNSs rather than using self-report measures (e.g., Forest & Wood, 2012; Szwedo et al., 2010). It will be important for research on SNS use and depression to do this as well, given evidence of biases in information processing among depressed individuals (for a review, see Mathews & MacLeod, 2005). This could shed light on whether people's actual behavior on SNSs is influencing their mental health or if their perceptions of their behavior are more important. Third, given that nearly all of the studies in this area have used self-report measures of depressive symptoms, it remains unclear if findings extend to clinical diagnoses of depressive disorders. Fourth, although research has begun to examine the extent to which different activities on SNSs contribute to depression, there are still numerous activities – many of which are social in nature – that have yet to be examined. For instance, Facebook allows users to post status updates for other users to see, which other users can then comment on or press a button to indicate that they like the status update. Some studies have examined the content of status updates (e.g., Forest & Wood, 2012) and people's responses to status updates (e.g., Chen & Lee, 2013), and it is possible that these processes are also related to depression. Fifth, as SNSs become more popular, additional venues for social networking continue to be created (e.g., Twitter, Instagram, Snapchat). As new SNSs are created, it will be important to continue to refine our understanding of the association between SNS use and depression. It is particularly important to gain a better understanding of how these processes impact children and teenagers who grow up using this technology throughout a critical developmental period. Thus, longitudinal research that examines the development of social networking use in childhood and adolescence may help shed light on how these problematic relationships emerge. Longitudinal designs will also allow for tests of bidirectional associations, which will help refine our understanding of the directionality of the association between SNS use and depression. Finally, it will be important for research to consider more diverse populations in an effort to understand demographic differences (e.g., age, gender, race/ethnicity) and other differences (e.g., personality traits, other mental health problems) in order to increase our understanding of for whom and under what circumstances SNS use is problematic.

Conclusion

In conclusion, the past decade has brought substantial advances in technology as well as our understanding of how technology use impacts well-being. Several conclusions can be drawn from the existing literature on social networking and depression. Contrary to initial speculation, simply spending a lot of time using SNSs does not appear to be a risk factor for depression. However, if an individual uses SNSs to the point that such use begins to impact his/her offline life in a negative way, then it has the potential to contribute to poorer well-being. In contrast to frequency, the quality of one's SNS experiences does appear to be related to well-being. Negative interactions on SNSs are associated with increases in depressive symptoms, similar to negative face-to-face interactions, and this appears to be particularly true for certain individuals (e.g., those who tend to ruminate, those with low self-esteem). Despite significant increases in our understanding of social networking and depression, additional research is needed to refine our understanding of these associations, particularly the mechanisms underlying the associations between SNS use and depression as well as individual differences that influence these associations.

References

Ahrens, A. H., & Alloy, L. B. (1997). Social comparison processes in depression. In B. P. Buunk & F. X. Gibbons (Eds.), *Health, coping, and well-being: Perspectives from social comparison theory* (pp. 389–410). Mahwah, NJ: Lawrence Erlbaum Associates.

Aldao, A., Nolen-Hoeksema, S., & Schweizer, S. (2010). Emotion-regulation strategies across psychopathology: A meta-analytic review. *Clinical Psychology Review, 30,* 217–237.

Bessière, K., Pressman, S., Kiesler, S., & Kraut, R. (2010). Effects of Internet use on health and depression: A longitudinal study. *Journal of Medical Internet Research, 12*(1), e6.

Bevan, J. L., Pfyl, J., & Barclay, B. (2012). Negative emotional and cognitive responses to being unfriended on Facebook: An exploratory study. *Computers in Human Behavior, 28,* 1458–1464.

Bhatia, V., & Davila, J. (2015). Bi-directional associations between depressive symptoms and problematic Internet use. Manuscript submitted for publication.

boyd, d. m., & Ellison, N. B. (2007). Social network sites: Definition, history, and scholarship. *Journal of Computer-Mediated Communication, 13*(1), article 11. Retrieved August 14, 2014, from http://jcmc.indiana.edu/vol13/issue1/boyd.ellison.html

Brandtzæg, P. B. (2012). Social networking sites: Their users and social implications – A longitudinal study. *Journal of Computer-Mediated Communication, 17,* 467–488.

Campbell, A. J., Cumming, S. R., & Hughes, I. (2006). Internet use by the socially fearful: Addiction or therapy? *CyberPsychology and Behavior, 9,* 69–81.

Chen, W., & Lee, K.-H. (2013). Sharing, liking, commenting, and distressed? The pathway between Facebook interaction and psychological distress. *Cyberpsychology, Behavior, and Social Networking, 16,* 728–734.

Cheung, M. S., Gilbert, P., & Irons, C. (2004). An exploration of shame, rank, and rumination in relation to depression. *Personality and Individual Differences, 36,* 1143–1153.

Chou, H. G., & Edge, N. (2012). "They are happier and having better lives than I am": The impact of using Facebook on perceptions of others' lives. *Cyberpsychology, Behavior, and Social Networking, 15,* 117–121.

Cotten, S. R., Ford, G., Ford, S., & Hale, T. M. (2012). Internet use and depression among older adults. *Computers in Human Behavior, 28,* 496–499.

Coyne, J. C. (1976). Depression and the response of others. *Journal of Abnormal Psychology, 85,* 186–193.

Darvell, M. J., Walsh, S. P., & White, K. M. (2011). Facebook tells me so: Applying the theory of planned behavior to understand partner-monitoring behavior on Facebook. *Cyberpsychology, Behavior, and Social Networking, 14,* 717–722.

Davila, J. (2011). The "Facebook depression" controversy. Retrieved August 14, 2013, from http://www.psychology.sunysb.edu/jdavila-/webpage/facebook%20depression%20controversy.htm

Davila, J., Hershenberg, R., Feinstein, B. A., Gorman, K., Bhatia, V., & Starr, L. (2012). Frequency and quality of social networking experiences: Associations with depressive symptoms, rumination, and co-rumination. *Psychology of Popular Media Culture, 1,* 72–86.

Davila, J., Stroud, C., & Starr, L. (2009). Depression in couples and families. In I. Gotlib & C. Hammen (Eds.), *Handbook of depression* (2nd ed.). New York, NY: Guilford Press.

Davis, R. A. (2001). A cognitive-behavioral model of pathological Internet use. *Computers in Human Behavior, 17,* 187–195.

Duggan, M., & Brenner, J. (2013, February 14). The demographics of social media users – 2012. Pew Internet & American Life Project. Retrieved November 30, 2014, from http://pewinternet.org/Reports/2013/Social-media-users.aspx

Feinstein, B. A., Bhatia, V., & Davila, J. (2014). Rumination mediates the association between cyber-victimization and depressive symptoms. *Journal of Interpersonal Violence, 29*(9), 1732–1746.

Feinstein, B. A., Bhatia, V., Hershenberg, R., & Davila, J. (2012). Another venue for problematic interpersonal behavior: The effects of depressive and anxious symptoms on social networking experiences. *Journal of Social and Clinical Psychology, 31,* 356–383.

Feinstein, B. A., Hershenberg, R., Bhatia, V., Latack, J. A., Meuwly, N., & Davila, J. (2013). Negative social comparison on Facebook and depressive symptoms: Rumination as a mechanism. *Psychology of Popular Media Culture, 2,* 161–170.

Finn, J. (2004). A survey of online harassment at a university campus. *Journal of Interpersonal Violence, 19,* 468–483.

Forest, A. L., & Wood, J. V. (2012). When social networking is not working: Individuals with low self-esteem recognize but do not reap the benefits of self-disclosure on Facebook. *Psychological Science, 23*, 295–302.

Fortson, B. L., Scotti, J. R., Chen, Y.-C., Malone, J., & Del Ben, K. S. (2007). Internet use, abuse, and dependence among students at a Southeastern Regional University. *Journal of American College Health, 56*, 137–144.

Griffiths, M. D. (2000). Does Internet and computer "addiction" exist? Some case study evidence. *CyberPsychology and Behavior, 3*, 211–218.

Haferkamp, N., & Krämer, N. C. (2011). Social comparison 2.0: Examining the effects of online profiles on social-networking sites. *Cyberpsychology, Behavior, and Social Networking, 14*, 309–314.

Hammen, C. (1991). Generation of stress in the course of unipolar depression. *Journal of Abnormal Psychology, 100*, 555–561.

Hammen, C. (2006). Stress generation in depression: Reflections on origins, research, and future directions. *Journal of Clinical Psychology, 62*, 1065–1082.

Hampton, K. N., Goulet, L. S., Her, E. J., & Rainie, L. (2009, November 4). Social isolation and new technology. Pew Internet & American Life Project. Retrieved November 30, 2014, from http://www.pewinternet.org/2009/11/04/social-isolation-and-new-technology/

Hampton, K. N., Goulet, L. S., Rainie, L., & Purcell, K. (2011, June 16). Social networking sites and our lives. Pew Internet & American Life Project. Retrieved November 30, 2014, from http://www.pewinternet.org/Reports/2011/Technology-and-social-networks.aspx

Huang, C. (2010). Internet use and psychological well-being: A meta-analysis. *Cyberpsychology, Behavior, and Social Networking, 13*, 241–249.

Jelenchick, L. A., Eickhoff, J. C., & Moreno, M. A. (2013). "Facebook depression?" Social networking site use and depression in older adolescents. *Journal of Adolescent Health, 52*, 128–130.

Joiner, T., & Coyne, J. (Eds.). (1999). *The interactional nature of depression: Advances in interpersonal approaches.* Washington, DC: APA.

Joiner, T. E., Jr., Metalsky, G. I., Katz, J., & Beach, S. R. H. (1999). Depression and excessive reassurance-seeking. *Psychological Inquiry, 10*, 269–278.

Kim, J., LaRose, R., & Peng, W. (2009). Loneliness as the cause and the effect of problematic Internet use: The relationship between Internet use and psychological well-being. *CyberPsychology and Behavior, 12*, 451–455.

Kowalski, R. M., & Limber, S. P. (2007). Electronic bullying among middle school students. *Journal of Adolescent Health, 41*, S22–S30.

Kraut, R., Kiesler, S., Boneva, B., Cummings, J., Helgeson, V., & Crawford, A. (2002). Internet paradox revisited. *Journal of Social Issues, 58*, 49–74.

Kraut, R., Patterson, M., Lundmark, V., Kiesler, S., Mukophadhyay, T., & Scherlis, W. (1998). Internet paradox: A social technology that reduces social involvement and psychological well-being? *American Psychologist, 53*, 1017–1031.

Kring, A. M., & Sloan, D. M. (2010). *Emotion regulation and psychopathology: A transdiagnostic approach to etiology and treatment.* New York, NY: Guilford Press.

Kross, E., Verduyn, P., Demiralp, E., Park, J., Lee, D. S., Lin, N., ... Ybarra, O. (2013). Facebook use predicts declines in subjective well-being in young adults. *PLOS ONE 8*(8), e69841.

La Greca, A., Davila, J., & Siegel, R. (2008). Peer relations, friendships, and romantic relationships: Implications for the development and maintenance of depression in adolescents. In N. Allen & L. Sheeber (Eds.), *Adolescent emotional development and the emergence of depressive disorders.* New York, NY: Cambridge University Press.

Lenhart, A., Purcell, K., Smith, A., & Zickuhr, K. (2010, February 3). Social media and mobile Internet use among teens and young adults. Pew Internet & American Life Project. Retrieved November 30, 2014, from http://www.pewinternet.org/~/media//Files/Reports/2010/PIP_Social_Media_and_Young_Adults_Report_Final_with_toplines.pdf

Lindsay, M., & Krysik, J. (2012). Online harassment among college students: A replication incorporating new Internet trends. *Information, Communication and Society, 15,* 703–719.

Locatelli, S. M., Kluwe, K., & Bryant, F. B. (2012). Facebook use and the tendency to ruminate among college students: Testing meditational hypotheses. *Journal of Educational Computing Research, 46,* 377–394.

Magid, L. (2011). "Facebook depression": A nonexistent condition. *The Huffington Post.* Retrieved November 30, 2014, from http://www.huffingtonpost.com/larry-magid/facebook-depression-nonexistent_b_842733.html

Manago, A. M., Graham, M. B., Greenfield, P. M., & Salimkhan, G. (2008). Self-presentation and gender on MySpace. *Journal of Applied Developmental Psychology, 29,* 446–458.

Marshall, T. (2012). Facebook surveillance of former romantic partners: Associations with postbreakup recovery and personal growth. *Cyberpsychology, Behavior, and Social Networking, 15,* 521–526.

Marshall, T. C., Bejanyan, K., Di Castro, G., & Lee, R. A. (2013). Attachment styles as predictors of Facebook-related jealousy and surveillance in romantic relationships. *Personal Relationships, 20,* 1–22.

Mathews, A., & MacLeod, C. (2005). Cognitive vulnerability to emotional disorders. *Annual Review of Clinical Psychology, 1,* 167–195.

McKenna, K. Y. A., & Bargh, J. A. (2000). Plan 9 from cyberspace: The implications of the Internet for personality and social psychology. *Personality and Social Psychology Review, 4,* 57–75.

Mishna, F., Cook, C., Gadalla, T., Daciuk, J., & Solomon, S. (2010). Cyber bullying behaviors among middle and high school students. *American Journal of Orthopsychiatry, 80,* 362–374.

Mitchell, K. J., Finkelhor, D., Wolak, J., Ybarra, M. L., & Turner, H. (2011). Youth Internet victimization in a broader victimization context. *Journal of Adolescent Health, 48,* 128–134.

Mitchell, K. J., Ybarra, M., & Finkelhor, D. (2007). The relative importance of online victimization in understanding depression, delinquency, and substance use. *Child Maltreatment, 12,* 314–324.

Morgan, C., & Cotten, S. R. (2003). The relationship between Internet activities and depressive symptoms in a sample of college freshmen. *CyberPsychology and Behavior, 6,* 133–142.

Muise, A., Christofides, E., & Desmarais, S. (2009). More information than you ever wanted: Does Facebook bring out the green-eyed monster of jealousy? *CyberPsychology and Behavior, 12,* 441–444.

Nie, N. H., Hillygus, D. S., & Erbring, L. (2002). Internet use, interpersonal relations, and sociability: A time diary study. In B. Wellman & C. Haythornthwaite (Eds.), *The Internet in everyday life* (pp. 215–243). Oxford, UK: Blackwell.

Nolen-Hoeksema, S., Wisco, B. E., & Lyubomirsky, S. (2008). Rethinking rumination. *Perspectives on Psychological Science, 3,* 400–424.

O'Keeffe, G. S., & Clarke-Pearson, K. (2011). The impact of social media on children, adolescents, and families. *Pediatrics, 127,* 800–804.

Rose, A. J. (2002). Co-rumination in the friendships of girls and boys. *Child Development, 73,* 1830–1843.

Rosen, L. D., Whaling, K., Rab, S., Carrier, L. M., & Cheever, N. A. (2013). Is Facebook creating "iDisorders"? The link between clinical symptoms of psychiatric disorders and technology use, attitudes and anxiety. *Computers in Human Behavior, 29,* 1243–1254.

Selfhout, M. H. W., Branje, S. J. T., Delsing, M., ter Bogt, T. F. M., & Meeus, W. H. J. (2009). Different types of Internet use, depression, and social anxiety: The role of perceived friendship quality. *Journal of Adolescence, 32,* 819–833.

Steinfield, C., Ellison, N. B., & Lampe, C. A. C. (2008). Social capital, self-esteem, and use of online social network sites: A longitudinal analysis. *Journal of Applied Developmental Psychology, 29,* 434–445.

Szwedo, D. E., Mikami, A. Y., & Allen, J. P. (2010). Qualities of peer relations on social networking websites: Predictions from negative mother–teen interactions. *Journal of Research on Adolescence, 21,* 595–607.

Tennant, C. (2002). Life events, stress, and depression: A review of recent findings. *Australian and New Zealand Journal of Psychiatry, 36,* 173–182.

Thompson, S. H., & Lougheed, E. (2012). Frazzled by Facebook? An exploratory study of gender differences in social network communication among undergraduate men and women. *College Student Journal,* 88–98.

van den Eijnden, R. M., Meerkerk, G., Vermulst, A. A., Spijkerman, R., & Engels, R. E. (2008). Online communication, compulsive Internet use, and psychosocial well-being among adolescents: A longitudinal study. *Developmental Psychology, 44,* 655–665.

Wang, H., & Wellman, B. (2010). Social connectivity in America: Change in adult friendship network size from 2002 to 2007. *American Behavioral Scientist, 53,* 1148–1169.

Wang, J., Tonja, R., & Iannoti, R. (2011). Cyber and traditional bullying: Differential association with depression. *Journal of Adolescent Health, 48,* 415–417.

Ybarra, M. L. (2004). Linkages between depressive symptomatology and Internet harassment among young regular Internet users. *CyberPsychology and Behavior, 7,* 247–257.

16

Sex, Alcohol, and Depression

Adolescent Health Displays on Social Media

Megan A. Moreno[1] and Megan A. Pumper[2]

[1] *University of Washington School of Medicine*
[2] *Seattle Children's Research Institute*

Social media, including social networking site use, among adolescents is nearly ubiquitous, and recent increases in smartphone ownership among adolescents have added to teens' daily social media diet (Lenhart et al., 2011; Smith, 2013). Smartphone ownership is rising not only in the United States, but among Asian countries; Singapore and Hong Kong have some of the highest rates of smartphone ownership in the world (Blodget, 2012). No longer is the use of social media just a phenomenon among teens – the past few years have seen increasing rates of social media use among adults (Lenhart, 2009; Lenhart, Purcell, Smith, & Zickuhr, 2010; Melamud & Otero, 2011). The uptake of social media among parents, teachers, and other adult role models means that content displayed by teens on social media may be viewed by a wide audience that may include friends, family, employers, or educators. Previous work has illustrated that social media are common online platforms in which adolescents choose to represent health behaviors and conditions such as alcohol, sexual behavior, and depression (Moreno, Jelenchick, et al., 2011; Moreno, Parks, Zimmerman, Brito, & Christakis, 2009). Offline, these behaviors are associated with increased rates of morbidity and mortality among teens. Thus, these displays may provide new opportunities and challenges in adolescent health.

We will begin this chapter with an understanding of how these health behaviors and conditions impact adolescent health. We will then consider how teens choose to represent behaviors such as alcohol use and conditions such as depression on social media. We will then consider two key areas of inquiry that present both challenges and opportunities for adolescent health. First, we will describe the *validity of these displayed health behaviors and conditions* to the profile owner. Before future interventions using social media displays can proceed, an understanding of what these displays mean to the adolescent profile owner is needed. Second, an understanding of the *influence of these displays on other teens* is needed to guide future educational efforts in teaching teens about how to interpret social media displays by peers. We end with a consideration of the myriad opportunities that social media displays provide toward improving adolescent health.

Morbidity and Mortality in Adolescent Health

It is well known that many of the most important causes of morbidity and mortality in adolescence are associated with health behaviors, particularly health risk behaviors such as sexual behavior, substance use, and violence (Baskin-Sommers & Sommers, 2006; Busen, Marcus, & von Sternberg, 2006; Camenga, Klein, & Roy, 2006; Centers for Disease Control and Prevention, 2005; DuRant & Sigmon Smith, 2002; Loeber et al., 2005; Stephens, 2006; Teplin, McClelland, Abram, & Mileusnic, 2005). Prevalence data suggest by 12th grade slightly more than half of adolescents have had sex, half currently drink alcohol, and 30% have been in a physical fight (CDC, 2005). Teens who engage in one risky behavior have a higher risk of engaging in others (Baskin-Sommers & Sommers, 2006; Camenga et al., 2006; Donenberg, Emerson, Bryant, & King, 2006; McClelland & Teplin, 2001). Other contributors to risk for morbidity and mortality in adolescence include mental illness, such as depression. Depression often has an onset during the adolescent years. One previous study of high school-age adolescents found that almost 10% met criteria for current depression and approximately one-third reported a lifetime history of depression (Lewinsohn, Hops, Roberts, Seeley, & Andrews, 1993). Depression is common and is associated with adverse outcomes such as increased rates of substance use, comorbid psychiatric conditions, and suicide (Bramesfeld, Platt, & Schwartz, 2006; Deas & Brown, 2006; Garlow et al., 2008; Kessler, Foster, Saunders, & Stang, 1995; Rao & Chen, 2009).

A challenge in preventing these causes of morbidity and mortality is that many teens do not go to the doctor for preventive health visits (Halpern-Felsher et al., 2000). In particular, adolescents who struggle with depression are frequently undiagnosed as many do not perceive a need for help and do not seek clinical services (Eisenberg, Golberstein, & Gollust, 2007; Zivin, Eisenberg, Gollust, & Golberstein, 2009). Barriers to help-seeking include lack of knowledge about available services, as well as concerns regarding stigma and privacy (Eisenberg, Downs, Golberstein, & Zivin, 2009; Hunt & Eisenberg, 2010). For adolescents who do visit the doctor, only a minority are asked about health risk behaviors such as alcohol use or sexual behaviors (Mangione-Smith et al., 2007). As current methods fail to identify many adolescents who are at risk for or engaging in health risk behaviors, innovative approaches are clearly needed (Halpern-Felsher et al., 2000; Lehrer, Pantell, Tebb, & Shafer, 2007; Mangione-Smith et al., 2007; McKee & Fletcher, 2006). Thus, social media may provide a new venue to learn about and identify teens who are considering or engaging in health risk behaviors, or struggling with depression.

Previous work has illustrated that social media are common places in which adolescents choose to represent these health behaviors and conditions (Moreno, Jelenchick, et al., 2011; Moreno, Parks, et al., 2009). As we consider what new opportunities and challenges these displays present to clinicians and researchers, two key areas of attention are needed. First, an understanding of the *validity of these displayed health behaviors and conditions* is necessary. Second, an understanding of the *influence of these displays on other teens* is needed.

Health and Health Risk Behavior Displays on Social Media

Social media displays include photographs, videos, and text created and displayed by peers, and viewed by peers. These displays can provide a rich contextual description of an adolescent's attitude, intention, behavior, or experience. Adolescents can determine how their peers interpret and support their displays by viewing comments and "likes" from other teens in response to what a teen posts online.

Several studies have illustrated that adolescents' displays on social media websites such as MySpace and Facebook frequently include health risk behaviors such as alcohol use, substance use, and sexual behaviors (Hinduja & Patchin, 2008; McGee & Begg, 2008; Moreno, Parks, & Richardson, 2007; Moreno, Parks, et al., 2009). Previous studies have found that alcohol displays are present on up to 80% of older adolescent Facebook profiles, sexual content is present on approximately 25% of older adolescent profiles, and that more than half of adolescents' MySpace profiles feature displayed references to one or more health risk behaviors (Egan & Moreno, 2011; Hinduja & Patchin, 2008; Moreno, Parks, et al., 2009).

Alcohol and Substance Use References

Displayed references to alcohol and substance use can include descriptions of attitudes, such as joining a Facebook group like "SHOT SHOT SHOT," "4.20 club," or "Drunk people taking care of drunker people." Positive attitudes toward alcohol may also manifest through "liking" or posting memes regarding favorite alcohol brands. Intention to drink alcohol may be displayed through accepting an invitation to a Facebook "event" that involves alcohol, or by posting about upcoming party plans such as "Can't wait for Friday night, beer pong and beer bongs!" Experiences with alcohol are commonly displayed through pictures at events featuring alcoholic drinks in hand, or even pictures of people in states of extreme inebriation. One controversial Twitter page depicts pictures of college students passed out drunk, often posed in embarrassing poses uploaded by friends.

References to substance use are also present on social media. A previous study described how psychostimulant drugs, specifically Adderall, were displayed on Twitter. Tweets about Adderall were highest during the time period when traditional university and college exams occurred (Hanson et al., 2013). The authors concluded that Twitter content tends to represent offline trends.

Sexual References

Displayed references to sexual health often fall into one of several categories. Revealing photographs are common sexual displays, often featuring adolescents partially undressed, showing cleavage or pelvic bones, or wearing lingerie. Sexual behavior references often include text descriptions of sexual experiences, or photographs that depict sexual acts or sexually suggestive poses. Sexual paraphernalia references often include sexual icons, such as the Playboy bunny. Sexual preference displays often include descriptions of sexual preferences for behaviors, partners, or genders. Personal sexual descriptions are references that highlight or emphasize sexual aspects of the profile owner, such as describing one's bra size, or photos taken focusing in on the profile owner's cleavage.

Social networking sites also provide a visual depiction of an adolescent's social network, and the ability to understand how attitudes, intentions, or behaviors are present or absent within particular peer groups. A 2010 study found that adolescents were more likely to display references to sexual behavior if a peer displayed similar references (Moreno et al., 2010). Social networking sites may provide a new lens through which we can better understand how particular risk behaviors diffuse within and beyond peer groups.

While displayed health risk behaviors are common on social media websites, displays of the negative consequences of these behaviors are less frequently noted. One study found that displays of negative consequences of alcohol use, such as hangovers or embarrassment, were rare (Moreno et al., 2010). This is important because adolescents are more likely to mimic risky behaviors if they do not perceive a consequence to it, as described in social learning theory (Bandura, 1977). For example, seeing a peer skateboard down a steep hill without harm may lead another teen to try this stunt.

Depression Displays on Social Media

References to depression symptoms on social media websites may be perceived as a rare phenomenon. Social media websites offer an individual the opportunity to selectively display one's identity, and further, depression is often considered a stigmatizing condition that an individual may wish to keep secret. These factors aside, depression is still commonly talked about on social media and depression symptoms are referenced.

A previous study examined Facebook profiles of older adolescents for depression symptom displays. Depression symptoms were present on 25% of the profiles examined (Moreno, Jelenchick, et al., 2011). This study used a codebook created using the clinical criteria for a Major Depressive Episode as described in the *Diagnostic and Statistical Manual for Mental Disorders* (DSM-IV; APA, 2000) to analyze the Facebook profile content. Posts such as "so, so unhappy" were identified as the symptom depressed mood. Further, Facebook posts such as "ugh I don't feel like getting up today or doing anything" were categorized under the symptom of decreased interest or pleasure in activities and "feeling absolutely useless today, I suck" as feelings of guilt, worthlessness, and negative self-appraisal.

References to depression symptoms are displayed on social media sites beyond Facebook. Some of the newer social media sites, such as Tumblr and Reddit, have a more flexible profile structure that allows for longer or more in-depth narratives. Entering a search term of "depression" on the site Tumblr may reveal concerning posts (i.e., "I really just need someone to talk to before I end up really, really hurting myself. But everyone I send a message to doesn't seem to care at all"). Tumblr allows for the capability to upload photos with text, which allows for a visual depiction of how a person is feeling (i.e., photograph of a person's open palm holding four pills, photograph caption reads "My new friends..."). The social media website Instagram allows for only uploading photos. Entering the search term "depression" on Instagram illustrated photographs that suggest depression highlighted by descriptions through the captions of the photographs. Some examples of Instagram posts that may suggest depression include a photograph of a person in a lake with text caption stating: "'What is depression like?' he whispered. 'It's like drowning. Except you can see everyone around you breathing.'" While some disclosures reveal symptoms or express challenges, other displays provide resources to share with others. Social support and messages of encouragement to those who have posted depression symptoms are seen as well in this context. Some examples of supportive posts include "Hang in there!" or "I've been through this too and you can make it through this." Thus, displayed depression references may include opportunities to share symptoms and experiences as well as to share resources or social support.

Positive Health Behaviors Displayed on Social Media

Few studies have examined the display of positive health behaviors, such as exercise or healthy eating, on social media. One study of college student Facebook profiles found that more than 70% of profiles had referenced one or more fitness behaviors. However, these behaviors included health approaches to diet and exercise as well as unhealthy behaviors such as crash diets or excessive exercise (Villiard & Moreno, 2012).

Validity of Displayed References on Social Media

In the early days of the Internet there were questions about whether the web was a place in which people would form new identities or behave in ways that were dramatically different from their offline selves. Similarly, with the rise of social media, social networking site profiles were suspected of being a shadowy reflection of a person's persona, rather than a portrayal of their identity.

While research in this area is still emerging, there are several areas of evidence that support displayed health references on social media as having face validity in the eyes of the profile owner who displays it. First, health risk behaviors are commonly displayed in patterns consistent with offline reporting, such as through survey research. For example, adolescents who display references to religious commitment are less likely to display references to sexual behavior (Gannon, Becker, & Moreno, 2013). Additionally, an adolescent who displays one health risk behavior such as sexual activity is more likely to display other behaviors such as alcohol or drug use (Moreno, Parks, et al., 2009). This suggests that patterns of adolescent behavior that have been researched and understood in offline life for decades are now being displayed online by adolescents.

Second, previous studies of Internet behaviors have shown that computer use encourages high levels of self-disclosure and uninhibited personal expression, which supports the validity of Internet self-report (Fleming, 1990; Newman, Consoli, & Barr, 1997; Wallace, Linke, Murray, McCambridge, & Thompson, 2006; Walther & Parks, 2002). In addition, most teens report that the majority of their online self-representation reflects their identity, but the presentation may not be entirely current (Caspi & Gorsky, 2006; Klein et al., 2007). Previous studies have also shown that even in websites designed to promote identity experimentation such as chat rooms, subjects generally evolved their online presentations to fit their own identities (Bechar-Israeli, 1996).

Finally, few studies have examined associations between displayed health behaviors and self-reported health behaviors. One study focusing on alcohol displays found that older adolescents who chose to display references to intoxication or problem drinking were more likely to score into the problem drinking category on a clinical screen (Moreno, Christakis, Egan, Brockman, & Becker, 2011). Further, these individuals were more likely to report a recent alcohol-related injury compared to those who did not display these behaviors. The authors concluded that displayed references to these problematic drinking behaviors may indicate older adolescents who would benefit from clinical screening for problem drinking.

Studies of sexual display on social media found that among older adolescents, these displays were not associated with behavior but with intention. Older adolescents who displayed sexual references were more likely to score high on a scale associated with intention to become sexually active in the next six months. The authors concluded that older adolescents who display sexual references may use these displays as a way of indicating that they are interested and ready to consider sexual behavior (Moreno, Brockman, Wasserheit, & Christakis, 2012).

Studies have also been conducted regarding the validity of displayed depression references on social media. In a study done in 2012, displayed depression references were found to be positively associated with self-reported depression symptoms using a clinical screen (Moreno, Christakis, et al., 2012; Richardson et al., 2010). The association was stronger among those who scored as having mild depression, suggesting that displayed depression symptoms may be a way for those with milder symptoms to express or moderate their symptoms and potentially prevent them from worsening.

Social media use characteristics, such as quantity of posts or number of connections made, can also offer a unique view of the health status of an individual. A study done in 2013 found that particular Facebook activities were predictive of those individuals who were depressed and those who were not (Park, Lee, Kwak, Cha, & Jeong, 2013). Investigators found that how an individual responded to tips and resources prompted by the researchers, friend count, and even location tags were related to whether or not the individual was depressed (Park et al., 2013).

Influence of Displayed References on Social Media

Previous research has established strong links between what adolescents observe and how they choose to behave (Bandura, 1986). The influence is particularly strong when it involves observing other adolescents, who can influence a given teen's own attitudes, intentions, and behaviors (Keefe, 1994; Wood, Read, Mitchell, & Brand, 2004). For example, adolescents who perceive that their peers are sexually active are more likely to report intention to become sexually active themselves (Kinsman, Romer, Furstenberg, & Schwarz, 1998).

Another strong source of influence on adolescent attitudes, intentions, and behaviors is the media (Dalton et al., 2003, 2009; Gidwani, Sobol, DeJong, Perrin, & Gortmaker, 2002; Titus-Ernstoff, Dalton, Adachi-Mejia, Longacre, & Beach, 2008). Many research studies have examined traditional media such as television and movies; findings have consistently shown that exposure to risk behaviors, such as alcohol use, tobacco use, or sexual behaviors, is associated with initiation of these behaviors (Dalton et al., 2009; Gidwani et al., 2002; Klein et al., 1993; Robinson, Chen, & Killen, 1998; Strasburger, Wilson, & Jordan, 2008). Thus, adolescents can learn these behaviors through media and be influenced to try out these behaviors.

Given the influence of both peers and traditional media on adolescent health risk behaviors, it is worth considering how social media may influence teens. Social media allow teens to be both creators and consumers of media, thus, social media combine both peer and media effects. Social media have been described as bringing together the power of interpersonal persuasion with the reach of mass media. B. J. Fogg described "mass interpersonal persuasion" as "the most significant advance in persuasion since radio was invented in the 1890s" (Fogg, 2008).

Social Media Displays May Influence Health Risk Behaviors

The potential source of influence on adolescent attitudes and behaviors from social media is supported through recent studies. One study found that adolescents who viewed alcohol references on their peers' Facebook profiles found these references to be believable and influential sources of information (Moreno, Briner, Williams, Walker, & Christakis, 2009). Another study found that adolescents who perceive that alcohol use is normative based on Facebook profiles are more likely to report interest in initiating alcohol use (Litt & Stock, 2011).

The influence of displayed social media content may also influence sexual expectations. One recent study investigated older adolescent males' perceptions related to viewing displayed sexual content on social media profiles of female peers (Moreno, Swanson, Royer, & Roberts, 2011). Males commented that they frequently view and attend to displayed sexual content displayed by females, such as revealing photographs or descriptions of "crazy nights" including "going whoring." Males explained that these types of displays may heighten personal expectations for sexual behavior from that female. One male explained, "if she's willing to put it up on Facebook, why wouldn't she be willing to give it to me?"

Social media displays related to depression may have influence in different ways. It has been hypothesized that the prevalence of displayed references to depression may contribute to a decreased stigma for depression (Moreno, Jelenchick, et al., 2011). On a more individual level, displayed social media references to depression may lead peers to provide increased attention or support to the person posting this content. One study investigated peer perceptions related to displayed social media depression references and found that many older adolescents interpreted these displays as "cries for help" (Egan, Koff, & Moreno, 2013). However, some peers reported that they viewed these references as "dramatic" or "attention-seeking," which would reduce their likelihood of reaching out.

The Facebook Influence Model

A 2011 summit convened by Rand concluded that new evaluation of existing health behavior theory models is needed to understand the role of social media (Collins, Martino, & Shaw, 2011). Thus, a recent study sought to determine young people's perceptions of Facebook that were influential. This mixed-methods study applied concept mapping methodology, a validated five-step method to visually represent complex topics. This approach allows the conceptual framework to be built from data based entirely on the views of key stakeholders. The outcome was a concept map, a visual representation of key concepts and their interrelationships.

The Facebook influence model includes 13 clusters; clusters include "influence on identity," "positive experiences," and "immersive environment" (Moreno, Kota, Schoohs, & Whitehill, 2013). These 13 clusters can be considered within four main concepts:

1 *Connection*: Facebook provides and enhances peer communication, networking, and connection.
2 *Comparison*: Comparison with peers has long been part of adolescence. Facebook allows this comparison to take place using tangible information such as photos, descriptions of behaviors, and peer comments.

3 *Identification*: Facebook allows a profile owner to develop an online identity through a profile. Profile owners can then revise that identity via feedback from peers' comments and "likes." The ability to develop one's identity in real time provides a unique multimedia view of the self.
4 *Immersive experience*: Facebook was described as a website that provided positive, negative, tool-based, and distracting features toward an immersive and powerful experience for users.

Thus, while Facebook provides a novel lens through which to consider behavioral influence, its influence can best be considered in the context of robust behavioral theory. Thus, each of the four cluster groups can best be considered alongside the framework of previous supporting work as synergistic or an expansion of previous theory. For example, the "identification" group describes the clusters regarding exploring and reflecting on one's identity using Facebook. The media practice model explains that users choose and interact with media based on who they are, and who they want to be at that moment (Brown, 2000). Facebook allows a profile owner to develop an online identity through a profile. Profile owners can then reflect and revise that identity via feedback from peers' comments and "likes," or by personal perusal through the Facebook "timeline." Young people can now develop an online identity in real time based on a vision of who one *wants to be*, as well as exposure to other media content and peer feedback. These 13 constructs and 4 groups suggest a comprehensive base for theoretical consideration to inform future work and the potential for intervention development using Facebook.

New Opportunities for Health Interventions on Social Media

Health Risk Behavior Displays

Parents are increasingly on Facebook, and many are likely "friends" with their older adolescent children, such as college students (Duggan & Smith, 2013). Parents or other caring adults who note references to health risk behavior displays may have unique opportunities to identify an adolescent who is at risk for morbidity or mortality. Among older adolescents, peer leaders such as church youth group leaders or dormitory resident advisors may be willing and able to approach adolescents when health risk behaviors are noted on social media (Kacvinsky & Moreno, 2014; Moreno, Grant, Kacvinsky, Egan, & Fleming, 2012).

Healthcare providers, such as physicians, nurses, and counselors, may be able to use social media to interact with adolescents in a clinical office setting. Some providers have proposed looking over a patient's profile page with the patient, as a novel way to take a social history (Moreno, 2010). There have been no research studies to date on how this would work in a clinical setting, or how providers may carve out time in a busy clinic schedule to pursue these activities.

Finally, organizations such as schools or universities may consider creating prevention messages and target them to students displaying references to health risk behaviors on social media. One approach may be to provide prevention messages linked to references suggesting intention. In a recent study, references to an alcohol-themed party were often present on Facebook profiles in the month prior to the event (Moreno, Kacvinsky,

Pumper, Wachowski, & Whitehill, 2013). These references included responding to a Facebook event invitation and displaying text suggesting excitement about or anticipation of the event (Moreno, Kacvinsky, et al., 2013). Another possible example may be providing pop-up advertisements distributed by campus health centers indicating availability of contraception options when a profile owner displays references to sex (Moreno, Brockman, et al., 2012). Overall, references indicating intention may represent new opportunities to provide prevention messages prior to a risky behavior taking place. Given the growing prevalence of cell phone use among older adolescents, these messages or interventions could be delivered by mobile device and reach adolescents in a timely manner.

Depression Symptom Displays

Two areas of potential intervention for adolescents with depression include benefits of social media use during periods of depression, as well as the potential for social media displays to identify adolescents who are at risk for or suffering from depression.

Benefits to social media use for adolescents with depression.   In 2006, Dutch researchers found that adolescents who had experienced a greater number of positive reactions to their SNS profile also experienced higher self-esteem and satisfaction with their life (Ahn, 2011). Comparably, in 2009, a study of college students in Texas demonstrated that Facebook usage was positively correlated with life satisfaction, social trust, and civic engagement (Ahn, 2011). There may be a limit in social network size for this benefit, as research suggests that those with extremely large social networks may have a decrease in the quality of their interactions with others, with superficial engagement substituting for meaningful relationships (Rajani, Berman, & Rozanski, 2011). Further, a recent controversy regarding use of social media by adolescents with depression was noted when the American Academy of Pediatrics suggested that time spent with social media may place adolescents at risk of "Facebook Depression" (O'Keeffe & Clarke-Pearson, 2011). However, an empirical study investigating this potential phenomenon did not find evidence of a relationship between time spent on Facebook and likelihood of depression (Jelenchick, Eickhoff, & Moreno, 2013).

Intervention Possibilities

When an adolescent chooses to display depression symptom references on a social media site, this action may open up opportunities for intervention messages from those who view the display. However, given that depression is an illness with the potential for patient to feel stigma, any intervention approaches must consider the privacy of the adolescent as well as appropriate language in communicating about the post. A previous study examined older adolescents' views regarding preferences for the person and the approach that would be recommended if a depression reference was noted on Facebook (Whitehill, Brockman, & Moreno, 2013). Study findings indicated that, perhaps not surprisingly, the ideal person to approach someone who displayed depression symptom references would be a friend. However, more than 90% of study participants would accept a known adult's approach, such as by a parent or teacher, so long as privacy, confidentiality, and non-judgmental communication were used. Having a stranger approach regarding a displayed depression reference was not well favored by participants. When addressing the manner of approach, older adolescents favored an in-person approach rather than communicating via social media. Thus, social media displays of depression may invite opportunities to inquire about well-being or provide support to an adolescent in a face-to-face setting.

Conclusion

Private and potentially stigmatizing information such as sexual behaviors or depression are commonly displayed on social media websites by today's adolescents. Previous studies have described that references to alcohol behaviors, sexual intentions, and depression symptoms provide rich data to understand adolescents' views and experiences. These displays often reflect attitudes, intentions, or experiences of the teens who choose to publicly display such references. Displayed references may be associated with individual behaviors such as with alcohol reference displays, intentions as with sexual reference displays, or current feelings as with depression reference displays. These references are influential to other teens and peers who may view them by suggesting that these behaviors are normative, or desirable. Thus, previous literature suggests that these references have both face validity and influence. The information that social media websites provide about these behaviors and experiences affords researchers and clinicians a better understanding of these behaviors and conditions, as well as opportunities to better target and treat these important causes of morbidity and mortality for this population.

References

Ahn, J. (2011). The effect of social network sites on adolescents' social and academic development: Current theories and controversies. *Journal of the American Society for Information Science and Technology, 62*(8), 1435–1445.

American Psychiatric Association (APA). (2000). *Diagnostic and statistical manual of mental disorders* (4th ed.) (DSM-IV). Washington, DC: Author.

Bandura, A. (1977). *Social learning theory.* New York, NY: General Learning Press.

Bandura, A. (1986). *Social foundations of thought and action: A social cognitive theory.* Englewood Cliffs, NJ: Prentice Hall.

Baskin-Sommers, A., & Sommers, I. (2006). The co-occurrence of substance use and high-risk behaviors. *Journal of Adolescent Health, 38*(5), 609–611.

Bechar-Israeli, H. (1996). From < Bonehead > to <cLoNehEAd>": Nicknames, play and identity on Internet relay chat. *Journal of Computer-Mediated Communication, 1*(2).

Blodget, H. (2012, September 13). Actually, the US smartphone revolution has entered the late innings. BI Intelligence. Retrieved February 20, 2014, from www.businessinsider.com/us-smartphone-market-2012-9

Bramesfeld, A., Platt, L., & Schwartz, F. W. (2006). Possibilities for intervention in adolescents' and young adults' depression from a public health perspective. *Health Policy, 79*(2–3), 121–131.

Brown, J. (2000). Adolescents' sexual media diets. *Journal of Adolescent Health, 27*, 35–40.

Busen, N. H., Marcus, M. T., & von Sternberg, K. L. (2006). What African-American middle school youth report about risk-taking behaviors. *Journal of Pediatric Health Care, 20*(6), 393–400.

Camenga, D. R., Klein, J. D., & Roy, J. (2006). The changing risk profile of the American adolescent smoker: Implications for prevention programs and tobacco interventions. *Journal of Adolescent Health*, *39*(1), 120.e1–10.

Caspi, A., & Gorsky, P. (2006). Online deception: Prevalence, motivation, and emotion. *CyberPsychology and Behavior*, *9*(1), 54–59.

Centers for Disease Control and Prevention (CDC). (2005). 2005 Youth Risk Behavior Survey. Retrieved October 1, 2007, from www.cdc.gov/yrbss

Collins, R., Martino, S., & Shaw, R. (2011). *Influence of new media on adolescent sexual health: Evidence and opportunities.* Rand Corporation Report. Retrieved November 30, 2014, from http://www.rand.org/pubs/working_papers/WR761.html

Dalton, M. A., Beach, M. L., Adachi-Mejia, A. M., Longacre, M. R., Matzkin, A. L., Sargent, J. D., … Titus-Ernstoff, L. (2009). Early exposure to movie smoking predicts established smoking by older teens and young adults. *Pediatrics*, *123*(4), e551–558.

Dalton, M. A., Sargent, J. D., Beach, M. L., Titus-Ernstoff, L., Gibson, J. J., Ahrens, M. B., … Heatherton, T. F. (2003). Effect of viewing smoking in movies on adolescent smoking initiation: A cohort study. *Lancet*, *362*(9380), 281–285.

Deas, D., & Brown, E. S. (2006). Adolescent substance abuse and psychiatric comorbidities. *Journal of Clinical Psychiatry*, *67*(7), e02.

Donenberg, G. R., Emerson, E., Bryant, F. B., & King, S. (2006). Does substance use moderate the effects of parents and peers on risky sexual behavior? *AIDS Care*, *18*(3), 194–200.

Duggan, M., & Smith, M. (2013, December 30) Social media update 2013. Pew Internet & American Life Project. Retrieved November 30, 2014, from http://www.pewinternet.org/2013/12/30/social-media-update-2013/

DuRant, R. H., & Sigmon Smith, K. (2002). Vital statistics and injuries. In L. S. Neinstein (Ed.), *Adolescent health care* (4th ed., pp. 126–169). Philadelphia, PA: Lippincott Williams & Wilkins.

Egan, K. G., Koff, R. N., & Moreno, M. A. (2013). College students' responses to mental health status updates on Facebook. *Issues in Mental Health Nursing*, *34*(1), 46–51.

Egan, K. G., & Moreno, M. A. (2011). Alcohol references on undergraduate males' Facebook profiles. *American Journal of Men's Health*, *5*(5), 413–420.

Eisenberg, D., Downs, M. F., Golberstein, E., & Zivin, K. (2009). Stigma and help seeking for mental health among college students. *Medical Care Research and Review*, *66*(5), 522–541.

Eisenberg, D., Golberstein, E., & Gollust, S. E. (2007). Help-seeking and access to mental health care in a university student population. *Medical Care*, *45*(7), 594–601.

Fleming, P. J. (1990). *Software and sympathy: Therapeutic interaction with the computer.* Norwood, NJ: Ablex.

Fogg, B. J. (2008). *Mass interpersonal persuasion: An early view of a new phenomenon.* Paper presented at the Third International Conference on Persuasive Technology, Berlin, Germany.

Gannon, K. E., Becker, T., & Moreno, M. A. (2013). Religion and sex among college freshmen: A longitudinal study using Facebook. *Journal of Adolescent Research*, *28*(5), 535–556.

Garlow, S. J., Rosenberg, J., Moore, J. D., Haas, A. P., Koestner, B., Hendin, H., & Nemeroff, C. B. (2008). Depression, desperation, and suicidal ideation in college students: Results from the American Foundation for Suicide Prevention College Screening Project at Emory University. *Depression and Anxiety*, *25*(6), 482–488.

Gidwani, P. P., Sobol, A., DeJong, W., Perrin, J. M., & Gortmaker, S. L. (2002). Television viewing and initiation of smoking among youth. *Pediatrics*, *110*(3), 505–508.

Halpern-Felsher, B. L., Ozer, E. M., Millstein, S. G., Wibbelsman, C. J., Fuster, C. D., Elster, A. B., & Irwin, C. E., Jr. (2000). Preventive services in a health maintenance organization: How well do pediatricians screen and educate adolescent patients? *Archives of Pediatrics and Adolescent Medicine*, *154*(2), 173–179.

Hanson, C. L., Burton, S. H., Giraud-Carrier, C., West, J. H., Barnes, M. D., & Hansen, B. (2013). Tweaking and tweeting: Exploring Twitter for nonmedical use of psychostimulant drug (Adderall) among college students. *Journal of Medical Internet Research*, 15(4), e62.

Hinduja, S., & Patchin, J. W. (2008). Personal information of adolescents on the Internet: A quantitative content analysis of MySpace. *Journal of Adolescence*, 31(1), 125–146.

Hunt, J., & Eisenberg, D. (2010). Mental health problems and help-seeking behavior among college students. *Journal of Adolescent Health*, 46(1), 3–10.

Jelenchick, L., Eickhoff, J. E., & Moreno, M. A. (2013). "Facebook depression?" Social networking site use and depression in older adolescents. *Journal of Adolescent Health*, 52(1), 128–130.

Kacvinsky, L. E., & Moreno, M. A. (2014). Facebook use between college resident advisors' and their residents: A mixed methods approach. *College Student Journal*, 48(1), 16–22.

Keefe, K. (1994). Perceptions of normative social pressure and attitudes toward alcohol use: Changes during adolescence. *Journal of Studies on Alcohol and Drugs*, 55(1), 46–54.

Kessler, R. C., Foster, C. L., Saunders, W. B., & Stang, P. E. (1995). Social consequences of psychiatric disorders I: Educational attainment. *American Journal of Psychiatry*, 152(7), 1026–1032.

Kinsman, S. B., Romer, D., Furstenberg, F. F., & Schwarz, D. F. (1998). Early sexual initiation: The role of peer norms. *Pediatrics*, 102(5), 1185–1192.

Klein, J. D., Brown, J. D., Childers, K. W., Oliveri, J., Porter, C., & Dykers, C. (1993). Adolescents' risky behavior and mass media use. *Pediatrics*, 92(1), 24–31.

Klein, J. D., Graff, I., Havens, C., Thomas, R. S., Wanja, K., & Morris, G. (2007). *The impact of cyberspace on teen and young adult social networks*. Paper presented at the Pediatric Academic Society, Toronto, Ontario, Canada.

Lehrer, J. A., Pantell, R., Tebb, K., & Shafer, M. A. (2007). Forgone health care among U.S. adolescents: Associations between risk characteristics and confidentiality concern. *Journal of Adolescent Health*, 40, 218–226.

Lenhart, A. (2009, January 14). Adults and social network websites. Pew Internet & American Life Project. Retrieved November 30, 2014, from http://www.pewinternet.org/2009/01/14/adults-and-social-network-websites/

Lenhart, A., Madden, M., Smith, A., Purcell, K., Zickuhr, K., & Rainie, L. (2011, November 9). Teens, kindness and cruelty on social network sites. Pew Internet & American Life Project. Retrieved November 30, 2014, from http://www.pewinternet.org/2011/11/09/teens-kindness-and-cruelty-on-social-network-sites/

Lenhart, A., Purcell, K., Smith, A., & Zickuhr, K. (2010, February 3). Social media and young adults. Pew Internet & American Life Project. Retrieved November 30, 2014, from http://www.pewinternet.org/2010/02/03/social-media-and-young-adults/

Lewinsohn, P. M., Hops, H., Roberts, R. E., Seeley, J. R., & Andrews, J. A. (1993). Adolescent psychopathology: I. Prevalence and incidence of depression and other DSM III-R disorders in high school students. *Journal of Abnormal Psychology*, 102(1), 133–144.

Litt, D., & Stock, M. (2011). Adolescent alcohol-related risk cognitions: The roles of social norms and social networking sites. *Psychology of Addictive Behaviors*, 25(4), 708–713.

Loeber, R., Pardini, D., Homish, D. L., Wei, E. H., Crawford, A. M., Farrington, D. P., ... Rosenfeld, R. (2005). The prediction of violence and homicide in young men. *Journal of Consulting and Clinical Psychology*, 73(6), 1074–1088.

Mangione-Smith, R., DeCristofaro, A. H., Setodji, C. M., Keesey, J., Klein, D. J., Adams, J. L., ... McGlynn, E. A. (2007). The quality of ambulatory care delivered to children in the United States. *New England Journal of Medicine*, 357(15), 1515–1523.

McClelland, G. M., & Teplin, L. A. (2001). Alcohol intoxication and violent crime: Implications for public health policy. *American Journal of Addiction*, 10, 70–85.

McGee, J. B., & Begg, M. (2008). What medical educators need to know about "Web 2.0." *Medical Teacher*, 30(2), 164–169.

McKee, D., & Fletcher, J. (2006). Primary care for urban adolescent girls from ethnically diverse populations: Foregone care and access to confidential care. *Journal of Health Care for the Poor and Underserved, 17*(4), 759–774.

Melamud, A., & Otero, P. (2011). [Facebook and Twitter, are they already in the pediatrician's office? Survey on the use of social networks]. *Archivos Argentinos de Pediatria, 109*(5), 437–444.

Moreno, M. A. (2010). Social networking sites and adolescents. *Pediatric Annals, 39*(9), 565–568.

Moreno, M. A., Briner, L. R., Williams, A., Walker, L., Brockman, L. B., & Christakis, D. A. (2010). A content analysis of displayed alcohol references on a social networking web site. *Journal of Adolescent Health, 47*, 168–175.

Moreno, M. A., Briner, L. R., Williams, A., Walker, L., & Christakis, D. A. (2009). Real use or "real cool": Adolescents speak out about displayed alcohol references on social networking websites. *Journal of Adolescent Health, 45*(4), 420–422.

Moreno, M. A., Brockman, L. N., Wasserheit, J. N., & Christakis, D. A. (2012). A pilot evaluation of older adolescents' sexual reference displays on Facebook. *Journal of Sex Research, 49*(4), 390–399.

Moreno, M. A., Christakis, D. A., Egan, K. G., Brockman, L. N., & Becker, T. (2011). Associations between displayed alcohol references on Facebook and problem drinking among college students. *Archives of Pediatric and Adolescent Medicine, 166*(2), 157–163.

Moreno, M. A., Christakis, D. A., Egan, K. G., Jelenchick, L. A., Cox, E., Young, H., ... Becker, T. (2012). A pilot evaluation of associations between displayed depression references on Facebook and self-reported depression using a clinical scale. *Journal of Behavior Health Services Research, 39*(3), 295–304.

Moreno, M. A., Grant, A., Kacvinsky, L., Egan, K. G., & Fleming, M. F. (2012). College students' alcohol displays on Facebook: Intervention considerations. *Journal of American College Health, 60*(5), 388–394.

Moreno, M. A., Jelenchick, L. A., Egan, K. G., Cox, E., Young, H., Gannon, K. E., & Becker, T. (2011). Feeling bad on Facebook: Depression disclosures by college students on a social networking site. *Depression and Anxiety, 28*(6), 447–455.

Moreno, M. A., Kacvinsky, L. E., Pumper, M. A., Wachowski, L., & Whitehill, J. M. (2013). Associations between social media displays and event-specific alcohol consumption by college students. *Wisconsin Medical Journal, 112*(6), 251–256.

Moreno, M. A., Kota, R., Schoohs, S., & Whitehill, J. M. (2013). The Facebook influence model: A concept mapping approach. *Cyberpsychology, Social Networking, and Behavior, 16*, 504–511.

Moreno, M. A., Parks, M., & Richardson, L. P. (2007). What are adolescents showing the world about their health risk behaviors on MySpace? *Medscape General Medicine, 9*(4), 9.

Moreno, M. A., Parks, M. R., Zimmerman, F. J., Brito, T. E., & Christakis, D. A. (2009). Display of health risk behaviors on MySpace by adolescents: Prevalence and associations. *Archives of Pediatrics and Adolescent Medicine, 163*(1), 35–41.

Moreno, M., Swanson, M., Royer, H., & Roberts, L. (2011). Sexpectations: Male college students' views about displayed sexual references on females' social networking web sites. *Journal of Pediatric Adolescent Gynecology, 24*, 85–89.

Newman, M. G., Consoli, A., & Barr, T. C. (1997). Computers in assessment and cognitive behavioral treatment of clinical disorders: Anxiety as a case in point. *Behavioral Therapy, 28*, 211–235.

O'Keeffe, G. S., & Clarke-Pearson, K. (2011). The impact of social media on children, adolescents, and families. *Pediatrics, 127*(4), 800–804.

Park, S., Lee, S. W., Kwak, J., Cha, M., & Jeong, B. (2013). Activities on Facebook reveal the depressive state of users. *Journal of Medical Internet Research, 15*(10), e217.

Rajani, R., Berman, D. S., & Rozanski, A. (2011). Social networks – are they good for your health? The era of Facebook and Twitter. *QJM, 104*, 819–820.

Rao, U., & Chen, L. A. (2009). Characteristics, correlates, and outcomes of childhood and adolescent depressive disorders. *Dialogues of Clinical Neuroscience, 11*(1), 45–62.

Richardson, L. P., Rockhill, C., Russo, J. E., Grossman, D. C., Richards, J., McCarty, C., … Katon, W. (2010). Evaluation of the PHQ-2 as a brief screen for detecting major depression among adolescents. *Pediatrics, 125*(5), e1097–1103.

Robinson, T. N., Chen, H. L., & Killen, J. D. (1998). Television and music video exposure and risk of adolescent alcohol use. *Pediatrics, 102*(5), E54.

Smith, A. (2013, June 5). Smartphone ownership 2013. Pew Internet & American Life Project. Retrieved November 30, 2014, from http://www.pewinternet.org/2013/06/05/smartphone-ownership-2013/

Stephens, M. B. (2006). Preventive health counseling for adolescents. *American Family Physician, 74*(7), 1151–1156.

Strasburger, V. C., Wilson, B. J., & Jordan, A. (2008). *Children, adolescents and the media.* Beverly Hills, CA: Sage.

Teplin, L. A., McClelland, G. M., Abram, K. M., & Mileusnic, D. (2005). Early violent death among delinquent youth: A prospective longitudinal study. *Pediatrics, 115*(6), 1586–1593.

Titus-Ernstoff, L., Dalton, M. A., Adachi-Mejia, A. M., Longacre, M. R., & Beach, M. L. (2008). Longitudinal study of viewing smoking in movies and initiation of smoking by children. *Pediatrics, 121*(1), 15–21.

Villiard, H., & Moreno, M. A. (2012). Fitness on Facebook: Advertisements generated in response to profile content. *Cyberpsychology, Social Networking, and Behavior, 15*(10), 564–568.

Wallace, P., Linke, S., Murray, E., McCambridge, J., & Thompson, S. (2006). A randomized controlled trial of an interactive web-based intervention for reducing alcohol consumption. *Journal of Telemedicine and Telecare, 12*, 52–54.

Walther, J. B., & Parks, M. R. (2002). Cues filtered out, cues filtered in: Computer mediated communication and relationships. In M. L. Knapp, J. A. Daly, & G. R. Miller (Eds.), *The handbook of interpersonal communication* (pp. 529–563). Thousand Oaks, CA: Sage.

Whitehill, J. M., Brockman, L. N., & Moreno, M. A. (2013). "Just talk to me": Communicating with college students about depression disclosures on Facebook. *Journal of Adolescent Health, 52*(1), 122–127.

Wood, M. D., Read, J. P., Mitchell, R. E., & Brand, N. H. (2004). Do parents still matter? Parent and peer influences on alcohol involvement among recent high school graduates. *Psychology of Addictive Behaviors, 18*(1), 19–30.

Zivin, K., Eisenberg, D., Gollust, S. E., & Golberstein, E. (2009). Persistence of mental health problems and needs in a college student population. *Journal of Affective Disorders, 117*(3), 180–185.

17

Exploring Disclosure and Privacy in a Digital Age

Risks and Benefits

Karin Archer,[1] Emily Christofides,[2]
Amanda Nosko,[1] and Eileen Wood[1]

[1]*Wilfrid Laurier University*
[2]*University of Guelph*

Creating and sustaining relationships with others is a critical component of healthy emotional and social well-being. To develop and sustain close, intimate relationships, individuals must strike a fine balance between sharing personal information and experiences and maintaining personal privacy and emotional distance (Altman & Taylor, 1973). The advent of online social media and social networking sites has challenged our ways of thinking and behaving when it comes to balancing disclosure and privacy because online platforms offer such a wide array of options (e.g., visual, verbal, creative) for depicting personal information as well as a distribution network that far exceeds traditional face-to-face interaction contexts. For example, users of social networking sites must ask themselves what information should or should not be shared (a task that is also true for traditional face-to-face and online contexts), and they must consider how best to share their highly personal information *as well as* who might be privy to the information they provide. These latter considerations make decisions about disclosure and privacy substantially more elaborate and complex than in traditional face-to-face interactions.

Researchers across a wide variety of disciplines including education, psychology, and business have investigated how individuals navigate the balance between sharing information and exercising control to avoid over-disclosure of information in online social media contexts. Overall, social media sites appear to present a paradox for users (Acoca, 2008; Coe, Weijs, Muise, Christofides, & Desmarais, 2011; Kogan, Schoenfeld-Tacher, Simon, & Viera, 2010; Nosko & Wood, 2011; Nosko et al., 2012). For example, even though users boast a strong desire for privacy (Tufekci, 2008), they often fail to employ available mechanisms to protect their personal information (Archer et al., 2014; Debatin, Lovejoy, Horn, & Hughes, 2009; Liu, Gummadi, Krishnamurthy, & Mislove, 2011; Nosko et al., 2012; Nosko, Wood, & Molema, 2010). In this chapter we will explore how this paradox between controlling privacy and using public,

The Wiley Handbook of Psychology, Technology, and Society, First Edition. Edited by Larry D. Rosen, Nancy A. Cheever, and L. Mark Carrier.

wide-distribution platforms arises. In addition, we will examine the social impact of disclosure online. Finally, we will review mechanisms that might resolve conflicts between the desire to engage fully with social media and yet protect individuals from the very real risks from over-disclosure.

In examining the issues of disclosure and privacy in online social networking contexts, it is important to understand what is meant by terms such as self-disclosure and privacy, and to identify key disclosure and privacy theories. After introducing the background, the evolution of these theories from traditional face-to-face contexts to online settings will be addressed. The benefits and risks associated with usage of social media and social networking sites will then be discussed in conjunction with disclosure and privacy attitudes and behaviors. Finally, suggestions will be made for interventions and educational programs designed to target over-disclosure and to encourage people to protect their privacy.

Self-Disclosure

Self-disclosure generally refers to any message conveyed about the individual, and can be subdivided into various types. First, there are two broad categories of self-disclosure. Self-disclosure that consists of general facts about a person, such as "My favorite color is blue," or "My family comes from Germany," is called *descriptive self-disclosure* (Derlega, Metts, Petronio, & Margulis, 1993). Messages that convey expressions about feelings and opinions are called *evaluative self-disclosures* and include statements such as "I hate writing exams," or "I feel angry that you said that to me." Aside from the two broad categories of self-disclosure, it is also useful to distinguish the type of self-disclosure based on the referent; that is, whether the disclosure involves divulging information about one's relationships and interactions with others (*relational* self-disclosure) or information about oneself (*personal* self-disclosure). Because of these distinctions, Petronio (2002) suggests that personal disclosure of private information should be conceived of in the more comprehensive fashion that includes all of the information above.

Information sharing is not just an important factor in social relationships; rather, it serves as a necessary foundation in the vast array of social relationships we encounter in our lives (Fisher, 1986). Disclosure builds trust and enhances a sense of understanding among disclosing partners (Laurenceau, Feldman Barrett, & Pietromonaco, 1998; Rubin, 1975). Typically, face-to-face communication involves a gradual increase in reciprocal disclosure among interaction partners (Emerson, 1976; Homans, 1958; Worthy, Gary, & Kahn, 1969), where the depth and intimacy of information shared increases as relationship closeness increases (Cozby, 1973; Taylor, Altman, & Sorrentino, 1969).

Although several theories have been derived with the purpose of characterizing and clarifying the self-disclosure process in face-to-face interactions (Altman & Taylor, 1973; Gouldner, 1960), the nature of online communication warrants consideration of alternative factors that might not have arisen in the past. For example, traditional face-to-face interactions occur in real time, are synchronous, include both verbal and body language communication, and typically involve one-on-one or small group contexts. Online contexts are not bound by these parameters. In online contexts, interactions are often text-based and asynchronous, and can involve large groups of individuals ranging from close friends to strangers. These important contextual differences between offline (traditional face-to-face) and online contexts spurred researchers to adapt existing theories and introduce new theories of disclosure. One of the forerunners, Walther (1992, 1996), developed two theories to explain disclosure in online media: social information processing (SIP) theory and hyper-personal theory. Although these theories were initially established at a time when online communication was more limited (often limited to communications such as email), more recently, these theories have been extended to include a broader scope of computer-mediated communications including social networking contexts (e.g., Tong, Van Der Heide, Langwell, & Walther, 2008; Walther, 2006, 2011; Walther, Van Der Heide, Kim, Westerman, & Tong, 2008). These two theories are outlined below.

Walther's Online Disclosure Theories

Social information processing (SIP) theory   Walther's (1992) SIP theory rests on the assumption that impression formation and the "getting to know" process is based on a small initial amount of information in text-based form. Walther argues that while there may be a lack of non-verbal cues (e.g., gestures) in online communication, this does not necessarily imply that online relationships are less meaningful or weaker than offline relationships. Impressions can still be made, and relationships can be formed based on the online verbal cues (Walther, 2006; Walther et al., 2008). Walther (1996; Walther et al., 2008) suggests that people are inherently good at assessing both verbal and non-verbal cues, and that people can establish affinity (liking) for their online partner, despite the lack of non-verbal cues. Finally, Walther (1996, 2006) asserts that while computer-mediated relationships develop at a slower pace, they are equally as strong as offline relationships.

Online hyper-personal theory   Following from social information processing theory, Walther (1996) established the hyper-personal theory of online relationship formation. Walther coined the term "hyper-personal" because he noted that, in some instances, communication online could surpass the level of intimacy found in traditional face-to-face interactions. This theory applies to relationships formed and maintained solely online, and focuses on electronic communication that is devoted to social or recreational interaction (e.g., email communication, chat rooms, social networking). Despite the argument that offline communication is far more intimate and of a higher subjective quality than online communication (e.g., via email) (Sproull & Keisler, 1986), Walther (1996, 2011) argued that online communication, and relationships formed as a result, are just as, and in some cases more, intimate than relationships offline.

Walther (1996, 2011) notes that "selective self-presentation" may occur online, whereby senders of information online may opt to convey more favorable aspects of the self. He identified two elements common in online interaction that may enhance self-presentation: *asynchronous communication* and *reduced cues*.

Asynchronous communication refers to interactions where there is a time lag between messages. Walther argued that the time lag makes this form of communication more relaxed, and thus allows for more efficient allocation of cognitive resources. In addition, he asserted that "asynchronous verbal communication is more inter-subjective and less egocentric than in unplanned (spontaneous) discourse" (Walther, 1996, p. 26).

For example, online users have more time to plan their responses and, as such, may reflect to a greater degree on how their responses may be perceived or affect the receiver of the information (Walther, 2011). In turn, communication may be more clear and respectful to the audience. Further, Walther posits that first impressions are highly controlled and manageable in online communication. Because information is verbal and conveyed through text in most cases and often lacks physical cues that users cannot otherwise control, editing and self-censorship occur more often. As a result, the receiver of the information may over-attribute the reduced cues provided by the sender, and form a more positive image of their partner (Spears & Lea, 1992). This "over-attribution" occurs when the receiver of information builds stereotypical impressions of the partner. Given minimal amounts of information to base impressions on, receivers over-rely on verbal cues in the absence of physical ones, and may idealize the interaction partner. While this may seem detrimental to relationship formation, Walther argued that hyper-personal interaction has the potential to be highly rewarding. Indeed, Schlenker (1985) suggests that individuals tend to experience more satisfaction with their relationships when "their desired identity images are supported, validated or elicited" (p. 93).

In summary, what is common across theories is that features available through online disclosure have the potential to foster the foundations of solid relationships even though the format of interactions may differ from traditional face-to-face interactions. In addition, online relationships may permit more control and consistency in the presentation of one's own identity and yield socially desirable and effective communications (Buote, Wood, & Pratt, 2009; Walther, 2011).

Privacy

Privacy can be thought of in a number of different ways, and indeed, there is no one universally accepted definition of privacy. Debates about the nature of privacy have become especially pronounced in countries such as the United States where lawmakers face the challenge of balancing individual privacy rights with legislation and controls intended to protect the public (Westin, 2003). Concerns such as those facing American lawmakers have encouraged discussions regarding what should constitute reasonable expectations of privacy – especially with respect to contexts involving technology and the Internet (Rosen, 2001; Steeves, 2008), whether privacy exists as a concept that is distinct from other related concepts (see DeCew, 2006), and whether consumers value their own private data (Rauhofer, 2008). Despite the breadth of these discussions, understanding privacy as the ability to control access to one's personal information has surfaced regularly in theories of privacy (Altman, 1975; Westin, 1967). These theories are explained in the following section.

Privacy Theory

Privacy regulation theory Privacy has been thought of primarily as either a process of regulating interpersonal boundaries (Altman, 1975) or as the management of one's information (Westin, 1967). Privacy as the regulation of interpersonal boundaries is an approach that was first explored by Altman in 1975 but has since been clarified and expanded (Petronio, 2002, 2010). Altman's theory of privacy describes how environmental and interpersonal circumstances motivate and, in turn, are affected by privacy-related behavior. Altman describes privacy as a dialectic process, whereby individuals seek an ideal balance between being open and closed to interactions with others at any given time. Dialectic in this case refers to the tension between the desire to be open with other people and the desire to be closed or private. Altman, Vinsel, and Brown's (1981) perspective on dialectic processes is that they involve three core components: *opposing factors* (such as the desire to be open and closed); together the factors are part of *a unified system*; and the system is *dynamic* (meaning that the balance of these factors may shift over time). Burgoon (1982) also believed that privacy is dialectic and found that in response to physical, interactional, psychological, and informational privacy violations, people use specific behaviors to restore privacy. For example, Burgoon and colleagues (1989) found that people were most likely to use tactics such as abbreviating a conversation, looking away, or changing the topic in order to return their privacy to a desired level.

Communication privacy management (CPM) theory Petronio's (2002, 2010) work on CPM draws on privacy regulation theory as well as Altman and Taylor's (1973) earlier research on the process of relationship formation. This theory approaches privacy as a process for managing people's interface between themselves and others. According to Petronio, people have privacy boundaries around themselves and their personal information. When the information is theirs alone, they set the terms of their boundaries and of how and when these boundaries can change. When information is shared, the privacy boundary changes such that the information becomes jointly owned. There may be rules for the way the information can be shared, how it can be discussed among those in the know, what can be shared with people outside the boundaries, and who can do the sharing. Social groups also have their own idiosyncratic privacy norms, which are quickly learned by new members of the group, though if these norms are not well understood these individuals may have disagreements, or experience *boundary turbulence*.

Child, Petronio, Agyeman-Budu, and Westermann (2011) found that people who write blogs sometimes post information only to regret it later as a result of the way the information might be perceived, fear of the possibility of revealing their identity, and potential relationship, legal, or employment consequences. These fears led people to remove posted information (called blog scrubbing) when they experienced *boundary turbulence*, which occurred when the privacy rules that individuals employed when posting on their blog no longer protected their privacy to the degree that they desired. As a result of this mismatch, bloggers changed their privacy rules and revised previous blogs according to the new privacy rules in order to better fit their new privacy needs.

Recent research confirms that there are a number of conscious, reflective ways in which people manage their privacy, including an assessment of the information to be revealed, the relationship within which the disclosure is to take place, the context, and the potential risks and benefits (Christofides, 2012). However, many of the decisions people make in regards to their privacy are largely impulsive or unplanned, and nonconscious influences also play a role. As a result, people sometimes make choices about their privacy based on how they feel in a particular situation or respond to another person, rather than using what they state as their approach to privacy. These unconscious influences help to explain the mismatch between beliefs and behavior, called the privacy paradox, which has so commonly been observed in the privacy literature (see Norberg, Horne, & Horne, 2007). However, it is important to note that impulsive disclosures are not always beneficial and can in fact be detrimental to people and to their relationships (Hawk, 2007).

Information privacy Westin (1967) examined the informational aspect of privacy, both in terms of what can be kept private and the purpose of doing so. Similar to the boundary views of privacy, this information control perspective approaches private information as something about which people want to make their own decisions regarding whether their information is shared or not. Westin was one of the first to outline the types and functions of privacy, a topic that was later researched by Pedersen (1979, 1997). Westin identified four types of privacy – solitude, intimacy, anonymity, and reserve – which differ in terms of who one is interacting with, and the level of openness. In solitude, the person is alone, and excludes others from their thoughts and personal space. In intimacy, the person is open, but they are only open with a specific person or target group of individuals. In anonymity, the person is in a public space and in the presence of other people but, because their identity is not known to these other people, they can experience a sense of privacy. With the final type of privacy, reserve, the person is in the company of other people, but they hold back certain information in order to maintain a desired level of privacy. In the online environment, all of these types of privacy apply, except perhaps for solitude. For example, Marwick and boyd (2010) describe how young people use specific language to direct comments to friends but make the meaning incomprehensible to strangers and parents, thereby creating a sense of intimacy in an environment that is normally considered public.

In addition to defining types of privacy, Westin (1967) also identifies the various functions of privacy. For example, he found that privacy provides personal autonomy, emotional release, self-evaluation, and limited or protected communication. Each type of privacy is thought to serve a different function for the person. According to Foddy and Finighan (1980), the purpose of privacy is related to the self and one's ability to maintain a specific role identity. The more two people interact, the more they develop ideas and expectations about each other's role and identity. The way a person is viewed is in a sense negotiated with the person with whom they are interacting, and must be negotiated with every new connection. In this way, privacy enables people to maintain an identity by controlling information that contradicts their expected role or desired identity. Thus, the purpose of privacy is to enable people to maintain specific identities and control information that might interfere with other people's acceptance of their identity claim. The information that people share is important in helping them define their identity, and what is kept private similarly helps by keeping identity-contradictory information out of view. For example, young adults with chronic illness have been found to keep information about their illness to themselves on social media in order to maintain the image of being a "regular" teenager to their online friends (Van der Velden & El Emam, 2013).

This desire to maintain different identities is one potential concern with social media, because open, available online outlets do not easily allow people to keep their different identities separate. This effect, called context collapse (Marwick & boyd, 2010), means that the various contexts that people inhabit are all merged into one online environment. In the offline world, privacy mechanisms help people to define their identity with specific others in the sense that they can keep private information that might be counter to their identity with that person but reveal it to others for whom it would not seem inconsistent. For example, a teenager may present one identity to a parent and another to a peer. However, online, it is difficult to separate information for different audiences and prevent unwanted sharing of information, which leads to some of the risks of revealing information online, a point we will return to shortly.

Benefits of Online Disclosure

People perceive many benefits in sharing information online, as evidenced by the growth and popularity in methods of online communication. For example, Facebook alone has more than 945 million active users, a figure that increases daily (Facebook, 2014). Nearly 80% of Internet users use social networks and blogs (Nielsen, 2013). This phenomenon is not limited to young people or to any specific country, as various forms of social communication media are becoming more commonly used worldwide and across ages. There are a number of reasons why people might find these environments so engaging. Nguyen, Bin, and Campbell (2012) identified context as an important factor that influences the degree of disclosure that occurs between communication partners. When compared to offline contexts, disclosure online initially involves a high frequency of information that is divulged over a short period of time (Joinson, 2001; Locke & Gilbert, 1995; Schouten, Valkenburg, & Peter, 2007; Tidwell & Walther, 2002; Walther, 1996; Wood, Nosko, Desmarais, Ross, & Irvine, 2006). Perceived psychological distance fostered by features of the online context (e.g., accessibility and asynchronicity of communication or a lag time between messages) may explain greater initial disclosure. Due to these features, online users may be less restrained and feel more relaxed, which may encourage less inhibition when sharing information (Suler, 2004).

Increased information sharing online can produce beneficial outcomes for people in their relationships with others. They are able to more easily access information, build and maintain relationships, explore their identity, and share information, pictures, and experiences (boyd, 2007; boyd & Ellison, 2007; Ellison, Steinfield, & Lampe, 2007). Just as increased access to information provides relationship benefits, it can also be instrumental to searching for and finding career-related information and opportunities. In addition, informal learning contexts, while often overlooked as credible and important learning environments, can promote cognitive and social development (Willoughby, Hui, & Wood, 2008). Social media encourage informal learning by providing a forum for collaborative learning, learning from peers, and providing and responding to peer feedback (Ajjan & Hartshorne, 2008; Bartlett-Bragg, 2006; Mason, 2006; Mejías, 2005; Selwyn, 2007). Many students view social media as safe, appealing, and an outlet that encourages active and engaged learning (Barrett, 2006; Willoughby & Wood, 2008). Benefits can also be found in formal learning contexts. In classrooms, for example, students have the opportunity to join discussion or interest groups on social networking sites, and share verbal and visual information, ideas, and opinions related to classroom material, which provides an ideal forum for learning from others (Bandura, 2001).

Risks of Online Disclosure

Not all outcomes of social networking are positive. Over-disclosing may place people at risk for a number of negative consequences (Gross & Aquisti, 2005; Nosko, Wood, & Molema, 2010). Social media and social networking sites rely heavily on self-disclosure and user openness. The success of these sites, including Facebook for example, is dependent on the user sharing as much information as possible, as quickly as possible (Schouten et al., 2007). In fact, users are prompted to divulge highly personal information when they first open a personal profile and they may not be able to experience the benefits of online social media without the corresponding risks (Christofides, Muise, & Desmarais, 2012b). The problem is that this highly encouraged disclosure may not be accompanied by considerations regarding privacy protection (Saint, 2010). In addition, there is evidence that increasing the ability to control disclosures, one of the foundational aspects of privacy, can actually lead people to disclose more information (Brandimarte, Acquisti, & Loewenstein, 2013). Therefore, even when users perceive that they control what they are sharing, they may be encouraged to over-disclose.

Given the vast array of information that can be shared and the number of users, concerns regarding security and privacy are a recurring issue (Acoca, 2008). Some concerns involve potential threats to personal safety from the abundance of information that is available and accessible about an individual on their online profile. Specifically, identity theft can become an issue if users provide too much information (e.g., birth date, address, phone, full name). Similarly, users can become targets or vulnerable to physical threats such as stalking, or the possibility of social risk as a function of self-identification with minority or stigmatized groups (Nosko et al., 2012).

A recent study of Facebook use among teenagers identified five key types of negative experiences resulting from their use of Facebook (Christofides, Muise, & Desmarais, 2012a). These experiences included interpersonal issues such as bullying and meanness, unwanted contact, over-exposure or accidental exposure, and misunderstandings. Youth and children have been shown to experience risks associated with being exposed to unwanted or inappropriate content or contact, or by engaging in inappropriate conduct themselves (Hasebrink, Livingstone, Haddon, & Ólafsson, 2009). While adults may also experience some of these negative consequences, they additionally have the potential for negative impacts on their professional and romantic relationships. The following sections provide a more detailed explanation of these risks.

Interpersonal relationships Disclosure and privacy behavior online has the potential to negatively impact people's interpersonal relationships. Individuals may experience conflicts with parents, with peers, or with their relationship partners. For example, Youn (2005) found that adolescents who disclosed information online sometimes regretted their disclosures, especially when they led to conflicts with their parents. The information that people disclose online may also negatively impact their romantic relationships. In a recent study of emerging adults, those who spent more time on Facebook were more likely to feel jealous in response to ambiguous information found on partners' profiles, and this jealousy, in some cases, negatively impacted their romantic relationships (Muise, Christofides, & Desmarais, 2009). The reasons for misunderstandings vary but one issue involves the availability of information presented. Each user may only have access to one side of an online conversation or one particular interaction within a relationship. This limited information can lead users to infer missing information or misunderstand the broader context.

The outlet or medium chosen to share information may also negatively impact interpersonal relationships. For example, in a recent study we examined how people judged potential student mentors when the mentor's information was disclosed through different media (Christofides, Wood, Benn, Desmarais, & Westfall, 2013).

When disclosures were presented in an offline format (in a paper diary), the mentors were judged to be significantly more private individuals than when the same disclosures were made in any of the online media tested (online diary, blog, or email). Interestingly, gender also had an impact on judgments about the discloser, with women giving more positive ratings than men, but only for more subjective measures such as the mentor's likeability, or how likely they would be to disclose in turn (no differences were found between the way men and women rated the other person's privacy). Judgments of likeability were important as qualitative findings indicated that once people decided that they did not like the discloser, they ceased to provide evaluations on the professionalism of the mentor (Christofides, Wood, Desmarais, & Nosko, 2013).

Together, the research suggests that the impact of sharing information via social media on interpersonal relationships is complex (Walther, 2011). Too much or too little disclosure or privacy can lead to misconceptions and negative evaluations of the discloser that may impact the development or maintenance of relationships (Marshall, Bejanyan, Di Castro, & Lee, 2013; Utz & Buekeboom, 2011).

Professionalism and employment   Increasingly, personal and professional identities are blurred when people use social media for both personal interactions and professional purposes and there may be negative consequences to these online disclosures. For example, in two recent studies of early-career veterinary professionals (Coe et al., 2011) and students in a professional veterinary program (Weijs, Coe, Christofides, Muise, & Desmarais, 2013), researchers found that most people shared more on their public profiles than would typically be expected in a veterinarian–client relationship and some of this information had the potential to reflect poorly on them as professionals and on the profession itself. Of the profiles the researchers attempted to view, 70–77% were publicly accessible and of those, 36% of students and 54% of veterinarians were classified as having medium levels of disclosure. Information in this category included home phone numbers, sexual orientation, and other personal details that clients would not generally know. Given that people use the Internet to search for information about the professionals they employ (Kogan et al., 2010), posting personal information in a publicly accessible forum might result in clients and potential clients making decisions about the professionals based on personal details that are not directly relevant to professional competence. People are unlikely to know that their clients are using this type of information to assess them because clients may simply choose to take their business elsewhere.

In addition, 21% of the professionals and 32% of the students posted information on their profiles that undermines their image as a professional and may even violate their code of ethics. This type of behavior potentially impacts their employment, as in recent news reports of professionals, such as teachers, losing their jobs over social media content (Alamenciak & Fong, 2012). In addition, over-disclosure of personal information may also impact the potential to be hired, as employers increasingly use social media content to assess employability (Jobvite, 2012).

Education   Cyberbullying, harassment, deliberate embarrassment, liability issues, and threats to academic integrity (i.e., cheating) are potential risks inherent in the integration of social media in educational contexts (Feinberg & Robey, 2008; King, 2002; Nixon, 2004). In some cases such violations may be a product of ignorance regarding expectations, especially as many educational institutions as well as students grapple to keep abreast of new technologies and their implications. For example, a Canadian university student created a Facebook study group that allowed other students to post homework questions and answers online and was subsequently accused of academic cheating (CBC News, 2008), even though the student argued that he did not know this was unacceptable. Whether transgressions are made through ignorance or intent, their increasing presence requires that educators provide students with explicit instructions regarding expectations as a prerequisite to using the Internet and social networking as part of their courses (Ribble, Bailey, & Ross, 2004). Setting "appropriate" expectations for social networking, however, is not a simple task as individuals vary in their comfort levels regarding privacy and disclosure, and monitoring students can be challenging. In an effort to assist educators in establishing rudimentary rules, some schools are creating common protocols regarding digital citizenship, or what is appropriate social behavior when online (Ribble et al., 2004). In many cases, students and parents are required to sign agreements acknowledging these protocols. Adherence to general principles of good conduct provides a safer, more explicit understanding for how social networking is to be integrated into the curriculum. These are first steps, however, and at present many schools do not have established protocols in place, leaving educators to develop and monitor online activities on their own.

Solutions to Problem Uses

Educators, businesses, and individuals clearly see a benefit in the use of social media (Youn, 2005). There are many ways in which users can be protected while using social media and social networking sites; however, any solution must address disclosure and privacy together. Avoiding disclosure altogether is neither possible nor appropriate in today's online world, nor would this solution be conducive to the many positive outcomes possible from social media. However, limited disclosure, particularly for sensitive information, is an important first step. In addition, once information is disclosed, mechanisms must be in place and utilized to allow users to maintain a level of privacy that is comfortable for them. Solutions that attempt to alter people's online experience, specifically toward disclosure and privacy, can come in a number of forms, including social solutions, technical solutions, and legal solutions (Barnes, 2006).

Social Solutions

Being aware of the risks and understanding consequences is a key in online protection. Research has shown that higher awareness of consequences contributes to less disclosure and more use of privacy settings (Christofides et al., 2012b). In one study, exposure to a news story of a young woman who was tracked down and approached by a news reporter using only information she had posted on Facebook was sufficient to limit people's disclosure when creating online profiles (Nosko et al., 2012). In a related study participants were twice as likely to change their privacy settings if they were victims of personal privacy invasion (Debatin et al., 2009). While actual exposure to harmful situations is, for obvious reasons, not ideal, it seems the sharing of other people's negative experiences can also be beneficial in changing online behavior.

Awareness can also be enhanced through direct instruction. For example, companies and school boards often hire internal personnel or external companies to conduct media safety training. This training provides instruction regarding risks associated with using social online media and steps that can be taken to protect against these risks. Effective instructional formats often employ direct and explicit instruction (Wood, Willoughby, Specht, Stern-Cavalcante, & Child, 2002). Direct/explicit instructional approaches use highly structured materials that are presented incrementally, accompanied by explanations, examples, and hands-on experience at each step (Rosenshine, 1987). Instruction can be face to face or through well-designed video-based presentations. We recently evaluated the effectiveness of a video-based presentation that employed a direct instruction approach to increase awareness of risks associated with disclosure and teach people how to use privacy settings for Facebook (Archer et al., 2014). Both experienced and novice Facebook users participated, with some being required to watch the presentation while others did not. Participants were then given time to create a new Facebook account or work on their existing account. Overall, participants who viewed the video materials increased their use of privacy settings. Clearly, providing basic information through short instructional interventions can be effective.

A number of online resources are already available for self-instruction. For example, the ad campaign "Social Media Survival" (Facecrooks, 2012) increases awareness of scams and spam, identity theft, cyberbullying, malware and viruses, and privacy. Similarly, several government sites provide Internet resources to educate people, especially children and parents, on Internet safety as well as assisting other organizations in doing so as well (e.g., www.cyber-safety.com).

Technical Solutions

There are a number of ways in which technology can be used to protect social network users from disclosure or privacy threats or violations. More drastic technical solutions involve disabling or banning social media/social networking. For example, some schools and workplaces place explicit restrictions or in some cases a complete ban on social networking sites and they are disabled at the IT level so that students or employees cannot access these sites. The problem with this solution is that the benefits of using these sites are also lost. Additionally, while this may prevent use of these sites during school or work hours, it has no impact on what is done after hours. The context collapse that occurs in an online environment (Marwick & boyd, 2010) blurs the line between people's professional and personal lives such that online information exchanges that occur outside of school or work hours impact people's lives at school or work. Therefore, employing these strategies is not necessarily effective in minimizing the potential risks overall.

Less drastic and highly relevant solutions are often being offered through social networking platforms themselves. For example, social networking sites such as Facebook have privacy settings that allow users to apply restrictions to specific pieces of information they disclose. The problem to date is not the lack of mechanisms to protect privacy but rather that users often fail to employ these settings (Gross & Acquisti, 2005). For example, one study found that from 800 randomly accessed profiles, approximately half were publicly accessible to anyone (Nosko et al., 2010).

Legal Solutions

The lack of geographical barriers online makes the enforcement of any laws regarding online activities very difficult. Online crimes can be committed from anywhere in the world and technology can allow perpetrators to hide their location and identity to avoid getting caught. Despite the challenges, various countries are beginning to form "cyberlaws" that govern online interactions. Also, many online sites, specifically social media sites, now have privacy policies in place to notify users of their legal rights and obligations. These documents are often lengthy and written in legal jargon, and the majority of users state that they do not read this policy (Acquisti & Gross, 2006).

Interestingly, social media sites are also being used as a new tool by police enforcement agencies for identifying and prosecuting criminals – even when the criminal actions do not involve online social networking *per se*. For example, police officers in Vancouver, Canada used images posted through social networking sites to identify and charge rioters in 2011. Researchers are not only examining the increased police surveillance but also the involvement of citizens through social media in conducting "pseudo-police work" (Crawford, 2012).

Some professionals are experiencing added legislation and rules by their colleges, governing bodies, and legal sources as a function of the challenges associated with maintaining a professional persona separate from a personal one in social networking contexts. For example, the Canadian Supreme Court ruled that teachers' actions off duty are relevant to their role as educators and, as a result of this ruling, a provincial teaching advisory board established social media guidelines for teachers to follow. These guidelines included not accepting or initiating "friend" requests with students or parents on any social networking site; avoiding behavior online that would be deemed inappropriate in person; and notifying parents in advance of any intended classroom use of social media (Council of the Ontario College of Teachers, 2011). Clearly, the increasing merging of online and offline contexts already has involved, and most likely will continue to involve, legislation that guides and protects users.

Responsibility for Safety in Social Networking Contexts

Already we have identified instructional interventions, technical interventions, legislation, and protocols all designed to encourage safer use of information distributed through social media. These interventions highlight a critical but controversial question – who is responsible for keeping people safe in online contexts? Research and evidence-based practice suggest that end users, the social media companies, the Internet service providers (ISPs), governments, and law enforcement agencies all impact on safety issues.

The Individual

While it is easy to lay the responsibility on the end users, often users' lack of knowledge leads them to over-disclose and fail to secure the privacy of their information. This lack of knowledge can include perceptions that the online environment is "safe" (Barrett, 2006; Brady & Libit, 2006; Hass, 2006; Kornblum & Marklein, 2006; McCarty, Prawitz, Derscheid, & Montgomery, 2011; Read, 2006), failure to read privacy policies (Acquisti & Gross, 2006; Cranor, Reagle, & Ackerman, 1999), and an inability to understand privacy policies (Berendt, Günther, & Spiekermann, 2005; Jensen & Potts, 2004; Micheti, Burkell, & Steeves, 2010; Milne & Culnan, 2004). With the rapid growth in technology there are generations of people for whom social media and social networking are completely new entities coupled with an online environment that is also unfamiliar. For many older adults, or newcomers to social networks, there is simply little or no awareness regarding potential risks from information disclosure and there is also a parallel lack of knowledge about how to maintain privacy of information (Nyemba, Mhakure, Chigona, Mukwasi, & Mosiane, 2011). Clearly, simple, explicit instructional interventions such as those noted above need to be available to ensure that individuals have the knowledge and skills to be able to make "safer" decisions when using social networking tools.

The Social Media Companies

Some activist groups believe social media companies are responsible for the safety of users. For example, The Red Hood Project (http://www.redhoodproject.com/) strives to hold the social media companies responsible for ensuring consumer protection. Social media companies and, more broadly, Internet-related companies have initiated attempts to increase consumer protection. For example, in 2011, the Coalition, comprising 28 Internet-based companies including social media companies such as Facebook and Google, expressed their commitment to taking positive action to make the Internet a safer place for children. Some actions listed in the Coalition's statement of purpose include simple and robust reporting tools for users, age-appropriate privacy settings, wider use of content classification, wider availability and use of parental control, and effective takedown of child abuse material (European Commission, 2011). Individual companies have also employed their own strategies. For example, Facebook has established an online safety center. This page has resources for parents, teachers, and teens on safe use of social media. They also describe how to use a new feature they call "social reporting." This allows users to report offensive material and encourages them to seek help from their friends or peers. In recent years social media companies have been taking steps toward online safety. However, it is still not clear how well these strategies work.

Internet Service Providers

ISPs' main response to the online issues is filtering. The major problem with filters is that none of them catches everything; therefore, solely relying on the ISP filter to catch any inappropriate material is not enough. In some countries, the United Kingdom for example, the possibility of an opt-in feature is being investigated, where the ISPs block inappropriate content in general unless the customer specifically asks for the block to be removed (CBC News, 2012). Requiring the customer to opt in to this content brings about obvious privacy issues in that customers are required to disclose that they would like access to this content. Such initiatives are promising but require more substantial investigation.

Police Force and Government

The United Kingdom has had a Child Exploitation and Online Protection Centre since 2006 through which they have urged online companies, such as social media companies, to install help buttons on their sites. These "help" buttons assist users by providing them with further advice about online security and making them aware of where they can report harassment. The Child Exploitation and Online Protection Centre is a national police agency that works with police officers and other child protection professionals in the community to keep children safe online (Sher, 2012).

The involvement of the government in regulating the Internet is not entirely supported either. For example, social media outlets such as Facebook were integral in Egypt's revolution, which is a prime example of where government involvement could be problematic for the public (Sutter, 2011). If governments determine what information is "potentially threatening" they may prevent the kind of social uprising and politically threatening material that was so critical for Egypt's revolution from being distributed. Overall, governments and policing agencies can provide some needed support while retaining the positive aspects of social media.

Conclusion

Social media clearly provide opportunities for initiating, developing, and maintaining social relationships. These relationships can foster individual growth and well-being, further education, and influence policy and government. However, among these tremendous possibilities for growth, there remain considerable concerns in ensuring the physical, emotional, and social safety of online users particularly when it comes to the fine balance between encouraging disclosure to build and sustain relationships and ensuring personal privacy.

Our summary of the extant research makes clear that although some offline and online disclosure and privacy concerns overlap, many do not. Hence, online disclosure and privacy need to be considered as unique entities that require unique solutions to ensure maximum positive benefits with minimal risks. Not surprisingly, the solutions to best minimize risk require multiple levels of integrated support including individuals, parents, academics, educators, businesses (especially social media providers), policymakers, and governments. This will not be achieved easily. As online social media tools and use continue to expand, and younger users grow up in a world where information is not only easily accessible but more easily shared, there will need to be ongoing evaluation of the impact of online social media tools as well as sensitivity to potential changes in what is perceived as over-disclosure and what is meant by privacy. Research will be needed to ensure that current models and theories continue to adapt and reflect both offline and online social contexts accurately.

In addition, although current research clearly indicates that our online disclosures have the potential to impact others both positively and negatively as well as perceptions about us as disclosers, more research is needed to understand the nuances that support these perceptions. Outcomes from research need to be accessible to government agencies, companies, educators, parents, and individuals to enable the construction of reasonable and flexible policies to protect people online as well as to provide information for users so they can better understand potential risks and mechanisms that will allow them to make informed decisions regarding their disclosure and privacy.

While it is important that end users are aware of the risks and take the steps necessary to protect themselves, it is not always reasonable to expect users to understand the intricacies of how their online data could be used against them currently or in the future. For this reason, it is also important that social media companies and ISPs also play a role in the education and safety of their consumers. Providing users with the tools and protection needed to allow them to use social media outlets with less risk of negative consequences will allow opportunities for individuals, educators, and businesses to harness the benefits associated with social media.

References

Acoca, B. (2008). *Scoping paper on online identity theft*. Ministerial Background Report DSTI/ CP (2007) 3/FINAL. Retrieved May 27, 2009, from http://www.oecd.org/dataoecd/ 35/24/40644196.pdf

Acquisti, A., & Gross, R. (2006). Imagined communities: Awareness, information sharing, and privacy on the Facebook. In *6th Workshop on Privacy Enhancing Technologies* (pp. 36–58). Berlin, Germany: Springer.

Ajjan, H., & Hartshorne, R. (2008). Investigating faculty decisions to adopt Web 2.0 technologies: Theory and empirical tests. *The Internet and Higher Education, 11*(2), 71–80.

Alamenciak, T., & Fong, P. (2012, October 16). Ontario man fired from job over comment posted on memorial page to Amanda Todd. *The Toronto Star*. Retrieved December 1, 2014, from http://www.thestar.com/news/canada/2012/10/16/ontario_man_fired_ from_job_over_comment_posted_on_memorial_page_to_amanda_todd.html

Altman, I. (1975). *The environment and social behavior*. Belmont, CA: Wadsworth.

Altman, I., & Taylor, D. A. (1973). *Social penetration: The development of interpersonal relationships*. Oxford, UK: Holt, Rinehart & Winston.

Altman, I., Vinsel, A., & Brown, B. B. (1981). Dialectic conceptions in social psychology: An application to social penetration and privacy regulation. In L. Berkowitz (Ed.), *Advances in experimental social psychology* (Vol. *14*, pp. 107–160). New York, NY: Academic Press.

Archer, K., Wood, E., Nosko, A., De Pasquale, D., Molema, S., & Christofides, E. (2014). Disclosure and privacy settings on social networking sites: Evaluating an instructional intervention designed to promote informed information sharing. *International Journal of Cyber Behavior, Psychology and Learning, 4*(2), 1–19.

Bandura, A. (2001). Social cognitive theory of mass communication. *Media Psychology, 3*(3), 265–299.

Barnes, S. B. (2006). A privacy paradox: Social networking in the United States. *First Monday, 11*(9). Retrieved December 1, 2014, from http://firstmonday.org/ojs/index.php/fm/ article/view/1394/1312

Barrett, H. (2006, March). Researching and evaluating digital storytelling as a deep learning tool. *Society for Information Technology and Teacher Education International Conference 2006*(1), 647–654.

Bartlett-Bragg, A. (2006). Reflections on pedagogy: Reframing practice to foster informal learning with social software. Retrieved October 2, 2008, from http://www.dream.sdu. dk/uploads/files/Anne%20Bartlett-Bragg.pdf

Berendt, B., Günther, O., & Spiekermann, S. (2005). Privacy in e-commerce: Stated preferences vs. actual behavior. *Proceedings from the ACM Conference, 48*(4), 101–106.

boyd, d. m. (2007). Social network sites: Public, private, or what? *Knowledge Tree, 13*. Retrieved December 1, 2014, from http://www.danah.org/papers/KnowledgeTree.pdf

boyd, d. m., & Ellison, N. B. (2007). Social network sites: Definition, history, and scholarship. *Journal of Computer-Mediated Communication, 13*(1), article 11. Retrieved November 30, 2014, from http://jcmc.indiana.edu/vol13/issue1/boyd.ellison.html

Brady, E., & Libit, D. (2006, March 9). Alarms sound over athletes' Facebook time. *USA Today*. Retrieved December 1, 2014, from http://usatoday30.usatoday.com/tech/news/ internetprivacy/2006-03-08-athletes-websites_x.htm

Brandimarte, L., Acquisti, A., & Loewenstein, G. (2013). Misplaced confidences: Privacy and the control paradox. *Social Psychological and Personality Science, 4*(3), 340–347.

Buote, V., Wood, E., & Pratt, M. (2009). Exploring similarities and differences between online and offline friendships: The role of attachment style. *Computers in Human Behavior, 25,* 560–567.

Burgoon, J. K. (1982). Privacy and communication. In M. Burgoon (Ed.), *Communication yearbook* (Vol. 6). Beverley Hills, CA: Sage.

Burgoon, J. K., Parrott, R., Le Poire, B. A., Kelley, D. L., Walther, J. B., & Perry, D. (1989). Maintaining and restoring privacy through communication in different types of relationships. *Journal of Social and Personal Relationships, 6,* 131–158.

CBC News. (2008, March 6). Ryerson student fighting cheating charges for Facebook study group. Retrieved from http://www.cbc.ca/news/canada/toronto/ryerson-student-fighting-cheating-charges-for-facebook-study-group-1.731823

CBC News. (2012, June 28). Should Internet service providers block pornography by default? Retrieved from http://www.cbc.ca/news/yourcommunity/2012/06/should-internet-service-providers-block-pornography-by-default.html

Child, J. T., Petronio, S., Agyeman-Budu, E., & Westermann, D. A. (2011). Blog scrubbing: Exploring triggers that change privacy rules. *Computers in Human Behavior, 27,* 2017–2027.

Christofides, E. (2012). *A grounded theory of psychology of privacy management.* [Doctoral dissertation]. University of Guelph, Guelph, Ontario, Canada.

Christofides, E., Muise, A., & Desmarais, S. (2012a). Hey mom, what's on your Facebook? Comparing Facebook disclosure and privacy in adolescents and adults. *Social Psychological and Personality Science, 3*(1), 48–54.

Christofides, E., Muise, A., & Desmarais, S. (2012b). Risky disclosures on Facebook: The effect of having a bad experience on online behavior. *Journal of Adolescent Research, 27*(6), 714–731.

Christofides, E., Wood, E., Benn, A. C., Desmarais, S., & Westfall, K. (2013). The impact of gender and context of disclosure on judgments of a discloser. Manuscript submitted for publication.

Christofides, E., Wood, E., Desmarais, S., & Nosko, A. (2013). Other people's disclosures: Judgments, feelings, and behaviors in response to the disclosure of private information. Manuscript submitted for publication.

Coe, J. B., Weijs, C. A., Muise, A., Christofides, E., & Desmarais, S. (2011). Teaching veterinary professionalism in the Face(book) of change. *Journal of Veterinary Medical Education, 38*(4), 353–359.

Council of the Ontario College of Teachers. (2011, February 23). Professional advisory: Use of electronic communication and social media. Retrieved from http://www.oct.ca/resources/advisories/use-of-electronic-communication-and-social-media

Cozby, P. C. (1973). Self-disclosure: A literature review. *Psychological Bulletin, 79,* 73–91.

Cranor, L. F., Reagle, J., & Ackerman, M. S. (1999). *Beyond concern: Understanding net users' attitudes about online privacy.* AT&T Labs-Research Technical Report.

Crawford, T. (2012, October 31). Online vigilantes can slow police investigations, UBC study on Stanley Cup riot concludes. *Vancouver Sun.* Retrieved from http://www.vancouversun.com/sports/golf/Online+vigilantes+slow+police+investigations+study+Stanley+riot+concludes/7478872/story.html

Debatin, B., Lovejoy, J. P., Horn, A.-K., & Hughes, B. N. (2009). Facebook and online privacy: Attitudes, behaviors, and unintended consequences. *Journal of Computer-Mediated Communication, 15,* 83–108.

DeCew, J. (2006). Privacy. *Stanford encyclopedia of philosophy.* Retrieved January 6, 2013, from http://plato.stanford.edu/entries/privacy/

Derlega, V. J., Metts, S., Petronio, S., & Margulis, S. T. (1993). *Self-disclosure*. Newbury Park, CA: Sage.

Ellison, N. B., Steinfield, C., & Lampe, C. (2007). The benefits of Facebook "friends": Social capital and college students' use of online social network sites. *Journal of Computer-Mediated Communication, 12,* 1143–1168.

Emerson, R. M. (1976). Social exchange theory. *Annual Review of Sociology, 2,* 335–362.

European Commission. (2011, December 1). Statement of purpose. *CEO coalition to make a better Internet for kids*. Retrieved November 30, 2014, from http://ec.europa.eu/digital-agenda/self-regulation-better-internet-kids

Facebook. (2014). Our mission. Retrieved December 1, 2014, from http://newsroom.fb.com/company-info/

Facecrooks. (2012, November 13). Facecrooks launches "Social Media Survival" campaign to raise safety awareness. Retrieved December 1, 2014, from http://facecrooks.com/Scam-Watch/Facecrooks-Launches-%E2%80%98Social-Media-Survival%E2%80%99-Campaign-to-Raise-Safety-Awareness.html/

Feinberg, T., & Robey, N. (2008). Cyberbullying. *Principal Leadership, 9*(1), 10–14.

Fisher, C. D. (1986). Organizational socialization: An integrative review. In K. M. Rowland & G. R. Ferris (Eds.), *Research in personnel and human resources management* (Vol. 4, pp. 101–145). Greenwich, CT: JAI Press.

Foddy, W. H., & Finighan, W. R. (1980). The conception of privacy from a symbolic interaction perspective. *Journal of the Theory of Social Behavior, 10*(1), 1–18.

Gouldner, A. W. (1960). The norm of reciprocity: A preliminary statement. *American Sociological Review, 25,* 161–178.

Gross, R., & Acquisti, A. (2005). Information revelation and privacy in online social networks. In *WPES '05: Proceedings of the 2005 ACM Workshop on Privacy in the Electronic Society*, 71–80.

Hasebrink, U., Livingstone, S., Haddon, L., & Ólafsson, K. (2009). *Comparing children's online opportunities and risks across Europe: Crossnational comparisons for EU Kids Online*. London, UK: LSE, EU Kids Online.

Hass, N. (2006, January 8). In your Facebook.com. *The New York Times*. Retrieved from http://www.nytimes.com/2006/01/08/education/edlife/facebooks.html?pagewanted=all&_r=0

Hawk, S. (2007). Disclosures of maternal HIV infection to seronegative children: A literature review. *Journal of Social and Personal Relationships, 24*(5), 657–673.

Homans, G. C. (1958). Social behavior as exchange. *American Journal of Sociology, 63,* 597–606.

Jensen, C., & Potts, C. (2004). Privacy policies as decision-making tools: An evaluation of online privacy notices. In *Proceedings of the SIGCHI conference on human factors in computing systems*, 477.

Jobvite. (2012, July 9). Jobvite social recruiting survey finds over 90% of employers will use social recruiting in 2012. Jobvite press release. Retrieved from http://recruiting.jobvite.com/company/press-releases/2012/jobvite-social-recruiting-survey-2012/

Joinson, A. N. (2001). Self-disclosure in computer-mediated communication: The role of self-awareness and visual anonymity. *European Journal of Social Psychology, 31,* 177–192.

King, K. P. (2002). Identifying success in online teacher education and professional development. *The Internet and Higher Education, 5*(3), 231–246.

Kogan, L. R., Schoenfeld-Tacher, R., Simon, A. A., & Viera, A. I. (2010). The Internet and pet health information: Perceptions and behaviors of pet owners and veterinarians. *Internet Journal of Veterinary Medicine, 8*(1). Retrieved December 1, 2014, from https://ispub.com/IJVM/8/1/12921

Kornblum, J., & Marklein, M. B. (2006, March 8). What you say online could haunt you. *USA Today*. Retrieved from http://www.usatoday.com/tech/news/internetprivacy/2006-03-08-facebook-myspace_x.htm

Laurenceau, J.-P., Feldman Barrett, L. A., & Pietromonaco, P. R. (1998). Intimacy as an inter-personal process: The importance of self-disclosure and perceived partner responsiveness in interpersonal exchanges. *Journal of Personality and Social Psychology, 74*, 1238–1251.

Liu, Y., Gummadi, K., Krishnamurthy, B., & Mislove, A. (2011). Analyzing Facebook privacy settings: User expectations vs. reality. In *Proceedings of the 2011 ACM SIGCOMM confer-ence on Internet measurement,* 61–70.

Locke, S. D., & Gilbert, B. O. (1995). Method of psychological assessment, self disclosure, and experiential differences: A study of computer, questionnaire, and interview assessment for-mats. *Journal of Social Behavior and Personality, 10*, 255–263.

Marshall, T. C., Bejanyan, K., Di Castro, G., & Lee, R. A. (2013). Attachment styles as predictors of Facebook-related jealousy and surveillance in romantic relationships. *Personal Relationships, 20*(1), 1–22.

Marwick, A. E., & boyd, d. (2010). I tweet honestly, I tweet passionately: Twitter users, context collapse, and the imagined audience. *New Media and Society, 13*(1), 114–133.

Mason, R. (2006). Learning technologies for adult continuing education. *Studies in Continuing Education, 28*(2), 121–133.

McCarty, C., Prawitz, A. D., Derscheid, L. E., & Montgomery, B. (2011). Perceived safety and teen risk taking in online chat sites. *Cyberpsychology, Behavior, and Social Networking, 14*(3), 169–174.

Mejías, U. (2005). A nomad's guide to learning and social software. In *The Knowledge Tree, 7.* Retrieved December 1, 2014, from http://knowledgetree.flexiblelearning.net.au/edition07/html/la_mejias.html

Micheti, A., Burkell, J., & Steeves, V. (2010). Fixing broken doors: Strategies for drafting privacy policies young people can understand. *Bulletin of Science, Technology, and Society, 30*(2), 130–143.

Milne, G., & Culnan, M. J. (2004). Strategies for reducing online privacy risks: Why consumers read [Or don't read] online privacy notices. *Journal of Interactive Marketing, 18*(3), 15–29.

Muise, A., Christofides, E., & Desmarais, S. (2009). More information than you ever wanted to know: Does Facebook bring out the green-eyed monster of jealousy? *CyberPsychology and Behavior, 12*(4), 441–444.

Nguyen, M., Bin, Y. S., & Campbell, A. (2012). Comparing online and offline self-disclosure: A systematic review. *Cyberpsychology, Behavior, and Social Networking, 15*(2), 103–111.

Nielsen. (2013). The paid social media advertising report 2013. Retrieved from http://www.nielsen.com/us/en/reports/2013/the-paid-social-media-advertising-report-2013.html

Nixon, M. A. (2004). Cheating in cyberspace: Maintaining quality in online education. *AACE Journal, 12*(1), 85–99.

Norberg, P. A., Horne, D. R., & Horne, D. A. (2007). The privacy paradox: Personal information disclosure intentions versus behaviors. *Journal of Consumer Affairs, 31*(1), 100–126.

Nosko, A., & Wood, E. (2011). Learning in the digital age with social networking sites: Creating a profile. In B. White, I. King, & P. Tsang (Eds.), *Social media tools and platforms* (pp. 399–418). New York, NY: Springer.

Nosko, A., Wood, E., Kenney, M., Archer, K., De Pasquale, D., Molema, S., & Zivcakova, L. (2012). Examining priming and gender as a means to reduce risk in a social networking context: Can stories change disclosure and privacy setting use when personal profiles are constructed? *Computers in Human Behavior, 28*(6), 2067–2074.

Nosko, A., Wood, E., & Molema, S. (2010). All about me: Disclosure in online social network-ing profiles: The case of Facebook. *Computers in Human Behavior, 26*, 406–418.

Nyemba, E., Mhakure, S., Chigona, W., Mukwasi, C., & Mosiane, S. (2011). Golden baby-boomers' perceptions of online social networking sites. *International Journal of Applications in Technology, 2*(3), 695–703.

Pedersen, D. M. (1979). Dimensions of privacy. *Perceptual and Motor Skills, 48*, 1291–1297.

Pedersen, D. M. (1997). Psychological functions of privacy. *Journal of Environmental Psychology, 17*, 147–156.

Petronio, S. (2002). *Boundaries of privacy: Dialectics of disclosure.* Albany, NY: SUNY Press.

Petronio, S. (2010). Communication privacy management theory: What do we know about family privacy regulation? *Journal of Family Theory and Review, 2*, 175–196.

Rauhofer, J. R. (2008). Privacy is dead, get over it! Information privacy and the dream of a risk-free society. *Information and Communications Technology Law, 17*(3), 185–197.

Read, B. (2006). Think before you share. *Chronicle of Higher Education, 52*(20), 4.

Ribble, M. S., Bailey, G. D., & Ross, T. W. (2004). Digital citizenship: Addressing appropriate technology behaviour. *Learning Leading Technology, 32*(1), 6–12.

Rosen, J. (2001). *The unwanted gaze: The destruction of privacy in America.* New York, NY: Vintage Books.

Rosenshine, B. (1987). Explicit teaching and teacher training. *Journal of Teacher Education, 38*(3), 34–36.

Rubin, Z. (1975). Disclosing to a stranger: Reciprocity and its limits. *Journal of Experimental and Social Psychology, 11*, 233–260.

Saint, N. (2010). Facebook's response to privacy concerns: "If you're not comfortable sharing, don't." Retrieved March 20, 2012, from http://www.businessinsider.com/facebooks-response-to-privacy-concerns-if-youre-not-comfortable-sharing-dont-2010-5

Selwyn, N. (2007). Screw Blackboard. Do it on Facebook! An investigation of students' educational use of Facebook. Retrieved September 30, 2013, from http://www.scribd.com/doc/513958/Facebookseminar-paper-Selwyn

Schlenker, B. R. (1985). Identity and self-identification. In B. R. Schlenker (Ed.), *The self and social life* (pp. 65–99). New York, NY: McGraw-Hill.

Schouten, A. P., Valkenburg, P. M., & Peter, J. (2007). Precursors and underlying processes of adolescents' online self-disclosure: Developing and testing an "Internet-attribute-perception" model. *Media Psychology, 10*, 292–315.

Sher, J. (2012, November 10). Bully button: U.K.-style social media hotline might have saved Amanda Todd. *The Star.* Retrieved from http://www.thestar.com/news/world/article/1285588---bully-button-u-k-style-social-media-hotline-might-have-saved-amanda-todd

Spears, R., & Lea, M. (1992). Social influence and the influence of the 'social' in computer-mediated communication. In M. Lea (Ed.), *Contexts of computer-mediated communication* (pp. 30–65). Hemel Hempstead, UK: Harvester Wheatsheaf.

Sproull, L., & Keisler, S. (1986). Reducing social context cues: Electronic mail in organizational communication. *Management Science, 32*, 1492–1512.

Steeves, V. (2008). If the Supreme Court were on Facebook: Evaluating the reasonable expectation of privacy test from a social perspective. *Canadian Journal of Criminology and Criminal Justice, 50*(3), 331–347.

Suler, J. (2004). The online disinhibition effect. *CyberPsychology and Behavior, 7*(3), 321–326.

Sutter, J. D. (2011, February 21). The faces of Egypt's revolution 2.0. *CNN.* Retrieved from http://www.cnn.com/2011/TECH/innovation/02/21/egypt.internet.revolution/index.html

Taylor, D. A., Altman, I., & Sorrentino, R. (1969). Interpersonal exchange as a function of rewards and costs and situational factors: Expectancy confirmation–disconfirmation. *Journal of Experimental Social Psychology, 5*, 324–339.

Tidwell, L. C., & Walther, J. B. (2002). Computer-mediated communication effects on disclosure, impressions, and interpersonal evaluations: Getting to know one another a bit at a time. *Human Communication Research, 28*, 317–348.

Tong, S., Van Der Heide, B., Langwell, L., & Walther, J. (2008). Too much of a good thing? The relationship between number of friends and interpersonal impressions on Facebook. *Journal of Computer-Mediated Communication, 13*, 531–549.

Tufekci, Z. (2008). Can you see me now? Audience and disclosure regulation in online social network sites. *Bulletin of Science, Technology, and Society, 28*(1), 20–36.

Utz, S., & Buekeboom, C. J. (2011). Social networking site or social surveillance site? Understanding the use of interpersonal electronic surveillance in romantic relationships. *Computers in Human Behavior, 27,* 705–713.

Van der Velden, M., & El Emam, K. (2013). "Not all my friends need to know": A qualitative study of teenage patients, privacy, and social media. *Journal of the American Medical Informatics Association, 20*(1), 16–24.

Walther, J. B. (1992). Interpersonal effects in computer-mediated interaction: A relational perspective. *Communication Research, 19,* 52–90.

Walther, J. B. (1996). Computer-mediated communication: Impersonal, interpersonal, and hyper-personal interaction. *Communication Research, 23,* 3–44.

Walther, J. B. (2006). Nonverbal dynamics in computer-mediated communication, or :(and the net :('s with you, :) and you :) alone. In V. Manusov & M. L. Patterson (Eds.), *Handbook of nonverbal communication* (pp. 461–479). Thousand Oaks, CA: Sage.

Walther, J. B. (2011). Computer-mediated communication and interpersonal relations. In M. L. Knapp & J. A. Daly (Eds.), *The handbook of interpersonal communication* (4th ed., pp. 443–479). Thousand Oaks, CA: Sage.

Walther, J. B., Van Der Heide, B., Kim, S., Westerman, D., & Tong, S. T. (2008). The role of friends' behavior on evaluations of individuals' Facebook profiles: Are we known by the company we keep? *Human Communication Research, 34,* 28–49.

Weijs, C. A., Coe, J. B., Christofides, E., Muise, A., & Desmarais, S. (2013). A study of Facebook use among early career veterinary professionals in Ontario, Canada [March to May 2010]. *Journal of the American Veterinary Medical Association, 242,* 1083–1090.

Westin, A. F. (1967). *Privacy and freedom.* New York, NY: Atheneum.

Westin, A. F. (2003). Social and political dimensions of privacy. *Journal of Social Issues, 59*(2), 431–453.

Willoughby, T., Hui, B., & Wood, E. (2008). Introduction to formal learning with technologies: Exploring the role of digital technologies. In T. Willoughby & E. Wood (Eds.), *Children's learning in a digital world* (pp. 131–140). Oxford, UK: Blackwell.

Willoughby, T., & Wood, E. (Eds.). (2008). *Children's learning in a digital world.* Oxford, UK: Blackwell.

Wood, E., Nosko, A., Desmarais, S., Ross, C., & Irvine, C. (2006). Online and traditional paper-and-pencil survey administration: Examining experimenter presence, sensitive material and long surveys. *Canadian Journal of Human Sexuality, 15*(3–4), 147–155.

Wood, E., Willoughby, T., Specht, J., Stern-Cavalcante, W., & Child, C. (2002). Developing a computer workshop to facilitate computer skills and minimize anxiety for early childhood educators. *Journal of Educational Psychology, 94*(1), 164–170.

Worthy, M., Gary, A. L., & Kahn, G. M. (1969). Self-disclosure as an exchange process. *Journal of Personality and Social Psychology, 13,* 59–63.

Youn, S. (2005). Teenagers' perceptions of online privacy and coping behaviors: A riskbenefit appraisal approach. *Journal of Broadcasting and Electronic Media, 49*(1), 86–110.

18

The Emergence of Mobile Social Network Platforms on the Mobile Internet

Andrew Richard Schrock

Annenberg School for Communication and Journalism and
University of Southern California

Mobile social network platforms (MSNPs) are social network sites (SNSs) (boyd & Ellison, 2007) that are accessed predominantly on mobile devices and gain new meaning through locative and mobile features. As of March 2013, more than half (751 million) of Facebook's overall users (1.11 billion) access the service on a mobile device each month (Espinosa, 2013). MSNPs are the second most popular use of a smartphone, following requests for directions (Zickuhr, 2012). MSNPs have arisen from a convergence of SNSs, the Internet, and mobile devices, or what Lee Rainie and Barry Wellman (2012) call the "triple revolution." The technology used to access MSNPs on mobile devices varies (Humphreys, 2013). Generally they are accessed through a mobile phone using a web browser or a specialty "app" (mobile software application). In the case of the "Facebook for Every Phone" effort, Facebook is accessed on feature phones, which are inexpensive cell phones that provide basic functionality for dialing numbers, playing games, and storing contacts but lack the storage capacity, speed, and features of "smartphones" such as the iPhone. The mobility and constant contact connectedness of MSNPs present a significant shift from SNSs as "web-based services" used for presenting one's identity and traversing social connections (boyd & Ellison, 2007, p. 211).

The current chapter summarizes the developments leading to current mobile social network platforms and addresses how these platforms represent a fundamental shift from desktop-based paradigms. Following this discussion, three particular characteristics of mobile social network platforms are considered: constant contact, the importance of place, and locational privacy. I will address particular issues of societal concern that emerge from devices being embedded into existing routines and habits, and will offer directions for future research.

Mobile social network platforms (MSNPs) emerged from the convergence of social network sites (SNSs) and locative and mobile social networks (LMSNs). SNSs are desktop-based websites that started in the late 1990s and allow individuals to "construct a public or semi-public profile ... articulate a list of other users ... and view and

---

The Wiley Handbook of Psychology, Technology, and Society, First Edition. Edited by Larry D. Rosen, Nancy A. Cheever, and L. Mark Carrier.

traverse their list of connections" (boyd & Ellison, 2007, p. 211). LMSNs peaked in popularity in the late 2000s and are mobile applications that are composed of networks, are formed through mobile usage, and leverage location to provide functionality not possible on desktop computers (de Souza e Silva & Frith, 2010, p. 487). The LMSN Foursquare, for example, structures activities around "check-ins" to locations, enabling users to see people and places around them on a map. While LMSNs presented a range of unique functions, they failed to gain a sufficient user base and advertising revenue, and most failed or were acquired by 2011 (Goggin, 2011). The companies behind SNSs were better financially and technically situated to gradually introduce mobile-specific features to a larger user base and take advantage of a gradual shift toward mobile devices. Thus, many of the features of LMSNs – geo-tagging, mobile image uploads, and "check-ins" – are now available on apps for MSNPs.

MSNPs such as Facebook and Twitter present a meaningful shift from desktop-based versions in several ways. First, they have shifted functionality from a focus on "profiles" as online identity on SNSs (Hinduja & Patchin, 2008; Jones, Millermaier, Goya-Martinez, & Schuler, 2008; Magnuson, 2008; Thelwall, 2008) to a constantly changing stream of information in the form of status updates and messages (Marwick, 2013). These features often mimic functionality of previous online media. Friends can reply to status updates leading to conversations springing up around particular topics similar to message boards. Facebook messaging is an anytime-anywhere tool that can be employed synchronously or asynchronously, similar to instant messaging services or SMS "texting." Mobile social media are adopted on a mass scope and serve various "post-mass media functions" of communication between individuals, communities, and groups (Lemos, 2010).

Second, these functions of MSNPs connect individuals constantly with egocentric social networks – depending on the platform, either based in shared history (friend and family) or shared interests – that are constantly in motion. While not all individuals who are on MSNPs are logged in on mobile devices, the switch to a mobile device is seamless. The default location for anyone logged into an SNS used to be at a confined set of locations: home, work, school, and perhaps at a coffee shop. The role of MSNPs in maintaining relationships likely has both positive and negative effects on psychosocial well-being based on changing contexts and locations. Communication on desktop-based SNSs helps to maintain relationships (Steijn & Schouten, 2013) and provide social support (Vitak & Ellison, 2012). It seems likely that a shift toward mobile versions enables a wider variety of social and instrumental support, such as asking for advice during a doctor's visit or posting pictures of friends immediately during a gathering. More on the negative end, the notion of "fear of missing out" describes the persistent feeling by individuals that when they put down their mobile social media they are neglecting vital opportunities to socialize.

Third, the mobile nature of MSNPs introduces new types of habits among this larger social network. Mobile media are frequently used for coordinating activities (Ling & Yttri, 2002; Ling, 2004) and congregating in particular locations (Humphreys, 2010; Rheingold, 2002), activities which were not possible with desktop computers. Locative and mobile social networks (de Souza e Silva & Frith, 2010, 2012; Hjorth, 2012) such as Foursquare encourage the creative reuse of public space. In these ways MSNPs disrupt easy compartmentalization of "online" and "offline" (Jurgenson, 2012; Papacharissi, 2005). In retrospect, "cyberspace" may have been the wrong metaphor for online sociality, as we are not transported to a different plane of existence when we use technology. Rather, time is fractured and we use mobile media across various devices and services throughout the day for just long enough to do what we want. For example, we are now acclimated to use our mobile devices for five minutes while standing in line at the grocery store. The frame of interaction shifts to one of networked individualism (Wellman, 1998, 2002) where people are constantly communicating with their networks through an always-on connection (Licoppe, 2004).

Given that mobile social network platforms are a convergence of social networks accessed on mobile devices, the current literature on SNSs and locative and mobile social networks is examined to consider the role MSNPs play in relationship formation and maintenance. In the following sections I will draw from three academic lineages: computer-mediated communication (Walther, 2011), micro-social studies in mobile communication (Smith, 2013), and social-psychological research on social network sites (boyd & Ellison, 2007). These three interdisciplinary clusters help illuminate areas of current academic interest as well as potential areas for problematic interactions in domains involving mobile social networking.

Social Network Sites

Social network sites are "web-services that allow individuals to (1) construct a public or semi-public profile within a bounded system, (2) articulate a list of other users with whom they share a connection, and (3) view and traverse their list of connections and those made by others within the system" (boyd & Ellison, 2007, p. 211). MSNPs go beyond "web-based services" with features that are accessed on mobile (smartphones, tablets) and semi-mobile (laptops) devices. As previously mentioned, mobile media also extend the reach of services from relatively immobile (desktops) computing devices. The constructing of a profile has been significantly downplayed in favor of communication that can be used synchronously or asynchronously, such as messages and status updates on a news feed. Finally, traversing a list of connections has become not as important as the content that comes through those connections.

MSNPs have become general-purpose socialization portals more closely linked in various ways with offline life. By late 2009 the number of SNS users had risen to 47% of American adults and 73% of online teens (Lenhart, Purcell, Smith, & Zickuhr, 2010), signaling a shift in usage toward the mainstream. Facebook, in comparison to competitors such as MySpace, emphasized features built around users' egocentric networks of known friends and family rather than "strangers" not met offline (Hampton, Goulet, Rainie, & Purcell, 2011). By early 2010 Facebook had edged out MySpace, which focused on media experiences such as television and music, and increasingly leveraged networked data sets to increase user interactions and advertising revenue. A wealth of SNSs in other countries exist, such as RenRen in China (Zhao & Jiang, 2011) and Orkut, which is popular in Brazil and India. However, their evolution to MSNPs in non-Western contexts remains understudied. Moreover, social networking is increasingly integrated into various platforms. Tumblr, for example, maintains a stripped-down interface and focuses on multimedia blogging on top of a social networking back-end where members can follow each other and repost media.

Social-psychological research on SNSs can generally be grouped into antecedents/ effects of usage (Anderson, Fagan, Woodnutt, & Chamorro-Premuzic, 2012), parental relationships (Rosen, Cheever, & Carrier, 2008), gender (Magnuson, 2008; Thelwall, 2008), and identity formation (Hinduja & Patchin, 2008; Jones et al., 2008; Magnuson, 2008; Sauter, 2014). Sociology has focused on the creation, maintenance, and dissolution of social relationships through social capital (Steinfield, Ellison, & Lampe, 2008; Wellman, Haase, Witte, & Hampton, 2007), and online communities (Reich, 2010). Sociological researchers often employed social network analysis on unobtrusive data sets retrieved from application programming interfaces (APIs) or "crawled" in a manner similar to search engines (Lewis, Kaufman, Gonzalez, Wimmer, & Christakis, 2008).

Blanket conclusions about the antecedents and effects of SNSs are difficult due to near ubiquitous usage (Espinosa, 2013), varying cultural contexts, and multiple types of SNSs. However, some basic practices can be noted. SNSs are important for instrumental purposes and for providing and receiving social support (Steijn & Schouten, 2013; Vitak & Ellison, 2012). They exist as an important site of social contact and sharing (Livingstone, 2008). While increased self-disclosure has been observed on SNSs, it is impacted by audience size, diversity, and user privacy concerns (Vitak, 2012). Although SNSs were popular among youth early on (boyd & Ellison, 2007), they have gained mainstream acceptance. The most feared types of online–offline relationships (e.g., kidnapping, solicitation) early on were found to be extremely rare (for a summary see Schrock & boyd, 2009). Less sensational but still troubling activities exist, many of which currently show conflicting results. For example, early findings show that use leads to increased psychological well-being (Ellison, Steinfield, & Lampe, 2007), but more recently concerns have emerged that users engage in comparisons with others leading to decreased happiness (Haferkamp & Kramer, 2011; Sueur et al., 2013). Communication on SNSs can be considered as a kind of paradox (Kraut et al., 1998; Kraut & Crawford, 2002) that requires further longitudinal research to connect individual psychologies and activities to societal ills and prosocial benefits.

Locative and Mobile Social Networks

Locative and mobile social networks leverage location and social networks to deliver location-specific experiences such as making visible services and social contacts around users. Interest in mobile social media began in earnest when GPS signals, previously limited in accuracy due to security concerns, were made more accurate by the Clinton administration in 2002. The first wave of locative media came from artists and hobbyists such as geocachers (Farman, 2012; Willis, 2010; Zeffiro, 2006). Cell phone-based games such as Sweden's *Botfighters* used GPS location as a variable for virtual battles in urban space. Generally these early uses were more performative and experimental than functional and service-based. More overt focus on local networks began over the time period of 2005–2009, driven by Google's focus on geolocative services and the rise of smartphones (Wilken, 2012). Locative and mobile social networks emerged during this time, starting with services such as Dodgeball, where users would text their location and receive a message in response about local venues and people around them. It was also the first service to offer "check-ins" to specific locations.

Dodgeball was founded in 2000, acquired by Google in 2005, and dissolved in 2009. Many similar LMSNs were founded between 2007 and 2010, including Gowalla and Whrrl, but few survived to the current day. The two Dodgeball founders – Dennis Crowley and Alex Rainert – left Google in 2007 and went on to create Foursquare, which is now the dominant LMSN with 45 million registered users.

The introduction of the smartphone, particularly Apple's iPhone in 2007 (Burgess, 2012) and an app development environment shortly after, signaled the interest of businesses in social experiences in urban spaces. The industry term for LMSN is social, locative, and mobile (SoLoMo). Both terms capture the underlying connectivity (social network), movement (mobile), and encounters within space (locative). The important technological shift driving both is location – coordinates that can be collected from satellites and used to connect local users to everything from retail establishments to individuals seeking romantic encounters (Crooks, 2013).

Visualizations of space figure prominently into the history of LMSNs. Location-based social networks "map social networks on physical space" (Sutko & de Souza e Silva, 2011, p. 4) and are also described as a kind of "hybrid space" (de Souza e Silva, 2006) where digital information intersects with the physical. Mobile communication scholarship has focused on bridging behaviors, often through map visualizations, that lead to new social relationships, particularly in urban spaces. LMSNs thus are generally thought to assist in the reinforcing of relationships and the forming of new ones (Campbell & Kwak, 2010; Humphreys, 2010; Luke, 2005; Wilken, 2010). Someone walking by a bar may use an app that displays a map of potential friends inside and decide to join them, for example. In this regard, mobile scholars are interested in urban communication that arises from a combination of communication and proximity in a pluralistic society (Park, 1915; Wirth, 1938).

New practices that have emerged on LMSNs include coordination (Humphreys, 2012), congregation (de Souza e Silva & Frith, 2012; Humphreys, 2011; Rheingold, 2002), and "geo-tagged" posting of media (Gordon & de Souza e Silva, 2011; Humphreys & Liao, 2011). However, initial interest in locative and mobile social networks may have overstated the degree to which location drives industry monetization strategies and user practices with mobile applications and services. Location by itself has not proven to be a powerful driver of social services, and MSNPs have eclipsed both user adoption and practices. For example, although 74% of smartphone owners used their phone to get real-time location-based information in 2012, only 10% had used a service such as Foursquare. In response to pressures to monetize, Foursquare moved its focus away from "gameified" check-ins and toward relationships with local vendors. Locative tagging proved easy to integrate with existing platforms such as Facebook and Twitter, reducing the uniqueness of LMSNs as specialty services. Individuals still have privacy fears, particularly of others being able to see their location (Humphreys, 2011). Locative media also implicitly assumed that there was a feature that, when combined with location, led to a kind of *flâneurism* (Luke, 2005). In this vision, individuals stroll the streets simply for the thrill of being seen and socializing with others. While LMSNs will continue to occupy a niche in the mobile marketplace, on the whole, users have not found these services particularly fun or useful. As will be described below, larger egocentric networks cultivated by Facebook and other SNSs present a host of different practices that align better with users.

Mobile Social Network Platforms

Mobile social network platforms combine the accessibility and mobility of LMSNs with the networked interactions possible on SNSs. They are multifunctional, ubiquitous, and serve to reinforce or create relationships. While much research has been conducted on LMSNs and SNSs separately, their convergence is understudied (Humphreys, 2013). This is a surprising omission, given the fascination among mobile communication scholars with the rise of services on the mobile Internet (Goggin, 2011). I use the term *platform* (Gillespie, 2010) to more productively focus on the combination of mobile media and social networks – social affordances (Wellman et al., 2006) – rather than overstating the importance of one device or other. For example, a MSNP may be accessed through a smartphone-based software application (or "app"), mobile website, or even feature phone.

A move to MSNPs opens up questions about other ways larger egocentric social networks are integrated into everyday interactions on the mobile Internet. First, individuals can better provide social support at a distance because they are more connected to a diversity of contexts. A computer would be impractical to use while on a bus, while waiting at a hospital, or while walking down a street. Second, proximity, the main attraction of LMSNs, still likely plays a central role in MSNPs, even as location is downplayed. LMSNs used maps of individuals' locations as a central feature, but this triggered fears of privacy or were tied to features that people did not care for (such as check-ins). Other modes of users signaling proximity include implicit cues ("I'm home") or micro-coordination that results from reporting of small movements ("Let's meet in the food court instead") while in persistent contact, leading to physical assembly (Ling & Yttri, 2002; Ling, 2004). Third, MSNPs are not separate from everyday life, but layered on top of it (de Souza e Silva, 2006). This may be a fun experience, as when friends share a particularly spicy status update while sitting together, or it can be quite dangerous, in the case of switching attention to and from a device while driving (Bayer & Campbell, 2012). Finally, media creation and viewing on mobile devices allows media (pictures, movies, and audio) to flow seamlessly to and from networked services.

Facebook's struggles in negotiating mobile experiences provide a lens through which to view the transition from SNSs to MSNPs as part of a mainstream mobile society. Facebook started to produce a mobile app starting with BlackBerry "smartphones" and grew to 63 million mobile users by 2009. While Facebook is guarded about publishing official statistics on growth of specific mobile platforms, a loophole allowed growth to be estimated between December 2011 and November 2012. Android apps increased from 66 to 193 million monthly average users while iPhone apps went from 91 to 147 monthly average users during the same period (Constine, 2013). As of June 2013, 819 million people, or well over half the 1.15 billion user base, access Facebook through a mobile device. Facebook's interest in mobile advertising revenue (Wilken & Sinclair, 2009a, 2009b) has considerably helped its valuation. Facebook accessed on a mobile device is, unlike "geo-locative" services such as Foursquare, not only defined by location. That is, you are not more likely to see posts by a neighbor just because she is closer by. Experiments with Facebook features such as "find friends nearby" resulted in objections among users, particularly due to privacy concerns (Lunden, 2012). Locative tagging is treated as one of many features rather than the only one. Humphreys (2013) recently observed that the scholarly focus on location as the central inroad to mobile communication meant that "non-location-based mobile social media have not been widely examined" (p. 22). While location may be employed through "check-ins" on MSNPs, this may primarily be popular among a minority of early adopters. Location can also be collected in other ways, such as detecting coordinates from image file headers and mentions of approximate location (at the city level) in status updates.

Emergent Issues on Mobile Social Network Platforms

Mobile social network platforms present a number of emergent issues. More than simply leading to more usage, mobile presents opportunities for fundamentally different experiences.

Constant Contact

The roots of constant social contact during everyday life can be traced to early work on *Keitai* in Japan among early adopters of the mobile Internet. Ito, Okabe, and Matsuda (2005) described how youth exhibited "selective sociality" with peer groups over mobile devices resulting in a "sense of being in psychological contact twenty-four hours a day" (p. 30). Mobile media provide a constant "connected presence" (Licoppe, 2004) where "copresent interactions and mediated distant exchanges seem woven into a single, seamless web" (p. 135). In other words, mediated and face-to-face interactions comprise relationships. Although mobile media are increasingly popular, Facebook users have met more than 89% of friends offline more than once (Hampton et al., 2011). Licoppe (2004) suggests stylistic differences as well, as maintaining mediated relationships at a distance requires "frequent small gestures" (p. 150) that tend to be more phatic (Malinowski, 1923) than informational. Mobile media fit into a continuous conversation in which each mediated interaction "reactivates, reaffirms, and reconfigures the relationship" (p. 138). Connected presence was successively used to describe negotiations of proximity (Licoppe, 2009), pragmatics of intimate relationships (Arminen & Weilenmann, 2009), and communication patterns of family members (Christensen, 2009). This symbolic interactionist and constructivist perspective differs from prevailing psychological notions of presence (Schroder, 2006) or automaticity (Bayer & Campbell, 2012).

MSNPs appear to be used for multiple types of activities related to maintaining relationships. Mobile devices are particularly embedded in everyday life from the moment of waking up to going to sleep at night. If the metaphor of the "social network site" in 2007 was the profile, the current one is the status update broadcast across news feeds (Marwick, 2013).

Importance of Place

History is littered with predictions of the negative effects of electronic media on place. According to many scholars, electronic media lead to time-space compression (Harvey, 1990) and even onerous "non-places" such as airports (Augé, 2008). Joshua Meyrowitz promoted the idea that we lose our "sense of place" with electronic media, referring to loss of contexts for interaction (Goffman, 1959). danah boyd, in a similarly neo-Goffmanian argument, described "context collapse" on SNSs – the combining of multiple groups for interaction into a single audience. Further, boyd notes how the online environment exacerbates problems of privacy and identity, as "in mediated spaces, there are no structures to limit the audience" (boyd & Ellison, 2007, p. 132). Context collapse generally stipulates that information being seen by unintended parties results in negative psychological effects and the attenuation of one's self. However, it has been criticized for assuming a dichotomy between online and offline, and a deterministic perspective on the impact of technical features (Beer, 2008). Communication research describes how online and offline are not separate entities (Baym, 2009; Papacharissi, 2005), and practices – rather than social affordances of platforms alone – impact subsequent effects.

Research from mobile communication describes how the complexity of mobile practices and social affordances of devices can have both positive and negative effects. On the positive side, practices with mobile media can imbue places with meaning and add a layer of sociality to physical spaces. Places can have emotional meaning to individuals (Canter, 1977; Gustafson, 2001; Manzo, 2005). Geo-tagging, a method of attaching location to particular media, can "allow users to create place-based narratives and engage in identity management" (Humphreys & Liao, 2011, p. 407). Ample interest in LMSNs clusters around proximity, or the ability to perceive those around you, resulting in interpersonal congregation (Rheingold, 2002) and creation of publics (de Souza e Silva & Frith, 2012; Sheller, 2004; Sheller & Urry, 2003). More negatively, scholars have long observed how mobile devices such as iPods encourage privatization, as they can be used to isolate one's self from others in public spaces (Bull, 2011). MSNPs exist alongside in-person interactions and can even compete with them, as "the social life of public space now competes with media technology that shifts interaction inward" (Kleinman, 2007, p. 19).

In retrospect, Meyrowitz's conclusions were too general (Kubey, 1992) and too deterministic (Williams, 2003). Place matters quite a bit for actions on mobile social networks that rely on proximity and mapping. Acknowledging a spatial dimension to online social networks provokes further questions about public and private life (Sheller & Urry, 2003) that are less about visibility of messages and more about the strategic use of mobile media to negotiate and augment interactions. For example, individuals carefully use mobile devices to separate work from home life, but are more forgiving in using them during family time (Wajcman, 2008). Foursquare users hold normative beliefs about how much cheating on check-ins is acceptable (Germaine, Leavitt, & Gray, 2013). Contrary to predictions, place has not been obliterated and has become increasingly important for negotiating online social relationships.

Locational Privacy

Solove (2008) described privacy as a pluralistic concept best considered within a framework of four general types that outline the current problem areas: information collection, information processing, information dissemination, and invasion. Other perspectives include behavioral (Margulis, 2003) and related to law or policy (e.g., Brandeis' assertion that privacy is a right). From an individual perspective, people constantly negotiate privacy as a dynamic and dialectical process (Palen & Dourish, 2003). Beliefs about privacy are also linked to culture (Hall, 1966), behavioral norms, age group, and cohort. A completely private or public life is impossible, so privacy is a kind of "balancing act" or negotiation between self and other (Altman, 1975). A challenge of considering privacy in online social networks is that normative beliefs about proper conduct are often not visible until they are violated (boyd, 2008). The paradox here is that individuals easily consent to giving information away, but are frequently surprised when it is used in ways they would not endorse (Barnes, 2006). These combinations of factors make it difficult to predict what will be an unsettling experience for a particular person (Nippert-Eng, 2010; Nissenbaum, 2011). Moreover, existing "notice-and-consent" models of obtaining permission to collect and store user data are poorly understood and arguably ineffective (Nissenbaum, 2011). The use of these data for targeted advertisements is even more confusing, involving vast advertising networks, tracking mechanisms, and industries (Turow, 2011). Helen Nissenbaum's (2010, 2011) notion of contextual privacy focuses on contexts of violations, as defined by specific roles, activities, norms, and values. Using this framework we can observe that individuals have quite different activities on mobile media and expectations about how reachable they are during these activities.

Privacy on LMSNs has been interpreted by users primarily as interpersonal rather than institutional (Humphreys, 2011; Marwick, 2012). In other words, they are mostly concerned with *who* can see their location and rarely understand the larger scope of data reuse and surveillance by corporations (Trottier, 2012). Most mobile users are surprised to hear about the way their locational data are collected and used by companies, and frequently object to the practice when asked (Fox, 2008). Users organize in response to over-reaches (boyd, 2008; Fernback, 2012) and change privacy settings to varying degrees (boyd & Hargittai, 2010). While the number of privacy violations on mobile social network platforms is unknown, several high-profile cases can be pointed to. Significant violations, such as the unlawful gaming of the mobile web browser Safari to track users that resulted in a $22.5 million fine against Google (Albanesius, 2012), show how companies can often outpace legal regulation. Privacy controls tend to be rudimentary, while other applications appear to collect information without their users' knowledge, such as by accessing contact information on address books.

Locational privacy, then, refers to how location is a special variable of concern on mobile devices (de Souza e Silva & Frith, 2012) related to fears of being seen or even stalked by unknown others. The ability to sense and view (and be sensed and viewed) is no longer circumscribed by the built environment, and mobile devices can be used in a variety of situations. Simply put, it is not currently known how often users post their location on MSNPs, although many are reluctant to share location information. Location slowly made its way back into mobile Facebook through the "Nearby" feature, which was eventually reduced to being a resource for local retail establishments similar to Yelp.

Discussion

MSNPs such as Facebook have received scant attention in the literature, yet they signal the first major shift in online social networks: a move from social networks being confined to the desktop to ubiquitous mobile presence. I have drawn on the concept of a platform (Gillespie, 2010) to refer to a relatively consistent experience and feature set across multiple devices that engenders constant contact (Katz & Aakhus, 2002;

Licoppe, 2004), blurring of place (Cresswell, 2006; Dourish, 2006; Wellman, 2001), and issues of locational privacy (de Souza e Silva & Frith, 2012; Humphreys, 2011). Overall concerns for this shift have been organized for researchers and society at large.

Research Implications

Future research agendas on antecedents of and effects from socialization through online communication should account for mobile practices and platforms. MSNPs have arisen from a combination of the massive connectedness of SNSs, mobility of mobile devices, and locative functionality of LMSNs. They are entering a phase of mainstream adoption (Rogers, 1995) and are embedded in everyday habits (Ling, 2012) among average Americans. A simple online–offline dichotomy (Papacharissi, 2005) is no longer the most accurate perspective for researching social media.

Mobile communication scholars have generally relied on qualitative methodologies (Büscher, Urry, & Witchger, 2011), illuminating the multifarious ways individuals strategically use mobile devices. They focus on descriptive research and outline various cultures and situations. However, few comparative studies exist that synthesize and test claims. In other words, mobile scholars "are not as engaged in systematically examining ways to probe, test, replicate, represent and generalize knowledge about mobility" (D'Andrea, Ciolfi, & Gray, 2011, p. 156). This dearth stands in contrast to rigorous work in computer-mediated communication (CMC) on interpersonal topics such as intimacy, self-disclosure, and trust (Walther, 2011) that is in-depth but tends to neglect mobility. Micro to macro linkages (Collins, 1983), whether theoretical or empirical, remain scarce. That is, mobile communication research has illuminated both individual habits and societal problems, but little to connect the two.

New developments in instrumentation provide inroads to address the above theoretical issues and suggest synergies with psychology and communication. Unobtrusive techniques based on mobile apps promise more accurate and granular data collection (Boase, 2013; Boase & Ling, 2013) than typical survey items such as user estimates of use (Anderson et al., 2012). Twitter's public API provides access to communications that can be retrieved and analyzed. These do not substitute for all self-reported data, such as relational satisfaction. However, they can enable more accurate predictions about relational outcomes. The scope of interactions on MSNPs and conflicting predictions regarding mobile communication also suggest a need for longitudinal data collection. For example, early proclamations of the Internet being related to negative effects related to social involvement and psychological well-being dissipated over three years (Kraut et al., 1998; Kraut & Crawford, 2002).

Societal Implications

The shift toward mobile and social media relates to the most pressing questions of society's integration of technology into the fabric of everyday life. MSNPs are the first significant shift in SNSs in the last decade. Scholars should be sensitive to these shifts without succumbing to the allure of the new (Marvin, 1988) or resorting to familiar tropes (Pool, 1982). Ample predictions exist on the emancipatory potential of SNSs and mobile devices (Benkler, 2007), as well as how they can distance us emotionally and physically from each other (Turkle, 2011). The combination of social media and mobile devices provokes a deeper consideration of the complex interplay between location, individual psychology, device affordances, networked interactions, and cultural context. This final section delves into specific debates around the impact of MSNPs for problematic uses.

Tele-cocooning Social networks (Christakis & Fowler, 2007) and how we attend to them (Hogan, 2009) have emerged as powerful predictors of behavior. One troubling prediction about MSNPs is that they will encourage "tele-cocooning" (Ito et al., 2005) or an over-reliance on existing social networks in urban space. If we carry our networks with us everywhere, we may rely on them rather than interact with new locations and individuals. This also encourages further homogeneity in network composition, because "urban space becomes ... a comfy echo-chamber of our own (commodified) profiles and those of our familiars" (Crawford, 2008, p. 81). This is particularly worrisome to mobile communication scholars who are interested in chance meetings that arise from the urban environment (see de Souza e Silva & Frith, 2012; Humphreys & Liao, 2011; Wilken, 2010). One result of tele-cocooning may be "fear of missing out" (FOMO) – the consumption of overly positive statements made through MSNPs resulting in a persistent feeling that others are enjoying life more than you. While it is currently unclear whether FOMO is a new trend, as a social phenomenon it speaks to the pervasiveness of MSNPs in everyday life. MSNPs are not just nice to have, but negative responses to their removal signal a dependency on them, because "the use of mobile phones by a critical mass of people facilitates the smooth functioning of everyday life" (Ling, 2012, p. 3).

Behavior in public space Norms of behavior with mobile social media in offline social situations are still emergent (Srivastava, 2005). Behavior in public spaces initially followed a displacement narrative. Rheingold (2002) noted a shift from voice to more data-dependent uses in how Tokyo residents were "staring at their mobile phones instead of talking to them" (Rheingold, 2002, p. xi). Push notifications can demand our attention, literally coming between in-person relations (Ling, 2008). However, successive research revealed further complexities. Mobile devices can also be shared locally and media observed together. Brown, Green, and Harper (2002) noted two forms of sharing: minimal sharing of content, and hands-on sharing where the phone was passed among youth. Acceptance of sharing phones relates to contextual privacy concerns, such as who is asking and type of application (Karlson, Brush, & Schechter, 2009). SMS texting follows similar "turn taking" as do conversations (Relieu, 2009).

Problematic usage of MSNPs Research on online harassment among youth has focused on distinctions between "schoolyard" bullying and the home environment (Beran & Li, 2007; Burgess-Proctor, Patchin, & Hinduja, 2009; Kowalski, Limber, & Agatston, 2007; Li, 2007; Patchin & Hinduja, 2006). MSNPs contribute to a blurring of place, making these distinctions permeable boundaries where parties are not always in the same place or communicating synchronously. Literature on "Internet addiction" has generally focused on online services (Byun et al., 2009; Ng & Wiemer-Hastings, 2005; Young, 1996), while problematic use of mobile phones has proceeded separately focusing on mobile devices (Billieux, 2012; Billieux, Van der Linden, & Rochat, 2008; Park, 2005). MSNPs combine device and service in increasingly powerful mobile devices that facilitate access to Internet services, provoking the need for a synthesis of which factors contribute to problematic overuse.

Conclusion

MSNPs are a meaningful shift in social media that combine the egocentric networks of SNSs, mobility of devices, and locative features of LMSNs. Constant contact, place, and privacy gain new dimensionalities as individuals employ mobile media for a range of activities that complicate earlier practices. Additionally, from a business perspective, mobile media have emerged as a central factor in platform monetization. Mainstream adoption of MNSPs has shown that early predictions about mobile media were exaggerated. For example, users on the whole do not take part in more creative types of consumption (*flâneurism*) or relish interactions with new parties ("strangers") in urban space. In fact, quite the opposite can be observed: the egocentric networks and controllable locative disclosure of MSNPs are a primary reason they were adopted over LMSNs, which were focused on locative functionality (such as check-ins) and triggered privacy concerns among users. These services will likely still continue, but remain of niche interest. Future research on online social media should focus on mobility as a default for many users and be innovative with methodologies and application of theory to capture flows of data. Particular care should be paid to the more onerous possibilities, such as mobile cocooning, as MSNPs are adopted across cultures and geographic boundaries.

References

Albanesius, C. (2012, August 9). FTC hits Google with $22.5 million fine over Safari tracking. Retrieved from http://www.pcmag.com/article2/0,2817,2408273,00.asp

Altman, I. (1975). *The environment and social behavior: Privacy, personal space, territory, crowding*. Monterey, CA: Brooks/Cole.

Anderson, B., Fagan, P., Woodnutt, T., & Chamorro-Premuzic, T. (2012). Facebook psychology: Popular questions answered by research. *Psychology of Popular Media Culture, 1*(1), 23–37.

Arminen, I., & Weilenmann, A. (2009). Mobile presence and intimacy: Reshaping social actions in mobile contextual configuration. *Journal of Pragmatics, 41*(10), 1905–1923.

Augé, M. (2008). *Non-places*. New York, NY: Verso.

Barnes, S. (2006). A privacy paradox: Social networking in the United States. *First Monday, 11*(9). Retrieved from http://firstmonday.org/article/view/1394/1312

Bayer, J. B., & Campbell, S. W. (2012). Texting while driving on automatic: Considering the frequency-independent side of habit. *Computers in Human Behavior, 28*(6), 2083–2090.

Baym, N. K. (2009). A call for grounding in the face of blurred boundaries. *Journal of Computer-Mediated Communication, 14*(3), 720–723.

Beer, D. (2008). Social network(ing) sites. Revisiting the story so far: A response to danah boyd & Nicole Ellison. *Journal of Computer-Mediated Communication, 13*, 516–529.

Benkler, Y. (2007). *The wealth of networks: How social production transforms markets and freedom*. New Haven, CT: Yale University Press.

Beran, T., & Li, Q. (2007). The relationship between cyberbullying and school bullying. *Journal of Student Wellbeing, 1*(2), 15–33.

Billieux, J. (2012). Problematic use of the mobile phone: A literature review and a pathways model. *Current Psychiatry Reviews, 8*(4), 299–307.

Billieux, J., Van der Linden, M., & Rochat, L. (2008). The role of impulsivity in actual and problematic use of the mobile phone. *Applied Cognitive Psychology, 22*(9), 1195–1210.

Boase, J. (2013). Implications of software-based mobile media for social research. *Mobile Media and Communication, 1*(1), 57–62.

Boase, J., & Ling, R. (2013). Measuring mobile phone use: Self-report versus log data. *Journal of Computer-Mediated Communication, 18*(4), 508–519.

boyd, d. (2008). Facebook's privacy trainwreck: Exposure, invasion, and social convergence. *Convergence, 14*(1), 13–20.

boyd, d., & Ellison, N. (2007). Social network sites: Definition, history, and scholarship. *Journal of Computer-Mediated Communication, 13*(1), 210–230.

boyd, d., & Hargittai, E. (2010). Facebook privacy settings: Who cares? *First Monday, 15*(8). Retrieved from http://firstmonday.org/article/view/3086/2589

Brown, B., Green, N., & Harper, R. (2002). Local use and sharing of mobile phones. In B. Brown, N. Green, & R. Harper (Eds.), *Wireless world: Social and interactional aspects of the mobile age* (pp. 92–107). London, UK: Springer.

Bull, M. (2011). *Sound moves: iPod culture and urban experience*. London, UK: Routledge.

Burgess, J. (2012). The iPhone moment, the Apple brand, and the creative consumer. In L. Hjorth & J. Burgess (Eds.), *Studying mobile media: Cultural technologies, mobile communication, and the iPhone* (pp. 28–43). New York, NY: Routledge.

Burgess-Proctor, A., Patchin, J., & Hinduja, S. (2009). Cyberbullying and online harassment: Reconceptualizing the victimization of adolescent girls. In V. Garcia & J. Clifford (Eds.), *Female crime victims: Reality reconsidered* (pp. 162–176). Upper Saddle River, NJ: Prentice Hall.

Büscher, M., Urry, J., & Witchger, K. (2011). *Mobile methods*. New York, NY: Routledge.

Byun, S., Ruffini, C., Mills, J. E., Douglas, A. C., Niang, M., Stepchenkova, S., ... Blanton, M. (2009). Internet addiction: Metasynthesis of 1996–2006 quantitative research. *CyberPsychology and Behavior, 12*(2), 203–207.

Campbell, S. W., & Kwak, N. (2010). Mobile communication and civic life: Linking patterns of use to civic and political engagement. *Journal of Communication, 60*(3), 536–555.

Canter, D. (1977). *Psychology of place*. London, UK: Architectural Press.

Christakis, N. A., & Fowler, J. H. (2007). The spread of obesity in a large social network over 32 years. *New England Journal of Medicine, 357*, 370–379.

Christensen, T. H. (2009). "Connected presence" in distributed family life. *New Media and Society, 11*(3), 433–451.

Collins, R. (1983). Micromethods as a basis for macrosociology. *Journal of Contemporary Ethnography, 12*(2), 184–202.

Constine, J. (2013, January 4). Facebook mobile user counts revealed: 192M Android, 147M iPhone, 48M iPad, 56M Messenger. *TechCrunch*. Retrieved from http://techcrunch.com/2013/01/04/how-many-mobile-users-does-facebook-have

Crawford, A. (2008). Taking social software to the streets: Mobile cocooning and the (un-) erotic city. *Journal of Urban Technology, 15*(3), 79–97.

Cresswell, T. (2006). *Place: A short introduction*. Oxford, UK: Blackwell.

Crooks, R. N. (2013). The rainbow flag and the green carnation: Grindr in the gay village. *First Monday, 18*(10). Retrieved from http://firstmonday.org/ojs/index.php/fm/article/view/4958/3790

D'Andrea, A., Ciolfi, L., & Gray, B. (2011). Methodological challenges and innovations in mobilities research. *Mobilities, 6*(2), 149–160.

de Souza e Silva, A. (2006). From cyber to hybrid: Mobile technologies as interfaces of hybrid spaces. *Space and Culture, 9*(3), 261–278.

de Souza e Silva, A., & Frith, J. (2010). Locative mobile social networks: Mapping communication and location in urban spaces. *Mobilities, 5*(4), 485–505.

de Souza e Silva, A., & Frith, J. (2012). *Mobile interfaces in public spaces: Locational privacy, control, and urban sociability*. New York, NY: Routledge.

Dourish, P. (2006). *Re-space-ing place*. Paper presented at the the 2006 conference on Computer-Supported Cooperative Work, New York, NY.

Ellison, N. B., Steinfield, C., & Lampe, C. (2007). The benefits of Facebook "friends": Social capital and college students' use of online social network sites. *Journal of Computer-Mediated Communication, 12*(4), 1143–1168.

Espinosa, J. (2013, May 1). Facebook grows to 1.1B MAU in Q1 2013, mobile up 124 percent year-over-year. *Inside Facebook.* Retrieved from http://www.insidefacebook.com/2013/05/01/facebook-grows-by-1-1b-mau-in-q1-2013-mobile-up-124-percent-year-over-year

Farman, J. (2012). Historicizing mobile media: Locating the transformations of embodied space. In A. P. Kavoori & N. Arceneaux (Eds.), *The mobile media reader.* New York, NY: Peter Lang.

Fernback, J. (2012). Sousveillance: Communities of resistance to the surveillance environment. *Telematics and Informatics, 30*(1), 11–21.

Fox, S. (2008, February 14). Privacy implications of fast, mobile Internet access. Retrieved December 2, 2014, from http://www.pewinternet.org/2008/02/14/privacy-implications-of-fast-mobile-internet-access/

Germaine, H., Leavitt, A., & Gray, M. (2013). *Jumping for fun? Negotiating mobility and the geopolitics of Foursquare.* Paper presented at the annual meeting of the International Communication Association, Phoenix, AZ.

Gillespie, T. (2010). The politics of "platforms." *New Media and Society, 12*(3), 347–364.

Goffman, E. (1959). *The presentation of self in everyday life.* Garden City, NY: Doubleday.

Goggin, G. (2011). *Global mobile media.* New York, NY: Routledge.

Gordon, E., & de Souza e Silva, A. (2011). *Net.Locality: Why location matters in a networked world.* Oxford, UK: Wiley Blackwell.

Gustafson, P. (2001). Meanings of place: Everyday experience and theoretical conceptualizations. *Journal of Environmental Psychology, 21*(1), 5–16.

Haferkamp, N., & Kramer, N. C. (2011). Social comparison 2.0: Examining the effects of online profiles on social-networking sites. *Cyberpsychology, Behavior, and Social Networking, 14*(5), 309–314.

Hall, E. T. (1966). *The hidden dimension.* New York, NY: Anchor.

Hampton, K., Goulet, L. S., Rainie, L., & Purcell, K. (2011, June 16). Social networking sites and our lives. Retrieved from http://www.pewinternet.org/Reports/2011/Technology-and-social-networks.aspx

Harvey, D. (1990). *The condition of postmodernity.* Oxford, UK: Blackwell.

Hinduja, S., & Patchin, J. (2008). Personal information of adolescents on the Internet: A quantitative content analysis of MySpace. *Journal of Adolescence, 31*, 125–146.

Hjorth, L. (2012). Relocating the mobile: A case study of locative media in Seoul, South Korea. *Convergence, 19*(2), 237–249.

Hogan, B. (2009). *Networking in everyday life.* [Doctoral dissertation]. University of Toronto, Toronto, Ontario, Canada. Retrieved from http://individual.utoronto.ca/berniehogan/Hogan_NIEL_10-29-2008_FINAL.pdf

Humphreys, L. (2010). Mobile social networks and urban public space. *New Media and Society, 12*(5), 763–778.

Humphreys, L. (2011). Who's watching whom? A study of interactive technology and surveillance. *Journal of Communication, 61*(4), 575–595.

Humphreys, L. (2012). Connecting, coordinating, cataloguing: Communicative practices on mobile social networks. *Journal of Broadcasting and Electronic Media, 56*(4), 494–510.

Humphreys, L. (2013). Mobile social media: Future challenges and opportunities. *Mobile Media and Communication, 1*(1), 20–25.

Humphreys, L., & Liao, T. (2011). Mobile geotagging: Reexamining our interactions with urban space. *Journal of Computer-Mediated Communication, 16*(3), 407–423.

Ito, M., Okabe, D., & Matsuda, M. (2005). *Personal, portable, pedestrian: Mobile phones in Japanese life.* Cambridge, MA: MIT Press.

Jones, S., Millermaier, S., Goya-Martinez, M., & Schuler, J. (2008). Whose space is MySpace? A content analysis of MySpace profiles. *First Monday, 13*(9). Retrieved from http://firstmonday.org/article/view/2202/2024

Jurgenson, N. (2012). When atoms meet bits: Social media, the mobile web and augmented revolution. *Future Internet, 4*(4), 83–91.

Karlson, A. K., Brush, A. J. B., & Schechter, S. (2009). *Can I borrow your phone?* Paper presented at the 2009 SIGCHI Conference on Human Factors in Computing Systems, Boston, MA.

Katz, J. E., & Aakhus, M. (2002). *Perpetual contact: Mobile communication, private talk, public performance.* Cambridge, UK: Cambridge University Press.

Kleinman, S. (2007). *Mobile communication in the twenty-first century, or "everybody, everywhere, at any time."* New York, NY: Peter Lang.

Kowalski, R. M., Limber, S. P., & Agatston, P. W. (2007). *Cyberbullying: Bullying in the digital age.* Oxford, UK: Wiley Blackwell.

Kraut, R., Patterson, M., Lundmark, V., Kiesler, S., Mukophadhyay, T., & Scherlis, W. (1998). Internet paradox: A social technology that reduces social involvement and psychological well-being? *American Psychologist, 53*(9), 1017–1031.

Kraut, S., & Crawford, A. (2002). Internet paradox revisited. *Journal of Social Issues, 58,* 49–74.

Kubey, R. (1992). A critique of No Sense of Place and the homogenization theory of Joshua Meyrowitz. *Communication Theory, 2*(3), 259–271.

Lemos, A. (2010). Post-mass media functions, locative media, and informational territories: New ways of thinking about territory, place, and mobility in contemporary society. *Space and Culture, 13*(4), 403–420.

Lenhart, A., Purcell, K., Smith, A., & Zickuhr, K. (2010, February 3). Social media and young adults. Retrieved from http://www.pewinternet.org/2010/02/03/social-media-and-young-adults/

Lewis, K., Kaufman, J., Gonzalez, M., Wimmer, A., & Christakis, N. (2008). Tastes, ties, and time: A new social network dataset using Facebook.com. *Social Networks, 30*(4), 330–342.

Li, Q. (2007). New bottle but old wine: A research of cyberbullying in schools. *Computers in Human Behavior, 23,* 1777–1791.

Licoppe, C. (2004). "Connected" presence: The emergence of a new repertoire for managing social relationships in a changing communication technoscape. *Environment and Planning D: Society and Space, 22*(1), 135–156.

Licoppe, C. (2009). Recognizing mutual "proximity" at a distance: Weaving together mobility, sociality and technology. *Journal of Pragmatics, 41*(10), 1924–1937.

Ling, R. (2008). *New tech, new ties: How mobile communication is reshaping social cohesion.* Cambridge, MA: MIT Press.

Ling, R. (2012). *Taken for grantedness: The embedding of mobile communication into society.* Cambridge, MA: MIT Press.

Ling, R., & Yttri, B. (2002). Hyper-coordination via mobile phone in Norway. In J. E. Katz & M. Aakhus (Eds.), *Perpetual contact: Mobile communication, private talk, public performance* (pp. 139–169). Cambridge, UK: Cambridge University Press.

Ling, R. S. (2004). The coordination of everyday life. In *The mobile connection: The cell phone's impact on society.* San Francisco, CA: Kaufmann.

Livingstone, S. (2008). Taking risky opportunities in youthful content creation: Teenagers' use of social networking sites for intimacy, privacy and self-expression. *New Media and Society, 10*(3), 393–411.

Luke, R. (2005). The phoneur: Mobile commerce and the digital pedagogies of the wireless web. In P. Trifonas (Ed.), *Communities of difference: Language, culture, and the media* (pp. 185–204). New York, NY: Palgrave Macmillan.

Lunden, I. (2012, June 24). "Find friends nearby": Facebook's new mobile feature for finding people around you. *TechCrunch.* Retrieved from http://techcrunch.com/2012/06/24/friendshake-facebooks-new-mobile-feature-for-finding-people-nearby-and-a-highlight-killer

Magnuson, M. (2008). Gender differences in "social portraits" reflected in MySpace profiles. *CyberPsychology and Behavior, 11*(2), 239–241.

Malinowski, B. (1923). The problem of meaning in primitive languages. In C. K. Ogden & I. A. Richards (Eds.), *The meaning of meaning: A study of the influence of language upon thought and of the science of symbolism* (pp. 296–336). New York, NY: Harcourt.

Manzo, L. C. (2005). For better or worse: Exploring multiple dimensions of place meaning. *Journal of Environmental Psychology, 25*(1), 67–86.

Margulis, S. T. (2003). Privacy as a social issue and behavioral concept. *Journal of Social Issues, 59*(2), 243–261.

Marvin, C. (1988). *When old technologies were new: Thinking about communications in the late nineteenth century.* New York, NY: Oxford University Press.

Marwick, A. (2012). The public domain: Social surveillance in everyday life. *Surveillance and Society, 9*(4), 378–393.

Marwick, A. (2013). *Status update: Celebrity, publicity, and branding in the social media age.* New Haven, CT: Yale University Press.

Ng, B. D., & Wiemer-Hastings, P. (2005). Addiction to the Internet and online gaming. *CyberPsychology and Behavior, 8*(2), 110–113.

Nippert-Eng, C. (2010). *Islands of privacy: Selective concealment and disclosure in everyday life.* Chicago, IL: University of Chicago Press.

Nissenbaum, H. (2010). *Privacy in context: Technology, policy, and the integrity of social life.* Stanford, CA: Stanford Law Books.

Nissenbaum, H. (2011). A contextual approach to privacy online. *Daedalus, 140*(4), 32–48.

Palen, L., & Dourish, P. (2003). *Unpacking "privacy" for a networked world.* Paper presented at the 2003 SIGCHI Conference on Human Factors in Computing Systems.

Papacharissi, Z. (2005). The real–virtual dichotomy in online interaction: New media uses and consequences revisited. *Communication Yearbook, 29*(1), 215–237.

Park, R. E. (1915). The city: Suggestions for the investigation of human behavior in the city environment. *American Journal of Sociology, 20*, 5.

Park, W. K. (2005). Mobile phone addiction. In R. Ling & P. E. Pedersen (Eds.), *Mobile communications: Re-negotiation of the social sphere* (pp. 253–272). Berlin, Germany: Springer.

Patchin, J., & Hinduja, S. (2006). Bullies move beyond the schoolyard: A preliminary look at cyberbullying. *Youth Violence and Juvenile Justice, 4*(2), 148–169.

Pool, I. de S. (1982). *Forecasting the telephone: A retrospective technology assessment of the telephone.* Westport, CT: Praeger.

Rainie, L., & Wellman, B. (2012). *Networked: The new social operating system.* Cambridge, MA: MIT Press.

Reich, S. M. (2010). Adolescents' sense of community on MySpace and Facebook: A mixed-methods approach. *Journal of Community Psychology, 38*(6), 688–705.

Relieu, M. (2009). Mobile phone "work": Disengaging and engaging mobile phone activities with concurrent activities. In R. Ling & S. W. Campbell (Eds.), *The reconstruction of space and time* (pp. 215–230). New Brunswick, NJ: Transaction Publishers.

Rheingold, H. (2002). *Smart mobs: The next social revolution.* Cambridge, MA: Perseus.

Rogers, E. M. (1995). *Diffusion of innovations* (4th ed.). New York, NY: Free Press.

Rosen, L. D., Cheever, N. A., & Carrier, L. M. (2008). The association of parenting style and child age with parental limit setting and adolescent MySpace behavior. *Journal of Applied Developmental Psychology, 29*(6), 459–471.

Sauter, T. (2014). "What's on your mind?" Writing on Facebook as a tool for self-formation. *New Media and Society, 16*(5), 823–839.

Schrock, A., & boyd, d. (2009). Internet threats to minors: Solicitation, harassment, and problematic content. In K. B. Wright & L. M. Webb (Eds.), *Computer-mediated communication in interpersonal relationships* (pp. 368–396). New York, NY: Peter Lang.

Schroder, R. (2006). Being there together and the future of connected presence. *Presence, 15*(4), 1–17.

Sheller, M. (2004). Mobile publics: Beyond the network perspective. *Environment and Planning D: Society and Space, 22*(1), 39–52.

Sheller, M., & Urry, J. (2003). Mobile transformations of "public" and "private" life. *Theory, Culture and Society, 20*(3), 107–125.

Smith, R. (2013). So what? Why study mobile media and communication? *Mobile Media and Communication, 1*(1), 38–41.

Solove, D. J. (2008). *Understanding privacy.* Cambridge, MA: Harvard University Press.

Srivastava, L. (2005). Mobile phones and the evolution of social behaviour. *Behaviour and Information Technology, 24*(2), 111–129.

Steijn, W. M., & Schouten, A. P. (2013). Information sharing and relationships on social networking sites. *Cyberpsychology, Behavior, and Social Networking, 16*(8), 582–587.

Steinfield, C., Ellison, N. B., & Lampe, C. (2008). Social capital, self-esteem, and use of online social network sites: A longitudinal analysis. *Journal of Applied Developmental Psychology, 29*(6), 434–445.

Sueur, C., Kross, E., Verduyn, P., Demiralp, E., Park, J., Lee, D. S., ... Ybarra, O. (2013). Facebook use predicts declines in subjective well-being in young adults. *PLOS ONE, 8*(8), e69841.

Sutko, D. M., & de Souza e Silva, A. (2011). Location-aware mobile media and urban sociability. *New Media and Society, 13*(5), 807–823.

Thelwall, M. (2008). Social networks, gender, and friending: An analysis of MySpace member profiles. *Journal of the American Society for Information Science and Technology, 59*(8), 1523–1527.

Trottier, D. (2012). *Social media as surveillance: Rethinking visibility in a converging world.* Burlington, VT: Ashgate.

Turkle, S. (2011). *Alone together: Sociable robots, digitized friends, and the reinvention of intimacy and solitude.* New York, NY: Basic Books.

Turow, J. (2011). *The daily you: How the new advertising industry is defining your identity and your worth.* New Haven, CT: Yale University Press.

Vitak, J. (2012). The impact of context collapse and privacy on social network site disclosures. *Journal of Broadcasting and Electronic Media, 56*(4), 451–470.

Vitak, J., & Ellison, N. B. (2012). "There's a network out there you might as well tap": Exploring the benefits of and barriers to exchanging informational and support-based resources on Facebook. *New Media and Society, 15*(2), 243–259.

Wajcman, J. (2008). Life in the fast lane? Towards a sociology of technology and time. *British Journal of Sociology, 59*(1), 59–77.

Walther, J. B. (2011). Theories of computer-mediated and interpersonal relations. In M. L. Knapp & J. A. Daly (Eds.), *The Sage handbook of interpersonal communication* (pp. 443–479). Thousand Oaks, CA: Sage.

Wellman, B. (1998). *Networks in the global village: Life in contemporary communities.* Boulder, CO: Westview Press.

Wellman, B. (2001). Physical place and cyberplace: The rise of personalized networking. *International Journal of Urban and Regional Research, 25*(2), 227–252.

Wellman, B. (2002). Little boxes, glocalization, and networked individualism. In T. Ishida & K. Isbister (Eds.), *Digital cities: Technologies, experiences, and future perspectives* (pp. 10–25). Berlin, Germany: Springer.

Wellman, B., Haase, A. Q., Witte, J., & Hampton, K. (2007). Does the Internet increase, decrease, or supplement social capital? *American Behavioral Scientist, 45*(3), 436–455.

Wellman, B., Quan-Haase, A., Boase, J., Chen, W., Hampton, K., Díaz, I., & Miyata, K. (2006). The social affordances of the Internet for networked individualism. *Journal of Computer-Mediated Communication, 8*(3). doi: 10.1111/j.1083-6101.2003.tb00216.x

Wilken, R. (2010). A community of strangers? Mobile media, art, tactility and urban encounters with the other. *Mobilities, 5*(4), 449–468.

Wilken, R. (2012). Locative media: From specialized preoccupation to mainstream fascination. *Convergence: The International Journal of Research into New Media Technologies, 18*(3), 243–247.

Wilken, R., & Sinclair, J. (2009a). Contests of power and place in mobile media advertising. *Australian Journal of Communication, 36*, 85–109.

Wilken, R., & Sinclair, J. (2009b). "Waiting for the kiss of life": Mobile media and advertising. *Convergence: The International Journal of Research into New Media Technologies, 15*(4), 427–445.

Williams, R. (2003). *Television: Technology and cultural form*. New York, NY: Routledge.

Willis, K. (2010). Hidden treasure: Sharing local information. *Aether: The Journal of Media Geography, 5*, 50–62.

Wirth, L. (1938). Urbanism as a way of life. *American Journal of Sociology, 44*(1).

Young, K. (1996). Internet addiction: The emergence of a new clinical disorder. *CyberPsychology and Behavior, 1*(3), 237–244.

Zeffiro, A. (2006). The persistence of surveillance: The panoptic potential of locative media. *Wi: Journal of Mobile Media, 1*.

Zhao, C., & Jiang, G. (2011). *Cultural differences on visual self-presentation through social networking site profile images*. Paper presented at the 2011 SIGCHI Conference on Human Factors in Computing Systems, Vancouver, BC.

Zickuhr, K. (2012, May 11). Three-quarters of smartphone owners use location-based services. Retrieved from http://www.pewinternet.org/2012/05/11/three-quarters-of-smartphone-owners-use-location-based-services/

19

Technology and Self-Presentation
Impression Management Online
Miriam Bartsch[1] and Kaveri Subrahmanyam[2]

[1]*University of Hamburg*
[2]*California State University, Los Angeles*

More than one-third of the world's population is currently online (Internet World Stats, 2014), including significant percentage of the population in North America (> 87%), Australia (> 72%) and Europe (>70%). With the emergence of Web 2.0 (e.g., O'Reilly, 2005), online contexts have increasingly become a venue for social activities (e.g., ComScore, 2012; Ellison & boyd, 2013) and content creation (Cormode & Krishnamurthy, 2008). In fact, on Web 2.0, also called the social web or social media, users can engage in a variety of activities including chatting, blogging, gaming, gambling, shopping, texting, and networking. Many of the more social, communication activities occur on social media sites such as Facebook, Twitter, and Instagram. With their visual (pictures and videos) and text-based spaces, they provide users a digital space for self-exploration, identity construction, or for interaction with other people without some of the constraints present in the offline world (Manago, Graham, Greenfield, & Salimkhan, 2008; Subrahmanyam, Reich, Waechter, & Espinoza, 2008).

In this chapter we focus on the need for self-presentation and the need for privacy. Self-presentation is defined as behaviors used for creating, modifying, and maintaining other people's impression about oneself (Brown, 2007). We focus on self-presentation and the need for privacy as they can be viewed as two sides of the same issue. Adopting a "historical" approach, we will show how the need for self-presentation and privacy is displayed in different online contexts – from early applications such as personal websites, multi-user dungeons (MUDs), and chat rooms to social networking sites (SNSs), which are the most popular social web applications at the time of writing this chapter.

We begin by describing the general technological affordances of online communication contexts, as these affordances have played an important role in our changing communication patterns and provide users with opportunities for self-presentation and exploration. But technological affordances also present challenges to privacy and so we also examine some privacy-related affordances that must be kept in mind. Then, we will outline impression management theory and describe research on self-presentation in social media. The third section will examine whether people present their "true

---

The Wiley Handbook of Psychology, Technology, and Society, First Edition. Edited by Larry D. Rosen, Nancy A. Cheever, and L. Mark Carrier.

self" online or whether they use affordances of online contexts such as anonymity (still found in some online contexts) to present idealized or false versions of themselves. In the last section, we will examine some of the privacy issues in social media such as SNSs.

Affordances of the Social Web

We begin by defining our use of the term affordances in the context of the social web. Affordances are the properties of an object (e.g., hammer) or environment (e.g., online chat room) that provide particular opportunities for action. Thus for instance, a hammer affords the property of banging a nail into a wall and an online text-based chat room affords the opportunity of interacting anonymously. Technology affordance has been defined as the "mutuality of actor intentions and technology capabilities that provide the potential for a particular action" (Faraj & Azad, 2012, as cited in Majchrzak, Faraj, Kane, & Azad, 2013). In this section, we describe the different online affordances that have been proposed by researchers. We focus on affordances that are relevant to emerging online communication patterns and in particular to self-presentation and privacy. The affordances themselves have changed as the Internet has moved from a more anonymous, text-based environment, where one was more likely to meet strangers and unknown others, to one that uses text, audio, and visual images, and where one can meet and interact with friends as well as unknown others.

In the early years of the Internet, when online communication tools first became available, Walther (1996) proposed a hyper-personal computer-mediated communication model that emphasized the technological affordances of online contexts (see also Walther, 2007). Some of the affordances he identified were as follows: (1) Editability of online messages and presentations – digital texts are editable, can be changed, and even erased and created anew before sending or making them public. (2) Thus, users can potentially have an unlimited amount of time to construct and refine a message before sending it. (3) These messages are conveyed without any physical cues – or, in other words, "in physical isolation from [the] receiver" (Walther, 2007, p. 2541); thus they are more "controllable and malleable than the less overtly controlled physical behavior of FtF [face-to-face] encounters" (Ekman & Friesen, 1969, as cited in Walther, 2007, p. 2541). (4) A user can concentrate on message construction unlike face-to-face communication, where a speaker has to monitor his/her non-verbal expressions or manage other relevant cognitive processes.

Resnick has similarly identified numerous social web affordances in his 2002 work. Technology, according to Resnick, can "remove barriers to interaction" (p. 11), making distant communication possible, such that the sender and receiver do not have to be at the same place or even in the same time zone; examples of such online communication include Internet chat rooms and instant messaging as well as asynchronous communication such as via email. Overlap between these categories is also possible with communication being both distant and asynchronous at the same time, as with instant messaging and email (Resnick, 2002). Of course, modalities are *restricted* in online communication, such that email messages can only include text (and now pictures), and video conferencing cannot entail smell and typically only provides information about the face and the upper part of speakers' bodies (Sherman, Michikyan, & Greenfield, 2013).

Other affordances (Resnick, 2002) of the social web include the potential for anonymity (e.g., via usernames or avatars in chat rooms, online games, bulletin boards, etc.), optimal maintaining ties (e.g., via SNSs), or multitasking (e.g., chatting online while doing homework and listening to music on YouTube). Yet another affordance according to Resnick (2002, p. 11) is the ability to send information to lots of recipients at once (*large fan-out*; e.g., postings on social network profiles or in blogs) or, conversely, to get information from a lot of sources simultaneously (*large fan-in*; e.g., "voting, shop bots" [p. 11] or various subscribed Twitter channels). boyd (2011) has pointed out that the potentially great *visibility* of users is an affordance of social network sites. Along with visibility, she has described three other affordances of social network sites: *persistence*, which is the idea that once information is expressed online it will be archived; consequently it can also be duplicated (*replicability*) and searched (*searchability*). boyd also wrote of *scalability*, and, like Resnick, has noted that large fan-out or "the potential visibility of content ... is great" (boyd, 2011, p. 46). Furthermore, *invisible audiences, collapsed contexts*, and the *blurring of public and private* (boyd, 2011, p. 49) result as "dynamics" from those affordances. Dynamics refer to the idea that when posting something within some online contexts, users do not know who is present and to whom they are posting their messages. She further notes that because of a lack of "spatial, social, and temporal boundaries ... it [is] difficult to maintain distinct social contexts" (p. 49).

To make information accessible to a broad audience is yet another affordance of the social web that is relevant to the notion of impression management (e.g., Krämer & Haferkamp, 2011). Krämer and Haferkamp (2011) have pointed out that it is not easy to create a (semi-)public profile for everybody who might catch a glimpse of it. One has to deal with questions such as: Who might see my profile information and what might s/he think about me afterwards? Do I want my colleagues to get the same information about me as my friends? What image do I want others to have of me? Although one can restrict one's audience through privacy settings and friends lists (see Krämer & Haferkamp, 2011) or via groups (Rui & Stefanone, 2013), there is as yet no technical option that allows users to create profiles for different audiences. Thus, users have to build a profile that *fits* all audiences in all contexts and this presents challenges to privacy, an issue we address in a later section. Finally, in a recent study of SNSs, Kuo, Tseng, Tseng, and Lin (2013) introduced three other affordances – *expressive information control, privacy information control,* and *image information control* – which allow profile owners to control the flow of verbal or non-verbal information revealed/expressed via their profile (see also Feaster, 2010), regulate privacy and self-disclosure in interpersonal interactions, and thus control the image they want to convey.

Impression Management Theory

In this section, we present the theoretical framework that we adopted to examine online self-presentation and privacy. The terms *self-presentation* and *impression management* are used interchangeably to describe the conscious or unconscious psychological process by which people present themselves to control the image other people perceive of them (e.g., Brown, 2007; Mummendey, 2006). The concept of impression management was first introduced by Erving Goffman in his 1959 work, *The Presentation of Self in Everyday Life*. About two decades after Goffman's seminal work, the scientific community had researched impression management theory thoroughly (e.g., Jones & Pittman, 1982; Leary & Kowalski, 1990; Schlenker, 1980). With the advent of the Internet, the study of impression management has been transferred and examined in the context of online communication contexts (e.g., Becker & Stamp, 2005; Haferkamp, 2010; Krämer & Winter, 2008; Kuo et al., 2013; Pearson, 2010).

Goffman (1972) used the metaphor of a theater with actors wearing masks to exemplify how people show different aspects of themselves toward different audiences and in different situations. The assumption is that self-presentation occurs in order to gain something, as for example in a job interview, where a person may *directly* present herself in a favorable way. Self-presentation in an *indirect* way is also possible, for example when talking (or backbiting) about others. It can occur in a *non-verbal* manner by apparel and posture as well as in a *verbal* manner, through one's language skills (Mummendey, 2006; see also Tedeschi, 1981).

Mummendey (2006) has identified both positive and negative impression management techniques. Positive techniques include the following: self-promotion (i.e., to show one's assets); entitlements (higher entitlements due to self-ascribed accomplishments); overstatements; basking in reflected glory (i.e., self-enhancement through contacts to important persons, groups, or events); boosting (i.e., evaluate others in a way to look good); competence/expertise; exemplification (i.e., act like a role model); credibility; trustworthiness, attractiveness, status/prestige (e.g., through apparel and other symbols); self-disclosure (i.e., be open-minded); and ingratiation/other-enhancement. Negative techniques include the following: self-handicapping (i.e., to hand over responsibility); understatements; supplication (i.e., to appear needy); show or emphasize symptoms of disease; intimidation of others or to slam someone (blasting). Additionally, Mummendey (2006) has listed tactics of impression management when in a predicament, such as: apologize for a mistake; defend one's innocence; make excuses; explain oneself (justification), and not allowing others to judge negatively (refusal). One can also use disclaimers to avoid bearing responsibility before predicaments take place (cf. Mummendey, 2006, pp. 53f.).

Online Impression Management

Just as individuals engage in impression management offline, they do so in online contexts as well. In this section, we discuss research that has shown that some of the aforementioned techniques have been used for online impression management. Research suggests that individuals reveal different aspects of their personality depending on the particular online setting, the people in the setting, and the situational demands. In online contexts, there is time to plan what to show and to whom, whereas in face-to-face situations, people have to do this in the moment (Walther, 2007). Walther (2007) has referred to the planned efforts typical of online contexts as hyper-personal communication. It allows for a more controlled self-presentation; because of the fewer cues available online, there are more possibilities to present oneself in an ideal and intended manner. Next we identify some of the general impression management techniques that have been found online and then discuss the more specific strategies adopted by users as they have adapted to the affordances of different online contexts.

Impression management techniques such as ingratiation and competence as well as supplication have been documented for online venues (Bortree, 2005; Trammell & Keshelashvili, 2005). For instance, in an analysis of a small sample of six blogs written by adolescent females, Bortree (2005) found the use of ingratiation, competence, and supplication. On MySpace, Kane (2008) found that users scored highest on ingratiation and competence. Intimidation (though those scores were lower) and behaviors indicating supplication were likewise found to be frequent on MySpace profiles. On Friendster, people formed friendships for reasons of impression management (Donath & boyd, 2004) – thus, they used the technique basking in reflected glory. On Facebook profiles, research suggests that participants implicitly present themselves as socially desirable, suggesting that they were using previously identified techniques such as basking in reflected glory or self-promotion (Zhao, Grasmuck, & Martin, 2008). These findings suggest that impression management theory as proposed by Goffman can be transferred and applied to self-presentation activities on Web 2.0.

In addition to adapting offline impression management techniques, people take advantage of technological affordances such as photographs for online self-presentation (Pearson, 2010; Salimkhan, Manago, & Greenfield, 2010; Siibak, 2009; Strano, 2008). Users report that they intentionally select photos for self-presentation (Bartsch, 2013; Ellison, Heino, & Gibbs, 2006; Siibak, 2009; Young, 2009), particularly attractive (e.g., Young, 2009) and sometimes even photoshopped ones (Whitty, 2008). Impression management is not only conveyed via photos. Research has also found evidence for self-presentation via status updates, (number of) friends, as well as wall posts and group membership (Haferkamp, Eimler, Papadakis, & Kruck, 2012; Haferkamp, Krämer, Drotner, & Schrøder, 2010; Tong, Van der Heide, Langwell, & Walther, 2008; Zhao et al., 2008). Such impression management is not only a motivator for using SNSs (e.g., Nadkarni & Hofmann, 2011), it may even be consciously planned and well maintained (Kuo et al., 2013). For instance, a participant in the focus group study by Manago et al. (2008) observed that, "Whenever you put any kind of information out there you have the intention of what you want people to think about you" (p. 450).

Users are also strategic about their impression management, especially when it comes to guarding their privacy. For instance, some users resort to communicating specific content via ambiguous images to an intended audience, which understands it exclusively; in their conclusion, Salimkhan et al. (2010, para. 6) note that "Youth's answer to the 'privacy paradox' ... may be to employ vague images to represent the self that only a subset of their social network will understand. In this way, they can still utilize social networks to validate and manifest possible selves as social reality without sacrificing privacy." Using self-report data from a survey of active Facebook users ($N = 684$) in Germany, Ruddigkeit, Penzel, and Schneider (2013) found that individuals use conditional self-disclosure in order to self-disclose without sacrificing all privacy. Thus they disclose some parts of the self while protecting others at the same time. Such selective information disclosure has also been found to be important for impression management when using instant messaging (Patil & Kobsa, 2004, 2005), which is similar to the chat tools found in social media such as Facebook.

Being Who You Are (or Want to be) Online

In the next subsections, we examine some of the more specific ways that users have engaged in impression management by engaging in self-presentation and self-disclosure in different online contexts. Adopting a historical approach, we start with the applications that emerged during the early years of the Internet and then examine more recently emerged applications. Note that some of these early applications are still in use, whereas others are used less frequently or hardly at all.

Webpages, MUDs, chatrooms, and blogs   Before the emergence of Web 2.0, home pages provided a venue for people to present themselves online (e.g., Döring, 2002; Papacharissi, 2002a, 2002b). Studies have suggested that self-presentation in personal home pages mirrored offline self-presentation; for instance, the self-presentation strategies (e.g., ingratiation, competence) observed on home pages were similar to those recorded in face-to-face encounters (Dominick, 1999; Machilek, Schütz, & Marcus, 2004). Owners of personal home pages were also found to present an authentic self rather than engaging in identity play (e.g., Döring, 2002; Machilek et al., 2004). In contrast to webpages, multi-user dungeons (MUDs) are text-based social environments where pretending and role-playing are the norm (Subrahmanyam & Šmahel, 2011); consistent with these technological affordances, gender-switching was found to be a vital aspect and frequent in MUDs (Roberts & Parks, 1999).

In the earlier days of the Internet, when it was easy to be anonymous in chat rooms, bulletin boards, or blogs and where one did not have to share details about one's identity and offline self, scholars suggested that people would experiment with different genders and identities while online (Hancock, 2007; Turkle, 1995). Research, however, suggests that identity play was not as widespread and frequent as predicted. In a study with a representative Czech sample, Šmahel and Machovcová (2006; cited in Subrahmanyam & Šmahel, 2011) found that only 15% of Internet users reported that they sometimes pretended to be someone else when online. Similarly, in her study of U.S. adolescents' home Internet use, Gross (2004) found that most online pretending was to play a joke rather than for identity play. Although identity play was not very prevalent, users capitalized on technological affordances to engage in self-presentation. For example, Shoham (2004) found that chat users presented themselves via nicknames, font color, and their comments. Research has also found that nicknames in chat rooms often revealed details such as gender, age, or location information (Subrahmanyam, Šmahel, & Greenfield, 2006). Such details are not readily available in online chat rooms compared to face-to-face encounters (Subrahmanyam et al., 2006), and thus usernames and even user pictures are used for self-presentation and impression management purposes.

Not only did chat users not consistently assume alternate identities, many presented their real name or even an actual photograph of themselves (Kapidzic & Herring, 2011; Qian & Scott, 2007). They were also found to be strategic in their online self-presentation. For instance, Kapidzic and Herring (2011) analyzed teen chat profiles with regard to messages and pictures and reported that "young females ... tended to present themselves as emotional, friendly, good listeners (reactive), sexually available and eager to please males ... while young males appear more assertive, manipulative, initiating, and visually dominant, while at the same time more distant" (p. 52). These studies suggest that rather than capitalizing on the anonymity afforded by online chat rooms, many users instead engaged in strategic self-presentation, such that they implicitly and explicitly presented key details of their identity such as their gender.

These results are not surprising, and Gies (2008) has suggested that assuming a fake identity requires a lot of work. He even argues that people may reveal more about their identity online compared to offline settings, where anonymity is not guaranteed. He has compared this with support groups, wherein one is supposed to be as open as possible about one's problems while at the same time revealing just as much as necessary and as little as possible about one's identity. Consequently, anonymity online (Gies, 2008) can lead to more openness and greater self-disclosure because of fewer cues that could lead to one's identity and thus to possible shame or harm.

Some evidence for this claim comes from a study of 207 bloggers by Qian and Scott (2007): the more identifying information a blogger revealed, the less s/he self-disclosed. This is likely because when a blog is linked to identity cues, it can be found more easily by search engines and thus personal information could be available for unintended audiences. Based on an online self-report survey, Bronstein (2013) found that most bloggers revealed authentic information (i.e., real name, actual photos) about themselves, but only 21% revealed "very personal information," 56% "somewhat personal information," and 18% did not disclose any personal information at all. Most of them also did not regret posting information that was "too personal" or "somewhat personal."

Consistent with the idea that the Internet helps with self-construction (Gonzales & Hancock, 2008), blogs have been found to be a venue for self-reflection and self-expression (McCullagh, 2008). This is particularly true of blogs written by adolescents and emerging adults (Mazur & Kozarian, 2010; Subrahmanyam, Garcia, Harsono, Li, & Lipana, 2009); based on a content analysis of teen blogs, Subrahmanyam and colleagues reported that adolescent bloggers used their entries to create narratives about themselves, as well as the people and events in their lives.

Not only do online users control their self-presentation consciously, they also self-present differently depending on the people and context of an online venue; participants in Brivio and Ibarra's (2009) study reported that they trusted their blog on the LiveJournal site more than the social network site MySpace. Additionally, they stated that on LiveJournal they had friends they were never likely to meet in offline life, and thus could be more open regarding their self-presentation. In contrast, on MySpace they were linked to people in their offline life, and thus they reported being more cautious about what information they revealed there. Similar findings were obtained by Trammell and Keshelashvili (2005), who measured self-presentation in their content analysis of 209 A-list blogs (i.e., very popular blogs with a broad audience) through self-revelation and use of impression management tactics. They found that the bloggers revealed a lot of personal information even though they could have been anonymous: 83% revealed their full real name and the majority (89%) shared some contact information, with email addresses being the most frequent information shared (99.5%). Interestingly, the bloggers in this study also shared personal information and over 68% revealed details about their occupation and biography.

Online games To examine self-presentation within disembodied environments such as online games, researchers have analyzed avatars, which are the "face and body" of the game player. Gender is an important element of self-presentation, and MacCallum-Stewart (2008) found gender-switching to be a common practice in MMORPGs (massively multiplayer online role-playing games). Such gender-bending reportedly occurs for the aesthetic pleasure an attractive persona implies. Even though MMORPGs are role-playing games, users identify with the avatar as an "aesthetic" or a "character", rather than as a "person" (MacCallum-Stewart, 2008, p. 36). They want to appear attractive, which leads to self-presentational aspects of avatar choice and thus suggests that players are engaging in impression management while role-playing in MMORPGs.

With regard to avatar creation, Trepte and Reinecke (2010) found that factors such as game type (competitive vs. non-competitive) and life satisfaction are relevant. The more competitive a game or the less satisfied a player is with his/her life, the bigger the difference between his/her and the avatar's personality attributes. That avatars have characteristics similar to players' own personality traits has also been found by Companion and Sambrook (2008). In contrast, Thomas and Johansen (2012) found that women created avatars that were thinner than their offline/physical appearance when they themselves would like to be thinner in reality. Using a self-report online survey, Bessière, Seay, and Kiesler (2007) found that players of World of Warcraft (the MMORPG with the most number of players worldwide) had self-idealized avatars. More precisely, the players' avatars were more conscientious, extraverted, and less neurotic than their offline physical selves, with the findings stronger in participants with lower self-esteem or higher depression. In contrast, combining self-reports and observer ratings, Wohn and Wash (2012) found that simulation game players created in-game virtual environments that made it possible to suggest the players' offline personalities rather than their ideal selves. Similarly, Yee, Ducheneaut, Nelson, and Likarish (2011) found that offline personality characteristics were represented in online characters of World of Warcraft.

Social networking sites   In contrast to online games and other early Internet contexts, online networks on SNSs overlap decisively with the offline community of a user (Subrahmanyam et al., 2008; Zhao et al., 2008). Even though social networking sites do not afford the kinds of identity play that are possible in anonymous contexts, they provide tools for users to explore their possible selves and present their ideal selves (Manago et al., 2008). It appears that such self-presentation may be more in tune with offline selves as research has found that the images generated by SNS users are closely related to who they are offline (Gosling, Gaddis, & Vazire, 2007). Using focus groups of Facebook users, Rosenbaum, Johnson, Stepman, and Nuijten (2010) identified their impression management goals and strategies. Their major goals were to create (1) an "authentic" and (2) a "current, positive, and professional presentation" as well as (3) to control for information they provide about themselves. Minor goals of self-presentation were to "ensure a good presentation through association and present oneself as socially literate" (p. 12).

To reach their goal of authenticity, the participants stated that they made sure the content of their profile (e.g., status updates) was an accurate reflection of "who they are, what they are thinking, and doing at that time" (p. 12). Similarly, another strategy was to post pictures that captured their physical appearance and personality (p. 12). However, focus group participants also reported that they had friends who posted pictures that showed self-enhancements of the profile owner. To make sure the provided self-presentation is always "up to date," participants identified strategies such as updating one's status daily, providing current information such as pictures, and responding promptly to comments. They reported that to appear in a positive light one has to post appealing pictures and provide positive profile content (via groups, self-descriptions, links, etc.).

An important part of the second goal (a current, positive, and professional self-presentation) was to have a somewhat professional self-presentation on Facebook, and to accomplish this participants reported that they monitored their Facebook walls for inappropriate posts by others and made postings related to their work/ organization.

The third goal (controlling information) dealt with privacy and users reported controlling what they post (and what others add to their profile) so they can determine what can be seen by whom as well as keep things completely off their profile. Receiving attention and getting recognition through status updates or comments on walls (by and of other users) was named as a minor goal. This is also a way of getting feedback about one's self-presentation, which seems to be highly appreciated. The second minor goal was to appear socially literate by "managing" contacts in accordance with socially accepted norms. The authors argue that "small social acts play a role in self-presentation" (p. 20) and thus self-presentation on Facebook is a dynamic process and is accomplished by a variety of goals and strategies (p. 22). Although exploratory, the study shows that users are consciously and laboriously managing their profiles to present an accurate picture of themselves.

Along similar lines, Back et al.'s (2010) study provides further evidence that Facebook users may present realistic self-displays. Using a combination of self-reports and observer ratings of 236 profiles (Facebook, StudiVZ, and SchuelerVZ), they found that profile owners "communicate their real personality" (p. 372) and did not find evidence that users create idealized profiles that do not reflect their actual personalities (p. 372). Walther, Van der Heide, Hamel, and Shulman (2009) additionally found that other-generated statements on Facebook are trusted more than self-generated content. This is because other-generated content might not be manipulated as easily as self-generated statements about oneself, thus those contents are seen to provide a more truthful picture of a person's real self rather than drawing an idealized one.

Further evidence that users do not restrict themselves to idealized self-presentation on SNSs comes from work by Moreno et al. (2011). These authors evaluated the status updates and comments in 200 publicly available Facebook profiles of their college-student sample and reported finding symptoms of depression in the online profiles. Interestingly, the profile owners were more likely to refer to symptoms of depression either when they were more active on Facebook or when they got at least one reaction to their comment suggesting they were using negative impression management tactics (e.g., to show or emphasize symptoms of disease) to appear needy or to seek attention.

Whether intentional or not, individuals' identity is typically behind a certain kind of self-portrayal. The construction of a coherent and stable identity is an important psychosocial task during adolescence and early adulthood (Erikson, 1959). Testing out different aspects of the self helps with this task and research indicates that youth use digital communication for such self-exploration (e.g., Subrahmanyam, Greenfield, & Michikyan, 2013). For instance, using participants' own descriptions of their photographs and wall posts/status updates, Michikyan, Subrahmanyam, and Dennis (2014b) found that users often presented their social and individual identity. Such self-presentation is quite fluid and Livingstone's (2008) interviews with 16 adolescents

(13–16 years) revealed that they often recreated their self-presentation. Such self-actualization is a social process and normative at this age, and Livingstone noted that younger teenagers changed the display of their online selves on SNSs more often than older teens. Thus, they showed their experimenting with different personality aspects "in real time" on their Facebook or MySpace profiles. Older adolescents preferred a plainer, less playful profile and presented their selves through other aspects, like links to their friends. The findings of Livingstone's study indicate that during adolescence youth may present a multifaceted self as they explore different selves in order to establish the one that they want to eventually live with.

Similarly, Michikyan, Dennis, and Subrahmanyam (2014) proposed that as they consolidate their self, emerging adults may present either a real, an ideal, or one of three different false selves (deception, impress/compare, and exploration) on their Facebook account. Using an online survey of 261 college students, they found that although the emerging adult participants did report presenting these different selves, they presented their real selves significantly more often than an ideal or false self. Even more interestingly, and in line with previously mentioned research, the false self that serves to try out different aspects of personality (and thus serves explorative functions) was used to a greater extent than the ideal self or a false self that is used for reasons of deception or impression/comparison. Michikyan, Dennis, and Subrahmanyam (2014) also examined the relation between online self-presentation and identity state, self-esteem, and depression and found that those who reported more coherent identity states also reported greater presentation of their real self on Facebook, and those reporting a less coherent sense of the self and lower self-esteem reported greater presentation of their false self on Facebook. There is some indication that such online self-presentation may be strategic. Using a web-based survey of Turkish students ($N=143$), Tosun (2012) examined motives for different levels of "true" self-presentation (high, medium, and low); results suggested that users reported presenting their true self to a higher level when they intended their Facebook use to create new friendships or to manage romantic relationships. Higher levels of true self on Facebook were also associated with maintaining long-distance relationships as well as with passive observation of other users' profiles.

Studies also have examined the relation between personality traits/factors like the Big Five and online self-presentation. It appears that narcissism is a personality trait that is related to self-promoting profile content; individuals who scored higher on scales of narcissism tended to upload more attractive (profile) photos as well as post status updates more frequently than those who scored lower (e.g., Amichai-Hamburger & Vinitzky, 2010; Buffardi & Campbell, 2008; Mehdizadeh, 2010; Ong et al., 2011; Wang, Jackson, Zhang, & Su, 2012). In a related vein, Michikyan, Subrahmanyam, and Dennis (2014a) found that emerging adults high in neuroticism reported greater extent of ideal and false self-presentation (to deceive as well as to impress/compare) on Facebook, whereas those low in extraversion reported greater levels of online self-exploratory behaviors.

To recap, in the previous sections, we examined the self-presentation and impression management that users engage in within different online contexts. We showed that self-presentation varied in different contexts and users did not always capitalize on the affordances of a particular tool. While MUDs are the venue for anonymity and role-playing, and players' avatars resembled their offline selves, nonetheless they were idealized versions of their real selves. Similarly, although users can be anonymous in chat rooms and blogs, research suggests that they often revealed information about themselves voluntarily, as for example when choosing a username that provides details about their gender, age, ethnicity, or location or when creating a profile. On SNSs, online self-presentation appears to overlap to a certain degree with offline aspects of the self. This is not surprising, given that online networks on SNSs often comprise people known from offline lives (Subrahmanyam et al., 2008), and thus it is easy for others to verify or provide feedback about information that is presented. Thus, telling lies is not very smart unless one wants to be unmasked by real-life contacts (Donath, 2007). Overall, we conclude that anonymity might still be possible on the web and sometimes it might be what users are looking for, but in the majority of online contexts examined here, individuals seem to present their true (at times somewhat idealized) selves and thus may be engaging in self-presentation rather than in self-exploration.

Risks and Privacy Online

With the many affordances of online environments and their use as a venue for identity exploration and self-presentation, there also come threats, including risks to privacy, Internet addiction (e.g., Kuss, Griffiths, & Binder, 2013; LaRose, Kim, & Peng, 2010; Rehbein & Mößle, 2013), and cyberbullying (e.g., Tokunaga, 2010). Here we mainly focus on the risks to privacy. As we noted earlier, self-presentation and maintaining one's privacy are two sides of the same coin. For instance, bloggers who disclose a lot of personal information in their blogs face the risk that the information presented could be seen by the wrong people at the wrong time. McCullagh (2008) suggests that potential employers could discover old blog posts that contain information/opinions that are not valid anymore and thus draw wrong conclusions. Privacy risks are not unique to blogs but are common in a variety of online contexts and activities (Wilson, Gosling, & Graham, 2012). When the desire for impression management is accompanied by the desire for privacy, it results in the selective presentation of the self (Kobsa, Patil, & Meyer, 2012). It should be noted that this chapter only examines risks to privacy in the context of the social web, and does not consider other privacy risks related to identity fraud, online banking, or shopping.

Facebook records and archives everything that is ever posted or uploaded to the site. For users, setting privacy restrictions to the highest possible security level is neither a default setting nor is it easy – according to an article in a German online newspaper, at the time of writing the article, 36 steps were required to "secure one's privacy on a Facebook profile" (Reißmann/dpa, 2012). Thus, many users might not change their privacy settings given the complexity and the time it takes to do so. In October 2013 Facebook changed its privacy settings for users 13 through 17 years of age, announcing that these users will now be allowed to set their profile to being publicly visible (note that the private setting is still the default for youth) (Facebook, 2013). With Facebook being currently the biggest SNS with more than 1.35 billion members worldwide (Facebook, 2014; Statista, 2015), this means that vast amounts of private information remain unsecured on the web.

Bartsch (2013) explored the privacy concerns of 532 participants and their self-presentation on Facebook via an online survey. About 96% of her sample reported that they had changed their privacy settings at least once and 70% reported that they had done so up to six times. Additionally there was a positive correlation between the need for privacy and the reported privacy behavior on Facebook, showing that people who were concerned about their privacy behaved accordingly. Bartsch's findings are consistent with other recent studies on the topic of privacy-related behavior (Patchin & Hinduja, 2010; Utz & Krämer, 2009; Wilson et al., 2012) and question the suggestion that while users might care about their privacy, they do not act accordingly (Acquisti & Gross, 2006; Barnes, 2006; Taddicken, 2011). In the same study by Bartsch (2013), 60% of the participants showed their offline first name and surname on their profile, while another 30% only revealed parts of their name, even though Facebook requires everybody to reveal their offline name (Reißmann, 2012). While the number of people (60%) that entered their full name was high, the finding that 30% only revealed part of their name suggests that at least some users were not blindly creating profiles but were thinking about possible issues when creating them. Surveying a sample of U.S. bloggers, Qian and Scott (2007) found that 30% of users partially entered their offline name, 12.6% revealed their full name, and 18.8% revealed other identifying information. In a Latin American sample (Bronstein, 2013), 48% stated that they revealed their real name, 11% revealed parts of their name, and 41% used a pseudonym. Bronstein (2013) argued that these percentages were probably because the bloggers felt secure in their blogging environment. Similarly, users' level of trust in the particular online environment is related to greater or lesser self-disclosure. Research suggests that users with greater privacy literacy (i.e., a better knowledge of how to restrict access to one's profile or to one's profile information) have a more restricted profile than those with a lower privacy literacy knowledge (Christofides, Muise, & Desmarais, 2012) and change their privacy settings more often (Bartsch, 2013). However, more frequent changes do not imply that the profile is more restricted and thus more secure in terms of privacy (Bartsch, 2013). Recall that in Bartsch's study a majority had made changes to their privacy settings, yet a little less than 50% revealed their contact information to someone other than themselves, 35% let their friends see it, and almost 2% let everybody see their current contact information. Similar results were found by Dey, Jelveh, and Ross (2012) in their long-term analysis of Facebook user profiles conducted in 2010–2011; they found that profile owners in New York City had become more aware of security risks and privacy issues as they restricted their profile to a greater extent. Relatedly, compared to profiles that were set to be public, profiles that were set to be private were found to be more often associated with the presentation of the real or ideal self (Michikyan, Dennis, & Subrahmanyam, 2014).

A recent article by Kisekka, Bagchi-Sen, and Rao (2013) showed that privacy information disclosure (PID) on Facebook may be affected by the access to the account: the authors examined the PID of users who accessed their account via smartphones and found that users disclosed less information when they either logged on via a mobile device or when they had more than one active SNS account. Females also disclosed less private information than males and greater difficulty in managing privacy controls led to an increase of PID in older (>55 years) participants. Overall, the above findings suggest that the rising awareness of privacy issues and the growing competencies regarding the Internet and mobile applications may in general be leading to safer interactions with social media.

Conclusion

During the early years of the Internet, the proliferation of disembodied and anonymous venues led scholars (e.g., Turkle, 1995) to speculate that users would engage in identity experimentation and create alternative selves online. Across a range of online contexts, there is little indication that adult users engage in such identity play. Instead, users, particularly adolescents and emerging adults, appear to use online venues to present different aspects of their self and identities (e.g., Livingstone & Bober, 2005; Subrahmanyam & Šmahel, 2011). The one consistent exception seems to be within online games, where a male gamer might choose a female avatar because he wants to play with an avatar that is more attractive (and presumably gets more attention) than the male ones. There are of course those who pretend to be someone else who do it for reasons that are not legal – such as with cyberbullying (e.g., ABC News, 2007; Tokunaga, 2010) or stalking (e.g., Gross & Acquisti, 2005). But as the studies described in our chapter suggest users of Web 2.0 engage in online self-presentation mostly for impression management. At the same time, although users seem to present aspects of their self that are true to their real self, they are also quite aware of privacy concerns. Their online privacy-seeking behaviors are by no means complete, but compared to the early years of the Internet, people have become much more sophisticated and strategic about their online impression management.

References

ABC News. (2007, November 19). Parents: Cyber bullying led to teen's suicide. Retrieved from http://abcnews.go.com/GMA/story?id=3882520&page=1

Acquisti, A., & Gross, R. (2006). Imagined communities: Awareness, information sharing, and privacy on the Facebook. In *6th Workshop on Privacy Enhancing Technologies* (pp. 36–58). Berlin, Germany: Springer.

Amichai-Hamburger, Y., & Vinitzky, G. (2010). Social network use and personality. *Computers in Human Behavior, 26*, 1289–1295.

Back, M. D., Stopfer, J. M., Vazire, S., Gaddis, S., Schmukle, S. C., Egloff, B., & Gosling, S. D. (2010). Facebook profiles reflect actual personality, not self-idealization. *Psychological Science, 21*, 372–374.

Barnes, S. B. (2006). A privacy paradox: Social networking in the United States. *First Monday, 11*(9). Retrieved from http://firstmonday.org/article/view/1394/1312

Bartsch, M. (2013). *Impressivacy – Or how to unite impression management and privacy concerns on Facebook*. [Unpublished thesis (Diplom)]. Department of Psychology, University of Hamburg, Germany.

Becker, J. A. H., & Stamp, G. H. (2005). Impression management in chat rooms: A grounded theory model. *Communication Studies, 56*, 243–260.

Bessière, K., Seay, A. F., & Kiesler, S. (2007). The ideal elf: Identity exploration in World of Warcraft. *CyberPsychology and Behavior, 10*, 530–535.

Bortree, D. S. (2005). Presentation of self on the web: An ethnographic study of teenage girls' weblogs. *Education, Communication and Information, 5*, 25–39.

boyd, d. (2011). Social network sites as networked publics: Affordances, dynamics, and implications. In Z. Papacharissi (Ed.), *A networked self: Identity, community, and culture on social network sites* (pp. 39–58). New York, NY: Routledge.

Brivio, E., & Ibarra, F. C. (2009). Self presentation in blogs and social networks. *Studies in Health Technology and Informatics, 144*, 113–115.

Bronstein, J. (2013). Personal blogs as online presences on the Internet: Exploring self-presentation and self-disclosure in blogging. *Aslib Proceedings: New Information Perspectives*, 161–181.

Brown, J. D. (2007). *The self*. New York, NY: Psychology Press.

Buffardi, L. E., & Campbell, W. (2008). Narcissism and social networking web sites. *Personality and Social Psychology Bulletin, 34*, 1303–1314.

Christofides, E., Muise, A., & Desmarais, S. (2012). Hey mom, what's on your Facebook? Comparing Facebook disclosure and privacy in adolescents and adults. *Social Psychological and Personality Science, 3*, 48–54.

Companion, M., & Sambrook, R. (2008). The influence of sex on character attribute preferences. *CyberPsychology and Behavior, 11*, 673–674.

ComScore. (2012). Year-on-year growth in unique visitors to leading social networks in Europe in March 2012, by platform (in percent). Retrieved from http://www.statista.com/statistics/280008/visitors-development-of-social-networks-in-europe-by-platform/

Cormode, G., & Krishnamurthy, B. (2008). Key differences between Web 1.0 and Web 2.0. *First Monday, 13*(6). Retrieved from http://firstmonday.org/ojs/index.php/fm/rt/printerFriendly/2125/1972

Dey, R., Jelveh, Z., & Ross, K. (2012). Facebook users have become much more private: A large-scale study. In *Proceedings of 4th IEEE International Workshop on Security and Social Networking (SESOC)*. Lugano, Switzerland.

Dominick, J. R. (1999). Who do you think you are? Personal home pages and self-presentation on the World Wide Web. *Journalism and Mass Communication Quarterly, 76*, 646–658.

Donath, J. (2007). Signals in social supernets. *Journal of Computer-Mediated Communication, 13*, 231–251.

Donath, J., & boyd, d. (2004). Public displays of connection. *BT Technology Journal, 22*(4), 71–82.

Döring, N. (2002). Personal home pages on the web: A review of research. *Journal of Computer-Mediated Communication, 7*(3). doi: 10.1111/j.1083-6101.2002.tb00152.x

Ellison, N. B., & boyd, d. m. (2013). Sociality through social network sites. In W. H. Dutton (Ed.), *The Oxford handbook of Internet studies* (pp. 151–172). Oxford, UK: Oxford University Press.

Ellison, N., Heino, R., & Gibbs, J. (2006). Managing impressions online: Self-presentation processes in the online dating environment. *Journal of Computer-Mediated Communication, 11*, 415–441.

Erikson, E. H. (1959). *Identity and the life cycle*. New York, NY: W. H. Norton.

Facebook. (2013, October 16). Teens now start with "friends" privacy for new accounts; adding the option to share publicly. Retrieved from http://newsroom.fb.com/news/2013/10/teens-now-start-with-friends-privacy-for-new-accounts-adding-the-option-to-share-publicly/

Facebook. (2014). Statistics. Retrieved from http://newsroom.fb.com/company-info/

Feaster, J. (2010). Expanding the impression management model of communication channels: An information control scale. *Journal of Computer-Mediated Communication, 16*, 115–138.

Gies, L. (2008). How material are cyberbodies? Broadband Internet and embodied subjectivity. *Crime, Media, Culture, 4*, 311–330.

Goffman, E. (1972). *The presentation of self in everyday life*. London, UK: Penguin. (Original work published 1959)

Gonzales, A. L., & Hancock, J. T. (2008). Identity shift in computer-mediated environments. *Media Psychology, 11*, 167–185.

Gosling, S. D., Gaddis, S., & Vazire, S. (2007, March 26–28). *Personality impressions based on Facebook profiles*. Paper presented at the ICWSM, Boulder, CO.

Gross, E. F. (2004). Adolescent Internet use: What we expect, what teens report. *Journal of Applied Developmental Psychology, 25*, 633–649.

Gross, R., & Acquisti, A. (2005). Information revelation and privacy in online social networks. In *Proceedings of WPES'05* (pp. 71–80). Alexandria, VA: ACM.

Haferkamp, N. (2010). *Sozialpsychologische Aspekte im Web 2.0. Impression Management und sozialer Vergleich* [Social psychological aspects of Web 2.0: Impression management and social comparison]. Stuttgart, Germany: Kohlhammer.

Haferkamp, N., Eimler, S. C., Papadakis, A. M., & Kruck, J. V. (2012). Men are from Mars, women are from Venus? Examining gender differences in self-presentation on social networking sites. *Cyberpsychology, Behavior, and Social Networking, 15*, 91–98.

Haferkamp, N., Krämer, N. C., Drotner, K., & Schrøder, K. (2010). Creating a digital self: Impression management and impression formation on social networking sites. In K. Drotner & K. C. Schrøder (Eds.), *Digital content creation: Creativity, competence, critique* (pp. 129–146). New York, NY: Peter Lang.

Hancock, J. T. (2007). Digital deception: When, where and how people lie online. In K. McKenna, T. Postmes, U. Reips, & A. N. Joinson (Eds.), *Oxford handbook of Internet psychology* (pp. 289–301). Oxford, UK: Oxford University Press.

Internet World Stats. (2014). Internet usage statistics: The Internet big picture. Retrieved from http://internetworldstats.com/stats.htm

Jones, E. E., & Pittman, T. S. (1982). Toward a general theory of strategic self presentation. In J. Suls (Ed.), *Psychological perspectives on the self*. Hillsdale, NJ: Lawrence Erlbaum Associates.

Kane, C. M. (2008). *I'll see you on MySpace: Self-presentation in a social network website.* [Masters thesis]. Cleveland State University, Cleveland, OH. Retrieved from http://academic.csuohio.edu/kneuendorf/c63309/Kane08.pdf

Kapidzic, S., & Herring, S. C. (2011). Gender, communication, and self-presentation in teen chatrooms revisited: Have patterns changed? *Journal of Computer-Mediated Communication, 17*, 39–59.

Kisekka, V., Bagchi-Sen, S., & Rao, H. R. (2013). Extent of private information disclosure on online social networks: An exploration of Facebook mobile phone users. *Computers in Human Behavior, 29*, 2722–2729.

Kobsa, A., Patil, S., & Meyer, B. (2012). Privacy in instant messaging: An impression management model. *Behaviour and Information Technology, 31*, 355–370.

Krämer, N. C., & Haferkamp, N. (2011). Online self-presentation: Balancing privacy concerns and impression construction on social networking sites. In S. Trepte & L. Reinecke (Eds.), *Privacy online: Perspectives on privacy and self-disclosure in the social web* (pp. 127–142). Berlin, Germany: Springer.

Krämer, N. C., & Winter, S. (2008). Impression management 2.0: The relationship of self-esteem, extraversion, self-efficacy, and self-presentation within social networking sites. *Journal of Media Psychology: Theories, Methods, and Applications, 20*, 106–116.

Kuo, F.-Y., Tseng, C.-Y., Tseng, F.-C., & Lin, C. S. (2013). A study of social information control affordances and gender difference in Facebook self-presentation. *Cyberpsychology, Behavior, and Social Networking, 16*, 635–644.

Kuss, D. J., Griffiths, M. D., & Binder, J. F. (2013). Internet addiction in students: Prevalence and risk factors. *Computers in Human Behavior, 29*, 959–966.

LaRose, R., Kim, J., & Peng, W. (2010). Social networking: Addictive, compulsive, problematic, or just another media habit. In Z. Papacharissi (Ed.), *A networked self: Identity, community, and culture on social network sites* (pp. 59–81). New York, NY: Routledge.

Leary, M. R., & Kowalski, R. M. (1990). Impression management: A literature review and two-component model. *Psychological Bulletin, 107*, 34–47.

Livingstone, S. (2008). Taking risky opportunities in youthful content creation: Teenagers' use of social networking sites for intimacy, privacy and self-expression. *New Media and Society, 10*, 393–411.

Livingstone, S., & Bober, M. (2005). *UK children go online: Final report of key project findings.* London, UK: LSE.

MacCallum-Stewart, E. (2008). Real boys carry girly epics: Normalising gender bending in online games. *Eludamos: Journal for Computer Game Culture, 2,* 27–40. Retrieved from http://www.eludamos.org/index.php/eludamos/article/viewArticle/vol2no1-5/51

Machilek, F., Schütz, A., & Marcus, B. (2004). Self-presenters, or people like you and me? Intentions and personality traits of owners of personal websites. *Zeitschrift für Medienpsychologie, 16,* 88–98.

Majchrzak, A., Faraj, S., Kane, G. C., & Azad, B. (2013). The contradictory influence of social media affordances on online communal knowledge sharing. *Journal of Computer-Mediated Communication, 19,* 38–55.

Manago, A. M., Graham, M. B., Greenfield, P. M., & Salimkhan, G. (2008). Self-presentation and gender on MySpace. *Journal of Applied Developmental Psychology, 29,* 446–458.

Mazur, E., & Kozarian, L. (2010). Self-presentation and interaction in blogs of adolescents and young emerging adults. *Journal of Adolescent Research, 25,* 124–144.

McCullagh, K. (2008). Blogging: Self presentation and privacy. *Information and Communications Technology Law, 17,* 3–23.

Mehdizadeh, S. (2010). Self-presentation 2.0: Narcissism and self-esteem on Facebook. *Cyberpsychology, Behavior, and Social Networking, 13,* 357–364.

Michikyan, M., Dennis, J., & Subrahmanyam, K. (2014). Can you guess who I am? Real, ideal, and false self-presentation on Facebook among emerging adults. *Emerging Adulthood* doi: 10.1177/2167696814532442

Michikyan, M., Subrahmanyam, K., & Dennis, J. (2014a). Can you tell who I am? Neuroticism, extraversion, and online self-presentation among young adults. *Computers in Human Behavior, 33,* 179–183.

Michikyan, M., Subrahmanyam, K., & Dennis, J. (2014b). Their photos, their words: A mixed-method approach to identity presentation and emotional disclosure on Facebook in a multi-ethnic sample of emerging adults. Manuscript submitted for publication.

Moreno, M. A., Jelenchick, L. A., Egan, K. G., Cox, E., Young, H., Gannon, K. E., & Becker, T. (2011). Feeling bad on Facebook: Depression disclosures by college students on a social networking site. *Depression and Anxiety, 28,* 447–455.

Mummendey, H. D. (2006). Selbstdarstellung [Self-presentation]. In H. W. Bierhoff & D. Frey (Eds.), *Handbuch der Sozialpsychologie und Kommunikationspsychologie* [Handbook of social psychology and communication psychology] (pp. 49–56). Göttingen, Germany: Hogrefe.

Nadkarni, A., & Hofmann, S. G. (2011). Why do people use Facebook? *Personality and Individual Differences, 52,* 243–249.

Ong, E. Y., Ang, R. P., Ho, J., Lim, J. C., Goh, D. H., Lee, C. S., & Chua, A. Y. (2011). Narcissism, extraversion and adolescents' self-presentation on Facebook. *Personality and Individual Differences, 50,* 180–185.

O'Reilly, T. (2005). What is Web 2.0? Retrieved from http://www.oreilly.de/artikel/web20.html

Papacharissi, Z. (2002a). The presentation of self in virtual life: Characteristics of personal home pages. *Journalism and Mass Communication Quarterly, 79,* 643–660.

Papacharissi, Z. (2002b). The self online: The utility of personal home pages. *Journal of Broadcasting and Electronic Media, 46,* 346–368.

Patchin, J. W., & Hinduja, S. (2010). Trends in online social networking: Adolescent use of MySpace over time. *New Media and Society, 12,* 197–216.

Patil, S., & Kobsa, A. (2004). Instant messaging and privacy. In A. Dearden & L. Watts (Eds.), *Proceedings of HCI* (pp. 85–88). Leeds, UK.

Patil, S., & Kobsa, A. (2005). Privacy in collaboration: Managing impression. In *Proceedings of the first international conference on online communities and social computing.* Mahwah, NJ: Lawrence Erlbaum Associates. Retrieved from www.ics.uci.edu/~kobsa/papers/2005-ICOCSC-kobsa.pdf

Pearson, E. (2010). Making a good (virtual) first impression: The use of visuals in online impression management and creating identity performances. In J. Berleur, M. D. Hercheui, & L. M. Hilty (Eds.), *What kind of information society? Governance, virtuality, surveillance, sustainability, resilience* (Vol. *328*, pp. 118–130). Berlin, Germany: Springer.

Qian, H., & Scott, C. R. (2007). Anonymity and self-disclosure on weblogs. *Journal of Computer-Mediated Communication, 12*(4), article 14. Retrieved from http://jcmc.indiana.edu/vol12/issue4/qian.html

Rehbein, F., & Mößle, T. (2013). Video game and Internet addiction: Is there a need for differentiation? *SUCHT-Zeitschrift für Wissenschaft und Praxis/Journal of Addiction Research and Practice, 59*, 129–142.

Reißmann, O. (2012, December 17). Klarnamen-Pflicht: Datenschützer Weichert stellt Facebook Ultimatum [Real name obligation: Security administrator Weichert issues Facebook an ultimatum]. *Spiegel Online Netzwelt*. Retrieved from http://www.spiegel.de/netzwelt/netzpolitik/klarnamen-pflicht-weichert-stellt-facebook-ultimatum-a-873411.html

Reißmann, O./dpa [Deutsche Presse-Agentur; German Press Agency]. (2012, August 27). Ärger um App Center – Verbraucherzentralen mahnen Facebook ab [Trouble about app center – consumer advice centers give Facebook a warning]. *Spiegel Online*. Retrieved from http://www.spiegel.de/netzwelt/netzpolitik/abmahnung-fuer-facebooks-app-center-kritik-auf-dem-sak12-a-852262.html

Resnick, P. (2002). Beyond bowling together: Sociotechnical capital. In J. M. Carrol (Ed.), *Human–computer interaction in the new millennium* (pp. 247–272). New York, NY: Addison-Wesley.

Roberts, L. D., & Parks, M. R. (1999). The social geography of gender-switching in virtual environments on the Internet. *Information, Communication, and Society, 2*, 521–540.

Rosenbaum, J. E., Johnson, B. K., Stepman, P. A., & Nuijten, K. C. (2010, April). *Just being themselves? Goals and strategies for self-presentation on Facebook*. Paper presented at the 80th annual conference of the Southern States Communication Association, Memphis, TN. Retrieved from http://www.benjaminkjohnson.com/wp-content/uploads/2010/09/Just_Being_Themselves_Final.pdf

Ruddigkeit, A., Penzel, J., & Schneider, J. (2013). Dinge, die meine Eltern nicht sehen sollten [Things my parents should not see]. *Publizistik, 58*, 1–21. doi: 10.1007/s11616-013-0183-z

Rui, J. R., & Stefanone, M. A. (2013). Strategic image management online: Self-presentation, self-esteem and social network perspectives. *Information, Communication and Society*, 1–20.

Salimkhan, G., Manago, A., & Greenfield, P. M. (2010). The construction of the virtual self on MySpace. *Cyberpsychology: Journal of Psychosocial Research on Cyberspace, 4*(1), article 1. Retrieved from http://cyberpsychology.eu/view.php?cisloclanku=2010050203&article=1

Schlenker, B. R. (1980). *Impression management: The self-concept, social identity, and interpersonal relations*. Monterey, CA: Brooks/Cole.

Sherman, L. E., Michikyan, M., & Greenfield, P. M. (2013). The effects of text, audio, video, and in-person communication on bonding between friends. *Cyberpsychology: Journal of Psychosocial Research on Cyberspace, 7*(2), article 1. doi: 10.5817/CP2013-2-3

Shoham, A. (2004). Flow experiences and image making: An online chat-room ethnography. *Psychology and Marketing, 21*, 855–882.

Siibak, A. (2009). Constructing the self through the photo selection: Visual impression management on social networking websites. *Cyberpsychology: Journal of Psychosocial Research on Cyberspace, 3*, 1. Retrieved from http://cyberpsychology.eu/view.php?cisloclanku=2009061501&article=1

Šmahel, D., & Machovcová, K. (2006). Internet use in the Czech Republic: Gender and age differences. In F. Sudweeks, H. Hrachovec, & C. Ess (Eds.), *Cultural attitudes towards technology and communication* (pp. 521–533). Murdoch, Australia: School of Information Technology, Murdoch University.

Statista. (2015). Anzahl der monatlich aktiven Facebook-Nutzer weltweit von 2008 bis zum 3. Quartal 2014 [Number of monthly active Facebook users worldwide from 2008 until third quarter of 2014]. Retrieved from http://de.statista.com/statistik/daten/studie/37545/umfrage/anzahl-der-aktiven-nutzer-von-facebook/

Strano, M. M. (2008). User descriptions and interpretations of self-presentation through Facebook profile images. *Cyberpsychology: Journal of Psychosocial Research on Cyberspace, 2*(2), article 1. Retrieved from http://cyberpsychology.eu/view.php?cisloclanku=2008110402&article=1

Subrahmanyam, K., Garcia, E. C., Harsono, L. S., Li, J. S., & Lipana, L. (2009). In their words: Connecting online weblogs to developmental processes. *British Journal of Developmental Psychology, 27*, 219–245.

Subrahmanyam, K., Greenfield, P., & Michikyan, M. (2013). Una actualización de las investigaciones acerca de la comunicación electrónica y relaciones adolescentes. *Ibero American Communication Review.*

Subrahmanyam, K., Reich, S. M., Waechter, N., & Espinoza, G. (2008). Online and offline social networks: Use of social networking sites by emerging adults. *Journal of Applied Developmental Psychology, 29*, 420–433.

Subrahmanyam, K., & Šmahel, D. (2011). Constructing identity online: Identity exploration and self-presentation. In *Digital youth: The role of media in development* (pp. 59–80). New York, NY: Springer.

Subrahmanyam, K., Šmahel, D., & Greenfield, P. (2006). Connecting developmental constructions to the Internet: Identity presentation and sexual exploration in online teen chat rooms. *Developmental Psychology, 42*, 395.

Taddicken, M. (2011). Selbstoffenbarung im Social Web [Self-disclosure on the social web]. *Publizistik, 56*, 281–303.

Tedeschi, J. T. (Ed.). (1981). *Impression management theory and social psychological research.* New York, NY: Academic Press.

Thomas, A. G., & Johansen, M. K. (2012). Inside out: Avatars as an indirect measure of ideal body self-presentation in females. *Cyberpsychology: Journal of Psychosocial Research on Cyberspace, 6*(3), article 3. doi: 10.5817/CP2012-3-3

Tokunaga, R. S. (2010). Following you home from school: A critical review and synthesis of research on cyberbullying victimization. *Computers in Human Behavior, 26*, 277–287.

Tong, S. T., Van der Heide, B., Langwell, L., & Walther, J. B. (2008). Too much of a good thing? The relationship between number of friends and interpersonal impressions on Facebook. *Journal of Computer-Mediated Communication, 13*, 531–549.

Tosun, L. P. (2012). Motives for Facebook use and expressing "true self" on the Internet. *Computers in Human Behavior, 28*, 1510–1517.

Trammell, K. D., & Keshelashvili, A. (2005). Examining the new influencers: A self-presentation study of A-list blogs. *Journalism and Mass Communication Quarterly, 82*, 968–982.

Trepte, S., & Reinecke, L. (2010). Avatar creation and video game enjoyment. *Journal of Media Psychology: Theories, Methods, and Applications, 22*, 171–184.

Turkle, S. (1995). *Life on the screen: Identity in the age of the Internet.* New York, NY: Simon & Schuster.

Utz, S., & Krämer, N. (2009). The privacy paradox on social network sites revisited: The role of individual characteristics and group norms. *Cyberpsychology: Journal of Psychosocial Research on Cyberspace, 3*(2), article 2. Retrieved from http://cyberpsychology.eu/view.php?cisloclanku=2009111001&article=2

Walther, J. B. (1996). Computer-mediated communication impersonal, interpersonal, and hyperpersonal interaction. *Communication Research, 23*, 3–43.

Walther, J. B. (2007). Selective self-presentation in computer-mediated communication: Hyperpersonal dimensions of technology, language, and cognition. *Computers in Human Behavior, 23*, 2538–2557.

Walther, J. B., Van der Heide, B., Hamel, L. M., & Shulman, H. C. (2009). Self-generated versus other-generated statements and impressions in computer-mediated communication: A test of warranting theory using Facebook. *Communication Research, 36*, 229–253.

Wang, J.-L., Jackson, L. A., Zhang, D.-J., & Su, Z.-Q. (2012). The relationships among the Big Five Personality factors, self-esteem, narcissism, and sensation-seeking to Chinese University students' uses of social networking sites (SNSs). *Computers in Human Behavior, 28*(6), 2313–2319.

Whitty, M. T. (2008). Revealing the "real" me, searching for the "actual" you: Presentations of self on an Internet dating site. *Computers in Human Behavior, 24*, 1707–1723.

Wilson, R. E., Gosling, S. D., & Graham, L. T. (2012). A review of Facebook research in the social sciences. *Perspectives on Psychological Science, 7*, 203–220.

Wohn, D. Y., & Wash, R. (2012). A virtual "room" with a cue: Detecting personality through spatial customization in a city simulation game. *Computers in Human Behavior, 29*, 155–159.

Yee, N., Ducheneaut, N., Nelson, L., & Likarish, P. (2011). Introverted elves and conscientious gnomes: The expression of personality in World of Warcraft. In *Proceedings of the SIGCHI conference on human factors in computing systems* (pp. 753–762). New York, NY: ACM.

Young, K. (2009). Online social networking: An Australian perspective. *International Journal of Emerging Technologies and Society, 7*, 39–57.

Zhao, S., Grasmuck, S., & Martin, J. (2008). Identity construction on Facebook: Digital empowerment in anchored relationships. *Computers in Human Behavior, 24*, 1816–1836.

20

Narcissism, Emerging Media, and Society

Keith W. Campbell[1] and Jean M. Twenge[2]

[1] *University of Georgia*
[2] *San Diego State University*

A few months ago one of us (WKC) saw two concerts. The first was dubbed the Americanarama Festival and featured Bob Dylan, Bob Weir, Wilco, and My Morning Jacket; the second headlined Keith Urban with My Little Big Town. Both concerts featured country music, acoustic guitars, and traditional themes, but they differed dramatically in their relationship with emerging media. At the Americanarama Festival, the crowd was told repeatedly that anyone seen taking videos with a cell phone would be removed from the concert. Before Bob Dylan came onto the stage, the audience was told again that they should watch the show in real life and not through a tiny screen. After the show, however, people still posted clips online – all the security and warnings did not stop the use of media.

The approach taken at the Keith Urban show was 180 degrees from this. Fans were encouraged to film and photograph the concert with their phones. At one point, a band member actually picked up a fan's phone and filmed the band from the stage. At another point, a fan was brought up and had her picture taken with Keith Urban in front of the audience. Finally, the audience was asked to turn on the lights on their phones during a particular song (as we used to do with lighters in the 1970s and 1980s and even into the 1990s). During the entire show fans were capturing images and presumably sending them to friends or uploading them online to sites such as Facebook or Twitter.

This tiny cultural snippet conveys some of the key issues around narcissism, emerging media, and culture. First, there is a huge pull to capture and broadcast experiences rather than directly experiencing them. The broadcasting gives people an opportunity for self-enhancement, potentially a narcissistic pursuit. Second, despite Bob Dylan's best efforts, emerging media are apparently going to win. When a security team cannot stop a behavior, you have lost. And, third, cultural pressures and emerging media each cause the other.

In the present chapter, we focus on the role of narcissism in emerging media use and culture. We begin by providing a description of narcissism as an individual trait and as a socio-cultural process. We then discuss the research findings on

The Wiley Handbook of Psychology, Technology, and Society, First Edition. Edited by Larry D. Rosen, Nancy A. Cheever, and L. Mark Carrier.

narcissism and emerging media. Finally, we will offer some ways to think about these issues going forward.

How Narcissism Works

Narcissism consists primarily of a grandiose/inflated self-image and a sense of entitlement coupled with lower levels of empathy and caring for others. A narcissistic individual thinks he or she is smarter, more important, or better looking than others and deserves to be treated as such. This individual can be charming, outgoing, and facile at starting relationships, but will do better with relationships that are shallow and lack emotional intimacy (Campbell & Miller, 2011).

Before delving into narcissism in more detail, we need to make an important conceptual aside. This description best fits what is often labeled *grandiose narcissism*. Two other forms of narcissism are commonly discussed. *Vulnerable narcissism* is linked to a sense of importance, but with much more fragility and vulnerability. People with high levels of vulnerable narcissism tend to be depressive, have low self-esteem, and think others are out to get them (Miller, Hoffman, et al., 2011). Second, *narcissistic personality disorder* (NPD) is the psychiatric variant, an extreme level of narcissism linked to significant problems in love and work. NPD is a mix of grandiose and vulnerable traits, but with more grandiosity (Miller, Gentile, Wilson, & Campbell, 2013). These three forms of narcissism – grandiose, vulnerable, and NPD – lead to much confusion in the literature. This is especially problematic because people in clinical settings see more of the vulnerable form of narcissism (Miller, Widiger, & Campbell, 2010), whereas the grandiose form is seen more in reality television stars (Young & Pinsky, 2006), business students (Westerman, Bergman, Bergman, & Daly, 2012), and criminal populations (Hepper, Hart, Meek, Cisek, & Sedikides, 2014). Our focus in this chapter will be on grandiose narcissism. There are far more data on this form, and it is more relevant to emerging media. In what follows, "narcissism" will refer to the grandiose form unless otherwise noted.

So, to the main question: How does narcissism work? Two prominent approaches to narcissism are likely to be of the most interest to researchers on emerging media. The first is a trait approach, which conceptualizes narcissism in terms of basic personality traits. This is most commonly done with the Big Five or Five Factor model (e.g., McCrae & Costa, 1987). Narcissism in Big Five terms is largely a combination of high extraversion and low agreeableness (Paulhus, 2001). The low agreeableness associated with narcissism is primarily in the area of grandiosity, so the negative correlation with narcissism and agreeableness is stronger with scales such as the NEO-PI that capture grandiosity than with the Big Five Inventory, which does not (Miller, Gaughan, Maples, & Price, 2011). Another alternative is to use the HEXACO six-factor scale that captures the dimension of honesty–humility, which is negatively correlated with narcissism (Jonason & McCain, 2012). A final useful trait model is an interpersonal circumplex with a power/agency dimension and friendliness/communion dimension. Narcissism is typically seen as high in power/agency and somewhat low in friendliness/communion (Miller, Price, Gentile, Lynam, & Campbell, 2012).

These same basic traits are seen in the newly proposed personality model of NPD as described in the fifth edition of the *Diagnostic and Statistical Manual of Mental*

Disorders (DSM-5; American Psychiatric Association, 2013). In this model, NPD is linked to the traits grandiosity and attention seeking, a finding that has been supported by research (Miller et al., 2013).

While the trait models are useful for understanding the personality structure of narcissism, dynamic models focus on the self-regulatory mechanisms involved in narcissism. In short, narcissistic individuals do or say things to keep themselves looking or feeling good. Two such models are the *dynamic self-regulatory processing model* (Morf & Rhodewalt, 2001) and the *agency model* (Campbell & Foster, 2007). These models differ in some ways but share an approach to understanding narcissism as part of an interactive system that includes self-conceptions, self-esteem, and social relationships. So, for example, John the narcissist thinks he is special and important. He starts a relationship with a beautiful woman. This makes him look and feel good (e.g., self-esteem) and reinforces his positive self-views (Campbell, 1999).

This narcissistic behavior is particularly dynamic because narcissistic individuals can be very attractive and likable when they are first encountered (Paulhus, 1998), especially when they are not aggressive (Küfner, Nestler, & Back, 2013). However, this likability can fade over time (Paulhus, 1998). This, in turn, causes the narcissistic individual to form new relationships or work harder at being seen as important and popular. This shifting dynamic – where narcissism works well in short-term, shallow, or emerging relationships but not so well in long-term, enduring, or emotionally deep relationships – has been captured in another dynamic model, the *contextual reinforcement model* (Campbell & Campbell, 2009).

Overall, narcissism can be conceptualized in trait terms as a mixture of grandiosity, entitlement, extraversion, and attention seeking. In dynamic terms, narcissism consists of grandiosity maintained through relationships that create status and esteem for the narcissistic individual, but that typically lack emotional depth or caring. These can be romantic relationships (like the one described above), friendships, or leader–follower relationships. In each case, the key is the drive for social status and esteem and the willingness to exploit others to this end.

Additionally, narcissism can be conceptualized as a socio-cultural variable. That is, some traits make a culture narcissistic, and these traits are linked to the levels of individual narcissism in the culture. One of the best models for this is the mutual constitution model of culture and the psyche (MCM; Markus & Kitayama, 2010). According to the MCM, large cultural values are linked to cultural institutions, and these to cultural products, then to interpersonal processes and behaviors, and finally to the individual self. This is described as mutual constitution because the causal arrows go in both directions – a culture is made of selves, but so too are selves made from culture. In the case of narcissism, the superordinate cultural value of individualism is linked to specific cultural institutions such as language (Greenfield, 2013; Twenge, Campbell, & Gentile, 2012a, 2012b, 2013) and cultural products such as popular music (DeWall, Pond, Campbell, & Twenge, 2011) to specific behaviors like naming practices (Twenge, Abebe, & Campbell, 2010) to psychological issues such as narcissism (Twenge & Campbell, 2009). This model is largely heuristic – that is, there have been no full tests of the MCM – but it is useful for conceptualizing the link between culture and the self/personality.

To be a little more specific in our conceptualization of narcissism and culture: Individualism is a – perhaps the – large and growing cultural value in the United States and many other cultures. We see narcissism as the dark side of individualism.

The bright sides of individualism are tolerance for individuals who are members of out-groups, reduction in prejudice, and women's rights and opportunities (Donnelly & Twenge, 2013; Twenge & Campbell, 2013). Many changes in cultural institutions and products reflect elements of individualism and narcissism such as uniqueness, self-esteem, and fame. For example, the use of pronouns in books has shifted toward a greater proportion of first-person singular and second-person pronouns (e.g., me and you) and fewer first-person plural pronouns (e.g., we; Twenge et al., 2012b). Self-esteem became a cultural movement starting in the early 1970s in the U.S., and increased dramatically after the mid-1980s when the movement reached schools and parents (Gentile, Twenge, & Campbell, 2010; Twenge & Campbell, 2001). Finally, fame has become a staple of television for young people (Uhls & Greenfield, 2011) and this is linked to narcissism (Greenwood, Long, & Dal Cin, 2013).

Specific behaviors have changed in the same direction. For example, more children receive unique or unusual names, and fewer receive common names. So, for example, in the 1940s about a third of baby boys in the United States were given one of the 10 most popular names; today under 10% are. These effects are independent of immigration rates and occur in both ethnically homogeneous and heterogeneous states. We, as a culture, act as if we want our children to be special and unique (Twenge et al., 2010). Likewise, suggestive of vanity, there has been a dramatic rise in cosmetic medical procedures performed for the sake of enhanced beauty (Twenge & Campbell, 2009). Finally, consistent with the MCM, individual psychology has changed along with the cultural changes. For example, narcissism has increased (Twenge & Foster, 2010), as has self-esteem (Gentile et al., 2010; Twenge & Campbell, 2001), positive self-views (Twenge, Campbell, & Gentile, 2012a), and extrinsic values such as money, fame, and image (Twenge, Campbell, & Freeman, 2012). In addition, empathy has decreased (Konrath, O'Brien, & Hsing, 2011), as have intrinsic values such as finding meaning and purpose in life (Twenge, Campbell, et al., 2012). Putting this together, we see a link between broad cultural values like individualism and individual traits like narcissism. We also have seen that these trends seem to be increasing. That is, markers of individualism and individual narcissism are on the rise.

What forces are driving the changes in narcissism? We argue that any force in society that allows an individual to present a grander image of his or her self than is actually warranted is a potential amplifier of narcissism. We term this the *fantasy principle* (Twenge & Campbell, 2009). Several cultural forces can drive fantasy forward. For example, the self-esteem movement in education along with specific behaviors such as grade inflation, overly generous award giving, and "all about me" projects allow young people to think they are more talented than they actually are. In some cultures – notably China – the one-child policy has had a similar effect, leading to what is sometimes labeled "Little Emperor Syndrome" (Cai, Kwan, & Sedikides, 2012). The massive credit bubble that began in the 1970s also allows people to behave as if they are far wealthier than they are. This bubble deflated somewhat a few years ago, but is now inflating again. There has also been a democratization of media that has opened up the possibility of fame to a far wider and less talented group of individuals. So rather than fame seen as a consequence of talent, success, or royal birth, it is available to those willing to step out and get noticed (Twenge & Campbell, 2009; Young & Pinsky, 2006).

Most germane to this chapter, emerging media also potentially play a role in increasing cultural narcissism by offering the possibility of grandiose self-presentation and self-esteem regulation to the broader culture. We want to be clear that emerging media are not the only or primary force behind increasing cultural narcissism. The narcissism trends began in the early 1970s – and likely even earlier – and emerging media did not really start pushing culture in a large way until the mid-2000s. That said, the link between narcissism, culture, and emerging media is important and one that will likely keep going. Before delving into this topic, we will briefly discuss what we mean by emerging media.

Emerging Media

Emerging media refers to a wide range of specific sites or platforms including Facebook, Instagram, LinkedIn, Twitter, Vine, Reddit, 4chan, YouTube, Pinterest, and so on. Additionally, it may include blogging, microblogging, online commenting, and online gaming. The distinctions between all these are not perfectly clear as, say, Facebook can be used to create an identity, microblog, and play online games.

Despite similarities and overlaps, these media differ in many important ways. These include:

- The ability to create and modify your own image – which you can do more extensively on Facebook than, say, Twitter.
- The reciprocity of relationships – Facebook and LinkedIn have reciprocity, while Twitter and YouTube do not.
- The anonymity of the posts – 4chan is more anonymous than, for example, Facebook.
- The general versus specific nature of the topics discussed – LinkedIn is commerce and organization focused, while Facebook is more general in its focus.
- Mainstream versus outside – Facebook is mainstream, while 4chan is outside.

Furthermore, each of these media has its own microculture with media-centered norms of behavior, beliefs, and so on. So, for example, it would be appropriate to show a picture of food on Facebook, but less appropriate on LinkedIn. Likewise, selfies are acceptable for Twitter (unless you are Geraldo Rivera) but, again, not for LinkedIn. Pornography would be tolerated on 4chan, but not Facebook.

Finally, emerging media are evolving. When we started working in this area, MySpace was a dominant media force. Now it is nowhere to be seen. It is likely that the emerging media landscape we see now will continue to change. Additionally, norms within individual sites may shift. For example, Facebook started off as a tool for college students; now it is a tool for individuals of many ages and, importantly, for business, governments, and other organizations. MySpace started as a music site, became a general site, and then went back to being a music site. This is a major problem for scientists because research and publication is slower than cultural changes in emerging media. We are often driving using the rear-view mirror. As we will see, one approach is to try to develop a general understanding of how narcissism works in emerging media, so that we can make reasonable predictions even in the face of rapid change in the media landscape.

Narcissism, Emerging Media, and Culture

Given what we know, the potential links between narcissism, emerging media, and culture can be vast. In purely mathematical terms, we have narcissism (high, low) × emerging media formats (20+). We then need to multiply that by the nature of the narcissism/emerging media relationship. The nature of the relationship between narcissism and emerging media can be broken down into several key research questions: Does narcissism lead to emerging media use? Does emerging media use lead to narcissism? And do emerging media play a role in the narcissistic culture more generally?

For example, we might want to know how narcissism is related to Reddit use and focus on several outcomes, such as desire to gain "karma," hostility or bullying in posts, topic of posts, etc. These questions are answerable, but there is a huge amount of research to be done – and to date there is no research we know of that links narcissism and Reddit, let alone looking at specific Reddit behaviors. And there are also the more indirect questions that are plausibly related to narcissism and emerging media, such as: Do emerging media lead to shallow or close social ties? Are they linked to empathy or concern for others? Does use of emerging media lead to loneliness or an experience of social acceptance? Some of these have been answered, but many have not. The bottom line is that there is a great deal of targeted research to do, and given the shifting nature of emerging media, specific findings will be a challenge. Thus, we think a far more fruitful approach is to start with what we know about narcissism and self-regulation and use this knowledge to better understand the role of narcissism in emerging media. In other words, we want to apply existing models of narcissism to the context of emerging media.

First, narcissism does predict behavior on emerging media. Most of the research is correlational, but given the general stability in narcissism it is likely that many of these effects suggest that narcissism drives behavior on emerging media. However, we do not know this for certain and a reciprocal effect may occur with emerging media use creating and/or reinforcing narcissism (or times where a third variable, such as becoming a celebrity, plausibly drives both narcissism and emerging media use).

Narcissistic individuals are good at beginning relationships, including dating relationships, friendships, and leadership positions. However, narcissists are better suited to shallow than emotionally deep relationships, and use relationships to boast their own self-esteem and social status. This is indeed the pattern we generally see online. For example, in several studies of Facebook, narcissistic individuals have a higher number of "friends" and social contacts (Buffardi & Campbell, 2008; Gentile, Twenge, Freeman, & Campbell, 2012; Mehdizadeh, 2010; Wang, Jackson, Zhang, & Su, 2012). Narcissists also use Facebook to self-enhance by, for example, displaying flattering or provocative photos of themselves (Buffardi & Campbell, 2008; Carpenter, 2012; Gülnar, Balcı, & Çakır, 2010; Kapidzic, 2013; Mehdizadeh, 2010; Nadkarni & Hofmann, 2012; Panek, Nardis, & Konrath, 2013; Rosen, Whaling, Rab, Carrier, & Cheever, 2013), and perhaps using more first-person pronouns in some contexts (DeWall, Buffardi, Bonser, & Campbell, 2011). There is mixed evidence, however, that narcissists use Facebook more than non-narcissists, with some finding this difference (e.g., Rosen et al., 2013; Ryan & Xenos, 2011) and some not (McKinney, Kelly, & Duran, 2012; Skues, Williams, & Wise, 2012). The way narcissists use Facebook seems to be the most robust feature; the link between narcissism and Facebook use likely has some important moderators.

The work on this topic outside of Facebook seems to show similar patterns. For example, narcissistic individuals have more friends and show greater self-promotion on MySpace (Gentile et al., 2012) and Twitter (McKinney et al., 2012; Panek et al., 2013). Some evidence suggests narcissistic individuals tweet more than less narcissistic individuals (Panek et al., 2013). Narcissistic individuals even have more salacious and self-enhancing personal email addresses (Back, Schmukle, & Egloff, 2008).

There is also work done on the other classic correlates of narcissism such as overconfidence (Campbell, Goodie, & Foster, 2004), or aggression following ego threat (Bushman & Baumeister, 1998; Twenge & Campbell, 2003). The work on overconfidence is very limited. In one study of online games, narcissism predicted overconfidence in males (Johnson et al., 2006). However, there is much more work on narcissism and aggression. On Facebook, narcissism predicts more aggressive language (DeWall, Buffardi, et al., 2011). Several studies show a link between narcissism and cyberbullying. This work primarily uses self-report data and has shown a link with cyberbullying assessments (especially with the more entitlement/exploitative factors of narcissism; Ang, Tan, & Mansor, 2011; Eksi, 2012) and with global bullying measures that include cyberbullying (Baughman, Dearing, Giammarco, & Vernon, 2012). Finally, some research shows a link between narcissism and violent video games, with narcissism related to amount of video game play and aggression levels in these games (Anderson et al., 2004).

Second, some (but less) evidence shows that emerging media use directly causes increases in narcissism. In one set of experiments, for example, individuals were asked to work on their personal webpage (Facebook or MySpace) or a control page (Google Maps). In both cases working on the personal webpage resulted in higher self-esteem, and on MySpace – but not Facebook – higher narcissism (Gentile et al., 2012). In other research, the link between Facebook and self-esteem is related to how close a person's friendships are with close ties resulting in higher self-esteem (Wilcox & Stephen, 2012). And this effect was shown again without the moderation of friendship ties (Gonzales & Hancock, 2011). Beyond this, however, the experimental data – or even longitudinal data – are very thin. One study shows that an increase in friendship networks over time on Facebook seems to elevate self-esteem in those with low self-esteem (Steinfield, Ellison, & Lampe, 2008), but no longitudinal study we know of has examined narcissism and emerging media.

Third, the broader relationship between emerging media use and narcissistic culture is difficult to pin down directly. At the cultural level, individual narcissism increased along with the rise in emerging media (Twenge & Campbell, 2009). We also know that the traits of self-promotion and self-enhancement shown by narcissistic individuals are transformed into cultural products via emerging media use. If you think of Facebook, for example, as an evolving cultural artifact akin to a massive Neolithic cave painting, the content of that cultural artifact is more self-promoting as a result of the narcissistic individuals doing the creating.

Finally, if narcissistic individuals on average have more links on major social network sites such as Facebook, and are likely more central in those networks (Clifton, Turkheimer, & Oltmanns, 2009), then when any member looks at his or her social network, he or she will see a higher level of narcissism than actually exists. So, an individual's view of culture will be distorted in the direction of narcissism by the overabundance of narcissistic individuals placing self-promoting posts online. This will influence the perception of culture and, by doing so, might change the culture. This process is perhaps easier to see in reality television. When people view "reality" television, what they see is not a random sample of real people, but an oversampling of narcissistic individuals often engaged in narcissistic or borderline pathological behavior (Young & Pinsky, 2006). Viewing the culture through the social networks of emerging media is akin to viewing the world through reality television.

To summarize the data thus far: Narcissism is related to activity on emerging media that parallels activity in the broader interpersonal domain. Narcissism predicts broad social media networks and using social media for self-enhancement purposes. Narcissistic aggression in emerging media is similar to the aggression narcissists display in other contexts. What we do not have is a fine-grained analysis of narcissism in the contexts of different media sites or various activities. It would be useful to see research examining narcissism across a broad swath of emerging media sites. The prediction would be that narcissism would work the same way in these various media cultures just like it seems to work the same way in different regional or national cultures (e.g., Tanchotsrinon, Maneesri, & Campbell, 2007). That said, the mean level of narcissism may differ across media cultures or platforms just as it does across regional cultures (Foster, Campbell, & Twenge, 2003). We also have a lack of experimental and longitudinal data. A number of interesting studies could be done with methods that go beyond the correlational model. Finally, much emerging media revolve around the idea of the social network. Looking at narcissism within the social network – especially across time – would be ideal.

The study of narcissism and culture is more challenging. One approach would be to examine emerging media use in cultures with different levels of narcissism. For example, do emerging media in Japan, where narcissism levels are relatively low, differ significantly from levels in China, where narcissism scores are higher (e.g., Fukunishi et al., 1996)? The ideal study here would use multiple measures of emerging media use and many cultures to try to tease apart the key variables.

Looking to the Future

Emerging media is one of the most interesting areas of contemporary research because it is both massive and rapidly evolving. The interesting question is what the future holds in terms of emerging media, narcissism, and culture.

If we begin with the fantasy principle, emerging media will theoretically be an avenue for increasing narcissism at the individual and cultural level if they allow people to present themselves in a way that inflates their self-esteem. The limit to this now seems to depend on the platform used. For example, the degree of self-inflation on Facebook is constrained by actual relationships (Gosling, Augustine, Vazire, Holtzman, & Gaddis, 2011). Thus, people can enhance themselves, but only to an extent. Other platforms where an individual is an anonymous actor interacting with other anonymous actors would allow for greater narcissism. In these contexts, narcissism could continually inflate. There are a few possible outcomes: The result would be either a mutual admiration society – we are all awesome – such as might occur on a forum where everyone shares the same opinion, or it could be a much more antagonistic space – we are all better than each other – filled with put-downs and dominance but with no reality against which to establish actual dominance. This process of ever-inflating narcissism could be extended using technology to create what would in psychodynamic terms be called a *narcissistic cocoon*: a space where a psychological state of esteem and status would be maintained without the constraints of reality (Masterson, 1985).

What is especially intriguing is the potential for narcissism expansion in the realm of emerging media while the traditional opportunities for narcissistic expansion are decreasing. The current economic climate provides fewer opportunities for young people to experience success by developing careers or starting families. Unemployment is up, family formation is down, and personal debt – especially student debt – is at a record high. At the same time, this generation of young people have been raised to see themselves as special and important and to have high expectations for the future (Twenge, 2006). In essence, we have created a massive cultural dissonance between young people's self-views and their social and economic reality. One reasonable response to this dissonance is for young people to migrate more and more of their lives online in order to gain and maintain esteem. The exemplar of this would be the young man living in his mother's basement and gaining a sense of esteem from his online life in fantasy gaming realms. We have coined the phrase *the great fantasy migration* (used here for the first time in print) to describe this plausible future.

Of course, the same emerging media that can be used to elevate narcissism could also be used to increase compassionate connections between people. The example of political activity on social networking sites is often suggested (Park, Kee, & Valenzuela, 2009). Unfortunately, the story is somewhat complicated by the finding that online media activism does not always result in actual political participation, as the experience with the famous Kony 2012 video showed (Drumbl, 2012).

What we know from social psychological research is that one way to reduce narcissism is to enhance similarity between people (Konrath, Bushman, & Campbell, 2006). This could conceivably be done on emerging media by making similarities between people salient. For example, LinkedIn highlights important similarities like shared friends and educational institutions. Another way to reduce narcissism is to increase feelings of compassion (Finkel, Campbell, Buffardi, Kumashiro, & Rusbult, 2009). This would be challenging, but sites like CaringBridge may well do that. CaringBridge is a social network site where individuals suffering severe medical conditions can both share their progress with friends and family and also receive messages of support from the same. All media can be used to differing ends, and the question is how to translate basic research into making emerging media into positive ends.

Conclusions

Narcissism predicts the use of the social and cultural environment to enhance and reinforce self-esteem and social status. This pattern has been found in a range of social contexts, from dating relationships to leadership. This same pattern occurs in the context of emerging media, where narcissism is associated with a large number of shallow relationships (e.g., Facebook friends) and the use of emerging media to enhance the self. This is often at the expense of others, as seen in work on narcissism and cyberbullying and aggression. The research on narcissism and emerging media, however, is still in its infancy. More work – especially using longitudinal and experimental methods – needs to be done. In addition, it remains to be seen what form narcissism and emerging media will take in the future.

References

American Psychiatric Association (APA). (2013). *Diagnostic and statistical manual of mental disorders* (5th ed.) (DSM-5). Arlington, VA: Author.

Anderson, C. A., Carnagey, N. L., Flanagan, M., Benjamin, A. J., Jr., Eubanks, J., & Valentine, J. C. (2004). Violent video games: Specific effects of violent content on aggressive thoughts and behavior. *Advances in Experimental Social Psychology, 36,* 199–249.

Ang, R. P., Tan, K. A., & Mansor, A. T. (2011). Normative beliefs about aggression as a mediator of narcissistic exploitativeness and cyberbullying. *Journal of Interpersonal Violence, 26*(13), 2619–2634.

Back, M. D., Schmukle, S. C., & Egloff, B. (2008). How extraverted is honey.bunny77@ hotmail.de? Inferring personality from e-mail addresses. *Journal of Research in Personality, 42*(4), 1116–1122.

Baughman, H. M., Dearing, S., Giammarco, E., & Vernon, P. A. (2012). Relationships between bullying behaviours and the Dark Triad: A study with adults. *Personality and Individual Differences, 52*(5), 571–575.

Buffardi, L. E., & Campbell, W. K. (2008). Narcissism and social networking web sites. *Personality and Social Psychology Bulletin, 34*(10), 1303–1314.

Bushman, B. J., & Baumeister, R. F. (1998). Threatened egotism, narcissism, self-esteem, and direct and displaced aggression: Does self-love or self-hate lead to violence? *Journal of Personality and Social Psychology, 75*(1), 219.

Cai, H., Kwan, V. S., & Sedikides, C. (2012). A sociocultural approach to narcissism: The case of modern China. *European Journal of Personality, 26*(5), 529–535.

Campbell, W. K. (1999). Narcissism and romantic attraction. *Journal of Personality and Social Psychology, 77*(6), 1254.

Campbell, W. K., & Campbell, S. M. (2009). On the self-regulatory dynamics created by the peculiar benefits and costs of narcissism: A contextual reinforcement model and examination of leadership. *Self and Identity, 8*(2–3), 214–232.

Campbell, W. K., & Foster, J. D. (2007). The narcissistic self: Background, an extended agency model, and ongoing controversies. *The Self,* 115–138.

Campbell, W. K., Goodie, A. S., & Foster, J. D. (2004). Narcissism, confidence, and risk attitude. *Journal of Behavioral Decision Making, 17*(4), 297–311.

Campbell, W. K., & Miller, J. D. (2011). *The handbook of narcissism and narcissistic personality disorder*. Hoboken, NJ: John Wiley & Sons.

Carpenter, C. J. (2012). Narcissism on Facebook: Self-promotional and anti-social behavior. *Personality and Individual Differences, 52*(4), 482–486.

Clifton, A., Turkheimer, E., & Oltmanns, T. F. (2009). Personality disorder in social networks: Network position as a marker of interpersonal dysfunction. *Social Networks, 31*(1), 26–32.

DeWall, C. N., Buffardi, L. E., Bonser, I., & Campbell, W. K. (2011). Narcissism and implicit attention seeking: Evidence from linguistic analyses of social networking and online presentation. *Personality and Individual Differences, 51*(1), 57–62.

DeWall, C. N., Pond, R. S., Jr., Campbell, W. K., & Twenge, J. M. (2011). Tuning in to psychological change: Linguistic markers of psychological traits and emotions over time in popular U.S. song lyrics. *Psychology of Aesthetics, Creativity, and the Arts, 5*(3), 200.

Donnelly, K., & Twenge, J. M. (2013). Change over time in Americans' attitudes towards women's roles, 1976–2012. Manuscript under review.

Drumbl, M. A. (2012). Child soldiers and clicktivism: Justice, myths, and prevention. *Journal of Human Rights Practice, 4*(3), 481–485.

Eksi, F. (2012). Examination of narcissistic personality traits' predicting level of Internet addiction and cyber bullying through path analysis. *Educational Sciences: Theory and Practice, 12*(3), 1694–1706.

Finkel, E. J., Campbell, W. K., Buffardi, L. E., Kumashiro, M., & Rusbult, C. E. (2009). The metamorphosis of Narcissus: Communal activation promotes relationship commitment among narcissists. *Personality and Social Psychology Bulletin, 35*(10), 1271–1284.

Foster, J. D., Campbell, W. K, & Twenge, J. M. (2003). Individual differences in narcissism: Inflated self-views across the lifespan and around the world. *Journal of Research in Personality, 37*(6), 469–486.

Fukunishi, I., Nakagawa, T., Nakamura, H., Li, K., Hua, Z. Q., & Kratz, T. S. (1996). Relationships between Type A behavior, narcissism, and maternal closeness for college students in Japan, the United States of America, and the People's Republic of China. *Psychological Reports, 78*(3), 939–944.

Gentile, B., Twenge, J. M., & Campbell, W. K. (2010). Birth cohort differences in self-esteem, 1988–2008: A cross-temporal meta-analysis. *Review of General Psychology, 14*(3), 261.

Gentile, B., Twenge, J. M., Freeman, E. C., & Campbell, W. K. (2012). The effect of social networking websites on positive self-views: An experimental investigation. *Computers in Human Behavior, 28*(5), 1929–1933.

Gonzales, A. L., & Hancock, J. T. (2011). Mirror, mirror on my Facebook wall: Effects of exposure to Facebook on self-esteem. *Cyberpsychology, Behavior, and Social Networking, 14*(1–2), 79–83.

Gosling, S. D., Augustine, A. A., Vazire, S., Holtzman, N., & Gaddis, S. (2011). Manifestations of personality in online social networks: Self-reported Facebook-related behaviors and observable profile information. *Cyberpsychology, Behavior, and Social Networking, 14*(9), 483–488.

Greenfield, P. M. (2013). The changing psychology of culture from 1800 through 2000. *Psychological Science, 24*(9), 1722–1731.

Greenwood, D., Long, C. R., & Dal Cin, S. (2013). Fame and the social self: The need to belong, narcissism, and relatedness predict the appeal of fame. *Personality and Individual Differences, 55*(5), 490–495.

Gülnar, B., Balcı, Ş., & Çakır, V. (2010). Motivations of Facebook, YouTube and similar web sites users. *Bilig, 54*, 161–184.

Hepper, E. G., Hart, C. M., Meek, R., Cisek, S., & Sedikides, C. (2014). Narcissism and empathy in young offenders and non-offenders. *European Journal of Personality, 28*(2), 201–210.

Johnson, D. D., McDermott, R., Barrett, E. S., Cowden, J., Wrangham, R., McIntyre, M. H., & Rosen, S. P. (2006). Overconfidence in wargames: Experimental evidence on expectations, aggression, gender and testosterone. *Proceedings of the Royal Society B: Biological Sciences, 273*(1600), 2513–2520.

Jonason, P. K., & McCain, J. (2012). Using the HEXACO model to test the validity of the Dirty Dozen measure of the Dark Triad. *Personality and Individual Differences, 53*, 935–938.

Kapidzic, S. (2013). Narcissism as a predictor of motivations behind Facebook profile picture selection. *Cyberpsychology, Behavior, and Social Networking, 16*(1), 14–19.

Konrath, S., Bushman, B. J., & Campbell, W. K. (2006). Attenuating the link between threatened egotism and aggression. *Psychological Science, 17*(11), 995–1001.

Konrath, S. H., O'Brien, E. H., & Hsing, C. (2011). Changes in dispositional empathy in American college students over time: A meta-analysis. *Personality and Social Psychology Review, 15*(2), 180–198.

Küfner, A. C., Nestler, S., & Back, M. D. (2013). The two pathways to being an (un-)popular narcissist. *Journal of Personality, 81*(2), 184–195.

Markus, H. R., & Kitayama, S. (2010). Cultures and selves: A cycle of mutual constitution. *Perspectives on Psychological Science, 5*(4), 420–430.

Masterson, J. F. (1985). *The real self: A developmental, self, and object relations approach.* New York, NY: Brunner/Mazel.

McCrae, R. R., & Costa, P. T. (1987). Validation of the five-factor model of personality across instruments and observers. *Journal of Personality and Social Psychology, 52*(1), 81–90.

McKinney, B. C., Kelly, L., & Duran, R. L. (2012). Narcissism or openness? College students' use of Facebook and Twitter. *Communication Research Reports, 29*(2), 108–118.

Mehdizadeh, S. (2010). Self-presentation 2.0: Narcissism and self-esteem on Facebook. *Cyberpsychology, Behavior, and Social Networking, 13*(4), 357–364.

Miller, J. D., Gaughan, E. T., Maples, J., & Price, J. (2011). A comparison of Agreeableness scores from the Big Five Inventory and the NEO-PI-R: Consequences for the study of narcissism and psychopathy. *Assessment, 18*(3), 335–339.

Miller, J. D., Gentile, B., Wilson, L., & Campbell, W. K. (2013). Grandiose and vulnerable narcissism and the DSM-5 pathological personality trait model. *Journal of Personality Assessment, 95*(3), 284–290.

Miller, J. D., Hoffman, B. J., Gaughan, E. T., Gentile, B., Maples, J., & Campbell, W. K. (2011). Grandiose and vulnerable narcissism: A nomological network analysis. *Journal of Personality, 79*(5), 1013–1042.

Miller, J. D., Price, J., Gentile, B., Lynam, D. R., & Campbell, W. K. (2012). Grandiose and vulnerable narcissism from the perspective of the interpersonal circumplex. *Personality and Individual Differences, 53*(4), 507–512.

Miller, J. D., Widiger, T. A., & Campbell, W. K. (2010). Narcissistic personality disorder and the DSM-V. *Journal of Abnormal Psychology, 119*(4), 640.

Morf, C. C., & Rhodewalt, F. (2001). Unraveling the paradoxes of narcissism: A dynamic self-regulatory processing model. *Psychological Inquiry, 12*(4), 177–196.

Nadkarni, A., & Hofmann, S. G. (2012). Why do people use Facebook? *Personality and Individual Differences, 52*(3), 243–249.

Panek, E. T., Nardis, Y., & Konrath, S. (2013). Mirror or megaphone? How relationships between narcissism and social networking site use differ on Facebook and Twitter. *Computers in Human Behavior, 29*(5), 2004–2012.

Park, N., Kee, K. F., & Valenzuela, S. (2009). Being immersed in social networking environment: Facebook groups, uses and gratifications, and social outcomes. *CyberPsychology and Behavior, 12*(6), 729–733.

Paulhus, D. L. (1998). Interpersonal and intrapsychic adaptiveness of trait self-enhancement: A mixed blessing? *Journal of Personality and Social Psychology, 74*(5), 1197.

Paulhus, D. L. (2001). Normal narcissism: Two minimalist accounts. *Psychological Inquiry, 12*(4), 228–230.

Rosen, L. D., Whaling, K., Rab, S., Carrier, L. M., & Cheever, N. A. (2013). Is Facebook creating "iDisorders"? The link between clinical symptoms of psychiatric disorders and technology use, attitudes and anxiety. *Computers in Human Behavior, 29*, 1243–1254.

Ryan, T., & Xenos, S. (2011). Who uses Facebook? An investigation into the relationship between the Big Five, shyness, narcissism, loneliness, and Facebook usage. *Computers in Human Behavior, 27*(5), 1658–1664.

Skues, J. L., Williams, B., & Wise, L. (2012). The effects of personality traits, self-esteem, loneliness, and narcissism on Facebook use among university students. *Computers in Human Behavior, 28*, 2414–2419.

Steinfield, C., Ellison, N. B., & Lampe, C. (2008). Social capital, self-esteem, and use of online social network sites: A longitudinal analysis. *Journal of Applied Developmental Psychology, 29*(6), 434–445.

Tanchotsrinon, P., Maneesri, K., & Campbell, W. K. (2007). Narcissism and romantic attraction: Evidence from a collectivistic culture. *Journal of Research in Personality, 41*(3), 723–730.

Twenge, J. M. (2006). *Generation me: Why today's young Americans are more confident, assertive, entitled – and more miserable than ever before*. New York, NY: Simon & Schuster.

Twenge, J. M., Abebe, E. M., & Campbell, W. K. (2010). Fitting in or standing out: Trends in American parents' choices for children's names, 1880–2007. *Social Psychological and Personality Science*, 1(1), 19–25.

Twenge, J. M., & Campbell, W. K. (2001). Age and birth cohort differences in self-esteem: A cross-temporal meta-analysis. *Personality and Social Psychology Review*, 5(4), 321–344.

Twenge, J. M., & Campbell, W. K. (2003). "Isn't it fun to get the respect that we're going to deserve?" Narcissism, social rejection, and aggression. *Personality and Social Psychology Bulletin*, 29(2), 261–272.

Twenge, J. M., & Campbell, W. K. (2009). *The narcissism epidemic: Living in the age of entitlement*. New York, NY: Free Press.

Twenge, J. M., & Campbell, W. K. (2013). Changes in tolerance for controversial beliefs and lifestyles in the U.S., 1972–2012. Manuscript under review.

Twenge, J. M., Campbell, W. K., & Freeman, E. C. (2012). Generational differences in young adults' life goals, concern for others, and civic orientation, 1966–2009. *Journal of Personality and Social Psychology*, 102(5), 1045.

Twenge, J. M., Campbell, W. K., & Gentile, B. (2012a). Generational increases in agentic self-evaluations among American college students, 1966–2009. *Self and Identity*, 11(4), 409–427.

Twenge, J. M., Campbell, W. K., & Gentile, B. (2012b). Increases in individualistic words and phrases in American books, 1960–2008. *PLOS ONE*, 7(7), e40181.

Twenge, J. M., Campbell, W. K., & Gentile, B. (2013). Changes in pronoun use in American books and the rise of individualism, 1960–2008. *Journal of Cross-Cultural Psychology*, 44(3), 406–415.

Twenge, J. M., & Foster, J. D. (2010). Birth cohort increases in narcissistic personality traits among American college students, 1982–2009. *Social Psychological and Personality Science*, 1(1), 99–106.

Uhls, Y. T., & Greenfield, P. M. (2011). The rise of fame: An historical content analysis. *Cyberpsychology: Journal of Psychosocial Research on Cyberspace*, 5(1), article 1. Retrieved from http://cyberpsychology.eu/view.php?cisloclanku=2011061601&article=1

Wang, J. L., Jackson, L. A., Zhang, D. J., & Su, Z. Q. (2012). The relationships among the Big Five Personality factors, self-esteem, narcissism, and sensation-seeking to Chinese University students' uses of social networking sites (SNSs). *Computers in Human Behavior*, 28(6), 2313–2319..

Westerman, J. W., Bergman, J. Z., Bergman, S. M., & Daly, J. P. (2012). Are universities creating millennial narcissistic employees? An empirical examination of narcissism in business students and its implications. *Journal of Management Education*, 36(1), 5–32.

Wilcox, K., & Stephen, A. (2012). Are close friends the enemy? Online social networks, self-esteem, and self-control. *Journal of Consumer Research*, 12–57.

Young, M. S., & Pinsky, D. (2006). Narcissism and celebrity. *Journal of Research in Personality*, 40(5), 463–471.

Part IV
Multitasking

21

Searching for Generation M

Does Multitasking Practice Improve Multitasking Skill?

L. Mark Carrier,[1] Mike Kersten,[2] and Larry D. Rosen[1]

[1] *California State University, Dominguez Hills*
[2] *Texas Christian University*

The purpose of this chapter is to explore the possibility that extensive practice in everyday multitasking is making young people especially good at that skill. Prior studies have noted the rampant multitasking among persons from the youngest generations (variously referred to as Generation M, the Net Generation, or digital natives), mostly predicated upon the frequent use of technological devices that either allow multitasking or encourage multitasking (Prensky, 2001; Roberts, Foehr, & Rideout, 2005; Tapscott, 1997). The results of a study are presented that asked people from several generations to rate their difficulty in combining tasks at home for multitasking. The self-report study queried people from the Net Generation, Generation X, and the Baby Boomer generation about how much they use technology at home and about how much they multitask with that technology. The general finding was that, in most cases, having extensive practice with everyday multitasking did not make a young person a better multitasker. In other words, for the most part, stubborn human mental limitations in the ability to simultaneously perform multiple tasks appear to exist even in this special population.

Literature Review

After collecting data from children about their technology use habits in the United States in 2004, the Kaiser Family Foundation referred to 8- to 18-year-olds as "Generation M" with the "M" standing for multitasking (Roberts et al., 2005). After a second wave of data collection, their analysis of data from 8- to 18-year-olds – now referred to as "Generation M^2" – showed that these American children and teenagers, on average, squeezed 10 hours and 45 minutes worth of daily media content into 7½ hours of media use (Rideout, Foehr, & Roberts, 2010). Further, Carrier, Cheever, Rosen, Benitez, and Chang (2009) found that younger generations of Americans

The Wiley Handbook of Psychology, Technology, and Society, First Edition. Edited by Larry D. Rosen, Nancy A. Cheever, and L. Mark Carrier.
© 2015 John Wiley & Sons, Ltd. Published 2015 by John Wiley & Sons, Ltd.

reported multitasking at home with a greater variety of tasks than older generations. They also found through self-report that the youngest generations reported a greater number of tasks combined at once than the oldest generations.

Studies report that college students also are frequent multitaskers. Jacobsen and Forste (2011) asked college students to complete an online questionnaire that included time-use diaries of media and other task use. They found that about two-thirds of the students reported using electronic media while in class, studying, or doing homework. Hammer et al. (2010) asked instructors and students from a technical college to complete a questionnaire that assessed practices and beliefs regarding cell phone and laptop use during lectures. The results showed that 91% of the students who owned laptop computers used the devices for non-academic reasons during lectures, possibly meaning that many of the students engaged in multitasking. Clayson and Haley (2012) found that almost all students in college marketing classes had received text messages during lectures and 86% had sent text messages. Tindell and Bohlander (2012) found that 91% of American college students in their study had sent or received a text message in their university class. Junco and Cotten (2011) administered an online questionnaire to college students from four universities that asked them to self-report their instant messaging (IM) use and their multitasking behaviors. The authors found high rates of multitasking while IMing. Rosen, Carrier, and Cheever (2013) found that American middle school, high school, and university students were prone to frequent task-switching while studying at home, presumably a part of a larger plan by the students to achieve multiple goals simultaneously. Baron (2008) found that American students multitask while using the computer for several reasons, including time pressure, boredom, and waiting during pauses in other computer-based tasks.

Intuitively, it would seem that all of this multitasking experience would have an effect upon multitasking efficiency. Some researchers have tried to measure the multitasking skills or abilities of the younger generations using self-report measures. In some cases, these persons appear to believe that they can indeed multitask efficiently. Carrier et al. (2009) asked three generations of Americans to indicate whether pairs of tasks were easy or difficult to combine at home. The results showed that members of the Net Generation (defined as individuals born after 1978) were less likely to find combinations difficult than Baby Boomers (born between 1946 and 1964). Members of Generation X were in between the other generations but not statistically different from them. Hammer et al. (2010) found that a subset of students believed that multitasking during lectures does not interfere with academic performance. On the other hand, Kinzie, Whitaker, and Hofer (2005) introduced handheld computers for use as synchronous chat devices during lectures in a college course and found through qualitative analysis of interview transcripts with participants (students and instructors) that both students and instructors did not recommend the simultaneous use of chatting devices and listening to lectures due to problems with dividing attention.

Other studies have used students as participants in situations where technology use must be combined with a key task. In these cases, young persons are not able to demonstrate that they can combine two tasks without a loss of performance. For example, Bowman, Levine, Waite, and Gendron (2010) found that college students asked to respond to IM requests while reading were significantly slower in their reading times compared to students who IMed prior to reading or who did not IM at all, although the comprehension scores on their reading did not suffer. Lee, Lin, and Robertson

(2012) asked students to read articles in a set amount of time and take quizzes on what they read either in a single-task condition ("silence") or while simultaneously having to watch videos, the contents of which would be tested later ("test"). The results showed significantly better reading comprehension in the silence condition than the test condition. Ellis, Daniels, and Jauregui (2010) found that texting lowered quiz scores based on an experiment in which business students either texted or did not text during a class lecture. Srivastana (2013) had American undergraduate students either listen to a podcast alone, read an article online alone, or do both together. The material from the podcast and from the article was tested using several different memory measures. Memory was reduced on all memory measures when the tasks were combined. Wood et al. (2012) examined the impact of technology use in the college classroom during lectures. Participants in their study – Canadian college students – were randomly assigned to one of several technology use or control conditions. For example, in one technology use condition, participants were required to use Facebook during lecture (three lectures were used). In another, students were required to do instant messaging. The key control condition was a paper-and-pencil note-taking condition. The results showed that, compared to the key control condition, students in the FB and IM conditions performed significantly worse on memory tests for lecture material; however, texting and emailing did not result in worse performance. However, post-hoc analyses comparing students who used technology during lecture to those who did not found that using technology reduced memory.

Self-report studies of everyday multitasking generally show no advantage for students with more media multitasking practice when it comes to multitasking skills. Levine, Waite, and Bowman (2007) administered questionnaires to college students about their self-described distractibility, reading patterns, and technology use patterns. The results showed a significant correlation between distractibility and IM use and a significant negative correlation between distractibility and reading time. Junco and Cotten (2011) found that the majority of the college students in their sample reported that IMing while doing homework interfered with homework completion. This was true whether the students were IMing while doing homework or IMing while doing non-computer tasks. Further, those who reported multitasking a great deal across all media were more likely to report that their homework had suffered.

When Carrier et al. (2009) asked Americans from three generations to indicate which tasks they choose to combine for multitasking at home, members of the Net Generation showed significantly more multitasking than other generations. Nevertheless, the authors found high levels of similarity of task combinations among the generations. Further, they found that the generations tended to agree on which combinations were difficult and which were easy. For example, all three generations reported that pleasure reading while talking to someone face to face was among the most difficult pairs to multitask. The researchers suggested that all people – regardless of their generation – choose tasks to combine based on the fact that certain tasks place a certain amount of cognitive load on general resources (Jeong & Fishbein, 2007; Jordan et al., 2005).

A few studies have tried to link everyday practice at multitasking with a direct measure of multitasking skill but there have not been consistent results. Alzahabi and Becker (2013) divided participants into heavy and light media multitaskers (using Ophir, Nass, & Wagner's, 2009, Media Multitasking Index). Then, the participants performed two tasks (classifying letters and classifying numbers on the screen) in dual-task conditions (simultaneously) or in task-switching conditions (switching rapidly between tasks). The results showed no difference between the groups in dual-task performance; however, there was a significant advantage in task-switching for the heavy media multitaskers in that they performed faster than the light media multitaskers when switching between tasks. In contrast, Ophir et al. (2009) found that heavy media multitaskers were slower than light media multitaskers were when switching between tasks. In addition, Minear, Brasher, McCurdy, Lewis, and Younggren (2013) tested heavy and light media multitaskers on several measures including attention tasks. They found that heavy media multitaskers performed no worse than light media multitaskers in task-switching.

In summary, it would seem that there is very little evidence to support the possibility that extensive multitasking practice in young persons is associated with increased multitasking efficiency. While it is clear that young persons engage in extensive everyday multitasking, only the self-report data from young persons who were asked to assess their own multitasking skills and the task-switching study in the laboratory by Alzahabi and Becker (2013) suggest an enhanced ability to multitask. Further, associations between amount of everyday multitasking and multitasking efficiency are negatively correlated or nonexistent.

So, why does extensive multitasking practice not lead to better multitasking? A number of structural factors have been proposed that could influence the inability of members of the younger generations to effectively multitask, including a natural human limitation in the level of general cognitive resources that can be allocated across multiple tasks (Jeong & Fishbein, 2007; Jordan et al., 2005), the existence of a fixed delay or bottleneck in switching between tasks (Bowman et al., 2010), a fixed amount of "cognitive capital" available for interactive tasks (Lee et al., 2012), neural limitations in retaining and retrieving information in dual-task conditions (Ellis et al., 2010), limits on how much simultaneous input one can receive (Kinzie et al., 2005), interference between essential learning processes and/or working memory processes (Junco & Cotten, 2011), and fixed demands on "cognitive load" by certain tasks that do not vary with practice or age (Carrier et al., 2009).

Although a small proportion of the population may be "supertaskers" capable of efficient multitasking, most people are not (Hammer et al., 2010) and instead will suffer from displacement of one task by another during multitasking (Levine et al., 2007) and ineffective processing due to keeping track of multiple tasks (Bowman et al., 2010). The appearance or self-perception of effective multitasking (i.e., parallel processing of information) might possibly arise from "negotiated interruption": using a processing "lag" in one task to get work done in another task (Bowman et al., 2010). A person's inclination to multitask, rather than being a means of increasing his or her cognitive efficiency, might be a well-developed habit (Junco & Cotten, 2011), a result of technology addiction (Hammer et al., 2010), a cognitive style developed as a result of quickly jumping around on tasks during technology usage (Levine et al., 2007), or even a way to satisfy a person's emotional needs (Wang & Tchernev, 2012).

Nevertheless, some authors have noted the essential role of *very extensive* practice in improving one's multitasking efficiency and the possibility that very high levels of practice are not being achieved in everyday life. Judd and Kennedy (2011) installed tracking software on computers in a laboratory at a university in Australia to identify instances of students' multitasking. The logs showed that multitasking was common but not at consistently high levels. The researchers noted that multitasking probably varies with characteristics of each situation that a person encounters, such that one's goal state dictates whether one needs to focus on just one task or is allowed to multitask, and time constraints affect whether one will multitask. Consequently, the first research question addressed in the present study is: What is the association between very high levels of everyday multitasking and multitasking efficiency?

The role of individual task practice also has been acknowledged as a potential factor since well-practiced tasks that can become "automatic" are more likely to be successfully paired concurrently with other tasks (Lee et al., 2012). Another hypothetically possible outcome of practice with individual tasks is that the component mental processes used to carry out the tasks could speed up. This would result in the total amount of time that the individual tasks tie up limited mental resources being reduced; hence, pairing the task with other tasks could become more efficient. Therefore, the second research question addressed in the present study is: What is the relationship between high levels of practice on individual everyday tasks and multitasking efficiency performing/practicing those tasks?

Following the methodology of Carrier et al. (2009), we administered an anonymous online questionnaire to more than 1,000 individuals of different ages. The questionnaires assessed baseline everyday technology usage, typical daily multitasking habits involving technology-related tasks, and self-assessments of the difficulty of combining specific pairs of everyday tasks for multitasking. Following the analyses of those authors, we used the self-rated difficulty levels as a measure of multitasking proficiency and we used comparisons across generations of individuals in these measures as evidence related to whether the youngest generation is behaving differently than other generations. Based on our research questions, we were interested in looking at the following outcomes.

Assessment of Multitasking Efficiency in Very Practiced Multitaskers

Are the members of the youngest generations with the most everyday multitasking practice finding it easier to multitask than other generation members? Since there is little evidence suggesting that extensive practice in younger individuals leads to a multitasking advantage, we should find the following:

Hypothesis 1a: Even the most extreme multitaskers in the youngest generation do not show a multitasking proficiency advantage in that the difficulty of combining tasks is not less than other individuals in that generation; and

Hypothesis 1b: The most extreme multitaskers among younger individuals should show the same pattern of difficulty ratings across task combinations as that of older generations (due to shared cognitive architectures).

Assessment of Multitasking Efficiency with Very Practiced Tasks

Do the younger persons who perform a particular everyday task extensively have an advantage over other young people when it comes to multitasking with that task? If it is true that prior experience with technology-based tasks is not benefiting the younger generation members, then:

Hypothesis 2:   Even extensive practice with a specific task should not allow multitasking with that task to be better (i.e., less reported difficulty) than in people without such practice.

Method

Participants

One thousand, one hundred, and sixty-four individuals, aged 18 to 69 years old (M= 35.4, SD= 13.2), participated in the study. Students from large general education courses at a Southern California university recruited the participants through word of mouth. Participants were entered into a lottery to win one of several $50 gift cards if they so desired. The sample consisted of 666 females (57.2%) and 498 males (42.8%). When divided into generations based on birth year, the sample comprised 328 Baby Boomers (born between 1946 and 1964) (28.1%), 339 members of Generation X (born between 1965 and 1979, henceforth "Gen Xers") (29.1%), and 472 members of the Net Generation (born between 1980 and 1999, and therefore including "Generation M" and "Generation M^2") (40.5%).

Materials

Several different measures related to the present study's goals were combined with demographic questions to form an online questionnaire administered via SurveyMonkey.com, a survey construction and response collection website. The measures included a measure of daily media usage, a measure of everyday multitasking, and items inquiring about several demographic factors (age, sex, ethnicity, and ZIP code). The web address for the questionnaire was provided to each participant, who was then allowed to access the questionnaire from a convenient location. No time constraint was placed upon completing the questionnaire but most participants completed it within 30 minutes.

Daily media usage measure   This measure was taken from Carrier et al. (2009). It consisted of 12 items asking about everyday tasks that might be performed at home. For each task, participants were asked to indicate approximately how much time they engaged in the task on a "typical" day at home. The 12 items were: surfing the web, offline computing (e.g., word processing), emailing, instant messaging (IMing), talking on the telephone, text messaging, playing video games, listening to music, watching television (TV), eating, pleasure reading, and talking face to face with someone. The eight-point response scale was: "not at all," "1 hour/day," "2 hours/day," "3 hours/day," "4–5 hours/day," "6–8 hours/day," "9–10 hours/day," and "more than 10 hours/day." The responses were converted into numerical values according to the response label, using the midpoint of a range if one was given.

Everyday multitasking measure   This measure was adapted from the one used by Carrier et al. (2009). A series of pages in the questionnaire addressed everyday multitasking activities. Each page presented the participant with an everyday task that might be performed at home. For each task, the participant was asked to indicate whether they perform the task (yes or no) and, if so, how difficult it was to pair that task with each of a series of other tasks on a list. For each potential pairing of tasks, the participant was asked to choose between "not paired," "difficult to pair," and "easy to pair." The tasks were pleasure reading, using a computer for reasons other than being online (e.g., word processing), playing video games, listening to music, eating, and talking to someone face to face. Since it was assumed that respondents eat and talk with other people, the questionnaire did not ask if the participant performed those tasks. The other tasks on the list were all of the above plus surfing the web, emailing, IMing/chatting, talking on the telephone, texting, and watching television.

Across all of the pages in the questionnaire related to everyday multitasking, there were 66 questions about specific pairings of tasks. Some pairs of tasks were queried two times due to the structure of the questionnaire items. For simplicity, only the first response to each pairing was scored. Thus, the data analysis utilized 51 unique potential pairings of everyday tasks. With respect to the amount of everyday multitasking, each "difficult" or "easy" response was scored as a 1 and each "not paired" response was scored as a 0. Then, the total number of 1s was computed and converted into a proportion of the maximum possible pairings. With respect to multitasking difficulty, each "difficult" response was scored as a 1 and each "easy" response was scored as a 0. Then, the total number of 1s was computed and converted into a proportion of the number of pairings for each participant.

Results

Hypothesis 1a: The most extreme multitaskers do not show a multitasking proficiency advantage over other young persons The first expected outcome from Hypothesis 1 is that the most extreme multitaskers will be no more proficient at multitasking than other members of the youngest generation. To assess this outcome, a measure of the amount of typical, everyday multitasking was calculated for each participant by computing the proportion of task combinations that were combined for multitasking. The mean proportion for all Net Generation students was .67 ($SD = .18$), indicating that the typical Net Gener used two-thirds of all of the possible task combinations for multitasking. In order to identify the most extreme multitaskers within the Net Generation sample, the respondents with the highest 20% of scores were used to form an extreme multitasker subgroup. The mean proportion of task combinations for this subgroup was .92 ($SD = .06$), indicating that members of this subgroup self-reported using nearly all of the possible task combinations during everyday multitasking at home.

Next, the multitasking proficiency of respondents was calculated by using the self-ratings of the pairings as "easy" or "difficult." The mean proportion of difficult pairings for all Net Generation members was .20 ($SD = .20$); this indicates that for the typical Net Generation member one-fifth of the pairings that they attempted were found to be difficult. The means for the extreme multitasker subgroup and the four other quintiles of multitasking subgroups are shown in Table 21.1. Visual inspection of the mean proportions shows that all means were in the range from .17 to .23, with no obvious order across conditions. Although the extreme multitaskers averaged a proportion of .17 of the pairings as difficult, compared to .22 for the lowest multitaskers, a one-way analysis of variance (ANOVA) revealed that there was not a significant effect of multitasking quintile upon multitasking difficulty, $F(4, 467) = 1.66$, $MSE = .04$, $p = .16$, $\eta^2 = .01$.

Table 21.1   Mean proportions of combinations young persons rated as "difficult" by multitasking level.

Multitasking subgroup	n	Mean proportion	SD
Lowest	95	.22	.29
Near lowest	101	.17	.16
Middle	83	.23	.20
Above average	104	.20	.17
Extreme	89	.17	.16

Hypothesis 1b: The most extreme multitaskers within the youngest generation should show the same pattern of difficulty ratings across task combinations as that of older generations   The second expected outcome from Hypothesis 1 is that the pattern of difficulty ratings across task combinations for the extreme multitaskers in the Net Generation should be the same as the patterns found in other generations. To assess this outcome, the average proportion of Net Generation extreme multitaskers who had difficulty in multitasking was calculated for each possible task combination. These values are shown in Table 21.2. Visual inspection of Table 21.2 reveals some patterns. Video gaming and talking face to face appear to be relatively difficult to pair with other tasks for the extreme Net Generation members while eating, listening to music, and emailing appear to not be very difficult. Values for the other generations (Generation X and Baby Boomers) were calculated in a similar fashion. The Pearson correlation coefficients were calculated to estimate the association between the extreme Net Generation member ratings and the ratings for the other two generations. There was a statistically significant positive relationship between the extreme Net Generation members and Generation X, $r(49) = .54$, $p < .001$, indicating that there was agreement between the patterns of difficulty ratings across the pairings. The correlation between the extreme Net Generation members and the Baby Boomers was $r(49) = .37$, $p < .01$, indicating a statistically significant positive relationship between the two sets of ratings.

Hypothesis 2: Even extensive practice with a specific task should not allow a member of the youngest generation to multitask with that task better than other people   The second expected outcome is that extensive practice with a skill that is a component of a multitasking pairing should not improve the success of pairing that skill with other skills. For the Net Generation members, the average number of hours spent each day on the 12 typical at-home tasks is shown in Table 21.3. The most frequently performed task was talking face to face; listening to music was the second most frequently performed task. The least frequently performed tasks were video gaming and reading for pleasure. The nine technology-based tasks were used in an analysis of the effect of task "practice" upon the difficulty of multitasking. For the Net Generation members, the associations between the amounts of time spent daily engaging in a particular task and the difficulty ratings of combining that task with other tasks were computed. The raw correlations are shown in Table 21.4. Hypothesis 2 predicted that the correlation between daily practice of a task and the difficulty of combining that task with another task should be close to zero and not statistically significant. In other words, having spent more time doing that task each day should not improve one's ability to combine that task with other tasks.

Table 21.2 Proportions of Net Generation extreme multitaskers reporting multitasking difficulty by task combination.

	Task 1					
Task 2	Reading	Offline	Gaming	Music	Eating	F2F
Offline computing	.29					
Video gaming	.47	.40				
Listening to music	.06	.03	.06			
Eating	.06	.09	.25	.01		
Talking face to face	.45	.39	.39	.17	.10	
Surfing the web	.13	.12	.35	.00	.03	.21
Emailing	.09	.08	.43	.00	.05	.19
IMing/chatting	.08	.10	.34	.01	.05	.21
Telephoning	.31	.23	.25	.19	.20	.45
Texting	.11	.05	.31	.00	.11	.21
Watching TV	.17	.19	.28	.15	.01	.21

Note. Computations include only those participants who paired the tasks together.

Table 21.3 Mean hours spent on everyday tasks at home on a typical day by Net Geners

Task	Mean hours	SD
Talking face to face	4.35	3.17
Listening to music	3.93	3.25
Texting	2.84	3.21
Offline computing	2.70	2.49
Surfing the web	2.64	2.20
Watching TV	2.56	2.19
Eating	2.40	1.95
IMing	1.82	2.68
Emailing	1.75	1.75
Telephoning	1.48	1.74
Reading	1.36	1.69
Video gaming	0.94	1.71

Note. Tasks are sorted from highest to lowest on mean hours performed.

Inspection of Table 21.4 reveals several interesting patterns. First, most of the correlations are not significant and are close to zero. Second, there are several significant, negative correlation values. In these cases, practice with a task was associated with less difficulty combining that component skill with another skill. This pattern was observed for the component skill of talking on the telephone, combining it with offline computing, video gaming, listening to music, and talking face to face. This pattern also was observed for the component skill of texting, when combining it with talking face to face. Further, more frequent use of two skills – video gaming and listening to music – was linked to improvement in multitasking with reading. Third, there are several cases in which more practice with the component skill is associated with *greater* difficulty in combining the task with another task. More practice at video gaming was associated with worse performance when combining gaming with eating,

Table 21.4 Correlations between daily use of skills and difficulty pairing with other skills in young persons.

| | | | | Daily Skill | | | | | |
Paired skill	Computing	Email	Gaming	IM/chat	Music	Surfing	Telephone	Texting	TV
Computing	—	.04	-.12	-.08	-.03	-.01	-.15**	-.09	-.09
Eating	-.01	.07	.14**	-.05	.00	-.02	-.02	-.01	.04
Email	-.05	—	.22***		.00				
Gaming	-.06	.00	—	.06	-.01	.20***	-.12*	-.07	.00
IM/chat	.01		.20***	—	-.08				
Music	-.01	-.04	.02	-.05	—	-.04	-.10*	-.04	-.09
Reading	-.12	-.07	-.19*	-.05	-.12*	-.05	-.10	-.05	-.04
Surfing	-.05		.18**		-.04	—			
Talking F2F	-.02	-.02	.30***	-.10	-.02	-.06	-.17**	-.19***	-.09
Telephone	.06		.22***		-.04				
Texting	-.01		.22***		.00				
TV	-.05		.23***		-.04				

Note. Not all possible pairs of tasks were measured (empty cells).

$*p < .05$

$**p < .01$

$***p < .001$

emailing, IMing, surfing the web, talking face to face, talking on the telephone, texting, and watching television. Additionally, more practice at surfing the web was associated with more difficulty combining surfing the web with video gaming.

Discussion

The purpose of this study was to investigate the relationship between everyday practice with technology-based tasks and multitasking efficiency in members of the youngest generation. Based on prior research showing mostly no advantage for everyday multitaskers in multitasking proficiency, it was hypothesized that Net Generation members with the most multitasking practice would have no advantage over Net Generation members with less practice. Also, it was hypothesized that the pattern of difficulty across task combinations experienced when multitasking would be the same for Net Generation members and for members of other generations. Further, it was expected that Net Generation members with more practice on particular technology-based skills would not have an advantage over other Net Generation members in combining that skill with other skills during multitasking. To test these hypotheses, an online questionnaire, administered to a large sample of Americans from all generations, assessed typical, at-home use of everyday tasks and subjective ratings of difficulty of combining those tasks with each other.

The results revealed that the members of the Net Generation with the most extreme level of at-home multitasking combined 92% of all possible combinations of the queried tasks: surfing the web, offline computing, emailing, instant messaging, talking on the telephone, text messaging, video gaming, listening to music, watching television, eating, pleasure reading, and talking face to face. However, those Net Generation members representing the most extreme 20% of multitaskers from that generation were no more likely to find combining tasks to be easy than the other four quintiles of Net Generation multitaskers. In other words, there was no evidence that extreme multitaskers in the Net Generation were any better at multitasking than other Net Generation members. Additionally, when looking at the patterns of which task combinations were reported as difficult and which as easy, the pattern for the extreme Net Generation members had a significant degree of overlap with the patterns for Generation X ($r = .54$) and for Baby Boomers ($r = .37$). So, the task combinations that older generations found difficult to perform tended to be the same task combinations that extreme Net Generation members found difficult to perform.

Finally, in most cases, practice with a component skill was not associated with better performance when combining that component skill with another skill for multitasking among the Net Generation members. In fact, for some cases, practice at a component skill was associated with *worse* performance when combining that skill with another skill. Most notably this happened for video gaming. Those Net Generation members who played more daily hours of video games showed worse performance when combining gaming with many of the other tasks, including emailing, IMing, surfing the web, talking face to face, using the telephone, texting, and watching television. Nevertheless, in a small number of cases (7 out of 69), practice on a component skill associated with better multitasking using that skill: (1) more talking on the phone was associated with better telephoning while performing offline computing, talking face to face, video gaming, and listening to music; (2) more texting was associated with better texting while talking face to face; and (3) more gaming and listening to music were associated with better multitasking with reading.

Overall, the three hypotheses generally were supported by the results. With everyday multitasking, the bulk of the present evidence does not support a link between more multitasking and better multitasking or between more practice with a task and better multitasking with that task. Two of the exceptions involved the component skills of talking on the phone and of text messaging. Structural factors that influence the ability of humans to combine more than one task for multitasking, including having fixed cognitive resources (Jeong & Fishbein, 2007; Jordan et al., 2005); fixed delays or bottlenecks in switching between tasks (Bowman et al., 2010); and/or limitations in retaining or retrieving information (Ellis et al., 2010), in processing input (Kinzie et al., 2005), and in learning and/or working memory (Junco & Cotten, 2011) do not appear to be avoided in most cases with extensive component skill practice or everyday multitasking by Net Generation members. The results tend to support the existence of fixed demands placed by particular tasks on our mental architecture (Carrier et al., 2009).

There are at least two possible cognitive explanations of the unexpected finding that practice at video gaming is associated with worse performance when combining gaming with other tasks. One possibility is that extensive video gaming changes the way in which video gaming is performed by someone in the Net Generation. Frequent video game players might use different strategies with respect to the allocation and use of specific mental processes compared to infrequent video game players. If so, then the different set of processes used by frequent gamers might make it more difficult for them to combine video gaming with other tasks. The new set of processes might improve video game performance while simultaneously decreasing the success of combining video gaming with other tasks. Video gaming is a complex task during which mental demands vary with the particular game played, the particular part of a game being played, and the particular difficulty level of the game being played. Thus, video gaming might be more likely to change in its mental subcomponents with practice than other tasks studied here. Another possible explanation for the findings with video gaming hinges on the complex, multitasking-like nature of the task itself. With video gaming practice, Net Generation members could become worse with managing multiple subtasks successfully because of the continuously interruptive nature of stimuli in the video gaming environment – stimuli that also tend to occur unexpectedly and unpredictably. The degeneration of general-purpose multitasking skills might thus make it more difficult for Net Generation members with extensive video gaming experience to combine video gaming with other tasks.

For some other task combinations, practice at a component task appeared to improve multitasking with that task. One possible explanation is that the component skill becomes automatic in the sense that it can be combined seamlessly with another task. However, that does not appear to be true in these cases. Talking on the telephone as a component skill was associated with improved performance combining telephoning with offline computing, with talking face to face, with video gaming, and with listening to music but not with the other tasks with which it was combined. Therefore, talking on the telephone did not become automatic in the sense that it could be combined with all other tasks. Furthermore, most people, including the Net Generation and Generation M participants, have extensive lifelong experience talking on the telephone, so it would be assumed that even the members of the youngest generation with relatively lower levels of telephoning practice would have achieved an "automatic" level of telephoning. The component skill of texting also was a task that did not seem to be automatic because it could not be combined with many other tasks without difficulty. Another possible explanation for these findings is that extensive telephoning and texting leads to qualitative changes in the mental resources or strategies that are used by the Net Generation members performing the tasks. Frequent talking on the telephone, to a degree even higher than other Net Generation members, might change the subset of cognitive processes that are used to perform the task or might change the strategy or style of task performance that then leads to greater success combining the task with offline computing and talking face to face. For example, it is possible that, in less extreme telephone talkers, processing a conversation requires deep processing of the conversational partner's message and reflective thought about the type of response required. In more extreme telephone talkers, learned expectations about the conversational topics, the conversational partner's style, and acceptable responses during conversations could reduce the need for analytical processing and increase the demands on timing, rhythm, and memory processes. The same could be true of extensive texting, even within a generation known for their texting prowess.

Limitations

One limitation of this study is that the data are from self-report measures, rather than a measurement of actual performance in multitasking situations. This self-report approach allowed for the collection of data from a large number of individuals – hundreds from each of the generations under investigation – but potentially suffers from the problems associated with self-report data such as incorrect recall by participants. Another limitation of the study is that the analyses were correlational and, thus, they cannot be used to infer cause and effect between the variables of multitasking practice, component skill practice, and multitasking efficiency. The approach used here limits the strength of the conclusions. Despite these limitations, the present results, when combined with the results of prior research on the topic, form a consistent body of knowledge that helps to answer the research questions posed.

Conclusion

The present study did not find significant evidence that Net Generation members' or Generation M members' practice at multitasking or practice at component technology-based skills improved their multitasking performance. The results are consistent with other studies related to this topic. Other self-reported multitasking research found that young people who multitask a lot show the same patterns of multitasking difficulties as people from other generations (Carrier et al., 2009) and that multitasking interferes with other important tasks (Junco & Cotten, 2011). In laboratory-based research, persons with extensive self-reported media multitasking were better at task-switching in one study (Alzahabi & Becker, 2013), but not in another (Ophir et al., 2009). Additionally, heavy multitaskers are not better at dual-task performance than light media multitaskers (Alzahabi & Becker, 2013). Also, young people tend to show interference when combining technology-based tasks with other tasks in laboratory settings (Bowman et al., 2010; Ellis et al., 2010; Lee et al., 2012). So, while multitasking is rampant in young people due to the technologies that are being used, on the whole, this multitasking madness does not appear to lead to an across-the-board improvement of multitasking skill.

References

Alzahabi, R., & Becker, M. W. (2013). The association between media multitasking, task-switching, and dual-task performance. *Journal of Experimental Psychology: Human Perception and Performance, 39*(5), 1485–1495.

Baron, N. (2008). Adjusting the volume: Technology and multitasking in discourse control. In J. E. Katz (Ed.), *Handbook of mobile communication studies* (pp. 177–193). Cambridge, MA: MIT Press.

Bowman, L. L., Levine, L. E., Waite, B. M., & Gendron, M. (2010). Can students really multitask? An experimental study of instant messaging while reading. *Computers and Education, 54*(4), 927–931.

Carrier, L. M., Cheever, N. A., Rosen, L. D., Benitez, S., & Chang, J. (2009). Multitasking across generations: Multitasking choices and difficulty ratings in three generations of Americans. *Computers in Human Behavior, 25*(2), 483–489.

Clayson, D. E., & Haley, D. A. (2012). An introduction to multitasking and texting: Prevalence and impact on grades and GPA in marketing classes. *Journal of Marketing Education, 35*(1), 26–40.

Ellis, Y., Daniels, B., & Jauregui, A. (2010). The effect of multitasking on the grade performance of business students. *Research in Higher Education, 8*(1), 1–10.

Hammer, R., Ronen, M., Sharon, A., Lankry, T., Huberman, Y., & Zamtsov, V. (2010). Mobile culture in college lectures: Instructors' and students' perspectives. *Interdisciplinary Journal of E-Learning and Learning Objects, 6*(1), 293–304.

Jacobsen, W. C., & Forste, R. (2011). The wired generation: Academic and social outcomes of electronic media use among university students. *Cyberpsychology, Behavior, and Social Networking, 14*(5), 275–280.

Jeong, S., & Fishbein, M. (2007). Predictors of multitasking with media: Media factors and audience factors. *Media Psychology, 10*(3), 364–384.

Jordan, A., Fishbein, M., Zhang, W., Jeong, S. H., Hennessy, M., Martin, S., & Davis, E. (2005, May). *Multiple media use and multitasking with media among high school and college students.* Paper presented at the International Communication Association, Annual Meeting, New York, NY.

Judd, T., & Kennedy, G. (2011). Measurement and evidence of computer-based task switching and multitasking by "Net Generation" students. *Computers and Education, 56*(3), 625–631.

Junco, R., & Cotten, S. R. (2011). Perceived academic effects of instant messaging use. *Computers and Education, 56*(2), 370–378.

Kinzie, M. B., Whitaker, S. D., & Hofer, M. J. (2005). Instructional uses of instant messaging (IM) during classroom lectures. *Educational Technology and Society, 8*(2), 150–160.

Lee, J., Lin, L., & Robertson, T. (2012). The impact of media multitasking on learning. *Learning, Media and Technology, 37*(1), 1–11.

Levine, L. E., Waite, B. M., & Bowman, L. L. (2007). Electronic media use, reading, and academic distractibility in college youth. *CyberPsychology and Behavior, 10*(4), 560–566.

Minear, M., Brasher, F., McCurdy, M., Lewis, J., & Younggren, A. (2013). Working memory, fluid intelligence, and impulsiveness in heavy media multitaskers. *Psychonomic Bulletin and Review, 20*, 1274–1281.

Ophir, E., Nass, C., & Wagner, A. D. (2009). Cognitive control in media multitaskers. *Proceedings of the National Academy of Sciences, 106*(37), 15583–15587.

Prensky, M. (2001). Digital natives, digital immigrants. *On the Horizon, 9*(5), 1–6.

Rideout, V. J., Foehr, U. G., & Roberts, D. F. (2010). *Generation M²: Media in the lives of 8- to 18-year-olds.* Menlo Park, CA: Henry J. Kaiser Family Foundation.

Roberts, D. F., Foehr, U. G., & Rideout, V. (2005). *Generation M: Media in the lives of 8–18 year-olds.* Menlo Park, CA: Henry J. Kaiser Family Foundation.

Rosen, L. D., Carrier, L. M., & Cheever, N. A. (2013). Facebook and texting made me do it: Media-induced task-switching. *Computers in Human Behavior, 29*(3), 948–958.

Srivastava, J. (2013). Media multitasking performance: Role of message relevance and formatting cues in online environments. *Computers in Human Behavior, 29*(3), 888–895.

Tapscott, D. (1997). *Growing up digital: The rise of the Net Generation.* New York, NY: McGraw-Hill.

Tindell, D. R., & Bohlander, R. W. (2012). The use and abuse of cell phones and text messaging in the classroom: A survey of college students. *College Teaching, 60*(1), 1–9.

Wang, Z., & Tchernev, J. M. (2012). The "myth" of media multitasking: Reciprocal dynamics of media multitasking, personal needs, and gratifications. *Journal of Communication, 62*(3), 493–513.

Wood, E., Zivcakova, L., Gentile, P., Archer, K., De Pasquale, D., & Nosko, A. (2012). Examining the impact of off-task multi-tasking with technology on real-time classroom learning. *Computers and Education, 58*(1), 365–374.

22

Multitasking and Attention
Implications for College Students
Laura L. Bowman, Bradley M. Waite, and Laura E. Levine

Central Connecticut State University

In this chapter, research relevant to college students' media multitasking behavior is reviewed. Multitasking refers to engaging in multiple activities simultaneously; media multitasking includes some form of media such as texting while driving. Media use, benefits to users, and the use of technology in the classroom are discussed. Media use, especially mobile media, has been strongly linked with multitasking especially among college students. The pervasiveness, perceived benefits, and impact of media multitasking in activities important to college students, including academic life, employment, driving, and pedestrian activity, are examined. A brief review of theory and research that help explain the possibilities and limits of multitasking due to cognitive and neurological abilities and constraints is included. In conclusion, ideas to help students manage multitasking to maximize both productivity and safety are discussed.

Media Use

The rapid adoption of mobile phone technology has been remarkable. Approximately 94% of Americans own a mobile phone (Nielsen, 2013) and about 61% of these are "smartphones" (i.e., devices with advanced operating systems; Smith, 2013). In 2012 Americans had 326 million wireless subscriber connections (e.g., smartphones, tablets), used 2.3 trillion minutes of wireless time, and sent 2.19 trillion text messages with reported wireless data traffic increasing 123% and 69% in the last two years (388 MB in 2010 to 867 MB in 2011 to 1468 MB in 2012) (Cellular Telecommunications Industry Association, 2013).

Rates of phone ownership vary around the world, within an overall high and growing rate. In countries studied by Nielsen (2013), phone ownership ranged from 81% in India to 99% in South Korea. Many people (from 7% in Turkey to 51% in Russia) reported owning more than one mobile media device, and in the majority of countries measured, smartphones were the most commonly owned type of phones.

The Wiley Handbook of Psychology, Technology, and Society, First Edition. Edited by Larry D. Rosen, Nancy A. Cheever, and L. Mark Carrier.

Benefits of Technology In and Out of Classroom Settings

Growth of mobile technology use in Asia, Europe, and the Americas has led to broader and deeper uses for these media devices. The benefits of modern mobile media technology are in many ways self-evident. The sheer adoption rates of the technology demonstrate the value ascribed to it by users. Common uses of media technology include communication activities such as text messaging, instant messaging (IM), emailing, social networking, web browsing, video, television, and music streaming, gaming, global position satellite services, commercial activities, such as shopping and banking, and increasingly educational activities in and out of the classroom. In combination with more traditional forms of Internet- and computer-based technology, these forms of electronic media devices offer powerful opportunities, convenience, and attractions for their users. In the United States, it has been estimated that young people spend over 7½ hours per day using all forms of electronic media and, with media multitasking considered, this translates into nearly 11 hours of media activity daily (Rideout, Foehr, & Roberts, 2010).

With the expanded availability and increased sophistication of portable media devices, educators have explored ways to take advantage of their power as educational tools. Computers and mobile technology devices are increasingly being deployed in educational settings and are transforming the way that teaching and learning take place in many schools and colleges. For example, social media, blogs, wikis, videos, and podcasts are being widely incorporated into the professional activities and classes of college-level instructors with 80% of a representative sample of U.S. college faculty indicating use of social media for some aspect of their course (Moran, Seaman, & Tinti-Kane, 2011). In one recent national survey of middle and high school teachers of advanced-level students, over 90% reported that the Internet has had a major impact on their teaching-related activities and the majority (57%) reported that technology has "enabled" their communications with students (Purcell, Heaps, Buchanan, & Friedrich, 2013). This same study found that three-quarters of the teachers reported that they or their students use mobile phones as part of class assignments and that 43% use tablet computers in class or for class assignments. Virtually all the teachers in one recent report indicated that they believe the Internet and related devices open up access for students to be able to obtain a wide range of resources, but many (76%) also strongly agreed that Internet search engines "have conditioned students to expect to be able to find information quickly and easily" (Purcell et al., 2012, p. 3). Most of these teachers reported having their students do online research (95%), and download or submit assignments online (79% and 75%, respectively). These researchers report that cell phones are becoming "particularly popular learning tools" (p. 4) with 72% of teachers saying they or their students use cell phones for class-related activities. However, this same group of teachers expressed agreement (88%) with the notion that students have "fundamentally different cognitive skills because of the digital technologies they have grown up with" (p. 7) and that "today's digital technologies are creating an easily distracted generation with short attention spans" (87%; p. 7). There is a clear trend for increased incorporation of technology-aided instruction inside and outside of the classroom but also concern for the implications of such instruction. Many instructors have reported concerns about this use, particularly relating to integrity of student work and privacy (Moran et al., 2011), the development of altered cognitive skills, and attentional problems (Purcell et al., 2012).

Advocates of technology-infused instruction cite the benefits of such teaching and learning as the potential to actively engage students in learning with mobile or portable devices and to create student-centered classrooms with "bring your own devices" models to open learning opportunities. In a nationally representative survey, parents reported that over half of all high school students in the U.S. carry a smartphone with them to school (Grunwald Associates LLC, 2013). This same survey found that parents are more likely to have positive evaluations of mobile media devices as educational tools when their children's school requires such use. However, whether technology-infused instruction leads to better learning outcomes or not is less than clear. Some reports and meta-analyses suggest positive outcomes (cf. Means, Toyama, Murphy, Bakia, & Jones, 2010).

Media Multitasking

Electronic media use provides many benefits, but there are risks from their use as well. One clear pattern is that these technologies offer the easy and continuous opportunity for multitasking. Though media multitasking can include activities that involve different cognitive systems activated concurrently (e.g., listening to music while driving), many media multitasking activities involve sequential processing or switching back and forth between tasks that involve the same system or modality (e.g., reading text messages while reading textbooks). Rideout et al. (2010) found that American youth use at least two different forms of media concurrently during about 29% of the time they are using media and 31% of students indicated that they multitask with media (e.g., texting and television viewing) most of the time when doing homework.

Multitasking with media may engender the perception that one is accomplishing more in a given period of time. Yet, the evidence suggests otherwise, at least with respect to academic tasks, as we discuss below. Reading with electronic devices does offer the opportunity to pursue linked information readily. This may lead the reader to make broad connections and explore context related to the reading immediately. However, it also has the potential to lead the reader to distraction from the primary source.

College Students' Use of Electronic Media During Academic Pursuits

The vast majority of American college students use electronic media on a regular basis and they are more likely to use it for multitasking than older adults (Carrier, Cheever, Rosen, Benitez, & Chang, 2009). Based on self-report, 28% used Facebook, 28% emailed, 21% searched the Internet, 10% used instant messaging (IM), and 69% (Junco, 2012) to 92% (Tindell & Bohlander, 2012) texted during class. The number who report multitasking while working on online courses was even higher. Burak (2012) found 63% used Facebook, 69% texted, 10% IMed, and 47% emailed. Fried (2008) found that students who brought laptops to class reported doing class-irrelevant activities for 17 minutes on average in a 75-minute class. Eighty-one percent checked email, 68% IMed, 43% surfed the net, 25% played games, and 35% reported doing other activities. Kay and Lauricella (2011) found that 60% of students were logged on to instant messaging most or all of the time when using a laptop computer, including during class time. Twenty-five percent of these students reported that they spent more than half of class time IMing with friends. In addition, almost half of students reported being distracted by other students' non-academic use of laptops during class, including 16% who were distracted by other students viewing pornography.

However, self-report may not be the most accurate way to assess media multitasking. Kraushaar and Novak (2010) used direct monitoring of student activity on laptop computers during a class that required students to use laptops. They found that students were involved in unrelated activities 42% of the time and opened, on average, 65 new sites during a 75-minute lecture, with twice as many non-course-related sites as course-relevant sites. In self-report, students vastly underreported the amount of distractive media they used; 61% of students IMed, but only 25% reported having done so. This may result from social desirability in self-reporting, but it may also be that people are simply unaware of how much multitasking they do. Brasel and Gips (2011) observed college students working on a computer while a television was playing in the same room. These students changed their focus of attention from computer to TV and vice versa 120 times per half hour but reported that they had done so on average 15 times.

Students also multitask with media while studying. Outside of class, the percent of students who report using IM while studying ranged from 62% (Bowman, Levine, Waite, & Gendron, 2010) to 93% (Junco & Cotton, 2011). Rosen, Carrier, and Cheever (2013) observed college students, as well as younger students, as they studied for 15 minutes in their homes to determine the nature of their use of electronic media. On average, college students switched tasks after about 6 minutes of work, usually to use technology. During a 15-minute study session they were on task 70–72% of the time. Students who had more clear-cut study strategies were less likely to switch from their studying than those who did not.

Academic Effects of Multitasking

Researchers have consistently found that the more students use electronic media in general, the lower their GPA tends to be (e.g., Harman & Sato, 2011; Walsh, Fielder, Carey, & Carey, 2013). The reasons for this correlation are not clear. Students may be multitasking and therefore paying less attention to their work, or they may be spending less time working and more time using media for social purposes, or it may be that poorer students are spending more time online.

Research in actual or simulated class environments as well as by self-report indicates that at least part of the reason for poor performance lies in direct distraction resulting from electronic media use while in class. Self-reported use of media while in class and while doing schoolwork has been related to lower GPA (Burak, 2012; Junco & Cotten, 2012). Fried (2008) found that students who reported more laptop use in class each week stated that they paid less attention to lectures, that lectures were unclear, and that they had less understanding of the material. Ellis, Daniels, and Jauregui (2010) found that students did more poorly on a quiz when they texted during class. Even the mere ringing of a cell phone in class has been found to disrupt note-taking and test performance (End, Worthman, & Matthews, 2010). In an experimental study, Rosen, Lim, Carrier, and Cheever (2011) found students who received and responded to 16 or more text messages during a 30-minute lecture did worse on a test of comprehension than those who received fewer than seven messages.

Rosen, Cheever, and Carrier (2012) found that some types of multitasking were more distracting than others. Use of Facebook was most distracting, but these researchers found an equal level of distraction if students were not allowed to check Facebook due to anxiety about what they were missing. Kraushaar and Novak (2010) found that IMing was the most distracting in their sample but there was no effect of using the Internet for surfing, entertainment, or emailing.

Wood and colleagues (2011) assigned different groups of students to text with a cell phone, or email, IM, or Facebook on a laptop during class lectures. Other students were instructed to use paper and pencil or word-processing for taking notes. Those students who used Facebook performed more poorly on a multiple choice exam on the material presented in the lectures than those who took notes on paper. Those who used no technology had higher test scores than those who did.

Studies that occur in a classroom type of setting have a clear time limit. In contrast, Bowman et al. (2010) and Fox, Rosen, and Crawford (2009) gave students unlimited time to read academic material. They found performance on comprehension tests did not differ between groups who were interrupted by electronic messaging, but time taken to complete this reading was considerably longer, even when the actual time spent messaging was subtracted from the total reading time (Bowman et al., 2010). Therefore, it takes students longer to achieve the same academic outcomes if they are distracted by media use while they are studying. In these experimental studies, the IMs sent to students were emotionally neutral. In real life, messages may be much more emotionally engaging. Shafer and colleagues (2012) found that highly emotional stimuli were more distracting than less emotional stimuli as assessed both behaviorally and neurologically.

Media multitasking has also been found to disrupt basic cognitive processes, which would likely result in lower academic performance. Cell phone conversations slowed reaction time and decreased accuracy on standardized cognitive measures of memory, discrimination, and attention (Kemker, Stierwalt, LaPointe, & Heald, 2009). College students' ability to recognize semantically related items on a list was poorer when they were interrupted with either a cell phone conversation or a text message exchange but there was no effect on false memory for related items that had not appeared on the list (Smith, Isaak, Senette, & Abadie, 2011).

Media Multitasking and Distractibility

There is clear research support for the relationship between direct distraction from media multitasking and poorer academic performance, but there is also evidence that greater media multitasking is related to general inattention, distractibility, and impulsivity. Ophir, Nass, and Wagner (2009) found that heavy media multitaskers had less ability to switch between tasks effectively and were more distractible due to both external and internal stimuli. Several studies have linked this outcome to problems with both memory and attention. For example, Cain and Mitroff (2011) found that heavy media multitaskers were less able to control their focus of attention when instructed to do so. Frein, Jones, and Gerow (2013) found lower performance on a memory test in individuals who used Facebook more often.

Individuals who multitask heavily with media report that they experience more inattention, distractibility, and impulsiveness, both in relation to academic tasks and as a general trait (Levine, Waite, & Bowman, 2007, 2013; Waite, Levine, & Bowman, 2009). Research that has come mainly from Asia has linked Internet addiction, defined as the "inability to control [one's] use of the Internet, which eventually causes marked distress and/or functional impairment" (Yoo et al., 2004, p. 487) with ADHD (Yen, Yen, Chen, Tang, & Ko, 2009; Yoo et al., 2004) and impulsivity (Lin, Ko, & Wu, 2011).

Multitasking and Work

College students are likely to continue multitasking behavior when employed outside of school. Media use can be helpful and required in some work environments, but safety risks and loss of productivity have been demonstrated during multitasking with media on the job. Safety issues include a range of problems, from transportation accidents (National Transportation Safety Board, 2010) to distractions during medical procedures (Smith, Darling, & Searles, 2011). In simulations of work situations productivity suffered as individuals took significantly longer to complete tasks (e.g., Nicholson, Nicholson, Parboteeah, & Valacich, 2009).

Driving and Distraction

Studies of media use while driving clearly demonstrate distraction caused by media multitasking. Naturalistic driving studies (e.g., Klauer, Dingus, Neale, Sudweeks, & Ramsey, 2006) that examine volunteers' driving habits by use of video cameras and other data recorders installed in vehicles during normal driving times have shown the distracting nature of multitasking with media while driving. These studies have demonstrated that nearly 80% of automobile accidents and 65% of near-crashes are due to driver distraction, with multitasking with wireless devices being the single most common multitasking distractor (Dingus et al., 2006; Klauer et al., 2006). The National Highway Traffic Safety Administration (NHTSA, 2010) reported that over 20,000 traffic accidents in a recent year were due to distraction caused by cell phone multitasking while driving. Crash and near-crash risk estimates increased twenty-threefold over baseline in one study of commercial vehicles (Olson, Hanowski, Hickman, & Bocanegra, 2009).

Controlled experimental laboratory research has also demonstrated clear patterns of distraction associated with multitasking. In general, these studies using computerized driving simulations (e.g., Drews, Yazdani, Godfrey, Cooper, & Strayer, 2009; Strayer & Johnston, 2001) have demonstrated that conversing on cell phones while (simulated) driving led to clear performance decrements (e.g., slower responses, missed traffic signals, more crashes) in over 97% of drivers (Watson & Strayer, 2010). Study results suggest that performance decrements were due to the diversion of attention resulting from the cognitive demands of the phone conversation itself and not solely from the driver looking away to manipulate a device (Strayer, Watson, & Drews,

2011). That is, conversations using "hands-free" devices were just as distracting in that they led to a similar level of driving performance decrement as did conversations using handheld devices. Strayer et al. (2011) note that cognitive distraction leads to inattentional blindness, leading drivers to miss important cues in their environment.

Multitasking and Pedestrian Activity

The latest report by the NHTSA (2013) indicates that the number of traffic fatalities involving pedestrians increased by 4% in 2010 and another 3% in 2011. This increase may be a result of a rise in distracted walking. The Liberty Mutual Insurance News (2013) reported on a national survey of over 1,000 adults, many of whom admitted texting or emailing (26%), talking on the phone (51%), and listening to music (34%) while crossing the street. In Delaware, decals warning texting pedestrians to "Look Up" were installed on the sidewalks of intersections (Glatter, 2012) and in some states pedestrians can be fined for distracted walking (Burke, 2012).

Most empirical research on walking behaviors has examined the impact of mobile devices such as cell phones or portable music devices. Results of studies conducted in naturalistic and experimental environments repeatedly show impairments (Hyman, Boss, Wise, McKenzie, & Caggiano, 2010; Schwebel et al., 2012). Nasar and Troyer (2013) found that young people (ages 16–25 years) were most likely to be involved in a pedestrian accident, most while talking on a cell phone. Using a simulated street-crossing task, Neider and colleagues (2011) found that both older adults ($M = 73$ years) and traditionally college-aged adults ($M = 22$ years) had slower crossing times when using a cell phone, further demonstrating the distracting nature of mobile media multitasking.

The multitasking distraction appears to work in both directions. That is, not only does the media use distract from walking performance, walking interferes with the intake of information from the media. For example, Doolittle and Mariano (2008) found that students' ability to recall information presented via video was worse when they were walking compared to when they were stationary. Coens, Degryse, Senecaut, Cottyn, and Clarebout (2011) found evidence that students' ability to learn information presented auditorily while moving was impaired. They had students listen to a podcast presentation via an iPod while sitting, walking, or jogging. Students who sat while learning performed better on a test than those who walked or jogged.

Theory and Basic Research on Divided Attention

Research demonstrating limitations on multitasking ability has theoretical underpinnings. Early theories of attention such as Broadbent's (1958) bottleneck model, Deutsch and Deutsch's (1963) late selection model, and Treisman's (1960) attenuation model proposed that attentional systems restrict the amount of information that can be processed. Treisman proposed that selection of information for processing was dependent on the physical characteristics of the stimulus (e.g., loudness, pitch, or brightness), but also relevance or meaning. Treisman found that when participants were instructed to shadow a meaningful message delivered to one ear in a dichotic listening task, participants followed the meaning when the message was changed to the ear they were supposed to ignore. Now referred to as the "cocktail party effect," Moray (1959) showed that participants heard their name spoken in the unattended channel when they were engaged in a selective attention task, i.e., focusing on one channel of information while ignoring another.

Later theories acknowledged that not only are stimulus properties important, but one's cognitive resources affect selective attention (e.g., Lavie, 2005; Norman & Bobrow, 1975). Kahneman (1973) argued that available cognitive resources are in part impacted by arousal levels as well as individual preferences, effort, and difficulty of the task. Lavie and Cox (1997) measured response time to identify a target (e.g., letter X or N) in either an easy condition (low cognitive load) in which the target was dissimilar to the distractors (e.g., X in a field of Os) or in a difficult condition (high cognitive load) in which the target was similar to the distractors (e.g., N among the letters W, H, M, and Z). When X was the target, participants pushed a specific key on a keyboard and were asked to ignore a possible second target (e.g., N). Under the low-load condition, participants took longer to identify the target (X), indicating that they also were attending to the potential target they were to ignore (N). Under the high-load condition, participants were faster to identify the real target (X), indicating that they were ignoring the potential target (N). This outcome suggests that when people are engaged in a demanding task, they are more likely to devote resources to that task, selectively attend to that task, and ignore the surrounding environment.

When people are attending to one task, they might not even perceive an unexpected novel stimulus. That is, they may experience inattentional blindness (Mack & Rock, 1998). A dramatic demonstration of inattentional blindness was performed by Simons and Chabris (1999). Participants in their study watched a film of a game involving basketball passing and were asked to count the number of passes made during the game. About mid-way through the game, a person dressed in a gorilla suit appeared in the film for a few seconds. After the film, participants were asked if they noticed anything unusual, and nearly half did not see the gorilla. In a different study, researchers found that participants failed to notice a unicycling clown when they were walking and talking on a cell phone (Hyman et al., 2010).

Though people *can* and *do* ignore irrelevant environmental stimuli, there are circumstances in which stimuli draw or hold attention (Yantis, 1996). Generally, attentional capture occurs for stimuli that have an abrupt onset or are visually salient (e.g., Yantis, 1993; Yantis & Jonides, 1984) or have high emotional impact. For example, participants had a more difficult time performing a Stroop test of selective attention when the stimulus words had emotionally negative connotations (e.g., rape; Pratto & John, 1991). Soares (2012) found that participants under a high cognitive load took longer to identify a target stimulus when fear-arousing stimuli such as snakes and spiders were included in the visual scene.

While people can selectively attend to stimuli under certain conditions, the more common state of the world is one in which people attempt to divide attention among simultaneous multiple streams of information. Though people can effectively multitask or handle many tasks at once (e.g., Spelke, Hirst, & Neisser, 1976), empirical evidence suggests that there are limits. For example, Neisser and Becklen (1975) found that participants were unable to follow the events of two superimposed visual images. Other research showed that performance declined when the tasks were demanding (Duncan, 1979; Hitch & Baddeley, 1976) or when task similarity increased

(Treisman & Davies, 2012). Schneider and Shiffrin's (1977) classic study demonstrated that participants could, with practice on an easy task, develop automatic processing skills in which attention could be efficiently divided. However, with a more demanding task, participants had to use controlled processing and even with practice were not able to efficiently divide their attention.

Not only do task characteristics impact successful division of attention, but cognitive structures restrict the amount of information that can be processed at once. Pashler (1993, 1998) described a psychological refractory period (PRP), in which attention to a second competing stimulus is delayed until after a period of time has passed. In a similar vein, Shapiro, Arnell, and Raymond (1997) described attentional blink (AB) as the failure to identify a second relevant target when presented less than 500 ms after the first target. When participants were engaged in a single-task activity such as looking for only one of the two targets, performance was not impaired. Both the PRP and AB phenomena, which show impairments with dual-task activities, differ in terms of methodological paradigms, but appear to share some of the same neural mechanisms at the early stages of processing (Marti, Sigman, & Dehaene, 2012). Evidence that different parts of the brain are involved in single- versus dual-task activities comes from Foerde, Knowlton, and Poldrack (2006) and Poldrack et al. (2005), who showed that the part of the brain associated with shallow processing (striatum) was involved when participants engaged in dual-task activities while the medial temporal lobe system associated with deeper processing was involved during single-task activities.

Desimone and Duncan (1995) proposed a (visual) model of attention known as biased or integrated competition. Their model takes into account bottom-up neural mechanisms and top-down mechanisms guided by situational task demands. Data from research studies measuring overt behavior and that of brain activity measures (e.g., ERP, PET) were considered. According to their model, the salience of the stimuli and the goals of the individual affect attention. Stimuli compete for attention and in general, more highly salient stimuli are selected for processing. However, competition among stimuli can be mediated by one's intentions.

The theories and research concerning attentional processes indicate that the ability to effectively divide attention is possible, but tenuous. The competing message could be delayed, processed shallowly, or suppressed and missed entirely, especially if cognitive load is high. At times a highly salient or emotional competing message can draw one away from focused tasks. Thus, research indicates that nearly all college students who believe they can successfully multitask while engaged in meaningful activities are mistaken.

Implications and Interventions for Students

Technology likely will continue to be an expanding presence in our lives. According to the concept of automaticity, one might predict that the more people multitask the better they get at it, but the research described earlier indicates limits to this notion. Those who multitask more with media seem to be less able to carry out their main task successfully. Therefore, how can one handle technology in a way that accords with the way one processes information and does not interfere with important tasks such as studying, driving, working, and even walking?

Interventions to Promote Academic Achievement

Many teachers limit their students' access to electronic media to reduce distraction. Rosen et al. (2013) found that over half of young people admitted to becoming highly or moderately anxious when they were not able to check their mobile devices. Limiting students' use of mobile media in class is not likely to improve attention for those students whose anxiety about what they were missing is as significant an internal distraction as the actual use of the devices. This is most likely to be true for students with high levels of Internet involvement.

The following are some ways that teachers may help students manage their use of technology:

1   Technology breaks: Rosen et al. (2012) found that when students were given one minute to use their electronic devices after 15 minutes of work they were better able to focus on subsequent class material.
2   Self-monitoring: Most people are unaware of how much they use technology and how frequently they switch tasks. Having students keep a log, or even videotape themselves as they work, can help them to become more aware of what they are doing so they can make conscious choices about what they want to do (Parry, 2013).
3   Promoting metacognitive skills: Teach students to regulate their use of electronic devices, or set boundaries, based on knowledge of when their use interferes with learning. In one study, students with greater metacognitive skills turned off the sounds on their IM and waited until break time to respond to messages. Students with lower metacognitive abilities responded to all incoming messages when they arrived (Wijekumar & Meidinger, 2005).
4   Meditation: Preliminary research has provided evidence that individuals who took part in brief periods of mindfulness meditation were subsequently less likely to switch between tasks and stayed with one task longer (Levy, Wobbrock, Kaszniak, & Ostergren, 2012) while another group was more efficient at switching between tasks than those who had spent the previous 10 minutes multitasking (McCarthy, 2013).
5   Positive use of technology: Instead of fighting students on the use of technology, use its capabilities creatively to engage students and enhance learning. For example, a teacher might set a task for students to explore online and then use the information to collaborate with others either online or in the classroom. Putting flashcards or even podcasts onto students' mobile phones might allow them to study during "down" times when they might otherwise be texting or playing a game.
6   Teaching technology literacy: Consider that technology will continue to be an issue for students after college. Therefore, teaching them how to use it well is an important goal. Rather than reacting to the students who are using it as distraction, use the opportunity to teach about controlling attention. Help students understand how, when, and why technology is controlling them rather than the other way around.

Interventions in Regard to Driving and Walking

Safety is the primary issue in regard to electronic multitasking while driving and walking. Eleven states prohibit all cell phone use while driving, while 37 states prohibit its use by new drivers (Governors Highway Safety Association [GHSA], 2013).

Forty-one states prohibit text messaging while driving, with six more prohibiting its use by new drivers (GHSA, 2013). Forty percent of teens report others driving dangerously due to cell phone use, but most believe their own use is not a problem (Tison, Chaudhary, & Cosgrove, 2011). In addition, 91% of teens report that their parent has talked on a cell phone while driving and 59% say their parent has texted while driving (Liberty Mutual & SADD, 2012).

The following interventions are designed to encourage young drivers not to use their cell phones while driving:

1   Do not model cell phone use while driving.
2   Do not call or text someone who is known to be driving.
3   Use an app (e.g., AT&T DriveMode™ or similar product) that lets incoming texters know the driver is unavailable and will respond later.
4   Help young drivers understand inattentional blindness: Ask them to describe verbally the road around them while they send a text as a passenger in a car.
5   Be sure young drivers know the risks and the laws concerning media device use while driving.

Interventions to promote awareness of the hazards of multitasking while walking include:

1   Installation of in-pavement signs or auditory signal devices (much like those for the hearing or visually impaired) to alert pedestrians of upcoming crosswalks and stop light changes.
2   Public service announcements and educational programs to alert pedestrians of the dangers of walking while distracted.
3   Modeling safe walking and texting behavior, by stopping and stepping off to a safe location to read and send text messages.

In conclusion, the potential benefits of technology and media with respect to learning, entertainment, social connection, and commerce are great. In order for individuals to use these technologies to their best potential and to minimize liabilities, it is recommended that teachers, parents, and students be aware of the limits of attentional cognitive systems. There are clear costs associated with multitasking. It is essential to understand when media multitasking is beneficial and when it is not. In this review, the evidence points to the benefit of limiting multitasking to superficial activities involving different cognitive systems that can be activated concurrently. Multitasking will interfere with performance on meaningful tasks such as studying, working, driving, and even walking, putting oneself and others at risk of reduced academic and work achievement and of physical harm to oneself or others.

References

Bowman, L. L., Levine, L. E., Waite, B. M., & Gendron, M. (2010). Can students really multitask? An experimental study of instant messaging while reading. *Computers and Education, 54,* 927–931.

Brasel, S. A., & Gips, J. (2011). Media multitasking behavior: Concurrent television and computer usage. *Cyberpsychology, Behavior, and Social Networking, 14,* 527–534.

Broadbent, D. E. (1958). *Perception and communication.* New York, NY: Pergamon Press.

Burak, L. J. (2012). Multitasking in the university classroom. *International Journal for the Scholarship of Teaching and Learning, 6*(2), 1–12.

Burke, M. N. (2012, May). Communities to start fine for texting and walking. Retrieved from http://usatoday30.usatoday.com/news/nation/story/2012-05-15/texting-while-walking-illegal/54979480/1

Cain, M. S., & Mitroff, S. R. (2011). Distractor filtering in media multitaskers. *Perception, 40,* 1183–1192.

Carrier, L. M., Cheever, N. A., Rosen, L D., Benitez, S., & Chang, J. (2009). Multitasking across generations: Multitasking choices and difficulty ratings in three generations of Americans. *Computers in Human Behavior, 25,* 483–489.

Cellular Telecommunications Industry Association. (2013). CTIA's semi-annual wireless industry survey. Retrieved from http://files.ctia.org/pdf/CTIA_Survey_YE_2012_Graphics-FINAL.pdf

Coens, J., Degryse, E., Senecaut, M., Cottyn, J., & Clarebout, G. (2011). Listening to an educational podcast while walking or jogging: Can students really multitask? *International Journal of Mobile and Blended Learning, 3,* 23–33.

Desimone, R., & Duncan, J. (1995). Neural mechanisms of selective visual attention. *Annual Review of Neuroscience, 18,* 193–222.

Deutsch, J. A., & Deutsch, D. (1963). Attention: Some theoretical considerations. *Psychological Review, 70,* 80–90.

Dingus, T. A., Klauer, S. G., Neale, V. L., Petersen, A., Lee, S. E., Sudweeks, J., ... Knipling, R. R. (2006). *The 100-Car Naturalistic Driving Study, Phase II – Results of the 100-Car Field Experiment* (Report No. DOT HS 810 593). Springfield, VA: National Technical Information Service. Retrieved December 3, 2014, from http://www.roadsafetyobservatory.com/Evidence/Details/11003

Doolittle, P. E., & Mariano, G. J. (2008). Working memory capacity and mobile multimedia learning environments: Individual differences in learning while mobile. *Journal of Educational Multimedia and Hypermedia, 17,* 511–530.

Drews, F. A., Yazdani, H., Godfrey, C. N., Cooper, J. M., & Strayer, D. L. (2009). Text messaging during simulated driving. *Human Factors, 51,* 762–770.

Duncan, J. (1979). Divided attention: The whole is more than the sum of its parts. *Journal of Experimental Psychology: Human Perception, 5,* 216–228.

Ellis, Y., Daniels, B., & Jauregui, A. (2010). The effect of multitasking on the grade performance of business students. *Research in Higher Education Journal, 8,* 1–10.

End, C. M., Worthman, S., & Matthews, M. B. (2010). Costly cell phones: The impact of cell phone rings on academic performance. *Teaching of Psychology, 37,* 55–57.

Foerde, K., Knowlton, B. J., & Poldrack, R. A. (2006). Modulation of competing memory systems by distraction. *PNAS Proceedings of the National Academy of Sciences of the United States of America, 103,* 11778–11783.

Fox, A., Rosen, J., & Crawford, M. (2009). Distractions, distractions: Does instant messaging affect college students' performance on a concurrent reading comprehension task? *CyberPsychology and Behavior, 12*(1), 51–53.

Frein, S., Jones, S., & Gerow, J. E. (2013). When it comes to Facebook there may be more to bad memory than just multitasking. *Computers in Human Behavior, 29,* 2179–2182.

Fried, C. B. (2008). In-class laptop use and its effects on student learning. *Computers and Education, 50,* 906–914.

Glatter, R. (2012, July). Texting while walking? Think twice. Retrieved from http://www.forbes.com/sites/robertglatter/2012/07/31/texting-while-walking-think-twice/

Governors Highway Safety Association (GHSA). (2013). Distracted driving laws. Retrieved from http://www.ghsa.org/html/stateinfo/laws/cellphone_laws.html

Grunwald Associates LLC. (2013). *Living and learning with mobile devices: What parents think about mobile devices for early childhood and K-12 learning.* Retrieved from http://www.grunwald.com/pdfs/Grunwald%20Mobile%20Study%20public%20report.pdf

Harman, B. A., & Sato, T. (2011). Cell phone use and grade point average among undergraduate university students. *College Student Journal, 45,* 544–549.

Hitch, G. J., & Baddeley, A. D. (1976). Verbal reasoning and working memory. *Quarterly Journal of Experimental Psychology, 28,* 603–621.

Hyman, I. R., Boss, S., Wise, B. M., McKenzie, K. E., & Caggiano, J. M. (2010). Did you see the unicycling clown? Inattentional blindness while walking and talking on a cell phone. *Applied Cognitive Psychology, 24,* 597–607.

Junco, R. (2012). In-class multitasking and academic performance. *Computers in Human Behavior, 28,* 2236–2243.

Junco, R., & Cotten, S. (2011). Perceived academic effects of instant messaging use. *Computers and Education, 56,* 370–378.

Junco, R., & Cotten, S. R. (2012). No A 4 U: The relationship between multitasking and academic performance. *Computers and Education, 59,* 505–514.

Kahneman, D. (1973). *Attention and effort.* Englewood Cliffs, NJ: Prentice Hall.

Kay, R. H., & Lauricella, S. (2011). Exploring the benefits and challenges of using laptop computers in higher education classrooms: A formative analysis. *Canadian Journal of Learning and Technology, 37,* 1–18.

Kemker, B. E., Stierwalt, J. A. G., LaPointe, L. L., & Heald, G. R. (2009). Effects of a cell phone conversation on cognitive processing performances. *Journal of the American Academy of Audiology, 20,* 582–588.

Klauer, S. G., Dingus, T. A., Neale, V. L., Sudweeks, J. D., & Ramsey, D. J. (2006). *The impact on driver inattention on near crash/crash risk: An analysis using the 100-Car Naturalistic Driving Study Data* (Report No. DOT HS 810 594). Washington, DC: National Highway Traffic Safety Administration.

Kraushaar, J. M., & Novak, D. C. (2010). Examining the affects (sic) of student multitasking with laptops during the lecture. *Journal of Information Systems Education, 21,* 241–251.

Lavie, N. (2005). Distracted and confused? Selective attention under load. *Trends in Cognitive Sciences, 9,* 75–82.

Lavie, N., & Cox, S. (1997). On the efficiency of visual selective attention: Efficient visual search leads to inefficient distractor rejection. *Psychological Science, 8,* 395–398.

Levine, L. E., Waite, B. M., & Bowman, L. L. (2007). Electronic media use, reading and academic distractibility in college youth. *CyberPsychology and Behavior, 10,* 560–566.

Levine, L. E., Waite, B. M., & Bowman, L. L. (2013). Use of instant messaging predicts self-report but not performance measures of inattention, impulsiveness and distractibility. *Cyberpsychology, Behavior, and Social Networking, 16,* 898–903.

Levy, D. M., Wobbrock, J. O., Kaszniak, A. W., & Ostergren, M. (2012). The effects of mindfulness meditation training on multitasking in a high-stress information environment. *Proceedings of Graphics Interface.* Retrieved from http://dmlevy.ischool.uw.edu/wp/wp-content/uploads/2013/03/Levy-Meditation-Multitasking.pdf

Liberty Mutual Insurance News. (2013, June 10). New study shows three out of five pedestrians prioritize smartphones over safety when crossing streets. Retrieved from http://www.libertymutualgroup.com/omapps/ContentServer?fid=3237831502381&pagename=LMGroup%2FViews%2FLMG&ft=8&cid=1240015377571

Liberty Mutual & SADD. (2012). Promoting responsible teen driver behavior. Retrieved from http://www.libertymutual.com/auto-insurance/teen-driving/articles-studies/articles-and-studies

Lin, M., Ko, H., & Wu, J. (2011). Prevalence and psychosocial risk factors associated with Internet addiction in a nationally/representative sample of college students in Taiwan. *Cyberpsychology, Behavior, and Social Networking, 14,* 741–746.

Mack, A., & Rock, I. (1998). *Inattentional blindness.* Cambridge, MA: MIT Press.

Marti, S., Sigman, M., & Dehaene, S. (2012). A shared cortical bottleneck underlying attentional blink and psychological refractory period. *Neuroimage, 59,* 2883–2898.

McCarthy, J. (2013, June 7). Enhanced media multitasking: The restorative cognitive effects of temporarily escaping the multitasking mindset. Thesis submission for the degree of Master of Arts in Communication, Stanford University. Retrieved from http://comm.stanford.edu/wp-content/uploads/2013/01/JordanMcCarthyMAThesis.pdf

Means, B., Toyama, Y., Murphy, R., Bakia, M., & Jones, K. (2010, September). Evaluation of evidence-based practices in online learning: A meta-analysis and review of online learning studies. [This report was prepared for the U.S. Department of Education under Contract number ED-04-CO-0040 Task 0006 with SRI International.] Retrieved from http://www2.ed.gov/rschstat/eval/tech/evidence-based-practices/finalreport.pdf

Moran, M., Seaman, J., & Tinti-Kane, H. (2011, April). Teaching, learning, and sharing: How today's higher education faculty use social media. Retrieved from http://www.babson.edu/Academics/Documents/babson-survey-research-group/teaching-learning-and-sharing.pdf

Moray, N. (1959). Attention in dichotic listening: Affective cues and the influence of instruction. *Quarterly Journal of Experimental Psychology, 11,* 56–60.

Nasar, J. L., & Troyer, D. (2013). Pedestrian injuries due to mobile phone use in public places. *Accident Analysis and Prevention, 57,* 91–95.

National Highway Traffic Safety Administration (NHTSA). (2010). *Distracted driving 2009: Traffic safety facts research note* (Report No. DOT HS 811). Washington, DC: Author. Retrieved from http://www.distraction.gov/research/PDF-Files/Distracted-Driving-2009.pdf

National Highway Traffic Safety Administration (NHTSA). (2013). *Traffic safety facts. 2010 data. Pedestrians* (Report No. DOT HS 811 748). Washington, DC: Author. Retrieved from http://www-nrd.nhtsa.dot.gov/Pubs/811748.pdf

National Transportation Safety Board (NTSB). (2010, January 21). NTSB determines engineer's failure to observe and respond to red signal caused 2008 Chatsworth accident; recorders in cabs recommended. Retrieved from http//www.ntsb.gov/news/2010/100121.html

Neider, M. B., Gaspar, J. G., McCarley, J. S., Crowell, J. A., Kaczmarski, H., & Kramer, A. F. (2011). Walking and talking: Dual-task effects on street crossing behavior in older adults. *Psychology and Aging, 26,* 260–268.

Neisser, U., & Becklen, R. (1975). Selective looking: Attending to visually specified events. *Cognitive Psychology, 7,* 480–494.

Nicholson, D. B., Nicholson, J. A., Parboteeah, D. V., & Valacich, J. S. (2009). Investigating the effects of distractions and task complexity on knowledge worker productivity in the context of mobile computing environments. *Journal of Organizational and End User Computing, 21,* 1–20.

Nielsen. (2013, February). The mobile consumer: A global snapshot. Retrieved from http://www.nielsen.com/us/en/reports/2013/mobile-consumer-report-february-2013.html

Norman, D. A., & Bobrow, D. G. (1975). On data-limited and resource-limited processes. *Cognitive Psychology, 7,* 44–64.

Olson, R. L., Hanowski, R. J., Hickman, J. S., & Bocanegra, J. (2009). *Driver distraction in commercial vehicle operations, final report* (Report No. FMCSA-RRR-09-042). Washington, DC: Federal Motor Carrier Safety Administration. Retrieved from http://www.fmcsa.dot.gov/factsresearch/research-technology/report/FMCSA-RRR-09-042.pdf

Ophir, E., Nass, C., & Wagner, A. D. (2009). Cognitive control in media multitaskers. *Proceedings of the National Academy of Sciences, 106,* 15583–15587.

Parry, M. (2013). You're distracted. *Chronicle of Higher Education, 59,* A26–A29.

Pashler, H. E. (1993). Doing two things at the same time. *American Scientist, 81,* 48–55.

Pashler, H. (1998). *Attention*. Hove, UK: Psychology Press.

Poldrack, R. A., Sabb, F. W., Foerde, K., Tom, S. M., Asarnow, R. F., Bookheimer, S. Y., & Knowlton, B. J. (2005). The neural correlates of motor skill automaticity. *Journal of Neuroscience, 25*, 5356–5364.

Pratto, F., & John, O. P. (1991). Automatic vigilance: The attention-grabbing power of negative social information. *Journal of Personality and Social Psychology, 61*, 380–391.

Purcell, K., Heaps, A., Buchanan, J., & Friedrich, L. (2013, February 28). How teachers are using technology at home and in their classrooms. Pew Internet & American Life Project. Retrieved from http://www.pewinternet.org/2013/02/28/how-teachers-are-using-technology-at-home-and-in-their-classrooms/

Purcell, K., Rainie, L., Heaps, A., Buchanan, J., Friedrich, L., Jacklin, A., … Zickuhr, K. (2012, November 1). How teens do research in the digital world. Pew Internet & American Life Project. Retrieved from http://www.pewinternet.org/2012/11/01/how-teens-do-research-in-the-digital-world/

Rideout, V. J., Foehr, U. G., & Roberts, D. F. (2010). *Generation M²: Media in the lives of 8- to18-year-olds*. Menlo Park, CA: Henry J. Kaiser Family Foundation. Retrieved from http://kaiserfamilyfoundation.files.wordpress.com/2013/01/8010.pdf

Rosen, L. D., Carrier, L. M., & Cheever, N. A. (2013). Facebook and texting made me do it: Media-induced task-switching while studying. *Computers in Human Behavior, 29*, 948–958.

Rosen, L. D., Cheever, N. A., & Carrier, L. M. (2012). *iDisorder: Understanding our obsession with technology and overcoming its hold on us*. New York, NY: Palgrave Macmillan.

Rosen, L. D., Lim, A. F., Carrier, L. M., & Cheever, N. A. (2011). An empirical examination of the educational impact of text message-induced task switching in the classroom: Educational implications and strategies to enhance learning. *Psicologia Educativa, 17*(2), 163–177.

Schneider, W., & Shiffrin, R. M. (1977). Controlled and automatic human information processing: I. Detection, search, and attention. *Psychological Review, 84*, 1–66.

Schwebel, D. C., Stavrinos, D., Byington, K. W., Davis, T., O'Neal, E. E., & de Jong, D. (2012). Distraction and pedestrian safety: How talking on the phone, texting, and listening to music impact crossing the street. *Accident Analysis and Prevention, 45*, 266–271.

Shafer, A. T., Matveychuk, D., Penney, T., O'Hare, A. J., Stokes, J., & Dolcos, F. (2012). Processing of emotional distraction is both automatic and modulated by attention: Evidence from an event-related fMRI investigation. *Journal of Cognitive Neuroscience, 24*(5), 1233–1252.

Shapiro, K. L., Arnell, K. M., & Raymond, J. E. (1997). The attentional blink. *Trends in Cognitive Sciences, 1*, 291–296.

Simons, D. J., & Chabris, C. F. (1999). Gorillas in our midst: Sustained inattentional blindness for dynamic events. *Perception, 28*, 1059–1074.

Smith, A. (2013, June 5). Smartphone ownership 2013. Pew Internet & American Life Project. Retrieved from http://www.pewinternet.org/2013/06/05/smartphone-ownership-2013/

Smith, T., Darling, E., & Searles, B. (2011). 2010 survey on cell phone use while performing cardiopulmonary bypass. *Perfusion, 26*, 375–380.

Smith, T. S., Isaak, M. I., Senette, C. G., & Abadie, B. G. (2011). Effects of cell-phone and text-message distracters on true and false recognition. *Cyberpsychology, Behavior, and Social Networking, 14*, 351–358.

Soares, S. C. (2012). The lurking snake in the grass: Interference of snake stimuli in visually taxing conditions. *Evolutionary Psychology, 10*, 187–197.

Spelke, E., Hirst, W., & Neisser, U. (1976). Skills of divided attention. *Cognition, 4*, 215–230.

Strayer, D. L., & Johnston, W. A. (2001). Driven to distraction: Dual-task studies of simulated driving and conversing on a cellular phone. *Psychological Science, 12*, 462–466.

Strayer, D. L., Watson, J. M., & Drews, F. A. (2011). Cognitive distraction while multitasking in the automobile. In B. Ross (Ed.), *The psychology of learning and motivation* (Vol. *54*, pp. 29–58). Burlington, VA: Academic Press.

Tindell, D. R., & Bohlander, R. W. (2012). The use and abuse of cell phones and text messaging in the classroom. *College Teaching, 60*, 1–9.

Tison, J., Chaudhary, N., & Cosgrove, L. (2011, December). *National phone survey on distracted driving attitudes and behaviors* (Report No. DOT HS 811 555). Washington, DC: National Highway Traffic Safety Administration.

Treisman, A. M. (1960). Contextual cues in selective listening. *Quarterly Journal of Experimental Psychology, 12*, 242–248.

Treisman, A., & Davies, A. (2012). Divided attention to ear and eye. In J. Wolfe & L. Robertson (Eds.), *From perception to consciousness: Searching with Anne Treisman* (pp. 24–31). New York, NY: Oxford University Press.

Waite, B. M., Levine, L. E., & Bowman, L. L. (2009). Instant messaging, multitasking and media use of college youth: Connections to impulsiveness and distractibility. *American Journal of Media Psychology, 2*(3/4), 126–146.

Walsh, J. L., Fielder, R. L., Carey, K. B., & Carey, M. P. (2013). Female college students' media use and academic outcomes: Results from a longitudinal cohort study. *Emerging Adulthood, 1*(3), 219–232.

Watson, J. M., & Strayer, D. L. (2010). Supertaskers: Profiles in extraordinary multi-tasking ability. *Psychonomic Bulletin and Review, 17*(4), 479–485.

Wijekumar, K., & Meidinger, P. (2005). Interrupted cognition in an undergraduate programming course. *Proceedings of the American Society for Information Science and Technology, 42*.

Wood, E., Zivcakova, L., Gentile, P., Archer, K., DePasquale, D., & Nosko, A. (2011). Examining the impact of off-task multi-tasking with technology on real-time classroom learning. *Computers and Education, 58*, 365–374.

Yantis, S. (1993). Stimulus-driven attentional capture. *Current Directions in Psychological Science, 2*, 156–161.

Yantis, S. (1996). Attentional capture in vision. In A. Kramer, M. Coles, & G. Logan (Eds.), *Converging operations in the study of visual selective attention* (pp. 45–76). Washington, DC: American Psychological Association.

Yantis, S., & Jonides, J. (1984). Abrupt visual onsets and selective attention: Evidence from visual search. *Journal of Experimental Psychology: Human Perception and Performance, 10*, 601–621.

Yen, J., Yen, C., Chen, C., Tang, T., & Ko, C. (2009). The association between adult ADHD symptoms and Internet addiction among college students: The gender difference. *CyberPsychology and Behavior, 12*, 187–191.

Yoo, H., Cho, S., Ha, J., Yune, S., Kim, S., Hwang, J., & Lyoo, I. (2004). Attention deficit hyperactivity symptoms and Internet addiction. *Psychiatry and Clinical Neurosciences, 58*, 487–494.

23

Understanding Multimedia Multitasking in Educational Settings

Eileen Wood and Lucia Zivcakova

Wilfrid Laurier University

Although the topic of multitasking has increasingly become evident in the media and among educational researchers, the act of multitasking is not a "new" phenomenon in society. Indeed, parents, teachers, and students have engaged in multitasking throughout the centuries. For example, parents have cared for their children while conducting their daily tasks; educators have supervised their class engaged in an exercise while marking papers, and students have attended to lectures while writing notes. All of these pairs of activities fall under the general definition of multitasking. That is, multitasking involves engaging in more than one task during the same period of time. What is new today, however, is that a vast array of portable, versatile, and powerful digital technologies afford us opportunities to multitask more frequently, more easily, and across a much greater array of activities (Pew Research Center, 2014; Rideout, Vandewater, & Wartella, 2003). For example, types of potential multitasking activities in which students and educators can engage include: entertainment, finances, social communication, research, and creative expression. This diverse array of activities can involve one person, or at the touch of a finger, learners can be connected with others close by and throughout the world. The flexibility of activities that can be performed with these new powerful and portable technologies offers the potential for less restricted, richer, and affordable e-learning experiences that can be tailored to the needs of individual learners as well as groups (Contreras-Castillo, Perez-Fragoso, & Favela, 2006; Gilbert, Morton, & Rowley, 2007; Hrastinski, 2006; Winter, Cotton, Gavin, & Yorke, 2010). For precisely these reasons, mobile technologies are being introduced to classrooms at all levels of education throughout the world (e.g., Higher Education Funding Council for England, 2005; National Committee of Inquiry into Higher Education, 1997; Winter et al., 2010). The introduction and use of technologies, however, is not without concern. Indeed, as one line of research grows to show the rich exploration, connectedness, and learning gains that can be achieved by introducing new digital technologies to the classroom, another line of research demonstrates restrictions, distractions, and lost learning opportunities. At the core of

The Wiley Handbook of Psychology, Technology, and Society, First Edition. Edited by Larry D. Rosen, Nancy A. Cheever, and L. Mark Carrier.

this latter line of inquiry is the issue of "costs" associated with multitasking or inappropriate multitasking. Given the seamless integration of digital technologies in today's society, the question for researchers today is not whether individuals multitask or not when technologies are used – we know they do, and this is especially the case among young people (Carrier, Cheever, Rosen, Benitez, & Chang, 2009). In fact, multitasking behaviors are so normative that many define it as a "way of life" (Rosen, 2007). Evidence supports this assertion even in the classroom. For example, students report multitasking 56.5% of the time when they use the Internet (Moreno et al., 2012). The questions of interest for researchers today, therefore, are directed at understanding how and when multitasking might affect classroom performance both positively and negatively.

Multitasking in Non-Educational Settings: Concerns and Necessities

Research documenting the negative impacts resulting from use of personal digital communication devices while engaged in other tasks is well established in a variety of non-educational domains. Specifically, performance, while multitasking, may not only be detrimental, but in some cases can be life threatening. For instance, cell phone use while driving has consistently yielded tremendous risk statistics, whereby one hour of driving, while using a cell phone, increases the risk of crashing by 400–900% (McEvoy et al., 2005; Violanti, 1998, Violanti & Marshall, 1996). Increased stress, loss of focus (Wallis & Steptoe, 2006), lowering of IQ (Freedman, 2007), and symptoms resembling those of attention deficit hyperactivity disorder (ADHD) also have been reported (Hallowell, 2005). Popular press reports also reveal a multitude of more sensational health risks associated with multitasking with mobile communication devices, including falling into sinkholes or off a pier, and even running into a black bear (The Week, 2012).

Despite these negative reports, there is also an acknowledgment that many situations in today's workforce require multitasking, and that multitasking with technologies is becoming an increasingly important and necessary skill (Appelbaum, Marchionni, & Fernandez, 2008; Freedman, 2007). Given the increasing demands to engage in multitasking and the increasing prevalence of portable digital devices that allow such multitasking to occur, multitasking in educational contexts is indeed an important issue to understand.

Setting the Stage for Multitasking in Educational Contexts

Developmentally, portable digital technologies are becoming increasingly evident in the lives and daily activities of young children both at home and in the formal educational system. Similarly, adult educational contexts, in response to the strain of physical space limitations on campus and the desire to make learning opportunities more accessible, have increasingly introduced new technologies as part of the learning environment. The prevalence of digital devices within and beyond the classroom presents an opportunity for technology-based multitasking to occur. How might we understand multitasking in an educational context? Is it detrimental, risky, and/or beneficial? These are the questions we will explore in the remainder of this chapter.

Multitasking: What is it?

Although earlier we noted that multitasking can be understood as engaging in more than one activity within the same time period (Lee & Taatgen, 2002; Pashler, 1994), the manner in which individuals engage in multitasking can vary. Specifically, three different forms of multitasking have been described in the literature: dual-tasking, rapid attention switching, and continuous partial attention. Dual-tasking (also referred to as divided attention or concurrent multitasking) occurs when we simultaneously pay attention to more than one stimulus (Kieras, Meyer, Ballas, & Lauber, 2000; Posner, 1990). This definition of multitasking is often what people imagine is occurring when the term multitasking is used. Specifically, we imagine an individual equally engaged in two different tasks. Within a research context, an experimental example of dual-tasking would be reading a paragraph on a computer screen, while keeping an eye on a letter placed at the top of the screen and indicating when the letter changes color (Schoor, Bannert, & Brunken, 2012). This example requires attention to the task of reading and monitoring the color of the letter at the same time. Dual-tasking is also evident in educational settings involving multimedia learning (Schuler, Scheiter, & van Genuchten, 2011), where the skills involved in navigating or utilizing multimedia are added to the primary task of learning.

Rapid attention switching occurs when we quickly switch our attention from one task to another (Posner, 1990). In this definition of multitasking, an individual dedicates their attention wholly to only one task/activity at a time, but cycles rapidly between the tasks. This iterative processing occurs so rapidly that both tasks are being engaged regularly and in quick succession. Continuous partial attention is a more recent conception of how multitasking occurs. Continuous partial attention involves paying partial attention to one or more tasks continuously, such as may occur when a student is engaged in web browsing while listening to a classroom lecture (Stone, n.d.).

Depending on the definition of multitasking that is assumed, different performance outcomes are expected, and in particular, different deficits in performance are predicted. For example, dual-tasking often results in slowed performance in at least one of the tasks that are being performed (e.g., Levy & Pashler, 2001; Levy, Pashler, & Boer, 2006). In rapid attention switching, performance in one of the two tasks may be impaired. For example, in an experiment where participants were asked to view one word quickly, followed by another (100 ms), the participants often forgot the second word when asked to recall both words (Enns, Visser, Kawahara, & Di Lollo, 2001). Less is known about the drawbacks associated with continuous partial attention, as its relatively new appearance means that more studies are required to fully understand how paying continuous partial attention impacts performance. However, dedicating only partial attention to two competing tasks would be expected to yield either slowing of tasks or detriments to performance on one or both tasks.

Theories to Explain How Multitasking Can Interfere With Learning

Slowing, errors, and other challenges associated with any multitasking activity are typically explained through the cognitive bottleneck theory. However, multitasking challenges associated with learning, and in particular multimedia learning, are often explained through one of two cognitive educational theories: cognitive load theory and the cognitive theory of multimedia learning.

The cognitive bottleneck theory assumes that our cognitive capabilities are limited and only allow us to complete tasks in a serial manner, one at a time. When we attempt to complete multiple tasks simultaneously, a constraint in decision-making, called a cognitive bottleneck, arises. This inability to process multiple decisions at a time causes cognitive slowing in order for the different decision-making tasks to be performed. This bottleneck in processing is also referred to as interference (Welford, 1967). The resulting cognitive bottleneck is analogous to a bottleneck on a highway, created by construction or a roadblock, in which two lanes of cars have to pass through a single lane, resulting in a slowing of traffic. Detrimental effects in the form of cognitive slowing are well evidenced (e.g., Borst, Taatgen, & van Rijn, 2010; McCann & Johnston, 1992; Pashler, Harris, & Nuechterlein, 2008; Pashler & Johnston, 1989; Welford, 1952) and have been shown in real-world contexts, such as driving a motor vehicle while conversing on a cell phone (e.g., Caird, Willness, Steel, & Scialfa, 2008), and in piloting an aircraft while conversing (e.g., Adams, Tenny, & Pew, 1991).

Both the cognitive load theory (Sweller, van Merriënboer, & Paas, 1998) and the cognitive theory of multimedia learning (Mayer, 2005) are based upon pre-existing information-processing theories in cognitive psychology. These theories assume that learning occurs through the interaction of long-term memory and working memory (Paas, van Gog, & Sweller, 2010). Long-term memory is vast and contains learned information and skills, as well as schemas and strategies that the learner can call upon to facilitate working memory. Working memory is a limited system that can be enlarged when schemas, automatized routines, and strategies are employed. Specifically, in one model of working memory, Baddeley (1999) posited that working memory is composed of three distinct subcomponents: the phonological loop, visuospatial sketchpad, and the central executive, each of which performs a specific function. More precisely, the phonological loop is involved in processing verbal information, whereas the visuospatial sketchpad is involved in the processing of visual and spatial information. Lastly, the central executive is basically the "brain" of the operation, performing multiple functions, including the coordination of tasks, switching attention between stimuli, as well as linking the information in each of the subsystems to long-term memory (Baddeley, 1999; Smith & Jonides, 1999).

The difference between cognitive load theory and the cognitive theory of multimedia learning is in the understanding of how limitations in working memory occur (Schuler et al., 2011). In cognitive load theory, learning is strongly impacted by the limited working memory. More specifically, the interaction of working memory and long-term memory is influenced by the type of learning task, the type of instruction, and the processing skills employed by the learner. These three elements represent different types of load on the system. The three types of load are: intrinsic, extraneous, and germane. Intrinsic load refers to the difficulty of the learning task, with challenging, novel tasks increasing the load for the learner. Extraneous load refers to additional demands placed on the learner resulting from the instructional design or presentation of the material (Sweller & Chandler, 1994). Germane load refers to the mental or cognitive processes that the learner can bring to the learning task, such as integrating new information with pre-existing prior knowledge (Kirschner, Ayres, & Chandler, 2011; Sweller, 1988). Although intrinsic load is presumed to be difficult to alter, both extraneous and germane loads can be altered through use of effective instructional designs and teaching methods, such as worked examples, which decrease working memory demands (Kirschner, Sweller, & Clark, 2006).

Cognitive load theory would predict deficits in performance when students engage in multitasking, because there would be an increase in extraneous load or intrinsic load. For example, when students use technology for off-task purposes, such as reviewing images on Facebook when they are supposed to be attending to lectures, the information presented using the technology imposes an added and unnecessary load to the instructional task at hand. Additionally, attempting to do more than one task reduces the amount of mental processing students can bring to each task, hence limiting the resources students can use for learning. Also, when exploring new technology platforms, games etc., intrinsic load is high, for example, because the user needs to acquire new rules and learn how to navigate the software, which also would reduce performance.

Similar to the cognitive load theory, the cognitive theory of multimedia learning (CTML) also operates on the assumption that the working memory presents limitations. However, the CTML adheres more closely to Baddeley's model of working memory and predicts that meaningful learning can occur only if visual and verbal information integrate together and combine with previous knowledge stored in long-term memory (Mayer, 2005). This prediction is well illustrated by the modality effect, where learning is improved when information is presented to learners in both verbal and visual modalities (spoken text and pictures) rather than when it is presented in a single, usually visual, modality (written text and pictures) (Ginns, 2005).

Overall, cognitive bottleneck theory, cognitive load theory, and cognitive theory of multimedia learning predict that learning challenging tasks, which overload our limited cognitive processing capacity, will result in decrements in performance.

The Exceptions: When Multitasking Does Not Detract from Performance

While the decrements in performance due to multitasking occur frequently, it is not always the case. Skills can play an important role in situations where multitasking is achieved successfully. Consistent with the theoretical foundations introduced above, when tasks are practiced to the point of automaticity, multitasking can occur without apparent risks to performance (Lee & Taatgen, 2002; Meyer et al., 1995; Oberauer & Kliegl, 2004; Schumacher et al., 2001). To date, experimental research demonstrating success with multitasking has employed very simple, highly controlled laboratory-based tasks (Lien, Ruthruff, & Johnston, 2006). To achieve success, the tasks must be practiced simultaneously in order to eliminate the dual-task slowing (Oberauer & Kliegl, 2004). Although one could imagine very simple daily tasks that might also yield these same effects, the complex daily activities people usually perform, especially those involved in educational environments, would seem to typically far exceed the types of automatized tasks that are likely to be executed simultaneously without interference (Pashler et al., 2008). However, some educational tasks involve several skills to be utilized simultaneously, and proficiency in the sub-skills of these tasks may reduce cognitive demands to permit multitasking to occur. For example, note-taking is a complex task which involves, as one sub-skill, handwriting or typing. Students with well-honed handwriting or typing skills are drawing upon highly automatized skills stored in long-term memory and, hence, are not imposing on the limited resources available in working memory (Gathercole & Alloway, 2008), leaving resources for other activities which may permit some level of multitasking. Overall, it appears that in some very highly practiced situations or in situations where tasks draw upon non-competing resources (Borst et al., 2010), multitasking may occur without deficit, but in novel, overlapping, or cognitively complex tasks (such as those found in many educational contexts), one would expect that some losses may be apparent.

Examining Research on Multitasking and Technology in Educational Contexts

One of the first steps in assessing the impact of multitasking with technology in the classroom is to understand how often students multitask followed by how that multitasking matches the goals of the instructional setting. A recent study yielded three categories of student study behavior when students were engaged in a self-directed learning situation where multiple tasks were to be completed. Multitasking, in the form of switching back and forth among the multiple activities, appeared most frequently (70% of sessions). Students rarely focused on a single task without interruptions (7% of sessions) or completed tasks in sequence without multitasking (10%), but rather preferred to shift among tasks (Judd, 2013). Clearly, when provided an opportunity to multitask, students do.

Students can either use technology as part of the learning task, or they may choose to use technology for non-relevant activities such as entertainment, keeping up to date with out-of-the-classroom events or occasions, or otherwise occupying themselves. In the research literature, these two uses are referred to as on-task and off-task (or disruptive) multitasking (e.g., Kay & Lauricella, 2011; Wood et al., 2011). The following sections review the current research regarding multitasking with technology within the classroom with sensitivity to the distinction between on- and off-task use.

On-Task Multitasking

Students' use of technology for on-task activities is diverse, including summarizing lessons, viewing course materials (such as video/audio files, spreadsheets, and PowerPoint slides), completing online tests and assignments, and searching the Internet (including the library website) for course-related materials, taking and sharing notes with other students, and asking questions regarding the learning material via texting (Hammer et al., 2010; Lindroth & Berquist, 2010; Winter et al., 2010). Whether students use laptops (Barak, Lipson, & Lerman, 2006; Lowerison, Sclater, Schmid, & Abrami, 2006), smartphones (Milrad & Spikol, 2007), or collaborative writing software (Rhine & Bailey, 2011), they report that using technology has a positive impact on their learning, especially if the instructor adapts his/her pedagogical style to take advantage of the technology's capabilities (Milrad & Spikol, 2007). For example, in one study, students reported improved integration and application of knowledge to novel contexts, deeper processing of the learning material, and improved collaborative learning (Lowerison et al., 2006). Moreover, learners who fully took advantage of technological resources as part of the learning task rated the effectiveness of the course more highly (Lowerison et al., 2006).

Students also report using digital computer technologies to support their in-class learning tasks *outside* of the classroom. Specifically, students use social media, email, and instant messaging to ask questions and receive answers, share important files and homework, coordinate group work and study groups, create social networks, and construct peer support contacts to improve motivation and to vent (Green & Bailey, 2010; Hrastinski & Aghaee, 2012; Timmis, 2012). Again, student's perceptions support the use of digital devices for learning. The particular means in which technology is seen to be advantageous among students is consistent with the wide body of research that views technology as a mechanism for providing flexible, innovative, rich, and individualized instruction (e.g., Gee, 2009; Schofield, 1994, 1997; Wood, Willoughby, Specht, Stern-Cavalcante, & Childs, 2002). Students' perceptions have been corroborated in descriptive research. For example, Barak and colleagues (2006) conducted observations of classroom engagement when technology was used as an instructional tool. Their results affirmed outcomes from survey and self-report studies that the use of laptops promoted student-centered, hands-on, exploratory, and collaborative learning with both classmates and instructors. Overall, these survey and observational research outcomes do not identify concerns regarding multitasking, nor do they note the concerns of slowing or performance decrements that would be predicted by the theories related to multitasking.

Outcomes employing other research methodologies, however, are less clear-cut and paint a much more complex picture with respect to when and how technology positively and negatively impacts on learning. For example, a series of experimental studies has examined the relative impact of technology use at different ages. Each of these studies assessed the added load of using technologies by employing an experimental laptop user group versus a no-technology control group design.

Lowther, Ross, and Morrison (2003) compared classroom laptop use versus a traditional technology-free classroom control group for fifth-, sixth-, and seventh-grade students' writing and problem-solving skills. Students in the laptop condition demonstrated greater writing as well as problem-solving skills than the students in the no-laptop control group.

Siegle and Foster (2001) examined the impact of laptop use in high school students. One group of students had full-time use of laptop computers for class and home use, while another group had no laptop use for the first half of the school year. The groups switched for the second half of the school year. While students self-reported that they benefited from using several types of software, including PowerPoint, actual benefits in terms of receiving higher grades merely approached significance (Siegle & Foster, 2001).

Among three studies at the university level, less positive outcomes were obtained. Specifically, in one study there were no significant differences in GPA performance between the laptop and no-laptop groups; however, students in the laptop group reported lower satisfaction with their education in comparison to the control group (Wurst, Smarkola, & Gaffney, 2008). In the two remaining studies, students not using technology outperformed those using technology (Hembrooke & Gay, 2003; Martin, 2011). Specifically, in the Hembrooke and Gay (2003) study, students who did not use laptops scored higher on memory measures of the lecture content than participants in the laptop condition, and in the Martin (2011) study, students in the no-laptop control group outperformed students in the laptop group with an average grade difference of a full letter grade.

Together, these studies suggest a pattern of decreasing positive effects and increasing negative effects when technology is used in higher education relative to earlier uses in the classroom. Why might this pattern occur? One possibility is that the integration of technology is more deliberately planned and more closely monitored in the younger grades than among the university groups. Given that technology use in elementary and high schools is often more constrained, involving booking equipment and meeting curricular goals (e.g., Mueller & Wood, 2012) than might be the case in university classrooms, where students bring their own devices and employ their own learning strategies to guide their use of the technologies, it may be that the gains associated with technology use in the younger groups studied reflect more instructionally relevant use of technology.

Some support for these suggestions is evident in recent correlational studies. For example, research examining the impacts associated with laptop ownership, frequency of computer use, and use of the Internet on test performance among fourth-, eighth-, and 11th-grade students resulted in mixed outcomes (Wainer et al., 2008). Consistent with the outcomes from student self-report studies and the experimental studies with younger students above, laptop ownership was associated with a small but positive effect on students' academic test performance. However, consistent with theories related to multitasking, greater computer use was associated with decreased performance overall, and this outcome was especially true for younger and more socio-economically disadvantaged students. These computer use outcomes appeared to be qualified by the type of computer use and grade level. Specifically, increased Internet use had a positive impact on learning outcomes for 11th-graders, but a negative impact for younger and more socio-economically disadvantaged students. Interestingly, when the Internet use was further examined, only with respect to when the Internet was used as a pedagogical tool, there was no significant impact on students' academic performance overall.

These variations point to important subtleties that must be considered when assessing potential benefits or losses associated with integrating technology as part of the learning task. Specifically, there is a need to be sensitive to characteristics specific to the learner (such as age), as well as what the student does when engaged with the technology. Additionally, just looking at amount of use does not give the best picture of whether multitasking is going to be a concern. Instead, amount and type of use both need to be considered. Whether technology enhances learning or detracts from it is not a simple question. Rather, cautious and careful exploration is needed to tease apart the circumstances that separate effective and ineffective use of technology in instructional settings, as well as which learners are most likely to perceive and show evidence of gains versus losses from the added "load" of technology as an instructional tool.

On the positive side, the above studies make clear that for many students, instructionally relevant uses of technology are perceived as positive additions to the learning environment, and multitasking is not singled out as a particular concern in these contexts. Instructionally relevant versus irrelevant uses of technology may be one key element in determining whether multitasking will impact on learning. In the next section we review recent research examining off-task (non-relevant) use of technology, which provides insight into the circumstances that lead to learning decrements when technology is used in the classroom.

Off-Task Multitasking

When asked, a majority of students (65%–93%) report using laptops and cell phones for off-task multitasking purposes during learning contexts (Fried, 2008; Hammer et al., 2010; Winter et al., 2010). The most frequent off-task behaviors are social networking (especially Facebook), instant messaging, texting, emailing, and web browsing (Fried, 2008; Hammer et al., 2010; Junco & Cotten, 2012; Levine, Waite, & Bowman, 2007; Zivcakova & Wood, 2012). Younger adults report engaging in more off-task multitasking behaviors than older adults (Winter et al., 2010; Zivcakova & Wood, 2012), and males report engaging in more off-task multitasking behaviors than females (Kay & Lauricella, 2011).

Much of the research that examines off-task multitasking involves university students. A negative correlation has been found between students' web browsing during classroom lectures and subsequent grades, with greater off-task web browsing associated with lower grades (Grace-Martin & Gay, 2001; Junco, 2012; Kraushaar & Novak, 2010). Interestingly, this multitasking outcome does not appear to be a function of limited resources being relegated to *navigation* skills, as Internet skills were not related to grade performance. Rather, the negative effects appear to be a function of amount of multitasking, as the students who engaged in more web browsing simply had lower GPAs (Junco, 2012). Fried (2008) also found that the more students use their laptops for off-task activities, the greater the learning decrements. Specifically, increased off-task multitasking was correlated with increased reports of difficulty in understanding course material, and lower perceptions of lecture clarity.

These correlational and self-report studies suggest amount of off-task multitasking *per se* is a key issue in understanding detriments to learning. Consistent with the outcomes found for on-task learning, it might also be the case that the type of multitasking students engage in when off task is also an important consideration. A recent experimental study provides insights on this issue. Specifically, university students were assigned to one of seven conditions for three consecutive lectures. These lectures were actual classes for an ongoing course and at the end of each a short quiz on content was given (Wood et al., 2011). Four groups of students were assigned to engage in one social communication activity throughout the three lectures (i.e., Facebook, email, MSN, or cell phone texting). Two groups were assigned to take notes, one with a laptop using a word-processing program, and another using handwritten notes and no technology. The last group was allowed to learn as they preferred using technologies as they wished.

Initial analyses detected a decrement in learning for students in the MSN and Facebook conditions relative to those in the handwritten note condition, suggesting that off-task use of these social communication outlets was particularly detrimental. However, a fidelity measure indicated that students who had access to technology did not fully adhere to the instructions for their experimental conditions. Instead, students engaged in more off-task technology-based activities than was specified for their condition. As a result, the participants were subsequently grouped into four categories of technology use: non-multitaskers, low, medium, and high-multitaskers according to the amount of multitasking they self-reported. Analyses among these groups indicated that non-multitaskers outperformed all other groups. In this case, even low levels of distracting use of technology during a lecture had a detrimental impact on learning (Wood et al., 2011).

The studies by Junco (2012), Fried (2008), and Wood and colleagues (2011) indicate that off-task multitasking impairs performance. However, the studies differ in that high amounts of web browsing or off-task behaviors were related to the level of learning losses in two studies, while the other found even lower levels of multitasking resulted in losses. One potential difference in these studies may be the types of off-task behavior in which the students were engaged.

Consistent with Wood et al. (2011), research indicates that engaging in social communication activities is particularly distracting. Specifically, a vast array of social networking alternatives, including Facebook, Twitter, instant messaging, and texting, are associated with substantial decreases in students' academic performance, including higher levels of unfinished assignments and lower GPA (Junco & Cotten, 2011, 2012; Karpinski, Kirschner, Ozer, Mellott, & Ochwo, 2013; Kirschner & Karpinski, 2010; Paul, Baker, & Cochran, 2012; Rosen, Carrier, & Cheever, 2013).

Students report frequently engaging social networking when they are studying. For example, Rosen, Carrier, and Cheever (2013) found that on average, students who engaged in task-switching spent only about six minutes focusing on studying before going off-task with their preferred social medium (i.e., Facebook, texting, etc.). In addition, these students reported having more technologies available and using those technologies for task-switching than students who did not express a preference for task-switching. Consistent with the previous studies mentioned, students who preferred to focus on a single task or use appropriate learning strategies tended to have higher GPAs in comparison to students who preferred task-switching.

Although use of social communication technologies is generally associated with higher performance decrements, recent research suggests that the pattern of decrements may not be universal. For example, Karpinski and colleagues (2013) compared grade point average outcomes for American and European students as a function of multitasking with social networking while engaged in academic tasks. Although in both samples use of social networking sites in the academic context predicted lower grade point averages, the relationship between use of social networking and grade point average was only moderated by multitasking for the American sample. This study highlights the need to be sensitive to cultural or individual differences in the way that multitasking may occur. In this study, for example, American students appeared to engage in more distracting multitasking behaviors, such as checking their text messages immediately after receiving them, where the European students delayed responding to incoming messages (Karpinski et al., 2013).

Sensitivity must also be extended to the context or degree of the distraction as a potential negative impact on learning. A study by Lin and Bigenho (2011) found that distracting learning contexts that place greater strain on cognitive resources do indeed create greater learning challenges. In their experimental study, they compared the relative impact of no distraction, an auditory distraction (competing word being spoken), and an auditory plus visual distraction, when learners attempted to learn lists of words. The learners were also assigned to take no notes, paper note-taking, or computer note-taking to determine the impact of distraction and note-taking on performance. Overall, there was a main effect for distraction with the combined auditory plus visual distraction leading to the greatest learning losses. There was no main effect for note-taking; instead, there was a significant interaction. This interaction showed that the best note-taking style in the no-distraction environment was taking notes on paper, as opposed to no note-taking or computer note-taking. Both computer-based and handwritten notes were equivalent in the auditory distraction environment. And lastly, in the audio-visual distraction environment, no note-taking led to better word recall than either paper note-taking or computer note-taking. Overall, as the level of distraction increased demands on cognitive resources, performance decreased, and fewer resources were available for learning. Interestingly, participants reported engaging in numerous effective cognitive strategies to enhance their learning, but these strategies also decreased as the distractions increased. The results in this study are consistent with assumptions of limited cognitive resources inherent in cognitive bottleneck theory, cognitive load theory, and the cognitive theory of multimedia learning. It appears that note-taking is helpful in environments with minimal distractions; however, when distractions are sufficiently demanding (such as might be the case when learners in the Wood and colleagues [2011] study were required to engage in social communication during lectures), insufficient resources are available for effective note-taking. Clearly, both the amount of off-task multitasking and the type of off-task multitasking impacts students' ability to learn.

Interestingly, when students are asked how their off-task behavior impacts their learning, they report that frequent switching between on-task and off-task behaviors is highly distracting. For example, students in one study indicated that they sometimes fail to complete assignments due to instant messaging (Junco & Cotten, 2011). In another study, more than 50% of participants reported that they learn best when they do not have access to digital technologies (Winter et al., 2010). In fact, students are quite accurate in their perception that off-task use of technology is problematic.

Moreover, off-task distractions need not be a result of personally engaging in off-task multitasking, as 64% of students indicate that they find other students' use of laptops distracting (Fried, 2008). This result is consistent with the findings of Hammer et al. (2010), who also found that students' in-class laptop use can pose a significant distraction to neighboring students. Surprisingly, students, especially younger students in the Hammer and colleagues (2010) study, nonetheless felt that such heavy engagement in off-task multitasking was an appropriate use of technologies in the classroom. On the other hand, the instructors, who accurately perceived student frequency of off-task multitasking, did not feel that such use of technologies was appropriate (Hammer et al., 2010). Given the prevalence of off-task multitasking and the misalignment in perceptions regarding the legitimacy of off-task multitasking, even when learning will be negatively impacted, educators may need to adopt more stringent controls to prevent or reduce off-task multitasking, or find new and creative ways of allowing students to use technology for off-task purposes in a controlled manner. For example, one such suggested method is to give students short "technology breaks" (Rosen et al., 2013).

Conclusion

The opportunity to provide individualized learning environments that promote self-regulated learning for every learner is one of the key reasons why technologies are so quickly being adopted in classroom (Mueller, Wood, De Pasquale, & Cruikshank, 2012). Successful e-learners possess many skills and characteristics that make them successful, including setting personal learning goals, engaging information-processing skills that promote deep processing, and metacognitive awareness. In addition, e-learners often engage in social aspects of learning that involve collaboration and decision-making skills (Cramphorn, 2004; Jong-Ki, 2008; Winter et al., 2010). Given the rate at which technologies are becoming integrated within educational contexts as active, motivating, instructional tools (Wurst et al., 2008), it is important to establish when and for whom multitasking demands are possible, and when they exceed capacity. We do not yet have all of the answers. It appears that multitasking, when relevant and well integrated into the learning context, is not only possible, but is appreciated and endorsed by students and results in increased motivation to learn, and, in some cases, enhanced learning outcomes. In contrast, there is substantial evidence that off-task use of technologies in the classroom results in learning decrements. Given that many students use technology inappropriately despite the distraction it poses to other students (Lowther et al., 2003), and the negative consequences it has for themselves, and that many students are unable to gauge their multitasking behaviors and instead underreport (Kraushaar & Novak, 2010) or over-report (Moreno et al., 2012) their multitasking behaviors, there is a need for educators and policymakers to set the criteria for successful use of technologies in the classroom. The findings summarized in the present chapter provide some provocative challenges for educators and policymakers at all levels of education, as it will be their task to determine how to best integrate technology into the classroom, and at the same time, ensure maximization of learning.

References

Adams, M., Tenny, Y., & Pew, R. (1991). State of the art report: Strategic workload and the cognitive management of advanced multitask systems. *SOAR CSERIAC*, 91–96.

Appelbaum, S. H., Marchionni, A., & Fernandez, A. (2008). The multitasking paradox: Perceptions, problems and strategies. *Management Decision*, 46(9), 1313–1325.

Baddeley, A. D. (1999). *Essentials of human memory*. Hove, UK: Psychology Press.

Barak, M., Lipson, A., & Lerman, S. (2006). Wireless laptops as means for promoting active learning in large lecture halls. *Journal of Research on Technology in Education*, 38(3), 245–263.

Borst, J., Taatgen, N., & van Rijn, H. (2010). The problem state: A cognitive bottleneck in multitasking. *Journal of Experimental Psychology: Learning, Memory and Cognition*, 36(2), 363–382.

Caird, J. K., Willness, C. R., Steel, P., & Scialfa, C. (2008). A meta-analysis of the effects of cell-phones on driver performance. *Accident Analysis and Prevention*, 40, 1282–1293.

Carrier, L. M., Cheever, N. A., Rosen, L. D., Benitez, S., & Chang, J. (2009). Multitasking across generations: Multitasking choices and difficulty ratings in three generations of Americans. *Computers in Human Behavior*, 25, 483–489.

Contreras-Castillo, J., Perez-Fragoso, C., & Favela, J. (2006). Assessing the use of instant messaging in online learning environments. *Interactive Learning Environments*, 14(3), 205–218.

Cramphorn, C. (2004, April 5–7). *An evaluation of the formal and underlying factors influencing student participation with e-learning web discussion forums*. Paper presented at the Networked Learning Conference, Lancaster, UK.

Enns, J. T., Visser, T. A. W., Kawahara, J., & Di Lollo, V. (2001). Visual masking and task switching in the attentional blink. In K. L. Shapiro (Ed.), *The limits of attention: Temporal constraints in human information processing* (pp. 65–81). New York, NY: Oxford University Press.

Freedman, D. H. (2007, February). What's next? Taskus interruptus. Retrieved from http://www.inc.com/magazine/20070201/column-freedman.html

Fried, C. B. (2008). In-class laptop use and its effects on student learning. *Computers and Education, 50*, 906–914.

Gathercole, S., & Alloway, T. (2008). *Working memory and learning: Practice guide for teachers.* Thousand Oaks, CA: Sage.

Gee, J. P. (2009). Digital media and learning as an emerging field, Part I: How we got here. *International Journal of Learning and Media, 1*(2), 13–23.

Gilbert, J., Morton, S., & Rowley, J. (2007). E-learning: The student experience. *British Journal of Educational Technology, 38*(4), 560–573.

Ginns, P. (2005). Meta-analysis of the modality effect. *Learning and Instruction, 15*, 313–331.

Grace-Martin, M., & Gay, G. (2001). Web browsing, mobile computing, and academic performance. *Educational Technology and Society, 4*(3), 95–107.

Green, T., & Bailey, B. (2010). Academic uses of Facebook: Endless possibilities or endless perils. *TechTrends, 54*(3), 20–22.

Hallowell, E. M. (2005). Overloaded circuits: Why smart people underperform. *Harvard Business Review, 83*(1), 55.

Hammer, R., Ronen, M., Sharon, A., Lankry, T., Huberman, Y., & Zamtsov, V. (2010). Mobile culture in college lectures: Instructors' and students' perspectives. *Interdisciplinary Journal of E-Learning and Learning Objects, 6*, 293–304.

Hembrooke, H., & Gay, G. (2003). The laptop and the lecture: The effects of multitasking in learning environments. *Journal of Computing in Higher Education, 15*(1), 46–64.

Higher Education Funding Council for England (HEFCE). (2005). HEFCE strategy for e-learning. Retrieved October 30, 2012, from http://www.hefce.ac.uk/pubs/hefce/2005/05_12/05_12.pdf

Hrastinski, S. (2006). The relationship between adopting a synchronous medium and participation in online group work: An explorative study. *Interactive Learning Environments, 14*(2), 137–152.

Hrastinski, S., & Aghaee, N. (2012). How are campus students using social media to support their studies? An explorative interview study. *Education and Information Technologies, 17*(4), 451–464.

Jong-Ki, K. (2008). The effects of LMS quality and e-learners' characteristics regarding e-learners' scholastic performance: A proposal for e-learning success model. *Proceedings from ASBBS, 15*(1), 34–45.

Judd, T. (2013). Making sense of multitasking: Key behaviors. *Computers and Education, 63*, 358–367.

Junco, R. (2012). In-class multitasking and academic performance. *Computers in Human Behavior, 28*, 2236–2243.

Junco, R., & Cotten, S. R. (2011). Perceived academic effects of instant messaging use. *Computers and Education, 56*, 370–378.

Junco, R., & Cotten, S. R. (2012). No A 4 U: The relationship between multitasking and academic performance. *Computers and Education, 59*, 505–514.

Karpinski, A. C., Kirschner, P. A., Ozer, I., Mellott, J. A., & Ochwo, P. (2013). An exploration of social networking site use, multitasking, and academic performance among United States and European university students. *Computers in Human Behavior, 29*, 1182–1192.

Kay, R. H., & Lauricella, S. (2011). Gender differences in the use of laptops in higher education: A formative analysis. *Journal of Educational Computing Research, 44*(3), 361–380.

Kieras, D., Meyer, D., Ballas, J., & Lauber, E. (2000). Modern computational perspectives on executive mental processes and cognitive control: Where to from here? In S. Monsell & J. Driver (Eds.), *Control of cognitive processes: Attention and performance XVIII* (pp. 681–712). Cambridge, MA: MIT Press.

Kirschner, P. A., Ayres, P., & Chandler, P. (2011). Contemporary cognitive load theory research: The good, the bad and the ugly. *Computers in Human Behavior, 27*, 99–105.

Kirschner, P. A., & Karpinski, A. C. (2010). Facebook® and academic performance. *Computers in Human Behavior, 26*, 1237–1245.

Kirschner, P. A., Sweller, J., & Clark, R. E. (2006). Why minimal guidance during instruction does not work: An analysis of the failure of constructivist, discovery, problem-based, experiential, and inquiry-based teaching. *Educational Psychologist, 46*, 75–86.

Kraushaar, J. M., & Novak, D. C. (2010). Examining the affects of student multitasking with laptops during the lecture. *Journal of Information Systems Education, 21*(2), 241–251.

Lee, F. J., & Taatgen, N. A. (2002). Multitasking as skill acquisition. *Proceedings of the 24th annual conference of the Cognitive Science Society* (pp. 572–577). Mahwah, NJ: Lawrence Erlbaum Associates.

Levine, L. E., Waite, B. M., & Bowman, L. L. (2007). Electronic media use, reading, and academic distractibility in college youth. *CyberPsychology and Behavior, 10*(4), 560–566.

Levy, H., & Pashler, H. (2001). Is dual-task slowing instruction dependent? *Journal of Experimental Psychology, Human Perception and Performance, 27*(4), 862–869.

Levy, J., Pashler, H., & Boer, E. (2006). Central interference in driving: Is there any stopping the psychological refractory period? *Psychological Science, 17*, 228–235.

Lien, M. C., Ruthruff, E., & Johnston, J. C. (2006). Attentional limitations in doing two things at once: The search for exceptions. *Current Directions in Psychological Science, 15*, 89–93.

Lin, L., & Bigenho, C. (2011). Note-taking and memory in different media environments. *Computers in the Schools, 28*(3), 200–216.

Lindroth, T., & Berquist, M. (2010). Laptops in an educational practice: Promoting the personal learning situation. *Computers and Education, 54*, 311–320.

Lowerison, G., Sclater, J., Schmid, R. F., & Abrami, P. C. (2006). Student perceived effectiveness of computer technology use in post-secondary classrooms. *Computers and Education, 47*, 465–489.

Lowther, D. L., Ross, S. M., & Morrison, G. M. (2003). When each one has one: The influence on teaching strategies and student achievement of using laptops in the classroom. *Educational Technology Research and Development, 51*(3), 23–44.

Martin, L. R. (2011). Teaching business statistics and a computer lab: Benefit or distraction? *Journal of Education for Business, 86*, 326–331.

Mayer, R. E. (2005). Cognitive theory of multimedia learning. In R. E. Mayer (Ed.), *The Cambridge handbook of multimedia learning* (pp. 31–48). New York, NY: Cambridge University Press.

McCann, R., & Johnston, J. C. (1992). Locus of the single-channel bottleneck in dual-task interference. *Journal of Experimental Psychology: Human Perception and Performance, 18*, 471–485.

McEvoy, S. P., Stevenson, M. R., McCartt, A. T., Woodward, M., Haworth, C., Palamara, P., & Cercarelli, R. (2005). Role of mobile phones in motor vehicle crashes resulting in hospital attendance: A case-crossover study. *BMJ, 331*, 428–430.

Meyer, D. E., Kieras, D. E., Lauber, E., Schumacher, E. H., Glass, J., Zurbriggen, N. E., ... Apfelblat, D. (1995). Adaptive executive control: Flexible multiple-task performance without pervasive immutable response-selection bottlenecks. *Acta Psychologica, 90*, 163–190.

Milrad, M., & Spikol, D. (2007). Anytime, anywhere learning supported by smart phones: Experiences and results from the MUSIS project. *Educational Technology and Society, 10*(4), 62–70.

Moreno, M. A., Jelenchick, L., Koff, R., Eikoff, J., Diermyer, C., & Christakis, D. A. (2012). Internet use and multitasking among older adolescents: An experience sampling approach. *Computers in Human Behavior, 28*, 1097–1102.

Mueller, J., & Wood, E. (2012). Patterns of beliefs, attitudes, and characteristics of teachers that influence computer integration. *Education Research International.* doi:10.1155/2012/697357

Mueller, J., Wood, E., De Pasquale, D., & Cruikshank, R. (2012). Examining mobile technology in higher education: Handheld devices in and out of the classroom. *International Journal of Higher Education, 1*(2), 43–54.

National Committee of Inquiry into Higher Education (NCIHE). (1997). *Higher education in the learning society: The Dearing report.* London, UK: HMSO.

Oberauer, K., & Kliegl, R. (2004). Simultaneous cognitive operations in working memory after dual-task practice. *Journal of Experimental Psychology, 30*(4), 689–707.

Paas, F., van Gog, T., & Sweller, J. (2010). Cognitive load theory: New conceptualizations, specifications, and integrated research perspectives. *Educational Psychology Review, 22,* 115–121.

Pashler, H. (1994). Dual-task interference in simple tasks: Data and theory. *Psychological Bulletin, 16,* 220–244.

Pashler, H., Harris, C. R., & Nuechterlein, K. H. (2008). Does the central bottleneck encompass voluntary selection of hedonically based choices? *Experimental Psychology, 55*(5), 313–321.

Pashler, H., & Johnston, J. C. (1989). Chronometric evidence for central postponement in temporally overlapping tasks. *Quarterly Journal of Experimental Psychology, 41A,* 19–45.

Paul, J. A., Baker, H. M., & Cochran, J. D. (2012). Effect of online social networking on student academic performance. *Computers in Human Behavior, 28,* 2117–2127.

Pew Research Center. (2014). Mobile technology fact sheet. Pew Internet & American Life Project. Retrieved December 3, 2014, from http://www.pewinternet.org/fact-sheets/mobile-technology-fact-sheet/

Posner, M. I. (1990). Hierarchical distributed networks in the neuropsychology of selective attention. In A. Caramazza (Ed.), *Cognitive neuropsychology and neurolinguistics* (pp. 187–210). Hillsdale, NJ: Lawrence Erlbaum Associates.

Rhine, S., & Bailey, M. (2011). Collaborative software and focused distraction in the classroom. *Journal of Technology and Teacher Education, 19*(4), 423–447.

Rideout, V. J., Vandewater, E. A., & Wartella, E. A. (2003). *Zero to six: Electronic media in the lives of infants, toddlers, and preschoolers.* Menlo Park, CA: Henry J. Kaiser Family Foundation.

Rosen, L. D. (2007). *Me, MySpace, and I: Parenting the Net Generation.* New York, NY: Palgrave Macmillan.

Rosen, L. D., Carrier, L. M., & Cheever, N. A. (2013). Facebook and texting made me do it: Media-induced task-switching while studying. *Computers in Human Behavior, 29,* 948–958.

Schofield, J. W. (1994). Barriers to computer usage in secondary school. In C. Huff & T. Finholdt (Eds.), *Social issues in computing: Putting computing in its place* (pp. 547–580). New York, NY: McGraw-Hill.

Schofield, J. W. (1997). Computers and classroom social processes: A review of the literature. *Social Science Computer Review, 15,* 27–39.

Schoor, C., Bannert, M., & Brunken, R. (2012). Role of dual task design when measuring cognitive load during multimedia learning. *Education Technology Research Development, 60,* 753–768.

Schuler, A., Scheiter, K., & van Genuchten, E. (2011). The role of working memory in multimedia instruction: Is working memory working during learning from text and pictures? *Educational Psychology Review, 23,* 389–411.

Schumacher, E. H., Seymour, T. L., Glass, J. M., Fencsik, D. E., Lauber, E. J., Kieras, D. E., & Meyer, D. E. (2001). Virtually perfect time sharing in dual-task performance: Uncorking the central cognitive bottleneck. *Psychological Science, 12*(2), 101–108.

Siegle, D., & Foster, T. (2001). Laptop computers and multimedia and presentation software: Their effects on student achievement in anatomy and physiology. *Journal of Research on Technology in Education, 34*(1), 29–37.

Smith, E. E., & Jonides, J. (1999). Storage and executive processes in the frontal lobes. *Science, 283,* 1567–1661.

Stone, L. (n.d.). Continuous partial attention. Retrieved December 3, 2014, from http://lindastone.net/qa/continuous-partial-attention/

Sweller, J. (1988). Cognitive load during problem solving: Effects on learning. *Cognitive Science, 12,* 257–285.

Sweller, J., & Chandler, P. (1994). Why some material is difficult to learn. *Cognition and Instruction, 12,* 185–233.

Sweller, J., van Merriënboer, J. J. G., & Paas, F. G. W. C. (1998). Cognitive architecture and instructional design. *Educational Psychology Review, 10,* 251–296.

Timmis, S. E. (2012). Constant companions: Instant messaging conversations as sustainable supportive study structures amongst undergraduate peers. *Computers and Education, 59*(1), 3–18.

Violanti, J. M. (1998). Cellular phones and fatal traffic collisions. *Accident Analysis and Prevention, 30,* 519–524.

Violanti, J. M., & Marshall, J. R. (1996). Cellular phones and traffic accidents: An epidemiological approach. *Accident Analysis and Prevention, 28,* 265–270.

Wainer, J., Dwyer, T., Dutra, R. S., Covic, A., Magalhaes, V. B., Ferreira, L. R. R., & Claudio, K. (2008). Too much computer and Internet use is bad for you, especially if you are young and poor: Results from the 2001 Brazilian SAEB. *Computers and Education, 51,* 1417–1429.

Wallis, C., & Steptoe, S. (2006). Help! I've lost my focus. *Time, 167,* 42–47.

The Week (2012, April 12). 6 embarrassing walking-while-texting fails. Retrieved on August 25, 2012, from http://theweek.com/article/index/226702/6-embarrassing-walking-while-texting-fails

Welford, A. T. (1952). The "psychological refractory period" and the review of high speed performance: A review and theory. *British Journal of Psychology, 43,* 2–19.

Welford, A. T. (1967). Single-channel operation in the brain. *Acta Psychologica, 27,* 5–22.

Winter, J., Cotton, D., Gavin, J., & Yorke, J. D. (2010). Effective e-learning? Multitasking, distractions and boundary management by graduate students in an online environment. *ALT-J, 18*(1), 71–83.

Wood, E., Willoughby, T., Specht, J., Stern-Cavalcante, W., & Childs, C. (2002). Developing a computer workshop to facilitate computer skills and minimize anxiety for early childhood educators. *Journal of Educational Psychology, 94*(1), 164–170.

Wood, E., Zivcakova, L., Gentile, P., Archer, K., De Pasquale, D., & Nosko, A. (2011). Examining the impact of distracting multitasking with technology on real-time classroom learning. *Computers and Education, 58,* 365–374.

Wurst, C., Smarkola, C., & Gaffney, M. A. (2008). Ubiquitous laptop usage in higher education: Effects on student achievement, student satisfaction, and constructivist measures in honors and traditional classrooms. *Computers and Education, 51,* 1766–1783.

Zivcakova, L., & Wood, E. (2012). *Students' natural use of technologies during a real-time classroom lecture.* Athens, Greece: ATINER'S Conference Paper Series, No. SOC2012-0066.

24

Multitasking, Note-Taking, and Learning in Technology-Immersive Learning Environments

Lin Lin[1] and Chris Bigenho[2]

[1] *University of North Texas*
[2] *Director of Educational Technology at Greenhill School*

Multitasking activities can appear as doing several things at the same time or switching rapidly between different tasks. Educators are concerned about the impact of multitasking on students' cognition and learning. With an increasing amount of technology in the learning environment, many educators are worried that students are too distracted to learn what they are supposed to learn (Healy, 1999; Oppenheimer, 2003).

The present chapter discusses the impact of technology integrations on multitasking and learning. In particular, it focuses on technology's impact on learners' cognitive load, note-taking abilities, study habits, and learning. The chapter will be organized as follows. We begin by looking at the benefits and drawbacks of technology-immersive learning environments. This brings forward discussions on different kinds of multitasking activities, with some more compatible while others more distracting to the intended learning. The compatibility of various activities is related to working memory, cognitive load, and multimedia design in learning. We highlight note-taking as a likely compatible multitasking activity in our discussions on working memory, cognitive load, and multimedia design. We conclude the chapter by discussing future studies to better understand the dynamics between multitasking, note-taking, and learning in today's technology-immersive classrooms.

Media Multitasking and Technology-Immersive Learning Environments

The rapid development of new media and technologies places pressure on schools and teachers to integrate them in classrooms. From computers in the classroom to one-to-one computing and laptop initiatives, there has been a rise of connected technologies in the classroom. Such connectivity has created new promises as well as challenges for learning.

The Wiley Handbook of Psychology, Technology, and Society, First Edition. Edited by Larry D. Rosen, Nancy A. Cheever, and L. Mark Carrier.
© 2015 John Wiley & Sons, Ltd. Published 2015 by John Wiley & Sons, Ltd.

The new learning opportunities range from self-directed learning to collaborative work afforded by the new media and technologies. With new technologies, students can use their social media and mobile devices to solve problems on their own or together with peers more easily. Instead of waiting for a teacher to provide the information or the answer, students can conduct their own searches online and find answers to problems. As a result, teachers may use the class time more effectively by discussing problem-solving skills instead of providing answers or drill-and-practice, as advocated by the Khan Academy (https://www.khanacademy.org/).

New technologies are advocated as a way to motivate students to learn (Prensky, 2001, 2012; Tapscott, 2009). For instance, young children are often attracted to the gestural interface of an iPad. Recent Horizon reports highlighted gesture-based computing as a promising learning technology (Johnson, Adams, & Cummins, 2012; Johnson et al., 2013; Johnson, Smith, Willis, Levine, & Haywood, 2011). Gesture-based systems – for example the Apple iPhone, iPad, Microsoft Kinect, and Nintendo Wii – are creating new opportunities for students to engage with information and learning materials through gestures such as touching, tapping, or swiping screens, jumping, or moving their bodies. By incorporating physical movements into learning environments, gesture-based technologies are helping to bridge educational theory and practice, and incorporate grounded cognition and embodied learning theories into teaching and learning practice.

Newer technologies are making significant gains in learning in the most fundamental ways. These advancements are occurring in the area of recursive content. That is, the technology-based activities and engagements not only help the learner obtain the content, but the activities also create a deeper understanding of the esoteric content in the process because of the new technologies. To put it simply, the "how" becomes the "what," and the "what" becomes the "how." The discussions about which is more important – the message or the medium (McLuhan, 1994) – or about which are more important for students to learn – the knowledge or the way to obtain knowledge – may become irrelevant in the near future.

Technology applications have an intrinsic potentiality to provide the learner with reinforcing activities that demonstrate the conceptual framework of the content, because they can be designed from the ground up with these learning connections in mind. An example of what is meant by this in practice: A 4-year-old is encouraged to trace the letters of the alphabet into an iPad application to learn his/her letters. By tracing the letters with fingers and changing colors to the letters traced, the child is learning to write the letters through more motivating practices. From a constructivist point of view, the selection of the required activities for the learner must always accomplish at least two things at once; it must convey the content (the what) using only the unique skill (the how) being taught. These "design for learning" vectors must be moving in the same direction. Further, the iterative nature of the collective tasks, and the variety of the methods of engagements, convey a body of knowledge that collectively further demonstrate the learner's appropriated knowledge. Since most of these learning applications are often repeated, the learner's repeated exposures afford discernment of the nuanced differences required in each individual task (what's required to write an "E" versus an "F," for example). Taken collectively, the recursion is complete when the activities or employed methods, applied consecutively, complete the body of knowledge to be conveyed. While the design of the content and tasks might be undertaken linearly, the engagement of the learner can be linear or global, depending on the desired learning outcome. Technology applications in their basic designs can choose whether conceptualization precedes visualization, whether visualization precedes conceptualization, or whether they arise simultaneously in the design (Davydov, 1990).

However, new technology opportunities come with new challenges. One of the challenges of new technologies in the classroom is the increased level of multitasking or distraction. When learning is distributed and diverse, and when students are allowed to explore freely, some students will be distracted, or be attracted to things that are different from what the teacher intends for them to be attracted to. Even in a structured lecture or learning activity, it is not uncommon to find students texting friends on their phones or updating their Facebook pages (Rosen, Carrier, & Cheever, 2013). Students can be seen to switch between computer programs and Internet browsers constantly when they are working on the computer. Instead of reading a story in a linear format, students often follow the hyperlinks and never seem to be able to complete one story anymore. In fact, students are on their phones or on their social media sites throughout the day whenever they are allowed to have access to their devices.

Compatible Versus Non-Compatible or Distracting Multitasking Activities

To simplify discussions, we will divide multitasking activities into two main groups. We name one group as "compatible multitasking activities" and the other as "non-compatible or distracting multitasking activities." By compatible multitasking activities we refer to the multiple tasks involved that are heading toward the same directions or goals. We can see such compatible or concerted effort in activities such as playing piano or basketball. A skillful pianist must coordinate eyes, hands, feet, and mind toward the same goal with multiple tasks (e.g., reading the music, playing the keyboard, pressing the piano pedal) in order to play a musical piece well. By non-compatible or distracting multitasking activities we refer to the activities that are not heading toward the same goal. For instance, checking postings on one's Facebook page is usually not related to or compatible with listening to a lecture in the classroom unless directed by the lecturer to do so; as such, it serves as a distracting activity from the intended goal. Below, we will briefly discuss the distracting multitasking activities, followed by the compatible multitasking activities.

Non-compatible or distracting multitasking activities   Research done on multitasking has mostly targeted the non-compatible multitasking activities. Studies show that our ability in multitasking is rather limited, if not impossible (Broadbent, 1957; Lang, 2001), that multitasking over different types of tasks reduces productivity (Just et al., 2001; Rubinstein, Meyer, & Evans, 2001), and that our ability to perform concurrent mental operations is limited by the capacity of the brain's central mechanism (Schweickert & Boggs, 1984). Burgess (2000) notes that three constructs support multitasking: retrospective memory, prospective memory, and planning. As such, the role of memory, expertise, and organization becomes critical. Klingberg and Roland (1997) observed that when people conduct two tasks that activate overlapping parts of the cortex, they experienced significant interference and increased reaction time to the tasks. Scholars believe that switching between tasks wastes precious time because the brain is compelled to restart and refocus (Just et al., 2001; Meyer & Kieras, 1997). According to Meyer and Kieras (1997), each time one has this alternation, there is a period in which one will make no progress on either task. The result is that it takes longer to finish any one chore, and that people do not do their task nearly as well as they would if they had given their full attention to the task at hand. A study by Ophir, Nass, and Wagner (2009) reported that heavy media multitaskers (HMMs) performed worse on task-switching than light media multitaskers (LMMs), likely due to HMMs' reduced ability to filter out interference from irrelevant stimuli and representations in memory.

Poldrack and Foerde (2007) found that people had a harder time learning new things when their brains were distracted by another activity. The functional magnetic resonance images (fMRIs) used by researchers showed that when people learned without distraction, an area of the brain known as the hippocampus was involved. This region of the brain is critical to the processing and storing of information. However, the hippocampus was not engaged when people learned while multitasking. Instead, the region of the brain called the striatum was activated. The striatum is activated by stimuli associated with reward or by stimuli associated with aversive, novel, unexpected, or intense experiences (Schultz, 2010). Results indicated that learning while distracted or multitasking would alter the brain's learning processes and change the way people learn (Poldrack & Foerde, 2007). Foerde, Knowlton, and Poldrack (2006) found that learning new things is dependent on working memory whereas habit learning is not as sensitive to working memory. Some tasks such as learning new skills may require high cognitive loads, while other familiar and automatic tasks may require lower cognitive loads. Studies on the impact of media multitasking on attention, cognitive load, and expertise (Lee, Lin, & Robertson, 2011; Lin, Robertson, & Lee, 2009) found that students were able to understand their reading materials well in silence and non-obtrusive background environments but they did poorly in the demanding multitasking environment. These results confirmed that working memory and cognitive load play an important role in determining how much information is retained when students perform more than one task at a time.

There have been claims that children who have grown up in environments rich in dual-task experiences can perform at higher levels in these situations than adults (Prensky, 2001). If the cognitive load for a task can shift toward the striatum (Schultz, 2010) because of practice forming habit-learned performances, then it might be possible that children have greater exposure to opportunities for dual-tasking and therefore develop greater habit learning (Poldrack & Foerde, 2007). However, studies looking at age differences related to dual-task coordination have returned differing results. For instance, Carrier, Cheever, Rosen, Benitez, and Chang (2009) investigated whether technological changes have resulted in changes in multitasking skills in the younger generation. They found that the younger generation exhibited similar mental limitations in multitasking as the older generation did, although members of the younger generation reported more multitasking activities. The studies conducted by Hartley and Maquestiaux (2007) and Hartley, Jonides, and Sylvester (2011) using fMRI showed no evidence that the management of central processing of dual tasks is qualitatively different in older adults than it is in younger adults. At the same time, we are seeing an increasing amount of psychological and cognitive issues that seem to be connected to the immersive use of new media and technologies and connected to media multitasking, ranging from stress and anxiety to various disorders (Rosen, 2012; Rosen, Carrier, & Cheever, 2011, 2013; Rosen, Whaling, Rab, Carrier, & Cheever, 2013).

Compatible multitasking activities   Compatible multitasking activities refer to the multiple tasks carried out together to help advance the intended goal. For instance, if the goal is to learn, then the compatible multiple tasks involved need to facilitate the learning process. Background music, note-taking, and real-time group work may belong to the set of compatible multitasking activities. In a study that was published in 2012 (Lin, Robertson, & Lee, 2012), we investigated undergraduate students' reading comprehension with different intentions and in different multitasking situations. We found that the addition of an unobtrusive video did not inhibit the processing of the primary reading task and that some participants actually benefited from the addition of the background video. We concluded that the unobtrusive video might have served as something to prevent the participants from daydreaming when they were completing their reading tasks. An analogy to this can be seen in people who prefer to study in a noisy café to a quiet library because the very quiet library may make them feel sleepy or mind-drifting. A study conducted by Andrade (2010) showed a similar result of the beneficial effect of a secondary task (doodling) on a primary task. According to Andrade, the act of doodling as the secondary task facilitated the primary task by reducing daydreaming. Such an effect may also be because people perform better in an environment where they have more control and flexibility, or in an environment which is more comfortable or familiar for them (Lin, 2009). In this case, the multitasking activity or habit may be part of the individual comfort or control for their learning.

Another potentially compatible multitasking activity might be back-channeling. Back-channeling has been enabled by the multiple converging technologies. For instance, it can occur when an attendee at a conference takes notes and immediately publishes their notes through social media such as Twitter or Facebook, making related comments about the presentation that is unfolding in real time. In this case, the back-channeling attendee is multitasking and works almost as a reporter. Other participants, onsite or offsite, read the comments of the "reporter" and offer their input. As a result, there may be a group of multitaskers sharing, communicating, and discussing the related topic while they are listening to the presentation at the same time. Obviously, the back-channeling attendees may take similar or opposing positions, may explain the topic with their own interpretations, and may point out unspoken aspects or undercurrents related to the topic at hand. What is interesting is that the back-channeling occurs while the event is unfolding. While it has the potential to sway the topic in a direction that is different from what was intended by the original speaker, it also has the potential to take advantage of multiple points of view and add to the richness of the topic.

Perhaps one of the most compatible multitasking activities in learning is taking notes while listening to a lecture. Note-taking, when defined broadly, may serve different purposes. For instance, drafting a shopping list is a note-taking activity just as jotting down notes while listening to a lecture is. Below, we will focus on the kind of note-taking activity that takes place while one is listening to a lecture or reading a text. This particular kind of note-taking usually requires comprehension, selection of information, and written production processes in a limited time or in a time-demanding environment (Bui, Myerson, & Hale, 2013; Piolat, Olive, & Kellogg, 2005). As a result, it is similar to a dual-tasking or multitasking activity.

Note-Taking, Multitasking, and Cognitive Load in Learning

In general, the main functions of note-taking are to encode and to store information externally for later review (DiVesta & Gray, 1972). Research shows that effective note-taking usually includes a great quantity of notes and that it captures the main or most important ideas (Einstein, Morris, & Smith, 1985; Kiewra & Fletcher, 1984). As a review tool, note-taking can be used to improve recall and retention (Hartley & Davies, 1978). In addition, note-taking may help increase a learner's attention when he or she is listening to a lecture or reading a text; as a result, it may help the learner integrate and elaborate upon what he or she hears, sees, or reads with prior knowledge.

Research on note-taking has produced mixed results. Some show that students improve their recollection of information when taking notes (Bligh, 2000; Howe, 1970; Johnstone & Su, 1994; Kiewra, DuBois, Christian, & McShane, 1988), while others indicate that there is no difference between taking notes and not taking notes (Kiewra, 1985). Some studies show that students fail to record the most important points when they take notes (Hartley & Cameron, 1967; Howe, 1970; Kiewra, 1985). Yet, in studies where note-taking-plus-review was compared to note-taking-only and no-notes, the note-taking-plus-review yielded better recall in general (Fisher & Harris, 1973; Richards & Friedman, 1978). Wittrock (1974, 1979) suggested that note-taking is beneficial when learners generate paraphrased notes which incorporate prior knowledge. Novellino (1985) compared note-taking on the computer to note-taking using pencil and paper in a lecture environment, and found that the participants who were poor typists did better with recall while taking notes using pencil and paper, and the skilled typists had better recall while taking notes on the computer.

Whether taking notes helps or not probably depends on the cognitive load that the students can handle in the note-taking process (Baddeley, Chincotta, & Adlam, 2001). Note-taking depends on the working memory (Baddeley, 2007). When taking notes, the learner needs to maintain a short-term memory in order to acquire, represent, select, and understand the continuous flow of incoming new information, and to update and interact with prior knowledge (Piolat et al., 2005). Studies show that learners who had greater working memory capacity benefited from note-taking while those who had less working memory capacity were impaired by taking notes (DiVesta & Gray, 1972). Katayama and Robin (2000) argued that the primary obstacle of good-quality notes was the amount of cognitive overload experienced by the students.

Our own research has also documented the complex relationships between note-taking and learning. In one study (Lin & Bigenho, 2011), we investigated undergraduate students' memory recalls in three different learning environments (no-distraction, auditory distraction, and auditory–visual distraction) and with three different note-taking options (no note-taking, note-taking on paper, and note-taking on computer). We found significant interactions between the different learning environments and note-taking options. In the no-distraction environment, the participants had better word recall taking notes on paper than taking notes on the computer or not taking notes. However, in the auditory–visual distraction environment, the participants had better word recall with no note-taking than taking notes on computer or taking notes on paper. The participants in the study indicated that when there was no distraction, note-taking, especially note-taking on paper, helped them remember and recall the words; however, when there were lots of distractions, note-taking served as another burden on their mental processing or recall.

In another study (Lin & Bigenho, 2013), we examined the extent to which high school students were capable of switching between different activities including watching a recorded lecture, taking notes, and chatting with a friend. We found that when chatting with friends, the students not only reduced the volume of notes by about 30% but also did worse in understanding or remembering the lecture. There were also interferences between notes and chat texts, resulting in mixed notes and chat messages in different places. Continued studies are being conducted to investigate interactions between different information delivery methods, patterns of notes, and patterns of chat activities. Note-taking, therefore, is a complicated process involving storing, comprehending, and producing information (Kiewra & Benton, 1988). According to Kiewra and Benton (1988), the "effective note-taker uses working memory capacity to attend, store, and manipulate information selected from the lecture simultaneously, while also transcribing ideas just previously presented and processed" (p. 35). While note-taking can be considered germane to many learning activities, it is clearly a dual task which can add to cognitive load and have a negative impact on short-term recall. With note-taking being a surrogate form of memory, it is important to understand how it plays with different memory structures and functions.

The Relationships Between Note-Taking, Memory, Cognitive Load, and Learning

If part of learning is the ability to place new information into long-term memory, then technology-immersed or multimedia learning must examine the process of adding to long-term memory. For the purposes of this chapter we will use Cowan's (2008) definitions to define the types of memory, which are long-term memory, short-term memory, and working memory.

Long-term memory refers to a large store of knowledge and a record of prior events. In general, a normal healthy person has a rich set of long-term memories. Short-term memory refers to a temporary storage of a limited and highly accessible amount of information (Cowan, 1993, 2008). One objective of learning is to encode memories worth recalling into the long-term store. This involves a transfer from the short-term store to the relatively permanent long-term store (Atkinson & Shiffrin, 1971).

Short-term memory is limited in both capacity and duration of store. Most people are limited to four to seven items in short-term memory without employing strategies such as chunking. Items in short-term memory rapidly decay with time, making room for shifts in attention and perception (Atkinson & Shiffrin, 1971; Baddeley, 1992; Cowan, 1993). Therefore, when making the distinction between long-term and short-term memory, we usually differentiate if the memory displays properties of memory decay and hits a chunk capacity limit (Cowan, 2008). If it exhibits these characteristics, we tend to categorize it as short-term.

While it is comparatively easy to differentiate the long-term memory from the short-term memory, it is a little more difficult to make the distinction between short-term and working memory. This is because they overlap (Baddeley & Hitch, 1974; Cowan, 2008). Baddeley and Hitch (1974) and Cowan (2008) found that working memory is made up of multiple components. Working memory is comprised of short-term storage components, activated memory, along with a focus of attention within it, and central executive processes that manipulate stored information. Both storage and processing are required to assess working memory capacity. Baddeley (1992) proposed a working memory model with three subcomponents composed of (1) the central executive, (2) the visuospatial sketchpad, and (3) the phonological loop. This model operates within the short-term memory system and requires "the concurrent storage and manipulation of information" (Baddeley, 1992, p. 556). The central executive serves as the attentional controller coordinating information from the visuospatial sketchpad and the phonological loop, while the visuospatial sketch-pad allows for cognitive manipulation of images. The phonological loop consists of a phonological store and an articulatory control. The phonological loop can be thought of as the region where self-talk takes place. Information entering the phonological loop comes from sensory receptors and long-term store where it is integrated with additional information. The central executive controls where the individual focuses their attention. This becomes important for learning, as tests of memory over the short term tend to correlate significantly toward cognitive aptitude. These also point to the importance of the attentional system (focus) used for both processing and storage.

There are a series of control processes operating within the short-term store that lead to either a response output or placement of the object in the long-term store. According to Atkinson and Shiffrin (1971), information follows in the process from sensory receptors to memory systems. That is, people acquire information through the process of environmental input, to sensory (visual, auditory, or haptic) registers, to short-term store/working memory (through rehearsal, coding, decisions, and retrieval strategies), and finally to long-term store or permanent memory. It is this process where our attention must focus if we are to understand how we can best use multimedia to increase learning outcomes. While there are distinct components to working memory, dual-task studies have demonstrated decreased performance under some conditions. Baddeley (1992) found "no disruption from the concurrent verbal task[s] but clear impairment from the tasks occupying the visuospatial sketch pad or the central executive" (p. 558). Baddeley (1992) also suggested it was possible to interfere with phonological coding of visual information, resulting in decreased ability to recall visual information.

Working memory is a complex process that exists at the junction of attention, perception, and memory. It is the gateway to learning. Any interference with the process of working memory disrupts learning. As input to working memory increases, cognitive load also increases. Exceeding the capacity of working memory leads to poor coding in long-term store. The phonological loop and the visuospatial sketchpad are the functional structures of working memory that allow a person to mentally manipulate visual representations of objects and memories, link phonological coding with visual coding, and mentally rehearse through inner voice. While these are separate systems, one can introduce interference between the systems through dual-tasking. This interference can also exist within the structures.

Cognitive load plays an important role in both hindering performance and enhancing experience. Ang, Zaphiris, and Mahmood (2007) identified five different forms of cognitive overload related to playing massively multiplayer online role-playing games (MMORPGs): (1) multiple game interactions, (2) multiple social interactions, (3) parallel game and social interactions, (4) interface overloads, and (5) identity construction overloads. They report a relationship between cognitive level and capacity to handle tasks. Generally, high cognitive levels result in low capacities. When a player exceeds cognitive capacities, his or her level of play decreases. However, "task[s] can be transferred from high to low level cognition by repetition" (Ang et al., 2007, p. 171). This implies that practice can improve a player's ability to work at higher cognitive levels. In fact, these authors reported that "expert users are almost immune to distractions" (p. 171). One explanation could be that repetitive practice stimulated activity in the striatum resulting in habit learning and lower cognitive loads.

Cognitive load theory (Sweller, 1988) suggests that a learner carries three forms of cognitive processing load: intrinsic load, extraneous load, and germane load. Intrinsic load is imposed by the nature and difficulty level of the new information; extraneous load is imposed by the methods and materials in the learning process; and germane load is the mental process of taking new information and integrating it with old information in order for the learning to occur. The total cognitive load of the three added together should not exceed the cognitive processing resources of the learner; otherwise, learning shuts down under excessive or overload. The intrinsic load tends to be fixed. Yet, the extraneous load and germane load can be manipulated through instructional design and note-taking strategies so as to maximize the cognitive resources available for the learner to process the intrinsic load and to improve learning outcomes (Kirschner, 2002).

Effective multimedia design to reduce cognitive load and to improve learning   Paivio (1986) presents a two-channel theory, which models information input to a learner as entering through two channels: a vocal channel (the processing of words) and an imagery channel (the processing of images). Paivio argues that it is easier for a learner to utilize attentive resources on two tasks differing in nature (one a word-task, the other an image-task) than on two similar tasks (two word-tasks or two image-tasks). Computer-based learning environments may incorporate text, video, and pictures to load the learner's input channels in a complementary manner and enrich the learner's experiences (Clark & Mayer, 2003). Yet, good multimedia design is necessary to minimize the extraneous cognitive load by filling multiple senses and channels of the learner with complementary information without redundancy, confusion, or an over-reliance on working memory (Miller, 1956; Sweller, 1988).

With the advent of netbooks and the iPad, along with the decreasing cost in computers, schools are moving fast in the direction of one-to-one computing, that is, a personal computer or laptop with the Internet and software for every student anytime and anywhere (Bebell & O'Dwyer, 2010). As a result, the technologies available to assist learning in the classroom are evolving. For instance, students are increasingly taking notes with their laptops instead of by paper and pencil. When they take notes, they may multitask, switching between word documents, chat windows, and the Internet on their computers. These multitasking activities may be interconnected and create a synergy to facilitate learning; yet they can also compete for attention and distract students from the learning task that they need to focus on. It does not happen that the more technologies there are, the better the learning. For effective learning to take place, it is necessary to integrate sound multimedia design with the learners' active engagement (Kozma, 1994; Lusk et al., 2009; Schnotz & Bannert, 2003).

Little research has been done to examine the relationship between working memory capacity as needed in note-taking and multimedia learning. Both working memory capacity and multimedia learning are influenced by attentional control (Mayer, 2001). Mayer (2001) describes multimedia learning as based on three essential processes requiring attentional control: selecting, organizing, and integrating relevant information. Note-taking requires similar processes of attentional control: the learner must attend to the goal and the available information, select and organize the relevant information, and integrate the working memory and long-term memory to achieve the learning goal. Given the potential overlap of the processes of multimedia learning and working memory required by note-taking, it is necessary to examine the effects of note-taking and learning in different media environments.

Multimedia environments present at least two different media concurrently. This is often visual and auditory but could also be haptic as well as multiple presentation of visual or auditory information. Care must be taken to assure that information assembled for presentation does not greatly increase cognitive load or create competing interference within working memory. Game developers recognize that one can vary the level of cognitive load to manipulate levels of engagement in the game (Ang et al., 2007). Games that are too easy or too difficult are seldom successful.

As designers work with multimedia, they can use cues to shift attention to relevant changes in the media environment. This could be an audio cue such as a chime, change in volume or music, or a change in pitch. Users can also be alerted to changes in the environment through visual cues such as change in color or location in the screen. The success of these alerts requires consistency in usage. Studies on flanker presentations illustrate the importance of location of presentation on a screen. Depending on the type of information and the task, poorly placed flankers can create unwanted increases in cognitive load, leading to inefficiencies in working memory and therefore learning.

These techniques are very important when working with parallel games, simulations that require parallel experiences and social interactions (Ang et al., 2007). There is considerable interest in virtual world video games and MMORPGs such as the World of Warcraft for learning. Cognitive overload may result from trying to keep track of multiple users in these multiplayer/multi-participant environments. Some environments use only visual cues of the avatar for identification, while others mitigate these effects by allowing users to place the avatar name above the character (Ang et al., 2007). These names may be fictitious, providing relative anonymity, or real-life references.

When designing multimedia systems for learning, there are several design principles related to cognitive theory that may be of assistance when trying to integrate verbal and visual information: (1) dual coding visual and verbal information; (2) remaining cognizant of the limited capacities of memory systems; and (3) using generative learning that requires the learner to "mentally select relevant information and build coherent connections" (Mayer, Moreno, Boire, & Vagge, 1999, p. 639). Mayer (2001) suggested seven principles for the design of multimedia learning (p. 184):

1   Students learn better from words and pictures than from words alone.
2   Students learn better when corresponding words and pictures are presented near rather than far from each other on the page or screen.
3   Students learn better when corresponding words and pictures are presented simultaneously rather than successively.
4   Students learn better when extraneous words, pictures, and sounds are excluded rather than included.

5   Students learn better from animation and narration than from animation and on-screen text.

6   Students learn better from animation and narration than from animation, narration, and on-screen text.

7   Design effects are stronger for low-knowledge learners than for high-knowledge learners and for high-spatial learners rather than for low-spatial learners.

The principle at play here is that construction of knowledge is facilitated when a learner can hold visual and verbal representations in working memory while relevant connections are created. Cognitive load can be "a major impediment to constructivist learning" (Mayer et al., 1999, p. 639). For this reason, how one assembles the audio and visual components is important. The designer needs to remain cognizant of other cognitive demands that are within the environment, remembering that he or she may not have control over all aspects of the learner's environment.

Mayer and colleagues (1999) found that learners were more effective at making referential connections associated with constructivist learning when visual and verbal presentations were constructed so that their respective representations were held in working memory concurrently. They reported that this effect was "maximized by concurrent presentation and ... minimized by successive presentation" (p. 643) so long as the capacity of working memory was not exceeded. This illustrates the importance of minimizing cognitive load demands within constructivist multimedia learning environments. Munyofu and colleagues (2007) discovered that chunking strategies can be effective in reducing the cognitive load in animated instructional environments, but that students need to have prerequisite knowledge before benefiting from animated instructions. McLaughlin, Rogers, Sierra, and Fisk (2007) underwent a different route examining the relationship between media and learning: they investigated the attributes of audio and video as instructional media and provided a basis for a taxonomy that would match the appropriate media to learning situations. They concluded that effective learning would not necessarily occur until there was an appropriate match between instructional media types and learning situations (McLaughlin et al., 2007).

However, it is not a simple task to control cognitive aspects or to match media with learning demands. It is important to keep in mind the intended audience as well as the expected outcomes. Every learner is different and some groups of learners require unique considerations. In a study looking at the use of color for attraction to relevant information in attention-problem children, Zentall and Kruczek (1988) found that it was important to apply discriminating use of color. They reported that "active attention-problem children performed better with relevant color than with non-relevant color. The educational implications of these findings are that color for active attention-problem children should be used to draw attention to relevant discriminative stimuli within tasks" (1988, p. 363). It is also possible that the use of color just to increase attractiveness of the task could actually disrupt performance for these children (Zentall & Kruczek, 1988). At the same time, color can be used to focus a learner's attention on new or relevant information. This form of instructional cueing might reduce cognitive loads, adding to the effectiveness of the multimedia lesson.

Finally, we must consider the nature of secondary interactions and secondary tasks performed during multimedia interactions. The literature on dual-tasking related to cellular phones and driving provides convincing evidence of the negative effect competing dual tasks can have on performance outcomes. The more complex the learning environment, the greater the likelihood for there to be interference between tasks. Interactive lessons delivered through learning management systems must be designed to minimize cognitive interference. This interference can result from interactions with a poorly designed learning environment, competing auditory or visual tasks, or extraneous visual or auditory characteristics of the course or multimedia environment. However, not all learning environments will result in the same cognitive levels for all students. While background music might serve as a major distraction for some, others would find that music increases their attention (Langer, 1997).

Future Research and Conclusion

It is clear that technology will continue to permeate our society in ways that exceed our imaginations. Advances in wearable technology and an emphasis on reduction in size with increases in performance ensure we will see smaller, less obvious and externally intrusive forms of technology entering our classrooms. With a major limiting factor to speed being the interface between human and machine, we will continue to explore new ways to directly interact with our devices. These ongoing advances make it important that we continue to explore active learning processes such as note-taking along with the various ways we interact with our technologies.

Future studies should explore the nature of note-taking compared to active dialogue, with note-taking being considered a surrogate discussion during the act of listening to a lecture. This would help us to better understand the role of technology in the note-taking process. What affordances do our existing technologies provide for effectively engaging in the process of learning and what are the cognitive costs of these uses? While multitasking has been demonstrated to have a large impact on psychological and cognitive processes (Rosen, 2010, 2012), it is clearly a functional part of our society and there is a need to better understand acceptable costs and useful forms of multitasking in learning environments. While increasing uses of fMRI technologies will help us to better understand multitasking in learning environments at a functional level, we must continue to explore educational multitasking *in situ*.

Learning environments today contain complex interactions, constantly evolving in structure and function. Educators must understand how to design learning environments that take advantage of the new media and technologies while minimizing negative cognitive impact from competing dual-task scenarios often encountered in media-rich learning environments. Controlling cognitive loads will rise in importance as these environments become more complex. A basic understanding of working memory, dual-tasking or multitasking, and cognitive load will help educators improve the efficacy of their multimedia-rich learning environments. The number of portable connective devices continues to increase in classrooms, resulting in a need to understand the effects of using these devices while attending to lessons in the classroom.

References

Andrade, J. (2010). What does doodling do? *Applied Cognitive Psychology, 24*, 100–106.

Ang, C. S., Zaphiris, P., & Mahmood, S. (2007). A model of cognitive loads in massively multiplayer online role playing games. *Interacting With Computers, 19*, 167–179.

Atkinson, R. C., & Shiffrin, R. M. (1971). The control of short-term memory. *Scientific American, 225*, 82–90.

Baddeley, A. D. (1992). Working memory. *Science, 255*, 556–559.

Baddeley, A. D. (2007). *Working memory, thought and action*. Oxford, UK: Oxford University Press.

Baddeley, A. D., Chincotta, D., & Adlam, A. (2001). Working memory and the control of action: Evidence from task switching. *Journal of Experimental Psychology: General, 130*(4), 641–657.

Baddeley, A. D., & Hitch, G. (1974). Working memory. In G. H. Bower (Ed.), *The psychology of learning and motivation: Advances in research and theory* (Vol. 8, pp. 47–89). New York, NY: Academic Press.

Bebell, D., & O'Dwyer, L. M. (2010). Educational outcomes and research from 1:1 computing settings. *Journal of Technology, Learning, and Assessment, 9*(1).

Bligh, D. (2000). *What's the use of lectures?* San Francisco, CA: Jossey-Bass.

Broadbent, D. (1957). A mechanical model for human attention and immediate memory. *Psychological Review, 64*, 205–215.

Bui, D., Myerson, J., & Hale, S. (2013). Note-taking with computers: Exploring alternative strategies for improved recall. *Journal of Educational Psychology, 105*(2), 299–309.

Burgess, P. W. (2000). Real-world multitasking from a cognitive neuroscience perspective. In S. Monsell & J. Driver (Eds.), *Control of cognitive processes: Attention and performance XVIII* (pp. 465–472). Cambridge, MA: MIT Press.

Carrier, L. M., Cheever, N. A., Rosen, L. D., Benitez, S., & Chang, J. (2009). Multitasking across generations: Multitasking choices and difficulty ratings in three generations of Americans. *Computers in Human Behavior, 25*(2), 483–489.

Clark, R. C., & Mayer, R. E. (2003). *E-learning and the science of instruction: Proven guidelines for consumers and designers of multimedia learning*. San Francisco, CA: Pfeiffer.

Cowan, N. (1993). Activation, attention, and short-term memory. *Memory and Cognition, 21*(2), 162–167.

Cowan, N. (2008). What are the differences between long-term, short-term, and working memory? In W. Sossin, J. C. Lacaille, V. F. Castellucci, & S. Belleville (Eds.), *Progress in brain research: The essence of memory* (Vol. *169*, pp. 323–338). Amsterdam, the Netherlands: Elsevier/Academic Press.

Davydov, V. V. (1990). *Types of generalization in instruction: Logical and psychological problems in the structuring of school curricula* (J. Teller, Trans.). Reston, VA: National Council of Teachers of Mathematics.

DiVesta, F. J., & Gray, G. S. (1972). Listening and notetaking. *Journal of Educational Psychology, 63*, 8–14.

Einstein, G., Morris, J., & Smith, S. (1985). Note-taking, individual differences and memory for lecture information. *Journal of Educational Psychology, 77*(5), 522–532.

Fisher, J. L., & Harris, M. B. (1973). Effects of notetaking and review on recall. *Journal of Educational Psychology, 65*, 321–325.

Foerde, K., Knowlton, B. J., & Poldrack, A. (2006). Modulation of competing memory systems by distraction. *Proceedings of the National Academy of Sciences of the United States of America, 103*(31), 11778–11783.

Hartley, A. A., Jonides, J., & Sylvester, C. (2011). Dual-task processing in younger and older adults: Similarities and differences revealed by fMRI. *Brain and Cognition, 75*, 281–291.

Hartley, A. A., & Maquestiaux, F. (2007). Success and failure at dual-task coordination by younger and older adults. *Psychology and Aging, 22*(2), 215–222.

Hartley, J., & Cameron, A. (1967). Some observations on the efficiency of lecturing. *Educational Review, 20*, 30–37.

Hartley, J., & Davies, I. K. (1978). Note-taking: A critical review. *Programmed Learning and Educational Technology, 15*(3), 207–224.

Healy, J. (1999). *Failure to connect: How computers affect our children's minds and what we can do about it.* New York, NY: Simon & Schuster.

Howe, M. J. (1970). Notetaking strategy, review and long-term retention of verbal information. *Journal of Educational Research, 63,* 285.

Johnson, L., Adams, S., & Cummins, M. (2012). *The NMC Horizon report: 2012 Higher Education edition.* Austin, TX: The New Media Consortium.

Johnson, L., Adams Becker, S., Cummins, M., Estrada, V., Freeman, A., & Ludgate, H. (2013). *NMC Horizon Report: 2013 Higher Education edition.* Austin, TX: The New Media Consortium.

Johnson, L., Smith, R., Willis, H., Levine, A., & Haywood, K. (2011). *The 2011 Horizon report.* Austin, TX: The New Media Consortium.

Johnstone, A. H., & Su, W. Y. (1994). Lectures – a learning experience? *Education in Chemistry, 31*(79), 75–76.

Just, M., Carpenter, P., Keller, T., Emery, L., Zajac, H., & Thulborn, K. (2001). Interdependence of nonoverlapping cortical systems in dual cognitive tasks. *Neuro Image, 14,* 417–426.

Katayama, A., & Robin, D. (2000). Getting students "partially" involved in note-taking using graphic organizers. *Journal of Experimental Education, 68,* 119–135.

Kiewra, K. A. (1985). Providing the instructor's notes: An effective addition to student note-taking. *Educational Psychologist, 20,* 33–39.

Kiewra, K., & Benton, S. (1988). The relationship between information-processing ability and notetaking. *Contemporary Educational Psychology, 13,* 33–44.

Kiewra, K., DuBois, N., Christian, D., & McShane, A. (1988). Providing study notes: Comparison of three types of notes for review. *Journal of Educational Psychology, 83*(2), 240–245.

Kiewra, K., & Fletcher, H. (1984). The relationship between levels of note-taking and achievement. *Human Learning: Journal of Practical Research and Applications, 3*(4), 273–280.

Kirschner, P. A. (2002). Cognitive load theory: Implications of cognitive load theory on the design of learning. *Learning and Instruction, 12*(1), 1–10.

Klingberg, T., & Roland, P. E. (1997). Interference between two concurrent tasks is associated with activation of overlapping fields in the cortex. *Cognitive Brain Research, 6,* 1–8.

Kozma, R. B. (1994). Will media influence learning? Reframing the debate. *Educational Technology Research and Development, 42*(2), 7–19.

Lang, A. (2001). The limited capacity model of mediated message processing. *Journal of Communication, 50*(1), 46–70.

Langer, E. (1997). *The power of mindful learning.* Boston, MA: Da Capo Press.

Lee, J., Lin, L., & Robertson, T. (2011). The impact of media multitasking on learning. *Learning, Media and Technology, 9*(1), 1–11.

Lin, L. (2009). Breadth-biased versus focused cognitive control in media multitasking behaviors. *Proceedings of the National Academy of Sciences, 106,* 15521–15522.

Lin, L., & Bigenho, C. (2011). Cognitive note-taking and memory in different media environments. *Computers in the Schools, 28*(3), 200–216.

Lin, L., & Bigenho, C. (2013). Chatting with friends online while watching a video: What and how much information is retained? *iConference 2013 Proceedings,* 433–436.

Lin, L., Robertson, T., & Lee, J. (2009). Reading performances between novices and experts in different media multitasking environments. *Computers in the Schools, 26*(3), 169–186.

Lin, L., Robertson, A., & Lee, J. (2012). The impact of outcome intentions on reading and multitasking performances. *Journal of Educational Technology Development and Exchange, 5*(1), 77–94.

Lusk, D., Evans, A., Jeffrey, T., Palmer, K., Wilstrom, C., & Doolittle, P. (2009). Multimedia learning and individual differences: Mediating the effects of working memory capacity with segmentation. *British Journal of Educational Technology, 40*(4), 636–651.

Mayer, R. E. (2001). *Multimedia learning.* New York, NY: Cambridge University Press.

Mayer, R. E., Moreno, R., Boire, M., & Vagge, S. (1999). Maximizing constructivist learning from multimedia communications by minimizing cognitive load. *Journal of Educational Psychology, 91*(4), 638–643.

McLaughlin, A., Rogers, W., Sierra, A., & Fisk, A. (2007). The effects of instructional media: Identifying the task demand/media match. *Learning, Media and Technology, 32*(4), 381–405.

McLuhan, M. (1994). *Understanding media: The extension of man.* Cambridge, MA: MIT Press.

Meyer, D. E., & Kieras, D. E. (1997). A computational theory of executive cognitive processes and multiple-task performance: Part 1. Basic mechanisms. *Psychological Review, 104,* 229–233.

Miller, G. A. (1956). The magical number seven, plus or minus two: Some limits on our capacity for processing information. *Psychological Review, 63,* 81–97.

Munyofu, M., Swain, W. J., Ausman, B. D., Lin, H., Kidwai, K., & Dwyer, F. (2007). The effect of different chunking strategies in complementing animated instruction. *Learning, Media and Technology 32*(4), 407–419.

Novellino, G. R. (1985). *Use of microcomputers to copy information: Effects on free recall.* [Unpublished doctoral dissertation]. University of Southern Mississippi.

Ophir, E., Nass, C. I., & Wagner, A. D. (2009). Cognitive control in media multitaskers. *Proceedings of the National Academy of Sciences, 106,* 15583–15587.

Oppenheimer, T. (2003). *The flickering mind: The false promise of technology in the classroom and how learning can be saved.* New York, NY: Random House.

Paivio, A. (1986). *Mental representations.* New York, NY: Oxford University Press.

Piolat, A., Olive, T., & Kellogg, R. T. (2005). Cognitive effort during note-taking. *Applied Cognitive Psychology, 19,* 291–312.

Poldrack, R. A., & Foerde, K. (2007). Category learning and the memory systems debate. *Neuroscience and Biobehavioral Reviews, 32,* 197–205.

Prensky, M. (2001). *Digital game-based learning.* Columbus, OH: McGraw-Hill.

Prensky, M. (2012). *Brain gain: Technology and the quest for digital wisdom.* New York, NY Palgrave Macmillan.

Richards, J. P., & Friedman, F. (1978). The encoding versus the external storage hypothesis in note taking. *Contemporary Educational Psychology, 3,* 136–143.

Rosen, L. D. (2010). *Rewired: Understanding the Net Generation and how they learn.* New York, NY: Palgrave Macmillan.

Rosen, L. D. (2012). *iDisorder: Understanding our obsession with technology and overcoming its hold on us.* New York, NY: Palgrave Macmillan.

Rosen, L., Carrier, M., & Cheever, N. (2011). An empirical examination of the educational impact of text message-induced task switching in the classroom: Educational implications and strategies to enhance learning. *Psicologia Educativa, 17*(2), 163–177.

Rosen, L., Carrier, M., & Cheever, N. (2013). Facebook and texting made me do it: Media-induced task-switching while studying. *Computers in Human Behavior, 29,* 948–958.

Rosen, L., Whaling, K., Rab, S., Carrier, L., & Cheever, N. (2013). Is Facebook creating "iDisorders"? The link between clinical symptoms of psychiatric disorders and technology use, attitudes and anxiety. *Computers in Human Behavior, 29,* 1243–1254.

Rubinstein, J. S., Meyer, D. E., & Evans, J. E. (2001). Executive control of cognitive processes in task switching. *Journal of Experimental Psychology: Human Perception and Performance, 27*(4), 763–797.

Schnotz, W., & Bannert, M. (2003). Construction and interference in learning from multiple representations. *Learning and Instruction, 13,* 141–156.

Schultz, W. (2010). Dopamine signals for reward value and risk: Basic and recent data. *Behavioral and Brain Functions, 6*(24).

Schweickert, R., & Boggs, G. J. (1984). Models of central capacity and concurrency. *Journal of Mathematical Psychology, 3,* 223–281.

Sweller, J. (1988). Cognitive load during problem solving: Effects on learning. *Cognitive Science, 12*(2), 257–285.

Tapscott, D. (2009). *Grown up digital: How the Net Generation is changing your world.* New York, NY: McGraw-Hill.

Wittrock, M. (1974). Learning as a generative process. *Educational Psychologist, 11*(2), 87–95.

Wittrock, M. (1979). The cognitive movement in instruction. *Educational Researcher, 8*(2), 5–11.

Zentall, S. S., & Kruczek, T. (1988). The attraction of color for active attention-problem children. *Exceptional Children, 54*(4), 357–363.

25

Multitasking and Interrupted Task Performance

From Theory to Application

Nicole E. Werner,[1] David M. Cades,[2] and Deborah A. Boehm-Davis[3]

[1] *George Mason University and Johns Hopkins University School of Medicine*
[2] *Exponent Failure Analysis Associates*
[3] *George Mason University*

On February 1, 1991, a Boeing 737 touched down on top of a 10-passenger Fairchild Metroliner, killing 34 people (National Transportation Safety Board, 1991). This incident started when an air traffic controller cleared a 10-passenger commuter aircraft to hold in take-off position on one end of the runway. Prior to clearing that aircraft for take-off, the same controller was interrupted by another aircraft that needed assistance re-establishing communications. The controller was then contacted by a large commercial jet on final approach asking for landing clearance. The controller issued the incoming aircraft clearance to land, and only too late realized that, after being interrupted, he never issued the take-off instruction to the 10-passenger commuter aircraft, which was now sitting on the same runway on which the large commercial jet had been cleared to land.

Though extreme, the story above illustrates the destructive potential of interruptions in safety-critical environments. Not every interruption leads to such destruction and loss of life, but interruptions do affect each and every one of us every day. They permeate our lives, which are filled with text messages, phone calls, emails, and instant messages (to name a few), constantly vying for our attention. By 2013, 91% of all adults in the United States had cell phones and 42% had tablet computers (Duggan & Smith, 2013). Thus, it is not surprising that in today's technology-driven world, from the time we wake up in the morning until we get into bed at night, we are bombarded by interruptions.

Other than the obvious annoyance factor at being disrupted, interruptions can have serious negative consequences, as illustrated in the first paragraph. Research has shown that when recovering from an interruption, it takes longer to complete a task and errors are more likely to be made on that task following the end of the interruption – if the task

The Wiley Handbook of Psychology, Technology, and Society, First Edition. Edited by Larry D. Rosen, Nancy A. Cheever, and L. Mark Carrier.
© 2015 John Wiley & Sons, Ltd. Published 2015 by John Wiley & Sons, Ltd.

is resumed at all (Gillie & Broadbent, 1989; Trafton, Altmann, & Brock, 2005; Trafton, Altmann, Brock, & Mintz, 2003). Thus, many of the tasks we perform daily – driving down the street or sending an email to your boss – are susceptible to errors due to interruptions.

Seminal work exploring interruptions indicated that they are disruptive to performance on a primary task (Cane, Cauchard, & Weger, 2012; Dismukes, 2012; Gillie & Broadbent, 1989; Jones, Gould, & Cox, 2012; Morgan & Patrick, 2013; Trafton et al., 2003, 2005). The disruptive potential of an interruption has typically been measured in terms of timing or accuracy. With timing, the time required to resume the primary task – known as the *resumption lag* – and the total time required to complete the primary task have both been shown to increase with interruptions. Accuracy, measured by the number of errors that occur when the primary task is resumed, typically also increases after interruptions. More recently, research has shown that interruptions also decrease the overall quality of the work produced when the process is interrupted (Foroughi, Werner, Nelson, & Boehm-Davis, 2014). With the proliferation of electronic communication devices such as cell phones, email, and instant messaging that continuously interrupt users, it is more important than ever to continue to develop a thorough understanding of the mechanisms underlying interruptions.

Interruptions at Work

Interruptions are pervasive in our everyday work environments. Research has suggested that interruptions cost the American economy $588 billion per year (Basex, 2006), occurring approximately 12.5 times per hour in some office settings (Cades, Werner, Arshad, & Boehm-Davis, 2010). The loss of productivity is not surprising given that another early study showed that in 40% of interrupted situations in an office environment, people failed to come back to their original tasks (O'Conaill & Frohlich, 1995). Recent research suggests that the problem of interruptions in the workplace persists, with one study showing that tasks performed with interruptions take one-third longer than those performed without interruptions (Marulanda-Carter & Jackson, 2012). Moreover, time effects have been shown to be most vulnerable to instant messaging-based interruptions (Mansi & Levi, 2013). However, other researchers have found hierarchical effects related to who is sending the instant message (Gupta, Li, & Sharda, 2013). A similar study showed that management-level employees experienced more and longer interruptions than other positions – up to six times as many lasting up to four times as long in some situations. These management-level employees also experienced over 120 interruptions in an 8-hour work shift, accounting for 71% of their daily activity (Sykes, 2011). This recent research suggests that interruptions are still a relevant and disruptive presence in the modern workplace. One potential cause of these interruptions is the proliferation of technologies and systems that can produce interruptions in this environment.

Because of the disruptive nature of interruptions and their potentially catastrophic effects, it is especially important to understand their impact in high-risk, safety-critical settings such as hospitals, aviation, and driving where interruptions occur at high frequencies and have potentially dire consequences. In the healthcare domain, interruptions and distractions have long been known to be a contributing risk factor for medical error. However, health care has only begun to investigate how the ever-increasing implementation of new technologies and countless interruptions healthcare providers must contend with are shaping the healthcare landscape.

Although some technologies such as electronic whiteboards have been shown to reduce the number of direct communication-based interruptions faced by healthcare providers (France et al., 2005), they can have the opposite effect as well, leading to more interruptions and phenomena such as *alarm fatigue*, in which healthcare providers ignore potentially important alarms due to oversaturation (Blake, 2014; Jones, 2014). One hospital that implemented web-based messaging to try to improve clinical communication found a 233% increase in interruptions (Quan et al., 2013). Unfortunately, most of the work to date on interruptions in healthcare environments has focused on interruption occurrence, with little attention paid to outcome, and even fewer studies examine the cognitive processes and implications underlying interrupted task performance (Grundgeiger & Sanderson, 2009; Rivera-Rodriguez & Karsh, 2010).

As detailed in our introductory story, the world of commercial aviation is by no means immune to the negative effects of interruptions. Interruptions on the flight deck are quite common and can lead to checklist steps being omitted (Dismukes, 2012). While not every interruption leads to a crash, the presence and commonality of them on the flight deck should be enough to show the importance of understanding their underlying mechanisms.

Driving – a task that most of us perform daily – is especially susceptible to the damaging effects of interruptions. A study conducted at the University of Utah found that driving while using a phone increases a driver's reaction time as much as being at the legal limit of alcohol consumption – a .08% blood alcohol level (Distraction.gov, 2008). Further, distracted driving is implicated in 20% of crashes with a result of 6,000 deaths and more than half a million injuries (Distraction.gov, 2012).[1] One study of iPhone use for navigation applications while driving showed that, even though this task was in support of the goal of driving, it was also distracting, with higher level of distractions associated with applications with multiple screens necessary for task completion (Quaresma, 2012). Similarly, Young and colleagues (2012) found that drivers in a simulated driving situation reduced speed and were unable to maintain a consistent lane position while selecting music from an iPod touch device. Research findings and a perception of a growing epidemic of mobile technology use in cars (for tasks both related and unrelated to driving) and distracted driving have led to the creation of the official U.S. government website for distracted driving in order to, according to Secretary of Transportation Ray LaHood, "raise awareness and provide information to people who want to get the facts on the issue [driver distraction], get involved in their communities, and help make our roads safer for all Americans" (LaHood, 2013). The National Highway Traffic Safety Administration (NHTSA) also recently released voluntary design guidelines for use in designing devices aimed at reducing visual–manual distraction to drivers that may be used while driving (NHTSA, 2012).

These are only a few reasons why it is important that research on interruptions explore how to better handle interruptions and mitigate the unfavorable consequences they create. To do this, we must first develop an understanding of the processes underlying interruptions and recovery. In other words, we must study the cognitive underpinnings of the interruption and recovery process.

Defining Interruptions

An interruption can be considered any secondary task that leads to the suspension of a primary task to which a person has the intention to return. Interruptions are considered as a form of multiple task management in the literature, but are considered different than distractions, multitasking, or task-switching. Although multitasking and task-switching have separate bodies of literature examining the underlying cognitive mechanisms and resulting behavioral effects, they share a considerable amount. One typically thinks of multitasking as performing more than one task concurrently. However, some would argue that dividing attention between more than one task is not possible and, thus, multitasking is simply a series of task switches (Borst, Taatgen & van Rijn, 2010; Monsell, 2003; Salvucci & Taatgen, 2008). Put simply, a distraction does not necessarily cause you to suspend the task you are working on. For example, an email chime either from your computer or the one in the next cubicle may be distracting in that it captures your attention. However, as a distraction, it would not cause you to stop what you are doing.

The interruption process consists of a series of discrete events unfolding in a particular order. As shown in Figure 25.1, a person first begins work on a primary task and then must, or chooses to, attend to a secondary task (Boehm-Davis & Remington, 2009). The secondary task may be presented without warning, or with some sort of alert calling attention to it. An alert can be anything from the ringing of your cell phone to signal a call to a chime from your computer reminding you to stand up and stretch. The time between the onset of an alert and the first step on the interruption task is called the *interruption lag*, the period of time during which a person disengages from the primary task. The person must then move focus to the interruption

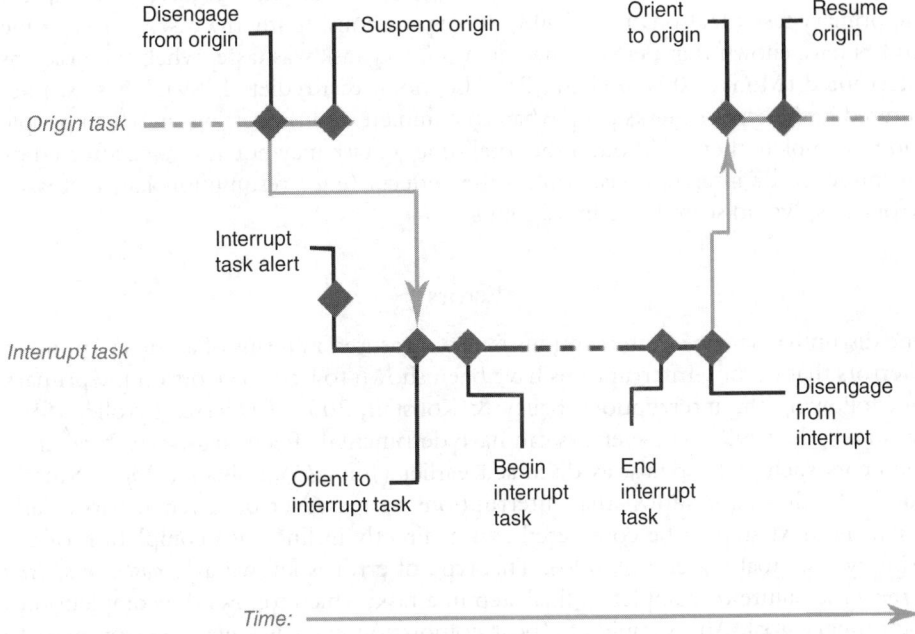

Figure 25.1 Anatomy of an interruption.

task and begin working on it. At some point while working on the interruption, the goal associated with the interruption will either be completed, or a decision will be made to switch back to the primary task. Once this occurs, a person must disengage from the interruption and reorient to the primary task. In order to successfully resume the primary task, a person must figure out what the next step is on that task. Following this *resumption lag* – the time between the last action on the interrupting task and the first action in resuming the primary task – a person can then resume the primary task.

One way in which the disruptive potential of an interruption is measured is in terms of the time lag to resume a primary task. This measure is then compared to the *interaction interval* – the time between two uninterrupted actions on the primary task – in order to determine whether or not and to what degree the interruption is disruptive. A longer resumption lag means that it took longer to resume the primary task following the interruption.

Impact of Interruptions on Performance

The impact that interruptions have on performance has been measured in a number of ways. Here, we will discuss the impact on time to complete the primary task, errors, and overall quality.

Increased Time to Complete the Primary Task

The disruptiveness of an interruption can be examined globally by measuring the effect of interruptions on the total time to complete the primary task. Although some researchers have found that interruptions slow the total time required to complete the primary task (Trafton et al., 2003), this is not consistently the case. In fact, some studies have shown that performance on a primary task was faster when the task was interrupted (Monk, 2004; Zijlstra, Roe, Leonora, & Krediet, 1999). These studies differed in the types of tasks people had to complete and the settings in which people had to complete them. Although the total time on task may not always be affected by the presence of interruptions, some other effects (e.g., resumption lag, increased error rates) would seem to be more robust.

Errors

The disruptive nature of interruptions is also measured in terms of accuracy (number of errors that occur). Interruptions have been shown to lead to errors on the primary task following the interruption (Bailey & Konstan, 2006; Cellier & Eyrolle, 1992; Zijlstra et al., 1999). These errors can have detrimental effects in safety-critical environments such as hospitals, as discussed earlier (Joint Commission, 2001; Santell, 2005). Studies have shown that interruptions increased errors overall, particularly when the next step to be completed is not directly in line with completion of the primary task goal (Li et al., 2006). This type of error is known as a *post-completion error* – the failure to complete a final step in a task, which follows the completion of the primary goal. An example of a post-completion error is when a person goes to the ATM to get money out, receives the money, but then leaves the ATM card in the machine because the goal of getting money has already been completed and there is a sense of the task being finished and the goal being achieved. An interruption just prior to a post-completion step (i.e., retrieving your ATM card) increases the likelihood that a post-completion error will occur (Li et al., 2006). Li et al. (2006) interrupted participants at various points during completion of a primary task that contained post-completion actions. Of particular interest was the interruption directly before the post-completion step. As suggested previously, the researchers found that an interruption directly before the post-completion step led to an increased rate of post-completion errors. Using data from these and related studies, and real-time eye movement data, Ratwani, McCurry, and Trafton (2008) were able to create a predictive model to help tell when people are more likely to make these types of errors. The goal would be to take such predictive models and use them to intervene.

Quality of the Work Produced

Speculation still exists about how interruptions affect the quality of our work. When Barack Obama became president and indicated that he planned to continue using his smartphone, there were concerns about an interruption in the Oval Office leading to a catastrophic event (Begley, 2009). More recently, radio talking heads and Internet bloggers alike have postulated that interruptions might have a detrimental impact on creativity (Smith, 2013). Currently, though, there is little to no empirical evidence to support those concerns.

Intriguingly, much of the research on interruptions suggests that even when people make errors upon resumption, they are able to recognize and correct those errors. Thus, it is not clear whether interruptions negatively affect overall performance other than by requiring additional time to correct errors and complete the task. Put simply, it seems previous research would suggest that given enough time, interruptions may not affect overall quality of performance.

Cades (2011) attempted to look at the effects of interruptions on overall quality by having students complete homework assignments either with access to the Internet, their mobile devices, and social media or without. Interestingly, this study showed that while all tasks performed with interruptions took longer, tasks that could be answered discretely (e.g., math problems, multiple choice questions) did not show quality decrements when performed with interruptions. Foroughi and colleagues (2014) sought to investigate this further and leveraged a more complex, creative thought task that mirrors a common real-world task – outlining and writing an essay. The goal was to examine whether interruptions lead to a decrement in overall quality of performance. The experiment consisted of a planning phase immediately followed by an execution phase. During the 12-minute planning phase, participants outlined their essay. During the 12-minute execution phase, participants typed their essay. Participants were either interrupted or not and interruptions occurred either during outline or while writing the essay. Individuals who were interrupted, either while out-lining an essay or while translating their outline into a final essay, had poorer-quality essays overall than those who were not interrupted. Moreover, participants who were interrupted during the outlining period but not during the execution period pro-duced the same number of words as when they were not interrupted, but the quality of their writing was reliably lower when they were interrupted during the planning process (Foroughi et al., 2014).

These results suggest that interruptions lead to an overall reduction in quality in a creative writing task when interrupted either while planning the essay or during the writing of an essay. Although this is focused on only one type of task, these results provide the first data pointing to the effect of interruptions on the overall quality of a task. Students and workers, plagued by constant interruptions to their work, tend to claim that given enough time to complete their tasks, they can compensate for delays caused by interruptions, and the work does not suffer. This work suggests otherwise.

Multitasking has become a covetable skill that is highlighted in cover letters and résumés. Yet no evidence has been documented to support these claims. In fact, recent reports suggest that high media multitaskers, in other words, those who attempted to complete more than four tasks at once, suffered negative consequences to cognitive control as well as in their ability to write essays when compared with low media multitaskers (Ophir, Nass, & Wagner, 2009). Although these studies employed a concurrent multitasking versus an interruption paradigm, they provide evidence that perceptions about multitasking ability and actual performance do not match. Similarly, Pool, Van der Hort, Beentjes, and Koolstra (2000) found that having spoken-word programs on in the background while students performed homework tasks led to slower performance and lower-quality work.

Theories of Interrupted Task Performance

Memory for Goals

The memory for goals model (Altmann & Trafton, 2002) is an activation-based model grounded in the adaptive control of thought–rational (ACT-R) computational modeling framework (Anderson, 2007; Anderson & Lebiere, 1998) that has been used to describe the cognitive processes that occur during the interruption of and recovery to a primary task. In ACT-R, information is stored in memory in chunks, and each of these chunks has a certain level of activation associated with it. The memory for goals model explains that the goal you are trying to retrieve (e.g., within the primary or interruption task) has a certain activation level associated with it. This activation level for the goal decays as a function of time. Therefore, longer interruptions lead to greater primary task goal decay. In turn, this leads to longer times to resume the primary task due to the lower activation levels of the to-be-retrieved goals.

The model specifies two constraints other than time that affect the activation level of a to-be-retrieved goal. The *strengthening constraint* deals with the frequency and/or recency with which a goal has been retrieved or attended. This constraint describes how consistent and multiple retrievals of a goal can boost activation. It also stipulates that the more recently a goal has been retrieved, the higher the activation level of that goal will be. The *priming constraint* suggests that environmental and mental contexts can also boost activation. One method by which goals can be strengthened is through rehearsal. In the case of interruptions, being able to rehearse (or think about) the primary task goal during the interruption period can lead to strengthening of that goal. This would then lead to an increase in the activation level of that goal and would facilitate fast and accurate retrieval of that goal following the interruption.

Threaded Cognition

Threaded cognition is a more recent theory of interrupted task performance that is also instantiated in the ACT-R cognitive architecture (Salvucci & Taatgen, 2008; Salvucci, Taatgen, & Borst, 2009). Initially a model of concurrent multitasking, Salvucci and colleagues (2008, 2009) have extended the memory for goals model and added their task thread and problem state components to attempt to more fully account for interrupted task performance (Salvucci & Taatgen, 2008, 2010). Threaded cognition theory adapts many of the same assumptions as the memory for goals model. However, each task or thought is represented as a thread. In contrast to memory for goals, threaded cognition does not talk about activation specifically, but rather describes tasks as *threaded*. Rather than modeling interruptions as involving suspension of a task, threaded cognition suggests that tasks occur on a continuum. Additionally, the model does not propose the lags described in memory for goals. Instead, the model purports that some processes, such as rehearsal of the primary task and secondary task actions, occur concurrently. This is possible because the theory assumes that threads will continue depending on the availability of resources in what is referred to as a greedy/polite manner – greedy because threads will use whatever resource they need, but polite because once a thread does not need the resource, it is returned to the general resource pool. Another assumption of threaded cognition is that there is a separate resource that is dedicated to remembering what you were doing on the primary task when you are working on a different task (Salvucci & Taatgen, 2010). This is known as the problem state, or in other words, the task goal. The problem state resource is where interference issues can occur. Because there is only one resource dedicated to the problem state of a task, if you are performing a primary task and a secondary task that each require a problem state, there will be interference and the theory predicts that an error is likely to occur as you try to resume the primary task.

Features Affecting Performance

The theories described make predictions about how individual features of tasks are likely to affect task performance. To date, researchers have focused on features such as interruption length (Hodgetts & Jones, 2006a; Iqbal & Bailey, 2005; Monk, Boehm-Davis, & Trafton, 2002), interruption complexity (Cades, Trafton, Boehm-Davis, & Monk, 2007; Cades, Ratwani, Boehm-Davis, & Trafton, 2008; Cellier & Eyrolle, 1992; Hodgetts & Jones, 2005, 2006a; Speier, Valacich, & Vessey, 1999; Zijlstra et al., 1999), similarities between the interrupting task and the primary task (Cellier & Eyrolle, 1992; Edwards & Gronlund, 1998; Oulasvirta & Saariluoma, 2004), the timing of the interruption (Latorella, 1998; Miyata & Norman, 1986; Monk et al., 2002), and interruption frequency (Monk, 2004; Zijlstra et al., 1999), to attempt to better understand the effects of interruptions on primary task performance and which theories can account for those findings.

Interruption Length

A relationship showing longer interruptions leading to longer resumption lags has been supported in several laboratory studies (Hodgetts & Jones, 2006a; Iqbal &

Bailey, 2005; Monk et al., 2002; Monk, Boehm-Davis, & Trafton, 2008). This has been termed the *interruption duration effect* (Hodgetts & Jones, 2006a; Monk et al., 2008), and although this effect has not been shown reliably across the board (Einstein, McDaniel, Williford, Pagan, & Dismukes, 2003), other studies have consistently found support for its existence (Hodgetts & Jones, 2006a; Monk et al., 2008). More recently, a study showed support for an interruption duration effect in conversations, with longer conversation suspensions requiring more effort to reinstate than shorter suspensions (Bangerter, Chevalley, & Derouwaux, 2010). Other recent work supporting the interruption duration effect found that although the incidence of error increased as interruption length increased, even a brief interruption led to a twofold increase in error on the primary task (Altmann, Trafton, & Hambrick, 2014).

Complexity of the Interruption

The effect of interruption complexity on primary task performance has been the focus of several studies (Cades et al., 2007; Cades, Werner, Trafton, Boehm-Davis, & Monk, 2008; Cellier & Eyrolle, 1992; Gillie & Broadbent, 1989; Hodgetts & Jones, 2005, 2006a; Speier et al., 1999; Zijlstra et al., 1999). The memory for goals model predicts that a more complex interruption should lessen the opportunity for strengthening of the primary task goal via rehearsal due to the higher cognitive demand of the interruption. This would, therefore, lead to greater goal decay and more difficulty in resuming the primary task than would a less complex interruption. Studies that have examined the effects of interruption complexity in terms of their effects on the resumption lag have supported this prediction (Cades et al., 2007; Cades, Werner, et al., 2008; Hodgetts & Jones, 2005, 2006a). Werner, Cades, and Boehm-Davis (under review) provide further support for this effect by defining complexity as the ability of the interruption task to inhibit ongoing processing of the primary task during an interruption. Based on this definition, the complexity of an interruption task was measured by a mental resources approach – analyzing the number of mental operators required to complete the task. The results suggested that an increase in the number of mental resources required to complete an interruption task increases complexity due to the increased inability to rehearse the primary task while performing the interruption.

Similarity of Tasks

The similarity of the interrupting task to the primary task has also been investigated (Cellier & Eyrolle, 1992; Czerwinski, Christman, & Rudisill, 1991; Edwards & Gronlund, 1998; Oulasvirta & Saariluoma, 2004). Oulasvirta and Saariluoma (2004) found that an interruption that was more similar to the primary task was more disruptive to primary task performance. For example, these results suggest that a person working on a word-processing task might find an instant message or email interruption more disruptive than a phone call. Aside from these tasks using the same modalities (visual, manual), depending on how a person's computer screen is arranged, the email or instant message might occlude the word-processing task, making encoding through visual rehearsal or using the word-processing task as a cue upon retrieval more difficult than a phone call, which, if answered with a hands-free option, would only need auditory resources.

Interruption Location

Another feature of interruptions that may affect performance is related to the point during a task at which the interruption occurs. Studies have shown that differential placement of an interruption during the primary task affects the ability to resume (Latorella, 1998; Miyata & Norman, 1986; Monk et al., 2002). In one study, participants were interrupted at different points throughout the completion of a primary task – the start, the middle, or the end (Monk et al., 2002). The results showed that interruptions caused longer resumption lags when the primary task was interrupted from the middle to the end of the task as compared to the beginning of a task. While this line of research may shed light on some of the cognitive processes involved in the suspension and resumption of an interrupted task, in today's world, it may be harder to take advantage of the less disruptive interruption points as interruptions have permeated the tasks we perform. Anyone who sits in front of a computer is constantly inundated with emails, instant messages, or social media alerts, which occur during all tasks.

Frequency of Interruptions

Zijlstra et al. (1999) examined the effects of interruption frequency on office workers. They generally showed that more frequent interruptions led to greater disruptions. Monk (2004) performed a study in which all participants received an average of 4.68 interruptions in the high-frequency condition. Surprisingly, the findings from this study showed that participants in the high-frequency condition resumed the primary task faster than those in the low-frequency conditions. The researchers proposed that the results of this study could be due to participants adapting to the more frequent interruptions by developing special strategies of goal maintenance. Interestingly, one study showed that instant messaging, a technology often associated with high levels of disruption, can be used to mediate disruptive effects. Garret and Danziger (2008) found that among a group of workers who regularly use computers, those who use instant messaging for work reported fewer interruptions and distractions than those who do not. Further analysis revealed that employees were able to use instant messaging to manage and triage interruptions by getting task-specific information and making others aware of their availability through status (e.g., "in a meeting," "do not disturb," "away," "available"). This is one example where people have been able to harness an otherwise distracting technology and use it to mitigate those same disruptive effects.

Mitigating Disruptions

As outlined above, the deleterious effects associated with interruptions, disruptions, and distractions come in many different shapes and sizes. Much research has been devoted to understanding various task aspects that affect the disruptiveness of interruptions (Cane et al., 2012; Dismukes, 2012; Jones et al., 2012; Morgan & Patrick, 2013; Trafton et al., 2003, 2005) as well as the relevant cognitive mechanisms underlying these effects (Altmann & Trafton, 2002; Oulasvirta & Saariluoma, 2004; Salvucci & Taatgen, 2008; Salvucci et al., 2009). As the understanding of interrupted task performance continues to grow, it is essential that these findings be used to assist in mitigating the relevant negative effects. In the following section, we provide an overview of some of these findings.

Training

Cades, Trafton, and Boehm-Davis (2006) and, more recently, Cades, Boehm-Davis, Trafton, and Monk (2011) investigated the potential effect of training with interruptions on primary task performance. In these studies, participants were trained on a number of computer-based tasks and were interrupted with other computer-based tasks that completely occluded the primary task. Participants were interrupted in either one, two, or three sessions of primary task performance, and performed either the same or different primary–secondary task pairs from session to session. The results showed that participants who were exposed to interrupting tasks more often across sessions were faster at resuming from the interruption than the participants who were exposed to interrupting tasks less often. Further, participants showed faster resumption when they were exposed to the same primary task–interruption task pair over repeated sessions. The implication for mitigating the deleterious effects of interruptions is that people may be able to better handle interruptions if exposed to them during the training of a task, and that this exposure may have task-specific facets. In light of these findings, it is possible that those who are working on the same task consistently may be able to mitigate the effects of interruptions such as email and social media over time.

Alerts

An interruption task can sometimes be preceded by an alert (Figure 25.1), which may allow a person to prepare prior to engaging the interruption. This preparation time, termed the *interruption lag*, is measured as the time from the onset of an alert to the first step on the interruption task. For example, when the phone starts ringing or you see a co-worker coming down the hallway toward your office, you might leave yourself a note or position the cursor where you left off as a cue to yourself upon return.

The memory for goals model suggests that an alert prior to the onset of an interruption would lead to a faster resumption of the primary task later because the alert would allow strengthening of the primary task goal prior to the interruption (Trafton et al., 2003). This effect is supported by research suggesting that an interruption lag only reduced the resumption lag when the environmental context is not changed (Hodgetts & Jones, 2006b). This idea is further supported by research on prospective memory (memory for doing something in the future, e.g., I have to remember to go to the store later). When interruptions allow time for planning the resumption step, or the goal-to-be-completed-later, people show fewer and less severe negative effects (Dismukes, 2012; Morgan & Patrick, 2013; Shum, Cahill, Hohaus, Gorman, & Chan, 2013).

Environmental Context and Cues

Access to environmental context and cues has been shown to improve interrupted task performance (Jones et al., 2012). One potential explanation for this is that availability of primary task context during the interruption strengthens activation of the primary task goal, which, according to memory for goals, can lead to a boost in the activation level of the primary task. For example, one study showed that auditory interruptions, which do not occlude the primary task screen, led to faster resumption than visual interruptions where the primary task was completely occluded (Ratwani et al., 2008). Hodgetts and Jones (2006b) found that a change in environmental context led to longer resumption times, demonstrating the importance of environmental context upon resumption.

An analysis of several published laboratory experiments and available naturalistic data further revealed the importance of the presence of environmental context and cues (Cades, Ratwani, et al., 2008). Using a *mega-analytic* technique (Carlson & Miller, 1987) to compare results from 15 published studies as well as 9 hours of naturalistic data from an office setting, researchers found that the interruption duration effect only held when there was no access to environmental context or cues during the interruption and upon resumption.

Cues also have been found to be useful upon resumption when they indicate what the next step on the primary task should be. In a complex computer interface task, participants' eye movements were tracked to see whether participants were looking at the correct location on the screen upon resumption (Ratwani et al., 2008). If participants did not look at the screen within a certain number of glances, the model predicted that an error was likely and provided support by displaying an explicit cue. This was found to reduce the number of errors made.

The Future

The prevalence of interruptions in everyday environments, coupled with their disruptive nature, continues to grow, especially due to the increased use of technology in our lives. While through research we have begun to learn about which types of interruption tasks are more disruptive than others and what types of theories might be used and advanced to help us understand the origin of those effects, there is still a lot we do not know. One important step in this work is that it has been leveraged to look at mitigations and mitigation strategies. For example, it was only after researchers developed a thorough understanding of how people resumed immediately following an interruption that they were able to use eye-tracking, as described above, to build a successful intervention (Ratwani et al., 2008).

Interestingly, the same technology that increases interruptions can also be tailored to help reduce the impact of interruptions. For example, Arroyo and Selker (2011) developed a framework, called Disruption Manager, which takes advantage of understanding a user's goals and tasks to assess when and how to present interruptions in order to minimize their disruptiveness. They have shown that Disruption Manager has led to a 26% performance increase for important tasks and a 32.5% increase for urgent tasks and that people using Disruption Manager were five times more likely to respond productively to instant messages. This is but one example of taking advantage of technology to facilitate interruption mitigation.

Work such as this is a good start. However, much is still unknown. It is critical that we conduct sufficient work to understand the nuances of how interruptions affect the quality of the products people produce before making recommendations to users and developing creative software solutions to aid performance in a world where interruptions are part of the permanent landscape. As just one small example, we still do not know whether the findings outlined generalize to all individuals or whether some individuals are more affected than others. Once we have this understanding, we can begin to develop tools for users based on specific tasks as well as individual cognitive differences to aid recovery from interruptions and improve productivity. The only thing we know for sure is that the hunger and need for instant access to information, coupled with the continued burgeoning of mobile technologies, make the investigation of the effects of these technologies ever more important.

Note

1   Statistics retrieved from http://www.distraction.gov/content/get-the-facts/facts-and-statistics.html

References

Altmann, E. M., & Trafton, J. G. (2002). Memory for goals: An activation-based model. *Cognitive Science, 26*(1), 39–83.

Altmann, E. M., Trafton, J. G., & Hambrick, D. Z. (2014). Momentary interruptions can derail the train of thought. *Journal of Experimental Psychology: General, 143*, 215–226.

Anderson, J. R. (2007). *How can the human mind occur in the physical universe?* Oxford, UK: Oxford University Press.

Anderson, J. R., & Lebiere, C. (1998). *Atomic components of thought.* Mahwah, NJ: Lawrence Erlbaum Associates.

Arroyo, E., & Selker, T. (2011). Attention and intention goals can mediate disruption in human–computer interaction. In P. Campos, N. Graham, J. Jorge, N. Nunes, P. Palanque, & M. Winckler (Eds.), *Human–computer interaction – INTERACT 2011, 13th IFIP TC 13 international conference (Lisbon, Portugal, September 5–9, 2011): Proceedings, Part II* (pp. 454–470). Heidelberg, Germany: Springer.

Bailey, B. P., & Konstan, J. A. (2006). On the need for attention-aware systems: Measuring effects of interruption of task performance, error rate, and affective state. *Computers in Human Behavior, 22*(4), 685–708.

Bangerter, A., Chevalley, E., & Derouwaux, S. (2010). Managing third-party interruptions in conversations: Effects of duration and conversational role. *Journal of Language and Social Psychology, 29*(2), 235–244.

Basex. (2006, January 9). Workplace interruptions cost US economy $588 bn a year. Retrieved from http://www.basex.com/press.nsf/0/E53F4C6142D119A6852570F9001AB0EC? OpenDocument

Begley, S. (2009). Will the BlackBerry sink the presidency? *Newsweek, 153*, 7.

Blake, N. (2014). The effect of alarm fatigue on the work environment. *AACN Advanced Critical Care, 25*(1), 18–19.

Boehm-Davis, D. A., & Remington, R. (2009). Reducing the disruptive effects of interruption: A cognitive framework for analysing the costs and benefits of intervention strategies. *Accident Analysis and Prevention, 41*(5), 1124–1129.

Borst, J. P., Taatgen, N. A., & van Rijn, H. (2010). The problem state: A cognitive bottleneck in multitasking. *Journal of Experimental Psychology: Learning, Memory, and Cognition, 36*, 2.

Cades, D. A. (2011). *Understanding the effects of interruptions on the quality of task performance.* [Dissertation]. George Mason University, Fairfax, VA. Retrieved from http://hdl.handle.net/1920/6338

Cades, D. M., Boehm-Davis, D. A., Trafton, J. G., & Monk, C. A. (2011). Mitigating disruptive effects of interruptions through training: What needs to be practiced? *Journal of Experimental Psychology: Applied, 17*(2), 97.

Cades, D. M., Ratwani, R. M., Boehm-Davis, D. A., & Trafton, J. G. (2008). Resuming from interruptions: Looking for common trends across multiple environments. Cognitive Science Society Conference, Washington, DC.

Cades, D. M., Trafton, J. G., & Boehm-Davis, D. A. (2006). Mitigating disruptions: Can resuming an interrupted task be trained? *Proceedings of the HFES 50th Annual Meeting* (pp. 234–238). Thousand Oaks, CA: Sage.

Cades, D. M., Trafton, J. G., Boehm-Davis, D. A., & Monk, C. A. (2007). Does the difficulty of an interruption affect our ability to resume? *Proceedings of the HFES 51st Annual Meeting* (pp. 368–371). Thousand Oaks, CA: Sage.

Cades, D. M., Werner, N. E., Arshad, Z., & Boehm-Davis, D. A. (2010, September). What makes real-world interruptions disruptive? Evidence from an office setting. *Proceedings of the Human Factors and Ergonomics Society Annual Meeting* (Vol. 54, No. 4, pp. 448–452). Thousand Oaks, CA: Sage.

Cades, D. M., Werner, N. E., Trafton, J. G., Boehm-Davis, D. A., & Monk, C. A. (2008). Dealing with interruptions can be complex, but does interruption complexity matter? A mental resources approach to quantifying disruptions. *Proceedings of the HFES 52nd Annual Meeting.* Thousand Oaks, CA: Sage.

Cane, J. E., Cauchard, F., & Weger, U. W. (2012). The time-course of recovery from interruption during reading: Eye movement evidence for the role of interruption lag and spatial memory. *Quarterly Journal of Experimental Psychology, 65*(7), 1397–1413.

Carlson, M., & Miller, N. (1987). Explanation of the relation between negative mood and helping. *Psychological Bulletin, 102*(1), 91.

Cellier, J.-M., & Eyrolle, H. (1992). Interference between switched tasks. *Ergonomics, 35*(1), 25–36.

Czerwinski, M., Christman, S., & Rudisill, M. (1991). Interruptions in multitasking situations: The effects of similarity and warning. Technical Report JSC-24757, NASA Johnson Space Center.

Dismukes, R. K. (2012). Prospective memory in workplace and everyday situations. *Current Directions in Psychological Science, 21*(4), 215–220.

Duggan, M., & Smith, A. (2013, December 30). Social media update 2013. Pew Internet & American Life Project. Retrieved from http://pewinternet.org/Reports/2013/Social-Media-Update.aspx

Edwards, M. B., & Gronlund, S. D. (1998). Task interruption and its effects on memory. *Memory, 6*, 665–687.

Einstein, G. O., McDaniel, M. A., Williford, C. L., Pagan, J. L., & Dismukes, R. (2003). Forgetting of intentions in demanding situations is rapid. *Journal of Experimental Psychology: Applied, 9*(3), 147.

Foroughi, C., Werner, N. W., Nelson, E. T., & Boehm-Davis, D. A. (2014). Do interruptions affect the quality of work? *Human Factors, 56*, 7, 1262–1271.

France, D. J., Levin, S., Hemphill, R., Chen, K., Rickard, D., Makowski, R., ... Aronsky, D. (2005). Emergency physicians' behaviors and workload in the presence of an electronic whiteboard. *International Journal of Medical Informatics, 74*(10), 827–837.

Garrett, R. K., & Danziger, J. N. (2008). IM = interruption management? Instant messaging and disruption in the workplace. *Journal of Computer-Mediated Communication, 13*(1), 23–42.

Gillie, T., & Broadbent, D. (1989). What makes interruptions disruptive? A study of length, similarity and complexity. *Psychological Research, 50*(4), 243–250.

Grundgeiger, T., & Sanderson, P. (2009). Interruptions in healthcare: Theoretical views. *International Journal of Medical Informatics, 78*(5), 293–307.

Gupta, A., Li, H., & Sharda, R. (2013). Should I send this message? Understanding the impact of interruptions, social hierarchy and perceived task complexity on user performance and perceived workload. *Decision Support Systems, 55*(1), 135–145.

Hodgetts, H. M., & Jones, D. M. (2005). Interrupting problem solving: Effects of interruption position and complexity. In M. Katsikitis (Ed.), *Past reflection, future directions: Proceeding of the 40th Australian Psychological Society Annual Conference, Melbourne, Australia.* Melbourne, Australia: Australian Psychological Society.

Hodgetts, H. M., & Jones, D. M. (2006a). Interruption of the Tower of London task: Support for a goal-activation approach. *Journal of Experimental Psychology: General, 135,* 103–115.

Hodgetts, H. M., & Jones, D. M. (2006b). Contextual cues aid recovery from interruption: The role of associative activation. *Journal of Experimental Psychology: Learning, Memory, and Cognition, 32,* 1120–1132.

Iqbal, S. T., & Bailey, B. P. (2005). Investigating the effectiveness of mental workload as a predictor of opportune moments for interruption. *CHI Extended Abstracts on Human Factors in Computing Systems,* 1489–1492.

Joint Commission on Accreditation of Healthcare Organizations. (2001). *A follow-up review of wrong site surgery.* Retrieved from http://www.jointcommission.org/sentinel_event_alert_issue_24_a_follow-up_review_of_wrong_site_surgery/

Jones, K. (2014). Alarm fatigue a top patient safety hazard. *Canadian Medical Association Journal, 186*(3), 178. doi: 10.1503/cmaj.109-4696

Jones, S. A., Gould, S. J. J., & Cox, A. L. (2012). Snookered by an interruption? Use a cue. In *People and Computers XXVI: Proceedings of the 26th Annual BCS Interaction Specialist Group Conference on People and Computers (BCS-HCI '12)* (pp. 251–256). Swindon, UK: British Computer Society.

LaHood, R. (2013). A message from Secretary LaHood. *Distraction.gov.* Retrieved from http://www.distraction.gov/content/about-us/message-from-secretary-LaHood.html

Latorella, K. A. (1998). Effects of modality on interrupted flight deck performance: Implications for data link. *Proceedings of the HFES 42nd Annual Meeting 1998.* Thousand Oaks, CA: Sage.

Li, S. Y. W., Cox, A. L., Blandford, A., Cairns, P., Young, R. M., & Abeles, A. (2006). *Further investigations into postcompletion error: The effects of interruption position and duration.* Paper presented at the 28th Annual Meeting of the Cognitive Science Society.

Mansi, G., & Levi, Y. (2013). Do instant messaging interruptions help or hinder workers' task performance? *International Journal of Information Management, 33*(3), 591–596.

Marulanda-Carter, L., & Jackson, T. W. (2012). Effects of e-mail addiction and interruptions on employees. *Journal of Systems and Information Technology, 14*(1), 82–94.

Miyata, Y., & Norman, D. A. (1986). Psychological issues in support of multiple activities. In D. A. Norman & S. W. Draper (Eds.), *User-centered system design* (pp. 265–284). Hillsdale, NJ: Lawrence Erlbaum Associates.

Monk, C. A. (2004). *The effect of frequent versus infrequent interruptions on primary task resumption.* Paper presented at the Human Factors and Ergonomics Society 48th Annual Meeting, Santa Monica, CA.

Monk, C. A., Boehm-Davis, D. A., & Trafton, J. G. (2002). The attentional costs of interrupting task performance at various stages. *Proceedings of the HFES Annual Meeting* (pp. 1824–1828). Thousand Oaks, CA: Sage.

Monk, C. A., Boehm-Davis, D. A., & Trafton, J. G. (2008). The effect of interruption duration on resuming suspended goals. *Journal of Experimental Psychology: Applied, 14*(4), 299–313.

Monsell, S. (2003). Task switching. *Trends in Cognitive Sciences, 7*(3), 134–140.

Morgan, P. L., & Patrick, J. (2013). Paying the price works: Increasing goal-state access cost improves problem solving and mitigates the effect of interruption. *Quarterly Journal of Experimental Psychology, 66*(1), 160–178.

National Highway Traffic Safety Administration (NHTSA). (2012). *Visual–manual NHTSA driver distraction guidelines for in-vehicle electronic devices* (Docket no. NHTSA-2010-0053). Washington, DC: U.S. Government Docket Management Facility.

National Transportation Safety Board (NTSB). (1991). Aircraft accident report. *Runway collision of USAir Flight 1493, Boeing 737 and SkyWest Flight 5569 Fairchild Metroliner, Los Angeles International Airport, Los Angeles, California, February 1, 1991* (Rep. No. NTSB-AAR-91-8). Washington, DC: Author.

O'Conaill, B., & Frohlich, D. (1995). Timespace in the workplace: Dealing with interruptions. In *Human Factors in Computing Systems: CHI '95 Companion* (pp. 262–263). New York, NY: ACM.

Ophir, E., Nass, C., & Wagner, A. D. (2009). Cognitive control in media multitaskers. *Proceedings of the National Academy of Sciences, 106*(37), 15583–15587.

Oulasvirta, A., & Saariluoma, P. (2004). Long-term working memory and interrupting messages in human–computer interaction. *Behaviour and Information Technology, 23*(1), 53–64.

Pool, M. M., Van der Hort, T. H. A., Beentjes, J. W. J., & Koolstra, C. M. (2000). Background television as an inhibitor of performance on easy and difficult homework assignments. *Communication Research, 27*(3), 293–326.

Quan, S. D., Wu, R. C., Rossos, P. G., Arany, T., Groe, S., Morra, D., ... Lau, F. Y. (2013). It's not about pager replacement: An in-depth look at the interprofessional nature of communication in healthcare. *Journal of Hospital Medicine, 8*(3), 137–143.

Quaresma, M. (2012). Assessment of visual demand of typical data entry tasks in automotive navigation systems for iPhone. *Work: A Journal of Prevention, Assessment and Rehabilitation, 41* (Suppl. 1), 6139–6144.

Ratwani, R. M., McCurry, J. M., & Trafton, J. G. (2008). Predicting post-completion errors using eye movements. *Proceedings of the SIGCHI Conference on Human Factors in Computing Systems* (pp. 539–542). New York, NY: ACM.

Rivera-Rodriguez, A. J., & Karsh, B. T. (2010). Interruptions and distractions in healthcare: Review and reappraisal. *Quality and Safety in Healthcare, 19*(4), 304–312.

Salvucci, D. D., & Taatgen, N. A. (2008). Threaded cognition: An integrated theory of concurrent multitasking. *Psychological Review, 115*(1), 101.

Salvucci, D. D., & Taatgen, N. A. (2010). *The multitasking mind*. Oxford, UK: Oxford University Press.

Salvucci, D. D., Taatgen, N. A., & Borst, J. P. (2009, April). Toward a unified theory of the multitasking continuum: From concurrent performance to task switching, interruption, and resumption. In *Proceedings of the SIGCHI Conference on Human Factors in Computing Systems* (pp. 1819–1828). New York, NY: ACM.

Santell, J. P. (2005). Medication errors: Experience of the United States Pharmacopeia (USP). *Journal of Quality and Patient Safety, 31*(2), 114–119.

Shum, D. H. K., Cahill, A., Hohaus, L. C., O'Gorman, J. G., & Chan, R. C. K. (2013). Effects of aging, planning, and interruption on complex prospective memory. *Neuropsychological Rehabilitation, 23*(1), 45–63.

Smith, K. (2013, March 31). The texting dead. *The New York Post*. Retrieved from http://www.nypost.com/p/news/opinion/opedcolumnists/the_texting_dead_MU5foa9q45bgg ABb122SxO

Speier, C., Valacich, J., & Vessey, I. (1999). The influence of task interruption on individual decision making: An information overload perspective. *Decision Sciences, 30*(2), 337–360.

Sykes, E. R. (2011). Interruptions in the workplace: A case study to reduce their effects. *International Journal of Information Management, 31*(4), 385–394.

Trafton, J. G., Altmann, E. M., & Brock, D. P. (2005). Huh, what was I doing? How people use environmental cues after an interruption. *Proceedings of the HFES 49th Annual Meeting*. Thousand Oaks, CA: Sage.

Trafton, J. G., Altmann, E. M., Brock, D. P., & Mintz, F. (2003). Preparing to resume an interrupted task: Effects of prospective goal encoding and retrospective rehearsal. *International Journal of Human-Computer Studies, 58,* 583–603.

Werner, N. E., Cades, D. M., & Boehm-Davis, D. A. (under review). Real world interruptions are complex: But what defines interruption complexity? *Theoretical Issues in Ergonomics Science.*

Young, K. L., Mitsopoulos-Rubens, E., Rudin-Brown, C. M., & Lenné, M. G. (2012). The effects of using a portable music player on simulated driving performance and task-sharing strategies. *Applied Ergonomics, 43*(4), 738–746.

Zijlstra, F. R. H., Roe, R. A., Leonora, A. B., & Krediet, I. (1999). Temporal factors in mental work: Effects of interrupted activities. *Journal of Occupational and Organizational Psychology, 72*(2), 164–185.

Part V

The Media's Impact on Audiences

26

Cultivation in the Twenty-First Century

Nancy Signorielli

University of Delaware

Television became a staple of life in the 1950s and by the end of that decade was a fixture in more than 90% of American homes. In the past 60-plus years television has become the most prominent of all mass media as well as one of the defining elements of modern life. Scholarly research and public debate on television has flourished and continues today even as newer technologies including the Internet, social media, video games, and smartphones have become part and parcel of the everyday life of most people.

Over the decades, television programming as well as its institutional structure and technology have undergone considerable change. Nevertheless, television still garners more of the public's time, and more of the advertisers' dollars, than any other medium. We are a long way from the 1950s, but television still remains the source of the most widely shared cultural stories, images, and lessons about life. While new technologies (online streaming, on demand, DVRs, smartphones, and tablets) make it easier to watch whenever, and wherever, we want, they only cement television's importance and centrality in our lives. At the same time, concerns about the "effects" of media portrayals of violence, sex, gender and racial/ethnic stereotypes, the family, medicine, politics, health, nutrition and weight, drugs and alcohol, mental illness, and much more, continue to motivate and frustrate researchers, parents, teachers, health professionals, and others.

In the 1960s, George Gerbner (1919–2005) devised a way of thinking about television and media effects that he called *cultivation*. Gerbner (1973) believed that storytelling, originally the domain of home and church, was the central component and served a distinct humanizing function in society. Stories today, however, are not the function of the home and church. Rather, today's stories are mass-produced by commercial conglomerates and mass-consumed to a historically unprecedented degree. Most of us cannot escape the most prevalent day-to-day mass-mediated messages of our society.

Gerbner's goal was to understand the consequences of growing up in a cultural environment dominated by mediated, profit-driven mass communication (Gerbner, 1973). He devised a research paradigm, called Cultural Indicators, to investigate (1) the institutional processes underlying the selection and production of media content

The Wiley Handbook of Psychology, Technology, and Society, First Edition. Edited by Larry D. Rosen, Nancy A. Cheever, and L. Mark Carrier.

(institutional process analysis), (2) the most prevalent, aggregate images in that content (message system analysis), and (3) the contribution of that content to audience beliefs and behaviors (cultivation analysis). While this model, its conceptual assumptions, and its methodological procedures can be applied to any dominant medium of communication (or any system of storytelling), cultivation analysis has largely focused on television, since no other medium has a greater and more profound hold on our time and attention, and most people watch television practically every day whether on a traditional set, a smartphone, computer, or other device. Indeed, no other medium garners as much consistent attention as television. In its simplest form, cultivation analysis asks if those who watch more television ("heavy viewers") have conceptions of social reality that are more reflective of what they see on television, compared to people who have similar demographic characteristics but who watch less television ("light viewers"). Cultivation analysis, then, examines how the stories we – as a culture – watch on television contribute to our beliefs and attitudes about the "real" world.

Cultivation was conceived as a critical alternative to traditional approaches to the study of media "effects." While the vast bulk of media effects research most often examines attitude or behavior change resulting from exposure to some type of media message, Gerbner did not believe that "changes" in outlooks due to viewing in the short term were the most important result of television watching. Such changes, he believed, were questions for persuasion and marketing research. Rather, Gerbner saw that television viewing resulted in shared cultural outlooks and assumptions that were nurtured, maintained, and reinforced by television's messages in large communities over long periods of time. All communication, he argued, cultivates the assumptions, points of view, and relationships on which it is premised. With mass communication, what is cultivated is standardized and more widely shared to a historically unprecedented degree. The common symbolic environment in which we grow up and live gives shape and meaning to all that we do; the more we "live" in that synthetic but coherent world, the more it cultivates our conceptions of social reality.

To some, this was a common-sense idea. However, many social scientists saw this as a too-simplistic explanation of television's effects or even a misuse of social science research methods; as a result, innumerable colloquies, critiques, revisions, and reappraisals appeared (see Shanahan & Morgan, 1999, for a review). But despite, or perhaps because of, the enormous amount of criticism leveled at cultivation, it is one of the most frequently cited theories of mass communication or media effects since the 1970s. Various studies of the literature regularly place cultivation, along with agenda setting and uses and gratifications, as one of the three most cited theories of media effects (Bryant & Miron, 2004). Indeed, one analysis of media effects research published between 1993 and 2005 found that cultivation was the *most* cited theory (Potter & Riddle, 2007). By 2013 more than 600 relevant studies had been published (two-thirds of which are extensions, replications, reviews, and critiques conducted by independent researchers not associated with Gerbner and the original research team).[1]

Cultivation is a worldwide phenomenon; studies have been carried out in Argentina, Australia, Belgium, Brazil, China, England, Germany, Hungary, Israel, Japan, Mexico, Russia, South Korea, Sweden, Thailand, and elsewhere. Clearly, such a large body of work – and all the complex issues and implications it raises – cannot be exhaustively treated here; this chapter attempts to provide only a general introduction to this area of research (a more extensive examination of the cultivation literature can be found in Morgan, Shanahan, & Signorielli, 2009, 2012; Shanahan & Morgan, 1999).

Cultivation Analysis Methods

Cultivation analysis typically begins by identifying the most common and stable patterns in television content, emphasizing the consistent images, portrayals, and values that cut across program genres. This is accomplished either by conducting a message system analysis (a content analysis) or by examining the results of existing content studies. Typical examples of consistent content patterns include the high levels of violence in prime-time TV programs (e.g., Gerbner, 1970; Signorielli, 2003) or under-representations of specific social groups (e.g., Signorielli, 1993a). Once those patterns are identified, the goal is to ascertain if those who spend more time watching television are more likely to perceive the real world in ways that reflect the particular messages and lessons seen on television. For example, do heavy viewers (having been immersed in the violent world of television) see the world as a more violent place, that more people are involved in violence, and that more people work in law enforcement occupations?

Cultivation hypotheses are most often tested using survey procedures to examine relationships between the amount of television viewing and conceptions of social reality. Several different types of questions are asked. Some juxtapose answers reflecting the statistical "facts" of the television world with those more in line with reality (often referred to as "first-order" cultivation measures). As an example, compared to light viewers, heavy viewers would be more likely to think that there are more agents of law enforcement in the workforce (Gerbner & Gross, 1976). Other questions examine symbolic transformations and more general implications of the message system data (often referred to as "second-order" cultivation measures). For example, questions about people's fear of victimization or the extent to which they think others can be trusted fall into this category. Finally, some questions simply ask about beliefs, opinions, attitudes, or behaviors. For instance, in many studies, heavy viewers have been shown to harbor more traditional beliefs about gender roles (Morgan, 1982; Signorielli, 1993a).

Studies use different types of samples (national probability, regional, convenience) of children, adolescents, or adults and assess the amount of viewing by asking how much time the respondent spends watching on an "average day." Although many investigators have operationalized amount of viewing in different ways, the key element is finding ways to differentiate those who watch more from those who watch less television. These data may be used in their original form (a ratio scale) or may be grouped by level of exposure ("light," "medium," and "heavy" viewing), on a sample-by-sample basis. People who regularly consume a great deal of television differ from light viewers in many ways besides simply how much time they spend watching. To deal with this, differences between the responses of light, medium, and heavy viewers are examined within specific demographic subgroups, statistically controlling for the effects of other variables.

As with many media effects studies, cultivation analyses typically generate small effect sizes. Even those who watch relatively little television may watch 7 to 10 hours a week and certainly interact with those who watch more. Thus, the cards can be statistically stacked against finding evidence of cultivation. Nevertheless, even small differences between light and heavy viewers may indicate far-reaching consequences. With very large audiences, a difference of a fraction of a percentage point in ratings can indicate the success or failure of a program (and be worth millions of advertising dollars), and a difference of a few percentage points in an election will determine who wins or who loses. Similarly, small relationships across large populations of heavy and light viewers may indicate profound social effects, particularly as they cumulate over time.

Critiques and Refinements

Few theories of media effects (and perhaps few areas of social research in general) have been critiqued as heavily and fiercely as cultivation. For some examples, see Doob and Macdonald, 1979; Hirsch, 1980; Hughes, 1980; Potter, 1993, 1994; Wober, 1990; see also Shanahan and Morgan, 1999. These critiques have focused on many issues, including cultivation's emphasis on overall amount of television exposure (as opposed to specific types of programs), the way television viewing is measured and divided into relative levels of exposure, justifications for interpreting television-world answers, the linearity of cultivation associations, and much more. Some of the most heated issues of contention have revolved around questions of spuriousness and the proper use of statistical controls.

Early analyses typically controlled one variable at a time. But several critics reanalyzing the same data argued that when multiple variables were controlled at the same time, the relationships between television viewing and attitudes mostly disappeared. This led them to conclude that there was no evidence to support the cultivation hypothesis.

Gerbner and his colleagues countered that even if a relationship disappears when controlling for multiple variables, significant patterns may still exist within specific subgroups, often reflecting a pattern they called "mainstreaming" (Gerbner, Gross, Morgan, & Signorielli, 1980). Specifically, mainstreaming shows that among light viewers, people who differ in terms of background factors such as age, education, social class, political orientations, and region of residence tend to have sharply different conceptions of social reality regarding violence, interpersonal mistrust, gender-role stereotypes, and a broad range of political and social outlooks. Yet, among heavy viewers in the same groups, those differences in conceptions tend to be much smaller or even to disappear entirely.

For example, Gerbner et al. (1980) found that low-income respondents were more likely than higher-income respondents to say that "fear of crime is a very serious personal problem." Among low-income respondents, amount of television viewing was not related at all to perceptions of crime. In contrast, although higher-income respondents, as a group, were less likely to think of crime as a serious personal problem, the heavy viewers with higher incomes were much more likely than the light viewers to be especially worried about crime. In other words, heavy viewers with higher incomes had the same perception as those with lower incomes; among heavy viewers, the difference stemming from income was sharply diminished. Similarly, among lighter viewers, those with more education have been found to express more "progressive" attitudes about gender roles, but this difference disappears among heavy viewers; more educated heavy viewers express the same "traditional" beliefs as heavy viewers with less education.

As research progressed a second process emerged to explain and predict how viewing may impact different viewers. This process noted that direct experience may be important for some viewers. Specifically, the phenomenon called *resonance* was proposed to illustrate how a person's everyday reality and patterns of television viewing may provide a double dose of messages that "resonate" and amplify cultivation. For example, those who live in high-crime urban areas often show stronger relationships between amount of viewing and self-reported fear of crime. Thus, in this case we see that both the "TV world" and the real world reinforce the impression that violence is widespread.

Much of this back-and-forth dialogue took place in the early to middle 1980s and from it emerged a few important theoretical outcomes. Nevertheless, cultivation theory and its basic research approaches flourished, even as the critiques also gained some level of acceptance among researchers. From these early debates, cultivation research grew and expanded. The overall focus of cultivation was broadened from its beginnings in violence to issues related to sex roles, aging, politics, health, science, religion, the family, the environment, and many other topics. Also, the study of cultivation was taken up by many individual researchers who had not worked or trained with the original Cultural Indicators research team, and it also became an international research phenomenon.

In short, during the past four decades close to 600 studies have (mostly) found relationships between television exposure and people's conceptions about the world. Exploring, comparing, detailing, and analyzing this research, Shanahan and Morgan (1999) reviewed over 20 years' worth of studies in a meta-analysis that found the body of cultivation research as a whole exhibited a small but persistent relationship between television exposure and beliefs about the world. In addition, the expansion of the study of cultivation led to important extensions and new strands of research, such as those focusing on the cognitive processes underlying cultivation (see, for example, Morgan et al., 2012, for the most up-to-date cultivation studies). But important questions remain: How large are these relationships, are they real, are some people more vulnerable to them than others, do they vary across different topics, and will we continue to find them as our media environments keep evolving?

Cultivation Findings

There have been many key areas in which cultivation research has been particularly relevant in helping us understand television's role in society. Early cultivation studies examined how television's extensive content of crime and violence contributed to people's conceptions about the world. More than five decades of message system analyses show that more than a third of television characters are involved each week in some kind of violent action. Although FBI statistics have clear limitations, they indicate that in any one year less than 1% of people in the United States are victims of criminal violence. Cultivation studies have found that those who spend more time with television are more likely to overestimate the amount of violence in society. They have exaggerated conceptions of danger, mistrust, and victimization, and they hold many inaccurate beliefs about crime and law enforcement (Gerbner et al., 1980; Shanahan & Morgan, 1999). This pattern of conceptions is known as the "Mean World Syndrome."

Message data say little directly about either the selfishness or altruism of people, and there are certainly no real-world statistics about the extent to which people can be trusted. Yet, cultivation studies show that long-term exposure to television tends to cultivate the image of a relatively mean and dangerous world. Compared to matching groups of lighter viewers, heavy viewers are more likely to say that most people "cannot be trusted," and most people are "just looking out for themselves" (Gerbner et al., 1980; Signorielli, 1990). Interestingly, those who see the world as a dangerous place may be more likely to hold strong views on law enforcement, to support punitive measures, and accept restrictions on civil liberties in the name of "security."

Other studies have dealt with assumptions about marriage and work. Signorielli (1993b) found that television cultivates realistic views about marriage but contradictory views about work. Heavy viewing adolescents were more likely to want high-status jobs and to earn a lot of money but also wanted to have their jobs be relatively easy with long vacations and time to do other things. In an earlier study, Signorielli (1991) found that television viewing cultivates conceptions that reflect the ambivalent presentation of marriage on television. Adolescents who watched more television were more likely to say they wanted to get married, to stay married to the same person for life, and to have children. Nevertheless, heavy viewers were more likely to believe that one sees so few good or happy marriages that one could question marriage as a way of life.

Cultivation is also relevant to politics and political communication. Entertainment-oriented programs (and indeed, most programs) have political implications that go beyond coverage of elections and campaigns. Fictional images of racial/ethnic minorities, sexual minorities, gender, corporations and other social institutions, politicians, the environment, and more, along with messages about individualism, consumption, materialism, equality, opportunity, power, and so on, are all relevant to understanding contemporary politics.

Cultivation theory argues that people "learn" a great deal both about politics and about issues with broad political relevance from television's stories. All programs are important, including political satire, because viewers do not necessarily make the distinction between sources of political information that may be considered legitimate (e.g., news) or illegitimate (e.g., comedy). Cultivation provides a mechanism whereby the totality of political information seen on television (and, theoretically, in blogs, on the Internet, etc.) can be related to people's conceptions about politics, in a broad sense. The findings of cultivation analysis tell us about the long-term, more general and pervasive consequences of cumulative exposure to television's messages, beyond those program elements typically defined as "political" (for example, how programs such as *Meet the Press*, *The Daily Show*, or *Saturday Night Live* influence people's ideas about politics or contribute to political knowledge) (Esralew & Young, 2012). In addition, a recent study found that films may contribute to people's political views (Adkins & Castle, 2014).

We thus find that today's combative environment of "in-your-face" politics on talk radio, cable news channels, Internet blogs, discussion boards, Facebook, Twitter, and YouTube videos may be cultivating a sense of political incivility that may ultimately impact policy and decision-making. It is not necessarily what is said, but how it is said that may cultivate people's views on politics. In addition, uncivil name calling, rather than thoughtful deliberation or understanding, is becoming the political norm (Hardy, 2012). Consequently, everything from political satire to strident talk shows seems to further polarize and fragment a highly divided electorate. Yet, cultivation analysis continues to find that heavy television viewers are more likely to say they are "moderate," and to avoid calling themselves either "liberal" or "conservative" (Gerbner, Gross, Morgan, & Signorielli, 1984).

Mainstreaming is particularly relevant for issues related to politics. For example, on many politically related topics, among light viewers the beliefs of liberals and conservatives are usually very different, and in expected ways. But when heavy television viewers are asked about these same topics, liberals tend to give responses that are more conservative and conservatives tend to give responses that are more liberal.

Even though heavy viewers are more likely to call themselves moderate (vs. liberal or conservative), their attitudes tend to converge toward conservative positions on social issues (such as gender, race, sexuality, freedom of speech, and so on) and toward liberal positions on economic issues. On economic issues, heavy viewers want the government to spend *more* on a variety of services and programs, even as they complain that their taxes are too high. In short, in relation to political issues, mainstreaming reflects the sense that television cultivates common perspectives, a relative homogenization that illustrates how television viewing has become the true melting pot of the American people and increasingly the world (Hardy, 2012).

Health is another area in which a cultivation approach is particularly relevant. Cultivation has typically focused on the long-term consequences of cumulative exposure to television's fictional messages and that most significant impacts of television involve stability, and resistance to change. Interestingly, in terms of health-related beliefs and behaviors, television's *lack* of change may be especially consequential. Over the years, content studies have shown that television characters are mostly healthy, that mental illness is a sign of deviance (and often accompanied by violence), that doctors are over-represented (and with many interesting and heroic characteristics), the miracles of medicine can easily and quickly cure any problem that arises, and that characters make very poor choices about the food they eat. Television's messages to children about nutrition are notoriously distorted toward bad options. Yet, television images show that despite the tendency toward consumption and promotion of unhealthy food options, television characters are sober, safe, and slim at all ages. Television's effects on health may be twofold. They may come from television's generally unhealthy messages but also reflect the physical impact of being a sedentary "couch potato" for many hours a day. For example, many studies have found strong relationships between amount of time spent watching television and obesity (Boulos, Vikre, Oppenheimer, Chang, & Kanarek, 2012; Carson & Janssen, 2012). Cultivation studies have also shown that those who watch more television are more complacent about food choices, drinking, and exercise.

The relationship between viewing and smoking is especially interesting. In the early days of television, programs included many images of people smoking and seemed to contribute to smoking adoption. Today, however, relationships are much less clear because smoking is less common on television (Kim & Shanahan, 2003; Shanahan & Scheufele, 2012). Studies have found that viewing of local TV news may promote fatalistic views about cancer and that spending a lot of time watching programs such as *Grey's Anatomy* shapes patients' predispositions about medical doctors (Quick, 2009). While there is little evidence that television viewing is a direct "cause" of disease, morbidity, or mortality, cultivation and related research have provided clear evidence of the importance of television for our perceptions about health, and often what we do as well. For instance, television viewing is associated with elevated risk of Type 2 diabetes (Allen, Melkus, & Chyun, 2011).

Once again the concept of *mainstreaming* suggests that television viewing may enhance similarities among otherwise divergent groups of people and may be particularly relevant for health-related conceptions. For example, those who watch more are generally more likely to say "I'm not concerned about weight; I eat and drink whatever I want," but this is much more pronounced among those who are least likely to express such nutritional complacency (younger or higher-income respondents). Those who are "already" complacent (lower-income, or older respondents) show weak or even negative associations. Television may therefore cultivate a neglect of good eating habits and healthy outlooks especially among those who "otherwise" are most attuned to healthier practices.

Recent Extensions of Cultivation

Today, there are many and various views about how cultivation should be studied, and include considerable ongoing exploration. This section briefly discusses some of these new developments and perspectives (for an extended treatment, see Morgan et al., 2012). Most of the studies and reviews reported here are supportive of the basic idea of cultivation, though many propose extensions and modifications to the methods originally suggested by Gerbner. Interestingly, there has been continued growth in the ways researchers conceptualize how we watch television and its consequences.

Cultivation studies have continued in the more traditional vein by updating and extending some of the classic dependent variables including images of crime (Custers & Van den Bulck, 2011) and sex roles (Harrison, 2003; Scharrer, 2012). Some of these studies have looked at the impacts of specific programs and genres, or the fear of events such as the 9/11 attacks. In addition, as perceptions and views about minorities have changed greatly during the past 40-plus years, the number of cultivation studies in this area has also grown (e.g., Mastro & Tukachinsky, 2012). For instance, Nisbet and Myers (2012), looking at the relationship between television viewing and views on homosexuality, utilized an innovative multi-level methodology that illustrates how social change, television depictions, and opinions can be analyzed over time. Along the same lines Hardy (2012), bringing a cultivation perspective to political communication, found that television viewing still tends to cultivate middle-of-the-road ideological self-perceptions.

One of the most fruitful and active areas of development in recent cultivation research has illuminated the cognitive mechanisms that "explain" the cultivation process. In an extensive series of studies, Shrum (see Shrum & Lee, 2012, for a comprehensive summary) has examined television's role in how people make first-order judgments (estimates of frequency and set size in the real world) and second-order judgments (attitudes, opinions, and feelings). Shrum and Lee (2012) posit that very different cognitive processes are at work when television viewing influences first- and second-order judgments. First-order cultivation judgments are memory-based, and formed through heuristic processes. Television images influence these judgments when someone recalls relevant information often seen in television programs. This occurs when people take cognitive short-cuts when forming a judgment; for heavy viewers, television-based information is more accessible, available, recent, and vivid. On the other hand, second-order cultivation judgments are formed in an "online" process, in which "the influence of television on judgment occurs during viewing, as information is processed" (Shrum & Lee, 2012, p. 162). Although "active" processing can counteract first-order cultivation (by making people aware of television as the source of their images), deep involvement or "transportation" in a story can enhance second-order cultivation.

Another issue in more recent cultivation research is whether the "realism" of television content matters for cultivation. Many scholars have examined the notion of "realism," particularly "perceived realism," as a critical component in understanding cultivation. While many researchers have assumed that only programs perceived as "realistic" would influence beliefs about the world, recent research shows that the situation is not that simple. For example, the research of Busselle and Bilandzic (2012) suggests that perceived realism is a default condition and that most content, even that recognized as fantasy, has some element of perceived realism. Consequently, the reasonable conclusion is that viewers carry impressions from television to their understanding of the real world.

"Classic" cultivation has always been concerned with the long-term and long-range effects of living with television in general. As Shanahan and Morgan (1999) note, it "is the pattern of settings, casting, social typing, action and related outcomes that cuts across program types and viewing modes and defines the world of television" (p. 30). Consequently, "orthodox" cultivation studies predict that those who watch more in general, television's heavy viewers, see more of these images and messages on a regular basis and that their views of social reality are influenced by the messages and images they see day in and day out, regardless of their individual selections or favorite programs.

Nevertheless, many researchers see genre as an important element in cultivation research. Some scholars, for example, believe that cultivation research should focus on different genres of programs because they assume that viewers watch more selectively than ritualistically (especially now that there are many more channels and many more options for viewing), and that different types of programs present diverse and distinct views of the world and social reality. Cohen and Weimann (2000) note that different genres, although typically driven by their own specific formulas, present viewers with diverse views about the world; crime dramas or action adventure programs, for example, focus on public life and the social order, while situation comedies, family dramas, and soap operas focus on domestic issues, family relationships, and friendships. Interestingly, Grabe and Drew (2007) suggest that one reason scholars examine possible genre-related differences in cultivation is that content analyses typically show variation in portrayals among genres. Situation and romantic comedies present different types of stories than crime dramas with the former genres having considerably less violence than the latter genres. In addition, Bilandzic and Busselle (2012) argue that genre's status as an important component of narrative implies that it is useful to look at cultivation within genres (such as crime programs). Among the many genres recently investigated are "sexually objectifying media" (Aubrey, 2006), music videos (Beullens, Roe, & Van den Bulck, 2012), and hospital dramas (Hetsroni, 2009).

Some researchers postulate that viewers' conceptions about fear and violence are specifically the result of viewing crime-related programming. Despite the knowledge that television's crime programs typically distort statistics about crime in society, several studies show relationships between conceptions about crime and the viewing of crime programs. For example, Holbert, Shah, and Kwak (2004), using a national probability sample, found that viewing television news and police reality programs was related to measures of fear of crime but that viewing crime dramas was not. This analysis also found that non-fiction viewing (such as police reality programs) was more strongly related to conceptions of social reality than the viewing of fictional crime dramas. They interpreted this difference as due to the increased perceived realism of the police reality programs. (Many other genre-based studies have produced a variety of genre-related findings.)

It may not be surprising that there are many instances in which exposure to very specific media, particularly specific genres of television programs, is related to having very specific views about the world and social reality. The cultivation perspective, however, focuses more on people's general viewing habits. Even in today's fragmented viewing world, viewing more television tends to mean greater exposure to what Gerbner conceived as the message "system," not just a collection of disparate and idiosyncratic viewing experiences. Patterns and similarities across all viewing genres are what matter most for the idea of cultivation. Even if people state that they have a preference for watching a specific genre (as we all do), overall media use normally encompasses viewing many different types of programs (as well as using other media such as magazines and newspapers). Although someone may profess to have a television diet consisting primarily of viewing crime programs, such as the *Law and Order* or *CSI* series, the images to which they are exposed may go far beyond just crime and violence. For example, while *Law and Order* and *CSI* are based primarily on the investigation of crime, these programs also offer images of interpersonal and family relationships as well as other thematic elements showing how the world works. Consequently, heavy viewers of these programs will not only learn about crime and violence, they will also learn important life lessons about how people interact with each other.

An interesting innovation in cultivation analysis comes from Riddle (2012), who has developed a measure to assess viewing across a person's lifetime. Her research posits that because cultivation is concerned with systematic, *long-term* exposure to television, it is critical to assess how people have watched television in the past, regardless of their current viewing habits. Riddle has developed a measure of past viewing practices and has found that measures of cumulative, lifetime exposure to television are more strongly related to conceptions and beliefs than are measures of current exposure levels. Consequently, the historical over-time dimension may turn out to be a very important component of cultivation research.

Among the more recent developments in cultivation research are interesting linkages of cultivation with other theories of mass communication. For example, Hetsroni and Lowenstein (2012) suggest a model to link cultivation with agenda-setting research. They look at both theories in terms of first- and second-order media effects, hypothesizing a single process that might unite the two. In addition, Diefenbach and West (2012) looked at the intersection of cultivation with the third-person effect. They posit that because cultivation is an example of a media effect that people can think about (thus generating possible expectations about how others might be affected), looking at these two approaches in tandem makes considerable sense, and they present data to support this view. Shanahan and Sheufele (2012) examine theoretical and empirical intersections between cultivation and the spiral of silence. Cultivation is also being examined through the lens of the critical cultural theorist. Ruddock (2012) links cultivation with ritual theory within the focus of digital sports media and fandom. Interestingly, Ruddock's work suggests that the idea of cultivation may become even more relevant as new media emerge.

Ruddock's argument notwithstanding, change in the media environment since cultivation was developed has been dramatic, and may seem to challenge or invalidate many fundamental assumptions of cultivation analysis. While the way we now receive our "stories" has changed, many aspects of their content have not and, in some ways, today's stories have become even more homogeneous. In short, media (no matter what the venue) are dominated by transnational, global conglomerates whose goal is to maintain a large share of the audience and increase profits. Indeed, as there are more and more channels and more and more outlets, the number of transnational companies continues to become smaller and smaller. Consequently, the smaller number of production venues may result in a more homogeneous than heterogeneous media environment. Cultivation has always been concerned with the broad underlying elements of content and how audiences interact with these messages. Indeed, as Shanahan and Morgan (1999) note, "the content of messages is more germane than the technology with which they are delivered" (p. 201). Watching a television program on a laptop, tablet, smartphone, or any other technology is still "watching television."

Cultivation continues to be a theory that is frequently tested, cited, and scrutinized, as it continues to evolve. Morgan et al. (2012) summarize the evolution of cultivation during the past 20 years. Many of the ideas for the future of cultivation suggested by Signorielli and Morgan (1990) have come to fruition (and many issues and problems they noted seem to be not so important anymore). Yet, as with any workable and viable theory, there are still important insights to be gained as to where cultivation research can go in the future. Cultivation's stature as one of the most well-known and well-used theoretical approaches in communication is justified, and this chapter should provide a useful view of where the research stands at this juncture. It will be interesting to see how research on cultivation will evolve in the next 20 years.

Note

1   A complete bibliography of cultural indicators work is located at http://people.umass. edu/mmorgan/CulturalIndicatorsBibliography.pdf

References

Adkins, T., & Castle, J. (2014). Moving pictures? Experimental evidence of cinematic influence on political attitudes. *Social Science Quarterly*, *95*(5), 1230–1244.

Allen, N. A., Melkus, G. D., & Chyun, D. A. (2011). Physiological and behavorial factors related to physical activity in Black women with type 2 diabetes mellitus. *Journal of Transcultural Nursing*, *53*(4–5), 299–302.

Aubrey, J. S. (2006). Effects of sexually objectifying media on self-objectification and body surveillance in undergraduates: Results of a 2-year panel study. *Journal of Communication*, *56*(2), 366–386.

Beullens, K., Roe, K., & Van den Bulck, J. (2012). Music video viewing as a marker of driving after the consumption of alcohol. *Substance Use and Misuse*, *47*(2), 155–165.

Bilandzic, H., & Busselle, R. (2012). A narrative perspective on genre-specific cultivation. In M. Morgan, J. Shanahan, & N. Signorielli (Eds.), *Living with television now: Advances in cultivation theory and research* (pp. 261–285). New York, NY: Peter Lang.

Boulos, R., Vikre, E. K., Oppenheimer, S., Chang, H., & Kanarek, R. B. (2012). ObesiTV: How television is influencing the obesity epidemic. *Physiology and Behavior*, *107*(1), 146–153.

Bryant, J., & Miron, D. (2004). Theory and research in mass communication. *Journal of Communication*, *54*, 662–704.

Busselle, R., & Bilandzic, H. (2012). Cultivation and the perceived realism of stories. In M. Morgan, J. Shanahan, & N. Signorielli (Eds.), *Living with television now: Advances in cultivation theory and research* (pp. 168–186). New York, NY: Peter Lang.

Carson, V., & Janssen, I. (2012). The mediating effects of dietary habits on the relationship between television viewing and body mass index among youth. *Pediatric Obesity*, *7*(5), 391–398.

Cohen, J., & Weimann, G. (2000). Cultivation revisited: Some genres have some effects on some viewers. *Communication Reports*, *13*(2), 99–114.

Custers, K., & Van den Bulck, J. (2011). Mediators of the association between television viewing and fear of crime: Perceived personal risk and perceived ability to cope. *Poetics*, *39*, 107–124.

Diefenbach, D. L., & West, M. D. (2012). Cultivation and the third-person effect. In M. Morgan, J. Shanahan, & N. Signorielli (Eds.), *Living with television now: Advances in cultivation theory and research* (pp. 329–346). New York, NY: Peter Lang.

Doob, A., & Macdonald, G. (1979). Television viewing and fear of victimization: Is the relationship causal? *Journal of Personality and Social Psychology*, *37*(2), 170–179.

Esralaw, S., & Young, D. (2012). The influence of parodies on mental models: Exploring the Tina Fay, Sarah Palin Phenomenon. *Communication Quarterly*, *60*, 338–352.

Gerbner, G. (1970, March). Cultural indicators: The case of violence in television drama. *Annals of the American Academy of Political and Social Science*, *388*, 69–81.

Gerbner, G. (1973). Cultural indicators: The third voice. In G. Gerbner, L. Gross, & W. Melody (Eds.), *Communications technology and social policy* (pp. 555–573). New York, NY: John Wiley & Sons.

Gerbner, G., & Gross, L. (1976). Living with television: The violence profile. *Journal of Communication*, *26*(2), 173–199.

Gerbner, G., Gross, L., Morgan, M., & Signorielli, N. (1980). The "mainstreaming" of America: Violence profile No. 11. *Journal of Communication*, *30*(3), 10–29.

Gerbner, G., Gross, L., Morgan, M., & Signorielli, N. (1984). Political correlates of television viewing. *Public Opinion Quarterly*, *48*(1), 283–300.

Grabe, M. E., & Drew, D. (2007). Crime cultivation: Comparisons across media genres and channels. *Journal of Broadcasting and Electronic Media*, *51*(1), 147–171.

Hardy, B. W. (2012). Cultivation of political attitudes in the new media environment. In M. Morgan, J. Shanahan, & N. Signorielli (Eds.), *Living with television now: Advances in cultivation theory and research* (pp. 101–119). New York, NY: Peter Lang.

Harrison, K. (2003). Television viewers' ideal body proportions: The case of the curvaceously thin woman. *Sex Roles: A Journal of Research*, *48*, 255–264.

Hetsroni, A. (2009). If you must be hospitalized, television is not the place: Diagnoses, survival rates and demographic characteristics of patients in TV hospital dramas. *Communication Research Reports*, *26*(4), 311–322.

Hetsroni, A., & Lowenstein, H. (2012). Cultivation and agenda-setting: Conceptual and empirical intersections. In M. Morgan, J. Shanahan, & N. Signorielli (Eds.), *Living with television now: Advances in cultivation theory and research* (pp. 307–328). New York, NY: Peter Lang.

Hirsch, P. (1980). The "Scary World" of the nonviewer and other anomalies: A reanalysis of Gerbner et al.'s findings of cultivation analysis, Part I. *Communication Research*, *7*(4), 403–456.

Holbert, R. L., Shah, D. V., & Kwak, N. (2004). Fear, authority, and justice: Crime-related TV viewing and endorsements of capital punishment and gun ownership. *Journalism and Mass Communication Quarterly*, *81*(2), 343–363.

Hughes, M. (1980). The fruits of cultivation analysis: A re-examination of the effects of television watching on fear of victimization, alienation, and the approval of violence. *Public Opinion Quarterly*, *44*(3), 287–302.

Kim, S., & Shanahan, J. (2003). Stigmatizing smokers: Public sentiment toward cigarette smoking and its relationship to smoking behaviors. *Journal of Health Communication, 8*, 347–367.

Mastro, D., & Tukachinsky, R. (2012). Cultivation of perceptions of marginalized groups. In M. Morgan, J. Shanahan, & N. Signorielli (Eds.), *Living with television now: Advances in cultivation theory and research* (pp. 38–60). New York, NY: Peter Lang.

Morgan, M. (1982). Television and adolescents' sex-role stereotypes: A longitudinal study. *Journal of Personality and Social Psychology, 43*(5), 947–955.

Morgan, M., Shanahan, J., & Signorielli, N. (2009). Growing up with television: Cultivation processes. In J. Bryant & M. Oliver (Eds.), *Media effects: Advances in theory and research* (3rd ed., pp. 34–49). Hillsdale, NJ: Lawrence Erlbaum Associates.

Morgan, M., Shanahan, J., & Signorielli, N. (Eds.). (2012). *Living with television now: Advances in cultivation theory and research.* New York, NY: Peter Lang.

Nisbet, E. C., & Myers, T. A. (2012). Cultivating tolerance of homosexuals. In M. Morgan, J. Shanahan, & N. Signorielli (Eds.), *Living with television now: Advances in cultivation theory and research* (pp. 61–80). New York, NY: Peter Lang.

Potter, W. J. (1993). Cultivation theory and research: A conceptual critique. *Human Communication Research, 19*, 564–601.

Potter, W. J. (1994). Cultivation theory and research: A methodological critique. *Journalism Monographs, 147*, 1–35.

Potter, W. J., & Riddle, K. (2007). A content analysis of the media effects literature. *Journalism and Mass Communication Quarterly, 84*(1), 90–104.

Quick, B. (2009). The effects of viewing *Grey's Anatomy* on perceptions of doctors and patient satisfaction. *Journal of Broadcasting and Electronic Media, 53*(1), 38–55.

Riddle, K. (2012). Developing a lifetime television exposure scale: The importance of television viewing habits during childhood. In M. Morgan, J. Shanahan, & N. Signorielli (Eds.), *Living with television now: Advances in cultivation theory and research* (pp. 286–306). New York, NY: Peter Lang.

Ruddock, A. (2012). Cultivation analysis and cultural studies: Ritual, performance, and media influence. In M. Morgan, J. Shanahan, & N. Signorielli (Eds.), *Living with television now: Advances in cultivation theory and research* (pp. 366–388). New York, NY: Peter Lang.

Scharrer, E. (2012). Television and gender roles: Cultivating conceptions of self and others. In M. Morgan, J. Shanahan, & N. Signorielli (Eds.), *Living with television now: Advances in cultivation theory and research* (pp. 81–100). New York, NY: Peter Lang.

Shanahan, J., & Morgan, M. (1999). *Television and its viewers: Cultivation theory and research.* Cambridge, UK: Cambridge University Press.

Shanahan, J., & Scheufele, D. (2012). Cultivation and the spiral of silence: Theoretical and empirical intersections. In M. Morgan, J. Shanahan, & N. Signorielli (Eds.), *Living with television now: Advances in cultivation theory and research* (pp. 347–365). New York, NY: Peter Lang.

Shrum, L. J., & Lee, J. (2012). Multiple processes underlying cultivation effects: How cultivation works depends on the types of beliefs being cultivated. In M. Morgan, J. Shanahan, & N. Signorielli (Eds.), *Living with television now: Advances in cultivation theory and research* (pp. 147–167). New York, NY: Peter Lang.

Signorielli, N. (1990). Television's mean and dangerous world: A continuation of the cultural indicators perspective. In N. Signorielli & M. Morgan (Eds.), *Cultivation analysis: New directions in media effects research* (pp. 85–106). Newbury Park, CA: Sage.

Signorielli, N. (1991). Adolescents and ambivalence towards marriage: A cultivation analysis. *Youth and Society, 23*(1), 121–149.

Signorielli, N. (1993a). Sex roles and stereotyping on television. *Adolescent Medicine: State of the Art Reviews, 4*(3), 551–561.

Signorielli, N. (1993b). Television and adolescents' perceptions about work. *Youth and Society*, *24*(3), 314–341.

Signorielli, N. (2003). Violence on television 1993–2001: Has the picture changed? *Journal of Broadcasting and Electronic Media*, *47*(1), 36–57.

Signorielli, N., & Morgan, M. (Eds.). (1990). *Cultivation analysis: New directions in media effects research*. Newbury Park, CA: Sage.

Wober, J. (1990). Does television cultivate the British? Late 80s evidence. In N. Signorielli & M. Morgan (Eds.), *Cultivation analysis: New directions in media effects research* (pp. 207–224). Newbury Park, CA: Sage.

27

Internet Addiction

Petra Vondráčková and David Šmahel

Masaryk University

Internet addiction can be defined as overuse of the Internet leading to impairment of an individual's psychological state (both mental and emotional), as well as their scholastic, occupational, and social interactions (Beard & Wolf, 2001). Young (1998b) describes Internet addiction as any online-related compulsive behavior that completely dominates the addict's life, interferes with normal living, and causes severe stress to family, friends, loved ones, and one's work environment. Other researchers, however, do not agree with using the term Internet addiction and use several other terms, such as Internet addiction disorder (Chou, Condron, & Belland, 2005), compulsive Internet use (Black, Belsare, & Schlosser, 1999), Internet pathological use (Davis, 2001; Morahan-Martin & Schumacher, 2000), problematic Internet use (Beard, 2005; Caplan, 2003), and Internet dependency (Chen, Chen, & Paul, 2001; Wang, 2001), each of which reflects a slightly different conception of this behavior. Starcevic (2013) asserts that the term Internet addiction should be abandoned because individuals do not usually get addicted to the Internet in general, but to specific online activities; therefore, being addicted to the Internet implies addiction to a delivery mechanism or to a medium for achieving something. He states that it would be more accurate and appropriate to refer to specific activities presumed to be addictive (e.g., online gaming addiction or cybersex addiction).

Some of the most typical online activities related to Internet addiction include online gaming such as massive multiplayer online role-playing games (MMORPGs), excessive online communication (email, chat rooms, social networking), cybersex activity overload (visiting online pornographic sites and initiating cybersex relationships), and online gambling (betting via the Internet) (Šmahel, Ševčíková, Blinka, & Veselá, 2009; Subrahmanyam & Šmahel, 2011). Due to limited space, this chapter does not focus specifically on any of these activities. Rather, we will first present a case study, which will provide a better understanding of the phenomenon of Internet addiction, followed by a historical overview of the Internet addiction phenomenon and its place in the context of mental health. Next, we will introduce the contributions of major researchers who, focused on defining its core components, designed measurement scales and diagnostic criteria focusing on the main areas of research in this field: the major surveys regarding prevalence rates and the correlates of Internet addiction. In the last section, we will introduce basic approaches to the treatment of Internet addiction.

The Wiley Handbook of Psychology, Technology, and Society, First Edition. Edited by Larry D. Rosen, Nancy A. Cheever, and L. Mark Carrier.

A Case Study of Internet Addiction

To provide an understanding of this topic, we present a short case study of a 35-year-old man ("Denis"), who sought the help of a clinical psychologist because of Internet addiction (Vondráčková, 2012). The immediate reason was constant quarreling with his wife over his playing of the online game *Wild Tribe*. Before the session, Denis completed an Internet addiction screening in a self-help program developed by the Department of Addictology.[1] He received a high score on general Internet use and also when answering questions concerning only the game itself. He set himself a target to stop or reduce his time spent playing the online game and to learn more about the potential reasons for his overuse of the Internet.

As an IT specialist, Denis spent a lot of time in front of the computer. He discovered the online game a year prior to his visit to the therapist, and continued playing since he found the game interesting. His goal was to understand the principle of the game, why others like playing it so much, and what the game's optimal economic strategies were. Initially, he created an account in one game world (the online environment where the online game takes place); later on he created accounts in two other game worlds. Even though he ultimately decided to leave one game world to have more time for his everyday life, he still spent a lot of time playing, the extent of which depended considerably on what was happening in the game. When it was necessary to resolve conflicts in the game, he could spend up to eight hours a day playing. His normal day with the game was as follows: in the morning he would spend between half an hour and one hour playing before going to work. At work he would check on the game's progress several times a day. Sometimes these checks would last up to 30 minutes, or even an hour, which would make him feel guilty since he then did not have enough time to take care of his work tasks. In the evening he would sit behind his laptop again for two to four hours. He would naturally spend a lot more time playing during the weekend. Logging into the game calmed him down and helped him forget about problems at work. He had frequent quarrels with his wife since he neglected his family and internal conflicts such as slacking at work. Denis also repeatedly tried to quit the game, but was always persuaded to return to the game by other online players. Denis reported that he sometimes felt grumpy or irritable if he was not able to be online, but he attributed these feelings to the fact that he promptly needed to solve some problem in the game rather than to withdrawal symptoms. When he was not online, he was often thinking about what was going on in the game, mainly the conflicts and strategies that would be the most important at that particular moment.

During his game play he met Linda, who took an important role in his online world. He was in close contact with her during his playing and gradually their relationship became quite strong. Every day they discussed not only the progress in the game but also their personal lives. Linda lived in another town, was married, and had three children. They even met once during one of Denis's business trips. They always remained just friends but their partners did not know about their meeting. What Denis probably liked the most about this relationship was that he had someone in this online game who listened to him, supported him, and accepted him. Several times he wanted to leave the game because of conflicts and lack of comprehension from other players, but Linda always managed to convince him to stay. He said that she was practically the last reason for him to stay in the game. About six months later Linda's husband found out about his wife's close online contact with Denis, which infuriated him, and Linda had to stop playing. Denis then lost his last motivation to stay in the game (Vondráčková, 2012).

Historical Background

The phenomenon of problematic computer use has been discussed since the late 1980s. In 1989, Margaret A. Shotton published the book *Computer Addiction? A Study of Computer Dependency*, presenting an investigation of the syndrome of computer addiction based on case studies of volunteers from throughout the United Kingdom who considered themselves to be dependent upon computers. She arrived at the conclusion that "computer dependency" existed but that it was not a clinical pathology, and that it did not constitute a threat to computer users themselves (Shotton, 2003).

The concept of Internet addiction was introduced by the New York psychiatrist Ivan Goldberg in 1995. Although his aim was to describe the diagnostic criteria of this new mental disorder as a joke for the amusement of the online community, the name and description of the disorder has been used ever since. In 1996, the American clinical psychologist Kimberley Young (1998a) published the results of a two-year study of Internet behavior and misuse, and was the first one to place the phenomenon of Internet addiction in a clinical context. This study received wide public attention, and the popular and professional debate surrounding Internet addiction grew (Reed, 2002). Young founded the Center for Internet Addiction, which studies various aspects of the condition. She investigated the basic aspects of Internet addiction, which were later further developed by other researchers. Young distinguished the following basic types of Internet addiction: online gaming, online gambling, online affairs, compulsive web surfing, and cybersex-cyberporn. She developed the Internet Addiction Test, designed the first diagnostic criteria of Internet addiction, and introduced treatment approaches based on cognitive-behavior principles (Young, 1998a, 1998b, 2007). Another important contribution to the concept of Internet addiction was made by Griffiths (2000a, 2000b), who defined the core components of Internet addiction: salience, mood modification, tolerance, withdrawal symptoms, conflict, and relapse. Both Young's test and Griffiths' components will be described in more detail in the next section of this chapter.

Since the 1990s, Internet addiction has attracted the attention of professionals around the world, mainly from developing and developed countries with wide Internet access. Some countries such as the United States, China, South Korea, and Germany even began developing the first specialized centers focused solely on this phenomenon (Block, 2008).

Internet Addiction and Diagnostic Mental Disorder Manuals

A majority of experts (psychologists, psychiatrists, and addiction-focused experts) include Internet addiction in the category of non-substance or behavioral addiction together with pathological gambling, compulsive shopping, sex addiction, and eating disorders, due to its similarities with drug addiction with respect to similar genetic

(Grant, Brewer, & Potenza, 2006; Potenza, 2006), neurobiological (Grant et al., 2006; Han, Kim, Lee, & Renshaw, 2012), personal (Goudriaan, Oosterlaan, de Beurs, & van den Brink, 2006; Potenza, 2006), and clinical characteristics (Blanco, Moreyra, Nunes, Sáiz-Ruiz, & Ibáñez, 2001; Grant et al., 2006; Hall & Parsons, 2001). All the above-mentioned addictions are included in DSM-5[2] or ICD-10,[3] except for compulsive shopping and Internet addiction. Internet addiction was considered for inclusion in the official DSM-5 diagnoses, but the final decision was not to include it. However, Internet gaming disorder (compulsive playing of online games) is classified in the DSM-5 appendix with a goal of encouraging additional research (APA, 2013). According to Pies (2009), the main reasons against Internet addiction's inclusion in the DSM-5's list of mental disorders are that symptoms of Internet addiction are likely to be the symptoms of other disorders, such as depression or obsessive-compulsive disorders, and that creating a separate category for this pathology will even further expand an already fast-growing list of supposed "disorders" and thus undermine the public's trust in psychiatric diagnosis.

Identification of Internet Addiction

In the last few years, there have been several proposals for standard diagnostic criteria for Internet addiction. In most cases, although some researchers have added or removed individual elements, most researchers have adapted the DSM pathological gambling criteria for identifying Internet addiction. The best-known diagnostic criteria of Internet addiction were proposed by Young (1998b). To confirm the presence of Internet addiction, five or more of the following points must be present: (1) The person is preoccupied with the Internet, thinks about online activities or anticipates the next session on the Internet; (2) the person needs to use the Internet for increasing amounts of time in order to achieve satisfaction; (3) the person has made unsuccessful efforts to control, cut back, or stop Internet use; (4) the person is restless, moody, depressed, or irritable when attempting to cut down or end Internet use; (5) the person stays online longer than originally intended; (6) the person has jeopardized or risked the loss of a significant relationship, job, educational or career opportunity because of Internet use; (7) the person has lied to family members or others to conceal the extent of their involvement with the Internet; (8) the person uses the Internet as a way of escaping from problems or of relieving a dysphoric mood (e.g., feelings of helplessness, anxiety, and depression).

Beard and Wolf (2001) proposed a modification to Young's criteria. They suggested that the first five criteria should be required for a diagnosis of Internet addiction, since these could be met without any impairment in the person's daily functioning. According to them, the last three criteria should be separated from the others since they impact the pathological Internet user's ability to cope and function and also influence her/his interaction with other people. Therefore at least one of the last three criteria should be present to diagnose Internet addiction. Griffiths (2000a) suggested the following six basic components of Internet addiction, where a high score in all six dimensions suggests that the person is addicted:

a   *Salience*: When the particular online activity turns out to be the most important activity in the person's life and governs their thinking (e.g., imagining being online when not), feelings (e.g., craving to play a particular online game), and behavior (e.g., chatting with online friends all the time, neglecting basic human needs such as eating and sleeping).

b   *Mood modification*: A subjective experience influenced by the pursued online activity (e.g., experiencing a tranquilizing feeling of "escape" or "numbing" and a feeling of irritation when it is not possible to be online).

c   *Tolerance*: The process whereby increasing amounts of the particular online activity are required to achieve the former effects.

d   *Withdrawal symptoms*: Unpleasant feelings, states, and/or physical effects (e.g., the shakes, moodiness, irritability) that come about when the specific online activity is discontinued or suddenly limited.

e   *Conflict*: Disagreements between the addicts and those around them (interpersonal conflict) or from within the individuals themselves (intrapersonal conflict) associated with the online activity.

f   *Relapse*: Tendency for repeated decline into earlier usage patterns of the online activity, and for even the most extreme patterns typical at the height of the addiction to be quickly restored after a period of relative control.

Inspired by the aforementioned core components and diagnostic criteria, experts have constructed various methods for assessing Internet addiction. The above-mentioned first effort to identify Internet addiction was made by Young (1998a), who developed a brief diagnostic questionnaire based on the DSM-IV criteria of pathological gambling. She later used the data gathered via this questionnaire to design the 20-item Internet Addiction Test (IAT) (Young, 1998a). There also exist other questionnaires, such as CIAS (the Chen Internet Addiction Scale), OCS (the Online Cognition Scale), and IRABI (Internet-Related Addictive Behavior Inventory) (Brenner, 1997; Davis, Flett, & Besser, 2002; Ko, Yen, Chen, Chen, & Yen, 2005). However, it is important to note that psychologists and counselors should be careful when using the questionnaires of Young and others, since these cannot reliably distinguish between addiction and excessive Internet use. The question of criteria objectivity and validity of self-reported questionnaires also remains open. Therefore the diagnosis of Internet addiction should be based mainly on a clinical interview (Young, 2011).

Prevalence Rates of Internet Addiction

Many surveys focusing on the prevalence of Internet addiction have been carried out, resulting in prevalence rates that vary widely from study to study, as can be seen in Table 27.1. The disadvantage of these surveys is that various definitions of Internet addiction were employed, different assessment methods were used, and the number and character of the surveys' participants also differed. In order to determine prevalence, many studies used samples of high school and college students (Cao & Su, 2007; Zhang, Amos, & McDowell, 2008) and some used Internet-based surveys (Wang, 2001; Young, 1998b). A possible explanation for measuring prevalence among adolescents may be the assumption that Internet addiction is primarily a problem affecting young people, as well as the fact that students are the most easily available group for researchers. Nevertheless, all the aforementioned facts strongly affect the validity of prevalence estimates.

Table 27.1 Review of surveys on the prevalence of Internet addiction.

Survey (year of publication)	Location	Internet addiction measures	Sample (years)	Prevalence (%)
Chou & Hsiao (2000)	Taiwan	Chinese-Internet-Related Addictive Behavior Inventory version II (C-IRABI-II)	910 college students	5.9
Johansson & Gotestam (2004)	Norway	Diagnostic Questionnaire for Internet Addiction (YDQ)	3,237 respondents (aged 12–18)	2
Niemz et al. (2005)	UK	Pathological Internet Use Scale	Online, 371 students	18
Aboujaoude et al. (2006)	U.S.	Questionnaire from diagnostic criteria for impulse control disorders, obsessive-compulsive disorder, and substance abuse	2,513 respondents (aged 18 or over)	0.3–0.7
Pallanti et al. (2006)	Italy	Internet Addiction Scale (IAS)	275 adolescents (aged 14–18)	5.4
Cao & Su (2007)	China	Diagnostic Questionnaire for Internet Addiction (YDQ)	2,620 students (aged 12–18)	2.4
Zhang et al. (2008)	China	Adapted questionnaire from already used questionnaires	143 college students	14
	U.S.		171 college students	4
Park et al. (2008)	South Korea	Internet Addiction Scale (IAS)	903 adolescents	10.7
Ni et al. (2009)	China	Internet Addiction Test (IAT)	3,557 first-year university students	6.44
Huang et al. (2009)	China	Diagnostic Questionnaire for Internet Addiction (YDQ)	4,400 college students	9.58
Bakken et al. (2009)	Norway	Diagnostic Questionnaire for Internet Addiction (YDQ)	3,399 respondents (aged 16–74)	1
Šmahel, Vondráčková, et al. (2009)	Czech Republic	Addiction scale derived from other questionnaires	1,381 respondents (aged over 12)	3.4
Fu et al. (2010)	Hong Kong	Diagnostic Questionnaire for Internet Addiction (YDQ)	Adolescents (aged 15–19)	6.7
Villella et al. (2011)	Italy	Internet Addiction Test (IAT)	2,853 high school students	1.2
Lin et al. (2011)	Taiwan	Chen Internet Addiction Scale – Revision (CIAS-R)	3,616 college students	15.3

Study	Region	Addiction scale	Sample	Prevalence
Šmahel & Blinka (2012)	Europe (survey in 25 countries)	Addiction scale derived from other questionnaires	19,834 children (aged 11–16)	1
Wu et al. (2013)	China	Young's Internet Addiction Test, Chinese version (YIAT-C)	1,101 adolescents (aged 12–14)	13.5
Tsitsika et al. (2013)	EU	Internet Addiction Test (IAT)	13,300 adolescents (aged 14–17)	1.2
Durkee et al. (2012)	EU	Questionnaire for Internet Addiction (YDQ)	11,956 adolescents (aged 14–15)	4.4
Wang et al. (2013)	China	Diagnostic Questionnaire (DQ) for Internet addiction	10,988 adolescents (aged 13–23)	7.5

Internet addiction prevalence rates among children and adolescents range from 1–2% (Šmahel & Blinka, 2012; Villella et al., 2011) to 15.3% (Lin, Ko, & Wu, 2011). In studies where representative samples of the whole population were selected, the prevalence rates tended to be lower, 0.3% to 0.7% (Aboujaoude, Koran, Gamel, Large, & Serpe, 2006) and 3.4% (Šmahel, Vondráčková, Blinka, & Godoy-Etcheverry, 2009), than in samples of children and adolescents. A high-quality study from Aboujaoude et al. (2006) in the United States involved a random telephone survey of 2,513 adults aged 18 and above. There the prevalence ranged from 0.3% to 0.7%. Representative studies also revealed that adolescents have higher scores in addiction tests than adults (Šmahel, Vondráčková, et al., 2009).

When looking at demographic characteristics, Internet addiction appears to be more common among men than women (Durkee et al., 2012; Niemz, Griffiths, & Banyard, 2005). Morahan-Martin and Schumacher (2000) explain the preponderance of men by the fact that men are more likely to express interest in information technologies in general, and furthermore to express interest in Internet applications with an addictive potential, such as games, pornography, and gambling. Among children and adolescents, a large European study (EU Kids Online, with more than 19,000 respondents) also revealed gender differences in terms of prevalence rates, but gender did not predict Internet addiction in linear regressions (Šmahel & Blinka, 2012). This means that gender differences could probably be often explained by other variables. Regarding age, as previously mentioned, the highest prevalence of Internet addiction is among the younger population, in particular those aged 16–29 years (Bakken, Wenzel, Gotestam, Johansson, & Oren, 2009; Šmahel, Vondráčková, et al., 2009).

Regarding prevalence across countries in the world, this is a difficult comparison to make due to different methodology used in individual studies. But it seems that the highest rates are among adolescents in Asian countries such as China, South Korea, or Taiwan where estimates are about 6–15% (Lin et al., 2011; Ni, Yan, Chen, & Liu, 2009), whereas in Europe and North America the estimates in this population are lower, specifically 1–5% (Durkee et al., 2012; Šmahel & Blinka, 2012; Villella et al., 2011). This has been confirmed in the study by Zhang et al. (2008), which was conducted on U.S. and Chinese students. Chinese students showed higher prevalence (14%) in comparison to U.S. students (4%). Unfortunately, it is hard to find studies in the aforementioned Asian countries carried out on the general population.

Three studies have been carried out which mapped the prevalence rates among adolescents in European countries. Durkee et al. (2012) mapped prevalence among 10 European Union (EU) countries and Israel and found that the highest prevalence was in Israel (11.8%) and Slovenia (5.8%), while the lowest prevalence was in Italy (1.2%) and Hungary (1.6%). Tsitsika et al. (2013) studied prevalence in seven EU countries and found that Spain and Romania showed the highest prevalence (1.5% and 1.7%), whereas the lowest prevalence was among adolescents in Germany and Iceland (0.9% and 0.8%). The aforementioned EU Kids Online study investigated children between 11 and 16 years of age in 25 countries and revealed that the highest pathological level of Internet addiction was in Cyprus (5%), but several countries had prevalence rates under 0.5% (Belgium, Estonia, France, the Netherlands, Finland, Poland, Slovenia, Spain, and Sweden).

Correlates of Internet Addiction

Research shows that Internet addiction is accompanied by problems in other areas of an individual's life such as school, work, relationships, health, and finances.

School or Work

Students with high online addiction scores showed learning difficulties, resulting in poor grades, missed classes, and problems paying attention during classes because of sleep deprivation (Chen & Peng, 2008; Douglas et al., 2008; Wainer et al., 2008). In the case of working people, Internet addiction occurred alongside lower efficiency, which in some cases resulted in job loss (Vondráčková, Vacek, & Svobodová, 2014; Young, 1998b).

Relationships

Individuals with symptoms of Internet addiction frequently reported low self-esteem, introversion, and extreme shyness, leading to low social skills, loneliness, and social isolation; the correlates connected to Internet addiction were high sensation seeking and deficient self-regulation (Caplan & High, 2011; Chen & Peng, 2008; Lam, Peng, Mai, & Jing, 2009; Mehroof & Griffiths, 2010; Morahan-Martin & Schumacher, 2000; Yang & Tung, 2007). Caplan (2003) and Liu and Kuo (2007) even claim that low social skills play the main role in the genesis and maintenance of Internet addiction. Some surveys have confirmed that Internet addiction could have an impact on relationships, as spending more time online may result in impatience, arguments, and strain in people's offline relationships (Lin & Tsai, 2002; Yang & Tung, 2007). A study on young people revealed associations between having online friendships and online addiction (Šmahel, Brown, & Blinka, 2012).

Mental and Physical Health

Chien Chou (2001), in his online interview study of college students, reported that the major physical complaints stemming from students' Internet use were eyesight deterioration and sleep deprivation. Among others, the college students mentioned sore shoulders, backs, hands and fingers, and fatigue. Suhail and Bargees (2006) focused on the effects of excessive Internet use in their study and found that students most frequently mentioned physical problems such as migraine/headaches, sleep disruption, and backaches because of Internet use. Vondráčková et al. (2014) added poor care of physical condition, such as eating irregularities and poor personal hygiene, to these negative consequences.

Studies focused on identifying psychiatric comorbidity of individuals with Internet addiction report high levels of anxiety, depression, and frequent incidents of mood disorders, anxiety disorders, impulse control disorders, substance disorders, and attention-deficit/hyperactivity disorders (Bozkurt, Coskun, Ayaydin, Adak, & Zoroglu, 2013; Jang, Hwang, & Choi, 2008; Ko, Yen, Yen, Chen, & Chen, 2012; Yoo et al., 2004). Some researchers suggest that Internet addiction can be associated with cyberbullying (Ko, Yen, Yen, Lin, & Yang, 2007), but also with other online risks, most typically with meeting strangers online, and less often with high sexual exposure (Šmahel & Blinka, 2012).

Financial Problems

In the context of financial losses, perpetual computer upgrades and phone bills related to Internet service fees were often mentioned (Douglas et al., 2008; Young, 1998b). This is probably an older problem, prior to "flat rates" and permanent online connections becoming widely available. Many reports mention great financial losses in the context of online gambling (Griffiths, 2000a) and cybersex addiction (Griffiths, 2011). Financial problems can also be caused by job loss, as pointed out above.

Treatment of Internet Addiction

With the increasing popularization of Internet addiction, health professionals have begun to publish treatment approaches for this target group (Kim, 2008; Orzack, Voluse, Wolf, & Hennen, 2006; van Rooij, Zinn, Schoenmakers, & van de Mheen, 2012; Young, 2007). Unfortunately, the design and reporting quality of Internet addiction treatment studies are not optimal due to various limitations, including inconsistencies in definition and diagnosis of problems, a lack of randomization, blinding techniques, and adequate controls as well as insufficient information concerning recruitment dates, sample characteristics, and treatment effects (King, Delfabbro, Griffiths, & Gradisar, 2011). All over the world, especially in the United States, Europe, Korea, and China, health professionals have begun to develop specialized treatment facilities for this target group (Block, 2008; Fackler, 2007; Huang, Li, & Tao, 2010). The South Korean government has established a network of more than 150 counseling centers and has introduced treatment programs for Internet addiction at almost 100 hospitals (Kim, 2008). Several boot camp-style programs for Internet-addicted adolescents have been set up in Korea and China (Koo, Wati, Lee, & Oh, 2011). In Western countries, clinics specializing in the psychological treatment of computer-based addictions have also emerged (e.g., the Outpatient Clinic for Computer Game and Internet Addictive Behavior in Mainz, Germany). Additionally, there are some online treatment services for Internet addiction (e.g., netaddictionrecovery.com; techaddiction.ca).

Most authors (van Rooij et al., 2012; Wieland, 2005; Young, 1998a) agree that lifelong abstinence from the Internet is not a treatment option, particularly because the Internet has become an indispensable part of modern life. Instead, it is recommended to focus on controlled use of the Internet. The aim is rather to interrupt problematic use of online applications while continuing to use those which are necessary for everyday life, e.g., email or browsing for information (Kim, 2008). In general, there is an agreement that the main treatment approach should be psychosocial, especially psychotherapy, which in more serious cases should be supplemented by pharmacotherapy. Many psychotherapeutic approaches can be used for the treatment of Internet addiction, as is the case in other mental disorders, and each of them stresses different aspects of the problem. In the literature, cognitive-behavioral approaches are prevalent (King, Delfabbro, Griffiths, & Gradisar, 2012), sometimes combined with elements of motivational interviewing

(Orzack et al., 2006; van Rooij et al., 2012). There also are published papers that focus on reality therapy (Kim, 2007, 2008), acceptance and commitment therapy (Twohig & Crosby, 2010), and family therapy (Yang, 2005) in the treatment of Internet addicts.

Specific Treatment Programs

In her specialized program for Internet addiction treatment, Young (1998b) offers methods based on cognitive-behavioral therapy (CBT). CBT views Internet addiction as a maladaptive cognitive coping style that can be modified by identifying the maladaptive thoughts, feelings, and behaviors causing the person to inappropriately use the Internet to meet their needs (Hall & Parsons, 2001; Wieland, 2005). She recommends the following interventions, using elements of the cognitive-behavioral approach aimed at reducing Internet addiction: practice the opposite Internet usage patterns; set goals determining the exact number of hours per day to be spent online; use of external stoppers as prompts to help log off; abstinence from the specific Internet application to which one is addicted; use of reminder cards with a list of the five major problems caused by Internet addiction and the five major benefits of cutting down or abstaining from a particular online application; making a list of every activity or practice that the addict has cut down on because of time spent online. She published a study examining the effects of online CBT interventions on 114 Internet addicts with the conclusion that clients reported CBT was effective at ameliorating the common symptoms of Internet addiction (e.g., motivation to quit, online time management, social isolation, sexual dysfunction, and abstinence from problematic online applications). Upon a six-month follow-up most clients were able to keep up symptom management and continued in their recovery (Young, 2007).

Van Rooij et al. (2012) introduced a cognitive-behavioral therapy and motivational interviewing-based treatment program that consists of 10 outpatient sessions within a six-month period. The program focuses on eliciting and strengthening motivation to change, choosing a treatment goal, gaining self-control, relapse prevention, and the training of coping skills. The evaluation study provided qualitative analysis of the experiences of the therapists with the treatment of 12 Internet addicts. Therapists reported that the program ordinarily used for substance dependence and pathological gambling fits well for Internet addiction, and further indicated that the treatment achieved some measure of progress for all of the 12 treated patients, while patients reported satisfaction with the treatment and actual behavioral improvements.

Kim (2007, 2008) has published two papers describing a program for students with Internet addiction. The program is based on the principles of William Glasser's reality therapy, which is widely used as a treatment for other addictive disorders. It is based on choice theory, which assumes that individuals are responsible for their own lives, for what they do, feel, and think, and that those who display addictive behavior should make the rational choice to achieve their goals. The program consists of 10 group sessions, in which the basic information about Internet addiction and the basic principles of reality therapy are explained. Results focused on the effectiveness of this program show that the program is able to reduce the level of Internet addiction while increasing self-esteem (Kim, 2008).

Future Research Directions

Since Internet addiction is a fairly new phenomenon, with the first studies appearing in the late 1990s, many questions remain unanswered, especially regarding clear terminology and diagnosis, prevalence, and treatment. Future research should focus on clarifying the concept of Internet addiction, related terminology, and creating a standardized instrument for measuring Internet addiction. Future studies are also needed to establish and compare the prevalence rates of Internet addiction in the general population across different countries, and to find possible different patterns in the causes of Internet addiction in different countries. Furthermore, almost nothing is known about possible Internet addictions among the elderly, which could become a problem in future years. There is a strong need for longitudinal studies on Internet addiction, which can reveal the causes and impacts of the addiction, and also the stability or instability of Internet addiction over time. Little is known about the natural history of this behavior, whether it is chronic, waxes and wanes in severity, or remits spontaneously. Therefore follow-up studies are necessary to track its emergence and determine its relationship to other disorders. In the clinical area, research should aim to clear up whether Internet addiction is a real clinical problem, to identify preventive measures, and find proven short- and long-term treatment strategies for Internet addicts. There is almost no information about treatment-seeking behavior, and how addicts who seek treatment differ from those who do not.

We can conclude that researchers have a long way to go in this area. More accurate definitions and also diagnostic criteria are required, including research with longitudinal perspectives. But with new technologies developing so quickly, new technical tools can bring new challenges in this area. Only a few researchers were aware of the phenomenon of online gaming 15 years ago and now there is almost a new generation of players addicted to these games. New technologies can create new challenges for scientists.

Acknowledgments

Petra Vondráčková and David Šmahel acknowledge the support of the Czech Science Foundation (GAP407/12/1831) and the Faculty of Social Studies, Masaryk University.

Notes

1　A self-help program for people with Internet addiction on the website of the Clinic of Addictology, First Faculty of Medicine, Charles University in Prague.
2　DSM-5 (Diagnostic and Statistical Manual of Mental Disorders) provides a common language and standard criteria for the classification of mental disorders and is published by the American Psychiatric Association.
3　ICD-10 (International Classification of Diseases) is a list published by the World Health Organization.

References

Aboujaoude, E., Koran, L. M., Gamel, N., Large, M. D., & Serpe, R. T. (2006). Potential markers for problematic Internet use: A telephone survey of 2,513 adults. *CNS Spectrums*, *11*(10), 750–755.

American Psychiatric Association (APA). (2013). Internet gaming disorder. Retrieved July 3, 2014, from http://www.dsm5.org/Documents/Internet%20Gaming%20Disorder%20Fact%20Sheet.pdf

Bakken, I. J., Wenzel, H. G., Gotestam, K. G., Johansson, A., & Oren, A. (2009). Internet addiction among Norwegian adults: A stratified probability sample study. *Scandinavian Journal of Psychology*, *50*(2), 121–127.

Beard, K. W. (2005). Internet addiction: A review of current assessment techniques and potential assessment questions. *CyberPsychology and Behavior*, *8*(1), 7–14.

Beard, K. W., & Wolf, E. M. (2001). Modification in the proposed diagnostic criteria for Internet addiction. *CyberPsychology and Behavior*, *4*(3), 377–383.

Black, D. W., Belsare, G., & Schlosser, S. (1999). Clinical features, psychiatric comorbidity, and health-related quality of life in persons reporting compulsive computer use behavior. *Journal of Clinical Psychiatry*, *60*(12), 839–844.

Blanco, C., Moreyra, P., Nunes, E., Sáiz-Ruiz, J., & Ibáñez, A. (2001). Pathological gambling: Addiction or compulsion? *Seminars in Clinical Neuropsychiatry*, *6*, 167–176.

Block, J. (2008). Issues for DSM-V: Internet addiction. *American Journal of Psychiatry*, *165*(3), 306–307.

Bozkurt, H., Coskun, M., Ayaydin, H., Adak, I., & Zoroglu, S. S. (2013). Prevalence and patterns of psychiatric disorders in referred adolescents with Internet addiction. *Psychiatry and Clinical Neurosciences*, *67*(5), 352–359.

Brenner, V. (1997). Psychology of computer use: XLVII. Parameters of Internet use, abuse and addiction: The first 90 days of the Internet Usage Survey. *Psychological Reports*, *80*(3), 879–882.

Cao, F., & Su, L. (2007). Internet addiction among Chinese adolescents: Prevalence and psychological features. *Child Care Health and Development*, *33*(3), 275–281.

Caplan, S. E. (2003). Preference for online social interaction: A theory of problematic Internet use and psychosocial well-being. *Communication Research*, *30*(6), 625–648.

Caplan, S. E., & High, A. C. (2011). Online social interaction, psychosocial well-being, and problematic Internet use. In K. S. Young & C. Nabuco de Abreu (Eds.), *Internet addiction: A handbook and guide to evaluation and treatment* (pp. 35–53). Hoboken, NJ: John Wiley & Sons.

Chen, K. C., Chen, I. J., & Paul, H. (2001). Explaining online behavioral differences: An Internet dependency perspective. *Journal of Computer Information Systems*, *41*(3), 59–63.

Chen, Y. F., & Peng, S. S. (2008). University students' Internet use and its relationships with academic performance, interpersonal relationships, psychosocial adjustment, and self-evaluation. *CyberPsychology and Behavior*, *11*(4), 467–469.

Chou, C. (2001). Internet heavy use and addiction among Taiwanese college students: An online interview study. *CyberPsychology and Behavior*, *4*(5), 573–585.

Chou, C., Condron, L., & Belland, J. C. (2005). A review of the research on Internet addiction. *Educational Psychology Review*, *17*(4), 363–388.

Chou, C., & Hsiao, M. C. (2000). Internet addiction, usage, gratification, and pleasure experience: The Taiwan college students' case. *Computers and Education*, *35*, 65–80.

Davis, R. A. (2001). A cognitive-behavioral model of pathological Internet use. *Computers in Human Behavior*, *17*(2), 187–195.

Davis, R. A., Flett, G. L., & Besser, A. (2002). Validation of a new scale for measuring problematic Internet use: Implications for pre-employment screening. *CyberPsychology and Behavior*, *5*(4), 331–345.

Douglas, A. C., Mills, J. E., Niang, M., Stepchenkova, S., Byun, S., Ruffini, C., & Atallah, M. (2008). Internet addiction: Meta-synthesis of qualitative research for the decade 1996–2006. *Computers in Human Behavior, 24*(6), 3027–3044.

Durkee, T., Kaess, M., Carli, V., Parzer, P., Wasserman, C., Floderus, B., & Wasserman, D. (2012). Prevalence of pathological Internet use among adolescents in Europe: Demographic and social factors. *Addiction, 107*(12), 2210–2222.

Fackler, M. (2007, November 18). In Korea, a boot camp cure for web obsession. *The New York Times*, p. 18.

Fu, K. W., Chan, W. S. C., Wong, P. W. C., & Yip, P. S. F. (2010). Internet addiction: Prevalence, discriminant validity and correlates among adolescents in Hong Kong. *British Journal of Psychiatry, 196*(6), 486–492.

Goudriaan, A. E., Oosterlaan, J., de Beurs, E., & van den Brink, W. (2006). Neurocognitive functions in pathological gambling: A comparison with alcohol dependence, Tourette syndrome and normal controls. *Addiction, 101*(4), 534–547.

Grant, J. E., Brewer, J. A., & Potenza, M. N. (2006). The neurobiology of substance and behavioral addictions. *CNS Spectrums, 11*(12), 924–930.

Griffiths, M. (2000a). Does Internet and computer "addiction" exist? Some case study evidence. *CyberPsychology and Behavior, 3*(2), 211–218.

Griffiths, M. (2000b). Internet addiction: Time to be taken seriously? *Addiction Research and Theory, 8*(5), 413–418.

Griffiths, M. (2011). Gambling addiction on the Internet. In K. S. Young & C. Nabuco de Abreu (Eds.), *Internet addiction: A handbook and guide to evaluation and treatment* (pp. 91–111). Hoboken, NJ: John Wiley & Sons.

Hall, A. S., & Parsons, J. (2001). Internet addiction: College student case study using best practices in cognitive behavior therapy. *Journal of Mental Health Counseling, 23*(4), 312–327.

Han, D. H., Kim, S. M., Lee, Y. S., & Renshaw, P. F. (2012). The effect of family therapy on the changes in the severity of on-line game play and brain activity in adolescents with on-line game addiction. *Psychiatry Research: Neuroimaging, 202*(2), 126–131.

Huang, R. L., Lu, Z., Liu, J. J., You, Y. M., Pan, Z. Q., Wei, Z., & Wang, Z. Z. (2009). Features and predictors of problematic Internet use in Chinese college students. *Behaviour and Information Technology, 28*(5), 485–490.

Huang, X.-Q., Li, M.-C., & Tao, R. (2010). Treatment of Internet addiction. *Current Psychiatry Reports, 12*(5), 462–470.

Jang, K. S., Hwang, S. Y., & Choi, J. Y. (2008). Internet addiction and psychiatric symptoms among Korean adolescents. *Journal of School Health, 78*(3), 165–171.

Johansson, A., & Gotestam, K. G. (2004). Internet addiction: Characteristics of a questionnaire and prevalence in Norwegian youth (12–18 years). *Scandinavian Journal of Psychology, 45*(3), 223–229.

Kim, J.-U. (2007). A reality therapy group counseling program as an Internet addiction recovery method for college students in Korea. *International Journal of Reality Therapy, 26*(2).

Kim, J.-U. (2008). The effect of a R/T group counseling program on the Internet addiction level and self-esteem of university students. *International Journal of Reality Therapy, 27*(2).

King, D. L., Delfabbro, P. H., Griffiths, M. D., & Gradisar, M. (2011). Assessing clinical trials of Internet addiction treatment: A systematic review and CONSORT evaluation. *Clinical Psychology Review, 31*(7), 1110–1116.

King, D. L., Delfabbro, P. H., Griffiths, M. D., & Gradisar, M. (2012). Cognitive-behavioral approaches to outpatient treatment of Internet addiction in children and adolescents. *Journal of Clinical Psychology, 68*(11), 1185–1195.

Ko, C. H., Yen, J. Y., Chen, C. C., Chen, S. H., & Yen, C. F. (2005). Proposed diagnostic criteria of Internet addiction for adolescents. *Journal of Nervous and Mental Disease, 193*(11), 728–733.

Ko, C. H., Yen, J. Y., Yen, C. F., Chen, C. S., & Chen, C. C. (2012). The association between Internet addiction and psychiatric disorder: A review of the literature. *European Psychiatry*, 27(1), 1–8.

Ko, C. H., Yen, J. Y., Yen, C. F., Lin, H. C., & Yang, M. J. (2007). Factors predictive for incidence and remission of Internet addiction in young adolescents: A prospective study. *CyberPsychology and Behavior*, 10(4), 545–551.

Koo, C., Wati, Y., Lee, C. C., & Oh, H. Y. (2011). Internet-addicted kids and South Korean government efforts: Boot-camp case. *Cyberpsychology, Behavior, and Social Networking*, 14(6), 391–394.

Lam, L. T., Peng, Z. W., Mai, J. C., & Jing, J. (2009). Factors associated with Internet addiction among adolescents. *CyberPsychology and Behavior*, 12(5), 551–555.

Lin, M. P., Ko, H. C., & Wu, J. Y. W. (2011). Prevalence and psychosocial risk factors associated with Internet addiction in a nationally representative sample of college students in Taiwan. *Cyberpsychology, Behavior, and Social Networking*, 14(12), 741–746.

Lin, S. S. J., & Tsai, C. C. (2002). Sensation seeking and Internet dependence of Taiwanese high school adolescents. *Computers in Human Behavior*, 18(4), 411–426.

Liu, C. Y., & Kuo, F. Y. (2007). A study of Internet addiction through the lens of the interpersonal theory. *CyberPsychology and Behavior*, 10(6), 799–804.

Mehroof, M., & Griffiths, M. D. (2010). Online gaming addiction: The role of sensation seeking, self-control, neuroticism, aggression, state anxiety, and trait anxiety. *Cyberpsychology, Behavior, and Social Networking*, 13(3), 313–316.

Morahan-Martin, J., & Schumacher, P. (2000). Incidence and correlates of pathological Internet use among college students. *Computers in Human Behavior*, 16(1), 13–29.

Ni, X. L., Yan, H., Chen, S. L., & Liu, Z. W. (2009). Factors influencing Internet addiction in a sample of freshmen university students in China. *CyberPsychology and Behavior*, 12(3), 327–330.

Niemz, K., Griffiths, M., & Banyard, P. (2005). Prevalence of pathological Internet use among university students and correlations with self-esteem, the General Health Questionnaire (GHQ), and disinhibition. *CyberPsychology and Behavior*, 8(6), 562–570.

Orzack, M. H., Voluse, A. C., Wolf, D., & Hennen, J. (2006). An ongoing study of group treatment for men involved in problematic Internet-enabled sexual behavior. *CyberPsychology and Behavior*, 9(3), 348–360.

Pallanti, S., Bernardi, S., & Quercioli, L. (2006). The Shorter PROMIS Questionnaire and the Internet Addiction Scale in the assessment of multiple addictions in a high-school population: Prevalence and related disability. *CNS Spectrums*, 11(12), 966–974.

Park, S. K., Kim, J. Y., & Cho, C. B. (2008). Prevalence of Internet addiction and correlations with family factors among South Korean adolescents. *Adolescence*, 43(172), 895–909.

Pies, R. (2009). Should DSM-V designate "Internet addiction" a mental disorder? *Psychiatry (Edgmont)*, 6(2), 31.

Potenza, M. N. (2006). Should addictive disorders include non-substance-related conditions? *Addiction*, 101, 142–151.

Reed, L. (2002). Governing (through) the Internet: The discourse on pathological computer use as mobilized knowledge. *European Journal of Cultural Studies*, 5(2), 131–153.

Shotton, M. A. (2003). *Computer addiction? A study of computer dependency*. London, UK: CRC Press. (Original work published 1989).

Šmahel, D., & Blinka, L. (2012). Excessive Internet use among European children. In S. Livingstone, L. Haddon, & A. Görzig (Eds.), *Children, risk and safety on the Internet: Research and policy challenges in comparative perspective* (pp. 191–204). Bristol, UK: Policy Press.

Šmahel, D., Brown, B. B., & Blinka, L. (2012). Associations between online friendship and Internet addiction among adolescents and emerging adults. *Developmental Psychology*, 48(2), 381–388.

Šmahel, D., Ševčíková, A., Blinka, L., & Veselá, M. (2009a). Abhängigkeit und Internet-Applikationen: Spiele, Kommunikation und Sex-Webseiten. In *Gesundheit und Neue Medien* (pp. 235–260). Berlin, Germany: Springer.

Šmahel, D., Vondráčková, P., Blinka, L., & Godoy-Etcheverry, S. (2009b). Comparing addictive behavior on the Internet in the Czech Republic, Chile and Sweden. In G. Cardoso, A. Cheong, & J. Cole (Eds.), *World Wide Internet: Changing societies, economies and cultures* (pp. 544–582). Macau, China: University of Macau.

Starcevic, V. (2013). Is Internet addiction a useful concept? *Australian and New Zealand Journal of Psychiatry, 47*(1), 16–19.

Subrahmanyam, K., & Šmahel, D. (2011). *Digital youth: Role of media in development.* New York, NY: Springer.

Suhail, K., & Bargees, Z. (2006). Effects of excessive Internet use on undergraduate students in Pakistan. *CyberPsychology and Behavior, 9*(3), 297–307.

Tsitsika, A., Janikian, M., Tzavela, E., Schoenmakers, T. M., Ólafsson, K., Halapi, E., & Richardson, C. (2013). *Internet use and Internet addictive behaviour among European adolescents: A cross-sectional study.* Athens, Greece: National and Kapodistrian University of Athens (NKUA).

Twohig, M. P., & Crosby, J. M. (2010). Acceptance and commitment therapy as a treatment for problematic Internet pornography viewing. *Behavior Therapy, 41*(3), 285–295.

van Rooij, A. J., Zinn, M. F., Schoenmakers, T. M., & van de Mheen, D. (2012). Treating Internet addiction with cognitive-behavioral therapy: A thematic analysis of the experiences of therapists. *International Journal of Mental Health and Addiction, 10*(1), 69–82.

Villella, C., Martinotti, G., Di Nicola, M., Cassano, M., La Torre, G., Gliubizzi, M. D., & Conte, G. (2011). Behavioural addictions in adolescents and young adults: Results from a prevalence study. *Journal of Gambling Studies, 27*(2), 203–214.

Vondráčková, P. (2012). *Addictive behavior on the Internet.* [PhD thesis]. Masaryk University, Brno, Czech Republic.

Vondráčková, P., Vacek, J., & Svobodová, K. (2014). Charakteristika uživatelů online svépomocného programu pro osoby se závislostním chováním na internetu: projevy, motivace, negativní důsledky a přínosy jeho omezení. *Adiktologie, 14*(1), 58–70.

Wainer, J., Dwyer, T., Dutra, R. S., Covic, A., Magalhaes, V. B., Ferreira, L. R. R., & Claudio, K. (2008). Too much computer and Internet use is bad for your grades, especially if you are young and poor: Results from the 2001 Brazilian SAEB. *Computers and Education, 51*(4), 1417–1429.

Wang, L. G., Luo, J., Bai, Y., Kong, J., Luo, J., Gao, W. B., & Sun, X. Y. (2013). Internet addiction of adolescents in China: Prevalence, predictors, and association with well-being. *Addiction Research and Theory, 21*(1), 62–69.

Wang, W. (2001). Internet dependency and psychosocial maturity among college students. *International Journal of Human-Computer Studies, 55*(6), 919–938.

Wieland, D. M. (2005). Computer addiction: Implications for nursing psychotherapy practice. *Perspectives in Psychiatric Care, 41*(4), 153–161.

Wu, X. H., Chen, X. G., Han, J., Meng, H., Luo, J. H., Nydegger, L., & Wu, H. R. (2013). Prevalence and factors of addictive Internet use among adolescents in Wuhan, China: Interactions of parental relationship with age and hyperactivity–impulsivity. *PLOS ONE, 8*(4).

Yang, F. (2005). The effect of integrated psychosocial intervention on 52 adolescents with Internet addiction disorder. *Chinese Journal of Clinical Psychology, 13*(3), 343.

Yang, S. C., & Tung, C. J. (2007). Comparison of Internet addicts and non-addicts in Taiwanese high school. *Computers in Human Behavior, 23*(1), 79–96.

Yoo, H. J., Cho, S. C., Ha, J. Y., Yune, S. K., Kim, S. J., Hwang, J., & Lyoo, I. K. (2004). Attention deficit hyperactivity symptoms and Internet addiction. *Psychiatry and Clinical Neurosciences, 58*(5), 487–494.

Young, K. S. (1998a). *Caught in the net: How to recognize the signs of internet addiction – and a winning strategy for recovery.* New York, NY: John Wiley & Sons.

Young, K. S. (1998b). Internet addiction: The emergence of a new clinical disorder. *CyberPsychology and Behavior, 1*(3), 237–244.

Young, K. S. (2007). Cognitive behavior therapy with Internet addicts: Treatment outcomes and implications. *CyberPsychology and Behavior, 10*(5), 671–679.

Young, K. S. (2011). Clinical assessment of Internet-addicted clients. In K. S. Young & C. Nabuco de Abreu (Eds.), *Internet addiction: A handbook and guide to evaluation and treatment* (pp. 19–34). Hoboken, NJ: John Wiley & Sons.

Zhang, L. X., Amos, C., & McDowell, W. C. (2008). A comparative study of Internet addiction between the United States and China. *CyberPsychology and Behavior, 11*(6), 727–729.

28

Smashing the Screen

Violent Video Game Effects

Ann Lewis, Sara Prot, Christopher L. Groves, and Douglas A. Gentile

Iowa State University

In 1965, Gordon Moore noted that computer processing power had roughly doubled every two years. He predicted that trend would continue for at least 10 years more (Moore, 1965). It turned out that prediction was much too conservative. In the twenty-first century, our technologies have become ubiquitous, yet are replaced in time spans that would have felt ludicrously short for scientists of 100, 70, or even 30 years ago.

One now-pervasive technology is video games. A far cry from the pixelated *Space Invaders*, or a jumping plumber (who became Italian because a fluffy mustache was the only way to distinguish his nose from his mouth), we have now brought our digitized entertainment to nearly full-immersion alternate-reality experiences. Co-emerging with the increasingly advanced art and storytelling has been the increasingly broad access to video games. Video games have moved from arcades to colonizing our homes and even our bodies, becoming available on the computers on our desks, the consoles in our entertainment centers, the tablets in our bags, and the smart-phones in our pockets.

Video games include varied applications from the educational to the professional to the entertaining. They cover a wide range of genres, and involve a wide spectrum of physical, emotional, and cognitive skill to use them effectively, and to compete with ourselves and others. Worldwide, over half a billion people play video games at least an hour a day (McGonigal, 2010). The average personal time spent gaming has gone up as well (Escobar-Chaves & Anderson, 2008; Gentile & Anderson, 2003; Rideout, Foehr, & Roberts, 2010). The average gamer spends eight hours a week in online play, virtually a part-time job (NPD Group, 2010), and the average young adult racks up 10,000 hours of game-playing by the time they turn 21, a nearly hour-for-hour equivalent to the time spent attending all of middle and high school (McGonigal, 2010). Collectively, we spend three billion hours a week playing video games.

Anything people do, however, has the opportunity to affect them. The violent content of many popular games has engendered particular concern. Of the top 10 most pre-ordered games of 2012, the primary method of game play centered on some form

The Wiley Handbook of Psychology, Technology, and Society, First Edition. Edited by Larry D. Rosen, Nancy A. Cheever, and L. Mark Carrier.

of combat (Welch, 2012). Five were first-person shooters, while the remaining five were in the more flexible adventure category, often combining their combat with world exploration. The number one most pre-ordered game, *Call of Duty: Black Ops II*, earned half a billion dollars in the first 24 hours following its release, and in less than a month it doubled that (Welch, 2012). *Black Ops II* is the ninth *Call of Duty* game. Across the franchise, players have spent 2.85 million years of collective game time playing (Fung, 2013), and yet *Call of Duty* is just one among many popular games.

We do not mean to vilify a single game, franchise, or producer, or to demonize video games. Although highly publicized violent events, particularly school shootings, have cast a spotlight on violent video game play as a possible contribution, there is no indication that playing a violent video game will turn a gamer from someone logging in to spend some digital time with friends into a mass murderer. But parents often underestimate how much exposure their children are getting to violence while playing video games (Funk, Hagan, & Schimming, 1999), and the violent content is commonly shown as justified, fun, and without negative consequences (Funk, Baldacci, Pasold, & Baumgardner, 2004). Assuming that violent game play is not predictive of mass murders does not mean that there is no reason to be concerned. There are several other effects that are of potential concern.

Repeated behavior, combined with regular rewards of fun and in-game accomplishments, may have a much more subtle effect than creating killers. Many researchers are more concerned with their relation to the types of aggression that children regularly come into contact with: verbal and relational aggression, bullying, and minor physical scuffles. Video games also deliver information on social roles and stereotypes. Some youth also appear to form addictive patterns with games, thereby damaging other areas of their functioning.

This chapter describes a theoretical framework for understanding effects of playing violent video games and then describes the current research covering those effects, including attentional, aggressive, prosocial, achievement, and other social-cognitive aspects.

Theoretical Frameworks

Nearly 50 years of research confirms that violent content in movies, television shows, and video games can serve as a causal risk factor for aggression (Anderson et al., 2003). However, understanding how this effect occurs and how seriously to take it is a complex task. Numerous theories of aggression exist, each of which provides a unique window of insight. However, when considered individually, each is only able to capture a fraction of the processes involved. For this reason, the general aggression model (GAM; Anderson & Bushman, 2002) was developed to provide an integrative framework through which these domain-specific theories are incorporated.

The general aggression model is considered a biosocial cognitive-developmental model, providing a theoretical framework through which all sources of aggressive behavior can be explained. Some of the influential theories that GAM incorporates include cognitive neo-association theory (Berkowitz, 1990, 1993), social learning theory (Bandura, 1977), script theory (Abelson, 1981; Huesmann, 1988), excitation transfer theory (Zillmann, 1971), and social interaction theory (Tedeschi & Felson, 1994).

Each of these theories is incorporated into both proximate and distal processes elucidated by GAM. Short-term processes are described by GAM's single episode cycle (see Figure 28.1), which begins with two forms of input. The first of these inputs consists of personal variables, which include personality constructs such as trait hostility and biological tendencies such as genetic dispositions toward aggression or high testosterone. These variables typically endure across situational episodes, but they also include the current state of the individual, such as mood or arousal. The second form of input is the situation itself, which may involve provocation, high temperatures, or exposure to content that primes aggression.

In the next stage of GAM's single episode cycle, these inputs influence several levels of the individual's internal state, including affect, cognition, and physiological arousal. Importantly, these three states both influence and are influenced by each other. For example, when aggressive cognitions are highly salient, individuals may begin to feel angry and experience increases in heart rate associated with anger. These internal state variables then inform decision-making processes when selecting a behavioral reaction. Decision-making can either be consciously deliberate and controlled (i.e., a thoughtful action) or impulsive and largely automatic. Once a behavior has been executed, it in turn influences the situation, which feeds into the next behavioral cycle.

Note that the single episode cycle most directly speaks to aggressive outcomes occurring within a given moment. However, it should also be noted that each social encounter can influence distal processes, such as learning about consequences or changes in the individual's predispositions to react aggressively. For example, when playing violent video games, aggression-related knowledge structures are learned, rehearsed, and reinforced. This leads to long-term changes in aggressive beliefs and

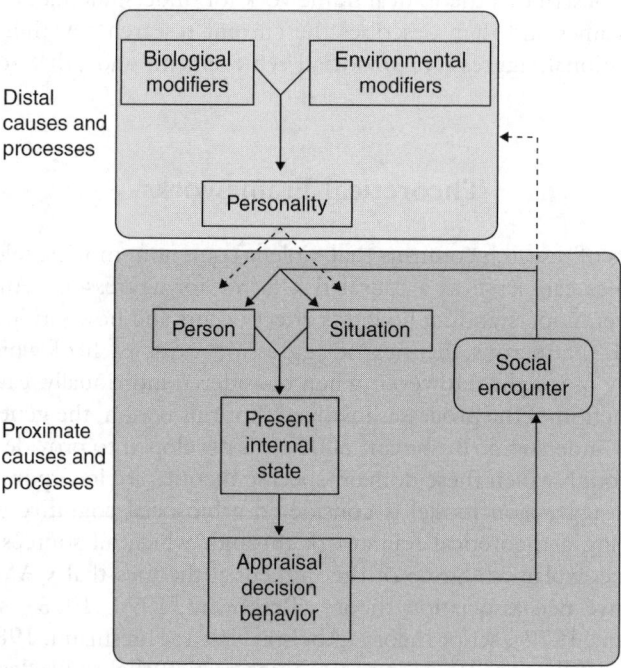

Figure 28.1 Single cycle within the general aggression model.

attitudes (Bryant, Carveth, & Brown, 1981; Crick & Dodge, 1994; Dodge, 2010), aggressive perceptual and expectation schemata (Dill, Anderson, Anderson, & Deuser, 1997; Moller & Krahé, 2009), aggression-related scripts (Huesmann, 1988), and desensitization to aggression and violence (Carnagey, Anderson, & Bushman, 2007; Mullin & Linz, 1995). In essence, what develop are the underlying psychological aspects that together influence aggressive personality, which in turn influences the types of situations that the individual may experience in the future.

Although violence in media has been the most heavily studied form of content, one should note that some video games clearly possess content that is not violent but also can influence thoughts, feelings, and behavior. For example, playing video games containing prosocial content leads players to increase helping behavior outside of the video game context (Greitemeyer & Osswald, 2010). For this reason, learning theories are best applied to understand the wider range of effects that video games can have beyond aggression. Similar to aggression, however, the literature devoted to learning is often fragmented into different levels of analysis, focusing on specific learning processes such as habituation, discrimination, classical conditioning, operant conditioning, observational learning, and cognitive and emotional learning. Although learning from games (or anything) can occur at each of these levels, they have also been integrated recently into a general learning model (Buckley & Anderson, 2006; Gentile, Groves, & Gentile, 2014). It is valuable to remember that basically every effect that video games can have on players is due to learning. People can learn from a single exposure to something, but they learn it especially well with repetition and rewards, both of which video games provide well.

Finally, although the general aggression model is widely accepted as an explanation of general learning processes in media-influenced aggression, additional processes may be involved. These include desensitization to violence, priming of aggressive thoughts, the development of aggressive scripts, excitation transfer, the modification of normative beliefs about aggression, and the reinforcement of hostile attribution biases. Groves, Prot, and Anderson (in press) discuss each of these processes in further detail and we encourage readers to visit this work for a more detailed theoretical account of such effects.

Empirical Findings

Aggressive Cognitions, Affect, and Behavior

Anderson et al. (2010) conducted a meta-analytic review of more than 130 studies in Western and Japanese sources published through 2008. They coded the material by methodology, participant characteristics, aggressive measure type, and game content, including whether the protagonist was a hero, criminal, or neither, and whether the violence targets were human, non-human, or both in experimental studies. Across the 130 studies reviewed, violent video game exposure was associated with an increase in both short-term and long-term aggressive cognition. Some interaction was found in culture and sex in some types of studies, although culture was confounded by type of measure involved.

This meta-analysis was an update to an earlier review by the same lead researcher. Both studies concluded that exposure to violent video games increased short-term and long-term aggressive thinking, aggressive feelings, and aggressive behavior.

Anderson and Bushman (2001) noted that the relationship between violent video game exposure and aggressive behavior was as strong as the relationship between condom use and HIV infection. Interestingly, several other meta-analyses have been conducted, and all of them find essentially the same empirical finding (an average significant effect size between 0.14 and 0.29) (Anderson, 2004; Anderson et al., 2004), but not all authors interpret it as important (Ferguson, 2007a, 2007b; Sherry, 2001). Although there is honest disagreement among researchers about whether an effect size of this magnitude is of practical significance, perhaps some of the difference in interpretation is due to the importance some researchers put on moderating factors. Several aspects of both games and gamers have been shown to either enhance or mitigate the effects of violent content.

Intent to commit aggressive actions within a game necessitates the activation of aggressive thoughts. However, the content of the game may influence the deliberative level of that intention. Subjects who played a game that rewarded violence displayed more hostile emotion, thinking, and behavior, while a game that punished violence resulted in more hostile emotion, but not thinking or behavior (Carnagey & Anderson, 2005). The level of player immersion or involvement in a game may also have an effect. For example, in one study aggressive behavior increased more in boys who played a violent video game compared to boys who just watched it being played (Polman, Orobio de Castro, & van Aken, 2008). Players who used a personalized character also exhibited increased aggression compared to those who used pre-programmed characters, although any violent game player was still subsequently more aggressive than those in the non-violent condition (Fischer, Kastenmüller, & Greitemeyer, 2010).

The greatest concern regarding video game play and real-life aggression may be in the long-term internalization of aggressive attitudes and desensitization to violence. Experienced players report less moral distress after playing violent games than inexperienced players do (Gollwitzer & Melzer, 2012). Players who self-reported more violent game play also demonstrated higher aggressive self-concept, and participants who played the violent video game *Doom* in an experimental context were faster to associate themselves with aggressive concepts than participants who played a non-violent game (Uhlmann & Swanson, 2004). Further, players who report higher levels of identification with violent characters are more aggressive after playing those games (Konijn, Nije Bijvank, & Bushman, 2007).

Ultimately, the research on violent video games and aggression fits very well within modern multi-causal theories of aggression, where media violence is considered just one among many risk factors for aggression (e.g., Gentile & Bushman, 2012). It is clearly not the largest; neither is it the smallest. This approach is useful for understanding why most people can play violent games and still not be particularly aggressive in their daily lives – aggression typically requires a confluence of multiple risk factors and very few protective factors. Within this framework, violent video games are simply one relatively small risk among many.

Empathy, Desensitization, and Helping

Most children initially respond to media violence with fear, disgust, and heightened arousal (Cantor, 1998). However, such aversive reactions gradually decrease with repeated exposure to violent images. Media violence consumers become desensitized not only to media images themselves but also to real-life violence (Mullin & Linz, 1995). There is research evidence of both short-term and long-term desensitization as a result of violent video game play. For example, even a brief, 20-minute episode of violent video game play can lead to reduced physiological responding to real-life violence (Carnagey et al., 2007). Such short-term desensitization dissipates quickly (Mullin & Linz, 1995). However, habitual media violence consumption can lead to more lasting effects. Several studies show evidence of chronic desensitization to violence through video game play (Bailey, West, & Anderson, 2011; Engelhardt, Bartholow, Kerr, & Bushman, 2011; Krahé et al., 2011). Habitual violent game players have reduced neural responses while viewing violent images (Bartholow, Bushman, & Sestir, 2006; Gentile, Swing, Anderson, Rinker, & Thomas, 2014). Chronic desensitization also has cognitive and affective consequences, such as increased positive attitudes toward violence and decreased empathy for violence victims (Bartholow, Sestir, & Davis, 2005; Funk et al., 2004).

Desensitization to violence is viewed as a key mediator that leads to increases in aggression and decreases in prosocial behavior as a result of violent video game play. Desensitization to violence leads to increases in aggressive cognitions and aggressive behaviors (Bartholow et al., 2005; Engelhardt et al., 2011; Krahé et al., 2011). Emotional numbing to sights of violence may also lead people to underestimate the severity of observed violence and reduce the likelihood of helping. Several studies support this prediction. For example, participants who just played a violent video game for 20 minutes are more likely to underestimate the severity of a fight they overheard and are less likely to help the injured victim (Bushman & Anderson, 2009). In the long term, violent video game play can lead to reductions in trait empathy and prosocial behavior (Gentile et al., 2009; Krahé & Möller, 2010).

Video Games and Sexual Socialization

As the adage says, sex and violence sell. In fact, they often sell together. Video games often combine sexual imagery with violent content. Fighting games have historically been seen as a male interest; a study of Norwegian youth found that 65% of boys had played first-person shooters, compared to only 8% of girls (Endestad & Torgersen, 2003). Female gamers are sometimes subject to sexual harassment when they enter this boys' club. In the highly publicized *Cross Assault 2012* controversy, a tournament coach who repeatedly sexually harassed one of his female players while he was being recorded (Crossassaultharass, 2012) defended sexual aggression in a statement claiming, "the sexual harassment is part of the culture. And if you remove that from the fighting game community, it's not the fighting game community" (O'Leary, 2012).

Whether a symptom or cause of the player imbalance, women are greatly underrepresented as characters in video games as well. In a study of video game covers, 90% of covers depicting humans portrayed men, while 43% portrayed women, and that ratio grew to 79% men to 21% women of the total 485 human characters coded across all covers (Burgess, Stermer, & Burgess, 2007). In a study examining 33 games' character content, only 15% of games depicted a female as an action character or hero, while 30% of games had no female characters at all (Dietz, 1998). Female characters are more likely to be sexualized than male characters (Ivory, 2006). As a class, female characters are mostly given accessory, supportive, or negative roles – goals, props, bystanders, obstacles, victims, or villains (Dietz, 1998; Glaubke, Miller, Parker, & Espejo, 2001).

Exposure to sexually aggressive or violent media is associated with several negative shifts in sexual attitudes, especially in men. Men who viewed a sexually aggressive film, as compared to a physically aggressive or neutral film, demonstrated more accepting attitudes toward sexual aggression, more attraction to the idea of sexual aggression, and less sympathy toward a rape victim than did women who viewed the same material (Weisz & Earls, 1995). Frequent gamers are more likely to condone stereotypes of hyper-sexualized women and violent men (Brenick, Henning, Killen, O'Connor, & Collins, 2007). Men who watched sexualized violent video games being played demonstrated a greater increase in rape myth acceptance than did women in the same study (Beck, Boys, Rose, & Beck, 2012). Images of sex-stereotyped female video game characters were shown to increase tolerance of sexual harassment in men, while the same caused a decreased tolerance in women (Dill, Brown, & Collins, 2008).

Video Games and Racial Stereotyping

Like women, racial minorities are also systematically underrepresented in video games. Recent content analyses demonstrate that more than two-thirds of video game characters are White (Burgess, Dill, Stermer, Burgess, & Brown, 2011; Dill, Gentile, Richter, & Dill, 2005; Williams, Martins, Consalvo, & Ivory, 2009). Non-White male characters are rare, whereas non-White female characters are almost nonexistent (Burgess et al., 2011). When racial minority characters are included, they are almost always portrayed in stereotypical (and often negative) ways. Black male characters are most often shown as street criminals or thugs (Burgess et al., 2011). Whereas violent acts performed by White protagonists are often depicted as heroic, violent acts performed by Black characters are predominantly shown as antisocial (Burgess et al., 2011; Dill et al., 2005). Arab video game characters are almost always portrayed as terrorists and are given the role of "the enemy" by American game designers (Sisler, 2008). Visual representations of such characters often contain stereotypical Arab facial features and clothing (e.g., turbans, dark skin, and facial hair; Sisler, 2008).

Social-cognitive models view media as powerful sources of social learning that can teach and reinforce beliefs about social groups (Saleem & Anderson, 2013). Thus, exposure to racial stereotypes in the media is expected to influence people's evaluations of minorities in real life. For example, stereotypical depictions of Blacks in television programs negatively influence viewers' perceptions of Blacks and reduce empathy toward this group (Dixon, 2007; Johnson, Olivo, Gibson, Reed, & Ashburn-Nardo, 2009). Recent research suggests that exposure to racial stereotypes in video games has similar effects on prejudice. For example, Saleem and Anderson (2013) demonstrated that playing a video game in which Arabs are shown as terrorists increases anti-Arab bias and perceptions of Arabs as aggressive.

Effects on Attention and Cognitive Control

A budding, and more optimistic, area of research regarding the influence of video games is that on attention and cognitive control. As noted, video game effects can be seen as essentially the result of learning processes. Critically, such effects can produce both negative and positive outcomes, as exemplified by the influence of violent media on aggression and prosocial media on helping. In line with this idea, video games have demonstrated both decrements and improvements on a number of visual attention-related tasks and measures.

Work by Boot et al. (2010) demonstrated that frequent video game players outperformed non-video game players on a battery of cognitive tasks including visual tracking of rapid moving objects, detecting visual changes in a complex array of items, task-switching, and mental rotation. These findings demonstrate improvements, not only in attentional tasks, but executive control and spatial information processing as well. However, in a training portion of their study, participants asked to play video games for a total of 21 hours did not outperform untrained participants on such cognitive tasks, suggesting either the presence of a selection effect, or a need for longer-term video game training. On the other hand, Green and Bavelier (2003) did find that participants trained to play a violent game demonstrated improved performance on perceptual and cognitive tests of functional field of view, attentional blink, and an enumeration task compared to those trained in *Tetris*. In other work, action video game players were better able to locate targets in visual search tasks (Wu & Spence, 2013) and demonstrate enhancements in drawing important information from visual stimuli (Applebaum, Cain, Darling, & Mitroff, 2013). Such findings are particularly interesting because it is rare that training techniques demonstrate transfer beyond the limited confines of the trained task itself (Boot, Blakely, & Simons, 2011). The focus of these studies is primarily on the effects of "action" video games, which tend to be violent first-person shooters. Ironically, these findings also hint at some potential negative effects on attention and executive functioning. It is possible, for example, that improving the ability to see into the periphery, to detect small movements, and to quickly reorient visual attention to the periphery may result in increased attention problems in the classroom, where children are expected to ignore the child fidgeting next to them.

The fast-paced nature of television and video games makes it possible for viewers to attend without the need to work hard at maintaining attention. In contrast, it takes substantially more effort to focus and sustain attention in classroom and home settings that are less exciting (Gentile, Swing, Lim, & Khoo, 2012). Indeed, several studies have found that television exposure is related to attention problems in childhood (Christakis, Zimmerman, DiGiuseppe, & McCarty, 2004; Landhuis, Poulton, Welch, & Hancox, 2007; Levine & Waite, 2000). Congruent findings exist for video game players (Gentile, 2009; Gentile, Swing, et al., 2012; Tolchinsky & Jefferson, 2011). Of particular interest is evidence that those with attention problems also tend to play more video games (Gentile, Swing, et al., 2012), suggesting a bi-directional relationship in which individuals with attention problems seek to play video games which potentially exacerbate their symptoms.

Other research has focused on the negative influence of video games on cognitive processes such as executive control. Bailey and colleagues (2011) demonstrated that frequent violent video game players exhibited reduced proactive control, a function involved in maintaining relevant information in memory to be used in a future task. Additionally, associations have been found between violent media use and executive control deficits measured by the Stroop task (Kronenberger et al., 2005; Mathews et al., 2005). Such findings are particularly informative considering attention disorders such as attention deficit hyperactivity disorder are considered to be partly a disorder of executive functioning (Willcutt, Doyle, Nigg, Faraone, & Pennington, 2005). Future research is necessary to examine the relations between media use, executive function deficits, and subsequent attention problems.

School Performance

A growing body of research also suggests that entertainment video game play (as opposed to educational game play) can have detrimental effects on school performance. For example, a recent survey of a nationally representative sample of American children and adolescents showed that almost half of heavy media users get poor grades, compared to 23% of light media users (Rideout et al., 2010). Longitudinal studies demonstrate that total screen time predicts lower future school performance, even while controlling for relevant covariates (Anderson, Gentile, & Buckley, 2007; Gentile et al., 2011). Perhaps the strongest evidence of a causal relationship between video game play and school performance comes from an experimental study by Weis and Cerankosky (2010). In this study, children were randomly assigned to receive a video game system immediately or after four months. Children who immediately received the video game system had lower reading and writing scores and greater teacher-reported academic problems than children in the control group did after the four-month period.

Why does video game play lead to lower school performance? According to the displacement hypothesis, video game play displaces time that would otherwise be spent in other activities that might have more educational benefit, such as reading or creating (Gentile, Lynch, Linder, & Walsh, 2004). Several studies support this view. For example, habitual video game players spend 30% less time reading and 34% less time doing homework than non-gamers (Cummings & Vandewater, 2007). In the study by Weis and Cerankosky (2010), time spent playing video games mediated the relationship between video game system ownership and school academic performance. These findings provide evidence of displacement. However, it is possible that mechanisms other than displacement are also involved in the association between video game use and school performance. For example, several studies suggest that video game play may exacerbate attention problems and harm executive control (Bailey, West, & Anderson, 2010; Gentile, Coyne, & Bricolo, 2012; Swing, Gentile, Anderson, & Walsh, 2010), both of which are important for school success. One longitudinal study also found evidence that the relation between amount of video game and television use and school performance was mediated by sleep (Barlett, Gentile, Barlett, Eisenmann, & Walsh, 2012). That is, children who spend more time with electronic media sleep less, which has a negative impact on their school performance. Further research is needed to establish whether and how mechanisms other than displacement mediate the relationship between video game use and school performance.

It is important to note that not all video game content has such negative effects on school performance. Whereas entertainment video games have negative effects on school performance, educational video games have been successfully used as teaching aids in a number of domains (Corbett, Koedinger, & Hadley, 2001; Murphy, Penuel, Means, Korbak, & Whaley, 2001).

Video Game Addiction

In recent years, there has been increased research interest in pathological video gaming, also termed video game addiction. Most researchers have defined video game addiction using criteria similar to those of pathological gambling – based on damage to multiple areas of functioning (e.g., academic, social, family, and occupational functioning; Sim, Gentile, Bricolo, Serpelloni, & Gulamoydeen, 2012). Video games are initially played for entertainment and relaxation. This behavior is not problematic at first, but may become pathological for some individuals when it disrupts functioning in different areas.

Studies conducted in different countries demonstrate similar prevalence of video game addiction across culture. Among youth in the United States, 8.5% of video game players fulfill diagnostic criteria for video game addiction (Gentile, 2009), compared to 12% in Europe (Grüsser, Thalemann, & Griffiths, 2007), 10% in China (Peng & Li, 2009), and 9% in Singapore (Choo et al., 2010). These findings suggest that video game addiction is not a trivial issue. It is a condition that can affect the well-being of a substantial number of people worldwide.

Pathological video gaming shows comorbidity with other mental health disorders, including anxiety disorders, mood disorders, substance use disorders, impulse control disorders, and personality disorders (Shapira et al., 2003). A key question in this area is whether video game addiction is a distinct disorder instead of just a symptom of other conditions. A two-year longitudinal study provides evidence that impulsivity and low social competence act as risk factors for developing video game addiction, whereas gaming addiction symptoms predict later depression, anxiety, social phobia, and poorer school performance (Gentile et al., 2011). This study provides strong evidence that video game addiction is at least a comorbid mental disorder, mutually reinforcing other disorders.

Recently, the American Psychiatric Association reviewed the evidence on pathological Internet and video game use, and concluded that there was sufficient evidence to include it in the updated *Diagnostic and Statistical Manual of Mental Disorders* (DSM-5; American Psychiatric Association, 2013). Before "Internet gaming disorder" will be widely accepted as a recognized mental health disorder, more research is needed concerning its prevalence, etiology, diagnosis, and treatment.

Age Effects

Finally, there has been discussion around possible age effects moderating these effects of violent video game play. Although learning processes are generally similar for both adults and children, potential age-related differences are a valid area of concern, particularly as children may experience greater media consumption than adults. Most studies on media violence are conducted using college-aged samples. However, early research found the same effects in children that the bulk of the research found in adults – that playing violent video games increased aggression and decreased prosocial behavior (Schulte, Malouff, Post-Gorden, & Rodasta, 1988; Silvern & Williamson, 1987). Other studies, some already mentioned in this chapter, also found consistent results using child or adolescent populations (e.g., Calvert & Tan, 1994; Gentile et al., 2004).

Other forms of childhood media consumption, namely television, have been shown to predict young adult aggression even 15 years later (Huesmann, Moise-Titus, Podolski, & Eron, 2003). Finally, Bushman and Huesmann (2006), in a meta-analysis of media violence studies on children and adults, found that, while both children and adults demonstrated significant effects of television, music, movie, video game, and comic book violence on aggression, short-term effects were greater for adults while long-term effects were greater for children.

Conclusions

The growing body of video game research, and its increasingly interdisciplinary nature, has given us greater insight into the nature of video game play. The early research found connections between violent game play and aggressive thinking, feelings, and behaviors (although at a level far lower than is often apparent from news headlines). More recent research has begun focusing on issues other than the violence itself, as researchers examine the roles the typically White male characters play vis-à-vis women and minorities. Extended violent video game play has been linked to desensitization, reduced empathy, and reduced helping behavior. Although playing video games in the violent video game genre has been linked to improvements in aspects of visual attention and executive control, extensive play is associated with poorer school performance, largely due to the amount of time taken from academic activities. For a minority of players, gaming can also take over so much of one's life that other areas are significantly damaged.

We openly acknowledge the limited category of video games this discussion covers. Although they are extremely popular, violent video games are neither the sole category nor the primary focus of the industry as a whole, and many non-violent games are being studied for possible beneficial effects. These games represent a fascinating and valuable area of application as social platforms, educational or training tools, and/or entertainment. Nonetheless, the effects of violence in video games are non-trivial, having both what might be considered "positive" and "negative" effects. As video games reach further into human life, becoming more pervasive and demanding more of our time, their cumulative effects may exert a great deal of influence.

References

Abelson, R. P. (1981). The psychological status of the script concept. *American Psychologist*, *36*(7), 715–729.

American Psychiatric Association (APA). (2013). *Diagnostic and statistical manual of mental disorders* (5th ed.) (DSM-5). Arlington, VA: Author.

Anderson, C. A. (2004). An update on the effects of violent video games. *Journal of Adolescence*, *27*, 113–122.

Anderson, C. A., Berkowitz, L., Donnerstein, E., Huesmann, R. L., Johnson, J., Linz, D., … Wartella, E. (2003). The influence of media violence on youth. *Psychological Science in the Public Interest*, *4*, 81–110.

Anderson, C. A., & Bushman, B. J. (2001). Effects of violent video games on aggressive behavior, aggressive cognition, aggressive affect, physiological arousal, and prosocial behavior: A meta-analytic review of the scientific literature. *Psychological Science*, *12*, 353–359.

Anderson, C. A., & Bushman, B. J. (2002). Human aggression. *Annual Review of Psychology*, *53*, 27–51.

Anderson, C. A., Carnagey, N. L., Flanagan, M., Benjamin, A. J., Eubanks, J., & Valentine, J. C. (2004). Violent video games: Specific effects of violent content on aggressive thoughts and behavior. *Advances in Experimental Social Psychology*, *36*, 199–249.

Anderson, C. A., Gentile, D. A., & Buckley, K. E. (2007). *Violent video game effects on children and adolescents: Theory, research, and public policy.* Oxford, UK: Oxford University Press.

Anderson, C. A., Shibuya, A., Ihori, N., Swing, E. L., Bushman, B. J., Sakamoto, A., … Saleem, M. (2010). Violent video game effects on aggression, empathy, and prosocial behavior in Eastern and Western countries. *Psychological Bulletin*, *136*, 151–173.

Applebaum, G. L., Cain, M. S., Darling, E. F., & Mitroff, S. R. (2013). Action video game playing is associated with improved visual sensitivity, but not alterations in visual sensory memory. *Attention, Perception and Psychophysics, 75*(4), 1161–1167.

Bailey, K., West, R., & Anderson, C. A. (2010). A negative association between video game experience and proactive cognitive control. *Psychophysiology, 47*, 34–42.

Bailey, K., West, R., & Anderson, C. A. (2011). The association between chronic exposure to video game violence and affective picture processing: An ERP study. *Cognitive, Affective, and Behavioral Neuroscience, 11*, 259–276.

Bandura A. (1977). *Social learning theory.* New York, NY: Prentice Hall.

Barlett, N., Gentile, D. A., Barlett, C. P., Eisenmann, J. C., & Walsh, D. A. (2012). Sleep as a mediator of screen time effects on U.S. children's health outcomes: A prospective study. *Journal of Children and Media, 6*(1), 37–50.

Bartholow, B. D., Bushman, B. J., & Sestir, M. A. (2006). Chronic violent video game exposure and desensitization: Behavioral and event-related brain potential data. *Journal of Experimental Social Psychology, 42*, 532–539.

Bartholow, B. D., Sestir, M. A., & Davis, E. (2005). Correlates and consequences of exposure to video game violence: Hostile personality, empathy, and aggressive behavior. *Personality and Social Psychology Bulletin, 31*, 1573–1586.

Beck, V. S., Boys, S., Rose, C., & Beck, E. (2012). Violence against women in video games: A prequel or sequel to rape myth acceptance? *Journal of Interpersonal Violence, 27*(15), 3016–3031.

Berkowitz, L. (1990). On the formation and regulation of anger and aggression: A cognitive neoassociationistic analysis. *American Psychologist, 45*, 494–503.

Berkowitz, L. (1993). Pain and aggression: Some findings and implications. *Motivation and Emotion, 17*(3), 277–293.

Boot, W. R., Basak, C., Erickson, K. I., Neider, M., Simons, D. J., Fabiani, M., … Kramer, A. F. (2010). Transfer of skill engendered by complex task training under conditions of variable priority. *Acta Psychologica, 135*, 349–357.

Boot, W. R., Blakely, D. P., & Simons, D. J. (2011). Do action video games improve perception and cognition? *Frontiers in Psychology, 2*, 226.

Brenick, A., Henning, A., Killen, M., O'Connor, A., & Collins, M. (2007). Social evaluations of stereotypic images in video games: Unfair, legitimate, or "just entertainment"? *Youth Society, 38*(4), 395–419.

Bryant, J., Carveth, R. A., & Brown, D. (1981). Television viewing and anxiety: An experimental examination. *Journal of Communication, 31*, 106–119.

Buckley, K. E., & Anderson, C. A. (2006). A theoretical model of the effects and consequences of playing video games. In P. Vorderer & J. Bryant (Eds.), *Playing video games: Motives, responses, and consequences* (pp. 363–378). Mahwah, NJ: Lawrence Erlbaum Associates.

Burgess, M. C. R., Dill, K. E., Stermer, S. P., Burgess, S. R., & Brown, B. P. (2011). Playing with prejudice: The prevalence and consequences of racial stereotypes in video games. *Media Psychology, 14*(3), 289–311.

Burgess, M. C. R., Stermer, S. P., & Burgess, S. R. (2007). Sex, lies, and video games: The portrayal of male and female characters on video game covers. *Sex Roles, 57*, 419–433.

Bushman, B. J., & Anderson, C. A. (2009). Comfortably numb: Desensitizing effects of violent media on helping others. *Psychological Science, 20*, 273–277.

Bushman, B. J., & Huesmann, L. R. (2006). Short-term and long-term effects of violent media on aggression in children and adults. *Archives of Pediatrics and Adolescent Medicine, 160*(4), 348–352.

Calvert, S. L., & Tan, S. (1994). Impact of virtual reality on young adults' physiological arousal and aggressive thoughts: Interaction versus observation. *Journal of Applied Developmental Psychology, 15*(1), 125–139.

Cantor, J. (1998). *Mommy, I'm scared! How TV and movies frighten children and what we can do to protect them.* San Diego, CA: Harvest/Harcourt.

Carnagey, N. L., & Anderson, C. A. (2005). The effects of reward and punishment in violent video games on aggressive affect, cognition, and behavior. *Psychological Science, 16*(11), 882–889.

Carnagey, N. L., Anderson, C. A., & Bushman, B. J. (2007). The effect of video game violence on physiological desensitization to real life violence. *Journal of Experimental Social Psychology, 43,* 489–496.

Choo, H., Gentile, D. A., Sim, T., Li, D., Khoo, A., & Liau, A. K. (2010). Pathological video-gaming among Singaporean youth. *Annals of the Academy of Medicine Singapore, 39,* 822–829.

Christakis, D. A., Zimmerman, F. J., DiGiuseppe, D. L., & McCarty, C. A. (2004). Early television exposure and subsequent attentional problems in children. *Pediatrics, 113*(4), 708–713.

Corbett, A. T., Koedinger, K. R., & Hadley, W. (2001). Cognitive tutors: From the research classroom to all classrooms. In P. S. Goodman (Ed.), *Technology-enhanced learning* (pp. 235–263). Mahwah, NJ: Lawrence Erlbaum Associates.

Crick, N. R., & Dodge, K. A. (1994). A review and reformulation of social information-processing mechanisms in children's social adjustment. *Psychological Bulletin, 115,* 74–101.

Crossassaultharass. (2012, February 28). Day 1: Sexual harassment on Cross Assault. Retrieved August 23, 2013, from https://www.youtube.com/watch?feature=player_embedded&v=0SLDgPbjp0M

Cummings, H. M. M., & Vandewater, E. A. P. (2007). Relation of adolescent video game play to time spent in other activities. *Archives of Pediatric and Adolescent Medicine, 161*(7), 684–689.

Dietz, T. L. (1998). An examination of violence and gender role portrayals in video games: Implications for gender socialization and aggressive behavior. *Sex Roles, 38*(5/6), 425–442.

Dill, K. E., Anderson, C. A., Anderson, K. B., & Deuser, W. E. (1997). Effects of aggressive personality on social expectations and social perceptions. *Journal of Research in Personality, 31,* 272–292.

Dill, K. E., Brown, B. P., & Collins, M. A. (2008). Effects of media stereotypes on sexual harassment judgments and rape supportive attitudes: Popular video game characters, gender, violence and power. *Journal of Experimental Social Psychology, 44,* 1402–1408.

Dill, K. E., Gentile, D. A., Richter, W. A., & Dill, J. C. (2005). Violence, sex, race and age in popular video games: A content analysis. In E. Cole & J. Henderson Daniel (Eds.), *Featuring females: Feminist analyses of the media.* Washington, DC: American Psychological Association.

Dixon, T. L. (2007). Black criminals and White officers: The effects of racially misrepresenting law breakers and law defenders on television news. *Media Psychology, 10,* 270–291.

Dodge, A. K. (2010). Social information processing patterns as mediators of the interaction between genetic factors and life experiences in the development of aggressive behavior. In P. Shaver & M. Mikulincer (Eds.), *Human aggression and violence: Causes, manifestations, and consequences* (pp. 165–185). Washington, DC: American Psychological Association.

Endestad, T., & Torgersen, L. (2003, November). *Computer games and violence: Is there really a connection?* Paper presented at Digital Games Research Conference, University of Utrecht, the Netherlands.

Engelhardt, C. R., Bartholow, B. D., Kerr, G. T., & Bushman, B. J. (2011). This is your brain on violent video games: Neural desensitization to violence predicts increased aggression following violent video game exposure. *Journal of Experimental Social Psychology, 47,* 1033–1036.

Escobar-Chaves, S. L., & Anderson, C. A. (2008). Media and risky behaviors. *Future of Children, 18*(1), Special issue on Media Technology in the Lives of Children. Retrieved December 6, 2014, from http://futureofchildren.org/futureofchildren/publications/journals/article/index.xml?journalid=32&articleid=60

Ferguson, C. J. (2007a). Video games: The latest scapegoat for violence. *Chronicle of Higher Education: Chronicle Review*, *53*(42), B20.

Ferguson, C. J. (2007b). The good, the bad and the ugly: A meta-analytic review of positive and negative effects of violent video games. *Psychiatric Quarterly*, *78*, 309–316.

Fischer, P., Kastenmüller, A., & Greitemeyer, T. (2010). Media violence and the self: The impact of personalized gaming characters in aggressive video games on aggressive behavior. *Journal of Experimental Social Psychology*, *46*(1), 192–195.

Fung, B. (2013, August 13). Humankind has now spent more time playing *Call of Duty* than it has existed on earth. *The Washington Post*. Retrieved from http://www.washingtonpost. com/blogs/the-switch/wp/2013/08/13/humankind-has-now-spent-more-time-playing-call-of-duty-than-it-has-existed-on-earth/

Funk, J. B., Baldacci, H. B., Pasold, T., & Baumgardner, J. (2004). Violence exposure in real-life, video games, television, movies, and the Internet: Is there desensitization? *Journal of Adolescence*, *27*(1), 23–39.

Funk, J., Hagan, J., & Schimming, J. (1999). Children and electronic games: A comparison of parents' and children's perceptions of children's habits and preferences in a United States sample. *Psychological Reports*, *85*(3), 883–888.

Gentile, D. A. (2009). Pathological video-game use among youth ages 8 to 18. *Psychological Science*, *20*, 594–602.

Gentile, D. A., & Anderson, C. A. (2003). Violent video games: The newest media violence hazard. In D. Gentile (Ed.), *Media violence and children* (pp. 131–152). Westport, CT: Praeger.

Gentile, D. A., Anderson, C. A., Yukawa, S., Ihori, N., Saleem, M., Ming, L. K., … Sakamoto, A. (2009). The effects of prosocial video games on prosocial behaviors: International evidence from correlational, experimental, and longitudinal studies. *Personality and Social Psychology Bulletin*, *35*, 752–763.

Gentile, D. A., & Bushman, B. J. (2012). Reassessing media violence effects using a risk and resilience approach to understanding aggression. *Psychology of Popular Media Culture*, *1*(3), 138–151.

Gentile, D. A., Choo, H., Liau, A., Sim, T., Li, D., Fung, D., & Khoo, A. (2011). Pathological video game use among youths: A two-year longitudinal study. *Pediatrics*, *127*, 319–329.

Gentile, D. A., Coyne, S. M., & Bricolo, F. (2012). Pathological technology addictions: What is scientifically known and what remains to be learned. In K. E. Dill (Ed.), *Oxford handbook of media psychology* (pp. 382–402). Oxford, UK: Oxford University Press.

Gentile, D. A., Groves, C., & Gentile, J. R. (2014). The general learning model: Unveiling the teaching potential of video games. In F. C. Blumberg (Ed.), *Learning by playing: Video gaming in education* (pp. 121–142). New York, NY: Oxford University Press.

Gentile, D. A., Lynch, P. J., Linder, J. R., & Walsh, D. A. (2004). The effects of violent video game habits on adolescent hostility, aggressive behaviors, and school performance. *Journal of Adolescence*, *27*, 5–22.

Gentile, D. A., Swing, E. L., Anderson, C. A., Rinker, D., & Thomas, K. M. (2014). Differential neural recruitment during violent video game play in violent- and nonviolent-video game players. *Psychology of Popular Media Culture*. doi: 10.1037/ppm0000009

Gentile, D. A., Swing, E. L., Lim, C. G., & Khoo, A. (2012). Video game playing, attention problems, and impulsiveness: Evidence of bidirectional causality. *Psychology of Popular Media Culture*, *1*(1), 62–70.

Glaubke, C. R., Miller, P., Parker, M. A., & Espejo, E. (2001). *Fair play? Violence, gender and race in video games*. Oakland, CA: Children Now.

Gollwitzer, M., & Melzer, A. (2012). Macbeth and the joystick: Evidence for moral cleansing after playing a violent video game. *Journal of Experimental Social Psychology*, *48*(6), 1356–1360.

Green, S., & Bavelier, D. (2003). Action video game modifies visual selective attention. *Nature*, *423*, 534–537.

Greitemeyer, T., & Osswald, S. (2010). Effects of prosocial video games on prosocial behavior. *Journal of Personality and Social Psychology*, *98*(2), 211–221.

Groves, C. L., Prot, S., & Anderson, C. A. (in press). Violent media effects: Theory and evidence. In H. Friedman (Ed.), *Encyclopedia of mental health* (2nd ed.). San Diego, CA: Elsevier.

Grüsser, S. M., Thalemann, R., & Griffiths, M. D. (2007). Excessive computer game playing: Evidence for addiction and aggression? *CyberPsychology and Behavior, 10*(2), 290–292.

Huesmann, R. L. (1988). An information processing model for the development of aggression. *Aggressive Behavior, 14,* 13–24.

Huesmann, R. L., Moise-Titus, J., Podolski, C.-L., & Eron, L. D. (2003). Longitudinal relations between children's exposure to TV violence and their aggressive and violent behavior in young adulthood: 1977–1992. *Developmental Psychology, 39*(2), 201–221.

Ivory, J. D. (2006). Still a man's game: Gender representation in online reviews of video games. *Mass Communication and Society, 9*(1), 103–114.

Johnson, J. D., Olivo, N., Gibson, N., Reed, W., & Ashburn-Nardo, L. (2009). Priming media stereotypes reduces support for social welfare policies: The mediating role of empathy. *Personality and Social Psychology Bulletin, 35,* 463–476.

Konijn, E. A., Nije Bijvank, M., & Bushman, B. J. (2007). I wish I were a warrior: The role of wishful identification in the effects of violent video games on aggression in adolescent boys. *Developmental Psychology, 43*(4), 1038–1044.

Krahé, B., & Möller, I. (2010). Longitudinal effects of media violence on aggression and empathy among German adolescents. *Journal of Applied Developmental Psychology, 31,* 401–409.

Krahé, B., Möller, I., Huesmann, L. R., Kirwil, L., Felber, J., & Berger, A. (2011). Desensitization to media violence: Links with habitual media violence exposure, aggressive cognitions, and aggressive behavior. *Journal of Personality and Social Psychology, 100*(4), 630–646.

Kronenberger, W. G., Mathews, V. P., Dunn, D. W., Wang, Y., Wood, E. A., Giauque, A. L., … Li, T. (2005). Media violence exposure and executive functioning in aggressive and control adolescents. *Journal of Clinical Psychology, 61*(6), 725–737.

Landhuis, C. E., Poulton, R., Welch, D., & Hancox, R. J. (2007). Does childhood television viewing lead to attention problems in adolescence? Results from a prospective longitudinal study. *Pediatrics, 120,* 532–537.

Levine, L. E., & Waite, B. M. (2000). Television viewing and attentional abilities in fourth and fifth grade children. *Journal of Applied Developmental Psychology, 21*(6), 667–679.

Mathews, V. P., Kronenberger, W. G., Wang, Y., Lurito, J. T., Lowe, M. J., & Dunn, D. W. (2005). Media violence exposure and frontal lobe activation measured by functional magnetic resonance imaging in aggressive and nonaggressive adolescents. *Journal of Computer Assisted Tomography, 29*(3), 287–292.

McGonigal, J. (2010). Gaming can make a better world. *Ted 2010.* Retrieved from http://www.iftf.org/our-work/people-technology/games/jane-mcgonigal-at-ted/

Moller, I., & Krahé, B. (2009). Exposure to violent video games and aggression in German adolescents: A longitudinal analysis. *Aggressive Behavior, 35,* 75–89.

Moore, G. E. (1965, April). Cramming more components onto integrated circuits. *Electronics,* 114–117.

Mullin, C. R., & Linz, D. (1995). Desensitization and resensitization to violence against women: Effects of exposure to sexually violent films on judgments of domestic violence victims. *Journal of Personality and Social Psychology, 69,* 449–459.

Murphy, R., Penuel, W., Means, B., Korbak, C., & Whaley, A. (2001). *E-desk: A review of recent evidence on the effectiveness of discrete educational software.* Menlo Park, CA: SRI International.

NPD Group. (2010, March 2). Number of digitally downloaded games purchased by online gamers rises for third consecutive year. Retrieved from https://www.npd.com/wps/portal/npd/us/news/press-releases/pr_100302/

O'Leary, A. (2012, August 1). In virtual play, sex harassment is all too real. *The New York Times.* Retrieved August 23, 2013, from http://www.nytimes.com/2012/08/02/us/sexual-harassment-in-online-gaming-stirs-anger.html

Peng, L., & Li, X. (2009). A survey of Chinese college students addicted to video games. *China Education Innovation Herald, 28,* 111–112.

Polman, A., Orobio de Castro, B., & van Aken, M. A. G. (2008). Experimental study of the differential effects of playing versus watching violent video games on children's aggressive behavior. *Aggressive Behavior, 34*(3), 256–264.

Rideout, V. J., Foehr, U. G., & Roberts, D. F. (2010). *Generation M²: Media in the lives of 8–18 year olds.* Menlo Park, CA: Henry J. Kaiser Foundation.

Saleem, M., & Anderson, C. A. (2013). Arabs as terrorists: Effects of stereotypes within violent contexts on attitudes, perceptions and affect. *Psychology of Violence, 3,* 84–99.

Schulte, N. S., Malouff, J. M., Post-Gorden, J. C., & Rodasta, A. L. (1988). Effects of playing videogames on children's aggressive and other behaviors. *Journal of Applied Social Psychology, 18*(5), 454–460.

Shapira, N. A., Lessig, M. C., Goldsmith, T. D., Szabo, S. T., Lazoritz, M., Gold, M. S., & Stein, D. J. (2003). Problematic Internet use: Proposed classification and diagnostic criteria. *Depression and Anxiety, 17*(4), 207–216.

Sherry, J. L. (2001). The effects of violent video games on aggression: A meta-analysis. *Human Communication Research, 27,* 409–431.

Silvern, S. B., & Williamson, P. A. (1987). The effects of video game play on young children's aggression, fantasy, and prosocial behavior. *Journal of Applied Developmental Psychology, 8*(4), 453–462.

Sim, T., Gentile, D. A., Bricolo, F., Serpelloni, G., & Gulamoydeen, F. (2012). A conceptual review of research on the pathological use of computers, video games, and the Internet. *International Journal of Mental Health and Addiction, 10*(5), 748–769.

Sisler, V. (2008). Digital Arabs: Representation in video games. *European Journal of Cultural Studies, 11,* 203–220.

Swing, E., Gentile, D. A., Anderson, C. A., & Walsh, D. A. (2010). Television and video game exposure and the development of attention problems. *Pediatrics, 126,* 214–221.

Tedeschi, J. T., & Felson, R. B. (1994). *Violence, aggression, and coercive actions.* Washington, DC: American Psychological Association.

Tolchinsky, A., & Jefferson, S. D. (2011). Problematic video game play in a college sample and its relationship to time management skills and attention-deficit/hyperactivity disorder symptomology. *Cyberpsychology, Behavior, and Social Networking, 14*(9), 489–496.

Uhlmann, E., & Swanson, J. (2004). Exposure to violent video games increases automatic aggressiveness. *Video Games and Public Health, 27*(1), 41–52.

Weis, R., & Cerankosky, B. C. (2010). Effects of video-game ownership on young boys' academic and behavioral functioning: A randomized, controlled study. *Psychological Science, 21*(4), 463–470.

Weisz, M. G., & Earls, C. M. (1995). The effects of exposure to filmed sexual violence on attitudes toward rape. *Journal of Interpersonal Violence, 10*(1), 71–84.

Welch, H. (2012, December 13). America's love affair with the first person shooter and the rise of "Call of Duty: Black Ops II." *ComplexGaming.* Retrieved from http://www.complex.com/video-games/2012/11/americas-love-affair-with-the-first-person-shooter

Willcutt, E. G., Doyle, A. E., Nigg, J. T., Faraone, S. V., & Pennington, B. F. (2005). Validity of the executive function theory of attention deficit/hyperactivity disorder: A meta-analytic review. *Biological Psychiatry, 57,* 1336–1346.

Williams, D., Martins, N., Consalvo, M., & Ivory, J. (2009). The virtual census: Representations of gender, race and age in video games. *New Media and Society, 11*(5), 815–834.

Wu, S., & Spence, I. (2013). Playing shooter and driving videogames improves top-down guidance in visual search. *Attention, Perception and Psychophysics, 75,* 673–686.

Zillmann, D. (1971). Excitation transfer in communication-mediated aggressive behavior. *Journal of Experimental Social Psychology, 7*(4), 419–434.

29

What is Known About Video Game and Internet Addiction After DSM-5

Christopher L. Groves, Jorge A. Blanco-Herrera,
Sara Prot, Olivia N. Berch, Shea McCowen,
and Douglas A. Gentile

Iowa State University

Over the past 10 years, there has been a rapid increase in video game and Internet use among children, adolescents, and adults. Nearly 91% of American children and teens play video games, and this proportion has increased over time (NPD Group, 2011). On average, children and adolescents spend almost two hours a day playing video games (Rideout, Foehr, & Roberts, 2010). A substantial number of males report playing much longer – four hours a day or more (Bailey, West, & Anderson, 2010). Although excessive time spent playing video games is not isomorphic with video game addiction (Choo et al., 2010; Hilgard, Engelhardt, & Bartholow, 2013; Spekman, Konijn, Roelofsma, & Griffiths, 2013), a high frequency of play can be considered a risk factor for developing a pathological level of play (Gentile, 2009; Spekman et al., 2013). Further, a number of news reports illuminate the severe consequences of video game addiction. Such cases have involved seizures, childhood neglect, and deaths after marathon sessions of game play during which people played for days at a time without sufficient sleep or food (Chuang, 2006; CNN, 2010; Reuters, 2007). These findings and events have led to growing public concerns about potential detrimental consequences of pathological video game play. Such concerns have led to an increased number of research studies examining gaming addiction in the past decade. However, studies examining what is now being referred to as Internet gaming disorder (IGD) began as early as 1983 (Soper & Miller, 1983).

The research literature has demonstrated that video game addiction can be reliably measured (Gentile, Coyne, & Bricolo, 2012). Most researchers have defined it based on damage to multiple areas of functioning, including psychological, social, school, family, and occupational performance (Sim, Gentile, Bricolo, Serpelloni, & Gulamoydeen, 2012). Researchers have also identified a number of risk factors and outcomes related to gaming addiction, including anxiety and mood disorders, social phobia, and poorer school performance (e.g., Gentile et al., 2011; Shapira et al., 2003). These findings

The Wiley Handbook of Psychology, Technology, and Society, First Edition. Edited by Larry D. Rosen, Nancy A. Cheever, and L. Mark Carrier.

provide evidence that gaming addiction is a major public health issue that affects the well-being of a substantial number of people worldwide. This apparent consensus notwithstanding, the research suffers from the lack of a common framework for defining the problem.

Recently, pathological video gaming was included as a potential formal disorder in the *Diagnostic and Statistic Manual of Mental Disorders* (DSM-5; American Psychiatric Association, 2013). The American Psychiatric Association (APA) reviewed the evidence concerning pathological Internet and video game use. A workgroup consisting of 12 experts and more than 20 outside advisors reviewed more than 240 publications in this area. They believed the evidence was strong enough to include IGD in the research appendix of the DSM-5 with the goal of encouraging additional research concerning its prevalence, etiology, risk factors, clinical course, and treatment (APA, 2013). Nonetheless, they noted that prior research did not have the framework of a common definition, which they now supplied as a way to guide further research. In addition, they recommended the name Internet gaming disorder to include the earlier research on the pathological use of both the Internet and video games.

This chapter examines how the prior research literature relates to the new DSM-5 criteria for diagnosing Internet gaming disorder. First, a brief overview is given of the nine DSM-5 criteria for Internet gaming disorder. Each of the cognitive and behavioral symptoms proposed in the DSM-5 are considered in turn and relevant research findings are reviewed. The overall fit between extant research findings and the DSM-5 criteria is discussed. Finally, recommendations are given for future research on Internet gaming disorder.

Overview of DSM-5 Criteria for Internet Gaming Disorder

Early studies on IGD focused mostly on defining it and demonstrating basic construct validity for the definitions. Some studies created scales based on Brown's addiction criteria (Brown, 1991), or were created based on a mixture of clinical observations and other addiction criteria (e.g., Young, 1996). Some studies adapted DSM criteria used to identify individuals with gambling disorder, on the basis that both would be considered behavioral addictions. Further, gambling and video game play share some remarkable similarities despite their apparent differences. For example, massive multiplayer online role-playing games (MMORPGs), which have received much focus in the IGD literature (e.g., Kuss, Louws, & Wiers, 2012; Šmahel, Blinka, & Ledabyl, 2008), often incorporate loot systems that closely resemble reward systems incorporated within gambling and lottery games. In many of these games, players progress through levels and game regions in which they must dispatch a variety of enemies. Each time one of these enemies is defeated, items that can be used by the player are usually looted from the enemy's body (small payout). On rare occasions, a highly valuable item is dropped (high payout). This process is highly analogous to pulling the slot machine lever each time an enemy is slain. For further discussion regarding the learning processes involved in these types of behaviorally addicting tasks, see Gentile, Groves, and Gentile (2014).

Despite its name, IGD does not require that individuals exhibit symptoms of addiction solely with online video games. Addictive video game play can occur in both offline and online settings (APA, 2013), though reports of video game addiction often involve online games such as MMORPGs. Importantly, frequent video game play cannot, alone, serve as the basis for diagnosis. The DSM-5 states that video game playing must cause "clinically significant impairment" in the individual's life in order to be considered a genuine disorder. Indeed, some studies have demonstrated that pathological video game use and high game play frequency are functionally distinct (e.g., Gentile, 2009).

Further, pathological use of Internet activities that are unrelated to video game playing cannot be considered as a basis for IGD diagnosis. Such activities include online shopping, social media use, web surfing, pornography use, or online gambling. Some of these activities do fall under other DSM-5 disorders (e.g., online gambling). A factor in determining whether these kinds of behavioral addictions can be considered a disorder is the availability of research illustrating the social, professional, educational, health, or personal impairments resulting from the addictive behavior. These related activities likely differ in a number of respects from IGD and the research was not deemed sufficient for DSM-5 inclusion.

The DSM-5 appendix presents nine criteria that should be used to identify possible IGD individuals. A total of five or more of each of these criteria must be met within a 12-month period before classification of IGD can be considered. These criteria are listed below (APA, 2013).

1   Preoccupation with Internet games. (The individual thinks about previous gaming activity or anticipates playing the next game; Internet gaming becomes the dominant activity in daily life.) *Note*: This disorder is distinct from Internet gambling, which is included under gambling disorder.
2   Withdrawal symptoms when Internet gaming is taken away. (These symptoms are typically described as irritability, anxiety, or sadness, but there are no physical signs of pharmacological withdrawal.)
3   Tolerance – the need to spend increasing amounts of time engaged in Internet games.
4   Unsuccessful attempts to control the participation in Internet games.
5   Loss of interest in previous hobbies and entertainment as a result of, and with the exception of, Internet games.
6   Continued excessive use of Internet games despite knowledge of psychosocial problems.
7   Has deceived family members, therapists, or others regarding the amount of Internet gaming.
8   Use of Internet games to escape or relieve a negative mood (e.g., feelings of helplessness, guilt, anxiety).
9   Has jeopardized or lost a significant relationship, job, or educational or career opportunity because of participation in Internet games.

Each of these criteria is discussed in more detail below.

Preoccupation

Preoccupation is the tendency to think excessively about video game playing in non-game contexts. Individuals experiencing this symptom are prone to intrusive cognitions related to the game and the video game becomes the most important area of life to the addicted player. These individuals will often think and fantasize about games to an extent that leads to distraction in other areas of life. This becomes troublesome when the preoccupation results in missed deadlines or appointments and other life domains suffer due to their preoccupation. Some studies measure preoccupation with questions also designed to capture cognitive salience. Items such as "I [often] think about playing Asheron's Call when I am not using a computer" capture how often players think about their games and how cognitively salient these games are to these players (Charlton & Danforth, 2007). Some studies multiple point scales to capture the severity of the player's preoccupation with the video game (Ko, Yen, Chen, Chen, & Yen, 2005). Studies that used criteria more similar to those proposed by the DSM-5 indicate that the prevalence of this symptom ranges from 5% to 25% (Bioulac, Arfi, & Bouvard, 2008; Choo et al., 2010; Desai, Krishnan-Sarin, Cavallo, & Potenza, 2010; Fisher, 1994; Salguero & Morán, 2002; Thomas & Martin, 2010).

Withdrawal

Withdrawal symptoms occur when one attempts to stop or reduce engaging in the addicted behavior. Withdrawal and tolerance are both features of physiological dependence, and can be evidence for a biologically based addiction. These withdrawal symptoms for gaming are specific to symptoms that arise when one is unable to initiate gaming. However, it is important to note that experiencing frustration (even extreme frustration) when, for example, an Internet connection is lost, cannot be considered as evidence for withdrawal.

Functional magnetic resonance imaging (fMRI) studies have shown that addicted gamers show similar brain activity to substance abusers when they crave the addicted behavior (Ko et al. 2009). Additionally, they also share similar benefits from drug treatments designed to help those with substance abuse (Han, Hwang, & Renshaw, 2010). These gamers reported fewer cravings and showed reduced brain activation in response to game cues. Among studies using a DSM-5 type definition, prevalence of this criterion ranges between 2% and 22% (Bioulac et al., 2008; Choo et al., 2010; Desai et al., 2010; Fisher, 1994; Gentile, 2009; Salguero & Morán, 2002).

Tolerance

Tolerance refers to a need for increasing amounts of the addicted activity in order to reach a desired level of satisfaction. In gaming this can refer to when the addicted individual needs to play for longer periods of time and more frequently in order to reach the same level of happiness and excitement they felt before. However, this does not refer to instances in which the individual engages in the game for longer than intended.

Tolerance can also be seen in players seeking additional video game content that they will find satisfying. This could come in the form of seeking more violent games, games with higher levels of complexity, or simply playing much longer to feel as rewarded as with previous play sessions. Endorsement of items measuring tolerance among video game players ranges between 6.7% and 9.8% (Bioulac et al., 2008; Choo et al., 2010; Fisher, 1994; Salguero & Morán, 2002).

Unsuccessful Reduction or Cessation Attempts

Among the most concerning of symptoms endorsed by video game addicts is an explicitly stated desire to cease or reduce playing regularly despite an inability to do so. When individuals begin to experience difficulties in daily life, and associate these problems with their game play, they may attempt to restore balance and improve life satisfaction by taking control of the time they spend playing. However, individuals who meet diagnostic criteria for IGD often experience difficulties in accomplishing this task, often citing that life seems "dark" or "boring" without playing (Wan & Chiou, 2006a).

Experiencing difficulties in reducing or ceasing frequency and duration of game play is not terribly surprising given that such games are designed to be compelling and motivating to play. Positive video game reviews are often littered with statements that the game is "impossible to put down," "will keep you coming back for more" (Parker, 2012), or even "incredibly addictive" (Gallegos, 2012). Not only can game features be designed to motivate play (such as variable reward schedules), Internet-connected games come with additional social motivations, including both social opportunities and social costs. Wang and Zhu (2011) cite players who note that "all my closest friends today are playing games." (p. 29). So then when they try to reduce their game habits they realize "it's hard to find new friends." (p. 26). The variety of apparent sources for this symptom underscores the power that such games have over the player's motivations to restore general life satisfaction. Unlike some other symptoms of IGD, the prevalence of this item has a relatively large range, between 2% and 36%, in studies that use criteria similar to those endorsed by the DSM-5 (Bioulac et al., 2008; Choo et al., 2010; Desai et al., 2010; Gentile, 2009; Salguero & Morán, 2002).

Loss of Interest in Previous Hobbies or Activities

This criterion describes gaming as a dominating force in the social and recreational life of the player. It is illustrated by significant reductions in previously enjoyed activities except for game play. This can manifest as less time or interest spent volunteering, playing sports, socializing with friends, or any other previously preferred activity in lieu of video game play.

Hussain and Griffiths (2008) found that video game addicts reported that loss of interest in previous hobbies occurred due to (among other reasons) adopting regular video game play. It is likely that this item reflects some of the motivations for addicts seeking to reduce or cease playing video games. It is likely that individuals who become addicted to video games feel as though other parts of their life have been lost, or that social aspects of their life that typically involve other activities are missing (e.g., the loss of sports-playing friends due to the addiction). This item has demonstrated a range of prevalence between 7% and 14.4% (Choo et al., 2010; Desai et al., 2010).

Excessive Gaming Despite Problems

One symptom that is closely related to the two previously discussed is the tendency for those addicted to games to continue to play excessively despite problems arising in life outside of the game. Trouble in one of these areas can also trigger problems in other areas, leading to a snowball effect in which general life disruption can become substantial. Significant correlations have been found with hours invested in a game and obsessive compulsiveness and interpersonal sensitivity (Pawlikowski & Brand, 2011). Other problems have been seen relating to marital or intimate relationship satisfaction. For example, addicted gamers may forgo communicating with their partner in order to spend more time playing. Indeed, among MMORPG players, nearly 20% reported that they believed their video game play had a negative effect on their relationships with non-playing partners (Cole & Griffiths, 2007). In 2010, Peng and Liu measured physical, personal life, and professional or academic problems – noting that video game dependency, but not weekly play time, was highly associated with problems in all three areas (Peng & Liu, 2010). Studies have reported the prevalence of this item is between 9% and 29% in the general population (Bioulac et al., 2008; Desai et al., 2010; Salguero & Morán, 2002).

Deceives Others About Gaming

Like other forms of addiction, friends and family members often express concern about their loved one's engagement with the addictive behavior. Individuals who meet the criteria for IGD are likely torn between playing games and maintaining their social relationships with those who are concerned. Unsurprisingly, this can lead the addicted player to deceive friends and family with the goal of satisfying both needs.

Forms of deception include lying about time spent playing games but could include lying about the number of obligations that the addict may have (e.g., stating that "my homework is finished," "I spend one hour a week playing video games," and "I am doing homework right now, not playing video games"). This item demonstrates dysfunctionality in relationships, as the trust within significant relationships is likely to be damaged by the deception. In contrast to many of the other symptoms, deception may not be observable by anyone other than the gamer (if he/she is good at lying). Studies have reported the prevalence of this item to be between 5% and 14% (Bioulac et al., 2008; Choo et al., 2010; Fisher, 1994; Gentile, 2009; Salguero & Morán, 2002).

Escape or Relief From a Negative Mood

Using video games to escape from daily concerns or to find relief from a negative mood such as anxiety, feelings of helplessness, or guilt is another criterion for IGD. In some sense, playing video games (or using any other form of media) to escape or relieve a negative mood is normative. Many individuals who engage in video game play are doing so to escape. However, addicted players often engage in this tendency so frequently that they have little or no opportunity to deal with problems in life that are creating a negative mood, effectively "hiding" from problems indefinitely rather than temporarily "escaping" from them.

Although escaping negative feelings may be a common use of video games, individuals also seek video games merely to experience the fun and pleasure associated with play. Some evidence suggests that those addicted to video games are more prone to seek game play to avoid discomfort, whereas non-addicted individuals play to seek satisfaction (Wan & Chiou, 2006b). Among studies using DSM-5 type methods for diagnosis, prevalence of this criterion ranges from 8% to 30% (Bioulac et al., 2008; Choo et al., 2010; Desai et al., 2010; Fisher, 1994; Gentile, 2009; Salguero & Morán, 2002; Thomas & Martin, 2010).

Jeopardized or Lost a Relationship, Job, or Educational or Career Opportunity

For several reasons, such as those described previously, video game addicts have difficulty curbing their time spent playing and therefore may spend much more time in the game than is warranted by the demands of their life. In one study, 23% of video game players reported skipping their homework to play instead, and 20% reported performing poorly on subsequent homework or tests because of playing (Gentile, 2009). Overall, video game players received poorer grades in school (Anand, 2007), skip school and get poorer sleep (Choo et al., 2010), and produce lower Scholastic Aptitude Test (SAT) scores (Anand, 2007) when compared to those who did not play video games or played less. Critically, pathological status predicted poorer school performance even after controlling for amount of time spent playing video games (Gentile, 2009). The prevalence rate of game players reporting this item ranges widely depending on the study and likely the populations under examination. These observed rates range from 5% to 48% (Bioulac et al., 2008; Desai et al., 2010; Fisher, 1994; Gentile, 2009; Salguero & Morán, 2002).

Review of Relevant Research

Section 3 of the DSM-5 is not intended for use as diagnostic criteria in clinical settings. It is designed to describe potential disorders for which there is sufficient research to suggest concern, and to stimulate additional research with the intent of informing decision-making regarding whether the condition should be included in a future edition of the DSM.

One factor that contributes to the likelihood of inclusion is the degree to which research regarding the disorder is standardized. This is one of the major purposes of Section 3 of the DSM-5 – to provide standardized criteria for future research which will establish prevalence of symptoms, temporal course of the disorder, etiology, biology, comorbidity, and treatment effectiveness.

DSM-based diagnoses tend to be based on the patient presenting a substantial number (usually half or more) of clinically relevant symptoms that demonstrate dysfunction. Each symptom is determined by a dichotomous (yes/no) decision (e.g., the patient has or has not deceived friends, family members, or co-workers regarding their video game play). Some studies have been used specifically to match these kinds of inclusion criteria. Many studies, however, use other methods of measuring whether an individual meets a given criterion. A common method in research is to rate these criteria on a scale, such as the relative frequency with which a given symptom is experienced, as opposed to determining whether it is or is not experienced at all. The inclusion of IGD in section 3 of the DSM-5 is intended to provide a standardized diagnostic method and definition for research use in future studies. With this in mind, the studies that have utilized a dichotomous criterion measurement and established cut-off values for classification are arguably the most relevant for informing the field about the characteristics of IGD. Such studies will hold value for future development of treatment plans, understanding etiology, estimating prevalence, and predicting the temporal course of the disorder.

The DSM-5 explicitly points out that "the literature suffers ... from lack of a standard definition from which to derive prevalence data" (APA, 2013, p. 796). Nonetheless, there are a number of studies that have used criteria very similar to those now established by the DSM-5. For example, Fisher (1994) found that 6% of children met 4 of 9 criteria for IGD. A study by Choo et al. (2010) found that 9% of video game players met 5 of 10 criteria for pathological video game use. A national study of American youth 8–18 reported 8.5% of players as addicted after meeting 6 of 11 criteria (Gentile, 2009). Thomas and Martin (2010) reported a slightly smaller prevalence rate at approximately 5% of video game players who met 4 of 9 criteria for addiction. In another recent study by Hilgard and colleagues (2013), 8% of individuals were classified as pathological gamers defined by an endorsement of 7 out of 14 total items. Although some range does exist, it appears that a general prevalence rate around 8% of video game players can be classified as addicted based specifically on studies that closely mirror the DSM-5 criteria and approach to classification.

The etiology and course of development of IGD are particularly understudied, especially in research utilizing criteria that closely mirror those proposed by the DSM-5. One study measured IGD-like gaming symptoms over a two-year period among more than 3,000 children in Singaporean elementary and secondary schools (Gentile et al., 2011). Of the roughly 9% of children who were classified as addicted at the beginning of the study, 84% remained addicted two years later. They also found that IGD individuals experienced greater levels of depression, had poorer grades, worsened relationships with parents, and demonstrated increased aggressive tendencies. Importantly, these comorbidities appeared for those who reached IGD status during the course of the study, and decreased for those who reduced their symptoms below the IGD threshold during the study. Further, Choo et al. (2010) found that pathological video game players scored no differently from non-pathological players on measures of intelligence or socio-economic status – further indicating the divergent validity of IGD. These trends suggest that IGD is not simply a consequence of other, established disorders such as depression, but is a unique or comorbid pathology. This is the only longitudinal study of which we are aware utilizing criteria that include both clinical cut-offs and dichotomous symptom measurements. It is worth considering, however, that similar results were found in a longitudinal study using a continuous scale measurement approach (Lam & Peng, 2010).

One area in which very little relevant research has been done is the etiology of IGD. In a study by Li, Liau, and Khoo (2011), participants were asked to report their endorsement of 10 total, yes/no/sometimes items derived from the DSM-IV-TR measure for pathological gambling. The authors were particularly interested in the reported discrepancies between individuals' ideal and actual selves, depression, and subsequent pathological game play. In this study, the authors found that individuals who felt that their ideal self was distant from their actual self experienced increased depression; in turn, this depression led to increased levels of self-reported escapism, and finally this heightened escapism led to increases in pathological video game use. However, it is important to note that actual–ideal self-discrepancies and escapism also had direct effects on pathological gaming – suggesting a complex, multi-causal etiology.

Among relevant studies, the findings that are perhaps the most motivating for producing future research are those indicating that IGD leads to a host of negative life outcomes for the individual. For example, Desai et al. (2010) found that pathological video game players were more likely to get into fights at school, experience depression, and smoke cigarettes. Choo et al. (2010) found that pathological status was associated with impulse control problems, social competence, hostility, and damage to social life. Pathological status had even been associated with increased frequency of borrowing money to support game-playing habits (Fisher, 1994), similar to co-dependency in other addiction disorders. But perhaps the negative outcome that has the greatest likelihood for long-term career damaging impact is that pathological video game users suffer from poorer academic performance (Anand, 2007; Choo et al., 2010; Gentile, 2009).

Future Directions and Conclusion

The inclusion of Internet gaming disorder in the DSM-5 represents a major advance for studying this complex issue. For the first time, we have a common definition and clinical framework within which to study it. Although there have been more than 100 published studies on gaming addiction, Internet addiction, or Internet gaming addiction, they used many different approaches to define and study these issues. On the one hand, this has been a real strength, because it demonstrated the robustness of the construct to measurement, which allowed the American Psychiatric Association to realize that the issue was substantial enough to include in the DSM. On the other hand, it has been difficult to make much progress without a common framework because most studies have had to propose and defend their approach. Nonetheless, most studies have found very similar results, regardless of approach.

This review focused particularly on those studies that hewed most closely to the DSM-5 definition of IGD. A substantial amount is known about IGD even when we limit the population of studies in this way. The definition appears to have: (1) strong internal reliability; (2) strong construct validity, as demonstrated by predictable patterns of comorbidities and negatively correlated outcomes; and (3) some evidence of predictive validity, as demonstrated by early IGD predicting later poor outcomes. Nonetheless, inclusion in the Appendix of the DSM-5 is intended to stimulate additional research, and a great deal remains to be known.

Four areas in particular have been under-studied, and we suggest here several research questions that deserve attention from researchers. First, almost nothing is known about the etiology of the disorder. Who is most at risk? What are the warning signs? Is there a typical set of steps that people go through as they develop the disorder? What is the time course for developing the problems?

Second, almost nothing is known about the general time course of the disorder. Two studies (Gentile et al., 2011; Lam & Peng, 2010) have demonstrated that it lasts for at least two years for a majority of those afflicted. We do not know how long it takes to develop, nor do we know how long it lasts without treatment.

Third, more research needs to focus on comorbidities and outcomes. The initial work suggests that IGD can be predicted from impulse-control problems, a lack of social skills, and an above-average amount of game play. IGD, in turn, predicts depression, social phobia, anxiety, and poorer school performance. It is likely, given how mental illnesses tend to work, that many of these issues are truly comorbid. That is, they influence each other. In our experience, people often wonder whether IGD is a "primary" or "secondary" problem. Our belief is that this is likely to be something of an irrelevant question. Even if depression is the initial problem to develop, which then causes increases in gaming, once the gaming begins to be problematic, it will likely influence the depression (as found by Gentile et al., 2011). From a treatment standpoint, knowing which of the comorbid issues came first can be valuable, but if only the "primary" problem is treated, then the patient will not improve as quickly as if all of the comorbid problems were treated concurrently.

Fourth, more study needs to focus on treatment. Several studies have found that IGD is treatable (Han et al., 2010; Young, 2007), but it is still unclear what types of treatments are likely to be most effective. Furthermore, we do not know if some types of patients would benefit from different types of treatments. It is likely that we may need to know more about patterns of comorbidities before we can answer this question. It is certainly possible that some people will develop distinct patterns of comorbidities, and these may need to be treated differently for maximum benefit.

It is our hope that inclusion of IGD in the DSM-5 will stimulate research under a common framework to answer these questions about the etiology, course, pattern, and treatment of the disorder. Once we know more about these issues, we will be able to distinguish whether IGD truly is a separate and independent disorder, and whether it should be included as such in the DSM-6.

References

American Psychiatric Association (APA). (2013). *Diagnostic and statistical manual of mental disorders* (5th ed.) (DSM-5). Arlington, VA: Author.

Anand, V. (2007). A study of time management: The correlation between video game usage and academic performance markers. *CyberPsychology and Behavior, 10*(4), 552–559.

Bailey, K., West, R., & Anderson, C. A. (2010). A negative association between video game experience and proactive cognitive control. *Psychophysiology, 47*, 34–42.

Bioulac, S., Arfi, L., & Bouvard, M. P. (2008). Attention deficit/hyperactivity disorder and video games: A comparative study of hyperactive and control children. *European Psychiatry, 23*, 134–141.

Brown, R. I. F. (1991). Gaming, gambling and other addictive play. In J. H. Kerr & M. J. Apter (Eds.), *Adult place: A reversal theory approach* (pp. 101–118). Amsterdam, the Netherlands: Swets & Zeitlinger.

Charlton, J. P., & Danforth, I. D. W. (2007). Distinguishing addiction and high engagement in the context of online game playing. *Computers in Human Behavior, 23*(3), 1531–1548.

Choo, H., Gentile, D. A., Sim, T., Li, D. D., Khoo, A., & Liau, A. K. (2010). Pathological video-gaming among Singaporean youth. *Annals of the Academy of Medicine Singapore, 39*(11), 822–829.

Chuang, Y. C. (2006). Massively multiplayer online role-playing game-induced seizures: A neglected health problem in Internet addiction. *Cyberpsychology, Behavior, and Social Networking, 9*, 451–456.

CNN. (2010, May 28). Jail for couple whose baby died while they raised an online child. *CNN.* Retrieved from http://edition.cnn.com/2010/WORLD/asiapcf/05/28/south.korea.virtual.baby/

Cole, H., & Griffiths, M. D. (2007). Social interactions in massively multiplayer online role-playing games. *CyberPsychology and Behavior, 10*(4), 575–583.

Desai, R. A., Krishnan-Sarin, S., Cavallo, D., & Potenza, M. N. (2010). Video-gaming among high school students: Health correlates, gender differences, and problematic gaming. *Pediatrics, 126*, e1414–e1424.

Fisher, S. (1994). Identifying video game addiction in children and adolescents. *Addictive Behaviors, 19,* 545–553.

Gallegos, A. (2012, May 14). Diablo III review. *IGN.* Retrieved November 16, 2013, from http://www.ign.com/articles/2012/05/14/diablo-iii-review-in-progress

Gentile, D. A. (2009). Pathological video game use among youth 8 to 18: A national study. *Psychological Science, 20,* 594–602.

Gentile, D. A., Choo, H., Liau, A. K., Sim, T., Li, D., Fung, D., & Khoo, A. (2011). Pathological video game use among youths: A two-year longitudinal study. *Pediatrics, 127,* e319–329.

Gentile, D. A., Coyne, S. M., & Bricolo, F. (2012). Pathological technology addictions: What is scientifically known and what remains to be learned. In K. E. Dill (Ed.), *Oxford handbook of media psychology* (pp. 382–402). Oxford, UK: Oxford University Press.

Gentile, D. A., Groves, C., & Gentile, J. R. (2014). The general learning model: Unveiling the teaching potential of video games. In F. C. Blumberg (Ed.), *Learning by playing: Video gaming in education* (pp. 121–142). New York, NY: Oxford University Press.

Han, D. H., Hwang, J. W., & Renshaw, P. F. (2010). Bupropion sustained release treatment decreases craving for video games and cue-induced brain activity in patients with Internet video game addiction. *Experimental and Clinical Psychopharmachology, 18*(4), 297–304.

Hilgard, J., Engelhardt, C. R., & Bartholow, B. D. (2013). Individual differences in motives, preferences, and pathology in video games: The Gaming Attitudes, Motives, and Experiences Scales (GAMES). *Frontiers in Psychology, 4,* 608.

Hussain, Z., & Griffiths, M. D. (2008). Gender swapping and socializing in cyberspace: An exploratory study. *CyberPsychology and Behavior, 11*(1), 47–53.

Ko, C. H., Liu, G. C., Hsiao, S., Yen, J. Y., Yang, M. J., Lin, W. C., … Chen, C. S. (2009). Brain activities associated with gaming urge of online gaming addiction. *Journal of Psychiatric Research, 43*(7), 739–747.

Ko, C. H., Yen, J. Y., Chen, C. C., Chen, S. H., & Yen, C. F. (2005). Gender differences and related factors affecting online gaming addiction among Taiwanese adolescents. *Journal of Nervous and Mental Disease, 193*(4), 273–277.

Kuss, D. J., Louws, J., & Wiers, R. W. (2012). Online gaming addiction? Motives predict addictive play behavior in massive multiplayer online role-playing games. *Cyberpsychology, Behavior, and Social Networking, 15*(9), 480–485.

Lam, L. T., & Peng, Z. W. (2010). Effect of pathological use of the Internet on adolescent mental health: A prospective study. *Archives of Pediatrics and Adolescent Medicine, 164*(10), 901–906.

Li, D., Liau, A., & Khoo, A. (2011). Examining the influence of actual–ideal self-discrepancies, depression, and escapism, on pathological gaming among massively multiplayer online adolescent gamers. *Cyberpsychology, Behavior, and Social Networking, 14*(9), 535–539.

NPD Group. (2011, October 11). The video game industry is adding 2–17 year old gamers at a rate higher than that age group's population growth. Retrieved August 14, 2014, from https://www.npd.com/wps/portal/npd/us/news/press-releases/pr_111011/

Parker, J. (2012). New addictive iOS games that are impossible to put down. *CNET.* Retrieved November 16, 2013, from http://reviews.cnet.com/8301-19512_7-57407407-233/new-addictive-ios-games-that-are-impossible-to-put-down/

Pawlikowski, M., & Brand, M. (2011). Excessive Internet gaming and decision making: Do excessive World of Warcraft players have problems in decision making under risky conditions? *Psychiatry Research, 188*(3), 428–433.

Peng, W., & Liu, M. (2010). Online gaming dependency: A preliminary study in China. *CyberPsychology and Behavior, 13*(3), 329–333.

Reuters. (2007, February 28). Online addict dies after "marathon" session. Retrieved from http://www.reuters.com/article/2007/02/28/us-china-internet-addiction-idUSPEK2677 2020070228

Rideout, V. J., Foehr, U. G., & Roberts, D. F. (2010). *Generation M²: Media in the lives of 8- to 18-year-olds.* Menlo Park, CA: Henry J. Kaiser Family Foundation.

Salguero, R. A. T., & Morán, R. M. B. (2002). Measuring problem video game playing in adolescents. *Addiction, 97*(12), 1601–1606.

Shapira, N. A., Lessig, M. C., Goldsmith, T. D., Szabo, S. T., Lazoritz, M., Gold, M. S., & Stein, D. J. (2003). Problematic Internet use: Proposed classification and diagnostic criteria. *Depression and Anxiety, 17*, 207–216.

Sim, T., Gentile, D. A., Bricolo, F., Serpelloni, G., & Gulamoydeen, F. (2012). A conceptual review of research on the pathological use of computers, video games, and the Internet. *International Journal of Mental Health and Addiction, 10*(5), 748–769.

Šmahel, D., Blinka, L., & Ledabyl, O. (2008). Playing MMORPGs: Connections between addiction and identifying with a character. *CyberPsychology and Behavior, 6*(11), 715–718.

Soper, W. B., & Miller, M. J. (1983, September). Junk-time junkies: An emerging addiction among students. *The School Counselor*, 40–43.

Spekman, M. L. C., Konijn, E. A., Roelofsma, P. H. M. P., & Griffiths, M. D. (2013). Gaming addiction, definition and measurement: A large-scale empirical study. *Computers in Human Behavior, 29*, 2150–2155.

Thomas, N. J., & Martin, F. H. (2010). Video-arcade game, computer game and Internet activities of Australian students: Participation habits and prevalence of addiction. *Australian Journal of Psychology, 62*(2), 59–66.

Wan, C., & Chiou, W. (2006a). Why are adolescents addicted to online gaming? An interview study in Taiwan. *CyberPsychology and Behavior, 9*(6), 762–766.

Wan, C., & Chiou, W. (2006b). Psychological motives and online games addiction: A test of flow theory and humanistic needs theory for Taiwanese adolescents. *CyberPsychology and Behavior, 9*(3), 317–324.

Wang, L., & Zhu, S. (2011). *Online game addiction among university students.* [Master's thesis]. Available from DiVA – Academic Archive Online database.

Young, K. S. (1996). Psychology of computer use: XL. Addictive use of the Internet: A case that breaks the stereotype. *Psychological Reports, 79*(3), 899–902.

Young, K. (2007). Cognitive behavior therapy with Internet addicts: Treatment outcomes and implications. *CyberPsychology and Behavior, 10*(5), 671–679.

30

The Future of Technology in Education

Candrianna Clem[1] and Reynol Junco[2]

[1] The University of Texas-Austin
[2] Iowa State University, Berkman Center for Internet and Society, and Harvard University

Higher education has faced many challenges in the early 2000s. Downturns in the national economy have often led to increased enrollments in higher education by people who lost their jobs and are looking to retrain for new careers (Carnevale, Jayasundera, & Cheah, 2012). However, the most recent downturn in the national economy saw with it a downturn in funding for higher education. Furthermore, college costs have outpaced inflation since the early 1980s (U.S. Bureau of Labor Statistics, 2010). The increased cost of attendance, especially at publicly funded institutions, has spurred increased scrutiny by politicians and society at large. These groups have called for greater accountability to show that higher education institutions are adding value to our students' lives.

The rise of for-profit institutions has intensified the call for accountability. Online-only programs and universities have seen sharp increases in enrollment. New models of course delivery, such as the MOOC (Massive Open Online Course), have grown in popularity. Sadly, many of these online service delivery models assume that *content delivery* is the key ingredient driving learning – that providing students with content knowledge is the sole requirement for improving educational outcomes. However, this is farthest from the truth. Student learning is not only measured in quiz scores but in domains that include psychosocial development, interpersonal skills, critical thinking, peer to peer learning, and learning how to be a lifelong learner. While new modes of online course delivery are growing in popularity, offline institutions have started to implement programs such as *flipped classrooms* in order to more fully engage students. In these classrooms, students use technologies like learning management systems to cover course material outside of class time and use class time to engage in active learning led by the instructor. Again, issues of accountability are in play for flipped classrooms have the potential to improve student retention and therefore to increase profits for educational institutions.

In their desire to provide the best learning experience for students, educators have also examined the viability of tablets to promote student learning. Many K-12 school districts have programs to provide iPads for students, identifying their ease of use and

The Wiley Handbook of Psychology, Technology, and Society, First Edition. Edited by Larry D. Rosen, Nancy A. Cheever, and L. Mark Carrier.

ability to help improve learning more so than laptops. However, laptops are different – they are a means of content production and used in just about every workplace setting in the industrialized world. They are the tools by which work happens and by which content is produced. Tablets, on the other hand, are unapologetically content consumption devices. That is, they are not designed to create content but to consume it. Unfortunately, while schools have done a great job providing tablets, they have done an unsatisfactory job integrating them into the curriculum and/or assessing the effectiveness of their integration. Rarely is professional development provided to ensure that teachers are using the tablets in meaningful ways. Even when professional development opportunities are provided, we have no way of knowing how best to train teachers to integrate tablets into the curriculum. This is because we have barely begun to scratch the surface of understanding how we can use new technologies to best support student learning, engagement, and motivation.

This chapter will review research on four technologies/processes that have popularly been thought to show great promise in helping support student learning: social media, MOOCs, flipped classrooms, and tablets. While other technologies and/or processes might have been included, these are the four that are most popular at the time of this writing. Educators are encouraged to maintain a critical eye on emerging technologies and evaluate their effectiveness. Of critical importance is the fact that technologies in and of themselves do not *magically* bring about learning; instead, how educators use those technologies matters a great deal in the outcomes achieved.

Social Media

While there are a number of popular social media sites and services among students, this section will focus solely on Facebook and Twitter because of the amount of research available on these two sites compared to other social media. Furthermore, Facebook and Twitter are the two most popular social media sites among college students as of this writing. It is worth pointing out that the social media landscape can and does change quite rapidly. MySpace was a perfect example – it was first an early competitor to Facebook and now is only used by 7% of teen social media users (Madden et al., 2013). While the sites and services will change and new ones will take their place as frontrunners on the social media scene, the educational processes examined in the following review can likely be applied to future technologies.

Facebook

Adoption and usage In a recent report by the Pew Internet & American Life Project, 94% of teens reported having a Facebook profile, with 81% using Facebook more than any other social networking site (Madden et al., 2013). Facebook is the most used social networking platform, with two-thirds of online adults claiming to be Facebook users, and women and younger adults (18–29) most likely to use the site (Duggan & Brenner, 2013). Women have more Facebook friends than men (Pempek, Yermolayeva, & Calvert, 2009), and are more likely to use the site for communication and relationship-building activities, to post photos and status updates, comment on content (Junco, 2013), and send private messages and friend requests (Muscanell & Guadagno, 2011). Latino students have been found to be less likely to use Facebook, while Asian

American students and students with college-educated parents were more likely to use Facebook (Hargittai, 2008). In addition, African American students have been found to be less likely to engage in social information-seeking activities such as checking up on friends and tagging photos, and students whose parents have lower levels of education are overall less likely to use Facebook for various activities (Junco, 2013).

Research on Facebook use has found that students use Facebook for around 30 minutes throughout the day and it is primarily used for social interaction with friends that the users had already established relationships with offline (Junco, 2013; Pempek et al., 2009). Almost 80% of students reported that none of their friendships on Facebook originated online, and few reported using Facebook to meet new people (9%) or find help with schoolwork (2%; Pempek et al., 2009). Selwyn (2009) found that university students used Facebook to reflect on their university experience, exchange information, and offer moral support, but only 4% of a total 68,169 wall postings were related to educational uses. Mazman and Usluel (2010) suggest that a user's perceived usefulness of Facebook is the most important factor in determining Facebook adoption, with ease of use, social influence, facilitating conditions, and community identity also being important factors in Facebook adoption processes.

Facebook as a learning management system   Facebook has been used as a replacement or supplement to traditional learning management systems (LMSs) due to many LMSs lacking tools for social interactions and personal profile spaces found on Facebook (Mazman & Usluel, 2010). Schroeder and Greenbowe (2009) compared activity in Facebook groups to a learning management system (i.e., WebCT), using it as a tool for generating student discussion. The results showed that the number of discussion posts in the Facebook groups was nearly four times more than on the WebCT discussion forum. Those who posted on Facebook raised more intricate topics and generated more detailed responses using complex communication patterns. Despite being more active on Facebook, students listed Facebook as one of the aspects of the course that they liked the least, indicating a discomfort with using it for traditional courses (Schroeder & Greenbowe, 2009; Vincent & Weber, 2011). However, Irwin, Ball, Desbrow, and Leveritt (2012) report that students found Facebook to be an effective learning tool due to enhanced interaction between students and instructors, as the social networking properties of Facebook make interaction with the page easier. In addition, students were able to receive updates and information, respond to questions, and participate in discussions more efficiently.

Using a Facebook group in a Chinese language learning class, Ooi and Loh (2010) found that the Facebook group allowed students to share course resources, provide comments, and participate in organized learning activities through Facebook events. McCarthy (2010), who studied the Facebook group as a blended learning environment, found increased course engagement, using activity logs as an indicator. In addition, 95% of participants felt that using Facebook as a learning management system helped them develop peer relationships, with 92% appreciating the interactive design of the course (McCarthy, 2010). Wang, Woo, Quek, Yang, and Liu (2011) found the Facebook group could be used as a course management system, because it has all of the basic functions of an LMS such as making announcements, sharing resources, and facilitating online discussion and weekly activities. In addition, they argued that the Facebook group can be used as a substitute or supplement to traditional LMSs, and can even be a fully functioning LMS in schools where LMSs cannot be afforded

(Wang et al., 2011). Wang, Scown, Urquhart, and Hardman (2014) also found that students were positive about using Facebook over traditional learning management systems, because it served as a useful platform for sharing information and ideas and to monitor and coordinate collaborative work. In a comparison of Facebook to Blackboard, Buzzetto-More (2012) found both systems to be rated equally when it came to hosting study sessions, supporting group projects, and providing answers to questions. Although Blackboard was considered to be better than Facebook for course announcements and providing links to course resources, learners thought Facebook was overwhelmingly better for socialization and strengthening interpersonal relationships, which is important for student persistence (Buzzetto-More, 2012). DiVall and Kirwin (2012) also found students to be more likely to be exposed to content when it is posted on Facebook instead of Blackboard. Lim and Ismail (2010) suggest that Facebook be used as an alternative to traditional learning systems for meaningful online academic discussions, but the quality of the outcome depends on the facilitator/instructor, the topic of discussion, and the timing and order of the posts (Lim & Ismail, 2010).

Facebook as a learning tool   Various researchers have explored students' usage and perception of Facebook (Ismail, 2010; Madge, Meek, Wellens, & Hooley, 2009; Ophus & Abbitt, 2009) as well as specific uses of Facebook in the classroom (Bosch, 2009; Irwin et al., 2012; Smith, 2011). In a survey of student Facebook use, Ophus and Abbitt (2009) found students to be largely supportive of using Facebook in their college courses. Communication with other students and family were among the most common activities, followed by accessing notes and course materials, and viewing the schedule. Most students indicated that they had never used Facebook to communicate with their instructor or for school tasks (Ophus & Abbitt, 2009). In a study of university students, Madge et al. (2009) reported that a majority of students used Facebook for primarily social purposes, with few students using it to discuss academic work (10%) or contact academic staff (<1%). Ismail (2010) found that students are likely to use a social networking site (SNS) if their friends do the same and that the technological support provided by the institution affects their intention more than their personal use does.

Bosch (2009) found that students used Facebook for finding learning materials, helping friends answer questions about course and assignment details, sharing information about projects, lectures, and study notes, and to communicate with the professor. In Bosch's (2009) study, one lecturer used Facebook as a convenient way of communicating information to students, while another lecturer felt that Facebook helped students overcome shyness and ask questions that they might otherwise feel uncomfortable asking in class (Bosch, 2009). In a study that used the Facebook Application Programming Interface (API) as an instructional tool to teach web programming, Smith (2011) found that Facebook gave students the ability to engage with a wider audience, allowing them to easily benefit from peer feedback and develop and refine their programming skills. In a study of the use of Facebook pages within university courses, Irwin et al. (2012) found that students initially felt that Facebook could be an effective learning tool, and believed increased interaction, participation in course discussion, and posted lecture notes and assessments to be the anticipated benefits of using Facebook within a course. However, post-course surveys showed that only half of the students felt that Facebook helped them learn course concepts, a perception resulting from the instructors' inconsistent course integration (Irwin et al., 2012).

Additional research has shown that Facebook has been proven to be an effective means of providing its users with external resources (Bahner et al., 2012; Pilgrim & Bledsoe, 2011), discussion and collaborative learning (Estus, 2010; McCarthy, 2010; Shih, 2011), and informal learning (Cain & Policastri, 2011; Robelia, Greenhow, & Burton, 2011). Pilgrim and Bledsoe (2011) also found that pre-service teachers used Facebook as a learning tool to gain knowledge about professional organizations and resources through social networks. In a study that used Facebook and Twitter to deliver curriculum to medical students, Bahner et al. (2012) found the social media platforms to effectively deliver descriptive educational content to students using "push technology."

In a study that used a Facebook group as a discussion tool, Estus (2010) found that students felt using Facebook for discussion was a valuable part of the course, because it encouraged healthy classroom discussion. Students supported its continued use in the course as well as the integration of additional Facebook capabilities when expanding into future course offerings (Estus, 2010). McCarthy (2010) found that Facebook acted as a space to mediate interaction between local and international students, increasing interactions by suppressing social inhibitions as well as intercultural and language barriers. Students reported improved academic relationships through rewarding academic discussions and increased interaction with the peer group (McCarthy, 2010). Shih (2011) examined the effect of integrating Facebook and peer assessment using a blended teaching approach. The findings suggest that incorporating Facebook and peer assessment in learning English writing can enhance knowledge construction and engagement and be effective when combined with collaborative learning (Shih, 2011).

In a study that sought to understand how Facebook could be used to support informal learning about environmental issues, Robelia et al. (2011) found that students who used the Facebook application "Hot Dish" increased their understanding of environmental issues. Participation on the site encouraged environmentally friendly behavior, and pushed participants to learn more about environmental issues through social and civic engagement (Robelia et al., 2011). Cain and Policastri (2011) studied the effectiveness of using Facebook as an informal learning tool, using a Facebook group to introduce students to issues outside of the course curriculum. Most students appreciated the lack of interaction requirements, making the use of Facebook as an informal learning environment a success (Cain & Policastri, 2011).

Facebook, student engagement, and grades   Positive correlations between Facebook use and college student engagement have been found, as students who spend more time on Facebook spend more time socializing with friends and engaging with student groups at their university (Heiberger & Harper, 2008). Contrary to the Higher Education Research Institute (2007) and Heiberger and Harper (2008), Junco (2012b) found time spent on Facebook to be negatively related to student engagement (as measured by an instrument based on the National Survey of Student Engagement), but commenting on content and creating or RSVPing to events was found to be stronger, a positive predictor of engagement score. Additional research has shown that using Facebook to check up on friends is positively related to building the social ties needed to maintain relationships as well as GPA, but this activity is negatively related to student engagement (Ellison, Steinfield, & Lampe, 2007, 2011; Junco, 2012a, 2012b).

Research on the impact of Facebook on academic outcomes has shown mixed results (Junco, 2012a; Kirschner & Karpinski, 2010; Kolek & Saunders, 2008; Pasek, More, & Hargittai, 2009). In a representative sample of college students, Kolek and Saunders (2008) found no correlation between Facebook use and GPA between users and non-users of Facebook. Using existing data sets, Pasek et al. (2009) also found mixed results on the relationship between Facebook and academic performance, finding no relationship between Facebook use and grades. Kirschner and Karpinski (2010) found a negative relationship between Facebook use and GPA, as Facebook users reported a lower average GPA than non-users. Junco (2012a) found that Facebook activities related to collecting and sharing information (checking up on friends and sharing links) are positively predictive of GPA, while social Facebook activities (status updates and chatting) are negatively predictive of GPA.

Twitter

Adoption and usage   Twitter, a microblogging tool and social networking site, is used for information sharing, information seeking, and interpersonal relationships, and offers a faster mode of communication, with the average blogger updating every few days to several times a day (Java, Song, Finin, & Tseng, 2007). Over the past few years, Twitter use has grown significantly, with currently 16% of adult Internet users on Twitter and 24% of online teens using the site. Younger adults (18–29), urban dwellers (Madden et al., 2013), and African Americans (Duggan & Brenner, 2013; Hargittai & Litt, 2011) are among the most likely to use Twitter.

Twitter as a learning tool   Various researchers have studied the effectiveness of Twitter as an instructional tool in the classroom (Al-Khalifa, 2008; Borau, Ullrich, Feng, & Shen, 2009; Clarke & Nelson, 2012; List & Bryant, 2009; Retelny, Birnholtz, & Hancock, 2012). Al-Khalifa (2008) sent course announcements using a third-party service called Twitterfeed to convert the RSS feed from the course blog into Twitter updates. He found that most of the students (93%) preferred receiving Twitter text announcements to visiting the course blog, and said they would subscribe to Twitter if offered in future courses (Al-Khalifa, 2008). Borau et al. (2009) used Twitter as a communication and cultural competence training tool in a blended English as a foreign language course. The authors found that 70% of the students felt that Twitter was effective in developing their English skills when used as a supplementary practice tool (Borau et al., 2009). List and Bryant (2009) also found Twitter to be an effective facilitator for student learning, because it allows for effective communication with other students and staff and access to archival logs to reference prior discussions regarding topics of interest. Retelny et al. (2012) used a Twitter page to involve students in the development of course materials, making lectures more relevant to students and improving student preparation and motivation. He found that a majority of his students felt the Tweets helped them grasp course concepts and would recommend the use of Twitter in the future (Retelny et al., 2012). In a study of Twitter use across two courses, Clarke and Nelson (2012) found that the course with heavier Twitter usage had a higher sense of classroom community and perception of course effectiveness, with pedagogical effectiveness rated more favorably among the course that used Twitter. Although there were not significant group differences in perceived learning, the course that used Twitter outperformed the other course in regards to measures of actual learning, such as final course grade and scores from a departmental learning assessment test (Clarke & Nelson, 2012).

Research has also shown that Twitter has a positive impact on student learning (Dunlap & Lowenthal, 2009; Kassens-Noor, 2012) and supports informal learning (Ebner, Lienhardt, Rohs, & Meyer, 2010). Dunlap and Lowenthal (2009) used Twitter as a course management system (CMS) to encourage an interactive social learning community. Learning management systems (LMSs) and CMSs both have online discussion boards, support for quizzes, course materials, and gradebooks; however, LMSs tend to be more comprehensive, allowing for administrative functions like enrollment-related tasks. The researchers suggest that the advantages of Twitter over a traditional CMS is that Twitter use addressed issues quickly, encouraged concise writing and writing to an audience, connected students to a professional community of practice, and supported informal learning (Dunlap & Lowenthal, 2009). Kassens-Noor (2012) divided a classroom into two groups: one group used Twitter for communication and information exchange and the other group kept a personal diary to discuss with group members at the end of the course. Kassens-Noor (2012) found that students using Twitter reported a higher level of team-created activities than the traditional group, because tweeting fosters team communication and continuous interactive engagement in the learning process. Twitter has also been found to support informal and collaborative learning, by facilitating a constant information flow between students and teachers. The transparent working process afforded by Twitter allows the teacher to intervene and guide student learning (Ebner et al., 2010).

Ally (2012) found increased levels of classroom participation, attentiveness, and engagement from students when using Twitter in the classroom, and a majority of the students were supportive of its use. In a study of Twitter usage across two groups, Junco, Heiberger, and Loken (2011) found that the GPAs of the group that used Twitter were significantly higher than the non-users. The authors found that Twitter use led to more frequent interaction and engagement, which in turn may have helped increase GPA. Twitter helped students build connections more quickly than classroom discussions, and improved instructor–student communication by providing a platform to ask probing questions (Junco et al., 2011). In a later study, Junco, Elavsky, and Heiberger (2012) found an increase in student engagement and grades in courses in which Twitter use was required compared to courses in which it was optional. This result shows that the way instructors integrate Twitter into the course is an important factor in the engagement and achievement gains received from Twitter (Junco et al., 2012).

Massive Open Online Courses (MOOCs)

What are MOOCs? "MOOCs," which stands for "Massive Open Online Courses," is a term coined by George Siemens and Stephen Downes in 2008, and an emerging method of online teaching (Fini, 2009). A MOOC is a large online course, consisting of several hundred to several thousand students, which offers open and often free registration, a publicly accessible online curriculum and resources, and social network integration. MOOCs are often facilitated by leading educators in the field of study, and have been offered both in conjunction with academic institutions and with independent providers (McAuley, Stewart, Siemens, & Cormier, 2010).

There are two pedagogically distinct types of MOOCs: *connectivist* MOOCs (cMOOCs) based on the connectivist theory of learning with informal networks (Siemens, 2005); and *content-based* MOOCs (xMOOCs), which follow more instructional and assessment-based teaching methods (Yuan & Powell, 2013). According to Siemens (2012), the cMOOC model "emphasizes creation, creativity, autonomy and social networking learning" while the xMOOC model "emphasizes a more traditional learning approach through video presentations and short quizzes and testing," suggesting that cMOOCs emphasize knowledge creation while xMOOCs focus on knowledge duplication. The major non-profit MOOC-style initiatives (e.g., edX, PSPU, and Coursera) have given learners from across the globe the opportunity to access learning materials for free, and commercial companies have also been set up to help universities offer for-profit xMOOCs (e.g., Coursera, Udacity, and Udemy) (Yuan & Powell, 2013).

Case studies of MOOCs   Research has been done on the effectiveness of the following cMOOCs: Connectivism and Connective Knowledge (CCK08) (Bell, 2010; Fini, 2009; Mackness, Mak, & Williams, 2010) and Personal Learning Environments Networks Knowledge (PLENK2010) (Kop, 2011; Stewart, 2010). Fini (2009) found that participants in CCK08 were able to participate in the course according to their own learning styles, goals, and availability, and use only the tools they felt were relevant to the course. In another study of CCK08, Mackness et al. (2010) suggest that CCK08 can support the connectivist principles of diversity, autonomy, openness, and emergent knowledge, but they need to be managed in order to avoid barriers to learning. Bell (2010) found that participants of CCK08 exhibited a high level of agency in connecting themselves, their work, and resources using the platform, and the high number of CCK08 participants and participant interactions suggests increased connections among students.

In a survey of the experiences of PLENK2010 participants, Stewart (2010) found that prior engagement with social media did not determine the MOOC participants' perception of course value (Stewart, 2010). Kop (2011) found that participants of PLENK2010 interacted with each other, gathered information and resources, and shared resources, but only a minority of students participated in the creation and distribution of content such as blog and video posts. Kop and Fournier (2010) also found that silent participants, "lurkers," did not produce course content, but participated in other course activities such as collecting and sharing information with others. Participants with previous MOOC experience more actively engaged in the course, and time management, goal setting, and time availability were the most important factors in influencing participation (Kop & Fournier, 2010). Kop, Fournier, and Mak (2011) also found that participants who were more confident with the MOOC technology were more likely to create content and learning networks, while MOOC novices were more likely to be consumers of the material. On a similar note, Kop and Carroll (2012) found that for some participants creating content and participating in discussion is not necessary to advance learning, while the creation of discussion among other participants inspired and motivated others to create their own original content.

Other studies of MOOCs include Future of Learning (Bremer, 2012) and MobiMOOC (DeWaard et al., 2011). In a study of the open course Future of

Learning, Bremer (2012) concluded that open online courses are appropriate for learners who are intrinsically motivated, well organized, and possess a certain level of digital literacy to be able to fully participate. In an analysis of MobiMOOC, a course that integrates mobile learning into a MOOC platform, DeWaard et al. (2011) found that 77.5% of the participants used mobile devices to access the course, suggesting the potential for mobile learning MOOCs in increasing and widening participation.

Flipped Classrooms

What are flipped classrooms? A "flipped classroom" is a pedagogical method that shifts learning outside of the classroom, and replaces the standard in-class lecture by providing students with the opportunity to review lecture materials outside of class in their own individual learning space, and then review and discuss course materials with the instructor in class (Hughes, 2012). Instructors use various technologies to create readily available course content for students to access whenever and wherever it is convenient, enabling them to come to class more prepared (Musallam, 2011). In a flipped classroom, students come to class prepared to engage with the instructor in guided learning activities such as question-and-answer sessions and problem-based small group activities. Flipping a classroom can serve as an effective way for instructors to add active learning to their classroom, and gives educators more time to integrate and apply student knowledge as well as gauge student understanding of course concepts (Hamdan, McKnight, McKnight, & Arfstrom, 2013).

Case studies of flipped classrooms Research has shown that flipped classrooms can help students learn more effectively than traditional class structures in both K-12 (Bergmann & Sams, 2012; Fulton, 2012; Green, 2012; Ruddick, 2012) and higher education (Moravec, Williams, Aguilar-Roca, & O'Dowd, 2010; Papadopoulos, Santiago-Roman, & Portela, 2010; Talbert, 2012; Warter-Perez & Dong, 2012; Zappe, Leicht, Messner, Litzinger, & Lee, 2009). Byron High School in Minnesota adopted the flipped learning model using open source materials to improve student math scores and replace outdated textbooks during a financial crisis. As a result, student engagement increased, state math test scores leaped from one-third of students passing three years earlier to nearly three-quarters, and ACT scores improved from 21.2 to 24.5 (Fulton, 2012). Students at Woodland Park High School in rural Colorado were missing too many classes, having to leave school early for extracurricular activities. In an attempt to solve this problem, Bergmann and Sams (2012) flipped their chemistry classrooms, recording and posting lectures so that absent students could have access to course materials. As a result, student peer interactions increased, and struggling students received the assistance they needed to better understand course concepts (Bergmann & Sams, 2012). After Detroit's Clintondale High School introduced flipped learning into all freshman classes, the school's failure rates dropped by as much as 33%. In addition, the number of student discipline cases dropped 74% in two years, from 736 in 2009 to 187 in 2011, and parent complaints from 200 to 7 (Green, 2012). In a study of college preparatory courses, Ruddick (2012) found that students in the flipped course had higher final exam scores than students in the lecture-based course, and students reported that the online resources were useful and helped them become more interested and less intimidated by chemistry. On the contrary, when comparing a flipped to a traditional class in a Kentucky high school, Johnson and Renner (2012) found no significant differences between the test scores of those who were in the flipped classroom and those who were not. The authors suggest, however, that the lack of benefits found in the flipped method of classroom instruction can be explained by the fact that the flipped classroom model was implemented without any perceived need for the intervention (Johnson & Renner, 2012).

In a flipped undergraduate architectural engineering course, Zappe et al. (2009) found that students felt the flipped classroom had a positive impact on student learning, thought it was a more effective method of teaching than lecturing, and benefited from having access to lecture videos outside of class. In a study of a flipped electrical engineering class at the University of Puerto Rico, Mayagüez, Papadopoulos and Roman (2010) found that students progressed through material faster and had a deeper understanding of course topics when they watched lectures on their own and worked on exercises and problems during class time. Additionally, three-quarters of students "frequently" or "always" helped their peers in class, 81% preferred the flipped class to the traditional format, and test scores in the flipped classroom exceeded those in the traditional classroom (Papadopoulos et al., 2010). When a traditional large-lecture introductory biology class was flipped at the University of California at Irvine, Moravec et al. (2010) found that students in the flipped classroom saw an increase of 21% on exam questions that were covered in pre-recorded videos and watched outside of class and then followed up with in-class exercises. In a digital engineering course at California State University, Los Angeles, Warter-Perez and Dong (2012) found that flipping the classroom was effective in helping students deepen their understanding of course materials and improving design skills. In a linear algebra class at Franklin College in Indiana, students were given the option of attending a traditional lecture or watching a pre-recorded lecture, then participating in group work during class. Talbert (2012) found that students exposed to the flipped class environment performed better on the exam than students in the traditional lecture setting.

Other research has shown that flipped classrooms provide a space for collaborative learning, despite dissatisfaction with the way the learning objectives were set up (Frederickson, Reed, & Clifford, 2005; Strayer, 2012). In an experiment at University College London, Frederickson et al. (2005) found that compared to students in traditional classrooms, students in the flipped classroom conditions were more aware of their own learning process, and recommended that students be given adequate space to reflect on course activities to make connections to the content. However, students in the flipped classrooms were less satisfied with the quality of instruction they received online, but were more satisfied with the opportunity to collaborate with peers that was stimulated by this learning environment. In addition, no significant difference in improvements in knowledge and levels of anxiety was found between the two versions of the course (Frederickson et al., 2005). Likewise, Strayer (2012) found that when comparing students in a flipped introductory statistics course to a traditional statistics course, students in the flipped course reported being less satisfied with the way the classroom structure prepared them for the learning tasks they were given in the course, but were open to cooperative learning and innovative teaching methods.

Tablets

Adoption and usage   Tablets have emerged as a new category of mobile device that blend the features of laptops and smartphones and have the ability to be personalized with thousands of applications (Johnson et al., 2013). The larger screen and gesture-based interface of tablets make them ideal tools for consuming and sharing content due to their ease of use and portability (Johnson, Adams, & Cummins, 2012). Among Americans over the age of 16, 43% own a tablet or an e-reading device, with higher ownership rates among those highly educated and upper-income households (Rainie & Smith, 2013). The popularity and portability of tablets have caused them to capture the attention of educators around the world, as mobile learning affords the opportunity to access information and knowledge and support learning anytime, anywhere (Traxler, 2007). The idea behind mobile learning is based on a social constructivist concept of learning that relies on the exchange and sharing of knowledge in social contexts (Bremer, 2012), and includes the process of knowledge acquisition "through continuous conversations and explorations across multiple contexts amongst people and interactive technologies" (Sharples, Taylor, & Vavoula, 2007, p. 244).

Tablets as a learning tool   In exploring the potential of tablets as a learning tool, many researchers have examined the attitudes and perceptions of students and faculty toward adopting tablet PCs in the classroom (El-Gayar, Moran, & Hawkes, 2011; Ifenthaler & Schweinbenz, 2013; Rossing, Miller, Cecil, & Stamper, 2012; Weitz, Wachsmuth, & Mirliss, 2006). In a study of the usefulness of tablets among faculty at Seton Hall University, Weitz et al. (2006) found that faculty were confident about the impact of tablets on learning but only a few were motivated to use them. More than 80% of faculty who used tablets in at least one of their courses would prefer to keep their tablet instead of going back to a standard laptop, and felt that the university should keep providing faculty with the option to use tablets in their courses. In addition, 90% of faculty felt that the tablet had positive value with regard to teaching and learning in their course (Weitz et al., 2006). When exploring the perception of learning and engagement from iPad use in graduate classrooms at Indiana University–Purdue University Indianapolis (IUPUI), Rossing et al. (2012) found that iPads provided easy access to information that encouraged students to apply course concepts to the real world as well as participate in collaborative learning and group work, improving the quality of class discussions. Students were also enthusiastic about using the iPad as a learning tool in a dynamic learning environment and felt that use of the tablet helped reinforce the concepts students learned in class and was particularly valuable for those who learned at a different pace. Features such as speed, portability, user-friendly interfaces, and comfortable design contributed to the iPad's convenience, and the visual learning opportunities afforded by the tablet were found to be useful in connected course content (Rossing et al., 2012). In a study of a tablet PC computing initiative at a Midwest university, El-Gayar et al. (2011) found that students' attitudes toward using tablets had the most direct influence on technology acceptance, followed by the availability and access to support mechanisms, the expected gain in school performance, and the social influence of peers and faculty. El-Gayar et al. (2011) suggest that instructors ensure that students continue to view tablets as easy to use, an important factor in influencing student intention to use technology, through continuous support and training throughout the year. In a contradictory study of middle school teachers' perceptions of tablet use in the classroom, Ifenthaler and Schweinbenz (2013) found that only a few respondents believed that tablets can improve learning outcomes, and most were unsure of specific ways that the technology could be used to facilitate learning and instruction. Even those with positive attitudes toward tablets had reservations about tablet use, but the respondents' negative attitudes were possibly influenced by other factors. Overall, all teachers expressed the need for a smoothly running technology infrastructure as a prerequisite for tablet use and when using it in the classroom (Ifenthaler & Schweinbenz, 2013).

Research has also studied the effectiveness of tablets as an instructional tool and learning aid in both K-12 and university settings (Enriquez, 2010; Galligan, Loch, McDonald, & Taylor, 2010; Keller, 2011; Kerawalla et al., 2007). Kerawalla et al. (2007) studied the effectiveness of teaching numeracy in elementary classrooms using a homework system on tablet PCs. The results showed that the homework system helped students better understand the learning materials, and got parents more engaged in their children's learning. The children were more enthusiastic, confident, and began to connect numeracy activities at school with activities at home. Tablets helped make schoolwork less of a chore and more of a seamless and transparent learning experience (Kerawalla et al., 2007). In a study of the usability and functionality of tablets in distance education mathematics courses at the University of Southern Queensland, Galligan et al. (2010) studied the effectiveness of tablets in teaching face-to-face and distance lectures, tutorials, and consultations. Using tablets in large lecture courses provided the ability for real-time modeling of math problems as a teaching tool, and gave the students opportunities for self-directed learning. Tablets used in smaller tutorial sessions personalize learning for each student, and can be used to provide timely feedback for both distance and face-to-face students. An advantage of using tablets in one-on-one consultations with students is that the session can be recorded and reused by the student for later reflection and/or use by other students as a reference (Galligan et al., 2010). In two case studies that used tablets and wireless technology to create interactive learning networks, Enriquez (2010) found that students in the courses with the tablets had higher attendance rates and spent more time on assignments outside of class, and performed better overall than students in traditional classes. The students reported that using tablets during lectures improved their ability to take notes, organize class materials, and integrate handwritten notes into course materials (Enriquez, 2010). Keller (2011) reported on pilot trials at Seton Hill University that integrated the iPad into classroom instruction as an e-textbook. The textbook software, Inkling, gave students the ability to add notes to the text as they read and comprehended the materials. Instructors can access these notes to gauge students' understanding of the readings, and correct a student's misunderstanding of a concept while remotely receiving and answering questions in real time (Keller, 2011).

Conclusion

Research has shown various affordances of using emerging technologies and processes to support learning. It is perhaps no surprise that technologies developed to help support social interactions (such as Facebook and Twitter) have been found to promote social interactions among students. Research showed that students felt positively about using social media in their courses, allowing instructors to *meet them where they are* and support their engagement in the learning process. Most students are familiar with social media and do not require the same kind of steep learning curve required by other types of learning management systems. Additionally, since these platforms are an engaging part of their digital worlds, there might be some intrinsic motivation that transfers when they are used in educational settings. While social media can easily facilitate student engagement, MOOCs, on the other hand, require experience with online learning models and a higher level of student motivation in order for them to be effective in supporting student learning. Perhaps along similar lines, the research on tablets shows that they are unlikely to be used in ways that improve learning outcomes and their use tends to be focused squarely on content delivery. This is in stark contrast to flipped classrooms, which tend to provide rich engaging experiences for students.

The research on flipped classrooms shows that they are effective ways to add active learning to classrooms. Students saw increased engagement, improvement in a wide range of educational outcomes (e.g., standardized test scores, pass rates, and disciplinary referrals). However, it seems that for some disciplines, flipped classrooms may not be an effective intervention. Of the technologies/processes discussed, it is no surprise that flipped classrooms seem to support the greatest amount and types of learning outcomes – this method was created to help support active learning and student engagement, both of which are directly related to student success. Extrapolating the flipped classroom movement, we can imagine that the classroom of the future will look like an engaging social space, bringing forth vigorous conversation and debate while using technologies to help students collaborate, communicate, and build a sense of classroom community.

There are two major themes that are highlighted in this review:

1 The affordances of the technologies matter in terms of outcomes. Those technologies that are aligned with course goals and used in ways that support them tend to see more beneficial outcomes. For instance, Facebook seems to be an effective replacement for a learning management system discussion board.
2 *How* the technologies are used makes a difference when evaluating educational outcomes. Using a tablet as a content consumption device, for instance, does nothing to promote critical thinking skills. Conversely, using Twitter to engage students in class discussions promotes offline discussions.

Educators are encouraged to think critically about new technologies that are promoted to support learning. As new technologies are adopted, it is essential for educators both to understand how they can be used to support learning based on learning theories and to collect data to evaluate their effectiveness. We have much more to learn about how these and future technologies will affect student learning. While some research is cited in this review, important questions remain about causal links between technology usage and particular outcomes. For instance, how do we know that social media themselves provided the catalyst for improved student engagement? Perhaps the increased engagement had much to do with the faculty member using the technology. Junco (2014) discusses how some faculty, by the nature of their personality style, are more likely to be engaging in the classroom and more likely to use technology in engaging ways. Therefore, we need to conduct research to answer these questions and to discover how much of the variance in outcomes is due to the technology, how much is due to how it is used, and how much is due to the educators using them.

References

Al-Khalifa, H. (2008). Twitter in academia: A case study from Saudi Arabia. *eLearn Magazine*, 9, 2.

Ally, M. (2012). Student attention, engagement and participation in a Twitter-friendly classroom. In *ACIS 2012: Location, location, location: Proceedings of the 23rd Australasian Conference on Information Systems 2012* (pp. 1–9). Geelong, Victoria, Australia: ACIS. Retrieved from http://eprints.usq.edu.au/22703/

Bahner, D. P., Adkins, E., Pate, N., Donle, C., Nagel, R., & Kman, N. E. (2012). How we use social media to supplement a novel curriculum in medical education. *Medical Teacher*, 34(6), 439–444.

Bell, F. (2010). Connectivism: Its place in theory-informed research and innovation in technology-enabled learning. *International Review of Research in Open and Distance Learning*, 12(3), 98–118.

Bergmann, J., & Sams, A. (2012). *Flip your classroom: Reach every student in every class every day*. Washington, DC: International Society for Technology in Education.

Borau, K., Ullrich, C., Feng, J., & Shen, R. (2009). Microblogging for language learning: Using Twitter to train communicative and cultural competence. *Advances in Web-Based Learning*, 78–87.

Bosch, T. E. (2009). Using online social networking for teaching and learning: Facebook use at the University of Cape Town. *Communication*, 35, 185–200.

Bremer, C. (2012). New format for online courses: The open course Future of Learning. *Proceedings of eLearning Baltics eLBa 2012*. Retrieved February 5, 2014, from http://www.bremer.cx/vortrag67/Artikel_elba2012_opco_bremer.pdf

Buzzetto-More, N. A. (2012). Social networking in undergraduate education. *Interdisciplinary Journal of Information, Knowledge, and Management*, 7, 63–90.

Cain, J., & Policastri, A. (2011). Using Facebook as an informal learning environment. *American Journal of Pharmaceutical Education*, 75(10), 1–8.

Carnevale, A. P., Jayasundera, T., & Cheah, B. (2012). *The college advantage: Weathering the economic storm*. Georgetown Public Policy Institute: Center on Education and the Workforce Report. Retrieved September 14, 2013, from http://www9.georgetown.edu/grad/gppi/hpi/cew/pdfs/CollegeAdvantage.ExecutiveSummary.081412.pdf

Clarke, T. B., & Nelson, C. L. (2012). Classroom community, pedagogical effectiveness, and learning outcomes associated with Twitter use in undergraduate marketing courses. *Journal for Advancement of Marketing Education*, 20(2), 29–38.

DeWaard, I., Abajian, S., Gallagher, M. S., Hogue, R., Keskin, N., Koutropoulos, A., & Rodriguez, O. C. (2011). Using mLearning and MOOCs to understand chaos, emergence, and complexity in education. *International Review of Research in Open and Distance Learning*, 12(7), 94–115.

DiVall, M. V., & Kirwin, J. L. (2012). Using Facebook to facilitate course-related discussion between students and faculty members. *American Journal of Pharmaceutical Education*, 76(2), 1–5.

Duggan, M., & Brenner, J. (2013, February 14). The demographics of social media users – 2012. Pew Internet & American Life Project. Retrieved January 31, 2014, from http://www.pewinternet.org/Reports/2013/Social-media-users.aspx

Dunlap, J. C., & Lowenthal, P. R. (2009). Tweeting the night away: Using Twitter to enhance social presence. *Journal of Information Systems Education*, 20(2), 129–135.

Ebner, M., Lienhardt, C., Rohs, M., & Meyer, I. (2010). Microblogs in higher education: A chance to facilitate informal and process-oriented learning? *Computers and Education*, *55*(1), 92–100.

Ellison, N. B., Steinfield, C., & Lampe, C. (2007). The benefits of Facebook "friends": Social capital and college students' use of online social network sites. *Journal of Computer-Mediated Communication*, *12*(4), 1143–1168.

Ellison, N. B., Steinfield, C., & Lampe, C. (2011). Connection strategies: Social capital implications of Facebook-enabled communication practices. *New Media and Society*, *13*(6), 873–892.

El-Gayar, O., Moran, M., & Hawkes, M. (2011). Students' acceptance of tablet PCs and implications for educational institutions. *Educational Technology and Society*, *14*, 58–70.

Enriquez, A. G. (2010). Enhancing student performance using tablet computers. *College Teaching*, *58*(3), 77–84.

Estus, E. L. (2010). Using Facebook within a geriatric pharmacotherapy course. *American Journal of Pharmaceutical Education*, *74*(8), 1–5.

Fini, A. (2009). The technological dimension of a massive open online course: The case of the CCK08 course tools. *International Review of Research in Open and Distance Learning*, *10*(5). Retrieved February 5, 2014, from http://www.irrodl.org/index.php/irrodl/article/view/643/141

Frederickson, N., Reed, P., & Clifford, V. (2005). Evaluating web-supported learning versus lecture-based teaching: Quantitative and qualitative perspectives. *Higher Education*, *50*(4), 645–664.

Fulton, K. (2012, April). Inside the flipped classroom. *The Journal*. Retrieved February 5, 2014, from http://thejournal.com/ articles/2012/04/11/the-flipped-classroom.aspx

Galligan, L., Loch, B., McDonald, C., & Taylor, J. A. (2010). The use of tablet and related technologies in mathematics teaching. *Australian Senior Mathematics Journal*, *24*(1), 38–51.

Green, G. (2012, July). *The flipped classroom and school approach: Clintondale High School*. Presented at the annual Building Learning Communities Education Conference, Boston, MA. Retrieved February 6, 2014, from http://2012.blcconference.com/documents/flipped-classroom-school-approach.pdf

Hamdan, N., McKnight, P., McKnight, K., & Arfstrom, K. M. (2013). A review of flipped learning. *Flipped Learning Network*. Retrieved December 7, 2014, from http://www.flippedlearning.org/cms/lib07/VA01923112/Centricity/Domain/41/LitReview_FlippedLearning.pdf

Hargittai, E. (2008). Digital reproduction of inequality. *Social Stratification*. Retrieved from http://communications.northwestern.edu/programs/phd_media_technology_society/publications/Hargittai.pdf

Hargittai, E., & Litt, E. (2011). The tweet smell of celebrity success: Explaining variation in Twitter adoption among a diverse group of young adults. *New Media and Society*, *13*(5), 824–842.

Heiberger, G., & Harper, R. (2008). Have you facebooked Astin lately? Using technology to increase student involvement. *New Directions for Student Services*, *124*, 19–35.

Higher Education Research Institute (HERI). (2007). College freshmen and online social networking sites. Retrieved March 7, 2010, from http://www.gseis.ucla.edu/heri/PDFs/pubs/briefs/brief-091107-SocialNetworking.pdf

Hughes, H. (2012). Introduction to flipping the college classroom. In T. Amiel & B. Wilson (Eds.), *Proceedings of the World Conference on Educational Multimedia, Hypermedia and Telecommunications 2012* (pp. 2434–2438). Chesapeake, VA: AACE. Retrieved from http://www.editlib.org/p/41097/

Ifenthaler, D., & Schweinbenz, V. (2013). The acceptance of tablet PCs in classroom instruction: The teachers' perspectives. *Computers in Human Behavior*, *29*(3), 525–534.

Irwin, C., Ball, L., Desbrow, B., & Leveritt, M. (2012). Students' perceptions of using Facebook as an interactive learning resource at university. *Australasian Journal of Educational Technology*, *28*(7), 1221–1232.

Ismail, S. (2010). International students' acceptance on using social networking site to support learning activities. *International Journal for the Advancement of Science and Arts, 1*, 81–90.

Java, A., Song, X., Finin, T., & Tseng, B. (2007). *Why we Twitter: Understanding microblogging usage and communities.* Paper presented at the Proceedings of the 9th WebKDD and 1st SNA-KDD 2007 Workshop on Web Mining and Social Network, Analysis, pp. 56–65.

Johnson, L., Adams, S., & Cummins, M. (2012). *The NMC Horizon report: 2012 Higher Education edition.* Austin, TX: The New Media Consortium. Retrieved from http://redarchive.nmc.org/publications/horizon-report-2012-higher-ed-edition

Johnson, L., Adams Becker, S., Cummins, M., Estrada, V., Freeman, A., & Ludgate, H. (2013). *NMC Horizon report: 2013 Higher Education edition.* Austin, TX: The New Media Consortium. Retrieved from http://www.nmc.org/pdf/2013-horizon-report-HE.pdf

Johnson, L., & Renner, J. (2012). *Effect of the flipped classroom model on secondary computer applications course: Student and teacher perceptions, questions and student achievement.* [Doctoral dissertation]. University of Louisville, KY.

Junco, R. (2012a). The relationship between frequency of Facebook use, participation in Facebook activities, and student engagement. *Computers and Education, 58*(1), 162–171.

Junco, R. (2012b). Too much face and not enough books: The relationship between multiple indices of Facebook use and academic performance. *Computers in Human Behavior, 28*(1), 187–198.

Junco, R. (2013). Inequalities in Facebook use. *Computers in Human Behavior, 29*(6), 2328–2336.

Junco, R. (2014). *Engaging students through social media: Evidence-based practices for use in student affairs.* San Francisco, CA: Jossey-Bass.

Junco, R., Elavsky, C. M., & Heiberger, G. (2012). Putting Twitter to the test: Assessing outcomes for student collaboration, engagement, and success. *British Journal of Educational Technology, 44*(2), 273–287.

Junco, R., Heiberger, G., & Loken, E. (2011). The effect of Twitter on college student engagement and grades. *Journal of Computer Assisted Learning, 27*(2), 119–132.

Kassens-Noor, E. (2012). Twitter as a teaching practice to enhance active and informal learning in higher education: The case of sustainable tweets. *Active Learning in Higher Education, 13*(1), 9–21.

Keller, J. (2011, May 8). The slow-motion mobile campus. *Chronicle of Higher Education.* Retrieved from http://chronicle.com/article/The-Slow-Motion-Mobile-Campus/127380/

Kerawalla, L., O'Connor, J., Underwood, J., du Boulay, B., Holmberg, J., Luckin, R., … Tunley, H. (2007). Exploring the potential of the homework system and tablet PCs to support continuity of numeracy practices between home and primary school. *Educational Media International, 44*(4), 289–303.

Kirschner, P. A., & Karpinski, A. C. (2010). Facebook® and academic performance. *Computers in Human Behavior, 26*, 1237–1245.

Kolek, E. A., & Saunders, D. (2008). Online disclosure: An empirical examination of undergraduate Facebook profiles. *NASPA Journal, 45*(1), 1–25.

Kop, R. (2011). The challenges to connectivist learning on open online networks: Learning experiences during a massive open online course. *International Review of Research in Open and Distance Learning,* Special issue: *Connectivism: Design and Delivery of Social Networked Learning, 12*(3). Retrieved from http://www.irrodl.org/index.php/irrodl/article/view/882

Kop, R., & Carroll, F. (2012). Cloud computing and creativity: Learning on a massive open online course. *European Journal of Open, Distance and E-Learning.* Retrieved from http://www.eurodl.org/?p=special&sp=articles&article=457

Kop, R., & Fournier, H. (2010). New dimensions to self-directed learning in an open networked learning environment. *International Journal of Self-Directed Learning, 7*(2).

Kop, R., Fournier, H., & Mak, J. S. F. (2011). A pedagogy of abundance or a pedagogy to support human beings? Participant support on massive open online courses. *International Review of Research in Open and Distance Learning,* Special issue: *Emergent Learning, Connections, Design for Learning, 12*(7), 74–93.

Lim, T., & Ismail, J. T. (2010). The use of Facebook for online discussions among distance learners. *Turkish Online Journal of Distance Education, 11*(4), 72–81.

List, J., & Bryant, B. (2009). Integrating interactive online content at an early college high school: An exploration of Moodle, Ning and Twitter. *Meridian Middle School Computer Technologies Journal, 12*(1). Retrieved from http://www.ncsu.edu/project/meridian/winter2009/List/index.htm

Mackness, J., Mak, S., & Williams, R. (2010). The ideals and reality of participating in a MOOC. In L. Dirckinck-Holmfeld, V. Hodgson, C. Jones, M. De Laat, D. McConnell, & T. Ryberg (Eds.), *Proceedings of the 7th International Conference on Networked Learning 2010, University of Lancaster,* Lancaster, pp. 266–275.

Madden, A., Lenhart, A., Cortesi, S., Gasser, U., Duggan, M., Smith, A., & Beaton, M. (2013, May 21). Teens, social media, and privacy. Pew Internet & American Life Project. Retrieved January 31, 2014, from http://www.pewinternet.org/Reports/2013/Teens-Social-Media-And-Privacy.aspx

Madge, C., Meek, J., Wellens, J., & Hooley, T. (2009). Facebook, social integration and informal learning at university: It is more for socialising and talking to friends about work than for actually doing work. *Learning, Media and Technology, 34*(2), 141–155.

Mazman, S. G., & Usluel, Y. K. (2010). Modeling educational usage of Facebook. *Computers and Education, 55*(2), 444–453.

McAuley, A., Stewart, B., Siemens, G., & Cormier, D. (2010). The MOOC model for digital practice, SSHRC Knowledge Synthesis Grant on the Digital Economy. Retrieved from http://www.elearnspace.org/Articles/MOOC_Final.pdf

McCarthy, J. (2010). Blended learning environments: Using social networking sites to enhance the first year experience. *Australasian Journal of Educational Technology, 26*(6), 729–740.

Moravec, M., Williams, A., Aguilar-Roca, N., & O'Dowd, D. K. (2010). Learn before lecture: A strategy that improves learning outcomes in a large introductory biology class. *CBE Life Science Education, 9,* 473–481.

Musallam, R. (2011). Should you flip your classroom? *Edutopia.* Retrieved April 3, 2014, from http://www.edutopia.org/blog/flipped-classroom-ramsey-musallam

Muscanell, N. L., & Guadagno, R. E. (2011). Make new friends or keep the old: Gender and personality differences in social networking use. *Computers in Human Behavior, 28*(1), 107–112.

Ooi, C. Y., & Loh, K. Y. (2010). Using online Web 2.0 tools to promote innovative learning. In Q. Y. Wang & S. C. Kong (Eds.), *Workshop proceedings of the 14th Global Conference on Computers in Education* (pp. 72–76). Singapore: National Institute of Education.

Ophus, J. D., & Abbitt, J. T. (2009). Exploring the potential perceptions of social networking systems in university courses. *Journal of Online Learning and Teaching, 5*(4), 639–648.

Papadopoulos, C., & Santiago-Roman, A. (2010). AC 2010-1868: Implementing an inverted classroom model in engineering statics: Initial results. *American Society for Engineering Education.*

Papadopoulos, C., Santiago-Roman, A., & Portela, G. (2010). Working in progress: Developing and implementing an inverted classroom for engineering statics. *Proceedings of 40th ASEE/IEEE Frontiers in Education Conference.*

Pasek, J., More, E., & Hargittai, E. (2009). Facebook and academic performance: Reconciling a media sensation with data. *First Monday, 14*(5). Retrieved from http://www.firstmonday.dk/ojs/index.php/fm/article/view/2498

Pempek, T. A., Yermolayeva, Y. A., & Calvert, S. L. (2009). College students' social networking experiences on Facebook®. *Journal of Applied Developmental Psychology, 30*(3), 227–238.

Pilgrim, J., & Bledsoe, C. (2011). Engaging pre-service teachers in learning through social networking. *Journal of Literacy and Technology, 12*(1), 2–25.

Rainie, L., & Smith, A. (2013, October 18). Tablet and e-reader ownership update. Pew Internet & American Life Project. Retrieved December 7, 2014, from http://www. pewinternet.org/2013/10/18/tablet-and-e-reader-ownership-update/

Retelny, D., Birnholtz, J., & Hancock, J. (2012). Tweeting for class: Using social media to enable student co-construction of lectures. In *Proceedings of the ACM 2012 conference on Computer Supported Cooperative Work Companion (CSCW '12)* (pp. 203–206). New York, NY: ACM.

Robelia, B. A., Greenhow, C., & Burton, L. (2011). Environmental learning in online social networks: Adopting environmentally responsible behaviors. *Environmental Education Research, 17,* 553–575.

Rossing, J. P., Miller, W. M., Cecil, A. K., & Stamper, S. E. (2012). iLearning: The future of higher education? Student perceptions on learning with mobile tablets. *Journal of the Scholarship of Teaching and Learning, 12*(2), 1–26.

Ruddick, K. W. (2012). *Improving chemical education from high school to college using a more hands-on approach.* [Unpublished doctoral dissertation]. University of Memphis, Memphis, TN.

Schroeder, J., & Greenbowe, T. J. (2009). The chemistry of Facebook: Using social networking to create an online community for organic chemistry. *Innovate: Journal of Online Education, 5*(4), 9.

Selwyn, N. (2009). Faceworking: Exploring students' education-related use of Facebook. *Learning, Media and Technology, 34*(2), 157–174.

Sharples, M., Taylor, J., & Vavoula, G. (2007). A theory of learning for the mobile age. In R. Andrews & C. Haythornthwaite (Eds.), *The Sage handbook of e-learning research* (pp. 221–247). London: Sage.

Shih, R. C. (2011). Can Web 2.0 technology assist college students in learning English writing? Integrating Facebook and peer assessment with blended learning. *Australasian Journal of Educational Technology, 27,* 829–845.

Siemens, G. (2005). Connectivism: A learning theory for the digital age. *International Journal of Instructional Technology and Distance Learning, 2*(1). Retrieved from http://www.itdl. org/Journal/Jan_05/article01.htm

Siemens, G. (2012, February 29). Massive open online courses as new educative practice. *Blog Elearnspace.* Retrieved from http://www.elearnspace.org/blog/2012/02/29/ massive-open-online-courses-as-new-educative-practice/

Smith, A. K. (2011). Web and software engineering the Facebook way: An undergraduate mini project. *ITALICS: Innovation in Teaching and Learning in Information and Computer Sciences, 10*(3). Retrieved December 7, 2014, from http://journals.heacademy.ac.uk/ doi/abs/10.11120/ital.2011.10030058

Stewart, B. (2010). Social media literacies and perceptions of value in open online courses. Retrieved December 7, 2014, from http://portfolio.cribchronicles.com/social-media-literacies-and-perceptions-of-value-in-open-online-courses/

Strayer, J. F. (2012). How learning in an inverted classroom influences cooperation, innovation and task orientation. *Learning Environments Research, 15*(2), 171–193.

Talbert, R. (2012). Learning MATLAB in the inverted classroom. *Proceedings of the ASEE Annual Conference and Exposition.*

Traxler, J. (2007). Defining, discussing and evaluating mobile learning: The moving finger writes and having writ … *Review of Research in Open and Distance Learning, 8*(2). Retrieved from http://www.irrodl.org/index.php/irrodl/article/viewArticle/346

U.S. Bureau of Labor Statistics. (2010, September). *Back to college.* United States Department of Labor. Retrieved January 31, 2014, from http://www.bls.gov/spotlight/2010/ college/

Vincent, A. H., & Weber, Z. A. (2011). Using Facebook within a pharmacy elective course. *American Journal of Pharmaceutical Education, 75*(1), 3.

Wang, Q., Woo, H. L., Quek, C. L., Yang, Y., & Liu, M. (2011). Using the Facebook group as a learning management system: An exploratory study. *British Journal of Educational Technology, 43*(3), 428–438.

Wang, R., Scown, P., Urquhart, C., & Hardman, J. (2014). Tapping the educational potential of Facebook: Guidelines for use in higher education. *Education and Information Technologies, 19*(1), 21–39.

Warter-Perez, N., & Dong, J. (2012, April). *Flipping the classroom: How to embed inquiry and design projects into a digital engineering lecture.* Paper presented at ASEE PSW Section Conference, California Polytechnic State University, San Luis Obispo, CA.

Weitz, R., Wachsmuth, B., & Mirliss, D. (2006). The tablet PC for faculty: A pilot project. *Educational Technology and Society, 9*(2), 68–83.

Yuan, L., & Powell, S. (2013). MOOCs and open education: Implications for higher education, A white paper. *Publications.cetis.ac.uk.* Retrieved from http://publications.cetis.ac.uk/wp-content/uploads/2013/03/MOOCs-and-Open-Education.pdf

Zappe, S., Leicht, R., Messner, J., Litzinger, T., & Lee, H. W. (2009). Flipping the classroom to explore active learning in a large undergraduate course. *Proceedings, American Society for Engineering Education Annual Conference and Exhibition.* Retrieved December 7, 2014, from http://www.researchgate.net/profile/Sarah_Zappe/publication/260201119_Flipping_the_classroom_to_explore_active_learning_in_a_large_undergraduate_course/links/0c96053021919ea91e000000

Index

Note: Page numbers in *italics* refer to Figures; those in **bold** to Tables.

The Wiley Handbook of Psychology, Technology, and Society, First Edition. Edited by Larry D. Rosen,
Nancy A. Cheever, and L. Mark Carrier.
© 2015 John Wiley & Sons, Ltd. Published 2015 by John Wiley & Sons, Ltd.